Ready-Made

Access 2.0 Applications

Ed Jones

Windcrest®/McGraw-Hill

New York San Francisco Washington, D.C. Auckland Bogotá
Caracas Lisbon London Madrid Mexico City Milan
Montreal New Delhi San Juan Singapore
Sydney Tokyo Toronto

Published by Windcrest, an imprint of McGraw-Hill, Inc.

pbk 2 3 4 5 6 7 8 9 10 DOC/DOC 9 9 8 7 6 5

Library of Congress Cataloging-in-Publication Data

Jones, Edward, 1952–
Ready-made access 2.0 applications / by Ed Jones.
p. cm.
Includes index.
ISBN 0-07-032774-2
1. Data base management. 2. Microsoft Access. I. Title.
QA76.9.D3J6457 1994
005.75'65—dc20 94-1200
CIP

Acquisitions editor: Brad Schepp
Editorial team: Robert Ostrander, Executive Editor
John C. Baker, Book Editor
Jodi L. Tyler, Indexer
Production team: Katherine G. Brown, Director
Tina M. Sourbier, Coding
Wanda S. Ditch, Desktop Operator
Patsy Harne, Desktop Operator
Lorie L. White, Proofreading
Marty Ehrlinger, Computer Illustrations
Design team: Jaclyn J. Boone, Designer
Brian Allison, Associate Designer
Cover design: Carol Stickles, Bath, Pennsylvania
Cover photograph: © Orion Press/Westlight

WU1
0327742

Dedication

To Ann Pharr

–En realidad, una amiga muy especial.

Contents

Part three: The Access applications

Introduction

Whether you are completely new to Access or have some experience with the program, you'll find useful points and techniques in this book for you. If you are just learning Access, you'll find that the hands-on examples, tips, and techniques detailed in Part Two of this book will help you quickly get up to speed and provide a foundation of skills that you can build on as you develop applications. If you already have some experience with Access and want to learn how to quickly use the object-oriented capabilities of Access to develop complete applications, the techniques covered in chapters 8 and 9 and in Part Three (chapters 10 through 18) will show how you can do this.

This book assumes that you are familiar with Windows and with using the PC. If this is not the case, you should at least take the Windows Tutorial before proceeding to work with Access (see your Windows documentation for details).

About this book

The book is divided into three parts. The first part of the book introduces the program and provides important guidelines for applications design. The second part of the book, "Putting Access to work," provides a brief overview of the basics of Access, such as designing and working with tables, forms, queries, reports, and macros. This part of the book better serves those whose only exposure to Access so far might have been the online help and the Microsoft documentation. The third part of the book details the different applications (which are provided on the accompanying disk). The different chapters in this section of the book are designed to highlight the different ways that you can quickly put Access to work in real–world applications.

How this book is organized

Chapter 1, "Introducing Access," shows how Access can meet your database management needs and gives an idea of the capabilities of Access.

Chapter 2, "What you can do," is provided as a brief guide to needed concepts, particularly for those whose only exposure to learning Access might have been the Microsoft documentation or the online help. In chapter 3, "Applications design," the major steps needed when designing an application in Access are outlined.

Chapters 4 through 7 cover the four significant Access objects of tables, queries, forms, and reports. In these chapters, you learn how to work with tables, how to establish the relationships that you'll need to support your applications, how to design efficient queries that get at the data you need, and how to design your forms and reports that will be needed by your applications.

Chapters 8 and 9 examine macros, which are at the heart of quick application development within Access. In these chapters, you'll learn how to create macros, how to attach them to other objects in Access, and how to structure complete menu-driven applications using macros.

Chapter 10 provides a brief introduction to Access Basic. While complex applications can be built without a single line of Access Basic code, there are specialized tasks for which Access Basic can come in handy.

Chapters 11 through 18 comprise Part 3 of the book. In this section are the ready-to-run applications (which also are contained on the accompanying disk). If you must develop applications of your own, you can examine the steps outlined in each of these chapters and use the techniques learned to design your own applications. Chapter 11 details assignment tracking; chapter 12 details a sales and order-entry system; chapter 13 details a time and billing system; chapter 14 details a mailing list application; chapter 15 details a real estate showcase system; chapter 16 details a personnel management system; chapter 17 details a payroll processing system; and chapter 18 details a system for tracking client contacts. Finally, an appendix covers hardware and software requirements and the installation process.

Getting the most from Access

The best way to effectively learn Access (or any program, for that matter) is to work with it. This book helps you to do that not only by showing how you can put Access to work in your own applications, but also in providing a variety of ready-to-run applications; chances are one of these is close to what you need to do specific jobs at your company. Copy the databases on the sample disk into your Access directory, and work with the sample applications. After getting familiar with the techniques in Part 2 of this book, try modifying the sample applications to handle specific tasks that you might have in mind. As you do so, you'll gain the real-world experience necessary to put Access to work within any database management task that comes your way.

Icons

The following icons are used throughout this book:

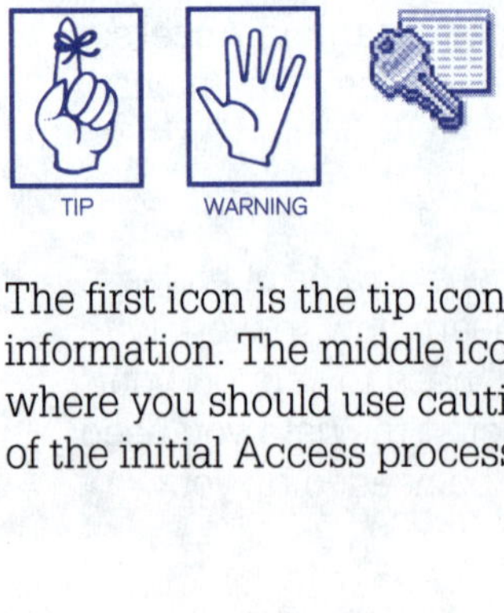

The first icon is the tip icon, which indicates tips and other helpful information. The middle icon is the warning icon. This icon identifies places where you should use caution. The last icon indicates where a continuation of the initial Access process breaks into substeps.

part 1

The basics of Access

1 What you can do

Welcome to Access, a remarkably powerful yet easy-to-use database manager for PCs running Windows. Virtually any task that lends itself to a database manager can be handled with Access. Figure 1-1 shows examples of business data stored within an Access database.

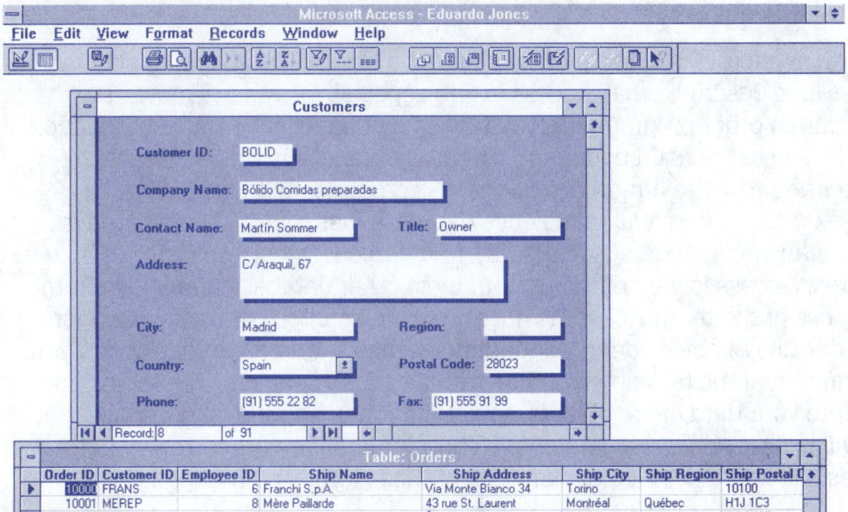

1-1
Access at work.

Business tasks that can be readily handled with Access include the following:

- Bookkeeping—Track the income and expenses of a business
- Sales/order entry and fulfillment—Manage and track orders and shipments
- Clients/contact management—Track client information and provide telephone "tickler" lists
- Mailing list—Manage lists of customers and print mailing labels
- Inventory—Track parts inventory and accounts receivables
- Assignment tracking—Track employee assignments, schedules, and progress

You will find examples of how you can implement all these applications, and more, in the pages of this book. One significant capability of Access is that, without writing program code, you can create and implement applications using Access macros. This book will show you how. The disk included with this book contains all of the applications highlighted in this text, along with sample data that you can use to immediately begin working with these applications. For those readers that do want to deal with programming, Access includes a powerful language known as *Access Basic*. An introduction to Access Basic is provided by this book; however, for all but the most complex or specialized applications, you will not need to know how to program in Access Basic.

About Access

According to Microsoft, Access is a *relational database manager*. This means that, besides being a database manager (a program that can manage your data in the form of tables), Access also is relational (meaning it simultaneously can deal with multiple tables and can draw relationships between those tables). However, if you're reading this book, you probably already have an idea as to the power of a relational database manager.

From an applications standpoint, perhaps the best way to begin explaining Access is to describe what Access is not, especially if you are moving to Access from other programmable database managers like dBASE or Paradox for DOS. Access is not a command-oriented database manager, which requires you to write hundreds of lines of program code to accomplish a complex task. Access will readily use database files that you've created in other database managers like dBASE or Paradox. However, in terms of how it operates, Access is very different from most other database managers. In the true sense of the term, Access is not an *object-oriented* database manager, but it does have object-oriented tendencies in many areas. Hence, it lets you perform numerous tasks by working with a series of objects. The tables that you store your data in are objects, as are the forms, reports, and queries that you will use to work with your data. (Those unfamiliar with forms, reports, or queries will find a detailed explanation of these terms in chapter 2.)

If your background includes experience programming with other relational database managers, a significant design aspect of Access that you might find difficult to become accustomed to is that complex tasks in Access do not require programming. While it is true that some very specific tasks might require programming (and Access has its own programming language called Access Basic for those tasks), in most cases, you can create complex applications without writing a single line of programming code. With Access, what is far more important than a knowledge of programming is a knowledge of how the objects in Access interrelate and how you can manipulate those objects using macros.

To utilize the "power without programming," you will need a thorough knowledge of how you can use the objects within Access, along with the capabilities of macros, to design and implement complete applications. The intent of this book is to provide that kind of knowledge, as well as examples that you can work with. While this book can help you to learn a great deal, you will not learn all there is to know about Access. In Access, Microsoft has created a flexible and complex database manager with a large number of options, and to cover them all in detail would likely triple the size of this book (and increase its cost accordingly). What this book will do is help you quickly become familiar with the major parts of Access. It will show you how you can quickly put Access to work in everyday business applications.

As a relational database management product, Access can work with multiple tables at the same time. Access uses common fields to draw relationships between multiple tables. Figure 1-2 shows an example of various related tables within a Query window.

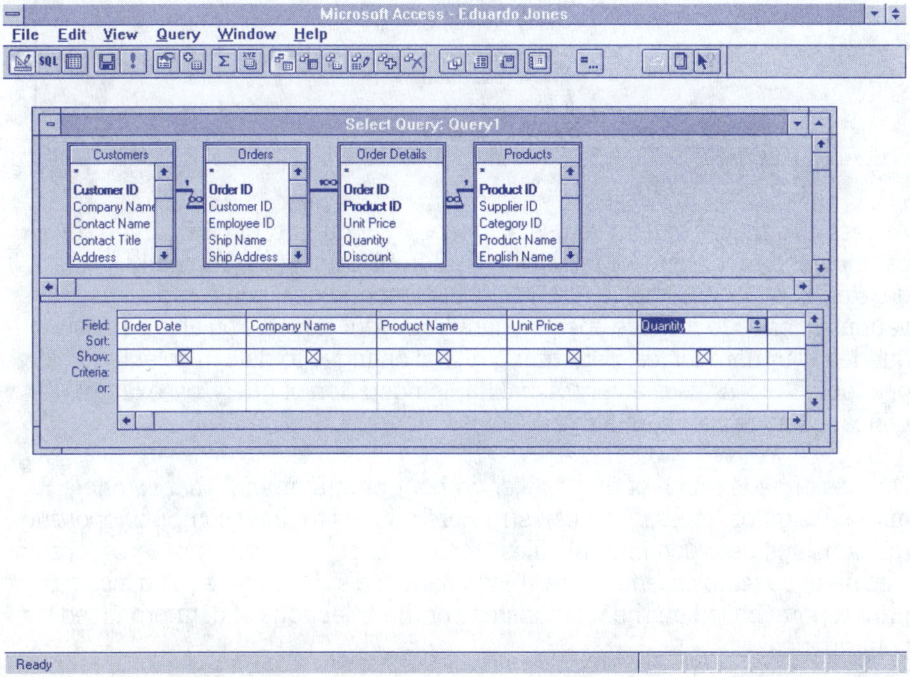

1-2
The Query window containing related files.

In the figure, a number of tables are related to form the basis of a sales tracking application. The lines that appear at the top of the window between the Orders table and the Customers table and between the Order Details table and the Products table denote relationships between those tables. With Access, you can perform queries, sort your data, and generate reports based on the fields in one or more related tables of a database. Using the relational capabilities of Access, you can generate relational reports like the one shown in FIG. 1-3 . The report in the example required no program code to create, and its data is based on the related contents of four tables.

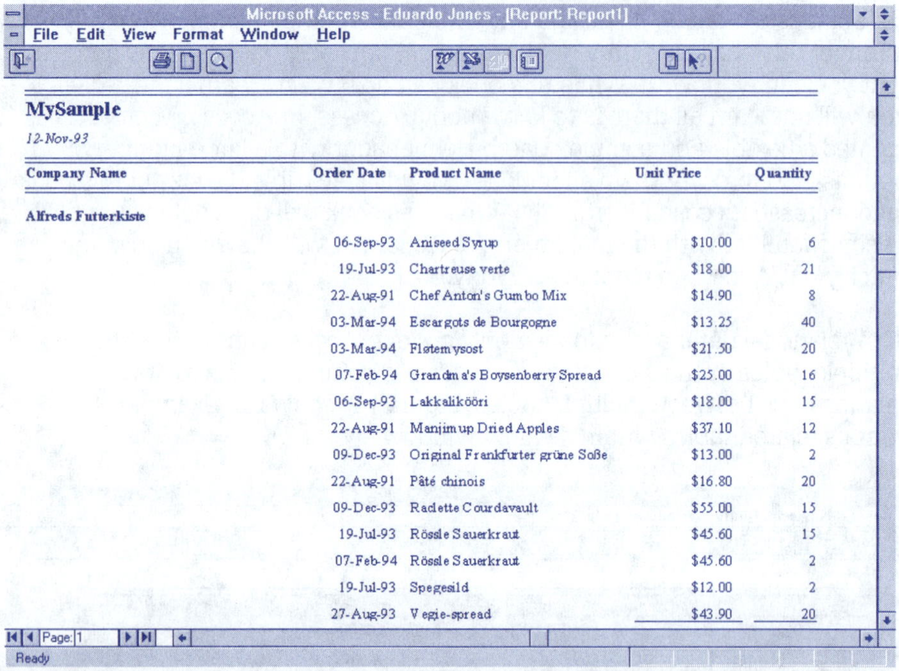

Company Name	Order Date	Product Name	Unit Price	Quantity
Alfreds Futterkiste				
	06-Sep-93	Aniseed Syrup	$10.00	6
	19-Jul-93	Chartreuse verte	$18.00	21
	22-Aug-91	Chef Anton's Gumbo Mix	$14.90	8
	03-Mar-94	Escargots de Bourgogne	$13.25	40
	03-Mar-94	Fløtemysost	$21.50	20
	07-Feb-94	Grandma's Boysenberry Spread	$25.00	16
	06-Sep-93	Lakkalikööri	$18.00	15
	22-Aug-91	Manjimup Dried Apples	$37.10	12
	09-Dec-93	Original Frankfurter grüne Soße	$13.00	2
	22-Aug-91	Pâté chinois	$16.80	20
	09-Dec-93	Raclette Courdavault	$55.00	15
	19-Jul-93	Rössle Sauerkraut	$45.60	15
	07-Feb-94	Rössle Sauerkraut	$45.60	2
	19-Jul-93	Spegesild	$12.00	2
	27-Aug-93	Vegie-spread	$43.90	20

1-3
A relational report.

Access also makes extensive use of Query-By-Example, or QBE. *Query-by-example* is a technique for retrieving data from databases, originally developed by IBM in the 1970s. Using QBE techniques, you can design various queries to retrieve specific data from your tables. You also can use queries to update tables, performing global changes to data in selected fields of a table. Access uses a very visual implementation of query-by-example; a typical query is shown in FIG. 1-4.

Queries provide much of the "power without programming" that is inherent in the design of Access. You can structure queries to draw complex reporting relationships between multiple files. You can design queries to select records that meet specific criteria or to provide data in a specific order. You also can print reports based on the relationships or the selections of data produced by your queries.

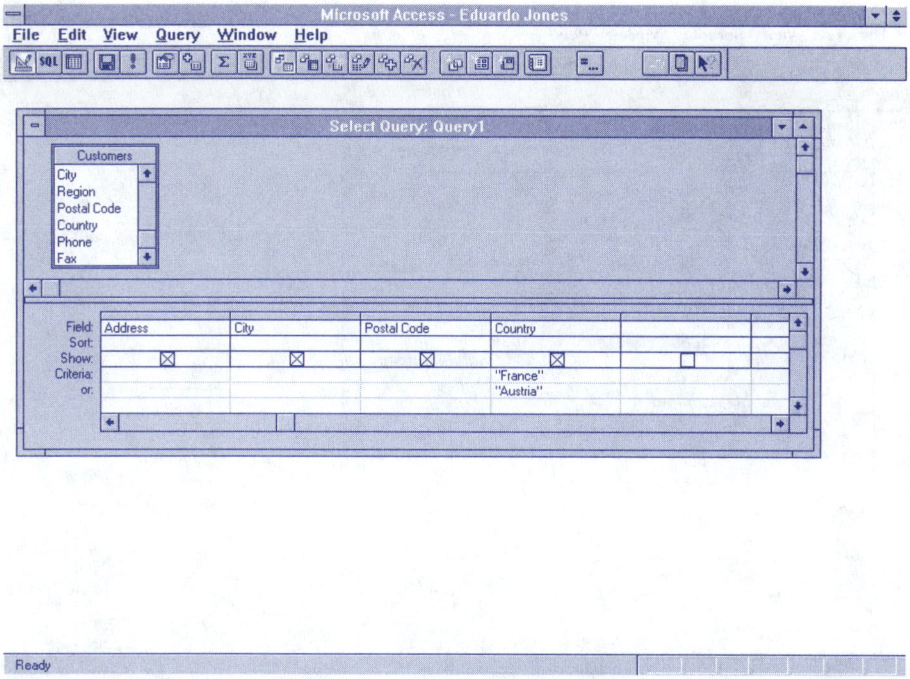

1-4
An example of a query in Access.

Access provides a number of "helpers" to assist you in getting your work done. Like most Windows products, there is an extensive, context-sensitive help system. However, Access provides more than just online help; there also are cue cards and wizards. *Cue cards* provide a type of online tutorial that you can refer to while you perform common database management tasks. *Wizards* also step you through the process of designing tables, queries, forms, reports, and graphs by asking you a series of questions, then creating the desired object for you. Wizards also can be used to create many design objects in Access forms and reports, such as list boxes, combination boxes, and graphs. The chapters in Part 3 of this book make extensive use of the wizards to aid in the fast creation of forms and reports. Figure 1-5 shows an example of a ReportWizard in use.

Once you have created tables; drawn relationships between related tables; designed queries to provide desired subsets of data; and designed forms and reports for the data entry, editing, and printing of data, you can use the menu options and dialog boxes within Access to manage your data. However, you'll need to be familiar with the various menu options in Access. At first, these can appear numerous and complex. If you want others to be able to use the power of Access without the learning curve inherent in acquiring such knowledge, you will need to build applications using macros. With such macros, you can present a user-friendly interface, such as the one shown in FIG. 1-6, to other users in your office or to other clients for whom you must develop complete systems.

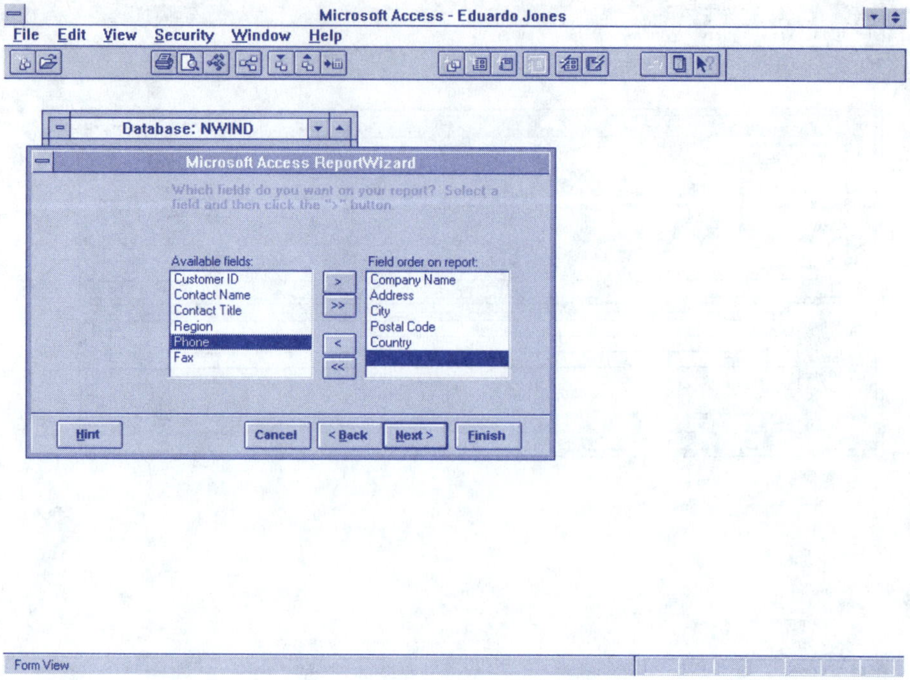

1-5
The ReportWizard used to quickly create a report.

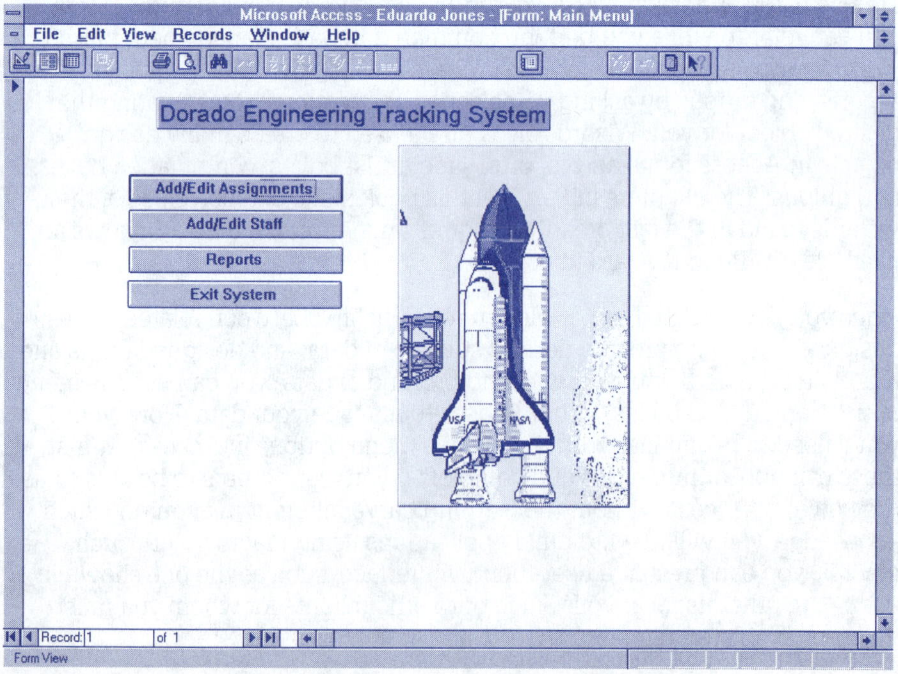

1-6
A main menu for a completed application.

Compared to the competition

Access is one of a new generation of relational database managers, written to take full advantage of the Windows environment. At the time of this writing, it is by no means the only Windows database manager; its competitors include Borland's Paradox for Windows, Approach Systems' Approach, Software Publishing's Superbase 4, and Microsoft's own FoxPro for Windows.

However, many of the competing products came with the built-in drawback of having to maintain compatibility with older, existing standards. In particular, Paradox for Windows and FoxPro for Windows needed to maintain strong compatibility with the file structure for earlier versions of those products, which operated in the DOS environment. To stick with the file formats originally designed for DOS products of an earlier age means that some of the limitations of those products appear in the newer Windows versions.

With Access, on the other hand, Microsoft was able to start with a clean slate. While compatibility with files created by products like dBASE, Paradox, and FoxPro is an integral part of Access, the clean slate approach to design means that Access does many things in a refreshingly different (and often less complicated) manner. Some of the noteworthy features that you'll find as you gain familiarity with Access are described in the following paragraphs.

All objects (such as multiple tables, queries, reports, and forms) are stored in a single database file. Not only does this vastly reduce the clutter of your hard disk, it enables Access to overcome the limitations of naming objects by DOS filenames. Where, in dBASE or Paradox, a table name would be limited to the DOS conventions of eight characters or less with no spaces, in Access, you can call tables whatever you want (of up to 64 characters in length), and you can include spaces.

Access provides a visual QBE (query-by-example). While QBE is nothing new to the database community, rarely has it been implemented in such a visual nature as with Access. With the QBE found in most competing database managers, you must manually type most or all expressions into the various fields of the query to tell the program what data you want to obtain. With Access, you can structure much of your query by dragging items with the mouse into the fields of the query.

Version 1.0 of Access lets you directly attach to files in dBASE, Paradox, and Btrieve file formats. In versions 1.1 and 2.0 of Access, you can attach to all of these formats and to FoxPro files. While virtually all modern database managers let you import and export to foreign file formats, the ability to attach to foreign files goes well beyond typical import/export capabilities. By attaching to a file, you can leave the file in its original foreign file format, and Access can continue to work with and manipulate the data. This is a significant capability in offices where you are sharing data stored using different database managers or in client-server applications where the data is stored on a file server. Access also has the ability to import and export files in FoxPro, Excel, Lotus 1-2-3, and ASCII and ANSI text formats.

Access is designed to operate on local area networks. You can design Access databases that are shared by members of work groups throughout an office. Also, you can use Access as a *front-end*, to work with data stored on a server using a *back-end* such as SQL Server. Security features are built into Access; you can encrypt databases, specify passwords, and identify permissions that will be granted to groups of users.

Object-orientation & applications design

Access applications operate differently than procedural languages in other database management programs in that many portions of an Access application are associated with individual objects in an Access database. Access makes use of *macros*—small, precise groups of directions that you attach to various objects in Access. In many cases, you can save time by using built-in features of Access to perform steps that would require programming in other database management programs.

As an example, to validate data entry with the programming language that is included with dBASE, you would need to write one long procedure to test the entry for each field in a table before the data is stored in the record. In Access, you can include built-in validation in the form of range checking within the definition of the field, and the validation will be automatically performed for any data that is entered in that field.

A suggestion . . .

This book is ideally suited for the user who wants to quickly put Access to work in real-world applications. A significant portion of this book details ways to perform common Access applications, such as designing tables, establishing relationships, entering and editing data, and creating queries, forms, and reports. If you already are familiar with Access and are looking to develop complete applications, you might want to review the information in chapters 2 through 7 and delve more deeply into the book beginning with chapter 8.

Given the complexity of harnessing the full power of Access, it helps to have a basic familiarity with Microsoft Windows before proceeding with this book. This book is written under the assumption that you already are familiar with basic Windows skills, such as sizing and moving windows, and switching between Windows applications. If you are completely new to the Windows environment, you should consider taking the Windows online tutorial before proceeding. (To start the Windows tutorial, from the Windows Program Manager, choose `Help`, then `Windows Tutorial`.)

About the Earth Aware example

Part 3 of this book contains a variety of applications for different business needs. If you are just getting up to speed with Access, you'll want to consider the material in Part 2 before moving on to Part 3. The examples in Part 2 of this book are based on the needs of a fictitious environmental organization called Earth Aware. As a nonprofit organization aimed at promoting environmental awareness, Earth Aware is dependent on the generosity of its members to accomplish its mandates. Two database tasks are of prime importance to an organization like Earth Aware: managing donations and keeping in touch with members. Because a small number of members also serve as volunteers on various projects, the organization also must manage its available volunteers as a resource.

As you work through Part 2 (chapters 4 through 9) of the book, you will be encouraged to work with the tables, queries, forms, and reports that will make up a complete application to manage the database needs of Earth Aware. The hands-on examples used throughout the chapters will demonstrate methods that you can use in designing a database for your specific application. Once you are familiar with databases and applications design in Access, you can use the applications presented in Part 3 as-is, or you can modify them to suit your own needs. (You'll find instructions at the start of chapter 4 on how you can copy the database used by Earth Aware from the accompanying disk onto your system.)

2 Access concepts

This chapter introduces some basic concepts that you will need to know as you work with Access. If you have been using Access for some time and intend to learn how to develop complete applications, you might want to skim over the material in this chapter. If you have worked with other database managers but are new to Access, you should carefully consider the material in this chapter, as many tasks you do in Access require a new way of thinking.

Access & object orientation

The significant difference between Access and most PC database managers that came before it is that Access posesses many *object-oriented* tendencies so that, in many cases, you work with objects to perform tasks. (In the true sense of the term, Access is not a completely object-oriented database manager; rather, it is a relational database manager with strong object-oriented qualities.) Objects in an Access database include your tables, forms, reports, and queries, as well as the macros that you create. Within many of these objects are additional objects; for example, when you manually create a form or a report, you place various objects, called *controls*, at various locations within the form or report. It's this object orientation that makes it possible to create sophisticated applications in Access without writing programs; as this book will show, you can quickly create applications in Access by creating and using various objects, including Access macros. The objects you'll use in Access to develop your applications include:

- Databases, which contain the objects (such as tables, forms, and reports) that you'll work with.
- Tables, which (as explained earlier) contain the individual records where your data is stored.
- Forms, which are used as a window to your tables and queries, to allow adding of new data and editing of existing data.
- Reports, which provide summaries of your data that can be displayed or printed.
- Queries, which are used to select specific sets of data from your tables, and to define relationships between tables.
- Macros, which store groups of instructions to automate tasks within Access.
- Modules, which are programs written in the language of Access Basic.

Databases defined

If you have ever used other PC database managers—particularly dBASE and its derivatives or Paradox—get ready for a fundamental difference when it comes to Access. In Access, a *database* is the collection of objects used to store your data. This differs radically from dBASE and Paradox, where a database is the file that contains an individual table and any forms, reports, or programming code exist apart from the database file. There are advantages to doing things the Access way, not the least of which is the ability to name objects (other than databases) without fighting the ridiculous limitations imposed by DOS filenames.

In computer terminology, a *database* is any collection of related information, grouped together. Often, when defining the concept of a database, it helps to compare computerized databases to the noncomputerized variety, such as filing cabinets of information or a box of 3-×-5" cards containing names and addresses. A random collection of information technically is not a database; what makes the information a database is the fact that the data is arranged in some type of logical order. With computers, information routinely is arranged and stored in the form of tables, with rows and columns in each table. One or more tables containing the data in an organized manner is considered to be a database. Access takes this common analogy further by adding the tools that you use to manage the data—such as queries, forms, and reports—to the database.

Tables defined

Access stores your data in the form of *tables*, which are collections of data arranged in rows of records and columns of fields. This arrangement, commonly used by spreadsheets, also is used by virtually every PC database manager on the market. Each row of the table contains one *record*, or one complete set of information, such as a person in a table of employees or a specific order in a table of customer orders. Each column of the table contains a separate *field*, or type of information, such as the street address of a person or a dollar amount of a particular sale. Figure 2-1 shows a simple mailing list using the popular Rolodex format applied to a table in Access.

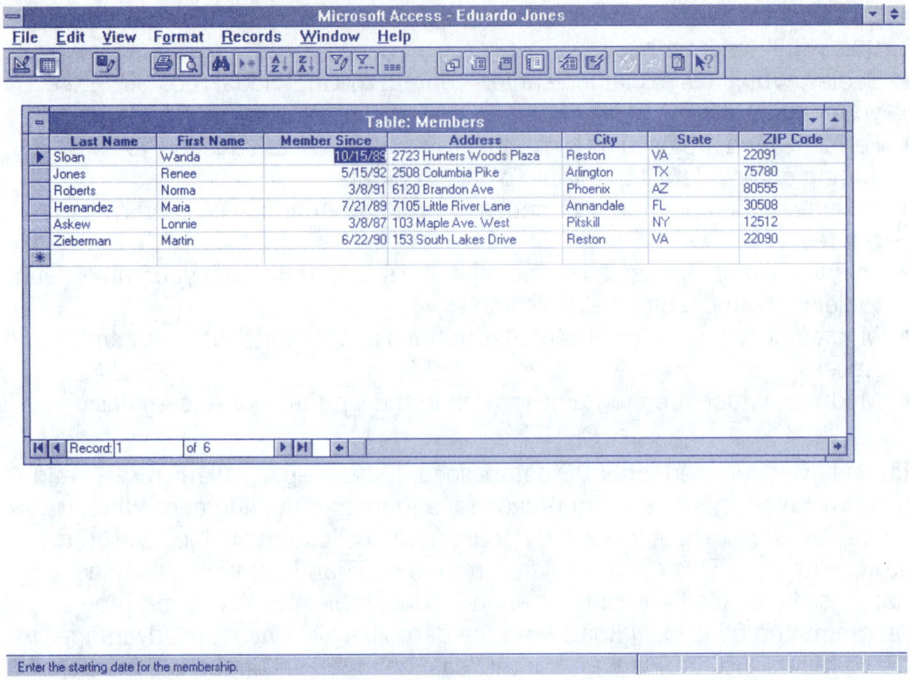

2-1
A mailing list stored as a table.

Queries defined

Once your data has been stored in the form of tables, you can obtain specific subsets of that data by using *queries*. The word *query* literally means "to ask," and Access queries provide a way of asking about your data. You can use queries to find a specific record (such as that of a person named Mary Smith), to print mailing labels for all persons living in a certain ZIP or postal code, or to display all employees who haven't had a performance review in 12 months.

Queries let you display and work with selected data from up to 16 tables at a time. (Queries can be based on other queries; therefore, in the unlikely event that you need to work with more than 16 tables at once, there are ways to do so in Access.) When you design your queries, you identify which records should be included in the results of the query and which fields should be included. You can specify *criteria*, which determine what records of the underlying tables appear in the query. The results of your queries can be used by the forms and reports you create. Access also lets you create *action queries*, which can be used to quickly modify or delete large amounts of data stored in tables.

Forms defined

In Access, you use *forms* to display the data that's stored in your tables or queries. If you haven't used forms in a computerized database before, you can think of them as being computerized equivalents of paper-based forms that are so familiar to businesses. Forms routinely are used for adding new data to a table and for editing or displaying existing data, usually in a one-record-at-a-time format. Using the FormWizards provided with Access, you can quickly create many variations of forms, or you can use the custom form design capabilities in Access to manually design any type of form desired. Forms can be designed to work with data that comes from more than one table at a time. In FIG. 2-2, the form shown is based on a relationship between multiple tables, displaying one record from a table of members along with all detail records showing contributions made by each member. (Chapter 6 details the design and use of forms.)

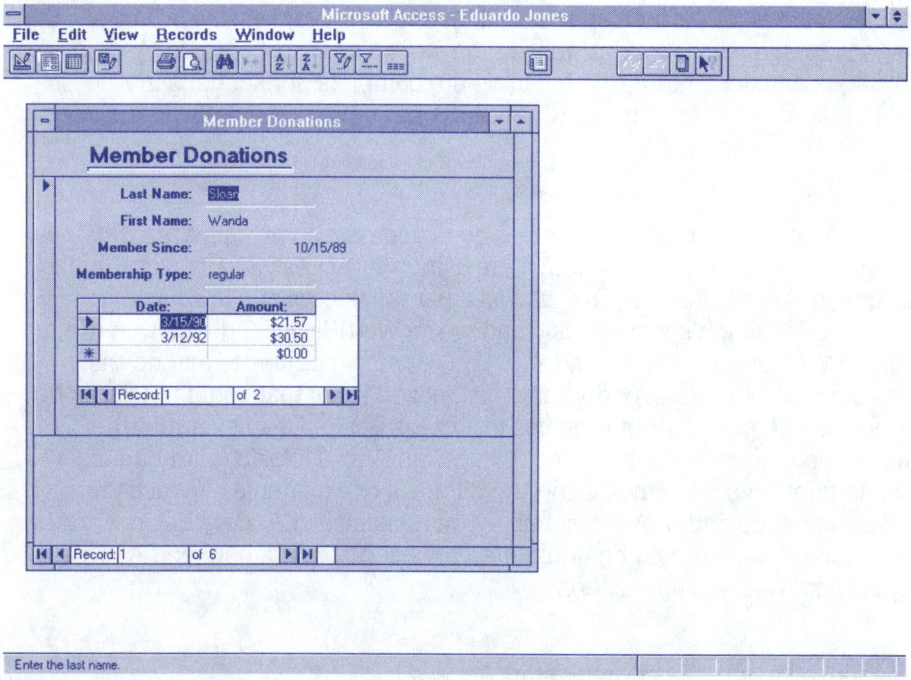

2-2
A form based on multiple tables.

Reports defined

The desired result of any database is to provide information in the form of *reports*, and Access is no slouch in this area. You can print reports from tables or from queries, in virtually any desired format. As with forms, you can design reports manually, or you can use ReportWizards to help you quickly design reports. Reports can contain graphics stored in Windows OLE (object linking and embedding) fields or graphics as decorative items stored in bitmap files by programs like Windows Paintbrush. (Chapter 7 details the design and use of reports.)

Macros defined

In many other programmable database managers, you design complete applications by writing hundreds of lines of program code to accomplish specialized tasks. In Access, you use *macros*, which are groups of instructions, to replace the hundreds of lines of program code required by similar products. When you run the macro, Access carries out the list of instructions. As an example, perhaps you routinely open two forms and a certain report and usually work with these throughout your day. You can create a macro that automatically opens the desired forms and reports and places them on your screen in the desired locations. As another example, if you run a query and export the results of that query to an Excel spreadsheet on a weekly basis, you can create a macro that handles this task.

One major purpose of this book is to show how you can create detailed applications, which will shield novice users from the complexities of Access and enable you to perform specialized tasks quickly and easily. In Access, the key to rapid applications design is in the extensive use of macros. As Part 3 of this book will demonstrate, you can create complete applications in Access with little or no programming. (Chapters 8 and 9 provide details on the use of macros in Access.)

Modules defined

In those rare cases where programming is necessary, you can write *modules*, which are collections of program code using the Access Basic programming language. Access Basic is provided as a part of Access and is similar in nature to Microsoft's Visual Basic and to the WordBasic language that is a part of Microsoft Word for Windows. You can use modules to extend the functionality of Access, performing specialized tasks that could not easily be performed (if at all) without the use of Access Basic. As an example, the application highlighted in chapter 13 uses an Access Basic routine to dial the phone through a modem. Dialing the phone is one example of a task that cannot be done within Access unless you make use of Access Basic. Another common use is in providing automated exchange of data between Access and other Windows applications.

Starting Access

Use the following procedure to start Access.

Step 1 Start Windows in the usual manner. In the Windows Program Manager, open the program group that contains Access (if it is not already open).

Step 2 Double-click the Microsoft Access icon. (See FIG. 2-3.) Access loads, and in a moment, you see the Microsoft Access Startup Window, as shown in FIG. 2-4. (*Note*: If you see a `Welcome to Microsoft Access` menu when you start the program, click the `Close` button to remove it and reveal the Microsoft Access Startup Window. With a newly-installed copy of Access, this welcome screen appears until you disable it by clicking the `Don't display this startup screen again` button.)

Step 3 From the menus, choose `File`, then `Open Database`. The Open Database dialog box (FIG . 2-5) appears. Click the desired database that you want to open, then click `OK`. The Database window appears, as shown in FIG. 2-6.

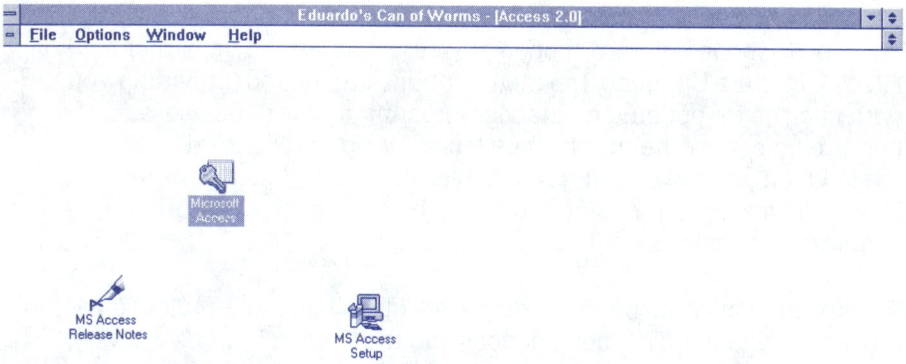

2-3
The Microsoft Access icon.

2-4
The Microsoft Access Startup window.

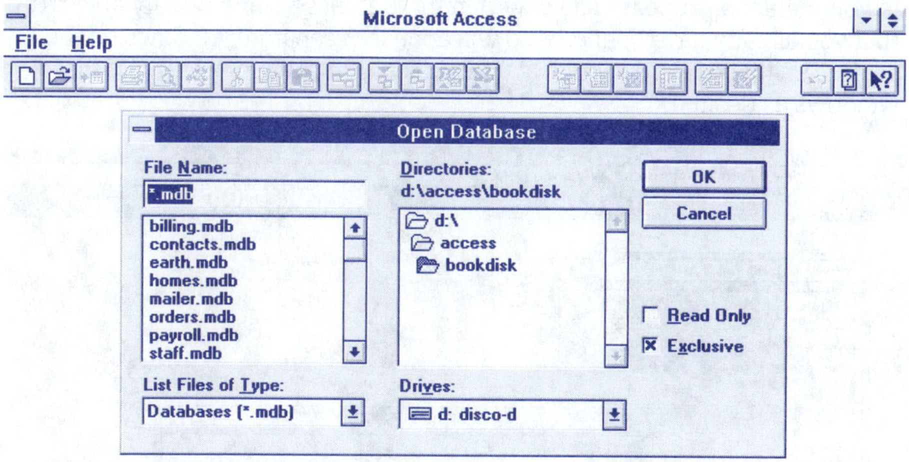

2-5
The Open Database dialog box.

From the Database window, you can create new objects, open existing objects, and design objects. Clicking any of the object buttons at the left side of the window causes existing objects of that type to appear. For example, if you click on the `Forms` button, you will see any forms that are stored in the current database.

The working environment

Once you open a database object (such as a table or form), Access takes on the appearance that it normally has when it is in *Run mode*. (Upcoming chapters will detail how you open and work with tables, forms, reports, and other objects in Access.) Access has three modes in which it operates; the appearance of the main window when Access is in Run mode is shown in FIG. 2-7.

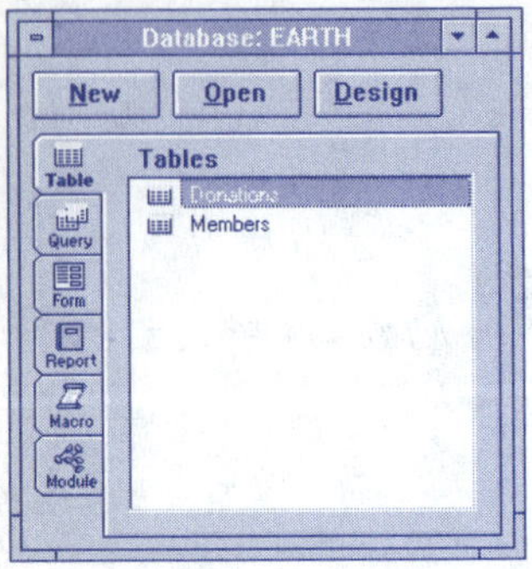

2-6 *The Database window.*

The three modes of Access are *Start-Up*, *Run*, and *Design*. Access is in Startup-Up mode before you open any database, as shown earlier in FIG. 2-4. In Start-Up mode, the menu options are limited, providing you with choices for opening a database, creating a new database, and performing some other utility-type tasks. Design mode is the mode you are in when you are creating new tables or designing forms or reports. How you can work in Design mode will be covered in appropriate chapters later in the book.

As illustrated in FIG. 2-7, Access displays a menu bar and a Toolbar (near the top of the window). The menu options and the Toolbar buttons will vary, depending on where you are in Access and depending on what objects you are working with at a given time. For that reason, various menu and Toolbar options will be explained as they are needed throughout this book. The Database window will be visible (unless you have hidden it with the `Hide` option of the Window menu). In addition, you will see any objects of the type currently selected by the object buttons in the Database window. For example, if the `Table` button is depressed in the Database window, all tables in your database appear in a list within the Database window. Any objects that you already have opened also will appear in separate windows on the screen. Using standard Windows techniques, you can move and size these windows as desired.

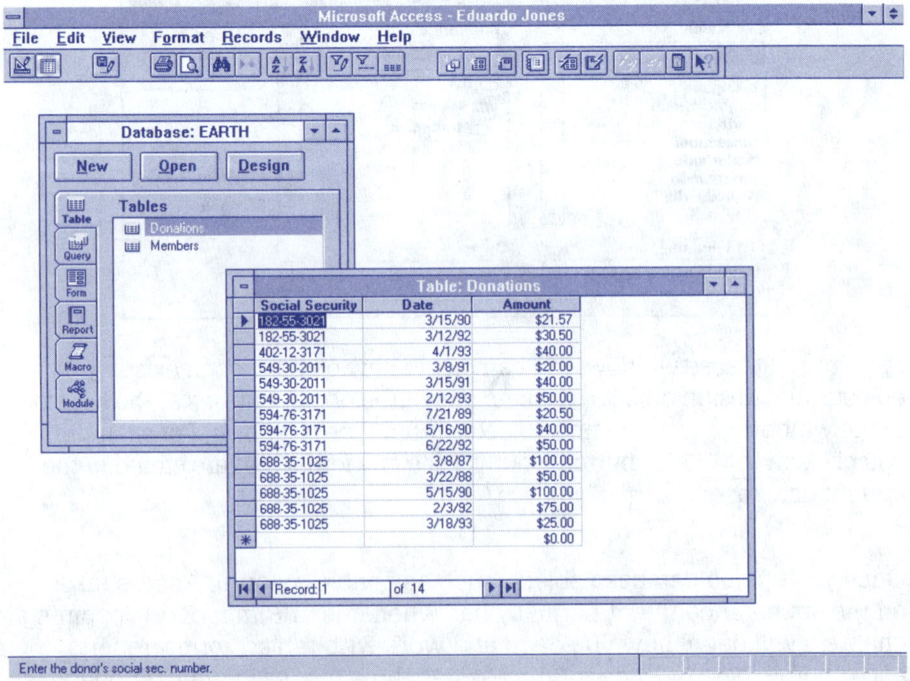

2-7
Access in Run mode.

Using online help

If you need help at any time, it is always available within Access by means of the online help System. If you have used other Windows products, you will find the help system to be familiar; it consists of a series of menus that aid you in finding the information you are looking for. (Access also provides *cue cards*, which is a separate system that helps you do certain tasks; the use of cue cards is discussed shortly.) You can access help by pressing F1, by choosing `Help`, then `Contents` from the menus, or by clicking the Help button (it's the one with the question mark) in the Toolbar.

Like other Windows products, the help system in Access is *context-sensitive*. In a nutshell, this means that Access tries to provide help with whatever you appear to be doing at the present time. For example, if you are designing a form and you press F1, Access will provide a help screen with information about forms. If you are in no particular area when you press F1 (or if you choose `Help/Contents` from the menus), Access displays the Help Table of Contents window, shown in FIG. 2-8. You can click on any of the underlined items to get information about a specific topic.

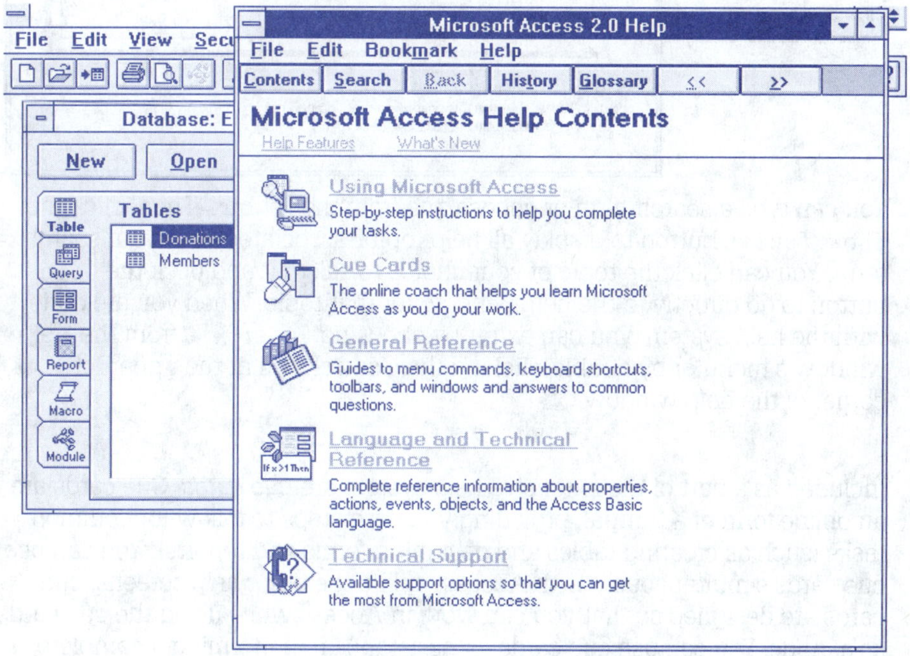

2-8 *The Help Contents window.*

One very useful feature of the help system is its ability to search for specific information. If you choose `Help/Contents` from the menus to display the window shown in the figure, then click the `Search` button, a Search dialog box appears, as shown in FIG. 2-9.

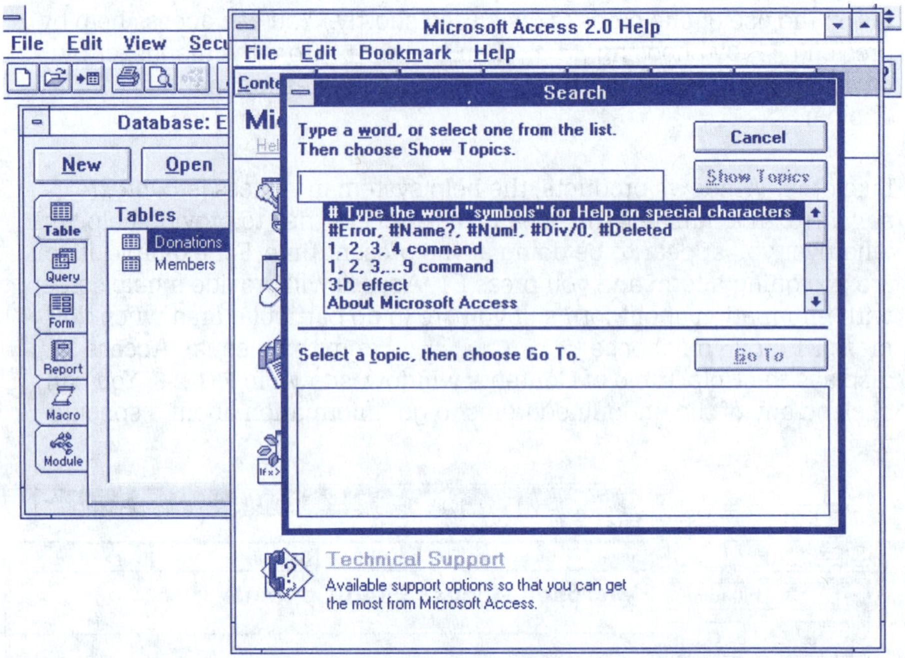

2-9
The Search dialog box.

You can type a search term or choose one from the list box. Then, click the `Show Topics` button to display all help topics associated with your search term. You can click the topic of your choice to select it and click the `GoTo` button to go directly to the help window for that topic. When you are done with the help system, you can exit it by choosing `File/Exit` from the Help window's menu or by double-clicking the Control icon at the upper-left corner of the help window.

Using cue cards

Included as a part of the extensive help system are *cue cards*. Cue cards are an online form of a tutorial, providing you with steps to follow for common tasks (such as creating tables and designing forms and reports). You can use cue cards simultaneously with Access; unlike the other help screens, cue cards are designed so that you can work in Access while using the cue cards as a guide. You can use cue cards for assistance in performing a complete procedure (such as creating a form) or for help with a specific task (such as calculating totals in a report). You can use the cue cards by choosing `Help/Cue Cards` from the menus or by clicking the Cue Cards icon in the Help Table of Contents window.

Exiting Access

When you are done with Access, you can exit the program by choosing `File/Exit`. (If the Database window is the only open window, you can press Alt–F4 to exit from Access.) Be sure to always exit Access in this manner; *never* exit Access, or any other Windows application, by simply turning off the computer while you still are in Windows. In Access, doing so can damage a database. (Note that Access includes a facility for repairing damaged databases; this topic is discussed in chapter 4.)

3 Applications design

This chapter outlines the major steps to follow when you design an Access application, from the planning stage through the process of documenting the application for other users.

Welcome to a brave new world

If you are completely new to applications development, don't feel disadvantaged. In many ways, you are at an advantage, because you have no old and ingrained habits to unlearn. If you are coming to Access from the xBASE (meaning dBASE and dBASE-compatible) world of applications design or from experience in building applications in Paradox or R:Base, you would do well to try to forget everything you've learned about writing applications. (One notable exception to this is Paradox for Windows, which does many things in a manner similar to that of Access.) The school of thought from the xBASE and Paradox for DOS world was similar to the following: after creating your tables, forms, and whatever reports could be managed with the built-in report writer, you sat down and proceeded to write hundreds of lines of program code. Most programmers started with the main menu and went from there, using a top-down approach. Perhaps you used a modularized design, or perhaps you were comfortable with the most nightmarish spaghetti code imaginable. You not only wrote code to handle menus and submenus, you also wrote code to print reports that you could not get the report writer to handle, you wrote code to validate entries typed into forms, you wrote code to handle queries, maintain indexes, search for data, display dialog boxes, and present error messages. In short, you wrote code for darn near *everything*.

If you've built any kind of experience level based on that common method of operation, you might be tempted to install Access, look at what needs to be done, and start using the same old techniques. The real danger is that you can do just that. Using Access Basic, you could write an application if you work long and hard enough at it. To do so, however, would be a phenomenal waste of your time. The object-oriented nature of Access and its flexible capabilities of macros make writing program code necessary in well over 90% of the cases where you had to write code when working with xBASE or PAL (Paradox) code. If there is one point you should try to remember when coming into the Access world as an applications developer experienced in other languages, it is this:

Program code is a necessary evil to be avoided at all costs.

As strange as this sounds, if you can take this rule to heart, you will easily make the jump to the new way of doing things that's required by Access. If you try to stick with the old ways, you will complicate your life unmercifully.

That much said, where should an experienced developer concentrate one's learning time? If you've done applications before and are comfortable with concepts of database design, working with tables and query-by-example, and reports, consider this advice: spend as much time as you can spare with *forms and macros*. Learn all you can about forms and macros (the extensive treatment of these items in this book is designed to aid you in that regard).

The nature of Access' design means that, once you know a great deal about forms, you automatically will know a great deal about reports, for Access uses the same techniques to lay out forms and reports. Macros, as stressed many places in this book, are your key to rapid development of applications in Access. Once you are comfortable with forms and macros, spend whatever time you can working with all the different types of queries available in Access. Armed with a knowledge of these objects, Access itself as a prototyping tool, and your previous experience in database design, you can take on the world's database application needs.

Database design & normalization

If you are unfamiliar with the nuances of database design, you should spend some time learning about proper database design and about normalization before you create your tables in Access. Any carefully-planned computer database involves three steps in the planning process: *data definition*, *data refinement*, and *normalization* (or the elimination of unnecessary redundancies). With relational databases, this process is important, because it helps you to determine when certain data should be stored in separate tables. When someone is new to database design, there is a tendency to create single tables that contain all the data associated with a task. This harmful tendency results in tables that are awkward to use, easy to damage, and wasteful in regard to disk space. The planning process using the steps described earlier helps avoid the kinds of problems associated with such databases.

Data definition

During the first step, *data definition*, you will want to define the categories, or fields, that will make up your database. As you do so, examine your needs carefully to determine the kinds of information that must be stored in your database. Because you initially do this on paper, it is not necessary to try to separate the fields into different tables, as you will tackle this in step 3 of the process. Because attributes are the groups of data that make up a database, any data that you can imagine within a column of a table is an individual attribute, or field. Names, addresses, customer numbers, stock numbers, descriptions, and item costs are common fields that your database might contain. As you plan for the required fields, it often helps to keep in mind what information is needed from the database, in the form of reports. Because the information that the reports provide will be based on the data that's placed in the fields, you will want to be sure that there are sufficient fields to provide the needed data.

As an example of a database, chapters 4 through 9 of this book use the needs of a fictitious environmental organization, Earth Aware, to demonstrate how data can be managed. Earth Aware is a Washington-based nonprofit organization and, like many nonprofit organizations, Earth Aware depends on contributions from its members to stay in existence. Keeping in touch with members (by means of a mailing list and the generation of form letters) is a prime task for the database application used by Earth Aware. In considering the needs for the organization, the staff members determined the need to store and retrieve specific information about each member; the name, address, date of the membership, amount of the donations; and the type of the membership. The initial list of attributes, which will later become the fields of various tables, is shown here:

- Member name
- Member address
- Date of membership
- Donation amounts
- Type of membership

One important point to keep in mind is that, during this phase of database design, it is a wise idea to list all the possible attributes needed by your application. You later might find that some of the categories are unnecessary, but any unneeded categories can be eliminated during the data refinement stage.

Data refinement

During the next step, *data refinement*, you will refine your list of categories so that it more accurately reflects the types of data that will be stored within your database. One tip that can significantly help in avoiding later troubles is to include suggestions from users of the application in the design process. The people who must use the database on a day-in and day-out process are likely to best know what kinds of information they must obtain from the database. As an example, when the staff of Earth Aware examined the initial list of categories, many of the refinements became apparent to them. For example, the staff realized that the old 3-×-5" file card system that had contained the membership names contained multiple occurrences of the same last name. To avoid confusion, the member name attribute was divided into two fields of last name and first name. It also was obvious that the address attribute needed to be divided into fields for street address, city, state, and ZIP or postal code. Because some members also serve as volunteers on certain projects within the organization, the suggestion also was made for the addition of a field that would indicate whether or not a member also was a project volunteer. After the refinement process was completed, the list of fields for Earth Aware looked like this:

- Last name
- First name
- Street address
- City
- State
- ZIP code
- Date of membership
- Donation amounts and dates made
- Type of membership
- Volunteer (yes/no)

In your case, some refinements will likely be obvious, and others might not be so obvious. One step that will help in identifying possible refinements is to go over your written list of fields that were compiled during the first step of the process.

Normalization

The last step, *normalization*, is the vitally needed step whenever you are working with relational databases. In a nutshell, normalization is a process by which data attributes (or fields) are grouped into individual tables. By performing this process, you eliminate any unnecessary redundancies between your tables. Remember that Access is a relational database, so the data stored in one table can be related to the data stored in another. It is important not to lose sight of this fact; it is all too common for users of database management software to create bulky, nonrelational databases. Such an approach can drastically increase the time involved in working with the data and can make the entire application difficult to use.

As an example, the currently proposed design for the Earth Aware database suffers from redundant data in the area of tracking donations. The hope at Earth Aware is that its members will continue to make donations on a regular basis—if this does not happen, Earth Aware won't be around for long. Because only a single amount can be entered into a field, how can the organization track the multiple donations made by most of its members? One way to do so would be to add a new record each time a member makes a donation. However, even the most novice of database users would recognize such a scheme as being terribly redundant, as you would need to enter a new name, address, and so forth for the same member each time a donation was made. Another approach might be to design a table with multiple fields to track donations, with attributes like these:

- Last name
- First name
- Street address
- City
- State
- ZIP code
- Date of membership
- Donation amount #1
- Donation amount #2
- Donation amount #3
- Donation amount #4
- Donation amount #5
- Type of membership
- Volunteer (yes/no)

At first glance, this might seem better, but there still is a problem with this approach. What happens when a long-time member makes a sixth (or seventh, or twelfth) donation? At some point either the staff stops tracking donations, or they overwrite previous donations with new data. The best way to resolve this design flaw is to apply the techniques of normalization to this proposed database and split the information into two tables. One table will contain membership information, and the other table will contain information about the donations made. When the staff refined the proposed data into two tables, this is the initial design that was achieved:

(members table)	*(donations table)*
1. Last name	1. Last name
2. First name	2. First name
3. Street address	3. Date of donation
4. City	4. Amount of donation
5. State	
6. ZIP code	
7. Date of membership	
8. Type of membership	
9. Volunteer (yes/no)	

While this approach presented a much better solution to the needs of the organization, a careful examination of the proposed design showed that redundancies still existed. In the donations table, there would be a need to enter both the last name and the first name of the member, as this would be the only way to link the records in the donations table with the records in the members table. This redundancy can be eliminated through the addition of an identifying field to both tables, containing a value that uniquely identifies each member of the organization. For ease of use, the staff at Earth Aware decided to use social security numbers as a form of membership ID to accomplish this task. Once the new field was added to the proposed design, the use of last name and first name fields in the donations table became unnecessary, and the final list of fields looked like this:

(members table)

1. Member ID
2. Last name
3. First name
4. Street address
5. City
6. State
7. ZIP code
8. Date of membership
9. Type of membership
10. Volunteer (yes/no)

(donations table)

1. Member ID
2. Date of donation
3. Amount of donation

Whenever you must have related tables, it helps to have a field that will always contain data that is unique to a record. Employee ID numbers, customer numbers, stock numbers, transaction numbers, and part numbers are examples of fields that commonly are used to establish relationships between tables. If the design of your application does not lend itself to a unique field, remember that Access lets you include a special field type, called *counter fields*, which contain numbers that Access automatically adds as you add new records. The values that Access places in counter fields will be unique. So, in many cases, you can use these as a means of identifying records in a unique fashion.

Remember that, even after you refine your database design and create the tables in Access, no database design is set in stone. If you later find that additional fields are needed, you can always add them. If you find redundant data that should be placed in multiple tables, you can create queries that will extract the data you need, then store that data into new tables. However, such steps represent work after-the-fact. The ideal is to take the time to plan your database from the start, so major changes later will not be needed.

Relationship types defined

If you plan on developing applications in Access, you also should be familiar with the types of relationships that must be established between tables of a relational database. In the world of PC-based relational database managers, there are three types of relationships that you must deal with: *one-to-one*, *one-to-many*, and *many-to-many*. (The names all refer to how many records in the first, or "parent," table are related to how many records in the second, or "child," table.)

One-to-one relationship

As an example, when a field in one record in a table relates specifically to a field in one record in another table, you have a *one-to-one* relationship. Figure 3-1 illustrates this concept.

Employee ID	Last name	First name	Salary	Hired
B101	Johnson	Ivan	402.80	3/22/86
D422	Klose	Hans	618.90	9/17/77
X297	Battle	Terence	592.85	6/22/83

Employee ID	Insurance	Cost
B101	Blue Cross	122.50
X297	Kaiser	97.50
D422	Prudential	117.50

3-1 *A one-to-one relationship.*

In this example, taken from a personnel database, one table contains employee names and addresses. Another table contains medical and dental benefit information for each employee. Each employee has one record detailing the health and benefit information, and each employee has one record detailing the name and address. The tables are linked by means of the Employee ID field. Because one record in the Medical table is related to only one record in the Names and Addresses table, we have a one-to-one relationship.

One-to-many relationship

By comparison, consider the example illustrated in FIG. 3-2. This figure illustrates a typical one-to-many relationship. In this case, a Customers table contains a list of names and addresses for customers of a mail-order company. A second table, Orders, contains a listing of all orders placed by a customer. Because customers (hopefully) will order products from the company regularly, each customer record can be related to many records in the Orders table. The result is a one-to-many relationship between the Customers table and the Orders table.

Many-to-many relationship

Finally, a type of relationship that is less common, but nevertheless possible, is the many-to-many relationship (illustrated in FIG. 3-3), where many records in one table can be related to many records in another table. A common example is that of student tracking at a university, where many students are assigned to many different classes.

Soc. Sec.	Last name	First name	Phone
121-55-8765	Smith	Susan	936-1212
155-90-2325	Robinson	Walter	555-2201
502-33-4567	Anderson	Benjamin	555-2310
900-55-2345	Hernandez	Maria	555-6271

Soc. Sec.	Matter	Description	Hours
121-55-8765	Avon Farms	electrical	20
121-55-8765	Fox Farm	electrical	12
900-55-2345	Wood Lakes	hvac	23
900-55-2345	Fox Farm	hvac	15
502-33-4567	Golden Pond	plumbing	27
502-33-4567	Fox Farm	plumbing	12
155-90-2325	Fox Farm	electrical	14
121-55-8765	Golden Pond	electrical	22
900-55-2345	Golden Pond	hvac	12

3-2
A one-to-many relationship.

Social	Last Name	First Name
123-44-5678	Johnson	Ivan
121-33-9876	Klose	Hans
232-55-1234	Battle	Natalie
901-77-3456	Hairston	Steve
121-90-5432	Edhardt	Ann

Class No.	Title	Room	Teacher
S100	EarthScience	204	Smith, R.
S101	Biology	210	Linder, B.
S102	Chemistry	205	Robbins, C.
H100	World History	114	Klein, N.
H101	Amer. History	121	Jones, R.
T100	Auto Repair	B14	Vasquez, J.
T101	Microcomputers	B12	Jones, E.

3-3
A many-to-many relationship.

For those just beginning to gain experience with relational database design, a common question is how does one determine where relationships are needed. There are no firm rules, but applying the concept of normalization (described earlier) can accomplish much in making relational needs more obvious. As always, analysis of the task at hand on paper can help to define the types of relationships needed.

Steps in system design

When you design a complex application, it's essential to follow some pattern of design steps to ensure that what the user gets will bear more than a passing resemblance to what the user actually wanted. This is true whether you are following guidelines in a college textbook or have these steps laid out in your head. Proper application design can be broken down into a series of specific steps. While different individuals might approach this task with some variation as to the exact steps and when they are performed, the following can serve as a guideline:

1. Obtain the design specification from the users (this process often is referred to as problem definition).
2. Define the output requirements.
3. Define the input requirements.
4. Define the tables and relationships needed.
5. Define the other objects (in the form of queries, forms, and reports) needed.
6. Outline the menu structure of the application.
7. Develop the application, using the object-oriented techniques of Access.
8. Test and debug the application.
9. Document the application for the users.

Step one

The first step is to obtain the design specification from the users. It can save you more wasted time than any other step in this entire process. To different developers, *design specification* means different things, and here is where you can quickly get into a morass of difficulties. To some programmers, a "design spec" is a one- or two-line statement, as when a user of a proposed application says, "Give us a program to handle our mailing list. Here are the categories we presently use." The programmer goes off and writes an application that he or she thinks is just what was needed and shows it to the users. After the users have asked for three dozen major changes to the application, it becomes evident that a more detailed design specification should have been requested in the first place.

Unfortunately, it is rare that users will provide a clear design spec from the start. More often than not, you must make an effort to get the users to give you a complete design spec. In a more complete design specification, each proposed field in each table is reviewed with the user. Here are some questions that you should consider asking if the users don't volunteer the information:

- Are sufficient fields noted in the design specification to perform the task?
- Are the right types of fields being used?
- What kinds of data entry screens do the users want to see?

If the application is for a work group, it makes sense to initially meet with both the person who requested the application and with the entire group. Effective problem definition is a repetitive process that calls for meeting with users, presenting proposed solutions, getting user suggestions, refining those proposed solutions, again meeting with users, and repeating the process until the users and the programmer are thinking along the same lines.

Step two

The second step is to define the output requirements. Starting with the application's output might seem like putting the cart before the horse, but the output of an application is what's important to the users. Data-entry is simply a means to an end. The whole purpose in purchasing Access (or any database management package) is to help gather and manipulate data so that it can be presented in some form of a report. The desired reports become critical in designing a system. Some questions you should ask include these:

- What will the users want from the report?
- How should the reports be formatted?
- What relationships must be drawn between multiple files to produce the desired reports?

Often, users aren't fully aware of what kind of reports they can get or whether they really even want printed reports as opposed to an onscreen response to a query. A recommended approach is to take the contents of sample reports based on sample data to show the users. (Here, the ability to rapidly prototype reports in Access will be a big help.) What's important is to create something that looks like what you think the finished product should represent. More often than not, the users will have something else in mind. By taking a red pencil to those sample reports, you can create more concise plans for the actual reports required by the application.

Step three

The third step is to define the input requirements. Armed with the output requirements, you can proceed to develop, on paper, pseudo data-entry screens that the users will use to enter the data. This will seem like a marginally useful task only to those who have not developed database applications for a wide range of users. Those who have developed applications in the past know that users will make seemingly nit picky requests for changes in the layout of data entry forms and that laying them out first on paper will save much time in redesign later.

Forms also should be designed clearly so that they minimize possible errors. Make entry forms as straightforward and as foolproof as possible. (Note the qualifier "as possible." For every designer who thinks he or she has designed a truly foolproof system, there is a fool lurking in the wings waiting to prove the designer wrong!) However, common-sense additions—clear messages, help screens, data validation, and error-handling—can do much to minimize possible user errors.

This also is the time to think about where all the data will come from and whether overall designs of the application can be adjusted to make the data-entry process simpler. If you are converting a manual system to computerization for the first time and printed forms have been used to record the information, it often makes sense to design your entry forms so that they mimic the existing paper-based forms.

If the data already exists in other, somewhat incompatible formats (such as on magnetic tape or in the form of printed reports from some outmoded time-sharing system no longer in use), don't be too quick to write off such data as unusable for your application. Scanners can read in hard copy, and there is no shortage of firms that will convert computer tapes of 8-inch floppy disks to ASCII text. Certainly your work will increase, as you must import the data into Access tables and clean up any unacceptable data. However, the potential savings in reduced data-entry time might far exceed your increased programming time.

Step four

The fourth step is to define the tables and relationships that are needed. Once the output and input requirements are stable, the design of the needed tables can be laid out. If you follow the initial steps in the process described in this chapter, it should be clear what fields and tables are needed to support the application. Relationships between multiple tables should be determined at this point, and any unnecessary fields that were suggested during the design specification phase should be eliminated. You also should consider what fields will be needed as key fields to better organize your files and provide the fastest sorting and reporting times. Also avoid the trap of duplicating unnecessary information in a table; instead, use the relational capabilities of Access to find the needed information in other tables.

Step five

The fifth step is to define the other objects (in the form of queries, forms, and reports) that are needed. Based on your feedback from the users of the system, you can proceed to design the forms and reports that will be needed, as well as the queries that will act as a source for the forms and reports. At this stage of the design process, it often is a wise idea to begin working with test data. Experimentation with the kinds of data that the users actually will enter will help refine your reports and ensure that your queries can provide the kinds of results that the users want.

Step six

The sixth step is to outline the menu structure of the application. Create a diagram showing the design of the menus needed to perform the application. If you are comfortable with computer flowcharts, they can prove useful for this purpose. Having a clear definition of the structure of the application taped to a nearby wall helps when you are hours into the design of a large application and trying to remember where report #14 must use query #4 as a record source. If you've developed applications in other languages, you are likely to be familiar with the benefits of modular program design. The object-oriented qualities of Access take this a step further; you can modularize your applications to a significant degree by copying, modifying, and reusing various macros, forms, reports, and queries throughout your application.

During the application design stage, a number of global decisions that will affect the individual parts of the application must be made. If the application is a transaction-based one (such as an inventory or a client-billing system), different parts of the application must share common tables and manipulate the same data in different ways. Because of such interactions, very complex applications first can appear to be massive tasks. However, any large application becomes manageable as a design task if it is broken down into a series of smaller steps.

Step seven

The seventh step is to develop the application, using the object-oriented techniques of Access. With all the pieces in place, you can proceed to develop the application. Most of your work here consists of designing macros that will link the needed actions with your various menu options. In a sense, Access lets you take a building-block design approach to creating applications, using the Access objects as the building blocks. If you are accustomed to top-down programming techniques, you can continue to use that basic methodology. (For nonprogrammers, *top-down coding* refers to the practice of starting an application's implementation with the overall part of the application that controls choices through the entire system. In most applications, this is the main menu.)

While a menu calling other menus might seem like the logical way to do things, don't get locked into a rigid design philosophy simply because it's the "way things have always been done." The event-driven nature of Access means that you often can provide more convenient ways for users to do things. For example, if a user wants to print a record after viewing that record through a form, it is somewhat ridiculous to make the user traverse through menu options to do this when a `Print` button on the form could accomplish the task in a single step.

An advantage of the object-oriented design inherent in Access that isn't readily apparent until you've written a few applications is that many of your macros can serve as part of your library of application development tools to be reused, with appropriate modifications, in future applications. You can create a library of your most commonly-used macros, then each time you design a new application, you can copy macros from the library as needed to handle common tasks in the new application. This drastically reduces the debugging time required for future applications and leaves you free to concentrate on improving applications in ways that you have not used before.

Step eight The eighth step is to test and debug the application. This obvious step is one that is all too often given the short shrift. Take the time to load tables with sample data and do all of the things that users will do when the application has been released to their use. Try to make the application fail and see if the results will be too much for the users to handle. Choose options that are invalid. Press the Enter key alone when data should have been entered into a dialog box. Users will do all of these things and more, and your application should be prepared to deal with these occurrences before its release.

Step nine The ninth and final step is to document the application for the users. Provide the users with documentation that describes the operation of the application. Include steps clearly detailing what users should do when things don't go as they should. If you are designing a major application, you owe your users clear documentation that includes both a description of how the application operates and a section that provides a reference guide for more experienced users. Your documentation is not likely to be as exhaustive as Microsoft's, but complex applications deserve more than a page of poorly written text that provides little more than a description of how to start the program. A sample of quality documentation might include the following:

- A table of contents
- Sections that explain how to add, edit, and delete records
- A section that describes how to print reports
- A section that describes how to search or query the database
- A section describing the use of any additional tools or utilities (such as routines for exporting files)

A real mark of quality documentation for novice users is the inclusion of a tutorial section. A well-written tutorial will contain examples of every common procedure the system requires (for example, how to edit records in the system).

None of the steps of application design outlined here should be considered significantly more important than the others. Application design is a multiple-step process that provides the best results if all of the steps are followed. Adherence to the complete design process will leave your users with an application that does the job and one they understand.

part 2

Putting Access to work

4 Working with databases & tables

This chapter will cover databases and tables with an emphasis on how you will use tables throughout Access.

Creating a database

As detailed in chapter 2, an Access database contains all the tables, forms, reports, queries, and macros associated with an application. Before you can create any tables to store your data, you first must create a database. You can create a database in Access by performing the following steps.

Step 1 Choose `File/New Database`. In a moment, the New Database dialog box (FIG. 4-1) appears.

Step 2 In the File Name text box, type the desired name for your database. Assuming you are running Windows 3.*x*, you must follow the DOS filenaming conventions when you choose a name: eight characters or less and no spaces. By default, Access adds an extension of .MDB to the filename that you enter.

If you want to save your database in a different directory than the current one, you can use the Directories list box within the dialog box to choose another directory. Double-click on the desired directory (you can click on the Drives list box to select a different disk drive). After selecting the desired directory, enter the file name for the database.

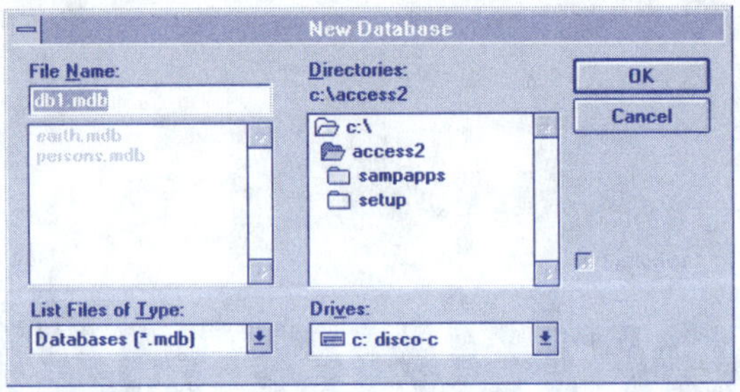

4-1 *The New Database dialog box.*

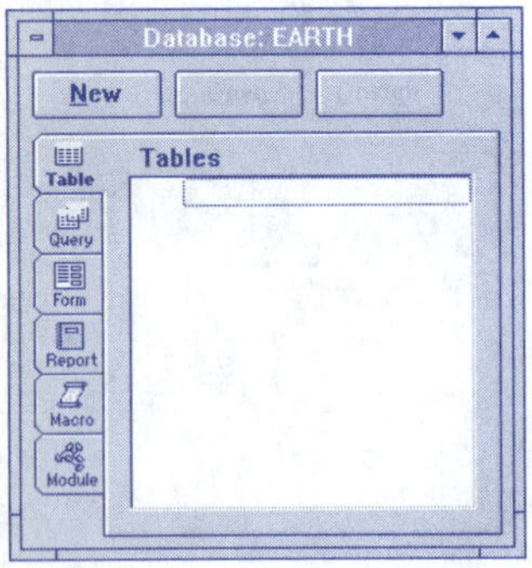

4-2 *The Database window.*

Step 3 Click OK. Access creates the database file within the specified directory. When this process is complete, Access displays the Database Window (FIG. 4-2). The Database window contains *object buttons*, for displaying the various objects that you'll create, and *command buttons* labelled New, Open, and Design.

Note that Access reserves 64K of disk space for each new database that you create. This might sound like a large amount, but much of this space is used to store data that helps Access manage all the objects that you will store in the database. As you add data and create forms, queries, and reports, the database size will grow as needed. In version 1.0 of Access, databases can be as large as 128Mb in size. In Access versions 1.1 and above, the maximum size of a database is 1 gigabyte.

Once you have created the database, the next step is to create the tables that will store your data. Once the tables have been created, you can proceed to create the queries, forms, and reports that you'll use to manage your data.

Hands-on practice: opening the example database

The database used in examples throughout Part 2 of this book, EARTH.MDB, is stored on the accompanying disk. If you want to work with this database rather than creating your own examples from scratch, you can copy it into your Access directory now by performing the following steps.

Step 1 Start Access, if you haven't already done so, and insert the accompanying disk into your disk drive. Press Ctrl–Esc to bring up the Windows Task List (FIG. 4-3).

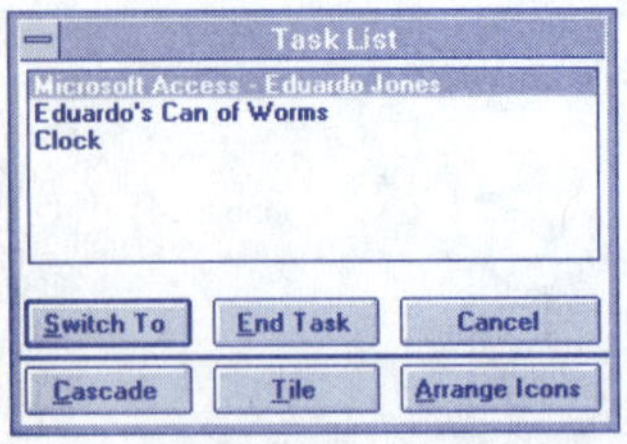

4-3 *The Windows Task List.*

Step 2 If File Manager is visible, choose it from the list. If File Manager is not on the list, choose Program Manager. Then, from the Program Manager window, find File Manager (by default, it is placed in the Main window) and double-click it to launch File Manager.

Step 3 With File Manager visible, click drive A or B as is appropriate. When you do so, EARTH.MDB appears among the files in the directory window. Click EARTH.MDB and, while holding the mouse button, drag it over to your current hard drive. For example, if Access is installed in your drive C:, you would click and drag EARTH.MDB over to the icon for drive C:.

Step 4 Windows will ask if you want to copy the file to the Access directory. Click `Yes`, and the file will be copied into your working Access subdirectory.

Step 5 Press Alt–F4 to put away the File Manager. Press Ctrl–Esc to bring up the Task List, and choose Microsoft Access to get back into Access.

Step 6 To open the database that you've copied from the disk, choose `File/Open Database` from the menus and select EARTH.MDB in the list box, then click `OK`.

Creating a table

As mentioned in chapter 1, Access stores all data in the form of tables. If you are importing or attaching to existing tables (such as from data in dBASE or Paradox format), you need not create new tables. However, if you are going to enter new data from scratch, you will need to create tables in Access to handle your data.

Access 2.0 offers two ways to create tables. You can do so manually, in which case you must tell Access how you want to design, or structure, the tables; what names you want for the fields, what sizes and data types the fields should be; and whether or not you want to apply any specific properties to the fields. (All of these topics are discussed further under "Creating a table manually" that follows.) You also can use the Table Wizards to create the table; if you use the Table Wizards, you choose from one of a number of common table designs (such as mailing lists, inventory, customer lists, or expense account transactions), and Access can automatically create the table for you. Users of version 2.0 of Access can use whichever method is preferable; users of earlier versions of Access must resort to creating the table manually.

Creating a table with the table wizards

To create a table using the table wizards, click the `Table` button in the Database window, then click `New`. In the New Table dialog box that next appears, click `Table Wizards`. In a moment, the Table Wizard dialog box appears, as shown in FIG. 4-4. If the table that you desire is to be based on a common business application; click the `Business` button underneath the Sample Tables list box. For tables based on personal applications, click the `Personal` button underneath the Sample Tables list box.

After choosing the desired type of application (business or personal), scroll up or down in the Sample Tables list box as is necessary and click a table that matches the type of job that you want to perform. Once you select a sample table in the Sample Tables list box, a list of suggested fields for that table will appear in the Sample Fields list box.

If you want to use all the fields in the Sample Fields list box in your table, click the double-right arrow button, and all the fields will appear in the list box titled `Fields in my new table`. You also can choose specific fields to be added, one at a time. Click any desired field in the Sample Fields list box to select it,

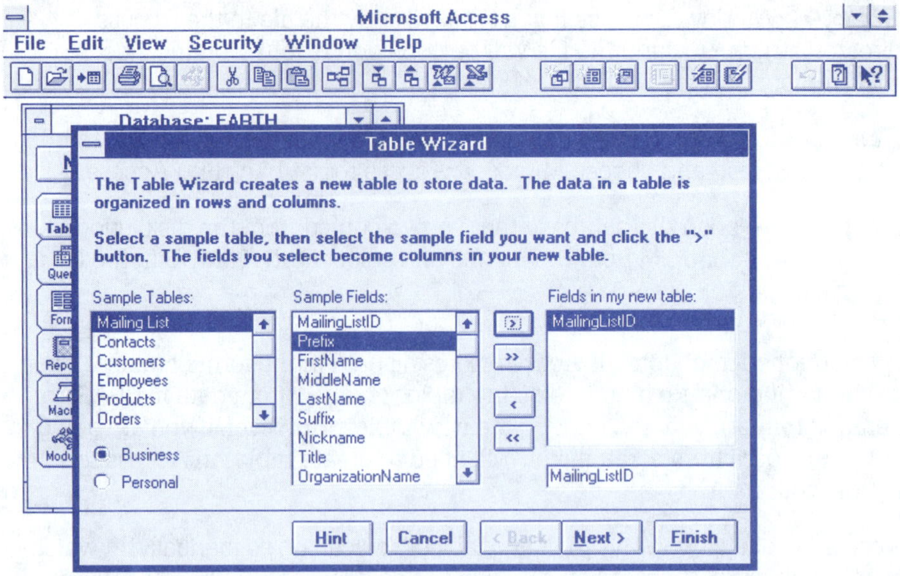

4-4 *The Table Wizard dialog box.*

then click the single-right arrow button to add just that field to the Fields In My New Table list box. Repeat this step for as many fields as are desired.

When you have finished choosing the fields that will be included in the table, click `Next`. The dialog box that now appears, as shown in FIG. 4-5, asks for a name for the table and whether you want Access to automatically define a primary key. (As explained further under "Creating a table manually," Access uses a primary key to uniquely identify each record in a table; this makes Access more efficient and speeds searches and sorts.) Enter a name for your table in the Table Name box, or accept the name that Access suggests. Leave the "Let Microsoft Access set a primary key" option turned on then click `Next`. The final dialog box to appear informs you that you have completed the process of designing the table. In this dialog box, you can click `Table Browse` to open the table in Datasheet view, or you can click `Form Browse` to automatically create and open a new form for adding data to the table. (Forms are discussed further in chapter 6.)

Creating a table manually

To create a new table without the aid of the wizards, click the `Table` button in the Database window, then click `New`. In the New Table dialog box which next appears, click `New Table`. This causes the Table window to appear in Design view, as shown in FIG. 4-6. (Along with the Table window, you might see a Table Properties window open. This will be detailed shortly.)

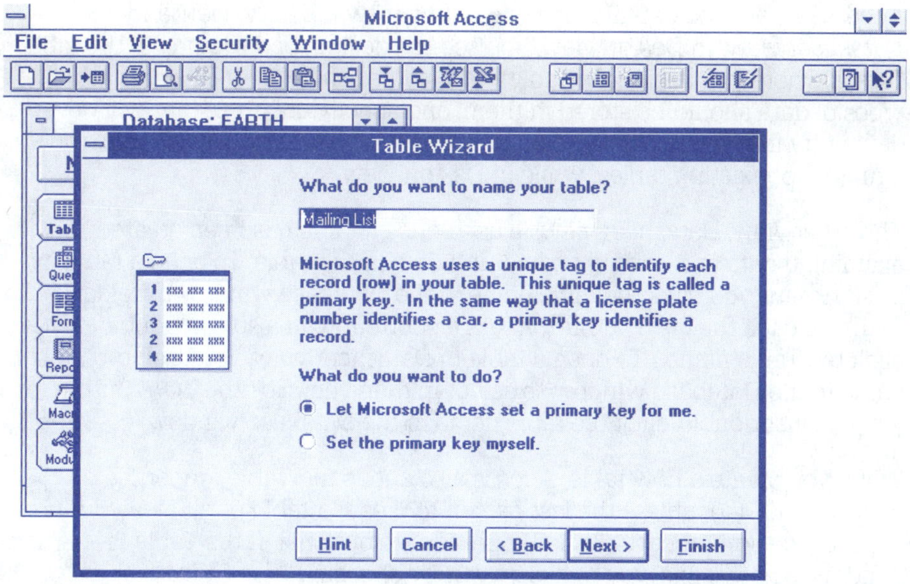

4-5
A prompt for a name in the Table Wizard dialog box.

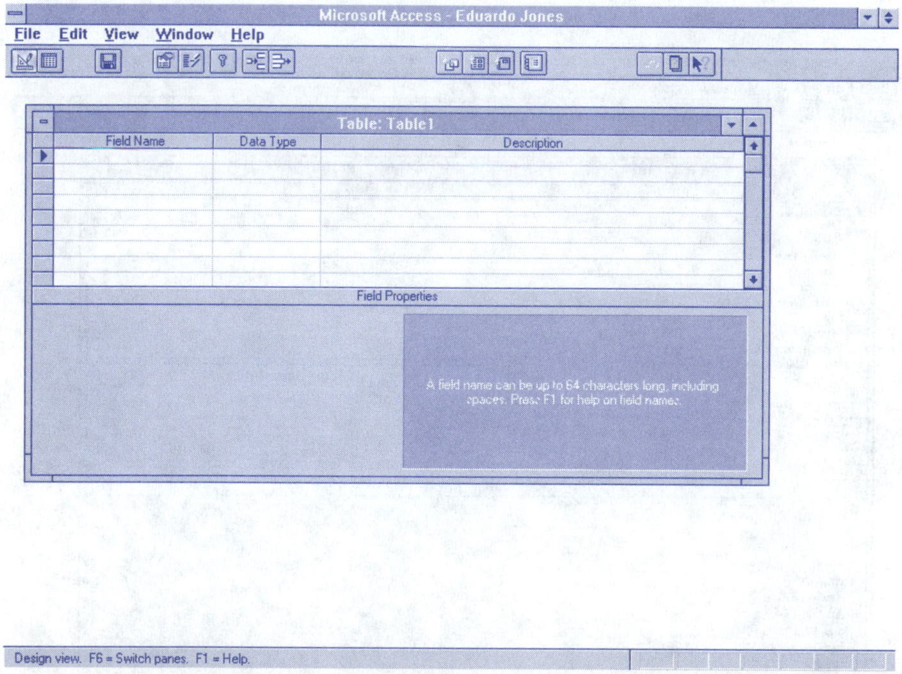

4-6
The Table window in Design view.

Access lets you look at tables in one of two views; *Design view* and *Datasheet view*. In Design view, you see the design, or structure, of the table. This is where you design the table—you name the fields, tell Access what types of data should be stored in them, and specify any rules that will govern data entry into the table. You can create new tables, as well as change the structure of existing tables, while in Design view.

The other view, Datasheet view, is used once a table has been created, for examining data and adding and editing data in the table. To open a table in Design view, you click the table name in the Database window to select it, then you click the `Design` button. (As a shortcut, you also can double-right-click the Table name.) To open a table in Datasheet view, you click the table name in the Database window to select it, then you click the `Open` button (or you can just double-click the table name in the Database window).

When you create a new table, Access also opens the Table Properties window (FIG. 4-7), unless the last person to create a table put it away during the table design process. Table Properties are optional. If the Table Properties window is not visible, you can display it by choosing `View/Table Properties` from the menus or by clicking on the Properties icon in the Toolbar. In the Table Properties window, you can enter an optional description of the table. Below the description (in version 2.0 and above) appear text boxes that let you enter Validation Rules and Validation Text. These entries can be used to perform validation before new data is accepted.

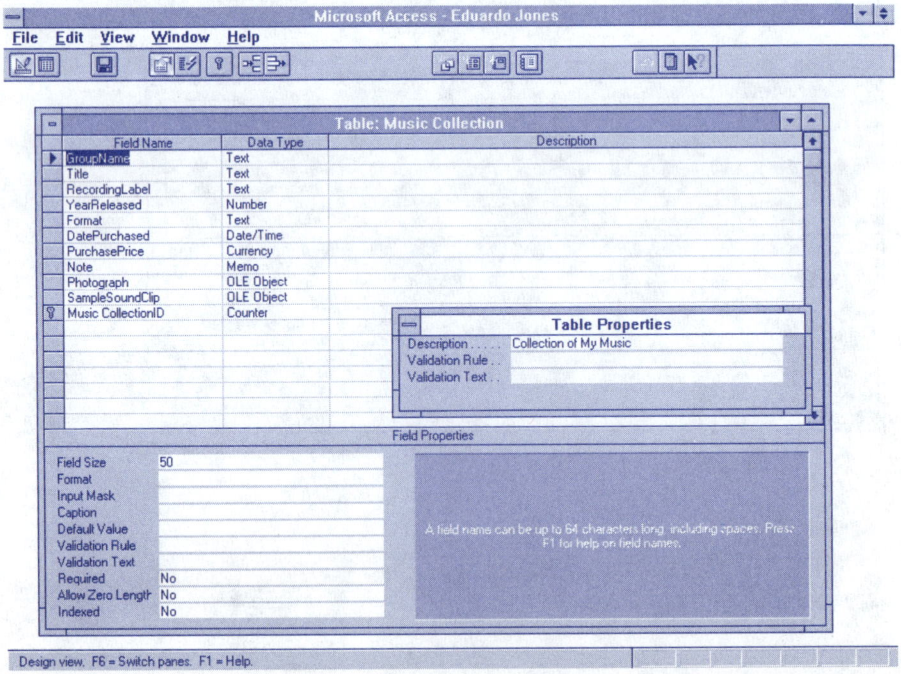

4-7
The Table Properties window.

You use the `ValidationRule` and `ValidationText` options to help the user enter valid data during the data-entry process. As an example, when a record is added for a new employee in a personnel table, you can require that the entry in a Date Hired field fall between the first date of operation for the company and today's date. In versions of Access prior to version 2.0, below the description, you will see the name of the primary key (if one has been assigned) and any secondary indexes that have been added. Primary keys and secondary indexes are both discussed later in this chapter.

The Table Window is divided into three columns: Field Name, Data Type, and Description. Under the Field Name column, you type the name for the field. Field names can be up to 64 characters in length and can include letters, numbers, spaces, or punctuation marks. Considering the flexibility of Access, it is a good idea to give fields descriptive names; for example, the name "Weekly Salary" might make more sense than a field name of "Wk Sal." However, avoid using field names that are overly long, as these can complicate matters when you are trying to design columnar reports. The field names might be so long that it becomes difficult to fit as many columns as you might prefer.

After entering the desired field name, press Tab, and the insertion pointer will move to the Data Type column. In this column, you specify the data type for the data that will be stored in the field. By default, Access assigns a data type of Text. You can change this default by clicking the arrow to cause the drop down list box of data types to open. (See FIG. 4-8.)

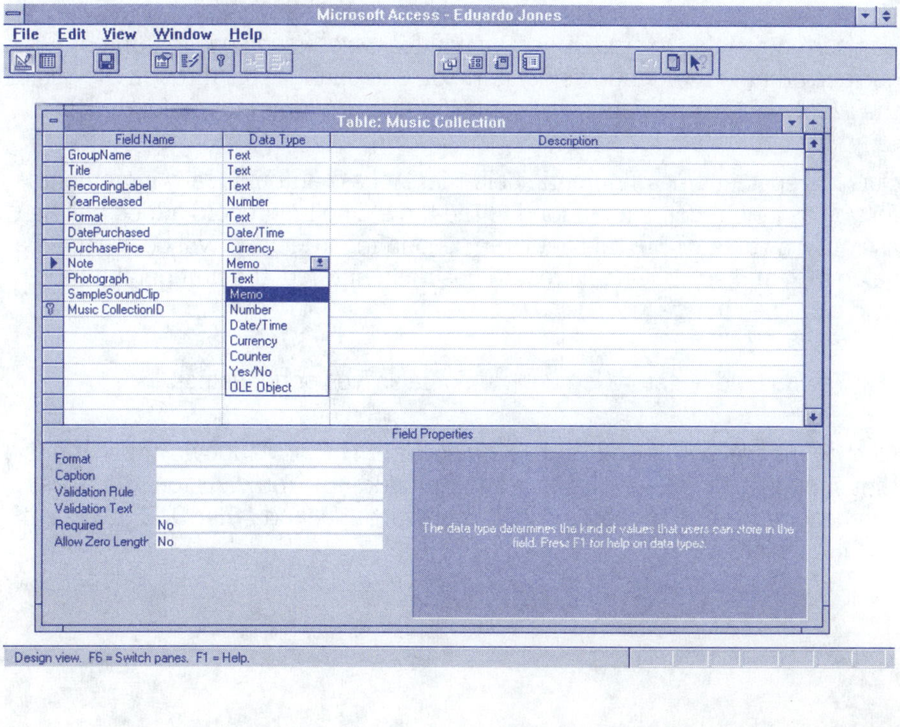

4-8
Drop-down text showing the data types.

Access allows a choice of eight types of fields. They are described in the following sections.

Text fields

Use text fields to store any combination of characters, including letters, numbers, any special symbols, and blank spaces. Up to 255 characters can be stored in a text field. Access defaults to a field size of 50 characters, although you can change this by clicking in the Field Size box and changing the default value to your desired value.

Memo fields

Memo fields are fields that you'll use to store large amounts of text (typically, text that is too large to fit in a text field). Up to 32,000 characters can be stored in a memo field for each record.

Number fields

Use number fields to store numbers other than currency, with or without decimal places. You'll want to use number fields for values that must be calculated. Numeric entries that are not calculated or that might contain hyphens (such as phone numbers, postal or ZIP codes, or part numbers) should be stored in text fields.

Date/time fields

These fields are used to store dates or times. Access will automatically reject invalid entries, such as dates that don't exist (13/34/99). You can use arithmetic with date/time fields. For example, you can subtract one date from another to display the number of days between two dates, and you can add a number of days to a date to display another date.

Currency fields

Use currency fields to store monetary values. Access will use the unit of currency that is the Windows default. You can change this through the use of the Windows Control Panel (see your Windows documentation for details).

Counter fields

This is a special type of numeric field that Access automatically increments for you as new records are added to the table. The first record added will be assigned a value of 1 in this field, the second record added will be assigned a value of 2, and so on. Once a record has been entered, the number in this field can't be changed.

Yes/no fields

Use Yes/no fields to store logical (true or false, yes or no) values.

OLE object fields

OLE object fields are used to store objects from other Windows applications that support OLE (Object Linking and Embedding). You can store graphics, spreadsheets, word processing documents, sound, and other OLE objects in an OLE Object field.

ress Tab again to move to the
ou can enter an optional description of
the field.

users, because they appear in the status
ough the form.

n for the field, press Tab again, and the
t field. You can continue entering field
or the remaining fields as desired.
mbers table from the sample database, in

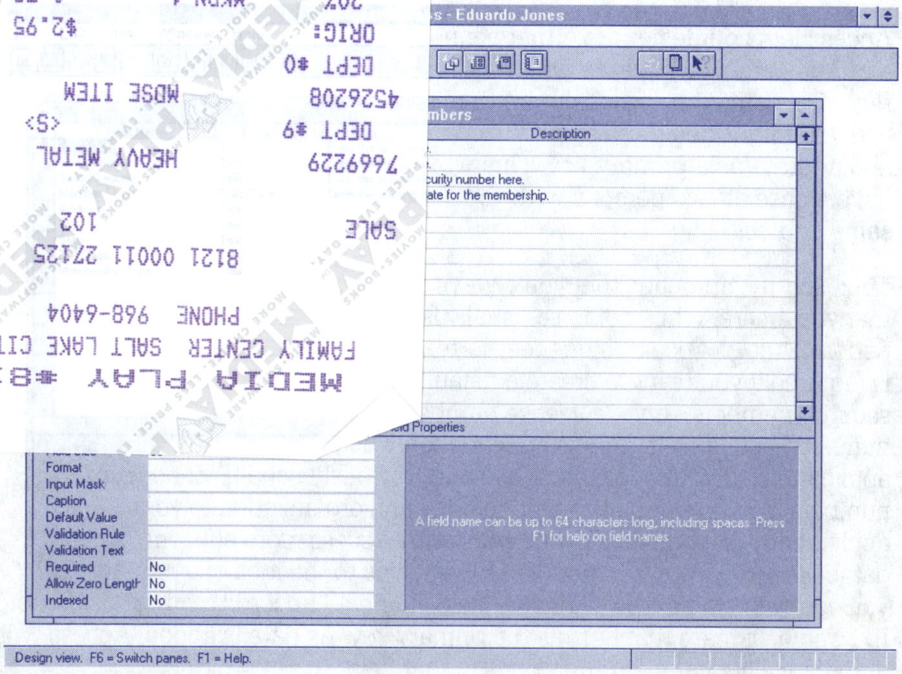

4-9
The Members table in Design view.

Field sizes & text fields

As mentioned, when you specify a field as a text field, Access defaults to a field size (in the Field Properties area of the window) of 50 characters. Note that this value is a maximum value, but Access does not use all of this space for the actual storage of records. Access uses *variable-length fields* to store textual data; therefore, unlike some database managers, if you enter a value that contains 12 characters, Access will use only 12 characters to store the data, and not 50. However, you should realize that the value in the Size properties box is a maximum value; if you leave it set to the default of 50 characters, you will not be able to store any more than 50 characters in that field within any given record. If you plan to store larger amounts of text, you might want to increase the size in the Properties box or consider using memo fields to store the text.

Adding a primary key

Access lets you define any field as a *primary key*. Simply put, a primary key is one or more fields that uniquely identify every record stored in the table. With primary keys, what is important to remember is that Access will not let you place the same data in the primary key field (or fields) of more than one record. For example, it would not be a wise idea to designate a "Last name" field as a primary key; if you then were to enter a record in the table with the last name of "Smith," you would never be able to enter another record in that table with that same last name.

Access lets you designate either a single field or a combination of fields as a primary key. So, in cases where no single field will serve as a unique record of data, you can use more than one field. For example, in a mailing list, you might decide to specify a combination of last name, first name, and address as a primary key. This would suffice, assuming that you never have a case of two persons with the same last and first names living at the same address.

Microsoft recommends that you always specify a primary key for the tables that you create. While doing so usually is not required, it will speed the performance of Access in queries, sorts, and other operations. (A primary key is required if you want to create a default relationship between tables.) Social security numbers, driver's license numbers, employee numbers, part numbers, or invoice numbers are commonly used as primary keys in business applications. If your application has not previously used ID or account numbers, now might be the time to add such organization to your application, as it will make your work with Access more efficient. When database applications do not lend themselves to the idea of a primary key, you can define a field as a Counter field, name it "Record Number" or "Record ID," and designate that field as the primary key. As data is added, Access will automatically increment the values in that field.

To set the primary key, perform the following steps.

Step 1 Click anywhere in the field that you want to use for the primary key. If you want to create a primary key based on more than one field, hold down the Ctrl key and click the field selector to the left of each field you want to include.

Step 2 Click the `Primary Key` button in the Toolbar or choose `Edit/Set Primary` key. When you do so, Access adds a primary key indicator to the left of the field or fields you've specified (FIG. 4-10).

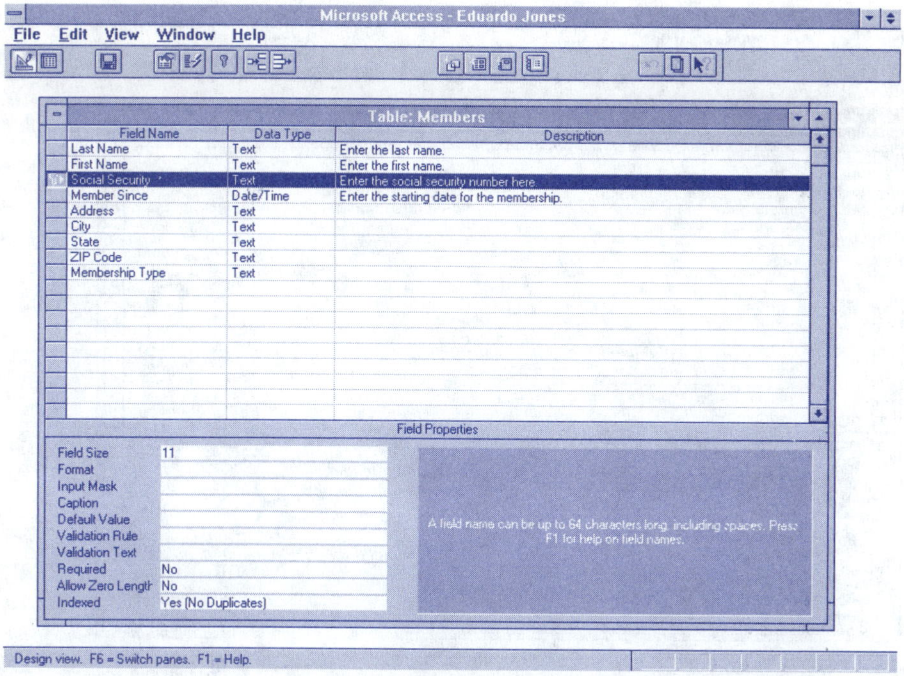

4-10
The primary key indicator.

Keep in mind that, unless you are using a sorted query, Access displays records in your table in primary key order. So, if there is a particular order you'll use most often when viewing or printing your data, it makes sense to try to design the table so that the primary key keeps the table in the desired order. (You can sort a table using any fields you want. See the end of this chapter for details.)

TIP

Using multiple-field primary keys

Where possible, it makes sense to specify a single field as a primary key. In some cases, however, this is simply not feasible. There might be no field in a record that is unique. If you can't convince your organization to add some kind of identifying field (such as a member number, stock number, or a customer identification number), you can create a key based on a combination of fields. As an example, consider the table structure shown in FIG. 4-11.

In this table, designed to store records of rented videos from a video store, there are fields for a customer ID number, the title of the video rented, and the date of the rental. None of these fields could be used alone as a primary key, for there will likely be duplicates in each of these fields. However, you could create a primary key, by selecting all three fields (to do so, you would hold the Ctrl key while clicking the Field Selector at the left edge of the fields), then you would click the `Primary Key`button on the Toolbar. As shown in the

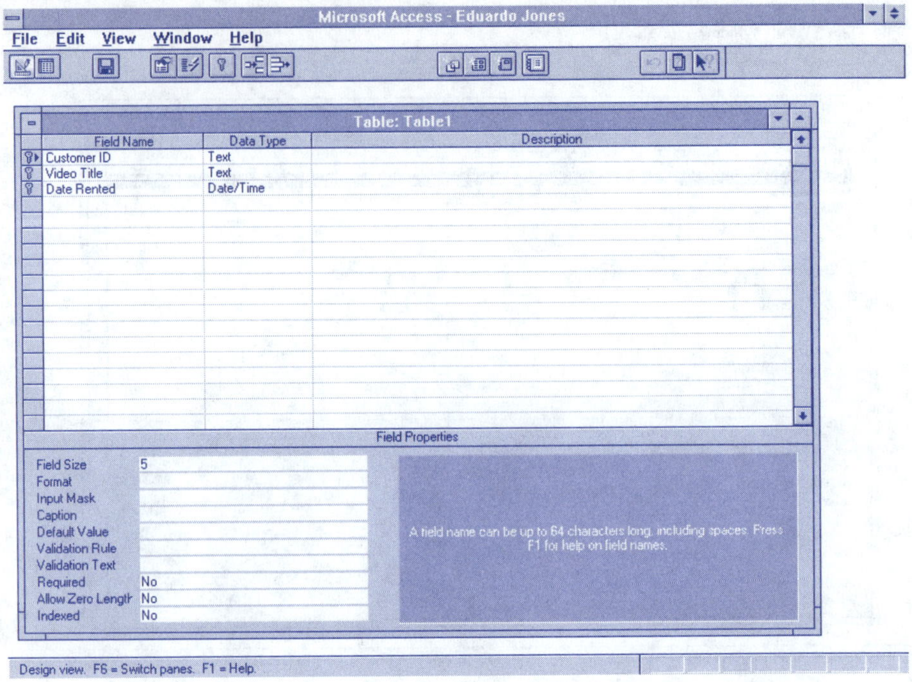

4-11
The table structure with the multiple primary keys.

figure, the key designations that would appear in the Field Selectors would show keys in each field, indicating that the fields combined serve as a primary key. This would suffice for this application, assuming the same customer never rents the same video twice in the same day.

Rearranging & deleting fields

"Nothing in life is permanent save change," the saying goes. You can easily change, rearrange, or delete fields as needed in any of your tables. To change a field, just click where the change is needed and make the desired change, using the Backspace or Del keys to delete existing characters.

To move a field, first select the field by clicking the Field Selector to the left of the field name, as shown in FIG. 4-12. Then, click the Field Selector again and, while holding the mouse button depressed, drag the field to the desired location.

To delete a field, first select the field by clicking the Field Selector. Then, press the Del key or choose `Edit/Delete Row`.

To insert a new field at a specific position in the table, place the insertion pointer anywhere in the desired row and choose `Edit/Insert Row`.

Saving the table

Once you've completed the process of defining a table's structure, you must save the table before data can be added to it. To save a table, perform the following steps.

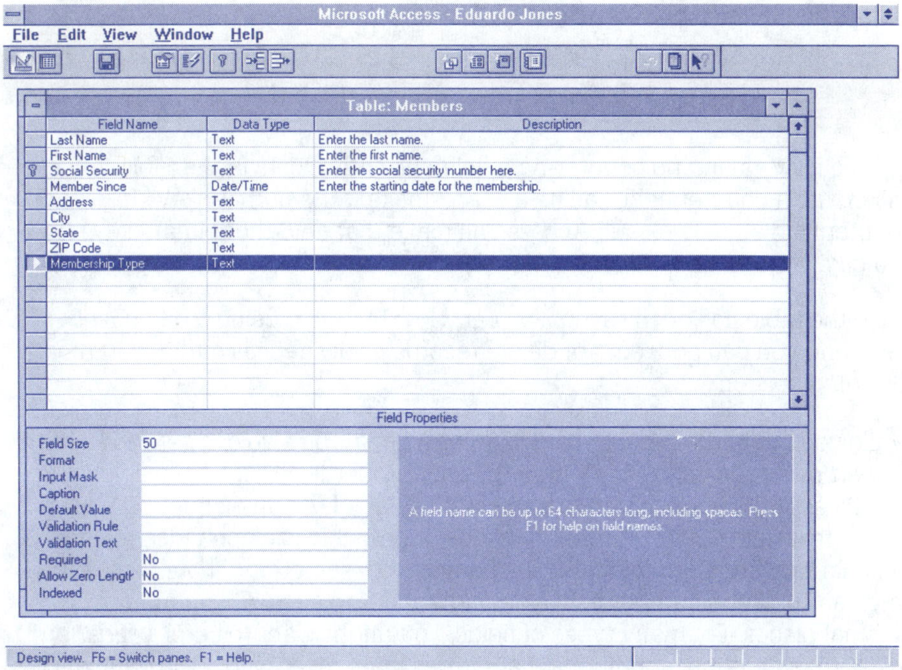

4-12
The Field Selector.

Step 1 Choose `File/Close` or double-click the Control menu icon (it's at the upper-left corner of the Table window). The dialog box shown in FIG. 4-13 appears. Click `Yes`. The Save As dialog box appears, as shown in FIG. 4-14.

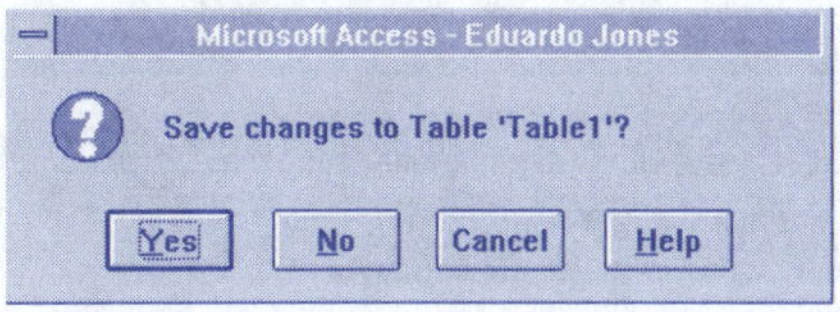

4-13
The save reminder dialog box.

4-14
The Save As dialog box.

Step 2 Type the desired name for the table. Note that you are *not* restricted to DOS filenames here; you can use any names up to 64 characters in length for your tables (as well as for your forms, reports, and queries that you create). Table names *cannot* contain periods, exclamation points, brackets, or leading blanks.

Step 3 Click `OK`. If you did not define a primary key for the table, Access will ask if you desire one now, by displaying the dialog box shown in FIG. 4-15.

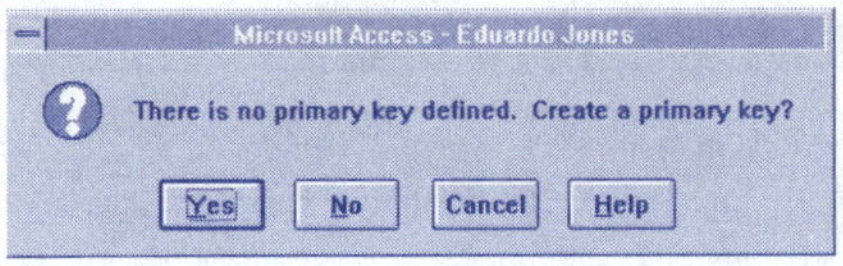

4-15
A dialog box for including a primary key.

If you click `Yes` and no counter-type field currently exists in the table, Access will create a counter field, call it "ID," and make it the primary key. (If a counter field already exists, Access will make that field the primary key.) If you click `No`, Access will save the table structure without a primary key.

Once the table has been saved, you can view the table using a datasheet view, and you can add, edit, or delete records as desired, as outlined in the following section.

Setting field properties

While you are in the process of designing a table, you also can set *field properties* for the table. Field properties are properties assigned to fields that tell Access how you want data stored or displayed. As an example, if you have a text field that will store ZIP codes, it probably is a good idea to change the field size from the default of 50 characters to something more reasonable (such as 10). For a number field, you might want to specify a number of decimal places. For many types of fields, you might want to enter *validation rules*, which identify conditions that entries must meet before the data will be accepted into the table.

During the design process, you can see the field properties for each field in the Table window; when you click in any field, the field properties for that field are visible in the bottom half of the Table window, as shown in FIG. 4-16.

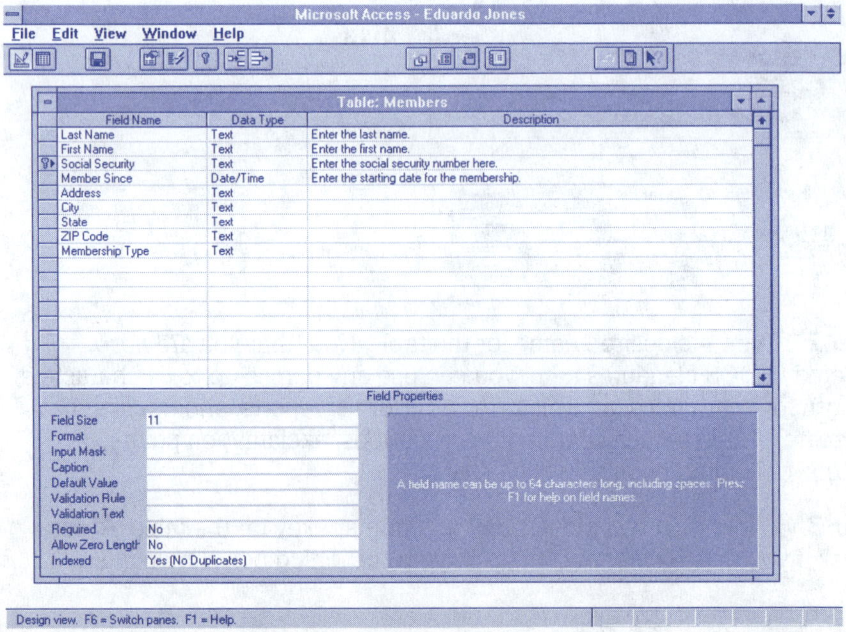

4-16
Field properties in a Table window.

The properties that you can define will vary, depending on what data type is chosen for the field; for example, number and currency fields let you specify a number of decimal places as a field property.

TABLE 4-1 details the field properties, and their uses.

Table 4-1
The property fields and their uses.

Property	Description
FieldSize	Maximum length of a text field, or limits a number field to data within the data type's range.
Format	Determines how data is displayed. You can use predefined formats or enter your own custom formats.
DecimalPlaces	Determines the number of places to the right of the decimal.
Caption	Specifies a default field label in new forms and reports.
DefaultValue	Specifies value that automatically appears in a field when new records are created.
ValidationRule	Limits entries in the field to data that matches specified data entry rules.
ValidationText	Specifies text that appears if invalid data is entered.
Indexed	Specifies single-field indexes to speed searches.

To set a property for a field, you perform the following steps.

Step 1 Open the desired table in Design mode (in the Database window, select the desired table, then click `Design`).

Step 2 In the upper portion of the Table window, choose the field whose properties you want to set by clicking anywhere in the field (or move to the field using the arrow keys, then press F6 to move to the lower portion of the Table window). Click the property that you want to set in the bottom portion of the window.

Step 3 If a down arrow appears in the box, click the down arrow and choose the desired property from the list that appears. If no down arrow is present, type the desired property into the text box.

If you are unsure about what to enter as a property, you can get help by first clicking the property in the bottom portion of the window, then pressing F1.

Using validation rules

A powerful feature of Access, called *validation rules*, lets you control how data can be accepted into the fields of a table. This is another area in which Access eliminates much of a need for writing program code in applications. In the dBASE dialects, you commonly validated data by writing programs to display data-entry forms and to validate the information. In Access, you can specify rules that the data must follow during the process of table design and can specify custom error messages that will be displayed if the data entered does not follow the rules.

To set validation rules, open the desired table in Design view. Click anywhere in the field that you want to set the validation rules for. Then, under Field Properties (at the bottom of the window), enter the desired validation rules and any validation text (the message that you want to appear if the data entered does not follow the rules).

You enter the validation rules as *expressions*. The expressions tell Access what is and is not acceptable. You can use standard math symbols with your expressions, and remember to include # symbols around dates. Examples of expressions and what they would mean are listed in TABLE 4-2.

Table 4-2
Expressions and what they mean.

Expression used	Means
`"USA" or "Mexico"`	Must contain entry of `USA` or `Mexico`.
`< > 0`	Must be less than or greater than zero ('Not' = 0).
`> 6.50 AND < 20.00`	Must be between 6.50 and 20.00. Must be greater than 6.50 and less than 20.00.
`< = #1/1/93#`	Must be equal to or earlier than Jan. 1, 1993.
`> = Date()`	Must be current date or later.
`< Date()`	Must be earlier than current date.
`Like "1R????"`	Must be 6 characters, starting with `1R`.

Note that you also can specify validation rules that are based on other fields. For example, assuming a table has a field named "Hire Date," another date field named "Vacation Start" might have a validation rule like the following:

```
> = [Hire Date] + 365
```

and the Vacation Start field would not accept a day that was within 364 days of the entry in the Hire Date field.

Note that you also can define validation rules in the forms that you create by opening the Properties window for a control on a form and entering the validation rule in the Validation Rule property box. However, an advantage to entering validation rules in the table is that they will always be in effect, whether you use a form to enter data or not. If you enter the validation rules in a form's design, the rules apply only when you are adding or editing data through that form.

Opening a table

To open a table for use, first click the `Table` button in the Database window to display all your tables, then click the desired table in the list box to select

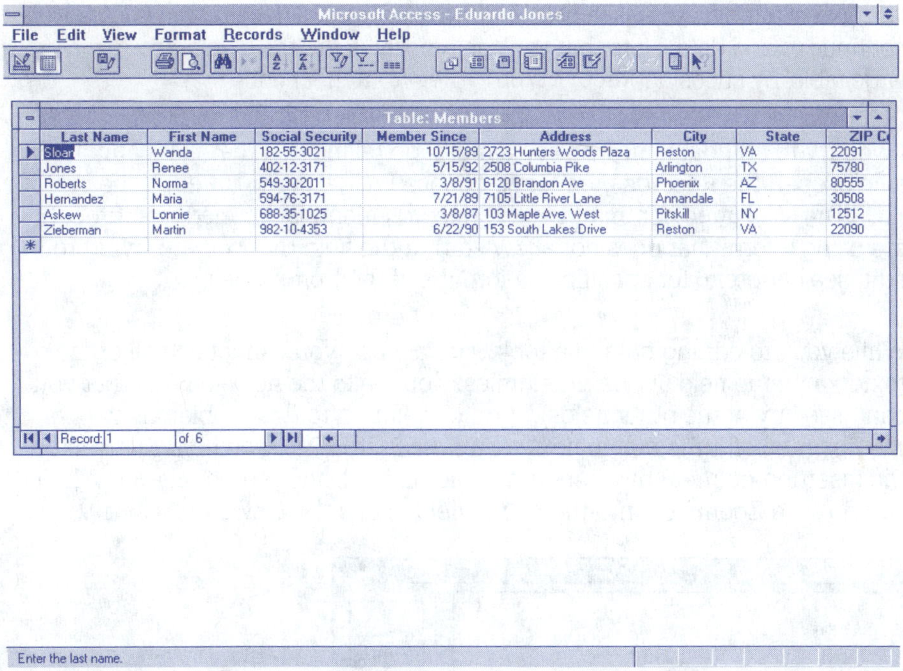

4-17
The Datasheet view.

it. Finally, click `Open`. The table opens in a *Datasheet view*, as shown in FIG. 4-17. (In this example, some records already have been added to the table.)

TIP

You also can open a table by double-clicking the table by name in the Database window.

In Access, you use the Datasheet view whenever you want to add, edit, or view the data in your table while it is displayed in this tabular form. (You also can add, edit, or view data through forms; the use of forms is detailed in chapter 6.) When in Datasheet view, you see your data in a tabular format with each record occupying one row and the fields placed as columns of the table.

Adding records

Once a table exists, you can add data to it or edit existing data by typing directly into the table's datasheet. In Access, every table has a blank record, located immediately after the last existing record, as shown earlier in FIG. 4-17. (In the figure, the empty row marked by an asterisk at the far left is the blank record.)

If there are no existing records in a table, the table will contain one blank record. The blank record always contains an asterisk in its record selector (to the immediate left of the record). As soon as you begin to type a record, a new blank record appears below your entry. Using the mouse or the Tab key, you can move the cursor to any of the fields of the record and type the desired data, using the Del or Backspace key to correct any errors. As you fill in each field with the desired value, press Tab to move to the next field. When you press Tab from the last field of a table, Access moves you to the next blank record, and you can continue to add data. Note that you can quickly get to the blank record in a large table, by choosing `Records/GoTo/New` from the menus.

TIP

If you try to edit data and you see a message telling you that you cannot edit a field, open the Records menu, and choose `Editing Allowed`. If the `Editing Allowed` command in the Records menu is dimmed, you probably are using a form that does not allow editing the field that you are trying to edit; see chapter 6 for specifics on forms and their properties.

Working with memo fields

While you are editing data in a table's datasheet, you cannot see all of the text in a memo field at one time (unless you make the field so wide that you can't see any of the other fields). A quick solution to this problem is to open the Zoom box for the memo field, using the Shift–F2 key combination. Place the insertion pointer anywhere in the memo field, and press Shift–F2. When you do so, a Zoom box into the memo field opens, as shown in FIG. 4-18.

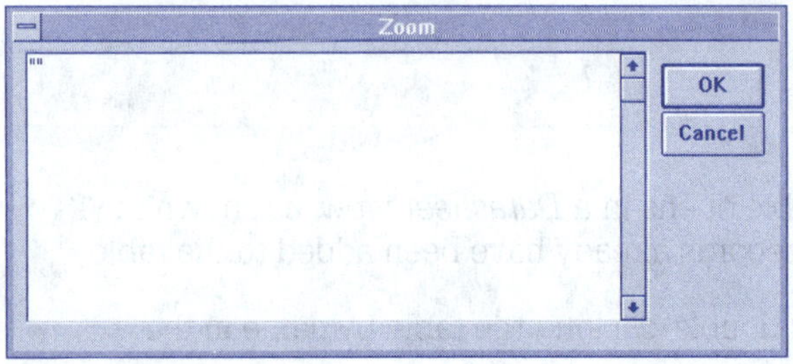

4-18
The Zoom box into a memo field.

You can make any desired changes to the memo field, then click the `OK` button to accept the changes. You can click `Cancel` to cancel any changes and return to viewing the datasheet.

Entering data in OLE fields

Access supports the use of OLE fields, which are containers that you can use to store data from other Windows applications. The most common use for OLE fields is to store graphics (such as pictures created in a program like Windows Paintbrush), but you can store other types of data, such as part of an Excel spreadsheet, a Word for Windows document, video, or sound. To insert OLE data into an OLE field in a table's datasheet, you perform the following steps.

Step 1 Start the other Windows application in the usual manner. Select the desired data in the other application, and choose `Edit/Copy` from the application's menus.

Step 2 Switch back to Access, and open the desired table. Tab to or click in the desired field of the table.

Step 3 From the menus, choose `Edit/Paste`. A copy of the data will appear in the field.

A note about saved data

If you are more accustomed to working with word processors and spreadsheets, you might wonder about a command to save your data after you've entered it. There actually is no need to save your data; Access automatically does so when you move to another record or when you close the table (or when you close a form that you might be using to enter or edit the data).

Using data entry to add records

While you can add data directly to an existing table, at times, you might prefer to add the data without having to view existing data. To accommodate such desires, Access provides the `Records/Data Entry` menu option. The difference between using this option and typing into the existing table is that, with `Records/Data Entry`, existing data is not displayed, so you could not accidentally edit or alter the existing table.

To add records with `Records/Data Entry`, first open the table that you want to add records to. Then, open the Records menu and choose `Data Entry`. Access will open an empty table with the same structure as the original table, and you can proceed to add the records as desired, as shown in FIG. 4-19.

When you are done, close the table (press Ctrl–F4, double-click the close icon in the window, or choose `File/Close` from the menus). The data entry table will close, and the new records automatically will be added to the original table.

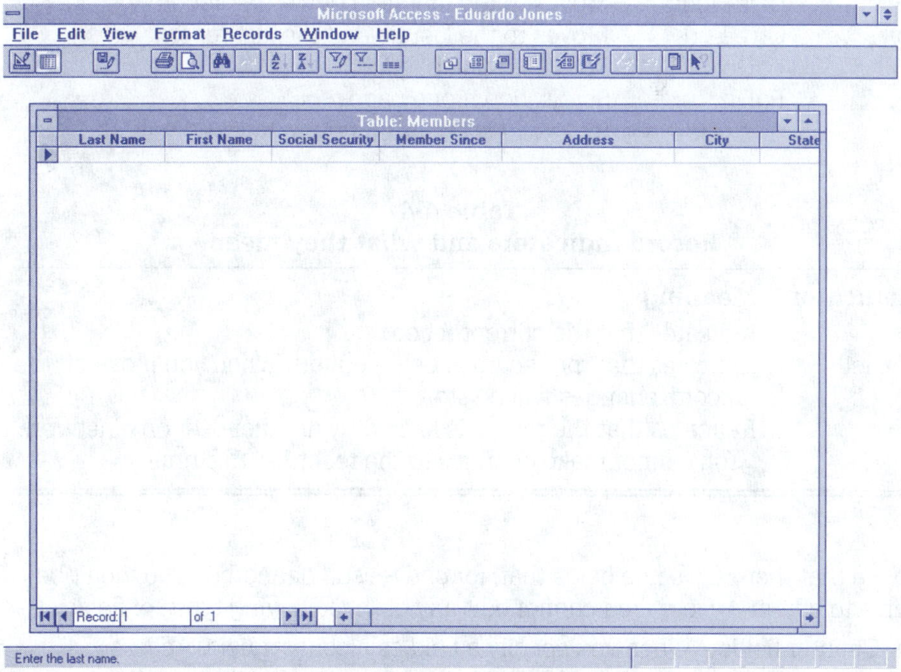

4-19 *The Members table after choosing* Records/Data Entry.

Editing data

As soon as you place the insertion pointer in a particular record, that record becomes the active, or current, record. If you select the data in a field and begin typing, the data replaces the existing data. If you want to make changes without replacing existing data, click in the existing text at the point where you want to make the change. The pointer takes on the shape of the insertion pointer, and you can insert or delete data as desired. TABLE 4-3 shows some useful keyboard navigation techniques that you can use while editing. Note that Access displays the *record indicators* to show the status of the current record. (See TABLE 4-4.)

Table 4-3
Navigation techniques used during editing.

Keystroke	Action
Left arrow	Moves left one character.
Right arrow	Moves right one character.
Down arrow	In a datasheet, moves to the next record.
Up arrow	In a datasheet, moves to the prior record.
Ctrl–PgDn	In a form, moves to the next record.
Ctrl–PgUp	In a form, moves to the prior record.
Tab	Moves to the next field.
Shift–Tab	Moves to the prior field.
Ctrl–Home	Moves to the first field of the first record.
Ctrl–End	Moves to the last field of the last record.
PgUp	Scrolls up one page.
PgDn	Scrolls down one page.

Table 4-4
Record indicators and what they mean.

Indicator	Meaning
>	Indicates that the current record.
pencil	Indicates that the record is being edited. When you move off the record, changes will be stored.
O	Indicates that the record is locked by another user on a network. You cannot make changes to the record at this time.

Fields you can't edit

Note that there are some fields that, for one reason or another, you won't be able to edit in Access. You cannot edit any of the following types of fields:

- Counter fields—When you specify a field as a counter field, Access automatically stores and increments the value as you add new records. You cannot change the value that Access stores in a counter field.

- Calculated fields—Because calculated fields are based on a calculated value, there is no actual data stored that can be edited.
- Locked fields—If a field's Locked property is set to `Yes` or its Enabled property is set to `No`, you cannot edit the field.
- Fields in certain kinds of queries—You can't edit totals in select queries, nor can you edit certain fields in queries that draw relationships between multiple tables.

Adding & editing data in forms

Adding and editing records directly into the datasheet of a table accomplishes the job at hand, but it often is not the most appealing way to work with your data. Often, a major drawback to this approach of adding and editing is that you cannot see most or all of the fields in a table (particularly if the table has a large number of fields). Most adding and editing of records is done through *forms*, because users of databases typically find it easier to work with single records through an onscreen form. Chapter 6 covers the topic of forms in detail, but you can use the following steps to create a form that you can use to add or edit records.

To quickly create a form you can use to add or edit data, perform these steps.

Step 1 In the Database window, click the `Form` button, then click `New`. This causes the New Form dialog box (FIG. 4-20) to appear. Click the down arrow next to Select A Table/Query. In the list box that opens, select the table you are working with. Click the `Form Wizards` button.

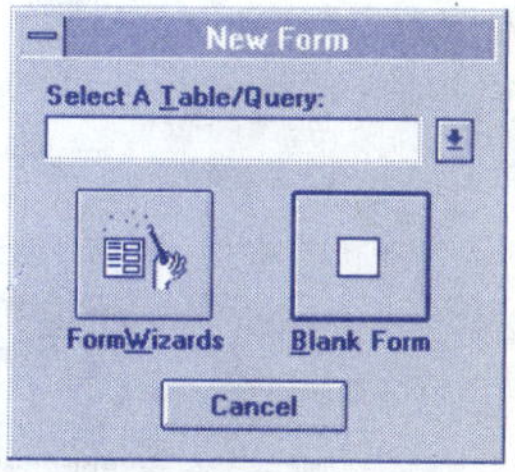

4-20 *The New Form dialog box.*

Step 2 In the next dialog box, click `OK`. (Users of version 2.0 and above can click `AutoForm` then click `OK`, and skip the next three steps.)

Step 3 In the next dialog box, click the double-arrow button to add all fields to the form, then click `Next`.

Step 4 In the next dialog box to appear, click a design of your choice for the form's appearance (`Standard`, `Chiseled`, `Shadowed`, `Boxed`, or `Embossed`), then click `Next`.

Step 5 In the next dialog box to appear, enter a title for the form, then click `Open`. The form will open, and you can begin adding and editing data through the form. Figure 4-21 shows a form for the Members table, created by using the previous steps.

For a more detailed explanation of the options that you see when you create the form, refer to chapter 6. Once the form has been created and opened, you can use the Ctrl–PgUp and Ctrl–PgDn keys or the navigation buttons at the bottom of the form to move throughout the table. (You also can choose `Records/GoTo` from the menus to move to the first, last, next, or previous record.) To search for a specific record, choose `Edit/Find` from the menus and fill in the search criteria in the dialog box that appears. (For more on this dialog box, see "Locating data" later in this chapter.)

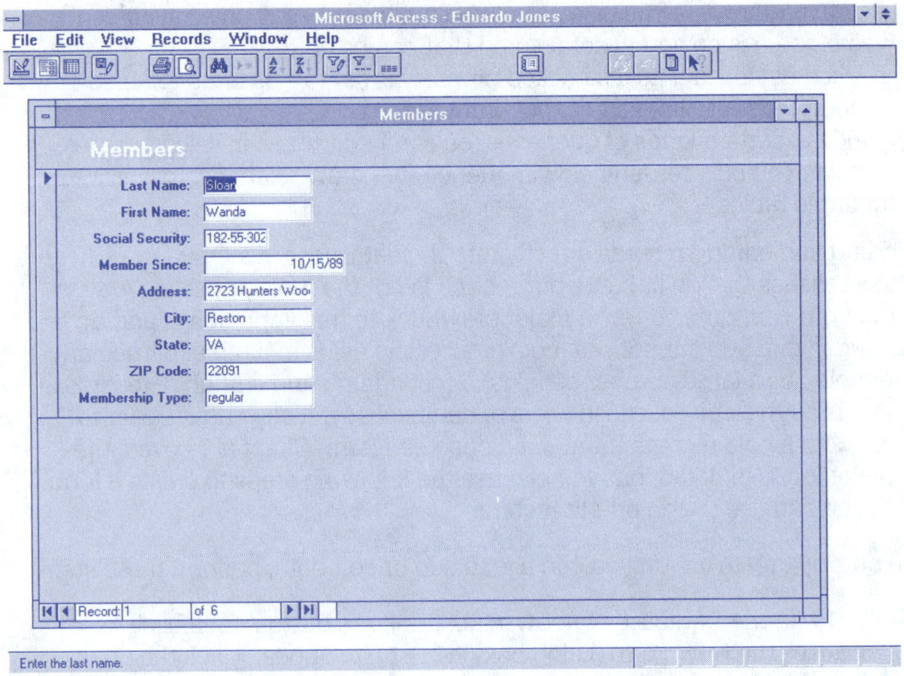

4-21
The form for editing in the Members table.

TIP

If your table contains memo fields or OLE fields, it is a wise idea to use forms to display your data. It is difficult to see much of the contents of memo fields (and impossible to see any of the contents of OLE fields) while viewing a table's datasheet. However, you can see the contents of memo fields and OLE fields through a form.

Deleting records

To delete a record, place the insertion pointer anywhere in the desired record and click the record selector at the left edge of the record or choose `Edit/Select Record`. Doing so will cause the entire record to be selected, as shown in FIG. 4-22.

Next, press the Del key or choose `Edit/Delete`. Access will display a confirmation box, asking if the deletion should be made permanent. Click `OK` if you want to delete the records; if not, click `Cancel`.

TIP

Deletions are permanent in Access. Once you've deleted a record, there is no way to get it back (short of reentering the entire record).

Changing a table's appearance

As you work with your data, you might find that you need to rearrange the way a table is displayed within a datasheet. Access is flexible in this regard; you can move columns, shrink or expand column widths, hide columns, or freeze columns so that they are visible at all times. You can change fonts used to display the data and can change the height of the rows in the

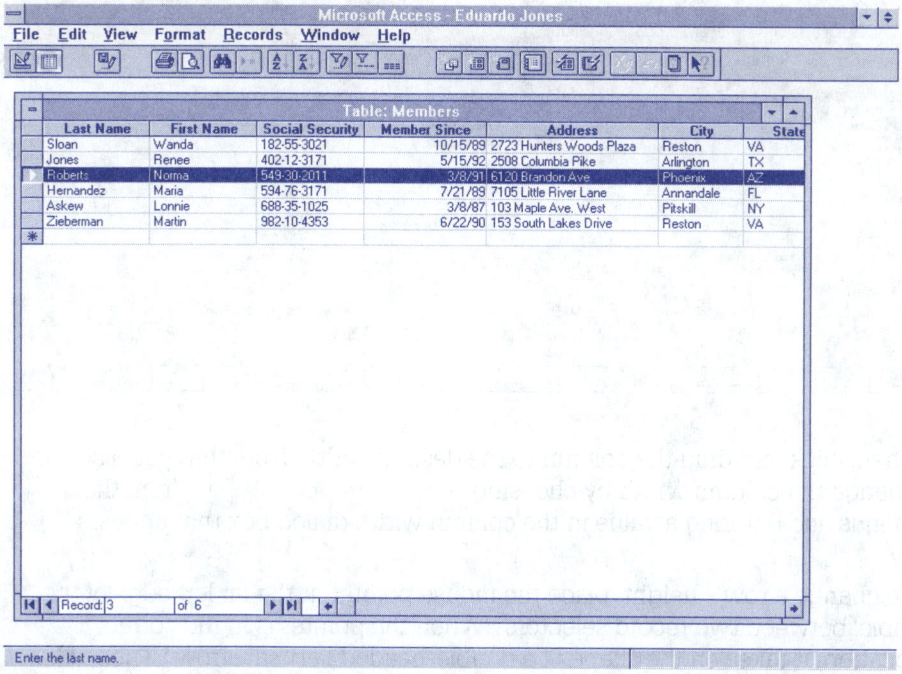

4-22
A selected record.

datasheet. The underlying data in the table never changes when you change the table's appearance; only the look of the table on screen is affected.

Many of the properties governing the appearance of the table in datasheet view can be changed using direct manipulation. In a nutshell, this simply means that you change an object by directly manipulating it with the mouse. As an example, you can move a column by clicking its field selector to select it, then clicking and dragging it to a new location. You can resize columns by clicking and dragging the right edge of the column and can change a row's height by dragging the line underneath the record selector (at the left edge of the datasheet window) to the desired size.

Moving columns

To move a column, first select the desired column, by clicking its field selector. With the field selected, click again and drag the column to the desired location. (As you drag, the new column's position will be indicated by a solid vertical bar, as shown in FIG. 4-23.)

TIP

You can move multiple columns at the same time if they are adjacent to one another. To select multiple columns for movement, click the first column to select it, then hold the Shift key depressed while you click additional columns.

Changing column widths

To change a column's width, place the mouse pointer at the right edge of the field selector for the field you want to move. (When the pointer is in the correct location, it takes on the shape of a double-headed horizontal arrow.)

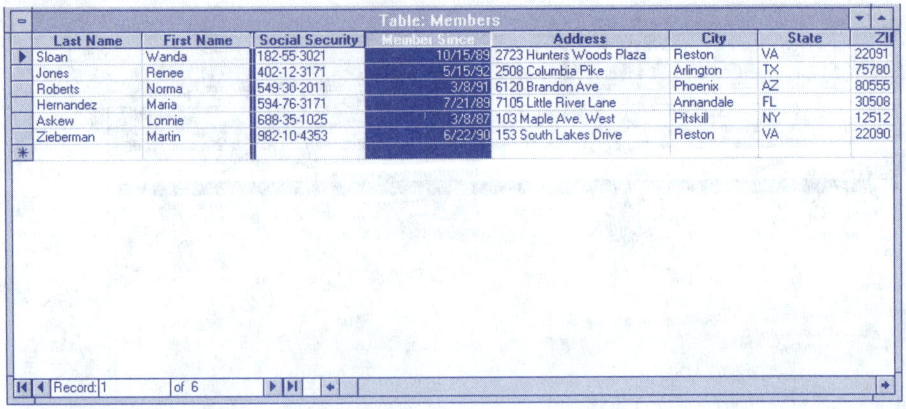

4-23
The vertical bar used to move columns.

Then, click and drag the column to the desired width. Note that you also can change the column width by choosing `Format/Column Width` from the menus and entering a value in the column width dialog box that appears.

Changing row heights

To change a row's height, place the mouse pointer at the far left edge of the table, between two record selectors. (When the pointer is in the correct location, it takes on the shape of a double-headed vertical arrow.) Then, click and drag the row to the desired height. Note that you also can change the row height by choosing `Format/Row Height` from the menus and entering a value in the row height dialog box that appears.

Changing fonts

To change the font used in a datasheet, open the Format menu and choose `Font`. When you do so, the Font dialog box appears, as shown in FIG. 4-24. Choose the desired font, font style, and size in the dialog box, then click `OK` for the changes to take effect.

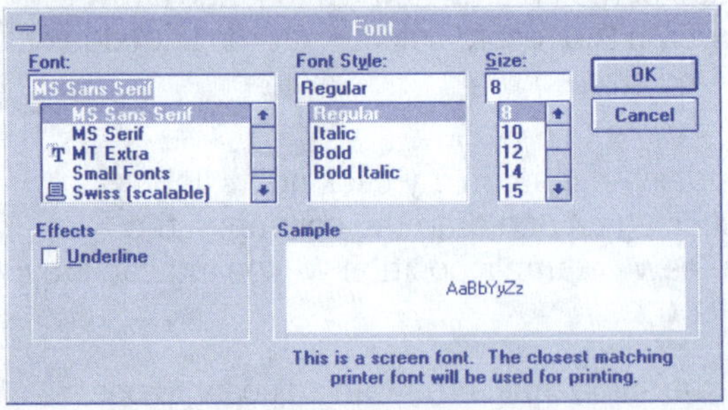

4-24
The Font dialog box.

Hiding & showing columns

You can hide columns from view with the `Hide Columns` option of the Format menu. To hide a column, first select the desired column by clicking its field selector, then choose `Format/Hide Columns` from the menus. To restore a hidden column to view, choose `Format/Show Columns` from the menus. When you do so, a Show Columns dialog box appears and you can choose the desired column to show, then click the Show button, followed by the Close button.

Freezing & unfreezing columns

If a table is too wide to be viewed entirely in datasheet view, you might want to freeze certain columns, so that they remain in view while other columns scroll off to the side. For example, in a table of customers, you might want to freeze the last name and first name columns, while allowing the remainder of the fields in the table to scroll. To freeze one or more columns, first select the desired column (or columns) to freeze. Click the field selector to select one column, then hold down the Shift key and click the field selector to select any additional columns. With the columns selected, choose Format/Freeze Columns from the menus. Once you have done this, the frozen column will remain visible when you scroll the table to the right to see additional fields.

Once you have frozen a column in place, you can unfreeze it by choosing Format/Unfreeze All Columns from the menus.

Saving changes

When you make changes to a table's layout and close the table, Access will ask if you want to save the changes to the table. If you respond with Yes (even though you might not have changed any of the actual data), the changes to the table's appearance will be saved.

Printing a table

One easy way to get a printed copy of the data in a table is to print the table while in Datasheet view. Note that you have far more flexibility in printing your data if you take the time to design a report, as outlined in chapter 7; however, if all you want is a fast copy of your data, printing the table will provide it. To print the records in a table, perform the following steps.

Step 1 Select the table in the Database window or open the table in a Datasheet view. (If you want to print a selected group of records, you must open the table in a Datasheet view and select the desired records by clicking and dragging at the left edge of the table.)

Step 2 Choose File/Print, or click the Print icon in the Toolbar. The Print dialog box (FIG. 4-25) appears.

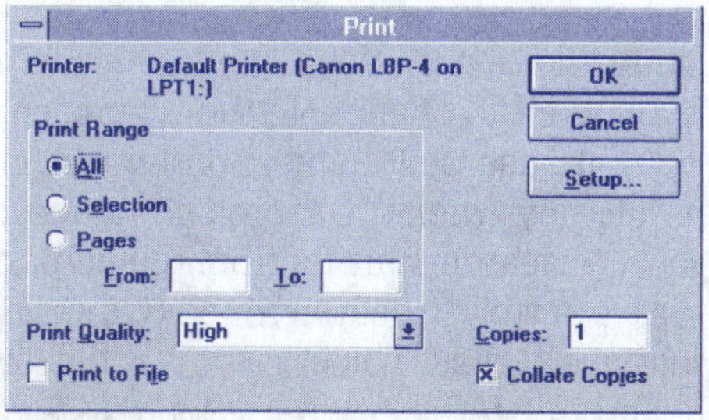

4-25
The Print dialog box.

Step 3 To print all the records, click `OK`. To print selected records, click `Selection` in the Print Range area of the dialog box, then click `OK`.

Once you click `OK`, the records will be printed and will appear in a tabular format, similar to the example of a Print Preview shown in FIG. 4-26.

Last Name	First Name	Social Security	Member Since	Address
Sloan	Wanda	182- 55- 3021	10/15/89	2723 Hunters Woods Plaza
Jones	Renee	402- 12- 3171	5/15/92	2508 Columbia Pike
Roberts	Norma	549- 30- 2011	3/8/91	6120 Brandon Ave
Hernandez	Maria	594- 76- 3171	7/21/89	7105 Little River Lane
Askew	Lonnie	688- 35- 1025	3/8/87	103 Maple Ave. West
Zieberman	Martin	982- 10- 4353	6/22/90	153 South Lakes Drive

4-26 *An example of the records shown in Print Preview.*

TIP

If you need to quickly print a table but you don't want all the columns included in the printout, use the `Format/Hide Columns` menu option, described earlier, to hide the unwanted columns, then print the report. Hidden columns will not appear in the printout.

Locating data

With a small table, you usually can find the records that you need to edit by looking for them. However, with a large table with hundreds of records, a visual search for a record becomes impractical. As an example, you could search within an employee ID number field for a specific employee. You can search for specific data by using the `Edit/Find` command from the menus, or the Find button on the Toolbar. To search for data using `Edit/Find`, you open the table that you want to search, then perform these steps.

Step 1 Click anywhere in the field (column) that you want to search, unless you intend to search all fields. (It is faster to search within a single field than to search all the fields in the table.)

Step 2 From the menus, choose `Edit/Find`, or click the `Find` button on the Toolbar. Access displays the Find dialog box (FIG. 4-27).

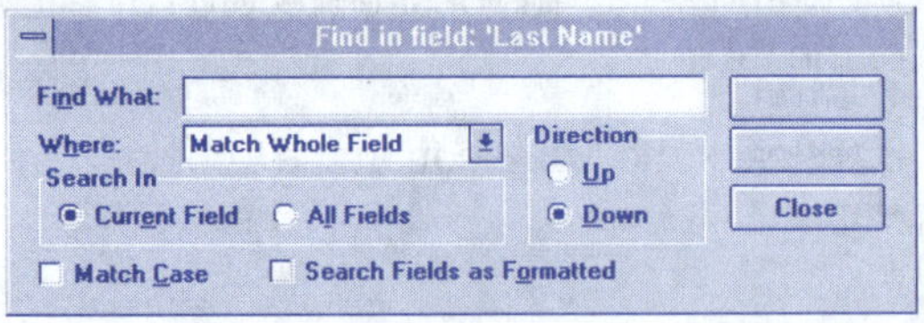

4-27 *The Find dialog box.*

Step 3 In the Find What box, enter the text that you want to find. Change any of the dialog box options that you want to change. In the Where list box, you can choose `Any Part of Field` (to search for any part of the string), `Match Whole Field` (to find a match only when the search string matches the entire field), or `Start of Field` (to search starting from the beginning of the field). Click the `Current Field` button to search in the current field, or click the `All Fields` button to search all fields. The `Direction` buttons specify the direction of the search, and the `Match Case` option tells Access to consider case as significant during the search (if the option is not turned on, Access treats upper-case and lower-case letters the same). Turn on the Search Fields As Formatted option if you want to search for data based on its display format.

Step 4 To find the first occurrence of the text, click the Find First button. To find the next occurrence of the text and all additional occurrences, click the Find Next button.

Step 5 When you are done with the search, click the Close button to put away the dialog box.

TIP

If you find yourself searching the same field repeatedly and it is not already defined as a primary key, you can speed performance of Access by adding an index to that field. See "Adding indexes" later in this chapter.

Because the Edit/Find command finds the first occurrence of what you are searching for by default, you might need to use the command repeatedly to find precisely what you are looking for. For example, if you search a table of customer names for a person with the last name of Johnson, you will find the first Johnson in the table, which might or might not be the one you are looking for. You can choose Edit/Find again, and this time click the Find Next button in the dialog box to find the next occurrence of the same search term. However, this might not be the most efficient method for finding data in large tables. If, for example, you are searching for a person named Wystina Smith in a large table with 320 Smiths, you might be in for a tedious search.

One way around this potential problem is to narrow your search by means of queries. With queries, you can specify search criteria for more than one field. (Queries are covered in detail in chapter 5.) Another trick that can speed your searches is to search based on a value in a unique field. For example, if a table of employees has a field for social security number, it makes sense to search on the basis of that field, because no two employees will ever have the same entry in that field.

Adding indexes

Access lets you add an *index* to a field of a table. (You cannot index on Yes/No, OLE, or memo fields.) Adding an index speeds the performance of searches on a given field. (Note that there is a drawback, as indexes slow the performance of Access when it comes to updating records.) You can add an index by performing these steps.

Step 1 Get into Design view for the table, and click the field that you want to index to select it.

Step 2 In the Indexed property box at the bottom of the window, choose Yes (Duplicates OK) or Yes (No Duplicates). If you choose Yes (Duplicates OK), you tell Access that the field can contain more than one record with the same data in this field. Choosing Yes (No Duplicates) prohibits duplicate records.

Note: Users of dBASE and similar products should note that indexes in Access are not added for the purpose of ordering records. If you want to place records in a certain order in Access, you do so by *sorting* the data, using the Toolbar's Sort buttons, or from within a query, or from within a form.

Multiple-field indexes

If you routinely search for data based on a combination of fields that aren't part of a primary key, you can speed such searches by adding a multiple-field index. As an example, consider the classic case of last and first names. If users of an application routinely search for records in a table based on a combination of last and first names, it would make sense to add a multiple field index based on a combination of those fields. You can create a multiple-field index with the following steps.

Step 1 Open the table in Design view.

Step 2 From the menus, choose `View/Indexes` (or click the `Indexes` button in the Toolbar) to open the Indexes window for the table. In a blank row under the Index Name column, enter any desired name for your index. Click in the Field Name column, and choose the first field that you want to base the index on from the list box; then, in the Sort Order column, choose Ascending or Descending, as desired. Click in the Field Name column of the next empty row, and again choose the first field that you want to base the index on from the list box; then, in the Sort Order column, choose Ascending or Descending, as desired. As an example, the multiple index shown in the properties window is based on a combination of last and first names. (See FIG. 4-28.) Keep in mind that the name for the multiple-field index should be included only in the row of the first field that you choose. In the Indexes dialog box, Access treats all rows as part of the same index, until it comes to a row containing another index name.

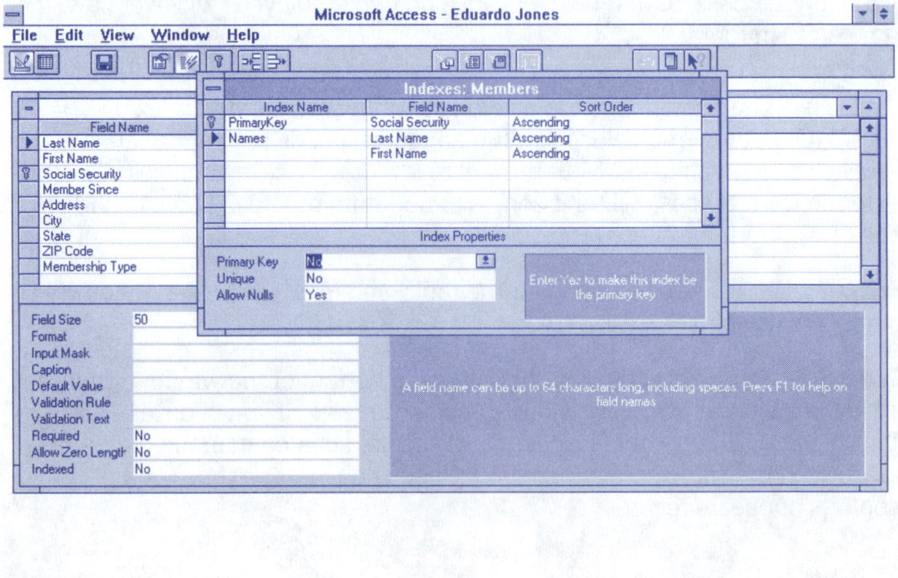

4-28 *A multiple index based on first and last names.*

Step 3 From the menus, choose `File/Save`. This causes the new index to be created.

Creating relationships between tables

Once you have more than one table in a database, you often will need to establish relationships between the tables. In Access, there are two ways that you can establish relationships. One way is to do so through *queries*, which will be discussed in chapter 5. The other way is to choose `Edit/Relationships` from the menus to open the Relationships window, and add the tables or queries that you want to relate to the window. Then, to define the relationship, you fill in the options in the Relationships dialog box that appears. To establish a relationship through the Relationships window, you perform the following steps.

Step 1 From the menus, choose `Edit/Relationships`. The Relationships window (FIG. 4-29) appears. (If you are establishing relationships for the first time with this database, the window will be empty, and the Add Table dialog box appears in the window, as shown in the figure.)

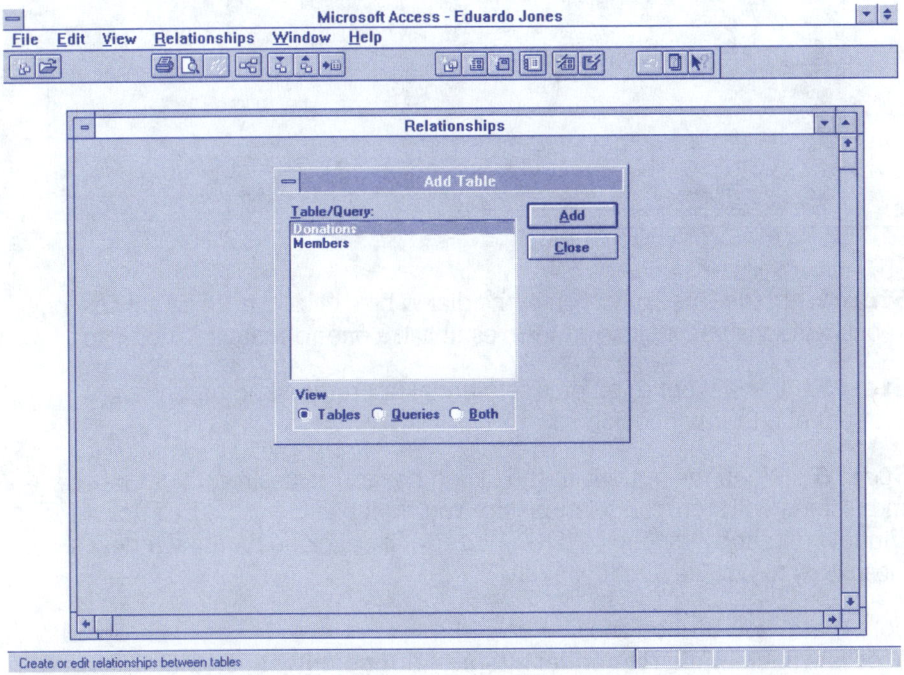

4-29
The Relationships window.

Step 2 In the Add Table dialog box, select the table or query that you want to create a relationship for, then click `Add`. (If the Add Table dialog box doesn't appear, choose `Relationships/Add Table` from the menus to display it.) Repeat this step for each table or query that you want to add to the window, then click `Close`.

Step 3 To create the relationship, drag the field or fields that you want to relate from the fields list of the primary table or query to the matching field or fields of the related table or query. When you do this, the Relationships dialog box appears, as shown in FIG. 4-30.

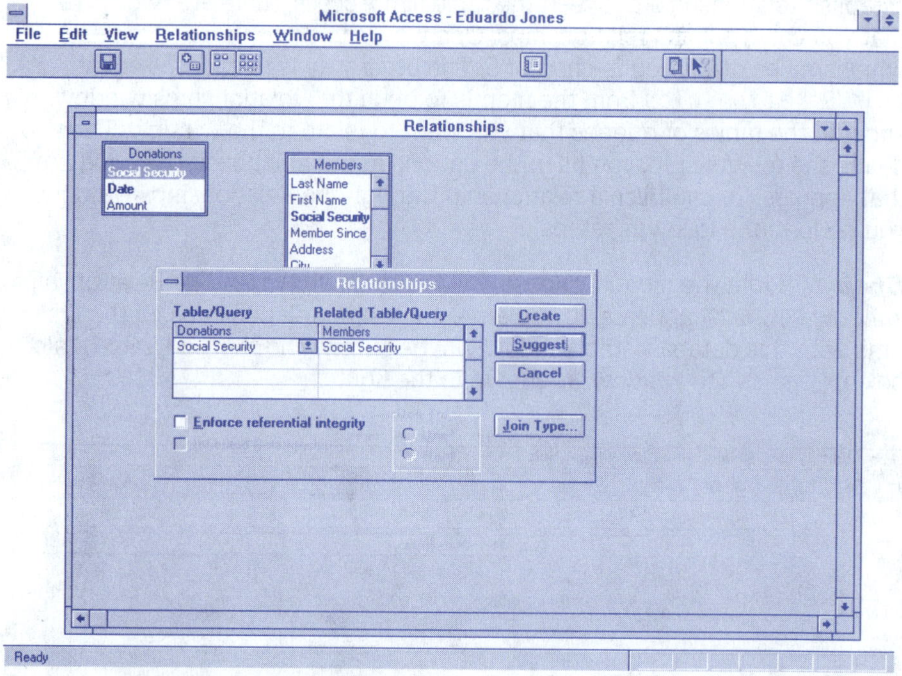

4-30 *The Relationships dialog box.*

Step 4 In the One To portion of the dialog box, click `One` (to establish a one-to-one relationship) or click `Many` (to establish a one-to-many relationship).

Step 5 If you want to enforce referential integrity, click the Enforce Referential Integrity check box.

Step 6 When the options in the dialog box are as desired, click `Create` and Access will store the relationship. You then can close the Relationships Window (either by choosing `File/Close`, or by clicking on the window's Close box) to put the window away.

Note that if you turn on the `Enforce Referential Integrity` option, Access will maintain referential integrity during operations that involve editing and deleting of records. In a nutshell, this means that you cannot add records to the related table if there is no corresponding entry for the matching field in the primary table, and you will not be able to delete a record from the primary table if doing so would leave "orphan" records in the related table.

Creating a many-to-many relationship

As chapter 3 mentioned, some database tasks require the defining of *many-to-many relationships*, where many records in one table relate to many records in another table. A common example is that of student tracking at a high school or college, where many students are assigned to many different classes. In Access, you can define a many-to-many relationship between tables with the following steps.

Step 1 If you haven't already done so, create the tables that you want to define the many-to-many relationship between.

Step 2 Create a third table, and include the primary key fields from each of the other two tables in this table. In the junction table, the primary key fields function as foreign keys.

Step 3 In the third table, set the primary key to include all the primary key fields from the other two tables.

Step 4 Define a one-to-many relationship between each of the two primary tables and the third table.

Copying tables to other databases

Because Access stores tables in databases, there are times when you might want to copy a table from one database to another. As an example, in a large company, different departments might want copies of a table containing personnel statistics, and each department might be using its own database. The table could be copied into the other databases on a regular basis. You can copy a table by performing the following steps.

Step 1 In the Database window, click the `Table` button. Click the desired table to select it.

Step 2 From the menu, choose `Edit/Copy`. Open the database that you want to copy the table to. (From the menus, choose `File/Open Database` and choose the desired database.)

Step 3 From the menus, choose `Edit/Paste`. Access displays the Paste Table As dialog box (FIG. 4-31). By default, the `Structure and Data` button is clicked, meaning the copied table will contain both the table structure and the actual data. You can click `Structure Only` to copy an empty version of the table, or you can click `Append Data to Existing Table`, in which case Access will add the copied data to the contents of an existing table. Enter a name for the copied table, then click `OK`.

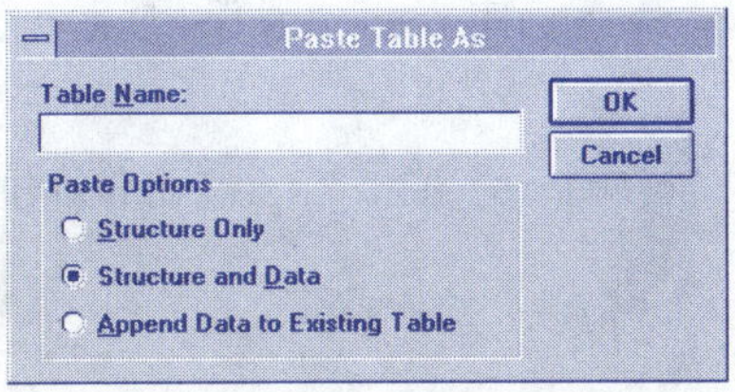

4-31
The Paste Table As dialog box.

Exporting data

As powerful and flexible as Access is, the program cannot be all things to all people. It is not a spreadsheet nor a word processor, but it excels at working side-by-side with your other programs like spreadsheets and word processors. You can use the Windows Clipboard and the cut-and-paste techniques of Windows to move data between Access and other Windows applications. You can use the `File/Export` command to export Access data so that it can be used both by Windows and non-Windows programs.

When you choose `File/Export` from the menus, the dialog box that appears can be used to copy data from an Access table into a new text file, spreadsheet, or database table. The very name "Access" implies easy access to other data, and Access is no slouch in this regard. In version 1.0 of Access, you can export data to the following file formats:

- Microsoft Access (to databases other than the open database)
- Delimited text (values separated by commas, tabs, or other characters)
- Fixed-width text (values arranged so that each field has a certain width)
- Microsoft Excel (versions 2.*x*, 3.0, and 4.0)
- Lotus 1-2-3 or 1-2-3/W (.WKS and .WK1 files)
- Paradox (.DB files)
- dBASE III and dBASE IV or Microsoft FoxPro (.DBF files)
- Btrieve (with Xtrieve dictionary file)
- Microsoft SQL Server

Version 1.1 of Access includes all of the previous formats and adds the following additional file formats:

- Sybase SQL Server
- Oracle Server

Version 2.0 of Access includes all of the previous formats and adds the Microsoft Word for Windows Merge Format.

Before exporting data, consider whether you want to first build a query. Access uses tables or queries as possible sources for your exported data; therefore, if you want just a selection of records or certain fields, you first should design a query that provides the desired data. You then can export the query to the file that will be used by the other software. (See chapter 5 for details on creating queries.)

To export data from Access, you perform the following steps.

Step 1 Click the Database window (or press F11) so that the Database window is the active window.

Step 2 From the menus, choose `File/Export`. The Export dialog box (FIG. 4-32) appears.

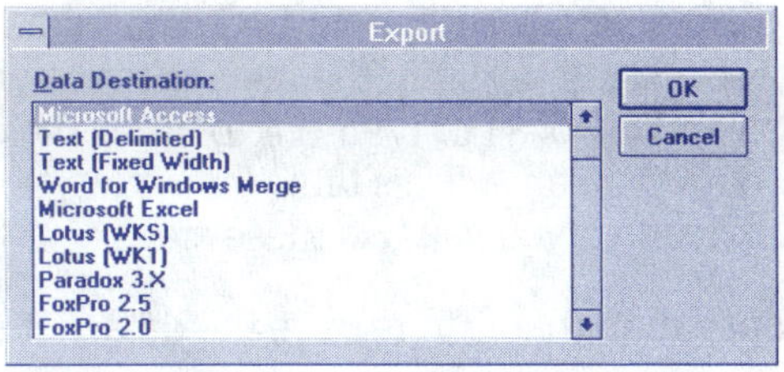

4-32
The Export dialog box.

Step 3 In the Data Destination list box, choose the desired file format for the exported data, then click OK. The Select Microsoft Access Object dialog box (FIG. 4-33) appears next. (Note that you can use the buttons at the bottom of this dialog box to see tables, or queries, or both.) Select the desired table or query to export, then click OK. The Export to File dialog box (FIG. 4-34) appears.

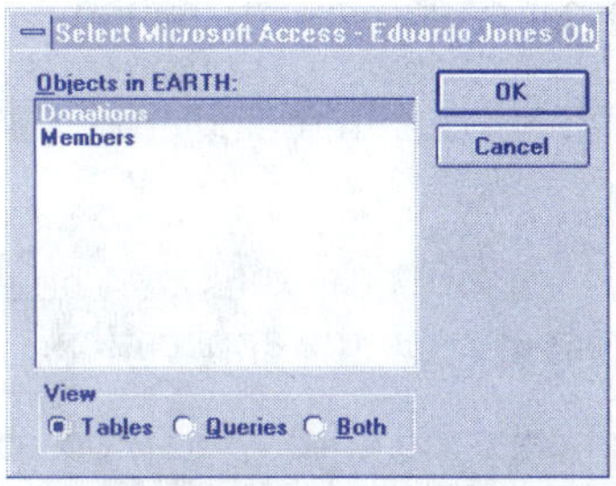

4-33
The Select Microsoft Access Object dialog box.

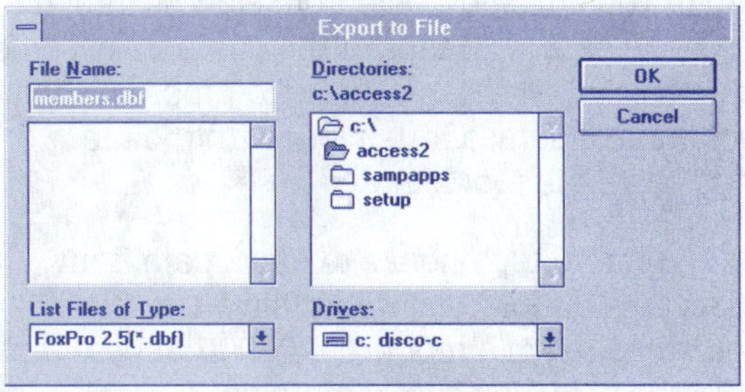

4-34
The Export to File dialog box.

Step 4 In the File Name text box, enter the name for the exported file. If you want to store the file in a different directory, you can click on the desired directory in the Directories box to open it. Click OK to export the file.

Moving data with windows cut-and-paste

If you need to place selected information from an Access table or a query into another Windows program, you often can obtain sufficient results with the cut-and-paste techniques that are designed into all Windows applications. With thousands of records, this technique gets somewhat awkward and unworkable; however, if all you need are a few dozen records or less, you might find it easier to use the clipboard than to export the data as a separate file. The procedure is simple; in effect, you select the desired data in the Access table or query, then choose `Edit/Copy` from the menus, then switch to the other Windows application and choose `Edit/Paste` to insert the data in the desired location. To copy data from an Access table (or a query's dynaset) to another Windows application, you can use these steps.

Step 1 Start the Windows application that is to receive the data, if it is not already running.

Step 2 In Access, open the table or query that contains the desired records and select the desired records. (You can select multiple records by clicking and dragging the mouse over the record selectors of the desired records. You can select all the records in a table by choosing `Edit/Select All Records` from the menus.)

Step 3 From the menus, choose `Edit/Copy`. Press Ctrl–Esc to open the Windows Task List, and switch to the other Windows application. Place the insertion pointer where the desired data is to appear. (If you are inserting the data into a spreadsheet, you can place the pointer in the desired cell of the spreadsheet.)

Step 4 From the application's menus, choose `Edit/Paste`. The Access data will appear at the insertion pointer location in the application.

This procedure works well with spreadsheets and with word processors. However, be aware that how the data appears in a word processor will depend on your tab settings. When you cut-and-paste from Access into a word processor, Access separates the data with tabs. If the contents of some of the fields are wider than the default tab stops in your word processor, you might wind up with irregular columns of data; a little work with the tab settings in your document should solve the problem.

You can use the same Windows Clipboard techniques to move data from other applications into Access. As an example, you might have text in a word-processing document that is needed in a memo field of an Access table. Rather than retyping the text into the field, you can get into your word processor, select the desired text and choose `Edit/Copy` to copy the data to the Windows Clipboard. Then, switch to Access, place the insertion pointer in the desired field of the table, and choose `Edit/Paste` to paste the data from the Clipboard into the field.

Hands-on practice: moving data from Access

If you have a Windows spreadsheet or a word processor, you can try the process detailed earlier to copy data from the Earth Aware database into a spreadsheet or a word-processing document. Perform the following steps.

Step 1 Start your Windows spreadsheet or word processor in the usual manner. Get into Access, and open the EARTH.MDB database, if it is not already open.

Step 2 In the Database window, click `Table`, then click `Donations`, then click `Open` to open the table in datasheet view.

Step 3 From the menus, choose `Edit/Select All Records` to select all the records in the table. Choose `Edit/Copy`. Press Ctrl–Esc, and choose your Windows spreadsheet or word processor by name from the Task List, then click `OK` to switch to the other program.

Step 4 Place the insertion pointer in an empty cell of the spreadsheet or at a blank location in the word-processing document, and choose `Edit/Paste` from the menus to paste the data into your spreadsheet or document. Figure 4-35 shows how the data appears in a spreadsheet in Microsoft Works, after the Social Security column of the spreadsheet has been widened. Figure 4-36 shows the data pasted into a document in Word for Windows.

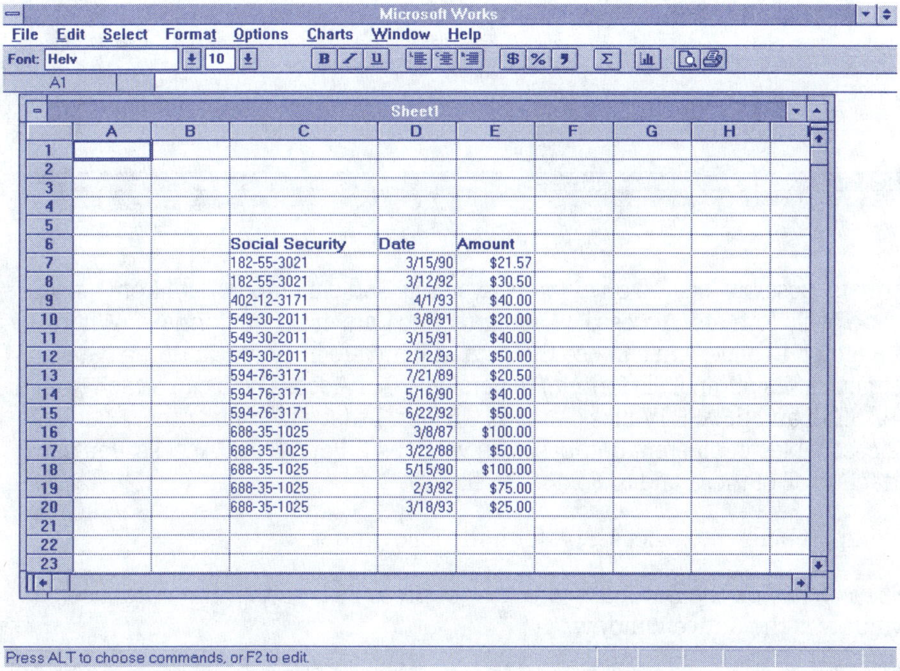

4-35
The results of data pasted into a Microsoft Works spreadsheet.

Keep in mind that, while the previous procedures work well with word-processing documents and spreadsheets, the same cannot be said for other database managers. Most Windows database managers are not designed to accept incoming Windows Clipboard data that fills more than a single field at a time. If you want to export data from Access to another database manager, use the `File/Export` command as described earlier in the chapter.

Importing & attaching tables

If your data already exists in another commonly-used file format, you need not rekey the data into an Access database. One of the strengths of Access (and, indeed, a reason for the program's name) is its ability to access data in different

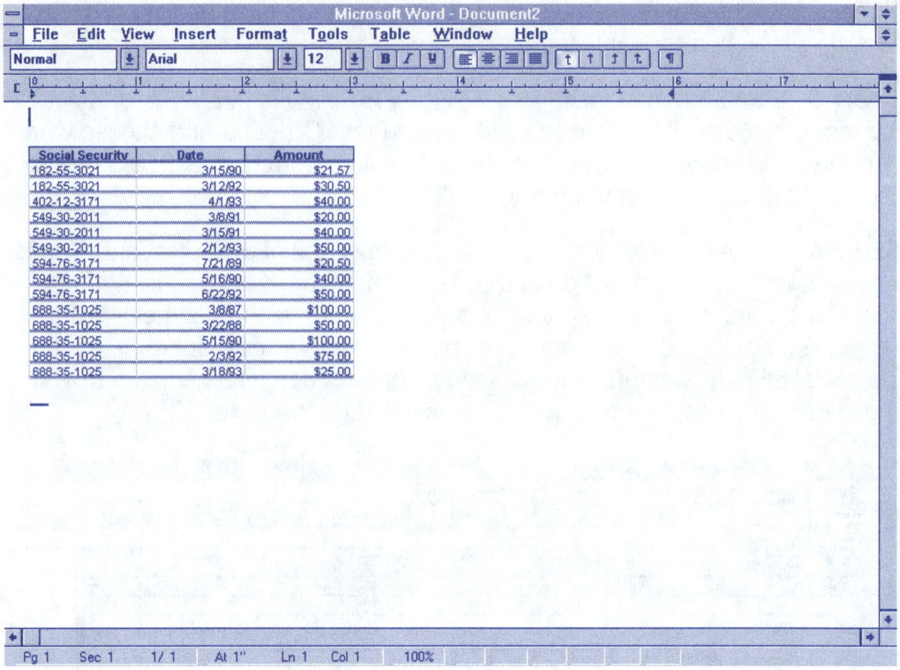

4-36
The results of data pasted into a Word for Windows document.

formats, possibly located on different systems. You can import data from a wide range of file formats. Access lets you *attach* to data in certain formats. (When you attach to a file, you can use the data as if it were in Access, but the data remains in its original file format.) In version 1.0 of Access, you can attach to dBASE III and dBASE IV files, Paradox 3.5 files, Btrieve files, and other Microsoft Access tables in different databases. In versions 1.1 and 2.0 of Access, you can attach to all of these and to FoxPro 2.*x* files.

Importing files

To import a file into Access, perform the following steps.

Step 1 Click the Database window (or press F11) so that the Database window is the active window.

Step 2 From the menus, choose `File/Import`. The Import dialog box (FIG. 4-37) appears.

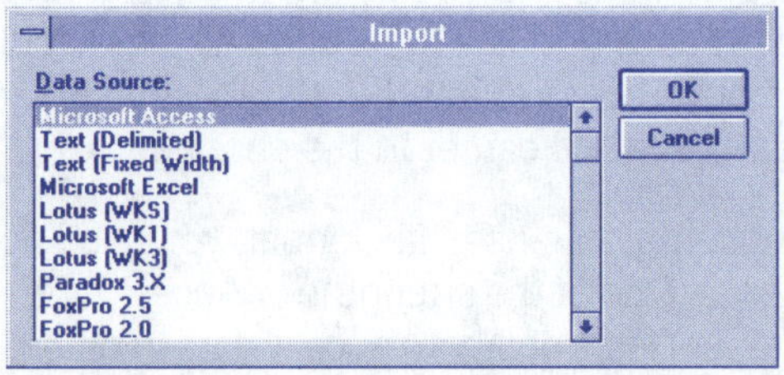

4-37
The Import dialog box.

Step 3 In the list box, click the desired data source, then click `OK`. A Select File dialog box (FIG. 4-38) now appears. Use the Drives and Directories list boxes to locate the desired file to import, then click the file to select it.

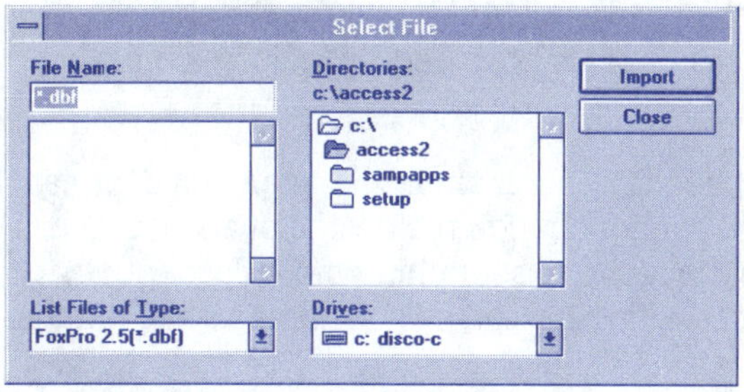

4-38
The Select File dialog box.

Step 4 Click the `Import` button. Access will proceed to import the file into a new Access table. When it is done, you will see a confirmation dialog indicating that the file has been successfully imported. Click `OK` to put away this dialog box, then click `Close` to close the Select File dialog box. You will see the new table in the Database window. (You might want to rename the table to something more descriptive than the DOS filename originally given it. With the table selected in the Database window, you can choose `File/Rename` from the menus to rename the table.)

Attaching tables

To attach a table in one of the acceptable formats, you use the following steps.

Step 1 From the menus, choose `File/Attach Table`. The Attach dialog box (FIG. 4-39) appears.

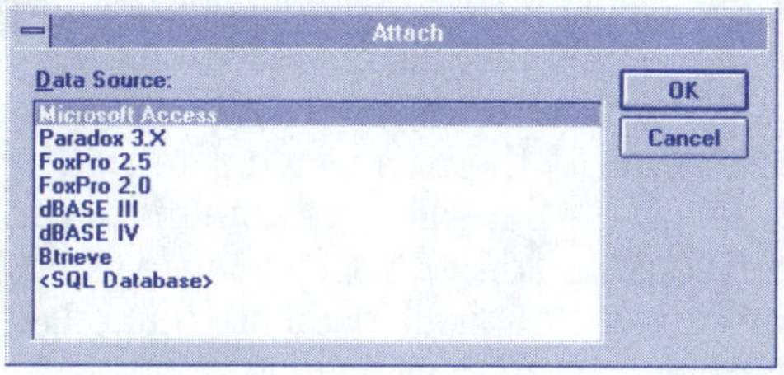

4-39
The Attach dialog box.

Step 2 In the list box, click the desired data source, then click `OK`. The Select File dialog box appears, as shown earlier. Use the Drives and Directories list boxes to locate the desired file to attach, then click the file to select it. Click the `Attach` button.

Step 3 In the case of dBASE files, the next dialog box to appear asks you to select any index files to attach. If you don't want to attach any index files, just click `Close`. If you want to attach to existing dBASE index files, click the desired index file to select it, then click `Select`. Repeat this step for any additional index files that you want to add.

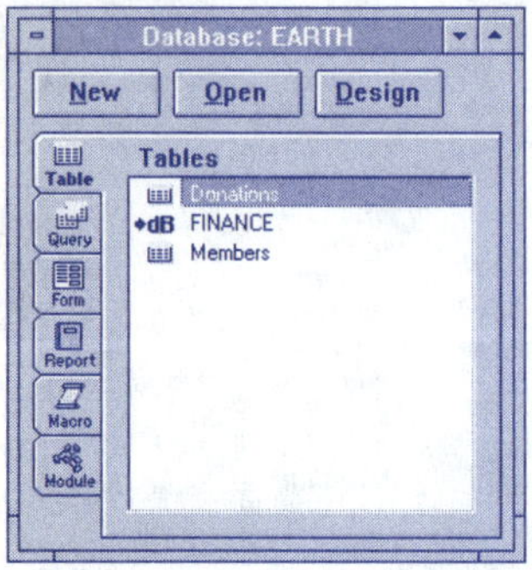

4-40 *An arrow indicating an attached table.*

Step 4 Click Close. Access will attach the file, and you will see a confirmation box indicating that the file was successfully attached. When you put away the Attach dialog box, you will see the attached table in the Database window (assuming the Table button has been pressed). Note the arrow that appears beside the table titled "FINANCE" in the Database window, as shown in FIG. 4-40. This arrow is how Access indicates that the table is an attached table.

Keep in mind that, because attached tables remain in the original file format, one major restriction applies: you cannot change the design of an attached table. However, you can change the name to something more descriptive; if you change the name in your Access database, the DOS name for the original file remains unchanged.

Compacting a database

Once you have been working with a database for some time, the database might use more disk space than it should and response time might not be as great as it could due to *fragmentation*. (Fragmentation is a process in which your database becomes stored in numerous clusters scattered over the surface of your hard disk.) There are commercial products available that will defragment your hard disk, but it is not necessary to resort to such if all you need is to defragment an Access database. You can use the File/Compact Database command to defragment a database. Compacting a database also removes any temporary or deleted objects that still might be in the database. (Note that you cannot perform this process while a database is open. The command does not appear on the menus unless no database currently is open.)

Before compacting a database, be sure that you have enough storage space on your hard disk for both the existing database and the compacted version. Access will compact the database and save it to disk before it deletes the older version of the database; therefore, for the time that the operation proceeds, you will need roughly twice as much disk space as is occupied by the database. (You can specify a different database name for the compacted database, in which case Access will not delete the old file but will leave both the old and the new versions of the database on your hard disk.) Also, if you are using Access on a network, note that you cannot compact a database that others are currently using. To compact a database, perform the following steps.

Step 1 From the menus, choose File/Compact Database. When you do so, Access displays the Database To Compact From dialog box, as shown in FIG. 4-41.

Step 2 Click the database that you want to compact, then click OK. When you do so, Access displays the Database To Compact To dialog box.

Step 3 Specify a name for the compacted database (remember to use acceptable DOS filenames), then click OK.

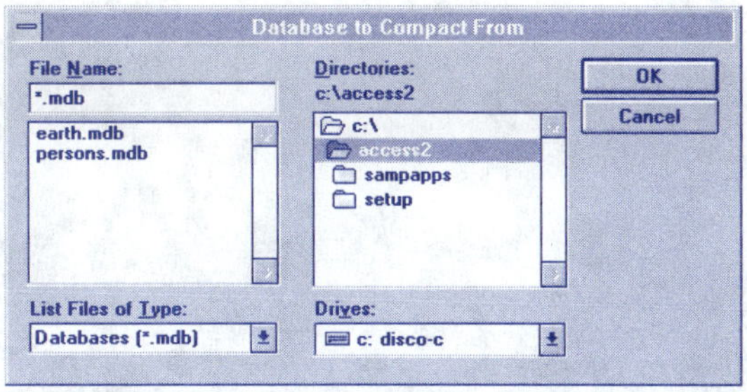

4-41
The Database to Compact From dialog box.

Damaged databases & a word of advice

It might be obvious that there are advantages and disadvantages to the Access method of storing everything associated with a database in a single file. The advantages are significant; there is no mammoth collection of files to clutter up your hard disk, and you need not struggle to remember (as with products like dBASE) what form or report goes with what table or query. The one notable disadvantage is only a disadvantage if and when something goes wrong. Because everything associated with a database is stored in a single file, if that file is damaged in any way, the potential for loss is great. People are people, computers are as imperfect as people, and files do get trashed from time to time, whether it's the fault of the hardware, the software, or the operator. The best insurance against losing data is to keep regular backups. Here is where the method of storage used by Access is again an advantage; you need copy only a single file to disk or tape backup, and you have an extra copy of your entire database.

If your machine shuts down in the midst of Access (such as when a power failure occurs), when the computer is restarted, you might find that Access is unable to open the database. If this is the case, a dialog box will appear advising you that the database has been damaged. The dialog box contains an `OK` button. Click `OK`, and Access will attempt to repair the database. (You also can choose `File/Repair Database` from the menus and choose a database by name in the dialog box that appears to attempt a repair on a damaged database.) Keep in mind that some data might be lost, particularly if the computer lost power in the midst of adding or editing records. If you made any changes to any objects (such as a table's design or the design of a form or report) and did not save them before the power failure occurred, those changes will be lost.

5 Working with queries

Chapter 4 detailed how data could be stored in Access tables, and that chapter also demonstrated how you could perform quick searches to find desired records. In the business world, however, what most often are needed from a database are sets of data that answer specific questions: Who are all members who donated more than $50.00 to the organization? How many employees live in a particular city where a commuter tax is about to take effect? Which salesrep sold more Caribbean vacations than any other this month? In Access, these kinds of questions are answered with *queries*. The word *query* literally means "to ask." When you run a query in Access, you are asking about your data.

This chapter explains in detail how you can use *graphical query-by-example*, or *graphical QBE*, to describe what data you're looking for and quickly obtain your desired results. Query-by-example is a term for a method of obtaining data pioneered by IBM in the 1970s, and graphical QBE is the method of query-by-example implemented by Microsoft in Access. With graphical QBE, you can perform most of the aspects of designing the query by dragging objects around a query form. Most queries that you'll perform in Access are likely to be *select queries*; these queries select desired information, based on how you structure the query. Select queries can display all fields in a table, certain fields, all records, certain records, or even a combination of selected portions of records from more than one table. Queries also can be used to sort your data, to ask questions about data stored in other file formats (such as

Paradox or dBASE files), and to calculate totals of numeric fields. You can base forms, reports, and even other queries on the results of queries.

As an example of the kind of task queries are needed for, using Earth Aware's tables introduced in the previous chapter, perhaps you want to see a list of donations made by each member in the organization. The member names are in one table, but the donations made by each member are in another table. To see the donations made by each member, you would need to examine data from both the tables, as illustrated in FIG. 5-1.

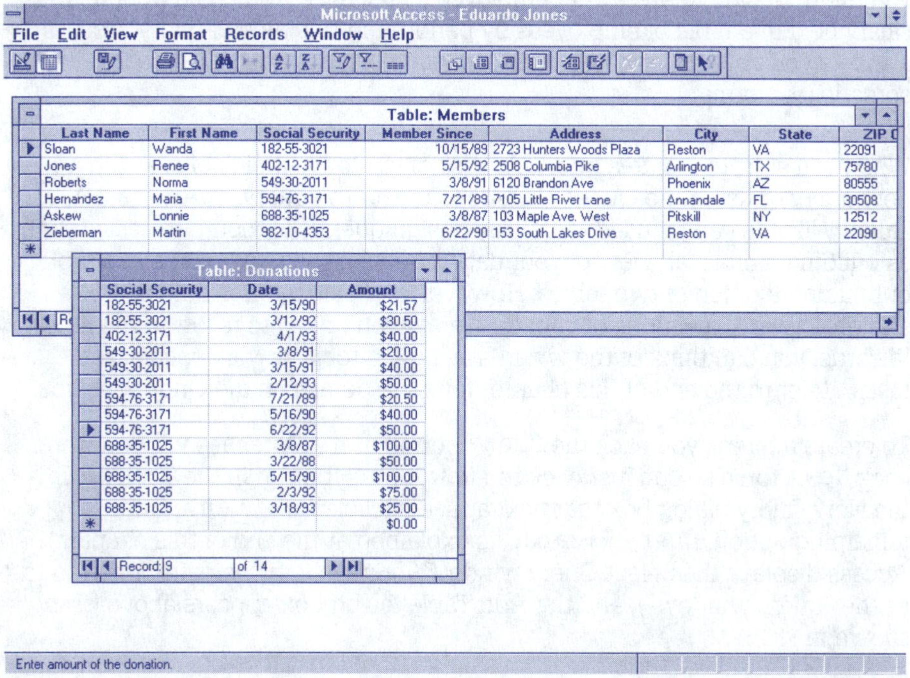

5-1
The concept of Select Query.

Once you run a select query, Access presents your data as a set of records in something called a *dynaset*. A dynaset strongly resembles a table, but it really isn't. Instead, it is a *dynamic* set of records from the table or tables the query is based on—hence the name, dynaset. For users of other PC-based databases, this is an important distinction to appreciate, because dynasets offer flexibilities that are not available in many other database managers. Some other database managers that use a form of query-by-example produce sets of data that are static, meaning they are a copy of the data in the original tables. If you make changes to the data in the answer provided by the query, you are not changing the data in the original tables.

In Access, because the answers to a table are dynamic and not static, you see the actual data in the answer to the query. If you make a change to the data in the dynaset, you are changing the data in the original table. An important plus for network users is that, because the data is dynamic, any changes made by others to the same table will be immediately apparent. Another significant plus of Access is that it lets you easily use queries as the basis for data shown in your forms or printed in your reports. You'll find additional details in chapters 6 and 7 on how you can base a form or a report on a query.

Select queries are not the only type of query that you can perform in Access; you also can perform *action queries*, which make changes to a group of records in a single operation. For example, in a moment of insane generosity, you might decide to give every employee a 20% raise. You could update a salary field in a table of employees by performing this type of query. Access also lets you perform *crosstab queries*, which present numeric data in spreadsheet format.

Creating a query

When you start to create a query, Access gives you a choice of creating a new query or using the Query Wizards to create the query. In Access 2.0, Query Wizards can be used to quickly design queries for complex tasks, such as building a crosstab view of your data, finding duplicate records in a table, or building a union of two tables. However, for basic queries that ask straightforward questions of your data, you won't need to resort to the Query Wizards; you can think of the wizards as power tools for very specialized tasks. Refer to the end of this chapter for more details on the Query Wizards.

To create a query, you click the `Query` button in the Database window, then click `New`. (You also can just click the `New Query` button in the Toolbar.) In the New Query dialog box that next appears, click `New Query`. (The remaining option, `Query Wizards`, is explained at the end of this chapter.) Access displays the Select Query window (for simplicity, hereafter referred to as the "query window"), and the Add Table dialog box appears above it, as shown in FIG. 5-2.

In the Add Table dialog box, you click the table or tables that you want to base the query on. (Queries also can be based on existing queries.) After clicking a table, click `Add`, and a list box of the table's fields appears in the query window. (If you are designing a relational query to access multiple tables, you can repeat this step for all tables that are to be used in the query. See "Using queries to draw relationships" later in this chapter for details.) When you are done adding tables to the query, click `Close` to put away the Add Table dialog box.

TIP

Another way to create a query is to click the `Table` button in the Database window, click the desired table to select it, then click the `New Query` button in the Toolbar, and in the dialog box that next appears, click `New Query`. Access opens a query window containing that table; you then can choose `Query/Add Table` if you want to add additional tables to the query.

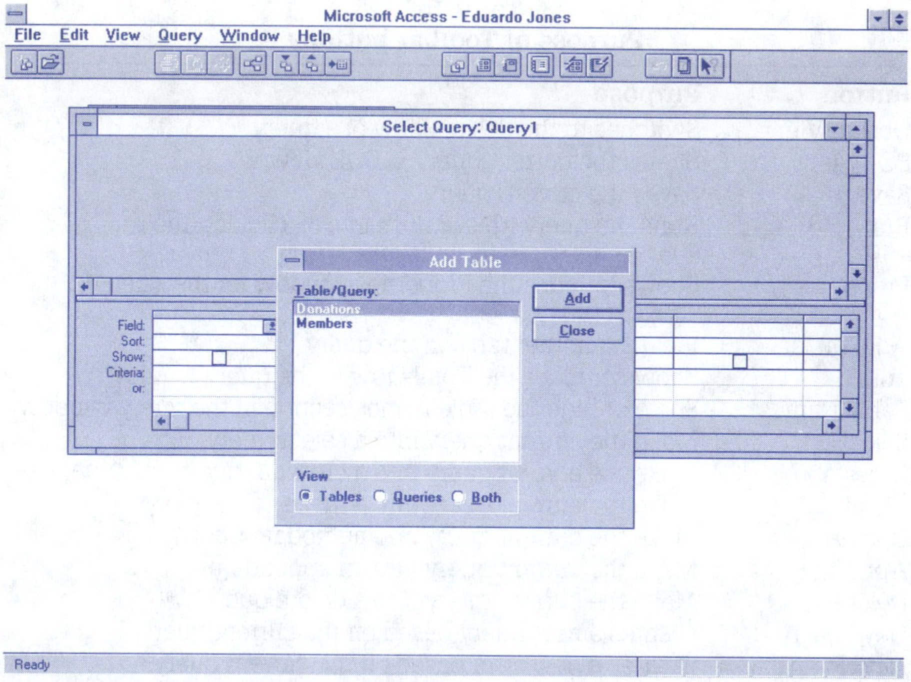

5-2
The Select Query window with the Add Table dialog box.

About the query window

The Query window is divided into two portions. The upper portion displays the field lists for all tables that you included in the query, and the lower portion displays the query form itself, where you will indicate which fields will be included in the query, how the records should be sorted, and any criteria that will select certain records from the tables.

Whenever a Query window is the active window, the Toolbar takes on an appearance specific to the use of queries. This Query Window Toolbar contains buttons that provide fast ways to perform common query operations, as shown in FIG. 5-3.

The purpose of the Toolbar buttons is outlined in TABLE 5-1.

Adding fields to the query

There are a number of ways that you can add fields to the query, depending on whether you want to add selected fields, or whether you want to add all fields to the query. To add selected fields to a query, you can click and drag each desired field from the Field List to the desired cell within the Field row of the query. As an example, you might create a query based on the Members table detailed in the previous chapter. To create a query containing the Last Name, First Name, City, and State fields, you would drag each of these fields to the Field row of the query form. Figure 5-4 illustrates this process.

Table 5-1
Purpose of Toolbar buttons.

Button	Purpose
Design View	Switches to the design view of a query.
SQL View	Shows the current query in SQL view.
Save	Saves the current query.
Run	Runs the query (this is the same as clicking the `Datasheet view` button).
Properties	Shows or hides the Properties window for the selected object.
Add Table	Include another table in the query.
Totals	Shows or hides the Totals row in the query window.
Table Names	Show or hide the table names section in the query window.
Select	Make the current query into a select query.
Crosstab	Make the current query into a crosstab query.
Make-Table	Make the current query into a make-table query.
Update	Make the current query into an update query.
Append	Make the current query into an append query.
Delete	Make the current query into a delete query.
New Query	Creates a new query based on the current query.
New Form	Creates a new form based on the current query.
New Report	Creates a new report based on the current query.
Show Database	Displays the Database window.
Invoke Builder	Displays the Expression Builder.
Undo	Undoes your last action.
Cue Cards	Displays Cue Cards.
Help	Opens a Help window.

You also can double-click a field name in the Field List; when you do this, it is added to the next blank column of the query grid. You also can just type the name of any field directly into the Field row of the query grid, although the click-and-drag methods generally are faster, and less error-prone, as you reduce the chances of typos using click-and-drag.

To add all fields to a query, you can either select them as a group and drag them all to the query grid, or you can drag the asterisk at the top of the Field List to the query grid. To select the fields as a group, just double-click the Title Bar at the top of the Field List. When you do this, Access selects all the fields. Then, click and drag any of the selected fields to the query grid.

To add all fields using the asterisk, drag the asterisk at the top of the Field List to the query grid or just double-click the asterisk. When you do this, the name of the table appears in the column of the query grid followed by an asterisk, indicating that all fields in the table will be included in the query, as shown in FIG. 5-5.

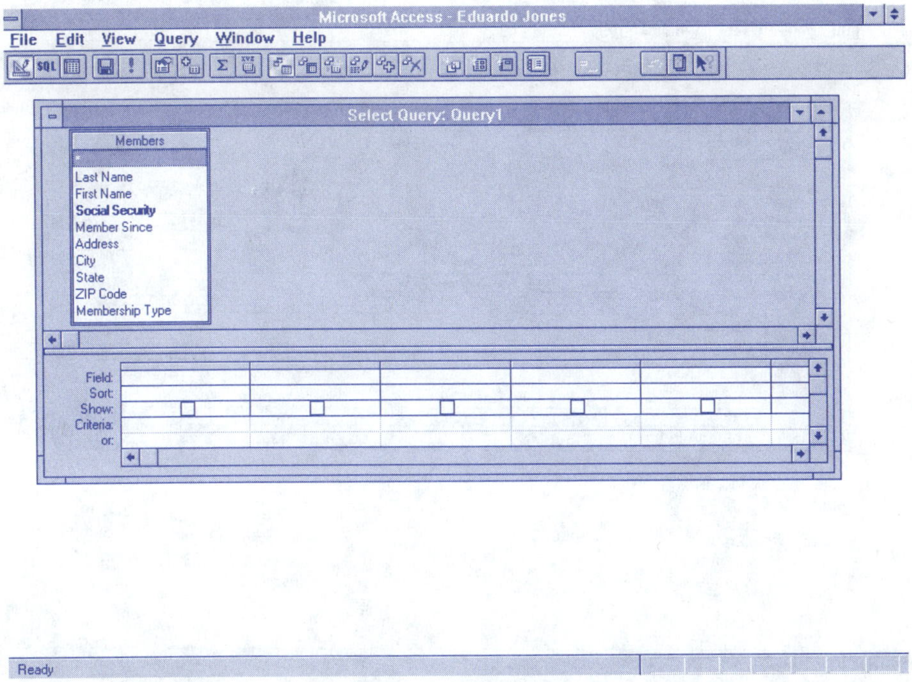

5-3
The Query Window toolbar.

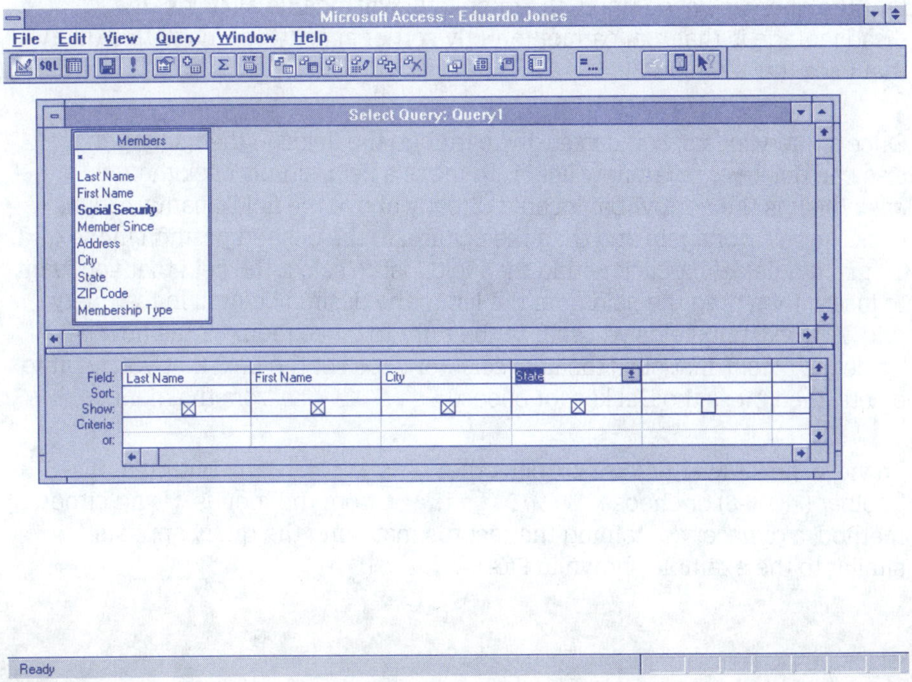

5-4
Adding fields to the query form.

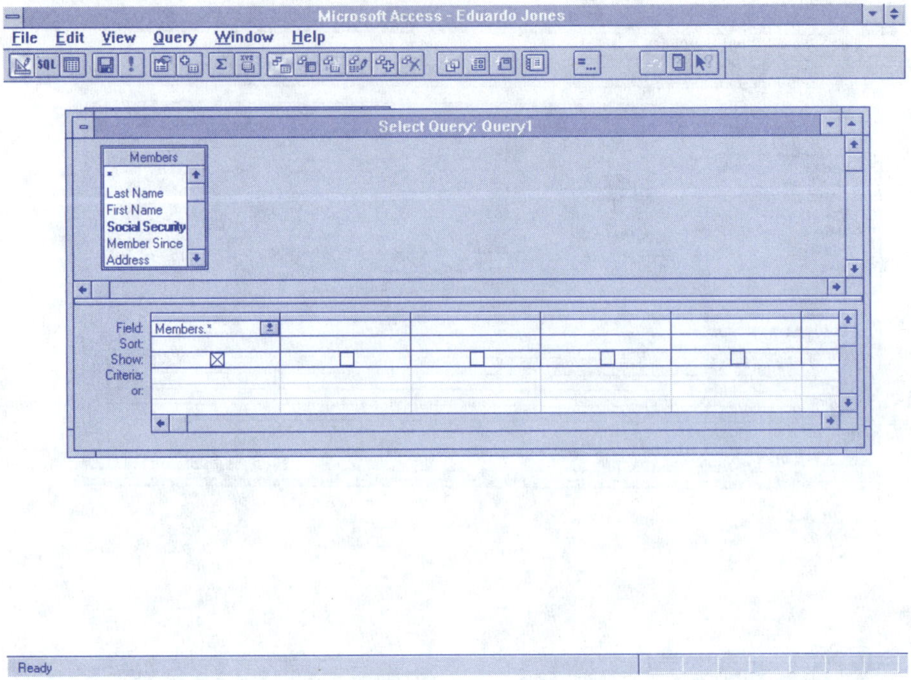

5-5
All fields added by dragging the asterisk.

There are advantages and disadvantages to using the asterisk to indicate all fields. An advantage is that, even if you later change the fields in the table that the query is based upon, the query still will include all fields. A disadvantage is that you cannot directly sort or specify criteria with a query that uses the asterisk.

Rearranging, inserting, & deleting fields

Once a query exists, you can easily rearrange the fields in the query grid; you also can delete or insert new fields. To move a field, simply click the *field selector* (it is the narrow bar located directly above the field's name). Then, click the selector again and drag the column to the desired position in the grid. To insert a field, first click within the Field List to select the field that you want to insert, then drag the field from the list to the desired column in the query grid. Any existing fields will shift to the right to make room for the new field. To delete a field, first click the field selector to select the field that you want to delete, then press the Del key (or choose `Edit/Delete` from the menus).

Viewing the dynaset

To view the answer to a query, click the `Datasheet View` button in the Toolbar (FIG. 5-6) or choose `View/Datasheet` from the menus. Using either method, a dynaset containing the records matching the query appears, similar to the example shown in FIG. 5-7.

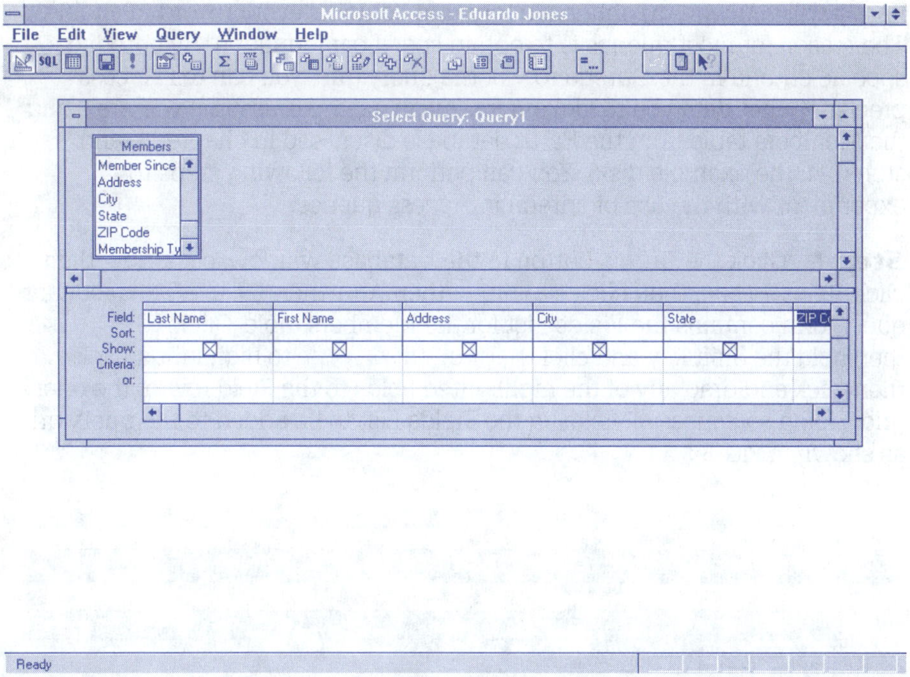

5-6
The Datasheet View *button in the Toolbar.*

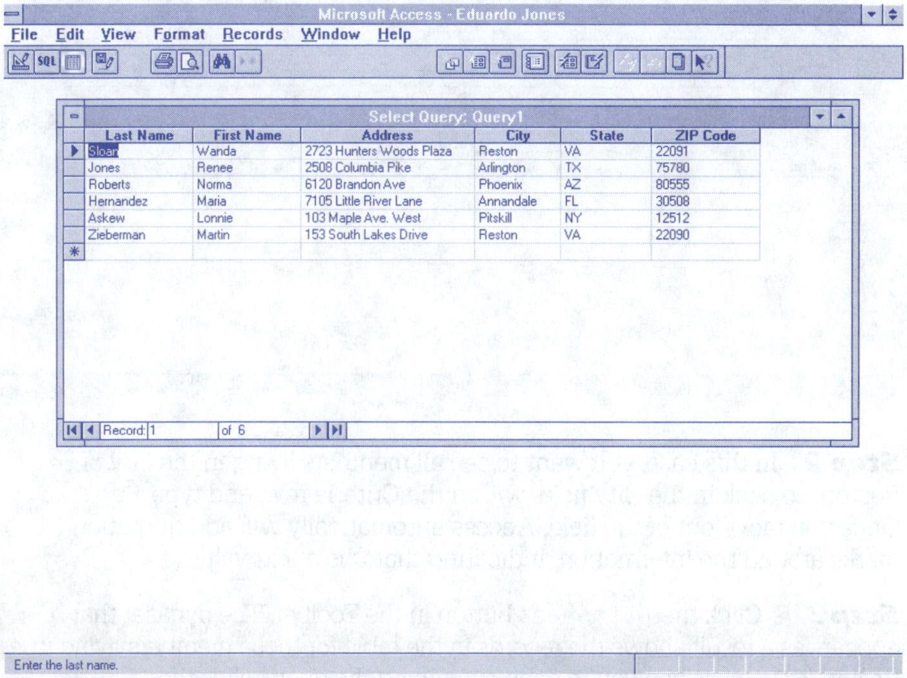

5-7
A response to a typical query.

Using criteria

Rarely will you want to obtain a query that contains every record in a table. The reason for most queries is to obtain specific information. By entering specific criteria in the Criteria row of the query grid, you can tell Access precisely what data you're looking for. As an example, assume you are using the Members table from the Earth database discussed in chapter 4 (and stored on the example disk). You can perform the following steps to experiment with the use of criteria in Access queries.

Step 1 Click the `Query` button in the Database window, click `New`, then click `New Query`, then click `Members`, then `Add`, then `Close`. The resultant query form contains the Fields List for the Members table. Click `Last Name`, then hold the Shift key and click `Membership Type` to highlight all fields, then click and drag any of the highlighted fields to the Field row of the query grid. Doing so causes all fields in the Fields List to be added to the query grid, as shown in FIG. 5-8.

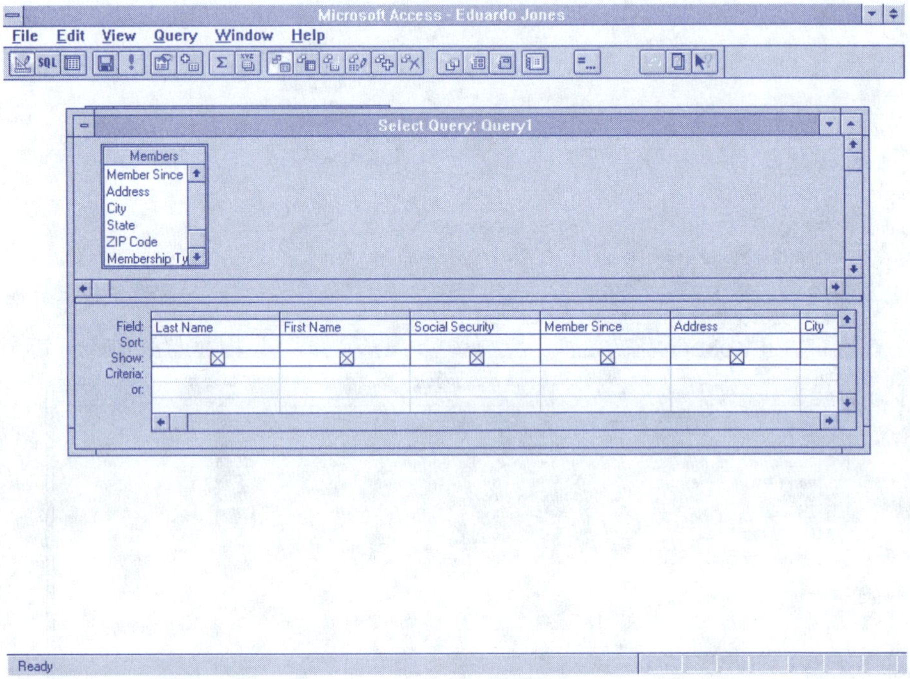

5-8
All fields added to the Members query.

Step 2 In this case, you want to see all members living in the city of Reston, so click in the City field, within the Criteria row, and type `Reston`. Once you move out of the field, Access automatically will add quotation marks around the information, indicating that it is a text value.

Step 3 Click the `Datasheet` button in the Toolbar. The dynaset that appears as a result shows the records in the table for those members living in Reston (FIG. 5-9). When you're done examining the query, click the `Design`

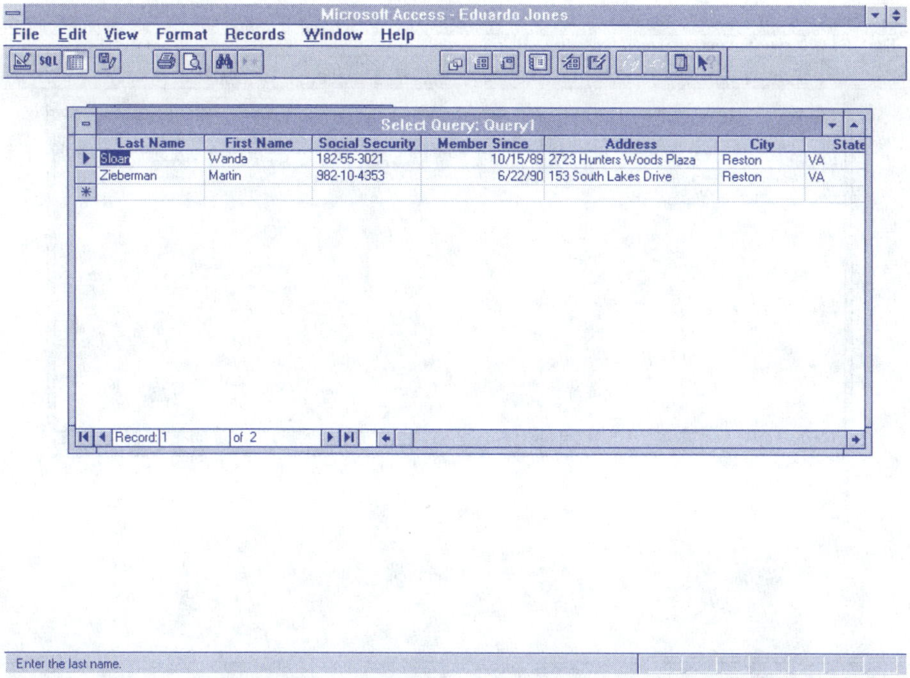

5-9
The results of a query containing a criteria.

button in the Toolbar to switch back to design mode, and delete the prior entry, `Reston`, from the query grid if you plan to duplicate the examples that follow.

As an example of a query using a range of dates, you could ask for all members whose membership began in the years 1990 or 1991 with the following steps.

Step 1 Click in the Member Since field, within the Criteria row, and type `Between 1/1/90 and 12/31/91`.

Step 2 Click the `Datasheet` button in the Toolbar. The dynaset that appears as a result shows the records in the table for persons who became members during the years 1990 and 1991 (FIG. 5-10). When done examining the query, click the `Design` button in the Toolbar to switch back to design mode, and delete the prior entries from the Criteria row of the query grid. (Additional details about date ranges and about symbols that you can use in constructing queries are provided in the next section of this chapter.)

Criteria matching on multiple fields

You can select records that meet criteria in two or more fields by simply entering the criteria in the desired format within each field of the query grid. As an example, if you wanted to see all members of the membership type "regular" who live in New York, the following steps would suffice.

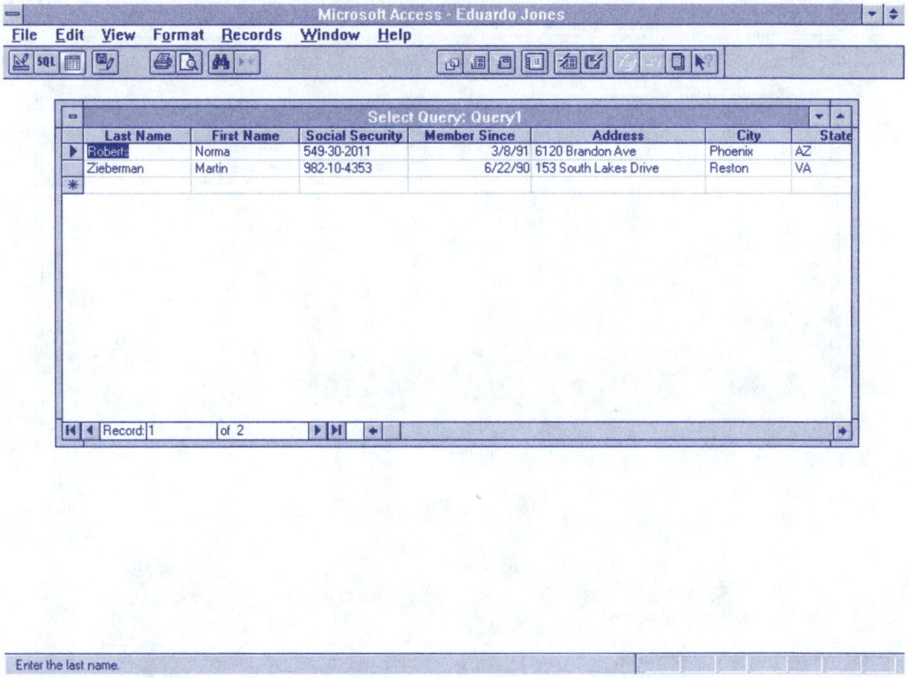

5-10
The results of a date-based query.

Step 1 Click in the State field, within the Criteria row, and type `NY`. Scroll the query window, if necessary, to bring the Membership Type field into view. Click in the Membership Type field, and type `student`.

Step 2 Click the `Datasheet` button in the Toolbar. The dynaset that appears as a result shows the records in the table for those members who live in New York and are of the "student" membership type (FIG. 5-11). When you're done examining the query, click the `Design` button in the Toolbar to switch back to design mode and delete the prior entries from the Criteria row of the query grid.

Building queries based on OR criteria

The types of queries described so far have either been queries selecting records based on a single criteria or have been "AND" queries, where data is selected based on one criteria *and* another criteria both being true. In the database world, this commonly is known as AND logic. In many cases, however, you will need another kind of logic, known as OR logic. In this case, records are qualified if any one of a group of conditions is met. As an example, perhaps you want to display all records of members living in New York or Texas. With the visual query-by-example of Access, OR logic is simple; you just add additional criteria on the lines below your first criteria, using as many lines as are necessary. As an example, consider the query shown in FIG. 5-12.

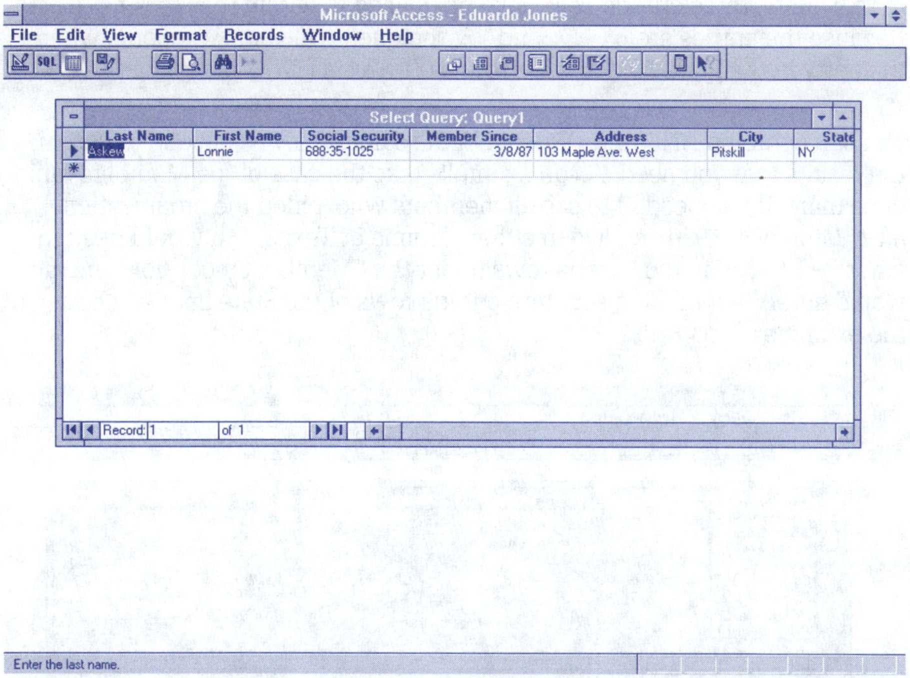

5-11
The results of a query containing multiple criteria.

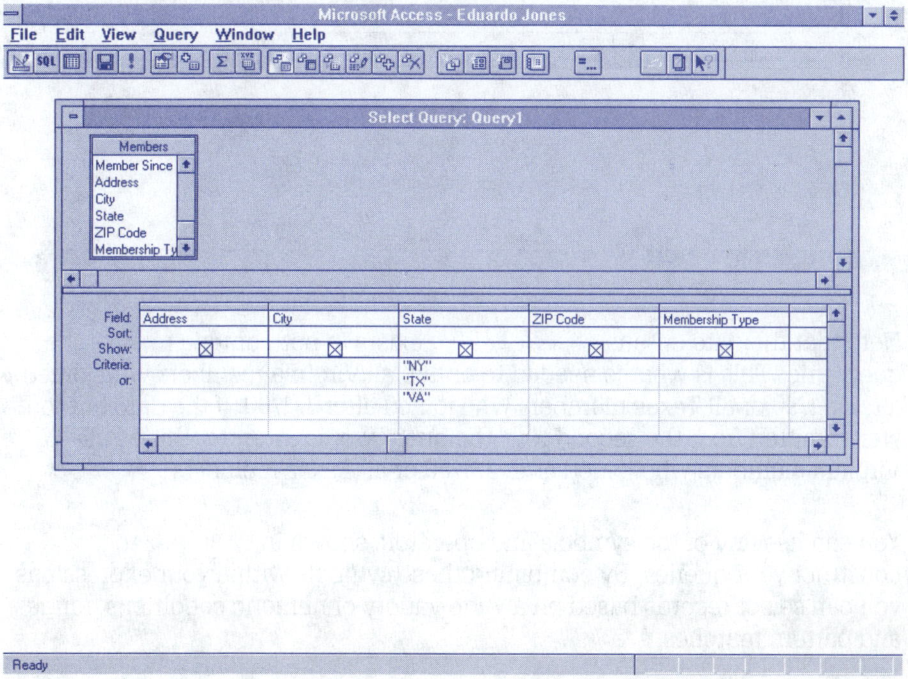

5-12
An example of a query using OR logic.

In this query, three criteria cells have been filled in within the State field. Because the entries are NY, TX, and VA, the query will extract records where the entry in the State field is New York (NY), Texas (TX), or Virginia (VA).

Combining AND & OR criteria

You can combine AND and OR logic in the same query as needed to obtain the results that you need. As an example, take the case of the Members table once more. If you needed to see all members who joined the organization after January 1, 1990 and live in either Virginia or Texas, you would need to enter >=1/1/90 in the criteria rows under the "Member Since" field, and you would enter VA and TX in separate criteria rows of the State field, as shown in the example in FIG. 5-13.

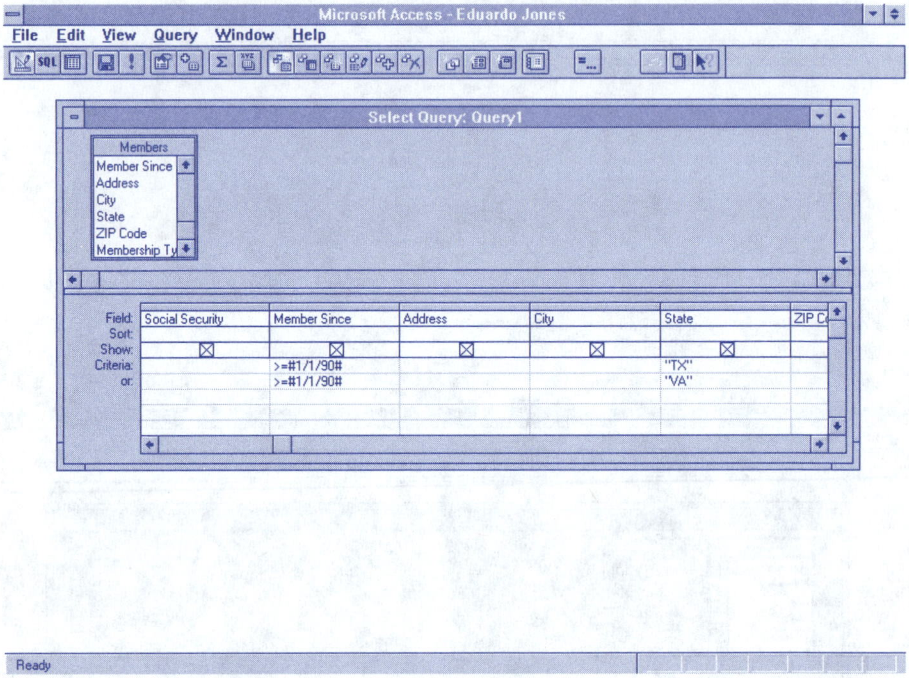

5-13 *A query combining AND and OR logic.*

Note that the date criteria, >=#1/1/90#, exists in both criteria rows of the query grid. This is what is needed to obtain all Virginia members who joined after 1/1/90 or all Texas members who joined after 1/1/90. If the date criteria were omitted from the second row, the query would interpret this as all Virginia members who joined after 1/1/90 or all Texas members.

Using query symbols & operators

You can use any of the symbols and operators shown in TABLE 5-2 to construct your queries. By combining these symbols within your expressions, you can select records based on a wide variety of numeric conditions, ranges, and pattern matches.

Table 5-2
Valid query operators.

Symbol or operator	Meaning	Example
=	Equals	= Robertson
>	Greater than	> 10.00
<	Less than	< 3000
> =	Greater than or equal to	> = 2/1/93
< =	Less than or equal to	< = 3000
< >	Not equal to	< > Texas
Between	Between two values, including the values	Between 10 and 80
In	Within a set of values	In (USA Mexico Canada)
Is Null	Field contains no data	Is Null
Is Not Null	Field contains data	Is Not Null
Like	Pattern matching	Like Jon*
And	Both expressions are true	> 2/1/90 AND < 2/28/90
Or	Either expression is true	USA Or CANADA
Not	Expression is not true	Not Jon*
?	Pattern matching for one character	= (212) 555-????
*	Pattern matching for any characters	Jon*

On occasion, you might need to locate a set of records in which characters match a given pattern. Access permits the use of certain "wildcards" as part of an expression in a query. The valid wildcard operators are the question mark, which represents a single character, and the asterisk, which represents any number of characters. As an example, for a date field, you could enter the expression:

```
LIKE * / * / 93
```

to query a date field for any dates in the year 1993. In a text field containing last names, you could use the expression,

```
LIKE "J*n"
```

to query a last name field for names that might include Joyton, Johnson, and James-Anderson.

Looking for embedded text

You can use the asterisk wildcard character to look for text that is embedded in a field by including an asterisk both before and after the desired search text. As an example, perhaps someone wants to find a member who lives "somewhere on Columbia Pike." In the Address field of the query, you could enter an expression like `"*Columbia Pike*"` and Access would include the desired records in the results. Note that you can use this technique with memo fields to find a text string that is somewhere in the memo text.

Querying for today's date

You can easily query a date field for records matching the current date or for records that match a calculation based on the current date. Simply use the date function in Access, which is DATE(). As an example, if you were to enter the expression:

```
date()
```

within the criteria cell for a date field, the query would select records where the entry in that field matches the current date (according to the computer's clock). You also could use an expression like:

```
between #1/1/92# and date()
```

to retrieve all records with a date falling between January 1, 1992 and the current date. You could retrieve all records falling within the past 30 days with an expression like:

```
between date() and date() - 30
```

Entering expressions

The query-by-example used by some database products (such as Borland's dBASE IV) requires that you enter expressions using a fairly precise syntax, particularly when working with dates. Access, on the other hand, offers quite a bit of flexibility in the manner in which you can enter expressions. Text can be entered with or without quotes and preceded or not preceded by an equal symbol. (When you move out of the field or when the query is run, Access automatically adds quotes around the text.) As an example, all four of the following expressions would mean the same thing in a text field of an Access query:

```
Texas
"Texas"
=Texas
="Texas"
```

Dates can be entered in nearly any date format. The # symbol surrounding dates is optional, but Access automatically will add this symbol around a date value that you enter into a query. As an example of dates, any of the following entries would be acceptable:

```
Apr 30 92
#4/30/92#
30 April 1992
4/30/92
30-Apr-92
```

Logical (yes/no) values can be entered as Yes or No, True or False, On or Off, or as numeric values of –1 (for yes) and 0 (for no).

Is Null & Is Not Null

If you need to locate a set of records where there is no entry in a specific field, you can use the term `Is Null` as an expression that tells Access to find records where no data is in the field. Note that this is not the same as simply leaving a field in the query grid empty. An empty field in the query grid tells Access that it does not matter what is in that field in a given record. The term `Is Null` indicates that the field must be blank (contain no data) before the record will appear in the dynaset in response to the query. The opposite expression, `Is Not Null`, can be used to indicate that the field must contain some kind of data.

Using the NOT operator

At times, you might want to query your database for records that do not match a particular value. For example, you might want to see all customers who do not live in Atlanta. You can do so by including the NOT operator within a query expression. For example, in a City field, you could enter the expression `Not "Atlanta"` to find all records from cities other than Atlanta.

Using ranges

The range operators (which are shown in TABLE 5-2) can be used to select records that fall within a certain range of values. Database users often think of numeric and currency values as falling within certain ranges, but you can use the range operators with text as well or with date values. You could design a query to select all records with last names from the letters *A* through *M*, or you could use a date field in a table of customer orders to show all orders processed between the first and last day of a certain month. As an example try using the range operators on the Members table, to obtain all members whose last names start with letters between *M* and *Z*. You can use these steps to try this.

Step 1 In the Database window, click the `Query` button, then click `New`, then click `New Query` to open a new query.

Step 2 In the Add Table dialog box, click `Members`, then click `Add`, then click `Close`. Click the Last Name field, then scroll down to the Membership Type field, then hold Shift and click it to highlight all the fields. Click and drag any field to the first empty cell of the Field row of the query grid to place all fields in the query.

Step 3 Click in the Criteria row of the Last Name field, and type the following criteria:

```
between "M" and "Zz"
```

Choose `Query/Run` (or click the Run Query icon in the Toolbar). Your results, shown in FIG. 5-14, contain all records falling in the range of letters specified.

In this example, notice the inclusion of the second letter *z*. It is important in this case, because if it were omitted, Access would retrieve all names up to *Z*, but none following the letter *Z* alone. This would have the effect of omitting

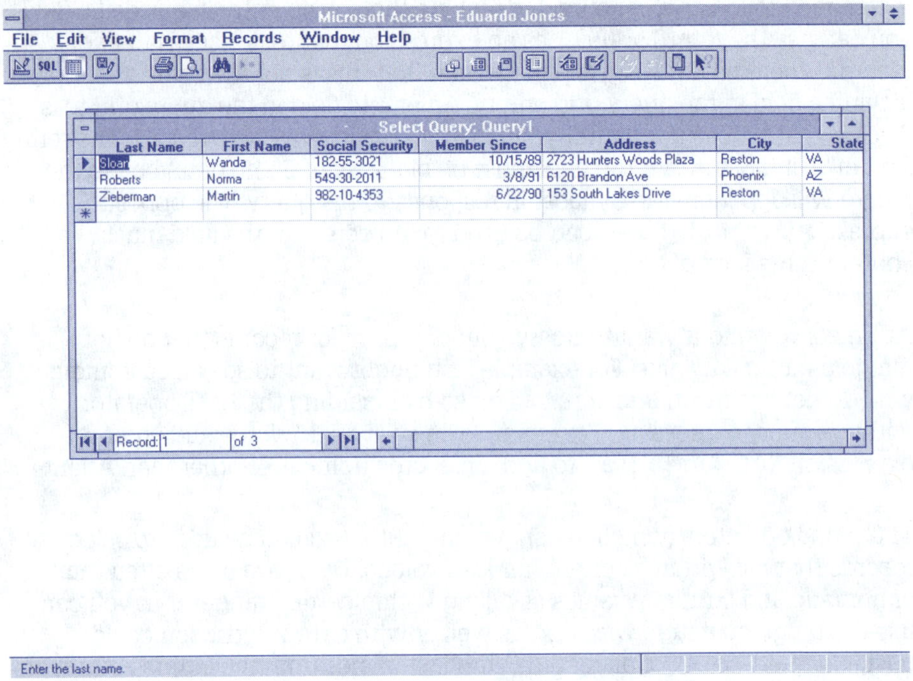

5-14
A query using a range to select names from M through Z.

all last names containing more than one character and beginning with *Z*. You can try a range criteria for a date field with the following steps.

Step 1 Choose `View/Query Design` (or click the Design icon in the Toolbar) to switch back to design mode for the existing query. Delete the existing criteria in the Last Name field.

Step 2 Click in the Criteria row of the Member Since field, and type the following criteria.

```
Between 1/1/90 And 12/31/91
```

Choose `Query/Run` (or click the Run Query icon in the Toolbar). Your results, shown in FIG. 5-15, contain all records where the date in the Member Since field falls between January 1, 1990 and December 31, 1991.

Omitting fields from the dynaset

Access gives you the ability to omit fields from the dynaset that results from your queries. As an example, you might want to display only those members living in Virginia, but you do not want the data from the State field included in the results of the query. To omit a field from the results, click the Show check box for that field to remove the `X` in the box. (By default, an `X` appears in the Show check box for any field included in the query, indicating that the field will be shown in the results.) As an example, in FIG. 5-16, the State field contains a criteria limiting the records to Texas (`TX`), but the `X` has been

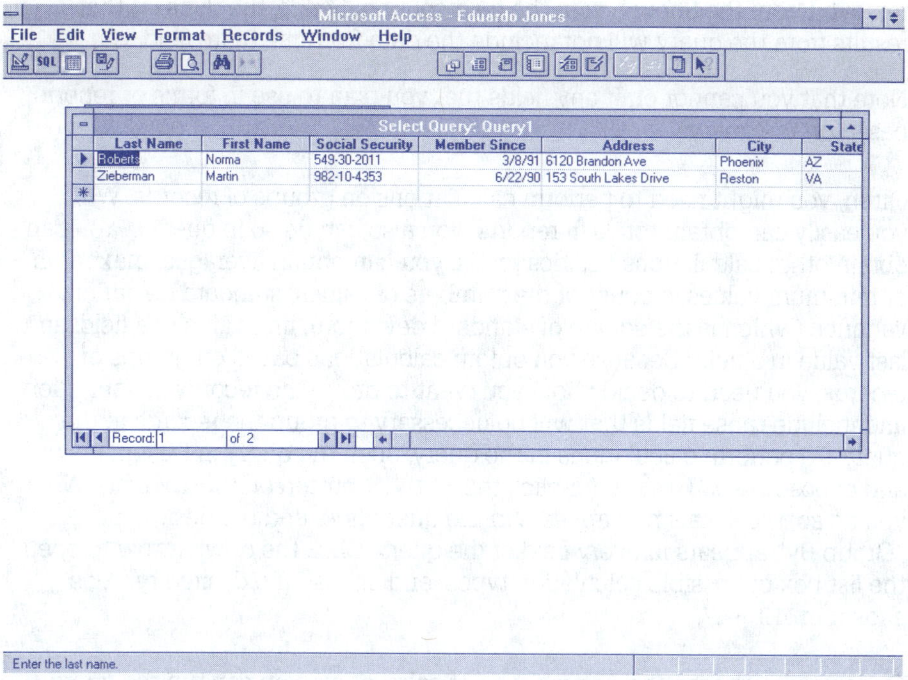

5-15
A query using a range to select dates in 1990 or 1991.

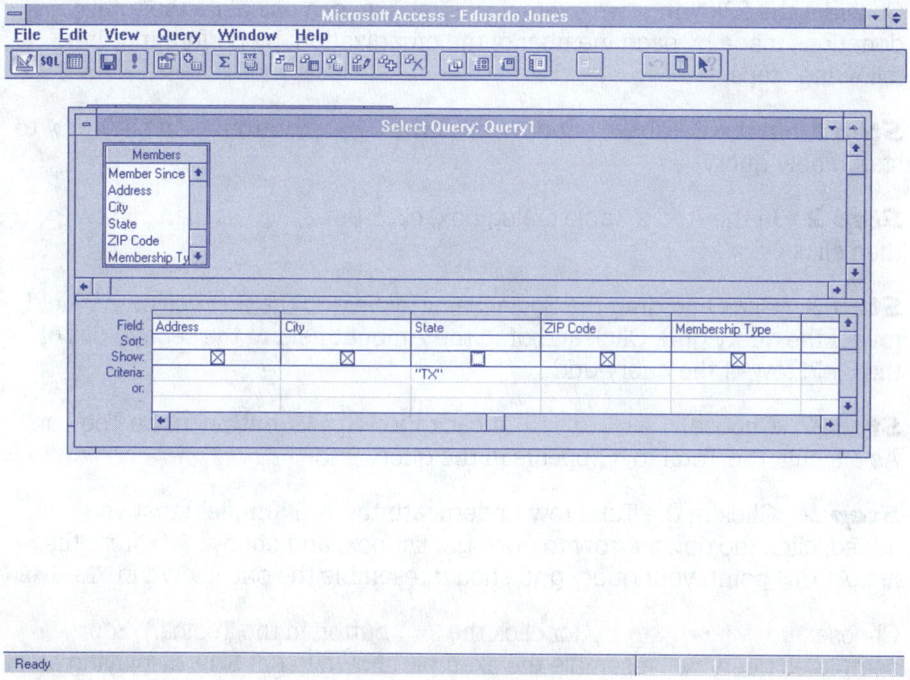

5-16
A query with a field omitted from the results.

removed from the Show box in the field column; hence, the dynaset that results from the query will not include the data from the State field.

Note that you cannot omit any fields that you plan to use in forms or reports based on the query.

Including calculations in queries

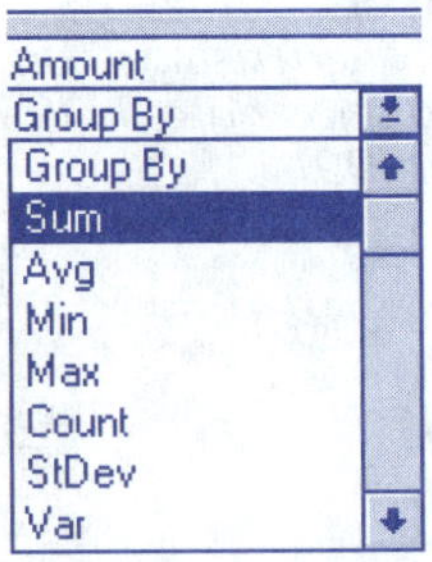

5-17 *The available types of queries.*

Often, you might need to perform calculations on groups of records. While you easily can obtain totals in reports, you also can do so in queries. You can obtain other calculations besides totals: you can obtain averages, maximum or minimum values, a count of the numbers of values, standard deviation, variance (which is the square of standard deviation), first value in a field, and last value in a field. Because you obtain calculations based on groups of records, you need to decide how you want to group the records in your query and include those fields that will be necessary to group the records in the query. To perform calculations in the query, open the query in Design view and choose `View/Totals` (or click the `Totals` button on the Toolbar). When you do so, the Totals row appears in the query grid, and the designation "Group By" appears in every field of the query. Click the down arrow to open the list box of possible calculation types, and choose the desired type, as shown in FIG. 5-17.

Once you've chosen the desired type of calculation, you can run the query, and the calculation will appear in the result.

Consider the following two examples. First, you can calculate the total donations made by each member of the organization, by performing the following steps.

Step 1 In the Database window, click the `Query` button, then click `New` to start a new query.

Step 2 In the Add a Table dialog box, click `Donations`, then click `Add`, then click `Close`.

Step 3 Click and drag the Social Security field to the first cell of the Field row of the query grid. Click and drag the Amount field to the second cell of the Field row of the query grid.

Step 4 Choose `View/Totals` or click the `Totals` button in the Toolbar. As a result, the Total row appears in the query grid.

Step 5 Click in the Total row underneath the Amount field that you've added, click the down arrow to open the list box, and choose `Sum` from the list. At this point, your query grid should resemble the one shown in FIG. 5-18.

Choose `Query/Run Query` (or click the `Run` button in the Toolbar). Your completed query will resemble the example shown in FIG. 5-19, displaying a sum of the donations for each member of the organization. (Ideally, you

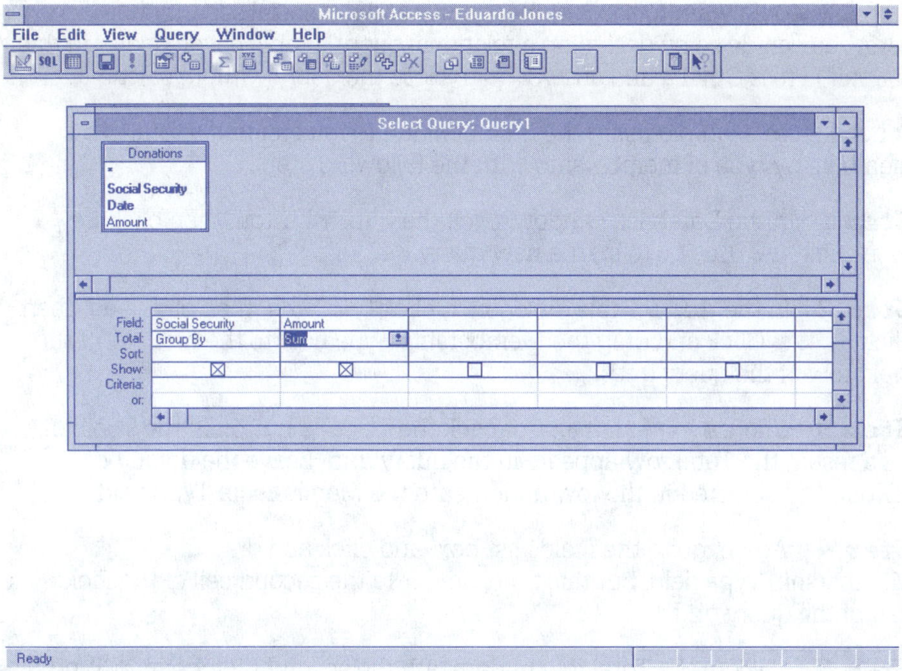

5-18
A query based on the sum of donations.

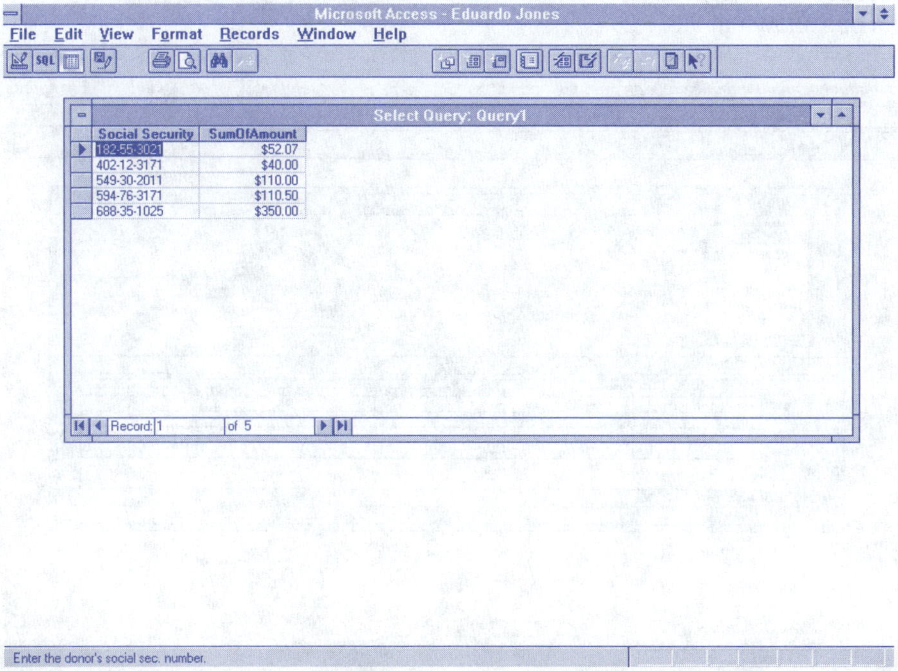

5-19
The results of a query based on the sum of donations.

probably would want to see member names and not social security numbers here; you can do so by designing a relational query, a topic covered later in this chapter.) Press Ctrl–F4 and answer No to close the query without saving it.

For one more example using the Members table, you can find a total of all members by type of membership with the following steps.

Step 1 In the Database window, click the Query button, then click New, then click New Query to start a new query.

Step 2 In the Add a Table dialog box, click Members, then click Add, then click Close. Click and drag the Membership Type field to the first cell of the Field row of the query grid.

Step 3 Choose View/Totals or click the Totals button in the Toolbar. As a result, the Total row appears in the query grid. Leave the default of "Group By" selected in the row underneath the Membership Type field.

Step 4 Again, go to the Fields list box, and click and drag the Membership Type field, but this time, drag it to the second cell of the Field row of the query grid.

Step 5 Click in the Total row underneath the second Membership Type field that you've added, click the down arrow to open the list box. This time, choose Count from the list. At this point, your query grid should resemble the one shown in FIG. 5-20.

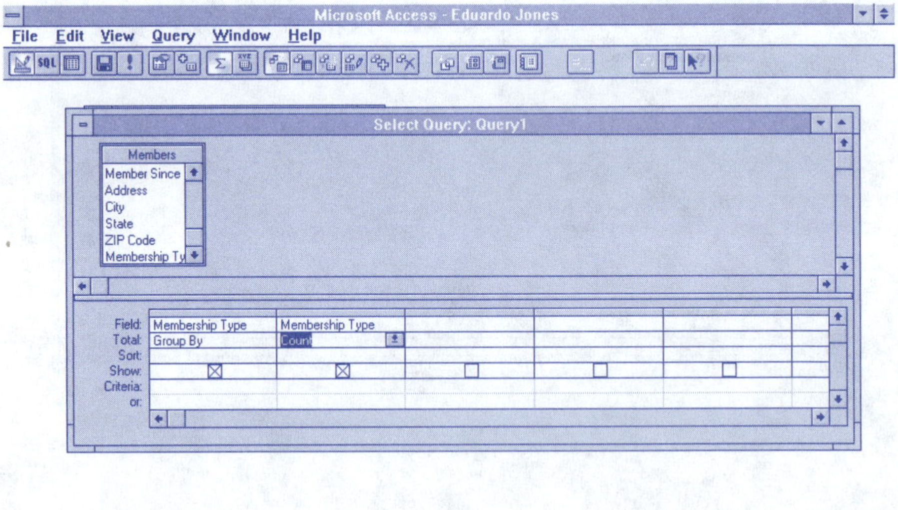

5-20
A query based on the count of groups of members.

Step 6 Choose Query/Run Query (or click the Run button in the Toolbar). Your completed query will resemble the example shown in FIG. 5-21, displaying a count of each group of records using the Membership Type field. (Press Ctrl–F4 and answer No to close the query without saving it.)

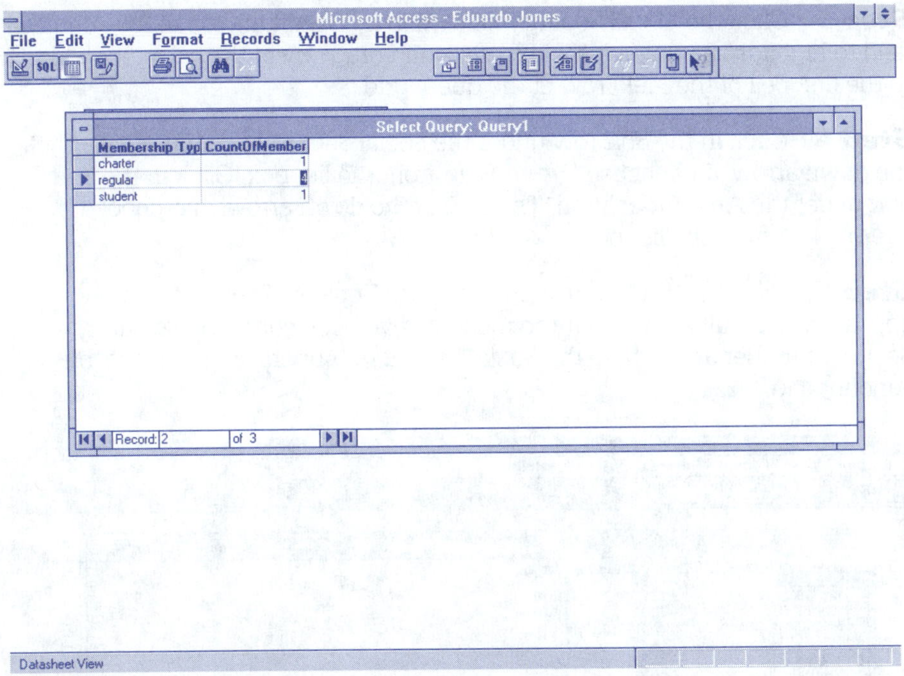

5-21
The results of a query based on the count of groups of members.

Sorting records

Another important use for queries is in the sorting, or arranging, of your data in the desired order. (By default, Access sorts tables in the order of the primary key; if you create a table that has no primary key, by default Access displays the data in the order in which the records were entered into the table.) Your data can be sorted alphabetically or numerically, in either ascending (A–Z, 0–9) or descending (Z–A, 9–0) order. You can sort on a single field (such as a Last Name field) or on a combination of fields (up to a maximum of 10 fields). To sort the records in a query, perform the following steps.

Step 1 Open the query in Design view. Click the Sort cell in the query grid for the field that you want to sort.

Step 2 Click the down arrow and select ascending or descending.

Step 3 To sort on additional fields, repeat steps 1 and 2.

To consider an example of a sort, you can sort the Donations table in the order of Social Security, then by Amount, by performing the following steps.

Step 1 In the Database window, click the `Query` button, then click `New` to start a new query.

Step 2 In the Add a Table dialog box, click `Donations`, then click `Add`, then click `Close`.

Step 3 Click the Social Security field, then hold Shift and click the Amount field to highlight all the fields. Next, click and drag any of the selected fields to the first cell of the Field row of the query grid.

Step 4 Click in the Sort row under the Social Security column. Then, click the down arrow, and choose `Ascending` from the list box. Click in the Sort row under the Amount column. Then, click the down arrow, and choose `Ascending` from the list box.

Step 5 Click the `Datasheet` button in the Toolbar. The dynaset that appears as a result shows that the records have been sorted by Social Security number and, where the Social Security numbers are the same, by Amount (FIG. 5-22).

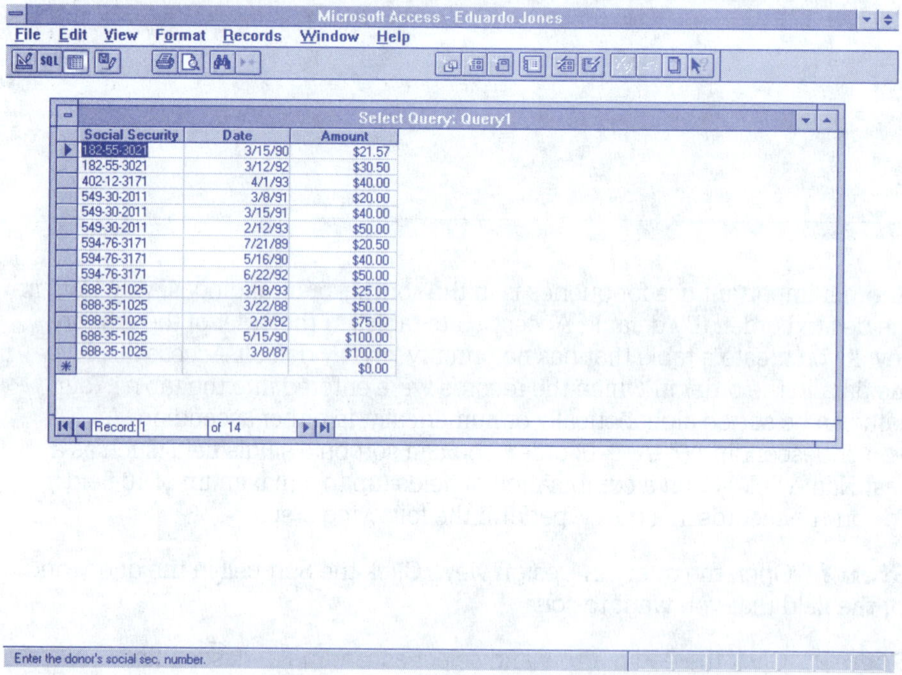

Social Security	Date	Amount
182-55-3021	3/15/90	$21.57
182-55-3021	3/12/92	$30.50
402-12-3171	4/1/93	$40.00
549-30-2011	3/8/91	$20.00
549-30-2011	3/15/91	$40.00
549-30-2011	2/12/93	$50.00
594-76-3171	7/21/89	$20.50
594-76-3171	5/16/90	$40.00
594-76-3171	6/22/92	$50.00
688-35-1025	3/18/93	$25.00
688-35-1025	3/22/88	$50.00
688-35-1025	2/3/92	$75.00
688-35-1025	5/15/90	$100.00
688-35-1025	3/8/87	$100.00
*		$0.00

5-22
The results of a query including a sort.

TIP

Queries are not the only way to sort your data within Access. You can quickly sort a table based on a field or a selected group of fields by using the Sort buttons on the Toolbar. You also can tell Access to sort within reports or in forms; see chapters 6 and 7 for details.

There are some important notes to remember when sorting within a query. The order in which you place your fields on the query grid is important when you are sorting on multiple fields. Once you've identified the fields to be sorted, Access sorts using the leftmost sort field first, then the next sort field to the right, and so on. Using the previous example, assuming that you wanted to sort on the Amount field first, then the Social Security field, the Amount field would have to be to the left of the Social Security field in the query grid. If the fields aren't in the order that you need, rearrange the fields before performing the query. (See "Rearranging, inserting, and deleting fields" earlier in this chapter for details on moving fields around in the query.)

Opening existing queries

To open an existing query, first click the `Query` button in the Database window; doing so causes all queries to be displayed. Next, either click the desired query in the list box and click `Open` or just double-click the desired query. Either method will cause the chosen query to open in a datasheet view.

To open an existing query in design view (where you can make changes to the design of the query), first click the `Query` button in the Database window. Next, click the desired query within the list box, then click `Design`. As a result, the query opens in the Design window, and you can make the desired changes to the query. (An alternate way to open a query in design view is to double-right-click the desired query in the Database window.)

Getting the latest data on a network

When you run a query while on a network, Access gives you the latest data based on the underlying tables at the time the query runs. It's always possible that if the query is open for some time, others might change the underlying data, and your query will no longer reflect reality. You can display the most current data at any time, by pressing Shift–F9.

Saving queries

To save a query, choose `File/Save` from the menus. If you are saving the query for the first time, Access will display a dialog box asking for a name for the new query. Enter the desired name (up to 64 characters in length, and spaces are allowed), then click `OK`.

TIP

You also can double-click the `Close` button of a query window to close the query; if it is a new query or an existing query that you have made changes to, Access will ask if you want to save the changes. Click `Yes` in the dialog box, and the query will be saved.

Printing queries

You can easily print the contents of your queries. This capability of Access provides an excellent way to get a fast report, although such a report will not contain the fancy formatting offered by reports that you design in Access. You can print a query by performing the following steps.

Step 1 Open the query in Datasheet view.

Step 2 If you desire only certain records in the datasheet, select those records.

Step 3 Choose `File/Print` from the menus, or click the Print icon in the Toolbar.

Step 4 When the Print dialog box appears, if you selected certain records, click the `Selection` button in the dialog box. Choose any other desired options in the dialog box, then click `OK`.

You'll find a more detailed explanation of the Print dialog box and details on the topic of designing and printing reports in chapter 7.

TIP

To obtain a fast, formatted report of your query data, use the ReportWizard to create a report and base it on your query. Create a new report using the ReportWizard (see chapter 7 for more details). In the Select A Table/Query list box (in the New Report dialog box), choose your query by name as the source of the records, then answer the remaining questions asked by the ReportWizard and save the report.

Using queries to draw relationships

Access lets you draw relationships between tables using either of two methods. One way is to set the relationships at the table level, using the `Edit/Relationships` command from the menus. (This technique was covered in the previous chapter.) The other method is to use queries to draw relationships between more than one table.

To build a relational query, open a new query and add the desired tables, using the techniques detailed earlier in the chapter. If you are using Access 2.0 and the tables share a common field name and field type, Access automatically will join them (a line appears between the field lists for the tables). You can manually join the tables in the query window. To join two tables, you simply click a field in one table and drag it to the equivalent field in the other table. (When you do this a *join line* appears between the tables, indicating that they have been joined.) You then can proceed to drag the desired fields into the query grid as detailed earlier in the chapter, add any desired selection or sorting criteria, and run the query to obtain your desired results. Figure 5-23 shows a query based on two tables, with a join established between the common Social Security field.

Five fields (Last Name, First Name, Member Since, Date, and Amount) have been added to the query, and a sort order has been specified for the Date field. Figure 5-24 shows the results when the query is run.

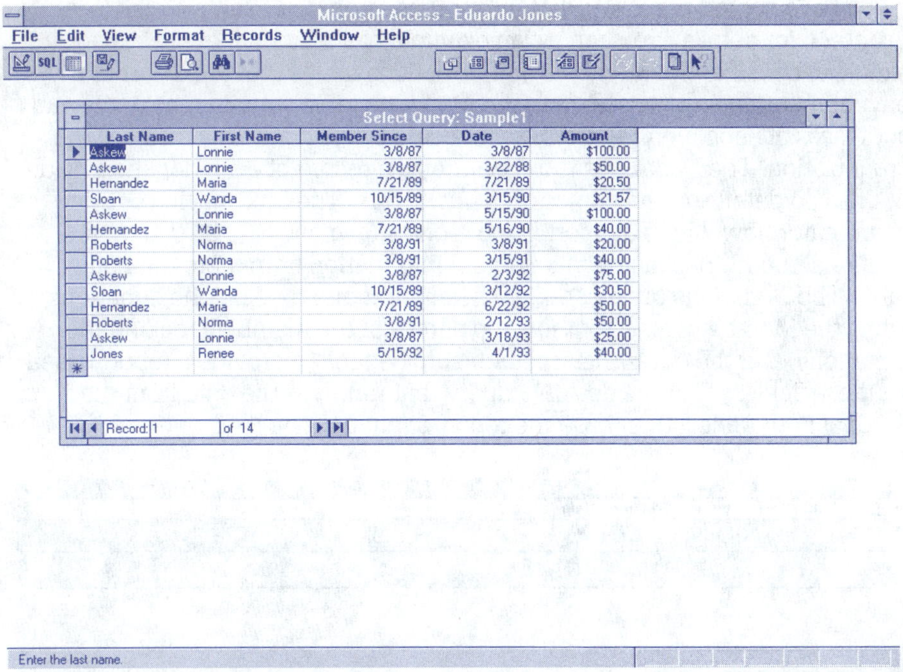

5-23
A query based on multiple tables.

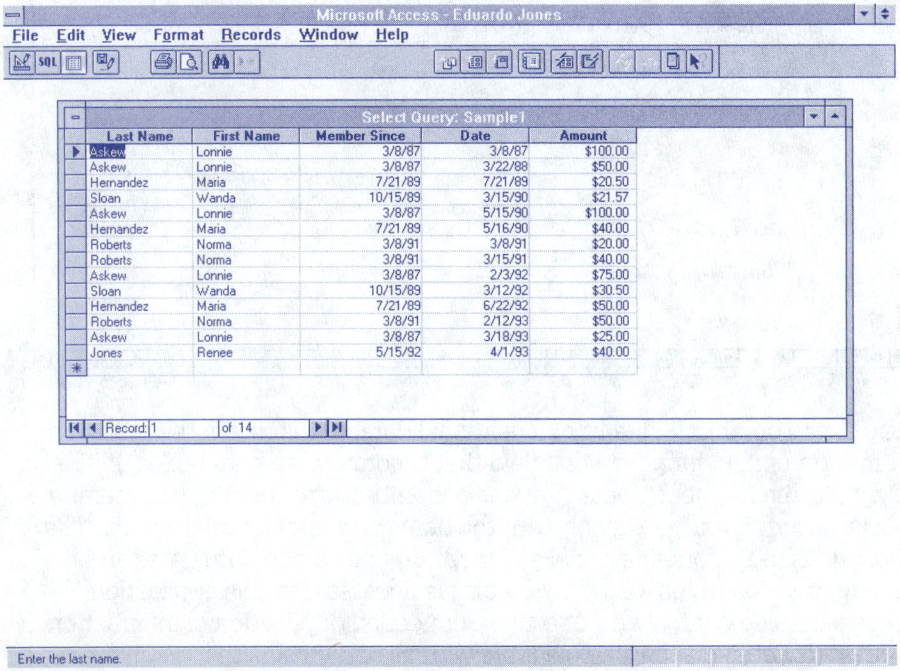

5-24
The results of a relational query.

Hands-on practice: a relational query

If you have copied the EARTH.MDB database from the example disk (see chapter 4 for details), you can try an example of a relational query. As an example, consider the Members and Donations tables that are a part of the environmental group's database. The Members table contains the name and addresses of each member but has no record of the donations made to the organization. The Donations table maintains a record of each donation made but has no details on the names of the members. The fund-raising coordinator now wants a report like the one shown in FIG. 5-25. This is a relational report, because it must obtain information from more than one table. The Donations table contains the amount and dates of the donations, while the Members table contains the names of the members making the donations, and the dates their membership began. To provide a report based on these fields, you must design a query that retrieves the data from the fields of both tables, then base the report on that query.

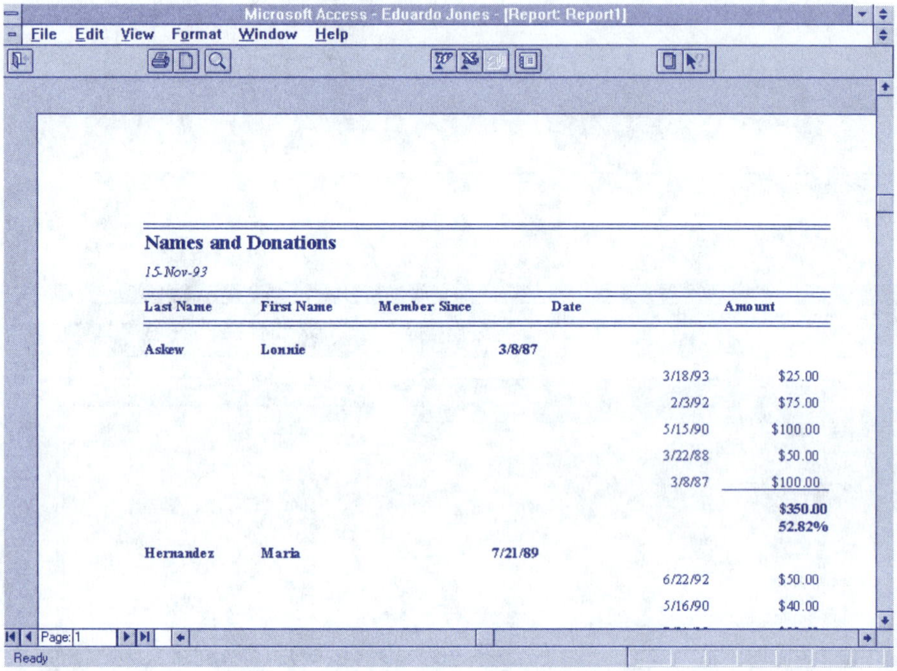

5-25 *An example of a relational report.*

The key to obtaining data from a relational database is to join the tables on some sort of matching field or a field that is common to both tables. In this example, the Members table contains a membership identifier (the member's social security number), along with the name and address information. The Donations table contains social security numbers, along with dates and amounts of donations. Using two tables is necessary in this application, because a single table would result in unneeded duplication of information. If you were working with a single table with all of the fields that are in these two tables, each time a member made a donation, you would need to reenter the name and address of that member. To avoid this kind of duplication, two tables are used, and the tables are joined together on the common field. It is important to note that without a field containing matching data in the tables, such a link is not possible. This is one reason that the design of complex, relational databases is not to be taken lightly. If you omit an important identifying field during the table design process, you might find it difficult or impossible to establish the needed relationships later.

To obtain a list with the member's name, date of the donation, and amount of the donation, perform the following steps.

Step 1 In the Database window, click the `Query` button, then click `New`, then click New Query to open a new query. The Add Table dialog box appears above the new query window.

Step 2 Click `Members`, then click `Add` to add the Members table to the query. Click `Donations`, then click `Add` to add the Donations table to the query. Then, click `Close` to put away the Add Table dialog box.

Step 3 If a line does not automatically appear between the Members and Donations field lists, click on the Social Security field in the Members table, and drag over to the Social Security field in the Donations table. When the mouse pointer changes to the shape of a small rectangle, release the mouse button. A join line will appear between the tables, as shown in FIG. 5-26.

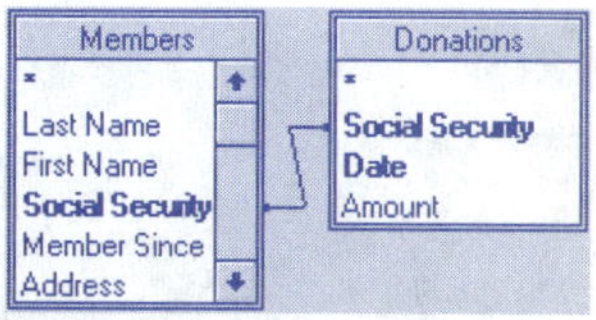

5-26 *The join line between the tables.*

Step 4 In the Members field list, click the Last Name field, and drag it down to the first empty cell in the Field row of the query grid.

Step 5 Click the First Name field, and drag it down to the next empty cell in the Field row of the query grid. Click the Member Since field, and drag it down to the next empty cell in the Field row of the query grid.

Step 6 In the Donations field list, click the Date field, and drag it down to the next empty cell in the Field row of the query grid.

Step 7 Click the Amount field, and drag it down to the next empty cell in the Field row of the query grid. At this point, your query window should resemble the example shown earlier in FIG. 5-23.

Step 8 To run the query, choose `Query/Run` from the menus (or click the Run icon in the Toolbar). The results should resemble those shown in FIG. 5-27.

Step 9 Press Ctrl–F4 to close the query window. Access will ask if you want to save the query; click `Yes`. When prompted for a name for the query, enter `Names and Donations`, then click `OK`.

You can see how you can use a ReportWizard to quickly design a report based on the relational query by performing the following steps. (For more details about reports, refer to chapter 7.)

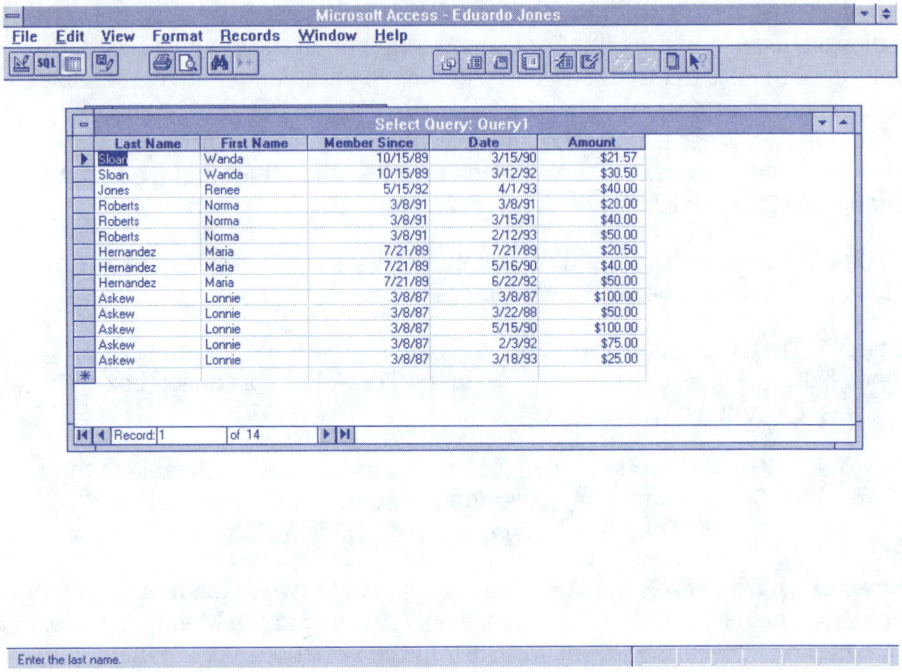

5-27 *An example of a relational query.*

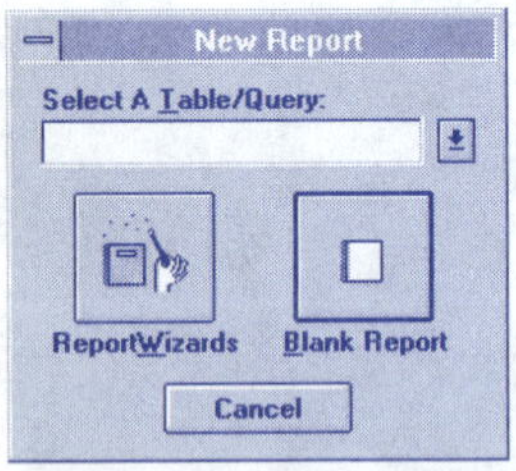

5-28 *The New report dialog box.*

Step 1 In the Database window, click the `Report` button, then click `New`. The New Report dialog box (FIG. 5-28) appears.

Step 2 Click the down arrow beside the Select A Table/Query box, and choose `Names` and `Donations` from the list box. Click the `ReportWizards` button. A dialog box appears, asking which Access Wizard you want to use. Click `Groups/Totals`, then click `OK`.

Step 3 The next dialog box to appear asks which fields you want on the report. Click the double-arrow button (`>>`) near the center of the dialog box, to place all fields in the report. Then, click `Next` at the bottom of the dialog box.

Step 4 The next dialog box asks which fields you want to group by. Double-click the Last Name field, then click `Next` at the bottom of the dialog box.

Step 5 The next dialog box asks how you want to group the data in each field. Leave the default of "Normal" selected at the right side of the dialog box, and click `Next`.

Step 6 The next dialog box asks which fields you want to sort by. Click `Next` at the bottom of the dialog box to ignore this question.

Step 7 The next dialog box asks which look you want for your report. Choose one of the three options that meets your fancy, then click `Next`.

Step 8 In the final dialog box to appear, Access asks for a name for the report, and by default, the same name as you assigned the query ("Names and Donations") appears. Click `Print Preview` to see a preview of the report; it should resemble the example shown in FIG. 5-29.

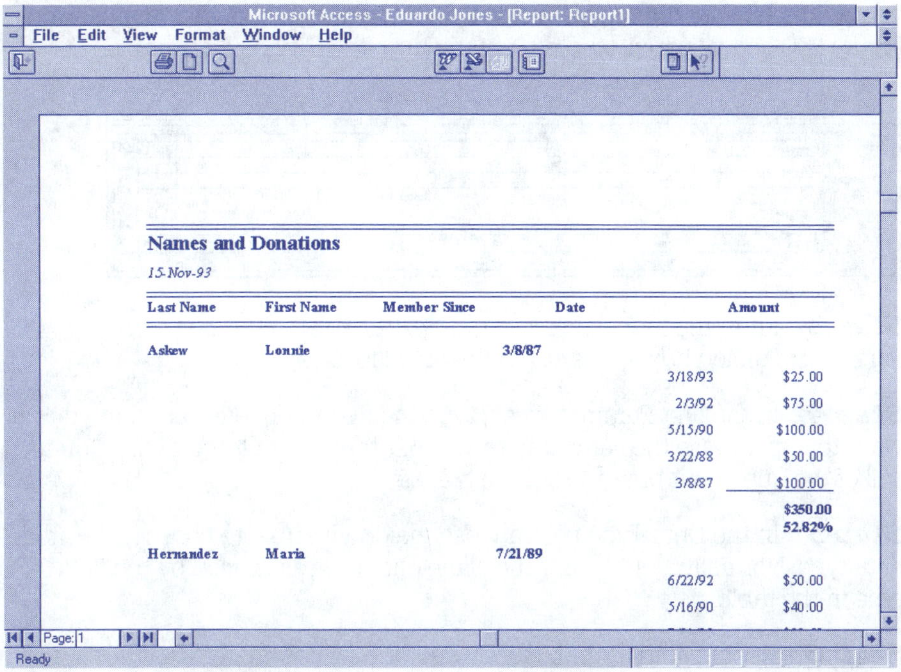

5-29 *The Print Preview of report.*

At this point, you could turn on your printer and click the `Print` button in the Toolbar to print the report. When you are done examining the report, press Ctrl–F4 to close the report window. (You can answer `No` in response to the `Save Changes` prompt, as this report will not be needed later in the book.)

Using parameter queries

If you find yourself often running the same query over and over and entering different criteria each time that you run the query, you should create a *parameter query* to save yourself time and effort. A parameter query is simply a query that automatically asks for needed criteria when it is run. You can use the same queries that you already have created as the basis for parameter queries. Instead of having to open the query window and type the new criteria into the query grid, Access will display dialog boxes with prompts, asking you for the criteria. Parameter queries are an important tool in designing complete applications, as they provide an easy way to prompt users of the application for needed information to obtain selective data. (In Part 3 of this book, many of the reports in the sample applications are based on parameter queries.) You can create a parameter query with the following steps.

Step 1 Create a query with the tables and the fields that you want.

Step 2 In the Criteria cells underneath the fields that you want to use as parameters, enter your parameter text, enclosed in square brackets. (This text will be used as a prompt in the dialog box that Access displays when the query runs.) Be careful to use text that is different than your field names. Figure 5-30 shows parameter text entered into the City field of a table.

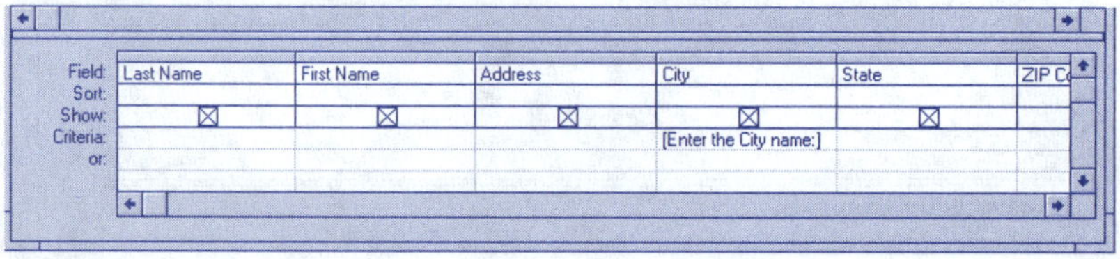

5-30 *The parameter text entered into City field of table.*

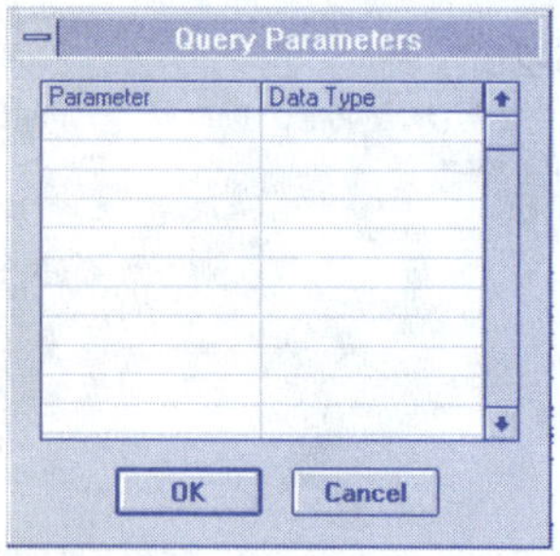

5-31 *The Query Parameters dialog box.*

Step 3 From the menus, choose `Query/Parameters`. The Query Parameters dialog box appears, as shown in FIG. 5-31.

Step 4 In the first Parameter cell, type the first parameter text that you want to appear (use the same parameter text that you entered in the Criteria cell of the query, but omit the square brackets).

Step 5 In the Data Type column, use the down arrow to choose a desired data type. Normally, you'll want the same data type as is used by the field type in the table.

Step 6 Repeat steps 4 and 5 for any additional parameters that you want the query to ask for. In the case of multiple parameters, Access asks for the data in a top-down order when you run the query.

Step 7 When you are done entering parameters, click `OK`. Save the query (you can press Ctrl–F4 and answer `Yes` to the save prompt, and supply a name when asked).

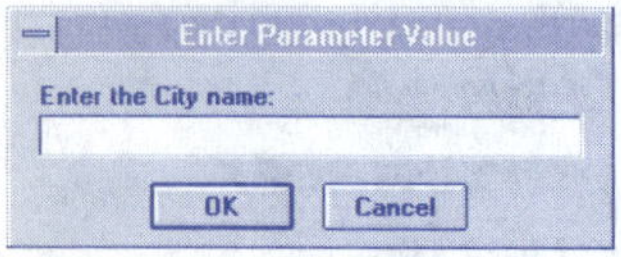

5-32 *A dialog box produced by a parameter.*

When you run the query, Access will display a dialog box asking for the parameter value. In the case of the example detailed earlier, the dialog box looks like FIG. 5-32. When you type in the data and click `OK`, the query runs and provides the data according to your criteria.

While the previous example made use of only a parameter with a single value, you are not limited to a single value in a parameter. One common use of multiple values in the same parameter is to prompt for a range of acceptable values. For example, consider the query designed earlier in the chapter for displaying names and donation amounts. If you want a parameter query that prompts for all donations made between two dates, you could enter:

```
Between [Enter the starting date] and [Enter the ending date]
```

in the Criteria cell of the query. When you run the query, Access first would ask for the starting date, then for the ending date. The resulting records shown in the query would contain only those records falling between the two dates.

Action queries

Select queries, which this chapter has examined until now, are just one type of query that Access can perform. You often will make use of *action queries*, which are queries that perform some type of task, such as updating a table, deleting a large group of records in a table, or appending records to a table. You create action queries by first creating a select query and running it to make sure that the records that it will contain are the records that you want to perform the action on. Then, while in Design mode, you change it into an action query, by clicking the appropriate Toolbar button, or by opening the Query menu and choosing one of the four options for action queries (Make Table, Update, Append, or Delete).

Appending records

Append queries can be used to append data from one table to another. The tables need not have the same structure, but the fields that you use as you append the data must be the same types of fields. Append queries are commonly used when you have data in one Access database and you want to add that data to a table in a different Access database. You can even append data from foreign tables that have been attached to your database. To perform an append query, you use the following steps.

Step 1 Design and test a select query that retrieves the records that you want appended to the table. (If the records are to come from an attached database, you must attach the database first.) Get into Design view if you are not there already.

Step 2 From the menus, choose `Query/Append` or click the `Append Query` button in the Toolbar to change the select query into an append query. When you do so, the Queries Properties dialog box appears, as shown in FIG. 5-33.

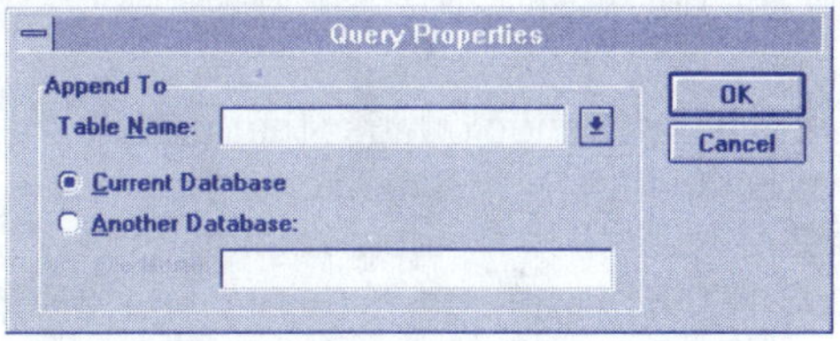

5-33
The Queries Properties dialog box for the Append Table query.

Step 3 In the Table Name box, type the name of the table that you want to append the records to or click the down arrow and choose a table name from the list. If you want to append to a table in a different database, click the `Another Database` button in the dialog box and enter the name of the database in the File Name text box. When you are done with the options in the dialog box, click `OK`. Access will add the Append To row to the query grid.

Step 4 Enter the field names from the table that you are appending records to in the Append To row, matching them to the existing fields in the Field row. (Where the field names are the same, Access automatically displays the field names in the Append To row.) *Note*: The Append To row and the Field row of your append queries must contain the same number of fields.

Step 5 Run the query by choosing `Query/Run` or clicking the `Run` button on the Toolbar. Access displays a confirmation dialog, telling you how many records will be added to the table. Click `OK` to run the query and append the records.

Deleting records

You can compose delete queries, which are action queries that delete all records meeting a specified criteria. As with other action queries, you first design a select query that obtains the records that you want to delete. While in Design view, you choose `Query/Delete` from the menus or click the `Delete Query` button in the Toolbar to change the type of query from a select query to a delete query. When you run the query, Access will warn you how many rows will be deleted. Once you click `OK` in the confirmation dialog box, the deletions will occur. You can use the following steps to perform a delete query.

Step 1 Design and test a select query that retrieves the records that you want deleted from the table.

Step 2 From the menus, choose `Query/Delete` or click the `Delete Query` button in the Toolbar. The query window's title will change to "Delete query" indicating that the query, when run, will delete the records.

Step 3 Run the query by choosing `Query/Run` or clicking the `Run` button on the Toolbar. Access displays a confirmation dialog, telling you how many records will be deleted from the table.

Step 4 If you do not want to delete the records, click `Cancel`. Otherwise, click `OK` to run the query and delete the records.

Updating records

You can compose update queries, which are action queries that update (or make specified changes to) all records meeting a specified criteria. Update queries are useful when you must change data in a global fashion. For example, you might need to give a new telephone area code to all residents living in a particular city, or in an employee table, you might want to increase all salaries of a given type of worker by $.50 per hour. As with other action queries, you first design a select query that obtains the records that you want to update. Then, you choose `Query/Update` from the menus or click the `Update Query` button in the Toolbar to change the type of query from a select query to an update query. Access adds an Update To row to the query, and you enter criteria in this row that specifies how you want to update the data. You can use the following steps to perform an update query.

Step 1 Design and test a select query that retrieves the records that you want deleted from the table.

Step 2 From the menus, choose `Query/Update`, or click the `Update Query` button in the Toolbar. Access adds the Update To row to the query grid.

Step 3 In the Update To cell for the field that you want to update, enter a desired expression or a value that will change the data. As an example, you could increase salaries by $.50 in a Salary field by entering `[Salary] + .50`.

Step 4 Run the query by choosing `Query/Run` or clicking the `Run` button on the Toolbar. Access displays a confirmation dialog, telling you how many records will be updated. Choose `OK` to run the query and update the records.

Creating new tables

Access lets you create new tables with make-table queries. This type of query creates a new table containing all the records selected by the query. Make-table queries can be useful for creating backup tables of your data or for storing data in tables that are contained in other Access databases. Make-table queries also are useful for exporting selective data to a foreign file format (such as dBASE). Here are the steps you can follow to create a make-table query.

Step 1 Design and test a select query that retrieves the records that you want inserted into the new table.

Step 2 From the menus, choose `Query/Make Table`, or click the `Make-Table Query` button in the Toolbar to change the select query into a make-table query. When you do so, the Queries Properties dialog box appears, as shown in FIG. 5-34.

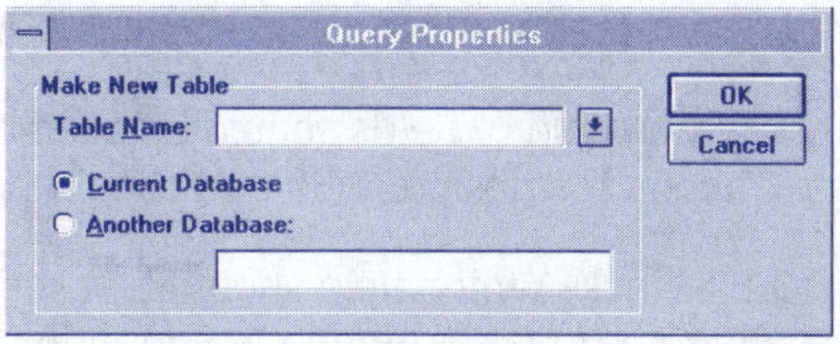

5-34
The Queries Properties dialog box for the Make Table query.

Step 3 In the Table Name box, type the name for the new table or click the down arrow and choose a table name from the list if you want to replace an existing table with the results of the query. If you want to append to a table in a different database, click the `Another Database` button in the dialog box and enter the name of the database in the File Name text box. When done with the options in the dialog box, click `OK`.

Step 4 Run the query by choosing `Query/Run` or clicking the `Run` button on the Toolbar. Access displays a confirmation dialog, telling you how many records will be added to the new table. Choose `OK` to run the query and create the new table.

Note: When Access creates a new table based on a make-table query, it does not transfer any key field specifications nor does it transfer any field properties to the new table. If you had specific field properties or key fields designated in the original table, you might want to designate the same information in the newly-created table.

Using the Query Wizards

With Access version 2.0, you are provided with Query Wizards, which are specialized tools that help you quickly design complex queries for specialized tasks. You can create the following types of queries with the Query Wizards: Crosstab queries, Find duplicates queries, Find unmatched queries, and Archive queries.

Creating Crosstab queries with the Query Wizards

Crosstab queries let you show your data with row and column headings, similar to the layout of a spreadsheet. Crosstab queries can be very useful for quickly summarizing large amounts of data. To create a crosstab query using the Query Wizards, you perform the following steps.

Step 1 Click the `Query` button in the Database window, then click `New`, then click `Query Wizards`.

Step 2 In the next dialog box which appears, click `Crosstab Query` as the desired type of query, then click `OK`.

Step 3 The Crosstab Query wizard dialog box appears (FIG. 5-35). This dialog box asks which table should be used as the basis for the crosstab. Click the desired table, then click `Next`.

Step 4 The dialog box now asks which field or fields should be used as the basis for the grouping. Choose the desired field or fields and click the right-arrow button to add the fields to the Row Headings list box, then click `Next`.

Step 5 The dialog box now asks which field or fields should be used as the basis for the column headings. Choose the desired field and click `Next`.

Step 6 The next dialog box (FIG. 5-36) asks which field should be used as the aggregate in the crosstab, and what aggregate function (count, minimum, maximum, first, or last) should be used. Make the desired selections in the dialog box, then click `OK`.

Step 7 The last dialog box to appear asks for a name for the query. Enter a name (or you can accept the default name proposed by Access). Then, click `Open` to run the query and display the data in a dynaset, or click `Design` to open the query in Design view. Figure 5-37 shows an example of a table of car sales and the resulting Crosstab query, when the Salesrep field was chosen as the basis for grouping, the Model Name field was chosen as the basis for the column headings, and the Price field was chosen as the aggregate, with a Sum function used.

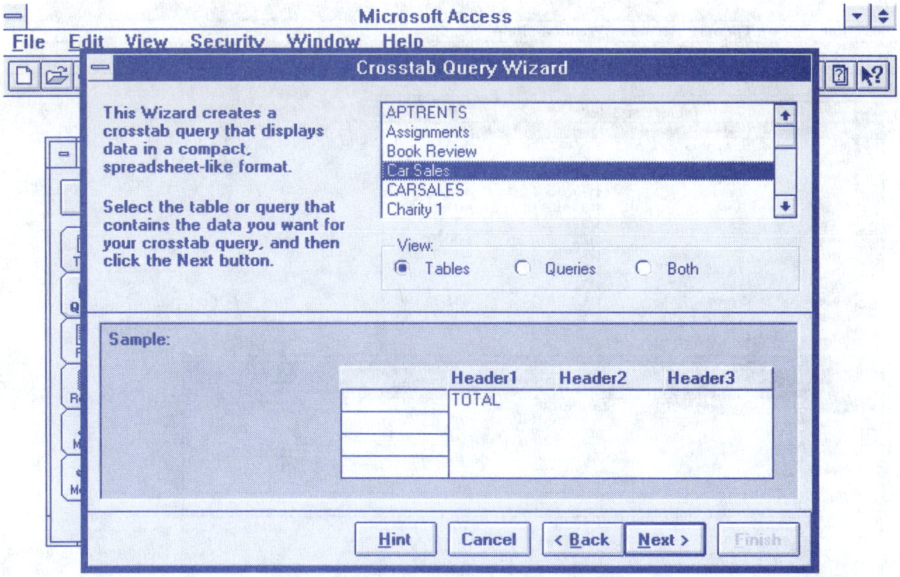

5-35
The Crosstab Query Wizard dialog box.

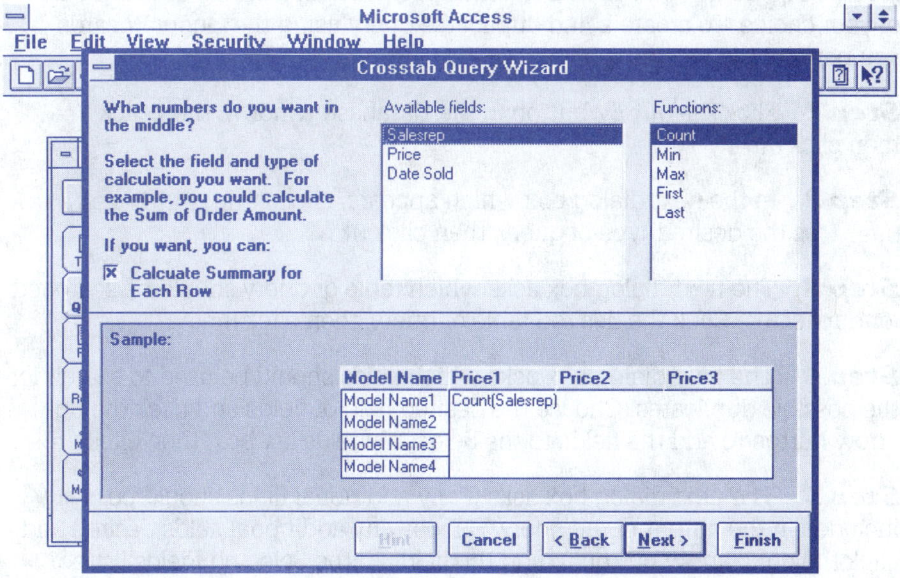

5-36
A Crosstab Query Wizard dialog box with fields chosen.

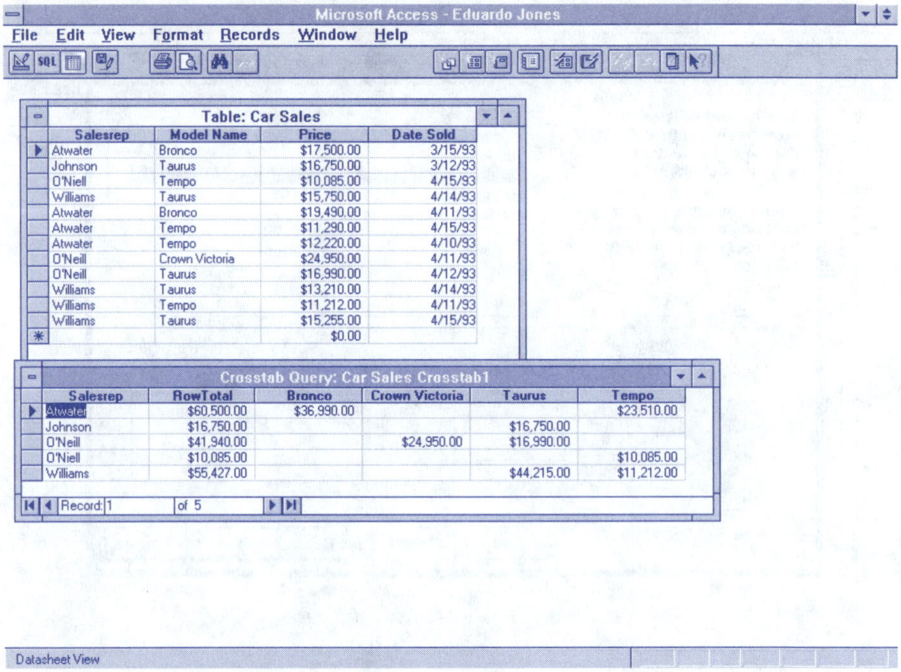

Salesrep	Model Name	Price	Date Sold
Atwater	Bronco	$17,500.00	3/15/93
Johnson	Taurus	$16,750.00	3/12/93
O'Niell	Tempo	$10,085.00	4/15/93
Williams	Taurus	$15,750.00	4/14/93
Atwater	Bronco	$19,490.00	4/11/93
Atwater	Tempo	$11,290.00	4/15/93
Atwater	Tempo	$12,220.00	4/10/93
O'Neill	Crown Victoria	$24,950.00	4/11/93
O'Neill	Taurus	$16,990.00	4/12/93
Williams	Taurus	$13,210.00	4/14/93
Williams	Tempo	$11,212.00	4/11/93
Williams	Taurus	$15,255.00	4/15/93
		$0.00	

Salesrep	RowTotal	Bronco	Crown Victoria	Taurus	Tempo
Atwater	$60,500.00	$36,990.00			$23,510.00
Johnson	$16,750.00			$16,750.00	
O'Neill	$41,940.00		$24,950.00	$16,990.00	
O'Niell	$10,085.00				$10,085.00
Williams	$55,427.00			$44,215.00	$11,212.00

5-37
An example of a car sales table and resulting crosstab query.

Creating Find Duplicate queries with the Query Wizards

As the name implies, Find Duplicates queries are used to find duplicate records in a table. You can search for duplicates based on the selected fields of your choice. To create a find duplicates query using the Query Wizards, you perform the following steps.

Step 1 Click the `Query` button in the Database window, then click `New`, then click `Query Wizards`.

Step 2 In the next dialog box which appears, click `Find Duplicates Query` as the desired type of query, then click `OK`.

Step 3 The next dialog box asks which table or query should be searched for duplicates. Click the desired table or query, then click `Next`.

Step 4 The next dialog box asks which fields should be used to search for the possible duplicates. Choose the desired field or fields and click the right-arrow button to add the fields to the Selected Fields list box, then click `Next`.

Step 5 The next dialog box asks if any additional fields should be included in the output of the query. Choose any additional fields desired and click the right-arrow button to add the fields to the Selected Fields list box, then click `Next`.

Step 6 The next dialog box asks for a name for the query. Enter a name (or you can accept the default name proposed by Access). Then, click the

Query Browse button to see the results of the query; any duplicate records found based on the fields you specified will appear in the results.

Creating Find Unmatched queries with the Query Wizards

You use Find Unmatched queries to find records in one table that have no related records in another table. As an example, you might have a table of customers, and a related table of orders for those customers. You could use a Find Unmatched query to find all customers who have no orders. To create a find unmatched query using the Query Wizards, you perform the following steps.

Step 1 Click the Query button in the Database window, then click New, then click Query Wizards.

Step 2 In the next dialog box that appears, click Find Unmatched Query as the desired type of query, then click OK.

Step 3 The Find Unmatched Query Wizard dialog box appears (FIG. 5-38). This dialog box asks which table or query contains the records that you want to see in the query's results. Click the desired table or query, then click Next.

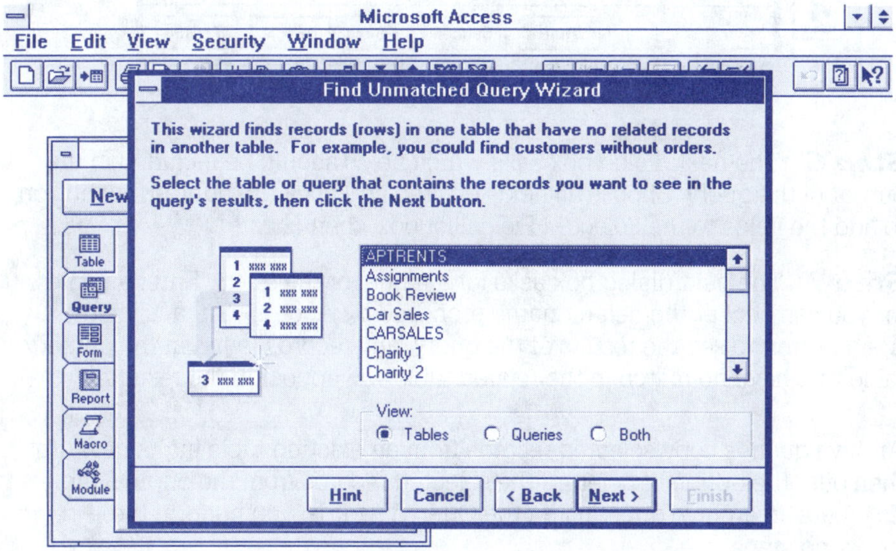

5-38
The Find Unmatched Query Wizard dialog box.

Step 4 The dialog box now asks which table or query contains the related records. Click the desired table or query, then click Next.

Step 5 The next dialog box (FIG. 5-39) asks which field is used as the matching field between both tables. Click a field in the first table, then click the matching field in the second table, then click the double-arrow button near the center of the dialog box. Finally, click `Next`.

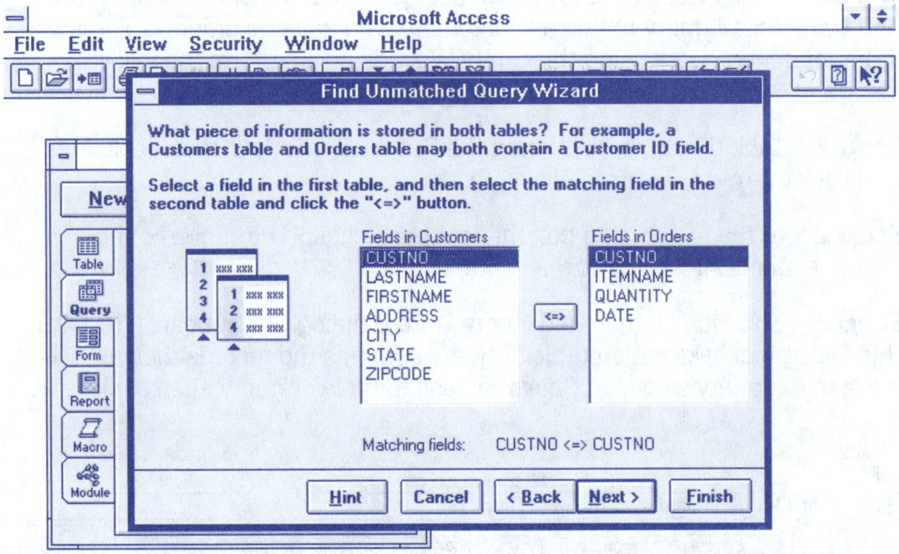

5-39
A Find Unmatched Query Wizard dialog box with matching fields chosen.

Step 6 The next dialog box asks which fields should be included in the output of the query. Choose all fields desired and click the right-arrow button to add the fields to the Selected Fields list box, then click `Next`.

Step 7 The next dialog box asks for a name for the query. Enter a name (or you can accept the default name proposed by Access). Then, click the `Open` button to see the results of the query; any records found in the primary table that have no match in the related table will appear in the results.

Creating Archive queries with the Query Wizards

Archive queries copy selected records from an existing table into a new table, then offer the option of deleting the selected records from the original table. To create an archive query using the Query Wizards, you perform the following steps.

Step 1 Click the `Query` button in the Database window, then click `New`, then click `Query Wizards`.

Step 2 In the next dialog box that appears, click `Archive Query` as the desired type of query, then click `OK`.

Step 3 The Archive Wizard dialog box (FIG. 5-40) asks which table contains the records you want to archive. Click the desired table, then click `Next`.

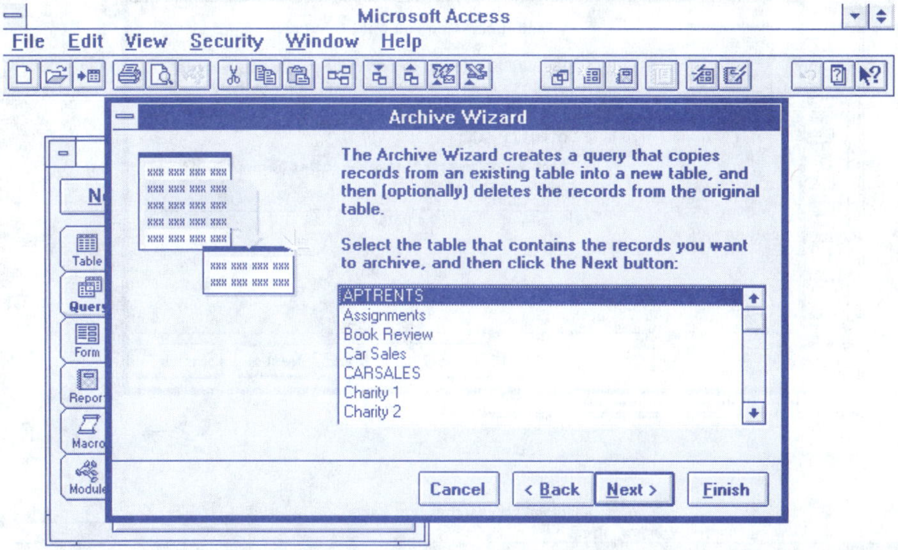

5-40
The Archive Query Wizard dialog box.

Step 4 The next dialog box that appears (FIG. 5-41) asks you to specify the criteria that determines which records should be archived. Enter the desired criteria in the dialog box, then click `Next`. As an option, you can check the box labelled "Archive All Records in the Table," and all the records will be archived.

Step 5 The next dialog box that appears (FIG. 5-42) shows you the records that will be archived (copied into a new table). Click the `Next` button to continue the process.

Step 6 The next dialog box which appears asks if you want to delete the archived records from the original table. Click `Yes` or `No` as desired, then click `Next`.

Step 7 The next dialog box asks for a name for the new table that will contain the archived records. Enter a name (or you can accept the default name proposed by Access), then click the `Archive` button to carry out the operation.

Viewing a query's SQL statements

If you are familiar with the database language known as SQL, you should know that Access interprets the queries that you design into SQL statements. (SQL is a database language originally developed by IBM in the 1970s for use on mainframe computers.) You can view and edit the SQL statements used by Access to process your queries. Open any query in Design mode, and

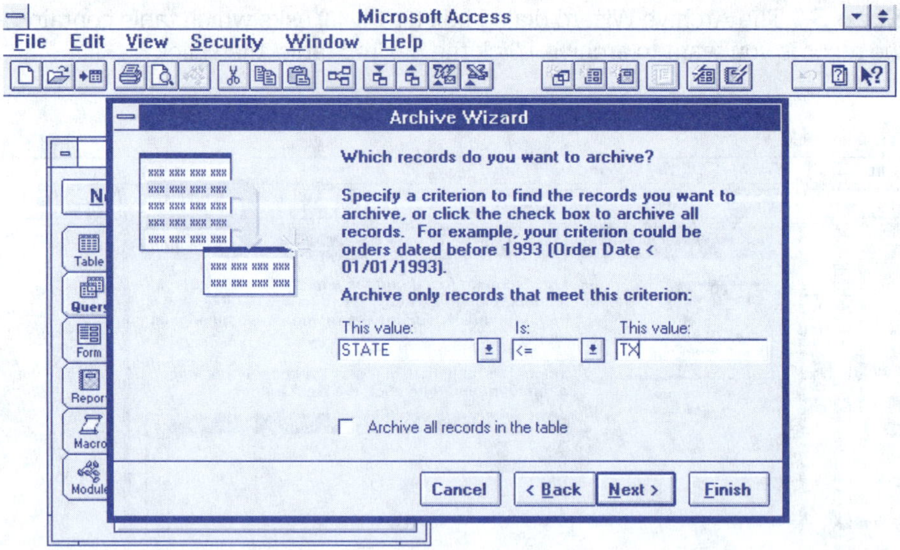

5-41
An Archive Query Wizard dialog box with filled-in criteria.

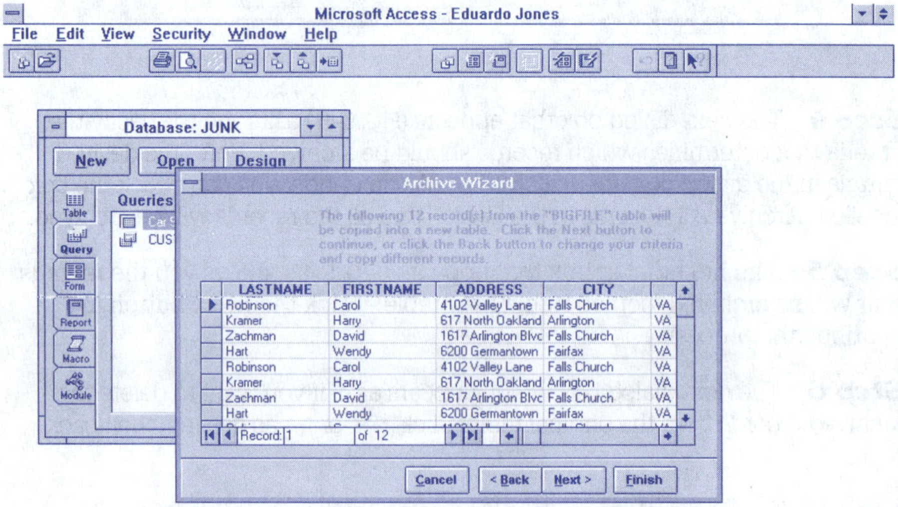

5-42
An Archive Query Wizard dialog box displaying records to be archived.

choose View/SQL from the menus (or click the SQL button in the Toolbar), and you will see the SQL statement in a window. An example of this window is shown in FIG. 5-43.

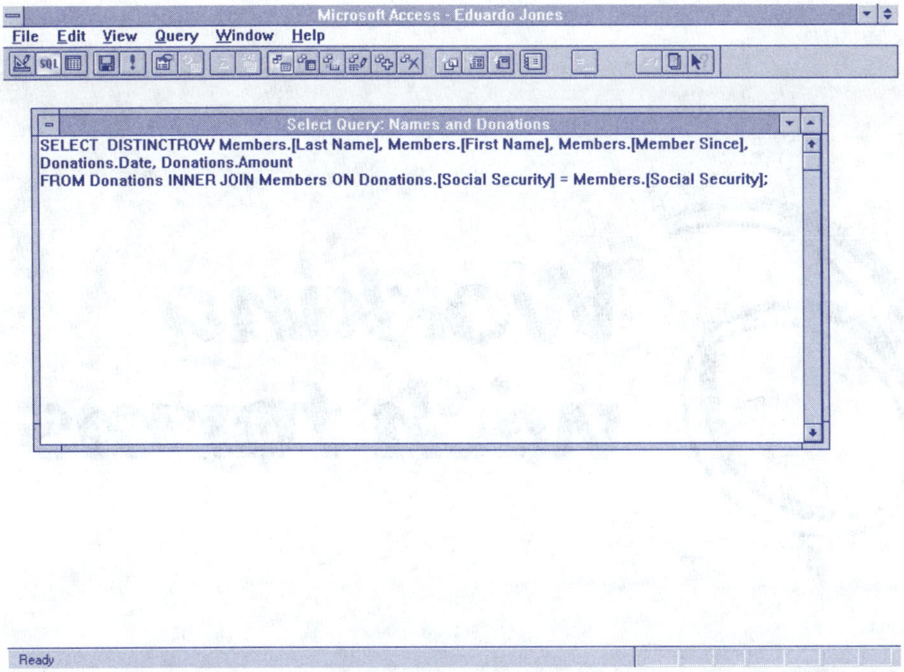

5-43
The View SQL dialog box.

The list box within the dialog box contains the SQL statement that is responsible for providing the results of your query. You can manually edit the query (assuming that you are familiar with the SQL language of database manipulation). Any changes that you make will be reflected in the query grid. Entering your own SQL statements is a topic beyond the scope of this book, and Microsoft recommends that you not make changes to the SQL statements unless you are intimately familiar with SQL.

6 Working with forms

As chapter 4 detailed, you can add data directly to a table by opening the table's datasheet, moving to the last record, and typing data into the fields. Data entry directly into a datasheet has its advantages. It is straightforward, and you can see a large number of records as well as many or all of the fields at the same time. However, such a straightforward approach to adding data to a table also can create problems.

One drawback is in the unfriendly screen presented to the computer user. If an employee does not know what is meant by a field name such as "Hourly Rate" at the top of a table, the help screens or the Access manual won't clarify matters. Yet another drawback is the lack of control that you have when editing a table through datasheet view; if for any reason you want to prevent the editing of a particular field, you cannot easily do so.

To overcome such limitations, Access lets you design *forms*. Forms are just like paper forms that you fill in with a pen. The form contains areas in which you can enter the data for a specific record; you can think of a form as something that shows a "snapshot" of one or more records in a table. Figure 6-1 shows an example of a form in Access.

Many forms are designed to show one record at a time, although you can easily design forms that show more than one record at a time. In Access, you can design forms that resemble the printed forms commonly used in your office. You also can restrict entry by omitting certain fields and including

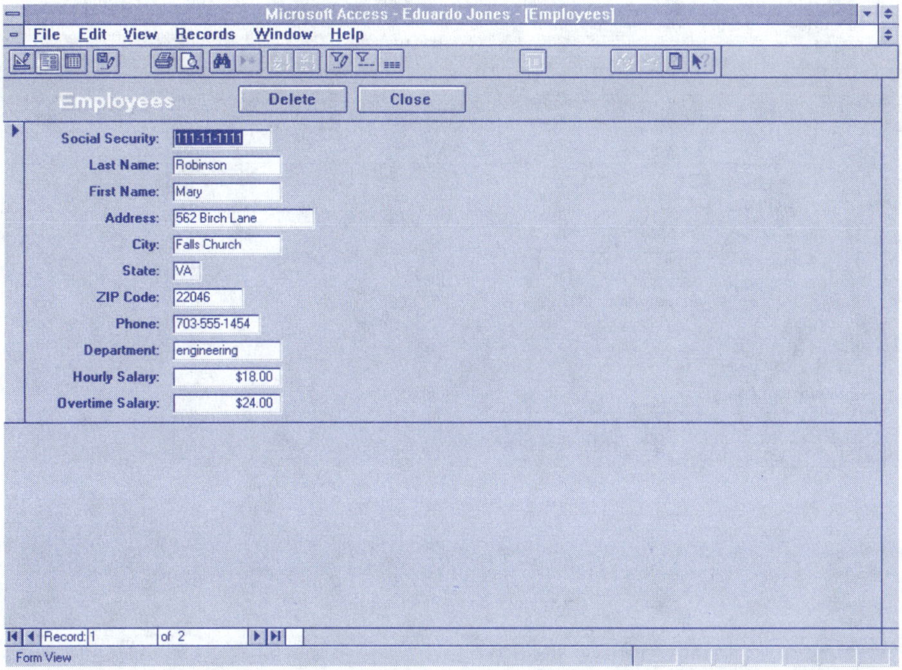

6-1
An example form.

other fields in the form. You can limit fields to accept certain types of data, such as amounts that fall within a predefined range. Using FormWizards, you can quickly create attractive forms with little or no specific design work. The forms that you create can be used for data entry, for viewing and editing data, or for printing data. There are two ways in which you can create forms in Access: you can use the FormWizards to quickly build a form by answering a series of questions, or you can create the form manually by starting with a blank form and placing fields, text, and graphics where desired. In many cases, you also can save time when designing forms by combining the two methods; you can use the FormWizards to create the form initially, then make changes to that form manually.

Creating forms with the Quick Form button

By far the fastest way to create a form is with the use of the `Quick Form` button on the Toolbar. (If you are using a version of Access prior to version 2.0, you will not have this feature.) The `Quick Form` button creates a single-column style of form for whatever table or query is selected or active at the time you click the button. The table (or query) can be the open, active window, or you can click the desired table or query in the Database window to select it. With the desired table or query selected or active, just click the `Quick Form` button in the Toolbar. Access creates and opens a form, without asking any questions about it's design. As an example, if you open the Earth Aware database provided on the sample disk, click the `Tables` button in the Database window and click Members to highlight it, then click the `Quick Form` button in the Toolbar, Access creates the form shown in FIG. 6-2.

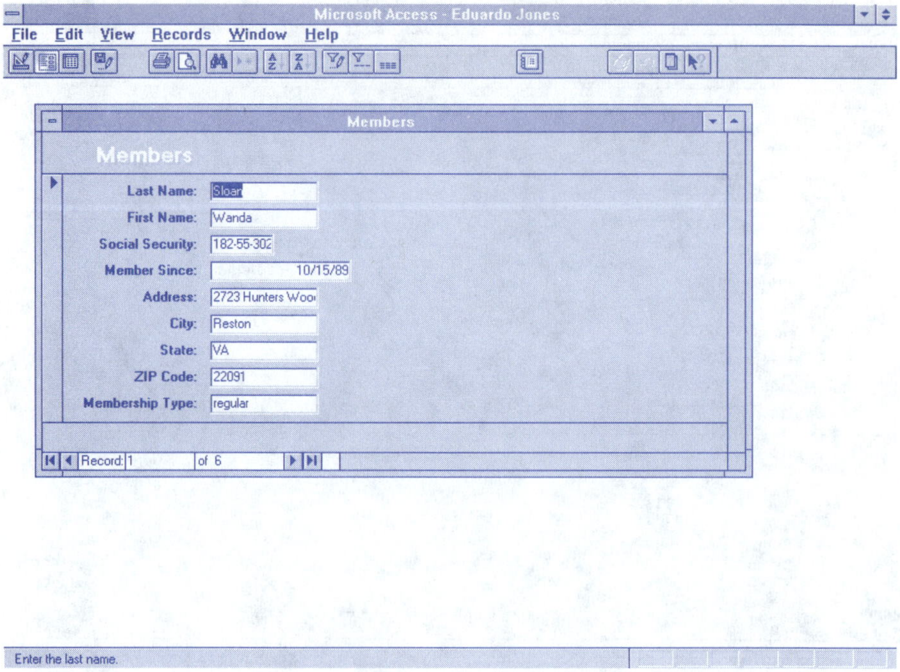

6-2
An example of a quick form created using the Members table.

Creating forms with FormWizards

Another fast way to create a form is to use the FormWizards. While this method is not as fast as the previous, it offers you more flexibility in that you are able to control many aspects of the form's appearance. The FormWizards help you create a form by asking you questions about the form (such as what type of form you desire and which fields should appear on the form). Once you answer the questions, the FormWizard automatically creates the form. You can use FormWizards to create single-column forms, tabular forms, main/subform forms, or graphs. The form shown earlier (in FIG. 6-1) is an example of a single-column form. In such forms, one column displays all the fields, with each field appearing on a single line. A tabular form displays your data in a table-like format, similar to that of a datasheet, as shown in FIG. 6-3.

A main/subform form is used to show data from two tables when the data has a one-to-many relationship (see chapter 4 for details on table relationships). As an example, there is a one-to-many relationship between the Members table and the Donations table detailed in chapter 4. For each member of the organization, there are one or more donations. With the main/subform, you can show the record from the "one" table in the main part of the form and display all associated records from the "many" table in the subpart of the form. Figure 6-4 shows an example of this type of form.

Finally, a graph form displays numeric data in the form of a graph. Figure 6-5 shows an example of this type of form.

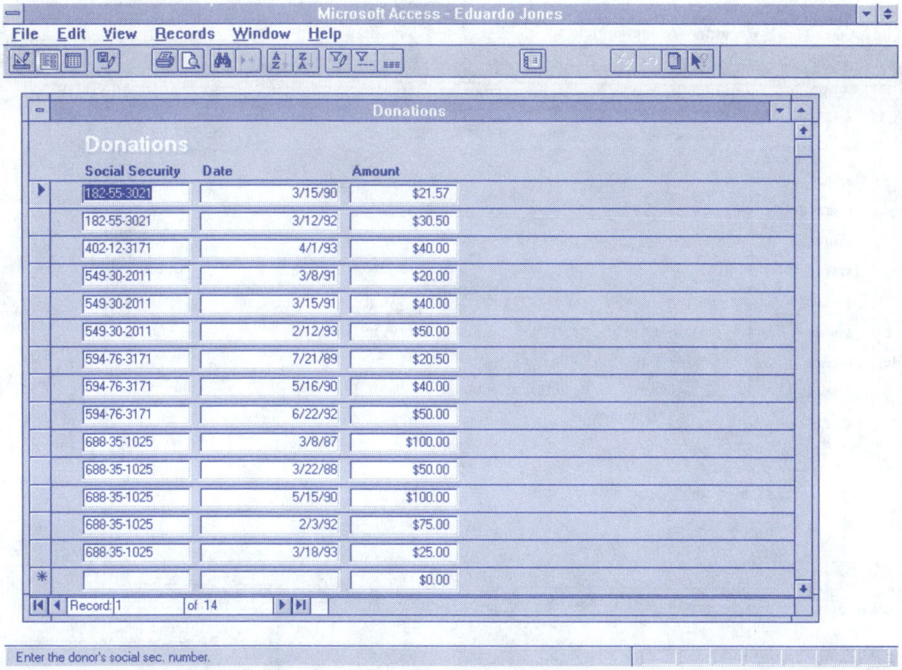

6-3
An example of a tabular form.

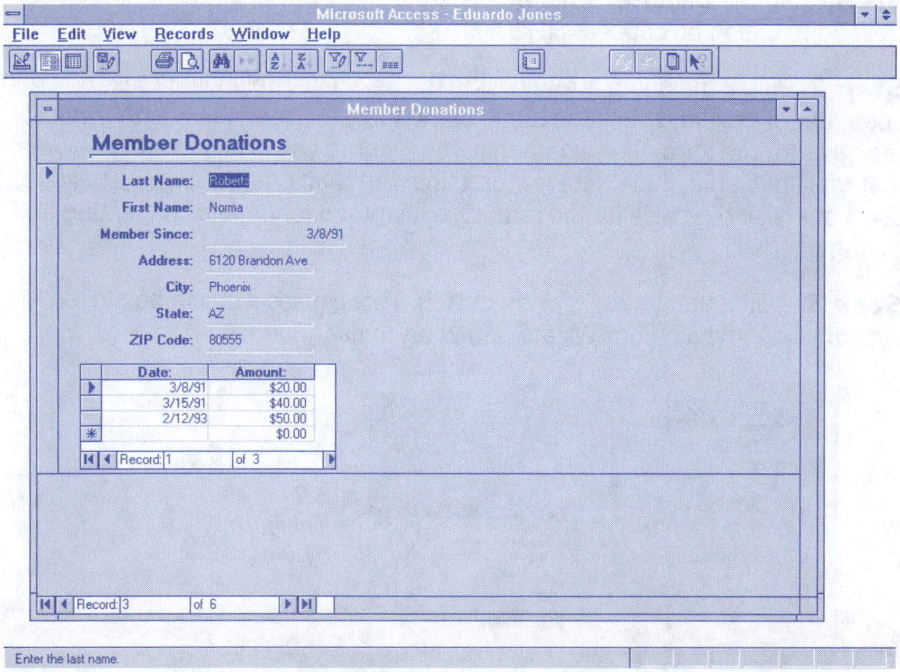

6-4
An example of a main/subform.

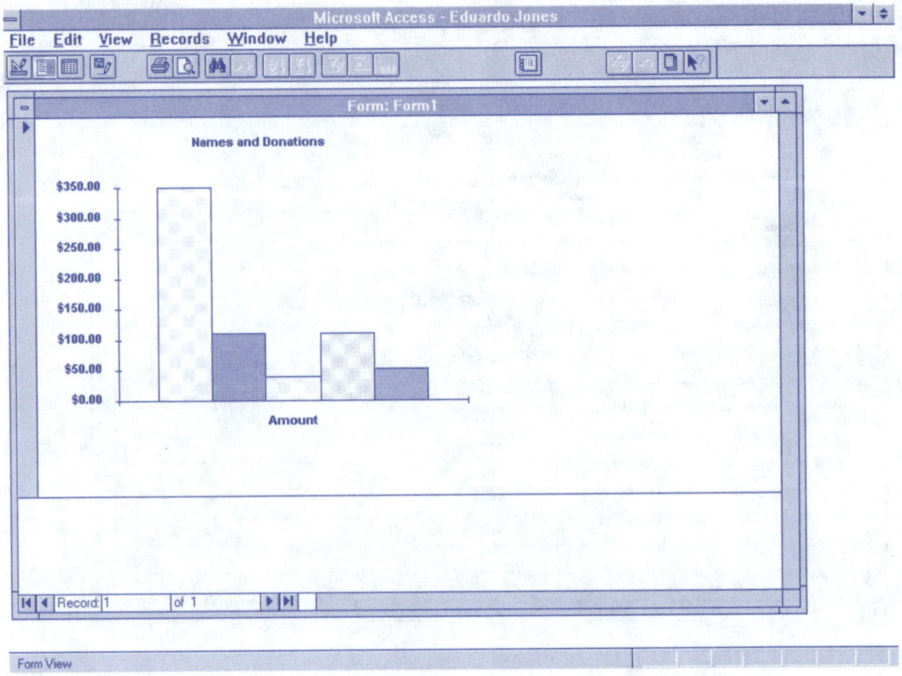

6-5 *An example of a graph form.*

To create a form with a FormWizard, perform the following steps.

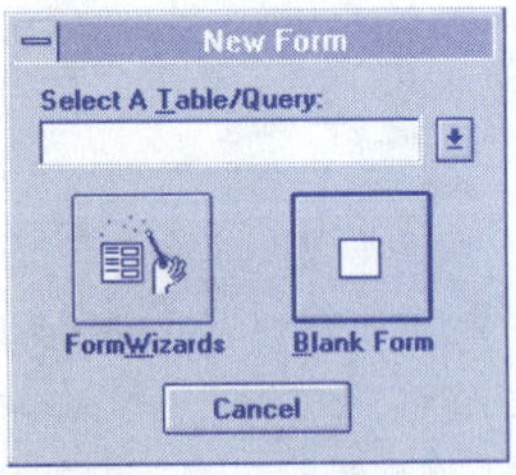

6-6 *The New Form dialog box.*

Step 1 In the Database window, click the `Form` button. Click `New`. The New Form dialog box appears (FIG. 6-6).

Step 2 Click the down arrow beside the Select A Table/Query text box to open the list box, and click the name of the table (or query) that is to serve at the basis for the form. (If the data that you want to use is in one table, choose that table by name; if the data is stored in more than one table, you'll need to use a query as the basis for the form. See chapter 5 for details on creating and saving queries.)

Step 3 Click the `FormWizards` button. This causes a dialog box to appear asking which FormWizard you want to use. (See FIG. 6-7.)

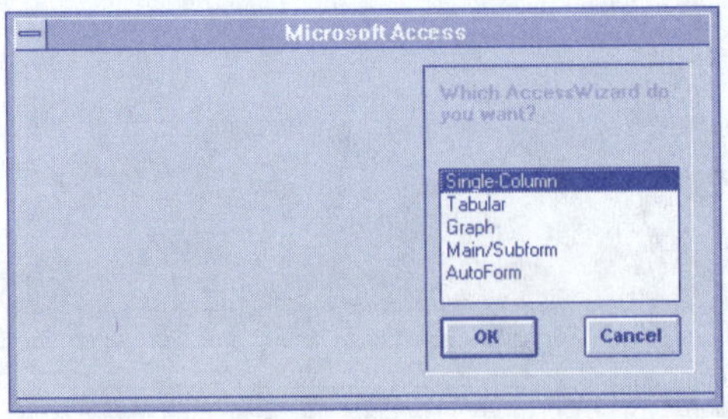

6-7 *The FormWizard dialog box.*

Step 4 Click single-column, tabular, main/subform, or graph, as desired. With single-column and tabular forms, the next dialog box to appear asks which fields you want included on the form. With main/subforms (also known as *multitable forms*), the dialog box asks which table or query contains the data for the subform, and the dialog box that follows will ask which fields are to be used for the form. With graph forms, the dialog box asks which fields you want used in the graph. The `Autoform` option is the equivalent of clicking the `Quick Form` button on the Toolbar; with this option, Access creates a single-column form without asking any further questions. Answer the questions asked for your particular type of form, then click `Next` to proceed.

Step 5 Once you have answered the questions about the tables and fields used as a basis for the form, Access will ask which type of look you want for the form, as shown in the dialog box shown in FIG. 6-8. Your choices here are standard, chiseled, shadowed, boxed, or embossed. After choosing your desired style, click `Next`.

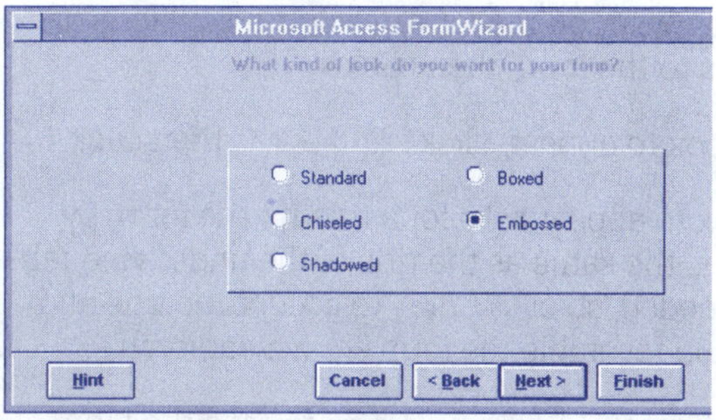

6-8
A dialog box used to determine the look for the form.

Step 6 The last dialog box to appear (FIG. 6-9) asks for a title for the form. You can accept the default title (which is always the same name as the underlying table or query), or you can enter a new title of your choosing. (This title will appear at the top of the completed form.) Then, click `Open` to open the form, or click `Design` to open the form in Design mode (where you can make additional changes to the form manually, if desired). The form shown earlier in FIG. 6-1 was created by choosing the single-column FormWizard along with the Members table, including all fields in the form, and selecting the embossed style for the form.

Hands-on practice: creating example forms

If you are experimenting with the sample database outlined in this part of the book, you can perform the following steps to create two forms. One will be used to add and edit records in the Members table, and the other will be used to add and edit records in the Donations table. Both forms will be needed to build the complete application outlined in chapter 9. (The forms also are contained in the EARTH.MDB database stored on the sample disk.) To practice creating the forms, perform these steps.

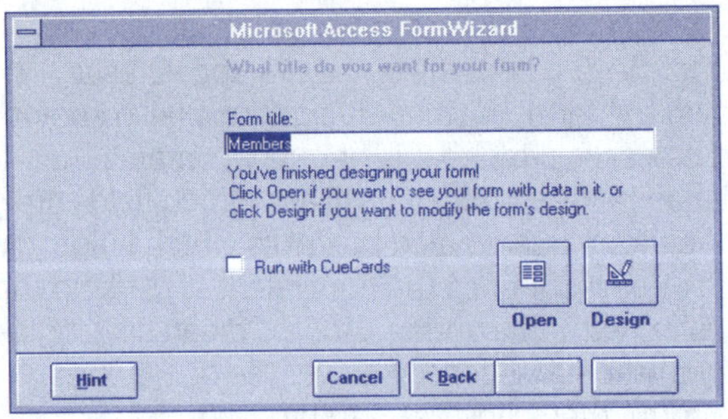

6-9
A dialog box used to determine the title for the form.

Step 1 In the Database window, click the `Form` button, then click `New`. The New Form dialog box appears. Open the list box under `Select A Table/Query`, and choose `Members`. Click the `FormWizards` button. The next dialog box that appears asks which wizard you want to use.

Step 2 With Single-column already selected as the default, click `OK`. You are next asked which fields you want on the form. Click the double-arrow button (`>>`) to add all the fields to the form, then click `Next`.

Step 3 In the next dialog box to appear, click `Embossed`, then click `Next`.

Step 4 The next dialog box to appear asks for a title for the form; by default, the title ("Members") is the same as the title of the underlying table. In this case, no changes are needed, so click `Open` to accept the title and open the form. Your form should resemble the form shown earlier in FIG. 6-1.

Step 5 From the menus, choose `File/Save Form` to save the form. When prompted for a title, enter `MEMBERS`. (If you copied the Earth Aware database from the accompanying disk, Access will ask you if you want to replace the existing form; click `Yes` in the dialog box if you are asked this question.) Press Ctrl–F4 to close the new form.

Now, continue with the following steps to create the form that will be used to add and edit records in the Donations table.

Step 1 In the Database window, click the `Form` button, then click `New`. The New Form dialog box appears. Open the list box under `Select A Table/Query`, and choose `Donations`. Click the `FormWizards` button.

Step 2 The next dialog box that appears asks which wizard you want to use. Click `Tabular` to select it, then click `OK`. You next are asked which fields you want on the form. Click the double-arrow button (`>>`) to add all the fields to the form, then click `Next`.

Step 3 In the next dialog box to appear, click `Embossed`, then click `Next`.

Step 4 The next dialog box to appear asks for a title for the form; by default, the title ("Donations") is the same as the title of the underlying table. In this case, no changes are needed, so click `Open` to accept the title and open the form. Your form should resemble the form shown earlier in FIG. 6-3.

Step 5 From the menus, choose `File/Save Form` to save the form. When prompted for a title, enter `DONATIONS`. (If you copied the Earth Aware database from the accompanying disk, Access will ask you if you want to replace the existing form; click `Yes` in the dialog box if you are asked this question.) Press Ctrl–F4 to close the new form.

You can use either of the forms by double-clicking the desired form in the Database window to open the form. Try adding and editing records in the Members and Donations tables to grow accustomed to the navigational techniques used within forms. For more details on navigating within a form, see the heading "Using a form" later in this chapter.

Creating forms manually

You can design your own forms without the aid of the wizards by choosing a blank form and placing any desired fields, text, and graphics on the form. To create a form manually, perform the following steps.

Step 1 In the Database window, click the `Form` button. Click `New`. The New Form dialog box appears (FIG. 6-10).

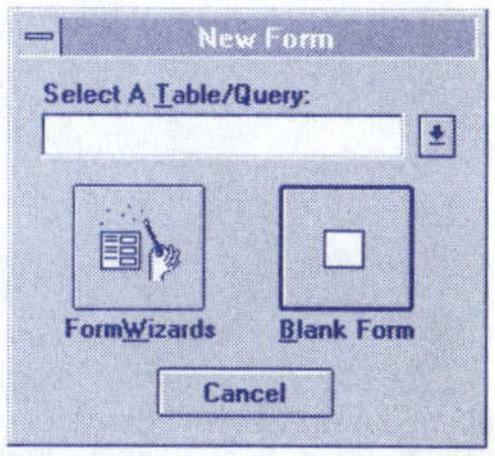

6-10 *The New Form dialog box.*

Step 2 Click the down arrow beside the Select A Table/Query text box to open the list box, and click the name of the table (or query) that is to serve as the basis for the form. (If the data that you want to use is in one table, choose that table by name; if the data is stored in more than one table, you'll need to use a query as the basis for the form. See chapter 5 for details on creating and saving queries.) Click the `Blank Form` button. Access displays the form in Design view, as shown in FIG. 6-11.

Step 3 Place the desired objects (fields, text, and any graphics) on the form, then save the form by choosing `File/Save`. The placement of objects on a blank form is covered in more detail in the pages that follow.

TIP

Keep in mind that you often can save time by using a wizard to create a form that is close to what you desire. Then, open the form, click the Design View icon in the Toolbar to enter design view, and make the desired changes to the form.

Design View window & form views

When you begin designing a form, you are placed in the Design View window, shown earlier in FIG. 6-11. You can think of this window as a "drawing area" where you can lay out your desired form. When you are designing a form, the Toolbar takes on the appearance shown in the figure. Note that the Toolbar contains three buttons at the left for three different types of views: design view, form view, and datasheet view.

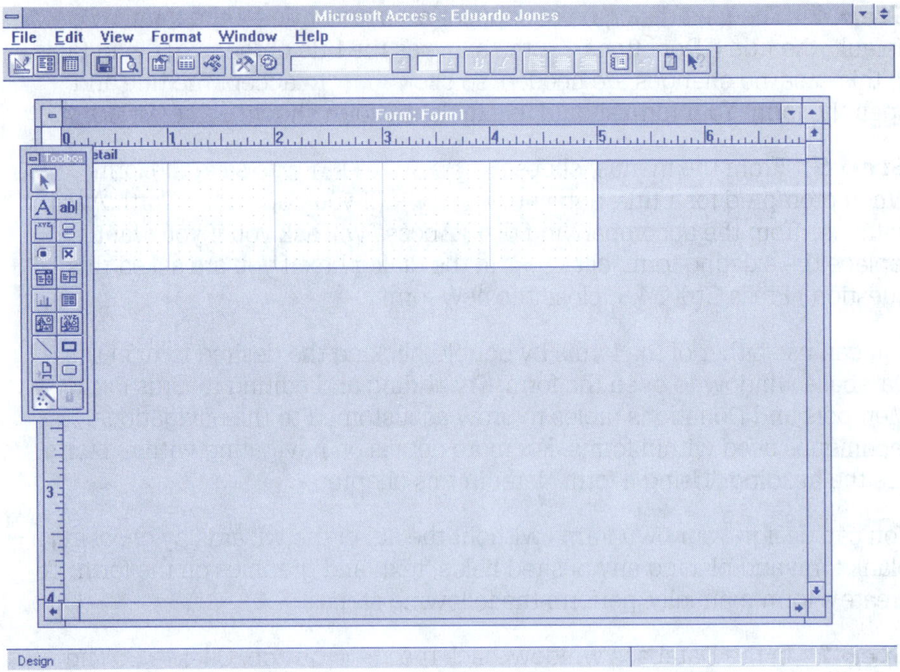

6-11
A blank form in design view.

These buttons control how you view the form. The `Design View` button places you in design view, where you can design the form. The `Form View` button switches you to form view, where you can add, edit, delete, and print the data in the underlying table (or query). The `Datasheet View` button displays the underlying datasheet (or in the case of queries, the dynaset).

In addition to the buttons just described, the Toolbar also contains buttons for performing a print preview, viewing properties of a selected object, displaying a list of fields that you can drag to your form, and displaying the Palette that can be used to change the appearance of an object.

TIP

Before you begin designing forms, remember the use of `Edit/Undo` from the menus. If you make a change or an addition to a form and you don't like the change, in most cases, you can choose `Edit/Undo` to reverse the action.

Working with controls

Access refers to most objects in a form (such as labels and fields) as *controls*. If you plan on designing your own forms and reports, you'll need to know how to select, size, and move controls within the Design View window. This knowledge will prove useful in designing your own reports, as Access uses the same techniques both in form design and in report design. Access makes use of three types of controls: *bound*, *unbound*, and *calculated*.

Bound controls are those controls that are tied (or "bound") to a particular field in a table or query. In FIG. 6-1, the fields from the table (Last Name, First Name, Address, and so on) are all bound controls. Unbound controls are controls that are not tied to a table or query in any way. In FIG. 6-1, the title "Members" at the top of the form is an unbound control. Calculated controls are controls that display a calculation based on a value in the underlying table or query. If you have worked with other database managers like dBASE or Paradox, these can be compared to calculated fields in those products.

Placing controls bound to fields The most common controls placed on most forms are those that are bound to a particular field of a table or query. These are the controls that allow for data entry and editing of records. You can add such controls to a form by dragging them from the field list to the desired location on the form. To add a field to the form, first click the `Field List` button in the Toolbar. (Doing so causes the field list to appear.) Then, click the desired field within the list and drag it to the desired location on the form. Figure 6-12 shows a blank form after three fields (Last Name, First Name, and Address) were dragged from the field list onto the form.

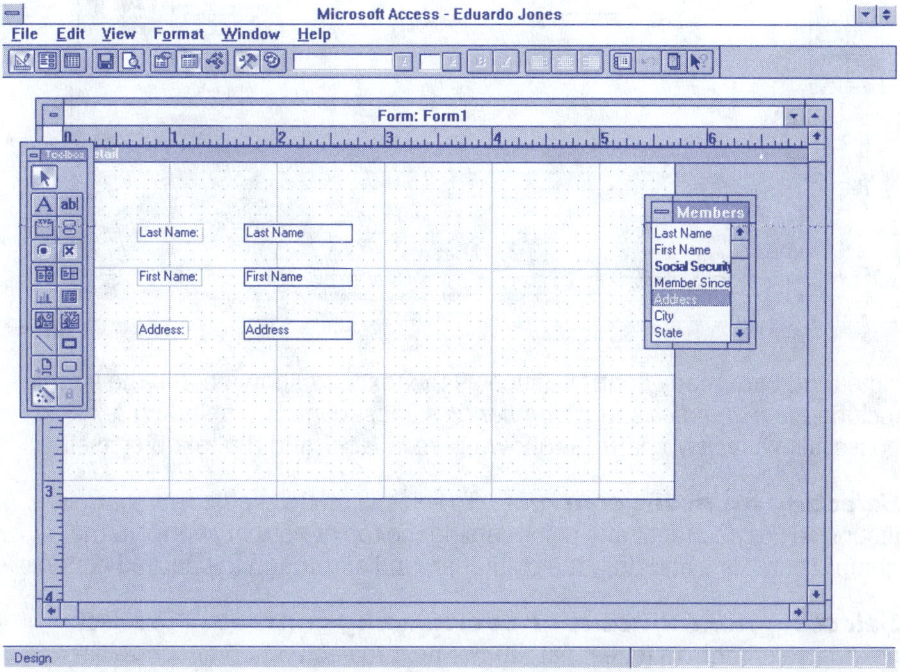

6-12
A blank form with the controls added from the field list.

Note that you can select and place multiple adjacent fields at one time by clicking the first field in the group, holding down the Shift key, and clicking the last field in the group. Then, click and drag the fields (as a group) to the desired location on the form. When you release the mouse button, all the fields will be placed on the form simultaneously. To select all the fields in the list at once, double-click the title bar of the field list. You can select nonadjacent fields by holding down the Ctrl key and clicking the desired fields.

Selecting controls Before you can make changes to a control—such as resizing or moving it—you first must select the control. To select a control, click anywhere in the control. When you do so, the control becomes surrounded by handles, indicating that it has been selected, as shown in the case of the Last Name field in FIG. 6-13.

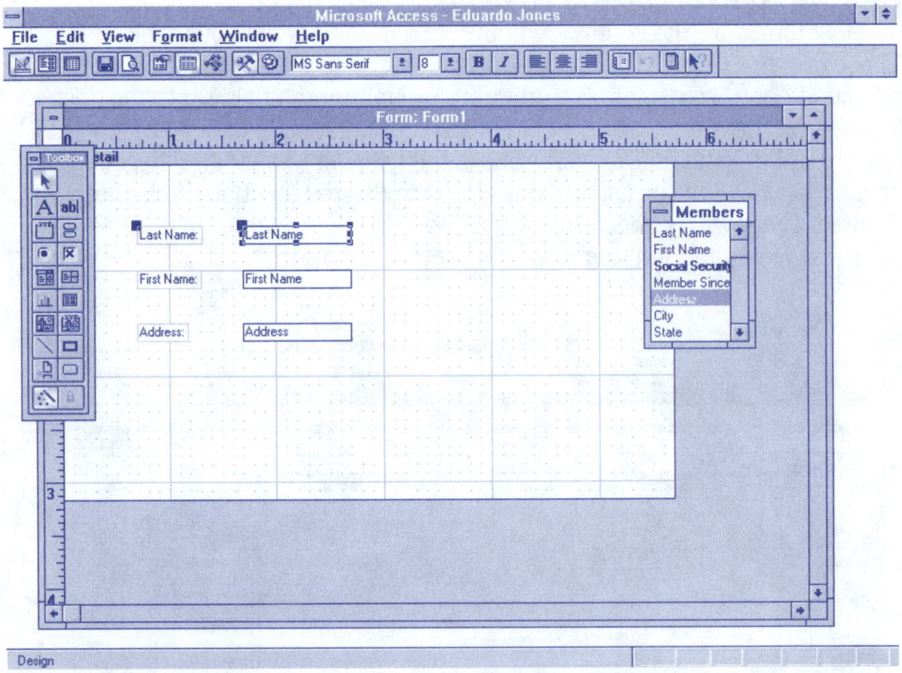

6-13
A selected control.

Note that, with many controls (such as the text box shown here), the handles include *move handles* and *sizing handles*. Most controls, including text boxes, also have two parts, as shown here: a *label*, and the text box itself.

Selecting adjacent controls To select a group of adjacent controls, first place the pointer at any point outside the top or bottom control in the group. Then, click and drag the pointer around or through the desired controls.

Selecting nonadjacent or overlapping controls To select nonadjacent controls (ones that are not next to each other) or controls that overlap, hold the Shift key depressed while clicking each control that you want to select.

Selecting all controls You can quickly select every control on a form by choosing `Edit/Select All` from the menus. (Note that you can deselect all selected controls by just clicking anywhere outside of a control.)

Moving and sizing controls To move a control, first select it (as detailed earlier), then move the pointer to the border of the control. When the pointer changes into the shape of an outstretched palm, click and drag the control to the desired location.

To move a control separately from any attached label, first select the control (or the label) by clicking it. Then, place the pointer on the move handle (it's in the upper-left corner of the control and is larger than the sizing handles) and click and drag the control to the desired location.

To resize a control, first select the control. Then, move the pointer to any of the control's sizing handles (where the pointer changes to a double arrow) and click and drag the control to the desired size.

Aligning controls You can maintain the alignment of controls as you move them with the use of the Shift key. Whenever you hold the Shift key depressed while moving a control, the control moves either horizontally or vertically in whatever direction you started, but not in both directions. Hence, if you wanted to maintain vertical alignment of a control while moving it horizontally, you would select the control, hold the Shift key depressed, and click and drag the control horizontally.

Copying controls At times, you might find it helpful to make duplicates of a control for use elsewhere in the form. To copy a control, first select the desired control. (If the control consists of a label attached to a text box, make sure you select the text box; otherwise, you will copy only the label.) With the control selected, choose `Edit/Duplicate` from the menus. Access will create a duplicate of the control, and you can use the movement methods described earlier to move the copy of the control to the desired location in the form.

Deleting controls To delete a control, first select the control, then press the Del key (or choose `Edit/Delete` from the menus). If you want to delete only the label, make sure that you have the label selected, and not the text box (click on the label to select it).

Changing labels If you want to change a label, first click the label to select it, then click the label again. When you click inside the label, an insertion pointer appears within the text of the label. You then can use the Backspace or Del keys as necessary to delete existing text and type the new text.

Creating controls with the Toolbox

The types of controls described so far have all been *bound controls*, or controls that are attached to a field in a table or query. Many times, you will need to add *unbound controls* to a form. Such controls would include graphics (that are not stored in any field of a table), descriptive text, or lines and rectangles. You also might need to add *calculated controls*, where the control displays a calculation based on a numeric field. To add unbound and calculated controls, you use the Toolbox, shown in FIG. 6-14.

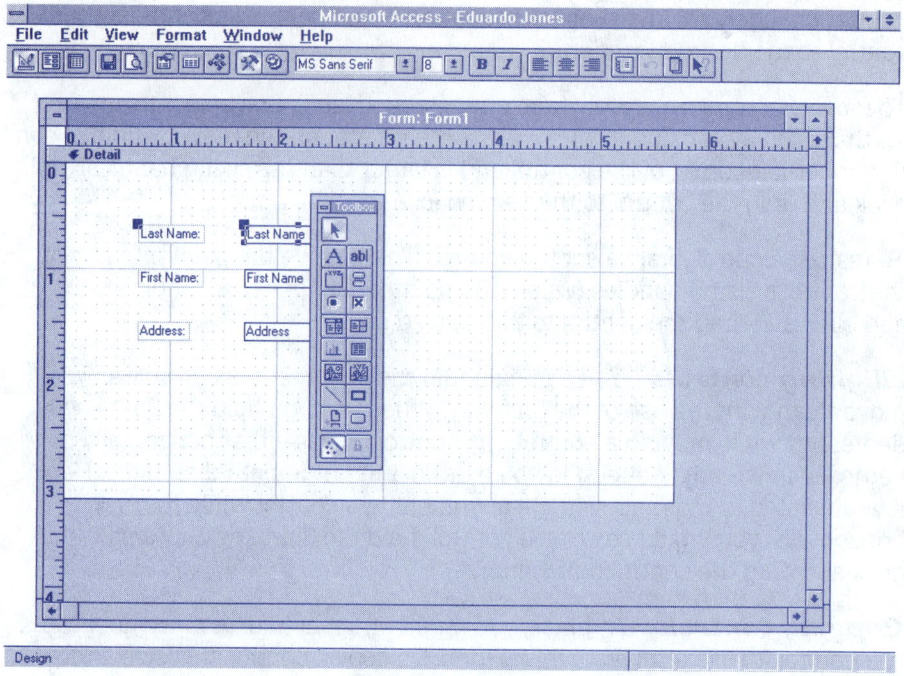

6-14
The toolbox.

Access normally displays the Toolbox when you open a form in Design View; however, if the last person using Access on your computer closed the Toolbox while in Design View, it might not be visible. If the Toolbox is not visible, choose `View Toolbox` to display it. To create a tool using the Toolbox, you perform the following steps.

Step 1 Click the tool for the desired type of control.

Step 2 Point to the place on the form where you want the upper-left corner of the control to begin, and click and drag down to the lower right corner.

You can use the Text Box tool to create a text box that is bound to a field; however, because this is the default control of the Toolbox, it is not necessary for you to use it before dragging a field from the Fields List to the form. The uses for all of the tools in the Toolbox are summarized here:

- Pointer—Use the pointer to select, move, size, or edit objects within the form.
- Label—Use the label tool to add a label; labels are convenient for titles, instructions, or descriptive text.
- Text Box—Use the text box tool to create a text box that is used to display the contents of a field (including fields that contain graphics).
- Option Group—Use the option group tool to add an option group to the form. Option groups contain check boxes, option buttons, or toggle buttons within a group. The user can select any single button or box in the group at a time.

- Toggle Button—Use the toggle button tool to add a toggle button. A toggle button can be used within an option group to chose one choice out of many, or it can be used individually to specify a yes/no choice.
- Option Button—Use the option button tool to add an option button. An option button (also known as a *radio button*) can be used within an option group to chose one choice out of many, or it can be used individually to specify a yes/no choice.
- Check Box—Use the check box tool to add a check box. A check box can be used within an option group to chose one choice out of many, or it can be used individually to specify a yes/no choice.
- Combo Box—Use the combo box tool to create a combination box. A combination box lets you select values from a predetermined list, or type in a value.
- List Box—Use the list box tool to create a list box. A list box lets you select values from a predetermined list.
- Graph—Use the graph tool to add a graph to a report. Using this tool starts the GraphWizard, which you can use to design a graph based on values in a table.
- Subform/subreport—Use the subform/subreport tool to add a subform to a form. As an example, if your form displayed the names of sales representatives, you might use a subform to display a detail table of all sales for that person. (Note that the subform must exist before you can use the tool to place it in the form.)
- Unbound Object Frame—Use the unbound object frame tool to add an OLE object created by another Windows application to the form.
- Bound Object Frame—Use the bound object frame tool to display the contents of an OLE field of a table or query in the form.
- Line—Use the line tool to draw lines in a form. (You can use the Palette to change the width and colors used by the lines that you add.)
- Rectangle—Use the rectangle tool to add rectangles or squares to a form. (You can use the Palette to change the width and colors used by the rectangles you add.)
- Page Break—Use the Page Break tool to insert a page break into the form. The page break will indicate the start of a new page on a form that uses multiple screens.
- Command Button—Use the command button tool to add a command button. You can use command buttons to carry out one or more commands.
- Control Wizards—Use the Control Wizards button to turn the Control Wizards on or off.
- Tool Lock—Use the Tool Lock to keep the current tool selected until you select a different one or until you click the pointer.

To close the Toolbox when you are done with it, choose `View/Toolbox` from the menus. (You also can double-click the Close icon in the Toolbox window or click near the top of the Toolbox to select it, then press Alt–F4.)

Changing properties for controls

As elsewhere in Microsoft Access, you use properties to determine how controls behave. While all controls have certain default properties, you often will want to change these. For example, you might want to change the font size or style used by a text box, or you might want to attach a macro to a control. To display the properties for a control, first select the desired control. Then, click the `Properties` button in the Toolbar or choose `View/Properties` from the menu. When you do so, the Properties window for the selected control appears (FIG. 6-15).

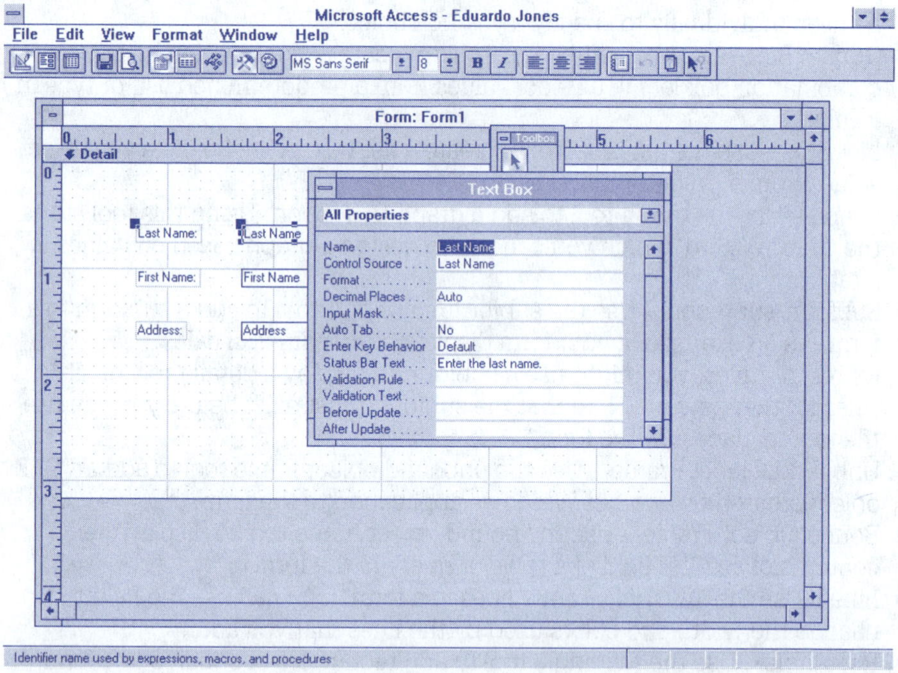

6-15
A Properties window for the selected control.

In the Properties window, click in the property that you want to change. If a down arrow appears, you can click the down arrow and choose the desired property from the list; otherwise, you type in an appropriate value for the property. If you need help on what kind of value to enter, first click in the property text box, then press F1 to see a help window that deals with that specific property.

Adding calculations to a form

You can add text boxes that display data based on a calculation. As an example, you might want to display a calculation that is 75% of the amount in an employee salary field, or you might want to display the current date. To create a text box that displays a calculation, perform the following steps.

Step 1 Click the Text Box tool in the Toolbar to select it. Click in the form at the upper-left corner where you want the text box to begin, and drag to the lower-right corner.

Step 2 Click in the text box, and type the desired expression starting with an equal symbol. For example, if you want the text box to display the contents of a field named "Salary" multiplied by 75%, you would enter `=Salary * .75` in the text box. If you wanted to display the current date, you would enter `=Date()` in the text box. (For more on expressions, see the following section.) When you enter an expression directly into the text box, you are placing the expression into the Control Source property for the control. Another way to do this is to select the control, open the Properties window with `View/Properties`, and enter the expression into the Control Source box.

Entering expressions

In forms (as in many other parts of Access), you will routinely need to enter *expressions* to provide data that can't be taken directly from a table. As mentioned earlier, expressions form the basis of calculations in text boxes, where the calculation provides a value (usually based on the contents of one or more fields in a table). Your expressions can be used in forms and reports. While the next chapter details the use of expressions in reports, many of the techniques for including expressions are the same whether you are designing forms or reports. When a form contains a control that is based on an expression, Access evaluates the expression each time the form is used. As you move from record to record within the form, the calculation reoccurs to provide the needed data.

Typically, text boxes are used to calculate values; however, in reality, Access lets you use any control that has a ControlSource property. When you use a text box, there are two ways of entering the expression. You can manually type it into the text box (beginning with an equal symbol), or you can use the Expression Builder. (The Expression Builder is a feature of Access 2.0, so if you are using an earlier version of Access, you must resort to manually typing the expression.)

To enter the expression directly into the text box, use these steps.

Step 1 Open the desired form, in Design view.

Step 2 Use the Toolbox to add a text box to the form, or select an existing text box.

Step 3 Click within the text box, and type an equal symbol followed by the desired expression.

To enter the expression using the Expression Builder, follow these steps.

Step 1 Open the desired form, in Design view.

Step 2 Use the Toolbox to add a text box to the form, or select an existing text box.

Step 3 With the text box selected, choose `View/Properties` (or click the `Properties` button) to open the Properties window for the selected text box.

Step 4 Using the right mouse button, click the ControlSource property in the Properties window.

Step 5 From the menu that appears, choose `Build`. When you do so, the Expression Builder appears (FIG. 6-16). In the Expression Builder, you select the table and field names, functions, and math or logical symbols to build the desired expression. (You can get help on the use of the Expression Builder by clicking the `Help` button in the Expression Builder dialog box.)

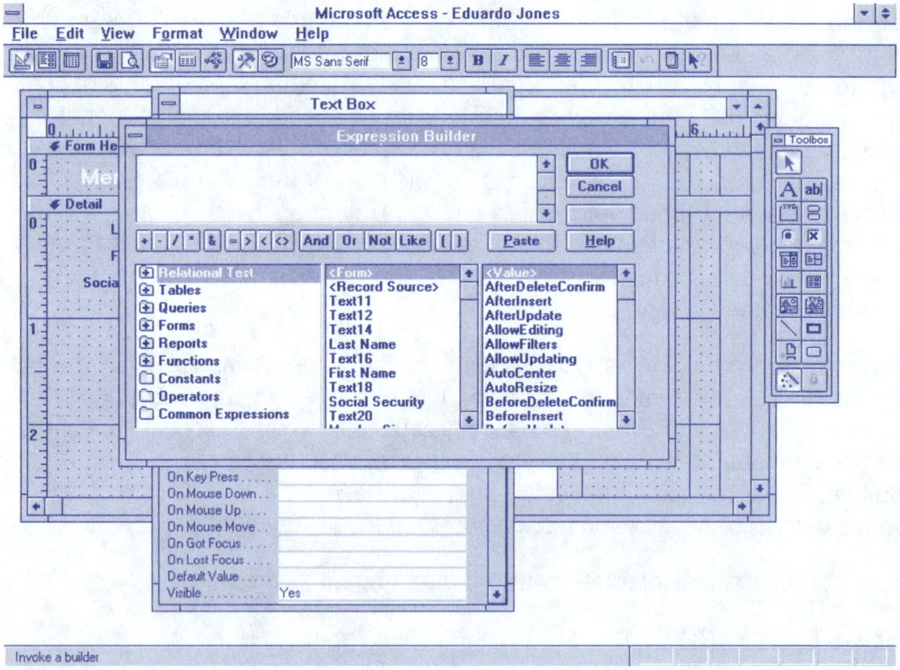

6-16 *The Expression Builder dialog box.*

Step 6 When done building the expression, click `OK`, and the expression appears within the text box.

When entering expressions manually, remember the use of the Zoom Box. If the expression is too long to view fully in the text box, you can type the expression in the Zoom box. To open the Zoom box, press Shift–F2 once the insertion pointer is where you want to place the expression.

Changing colors & effects

You can use the *Palette* to change the colors and effects associated with an object. To do so, first select the desired object, then click the `Palette` button in the Toolbar or choose `View/Palette`. With either method, the Palette appears, as shown in FIG. 6-17.

You can click among the colors within the Palette to change the colors for text, the fill color, and the border color. (Some of these options might be dimmed if they do not apply to the object. For example, the overall form will have only the Fill colors enabled, because the overall form does not have text or borders.) If you are working with a control and you want to hide its border, click the `Clear` button beside the Border row of colors. Also, when working with any objects that have a visible border, you can change the size of the border by clicking on the desired `Width` button at the top of the Palette. Use the `Appearance` buttons to choose a normal, raised, or sunken look for the selected object.

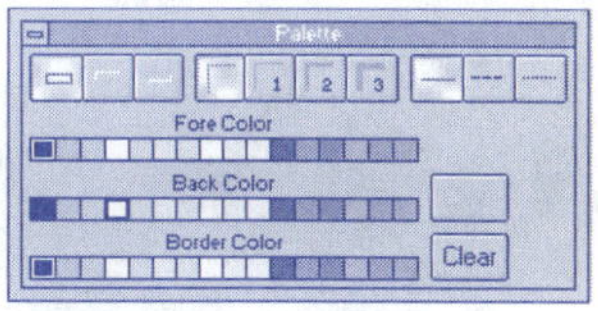

6-17 *The Palette.*

You often can improve the appearance of a form by clicking anywhere in the form away from an object (to select the overall form), opening the Palette, and changing the fill color. The FormWizards make use of the soft cyan, but you might find other colors more to your liking.

TIP

Changing fonts & justification

You can change the fonts and the justification for objects that contain text or data. First, select the desired object. When you do so, list boxes and buttons that control the fonts, point size, and justification are added to the Toolbar. These are identified in FIG. 6-18.

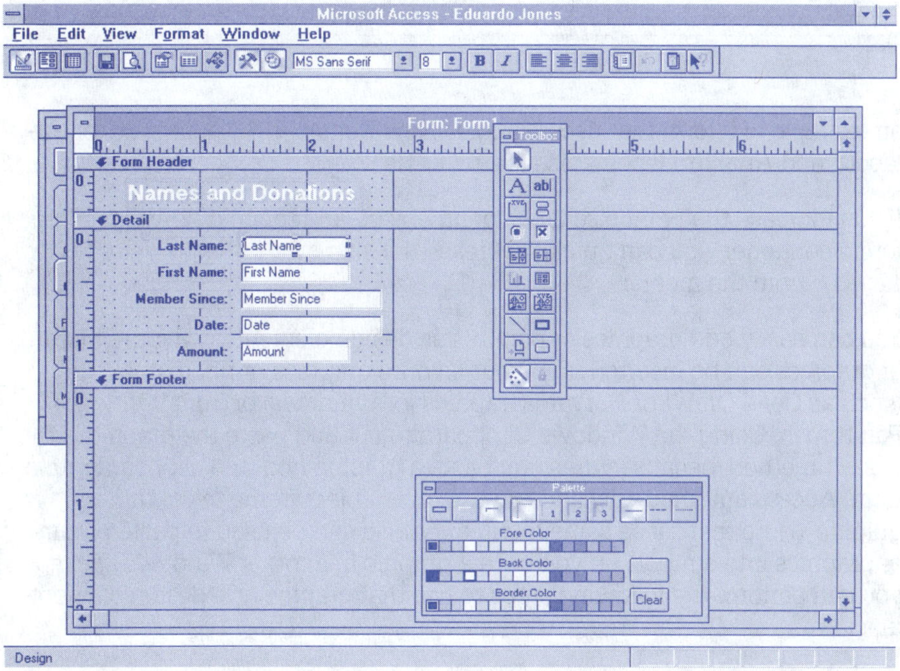

6-18
The Toolbar with added buttons.

With the object still selected, use the Toolbar options to change the font and point size, to select boldface, italics, or underlining, and to choose desired justification. The available fonts and point sizes will depend on what fonts and point sizes are available with your version of Windows. Figure 6-19 shows

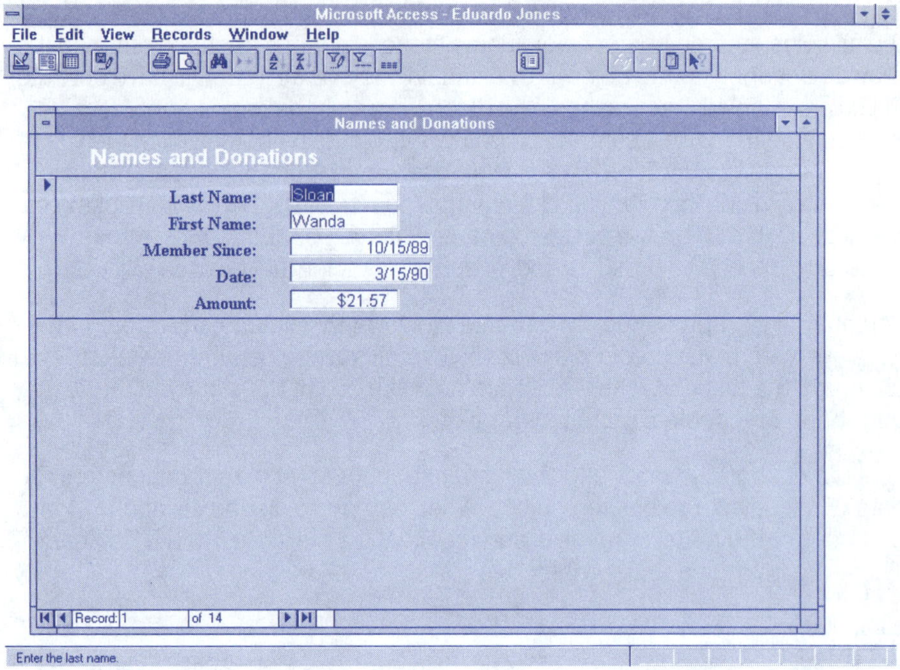

6-19
An example of different fonts and point sizes in a form.

an example of a form that uses Timxxes New Roman in 12-point size for the labels, and Arial in 11-point size for the fields.

If you increase the point size used for an object, and the text now is too large for its container, you can quickly increase the size by choosing `Layout/Size to Fit` from the menus.

Adding pictures & graphics

You can easily add graphics or pictures as design elements in a form. Pictures or graphics can be inserted from your favorite graphics or photo package (such as Corel Draw! or Harvard Graphics for Windows) or from Windows Paintbrush. Using the Windows Clipboard to cut and paste the graphic is the easiest method, because when you paste a graphic from the clipboard into a form, Access automatically adds an unbound object frame to contain the graphic. (Note that these same techniques also can be used to paste pictures or graphics into a report.) If you have a graphic in another Windows package, you can perform the following steps to use that graphic as a design element in a form.

If you are running Access and your graphic program simultaneously, one easy way to switch between them is to press Ctrl–Esc to display the Windows Task Switcher. Then, choose the desired application from the list. Follow these steps.

Step 1 Open the desired form in Access, and get into Design View.

Step 2 Start your graphics program under Windows, and design or load the graphics image that you want to use.

Step 3 Using Windows selection techniques applicable to your package, select the portion of the graphic that you want to place in the form in Access. (Figure 6-20 shows a portion of an image selected in Windows Paintbrush.) Choose `Edit/Copy` from the application's menus.

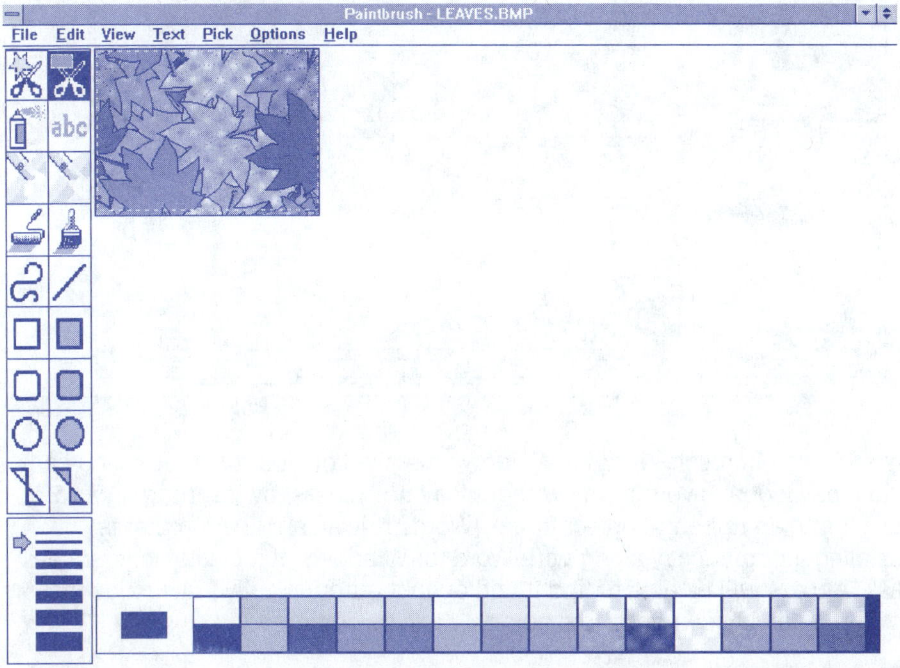

6-20
Part of a graphic selected in Windows Paintbrush.

Step 4 Press Ctrl–Esc to bring up the Windows Task Switcher, and choose Microsoft Access from the list.

Step 5 From the menus in Access, choose `Edit/Paste`. When you do so, the graphic appears in the form. (Figure 6-21 shows the graphic shown earlier, pasted into a form.)

Step 6 Using the move and sizing techniques detailed earlier, place the graphic in the desired location on the form.

Once a graphic has been placed, you can modify it in the original application by double-clicking the graphic, assuming the original application that you used to create the graphic supports Windows OLE (object linking and embedding) as an OLE server.

TIP

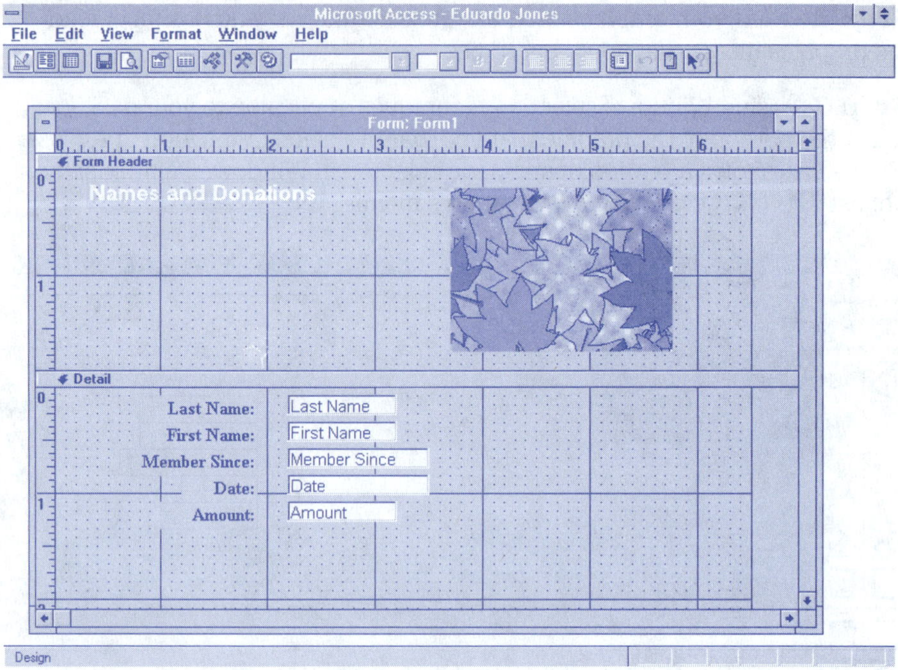

6-21
A Windows Paintbrush graphic in a form.

Adding a WordArt logo

If you have Microsoft Word for Windows installed on your computer, you can add fancy logos to your forms without leaving Access, by inserting a WordArt object into an unbound object frame. (WordArt is an application that is installed automatically along with Word for Windows; if it exists on your hard disk, Access will be able to find it and open it automatically.) The following example quickly demonstrates how this can be done.

Step 1 Open the form that you want to add the graphic to in Design View.

Step 2 If the Toolbox is not visible, choose `View Toolbox`. Click the `Unbound Object Frame` button in the Toolbox.

Step 3 Click and hold the mouse button at the upper-left corner of where you want the logo to start, and drag down to the lower-right corner. The Insert Object dialog box appears (FIG. 6-22).

Step 4 Click `MS WordArt`, then click `OK`. (If `MS WordArt` does not appear in the dialog box, it does not exist on your system.) A window to WordArt opens, as shown in FIG. 6-23. Replace the text `Your Text Here` in the text box with the text of your desired logo. Remember that you can use more than one line, although too many lines become impractical in a company logo.

Step 5 Choose a desired font, size, style, fill, and alignment from the dialog box. As you make various selections, they will appear in the Preview portion of the dialog box.

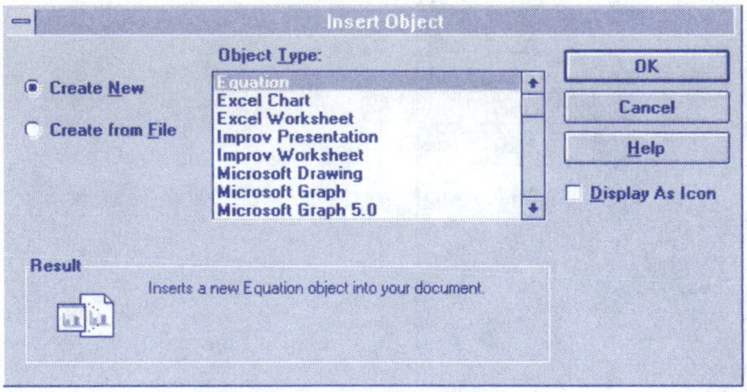

6-22
The Insert Object dialog box.

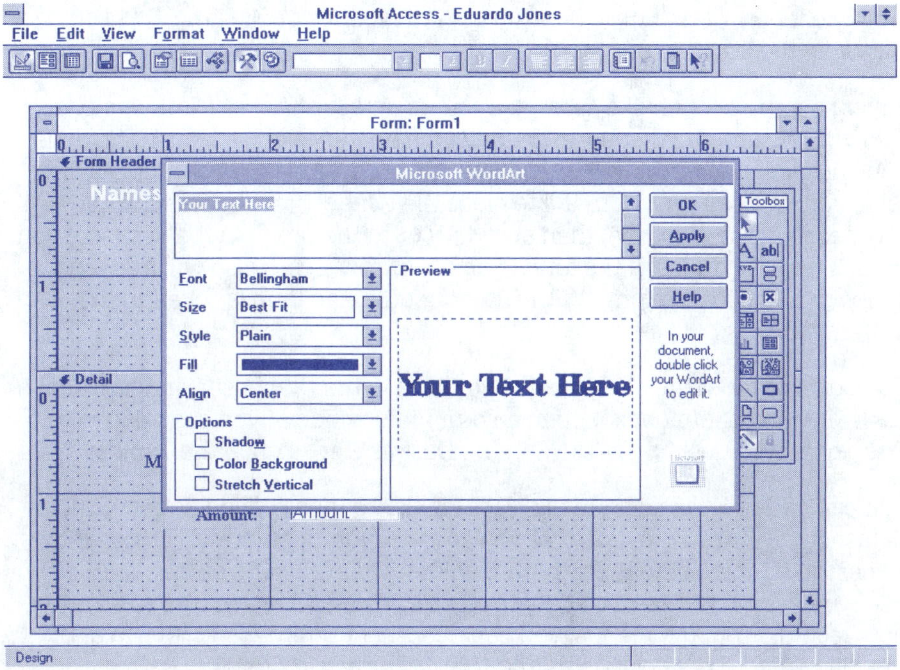

6-23
MS WordArt in a window.

Step 6 Click `OK` to close the WordArt window and place the completed WordArt object in the form. Figure 6-24 shows a WordArt object placed in a form for the Members table. While using WordArt, you can click the `Help` button for specific help with WordArt, or you can refer to your Word for Windows documentation for more information about WordArt.

Note that you can use these same techniques to paste elements created with WordArt into a report; see the next chapter for details on designing reports.

Previewing the form

You can test the form during the design process, by choosing `View/Form` from the menus or by clicking the `Form` button in the Toolbar. A record will appear in the form, and you can use the PgUp and PgDn keys to view additional records. You can return to the form design process at any time;

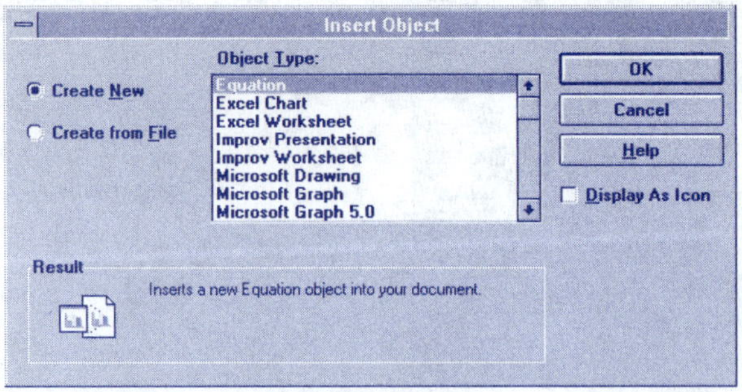

6-24
The WordArt object in a form.

simply choose `View/Form Design` from the menus or click the `Design` button in the Toolbar.

Saving a form

Saving a form is much like saving any other object in Access. You can choose `File/Save` from the menus, and supply a name (if asked) for the form, then you can close the form by pressing Ctrl–F4 or clicking on the window's close icon. You first can press Ctrl–F4 to close the window (or double-click the Close icon in the window), then answer `Yes` to the prompt when asked if you want to save changes. If the form is a new form, Access also will ask you to supply a name for the form. With either method, the form is saved to the current database.

Opening a saved form

To open a saved form, click the `Form` button in the Database window, then click `Open`. The form will open in a Form View window; you can change to Design View, if desired, by clicking the Design View icon in the Toolbar.

Using a form

You can add records using techniques similar to those of adding records in a datasheet. Because the data that you add through the form still is stored by Access in a table, there is always a blank record at the end of the table, and you can reach this blank record while in the form and type in the data for the new record. From the menus, you can choose `Records/GoTo/New` to get to the blank record or choose `Records/Data Entry` to drop into data entry mode and begin adding records. You also can use the navigation buttons that appear by default at the bottom of the form; you can click the last record button, then click the next record button to move to the blank record.

Editing of data is a simple matter; just click in the desired field or the Tab and Shift–Tab key combinations to move between fields and make the desired edits. Any changes that you make are saved when you move to another record, close the form, or choose `File/Save` Record. As with tables, you cannot edit some types of fields, including counter fields, fields that have been locked, fields based on a calculation, and certain fields in relational queries.

Key combinations for navigating within a form

You can use the GoTo command on the Records menu, the Up and Down Arrow keys, PgUp and PgDn, or the vertical scroll bar to move between records in a form. However, likely the easiest way to move between records when you are working with large tables is by using the navigation buttons in the lower-left corner of the form window.

To navigate in forms containing more than one page, you can use the PgUp and PgDn keys to move between pages. You also can use the F5 key to go to a specific record; press F5 to move to the record number box, then type the number of the record that you want to go to and press Enter. You can use the Tab and right-arrow keys to move to the next field; use Shift–Tab or the left-arrow keys to move to the prior field.

Entering data in OLE fields

Access lets you insert data into OLE fields in a form using the same cut-and-paste methods described for entering OLE data into a table's datasheet (see chapter 4). However, in forms, you also can use the Edit/Insert Object command to insert objects that you already have created and stored in other Windows software. To insert OLE data into an OLE field in a form, you perform the following steps.

Step 1 Tab to or click in the desired field of the table.

Step 2 From the menus, choose Edit/Insert Object. The Insert Object dialog box appears (FIG. 6-25). Scroll down the list if necessary, and click on the object type that you want to insert. (The list that you see is based on the Windows programs supporting OLE that have been installed on your computer.)

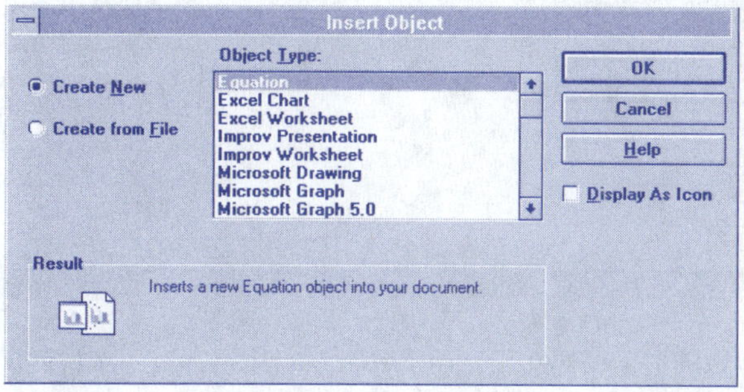

6-25 *The Insert Object dialog box.*

Step 3 If you want to create a new object of the selected type, click OK. If you want to insert the selected type of object from an existing file, click the Create from File button, choose the desired file from the dialog box that appears, then click OK.

If you click the OK button while Create is selected (as opposed to the Create from File button being selected), the application responsible for the type of object that you've selected opens, and you can create the object. When you are done, choose File/Exit from the application's menus. When you do so, a dialog box appears, asking if you want to update the embedded objects. Click `Yes`, and you will be returned to Access with the OLE object stored in the field.

Applying a filter

While you are using a form, you can apply a filter criteria to the form to limit the records that will be visible. This is quite helpful if you want to edit a selected group of records. For example, you might need to edit all employees assigned to a specific department. (You can accomplish the same results by designing a query, then basing a form on the query's records, but applying a filter often is faster.) Once you are familiar with queries (covered in the prior chapter), you will find form filters a simple matter, because they use a criteria grid based on the query grid. When you are using a form, the Toolbar contains three buttons not seen elsewhere, as shown FIG. 6-26.

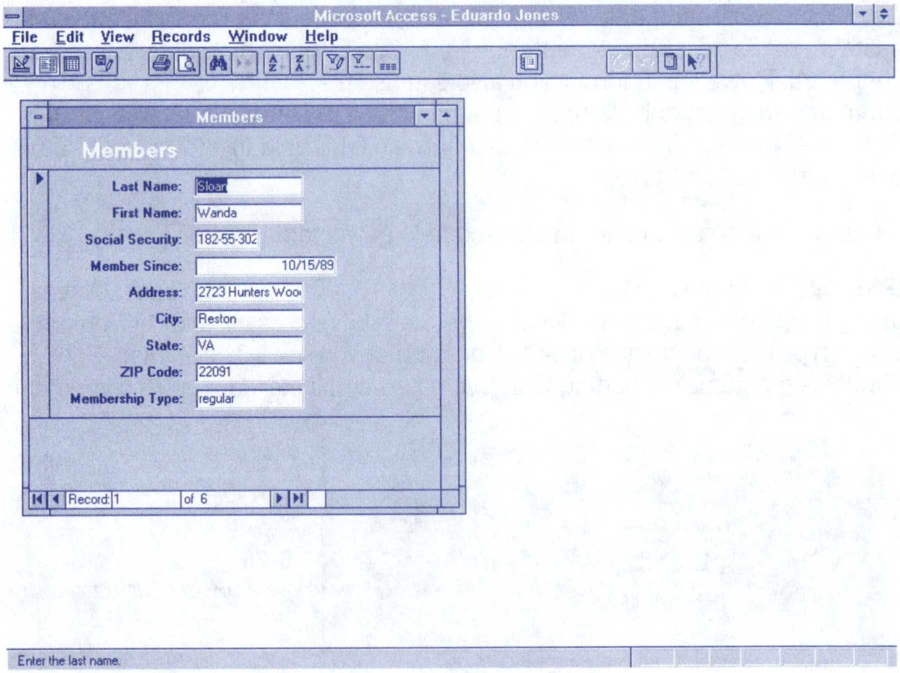

6-26
The Toolbar with filter buttons added.

These three buttons are the `Edit Filter/Sort`, `Apply Filter/Sort`, and `Show All Records` buttons. You first specify the filter to be used to select records visible in the form, then you use the `Apply Filter/Sort` and `Show All Records` buttons to apply and remove the effects of the filter, as desired. (Keyboard users should note that the menu equivalents of these buttons are `Records/Edit Filter/Sort`, `Records/Apply Filter/Sort`, and `Records/Show All Records`.)

To specify a filter, click the `Edit Filter/Sort` button or choose `Records/Edit Filter/Sort`. When you do so, a window containing a form that resembles the query grid appears, as shown in FIG. 6-27.

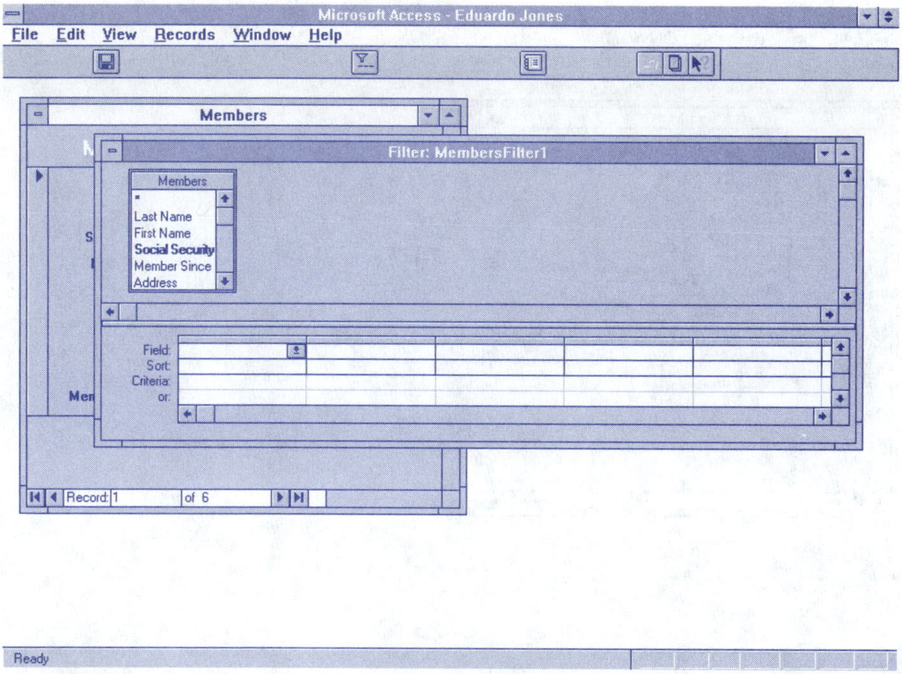

6-27
A filter window.

Drag the fields that you want to use to specify the filter conditions to the empty cells of the Criteria row. You need not drag every field; drag only those fields that are needed to filter the records. For example, if you wanted the form to show only those members living in a certain city in a certain state, you would drag the City and State fields to cells in the Criteria row of the filter.

After placing the needed fields, type the criteria used to specify the records in the Criteria rows of the filter. (You use the same techniques as were used for entering criteria in queries; refer to chapter 5 for more specifics.) As an example, the filter shown in FIG. 6-28 would filter entries for members living in Washington, North Carolina. In this case, having both the "City" and "State" fields in the filter avoids getting the wrong city named "Washington."

After entering the desired conditions, close the filter window by pressing Ctrl–F4 or by double-clicking the window's Close icon.

To apply the filter, click the `Apply Filter/Sort` button in the Toolbar or choose `Records/Apply Filter/Sort` from the menus. As you try navigating through the form, you will see that only those records that meet the criteria specified are available. Also, you might notice that the abbreviation "FLTR" appears in the Status Bar at the bottom of the main Access window, indicating that the filter is in effect.

To cancel the effects of the filter, click the `Show All Records` button in the Toolbar or choose `Records/Show All Records` from the menus.

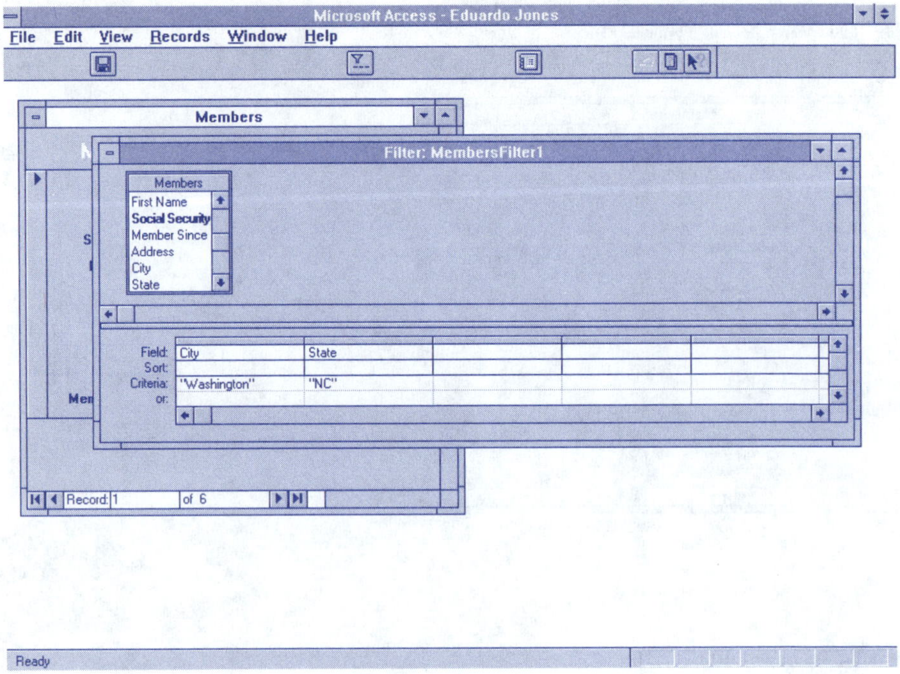

6-28
A filter window containing fields and sample criteria.

TIP

Filters are temporary; once you close the form, the filter is lost. If you find yourself repeatedly using the same filter, you should design and save a query that will accomplish the same task. You then can use that query as a basis for your form. For further details on queries, see chapter 5.

Printing a form

You can print a form; this often is handy when you want a printed copy of a single record. (You can print just one record or every record in a table.) To print using a form, perform the following steps.

Step 1 Open the desired form (or you can just select the form in the Database window).

Step 2 If you want to print just a single record, find the desired record, then choose `Edit/Select Record` from the menus (or click the Record Selector bar at the left edge of the form).

Step 3 From the menus, choose `File/Print`. This causes the Print dialog box to appear (FIG. 6-29).

Step 4 If you selected a single record to print, click `Selection` in the Print Range portion of the dialog box. For all records, leave the `All` option selected in the Print Range dialog box. Make any other desired selections in the dialog box, then click `OK` to begin printing.

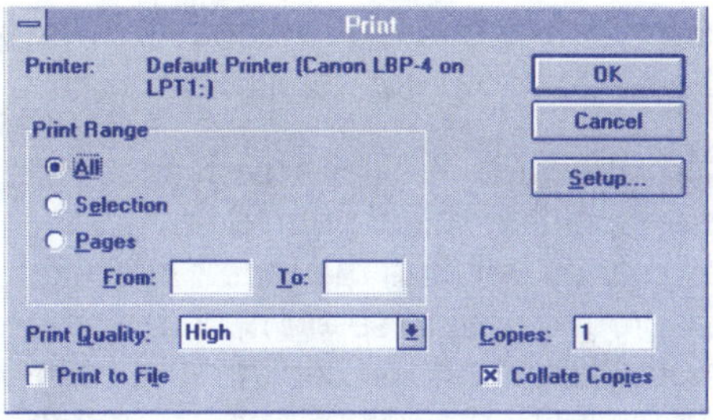

6-29
The File/Print dialog box.

Making a form read-only

You can make a form read-only, which will prevent its use for adding or editing records. Users will be able to view data in the form, but they will be unable to make any changes. To make a form read-only, perform these steps.

Step 1 Open the form in Design view. Choose `Select Form` from the Edit menu, then choose `View/Properties`.

Step 2 Change the Default Editing property to `Read Only`. Change the Allow Editing property to `Unavailable`. (Doing so disables the Editing Allowed command.)

Note that you can make individual fields on a form read-only by changing the Enabled and Locked properties for the fields (click the desired field, then choose `View/Properties` to open the property window for the field).

Deleting forms

If a form is no longer needed, you can delete it from the database. To delete a form, first click the `Forms` button in the Database window, then click the desired form to select it. Next, press the Del key (or choose `Edit/Delete` from the menus). Access will display a dialog box asking for confirmation, and you must click `Yes` before the form will be deleted.

Converting a form into a report

In some cases, you might need to create a report that is similar in design to an existing form. You often can save time by opening the form in Design view, then saving the form as a report. You then can proceed to use the techniques for modifying reports (discussed in the following chapter) to make any needed changes to the report. To save a form as a report, perform these steps.

Step 1 Open the form in Design view.

Step 2 From the menus, choose `File/Save As Report`. The Save Form As Report dialog box appears (FIG. 6-30).

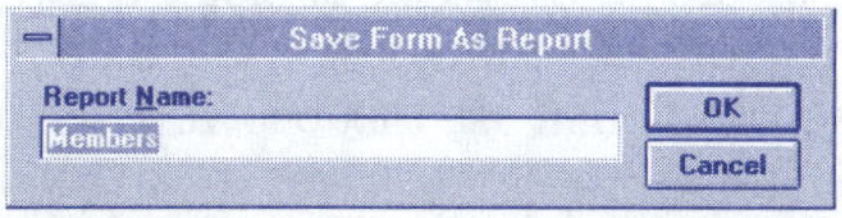

6-30
The Save Form As Report dialog box.

Enter a name for the report, then click OK. You can proceed to use the report as you would use any report; see the next chapter for details.

Note: If you create forms with the FormWizards and save them as reports, the background color used might not be appealing when printed on most printers. You can easily change the color by opening the report in design mode, clicking anywhere in the background area to select it, choosing View/Palette to open the Palette, and changing the background color to white. (See "Changing colors and effects with the Palette" earlier in this chapter for details on the Palette.)

Creating multipage forms

When designing your forms, you might find that there is too much data to comfortably fit on a single page of a form. When this is the case, you can easily add page breaks to mark the start of a new screen; in effect, what you create is a *multipage form*. To create a multipage form, use these steps.

Step 1 In the Design view of your form, display the toolbox and property sheet if they aren't already displayed.

Step 2 Choose the page break tool in the toolbox, then click the form where you want a new screen or page to start.

Note that page breaks don't control how much of the form is displayed in a window. If you want each window to show only one page at a time, design the form so each page break is an equal distance apart from the others. (Use the vertical ruler when positioning your page breaks to space them evenly.)

Creating multitable forms with subforms

Access lets you design forms within forms. The most common use for this technique is in the creation of multitable forms, which are forms with records from more than one table. For example, a sales application might need to display a customer record and all orders placed for that customer. Assuming the details concerning the customer are stored in a customer table and the details concerning the orders are stored in an orders table, you can display the data in a multitable form. Keep in mind that you can easily accomplish such a task using the FormWizards. However, if you prefer to create such forms manually, you can do so.

Note: Any multitable form consists of a subform bound to a master, or main form. The relationship between the underlying tables can be either a one-to-many relationship, in which one record in the main form relates to one or more records in the subform or a one-to-one relationship, in which one record in the main form matches only one record in the subform. When manually creating a multitable form, you must create and save the subform before designing the main form. Use the techniques for form design described earlier in this chapter to create the subform, then use the following instructions to create the multitable form.

Step 1 Open the main form in Design view. (If necessary, move the Form window so that you can see the Database window. Also, size the form so that it contains sufficient room to place the subform.)

Step 2 In the Database window, click the `Form` button to display the list of forms.

Step 3 In the list box, find the form that you want to use as a subform and click and drag it from the Database window to the main form. When you release the mouse button, a subform control appears within the main form, as shown in FIG. 6-31. Move the subform as desired to its location in the main form.

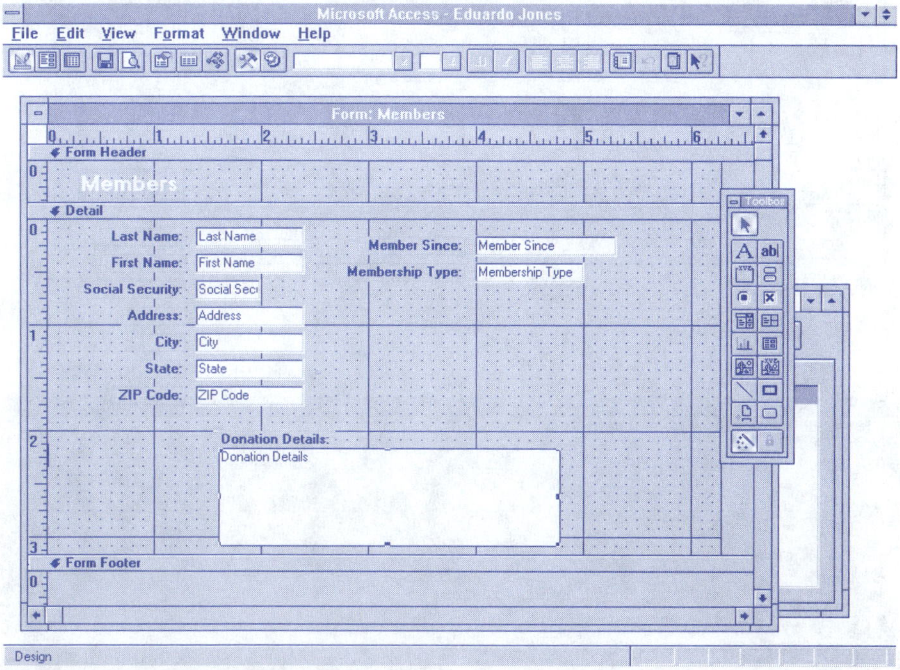

6-31
A subform control in a main form.

Step 4 With the subform selected, choose `View/Properties` from the menus to open the Properties window for the subform, as shown in FIG. 6-32.

Step 5 Click the LinkMasterFields property. If it contains an entry already, verify that Access has created the relational link on the fields that you had in mind (see the next section). If Access has not established a link, you must type the name of the field in the main form that will be used as a link to the records shown in the subform.

Step 6 Close the form and save it when prompted, using the methods described earlier in the chapter. When you open the form in Form view, the records for the table that you've used for the main form appear and the associated records from the related table appear within the subform. Figure 6-33 shows a form designed using these steps.

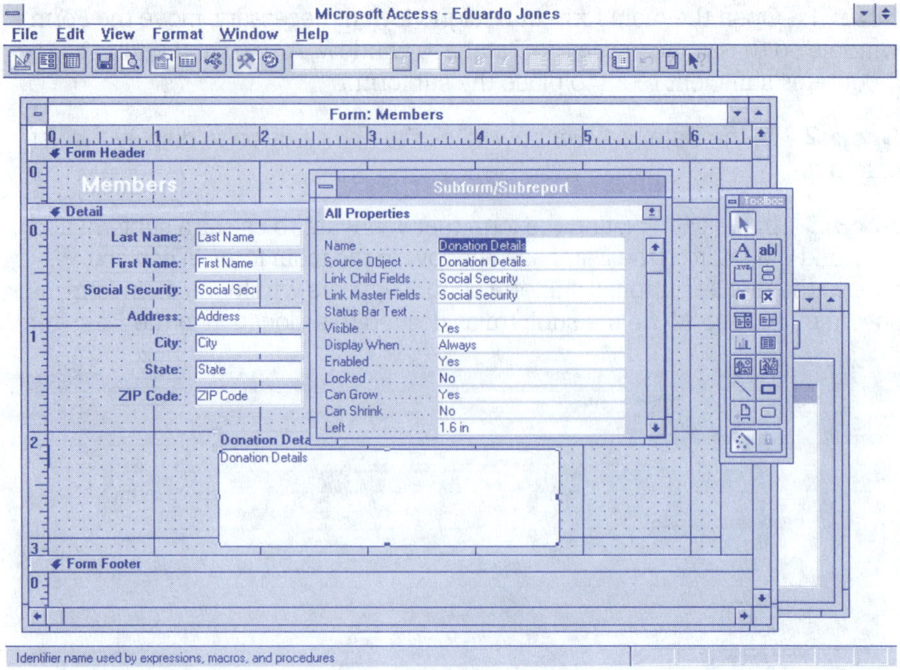

6-32
A properties window for a subform.

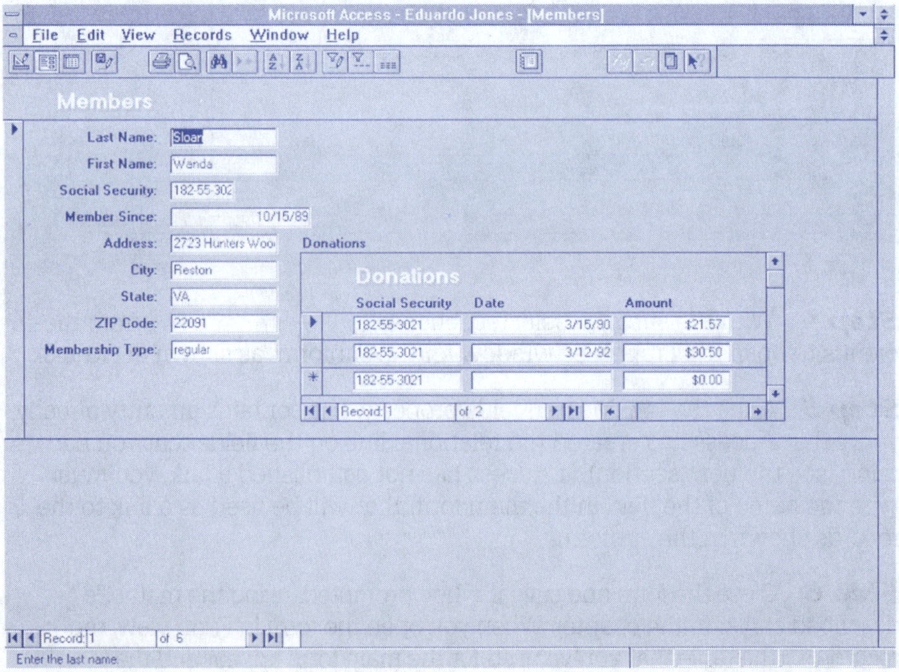

6-33
An example of a form containing a subform.

Linking subforms to main forms

As shown earlier, when you create a multitable form manually, you must verify that Access has established the proper link between the table used by the subform and the table used by the main form. You do so by opening the Properties window for the subform and verifying that Access has correctly established the relationship between the tables used by the subform and the main form. Access will establish the link successfully if both forms are based on tables and a relationship between them has been defined with the Relationships command or if the main form and subform contain fields with the same name and data type and the field on the main form is the primary key of the underlying table.

If no predefined relationship or same field names and types exist, Access cannot establish a link automatically, and the LinkMasterFields property will be blank. In such cases, you must type in the name of the field that will establish the link between the subform and the main form. For the relationship to make sense, the data types and the data must match, but the field names can be different.

Hands-on practice: manually creating a multitable form

If you want to see how you can use the techniques that were described earlier to create a multitable form, you can use the Members and Donations forms created earlier in the chapter to build a single form that simultaneously displays a member and all the donations associated with that member. Perform the following steps to do so.

Step 1 In the Database window, click the `Form` button to display the list of forms, then click `Members` to select it, then click `Design`. Click the right edge of the drawing area, and drag the right edge out to the 6½" mark on the horizontal ruler (this will provide sufficient room to place the subform).

Step 2 In the Database window, find the Donations form and click and drag it from the Database window to the existing Members form. When you release the mouse button, a subform control appears within the main form, as shown earlier in FIG. 6-31. Move the mouse pointer to the edge of the Donations subform until it takes on the shape of a palm, and click and drag the subform as far to the left as possible (without covering the existing fields of the Members table).

Step 3 Click the `Maximize` button so that you have more room to work with the form. Use the scroll bars if necessary to find the right edge of the Donations subform, click at the lower right corner, and make the subform roughly 4"×2". (You might have to drag the form footer down to provide sufficient room.)

Step 4 With the subform still selected, choose `View/Properties` from the menus to open the Properties window for the subform. Notice that the "Social Security" field already appears under "Link Child Fields" and "Link Master Fields." In this case, because the two forms are based on tables having an equivalent field, Access already has established the needed link.

Step 5 Do *not* choose `File/Save`; instead, from the menus, choose `File/Save As`. When prompted for a name, enter `Members and Donations`, and click `OK`.

Step 6 From the menus, choose `View/Form` to examine data within the form. The results should resemble those shown earlier, in FIG. 6-33.

Creating graphs

In Access, graphs are just one more type of form that you create. As with other forms, you can create graphs in one of two ways: with the FormWizards or by manually designing the form that contains the graph. Because a graph is a type of form, you can base the graph on a table or on a query. Before creating the graph, you'll want to determine what fields the data used to construct the graph must come from. If a specific query is needed to limit the graphed data in some way, you'll want to create and save the query before you design the graph.

Creating a graph with the FormWizard

The easiest way to create a graph is through the use of the FormWizard. To create a graph, you can use these steps.

Step 1 In the Database window, click the `Form` button, then click `New`. This causes the New Form dialog box to appear.

Step 2 In the Select a Table/Query list box, choose the table (or query) that will provide the data for the graph.

Step 3 Click the `FormWizards` button. The dialog box that appears asks which type of wizard you want to use. Click `Graph`, then click `OK`. The GraphWizard dialog box (FIG. 6-34) asks which type of graph you want to use. Click the desired graph type, and click the `Sum` or `Average` button to indicate whether totals should be a sum of values or an average of values. Then, click `Next`.

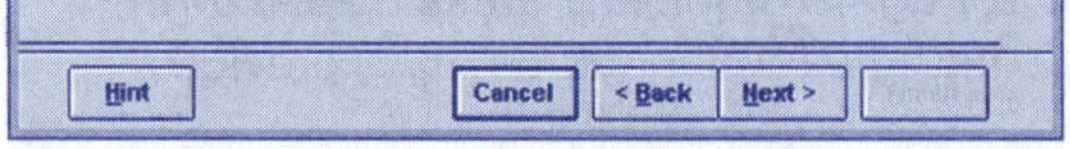

6-34 *The GraphWizard dialog box.*

Step 4 The next dialog box (FIG. 6-35) asks which fields you want to graph and use for the labels of the graph. Click the desired fields to use, then click `Next`.

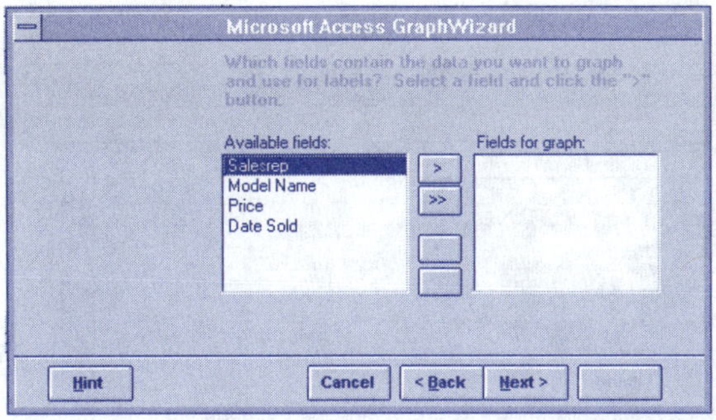

6-35
A dialog box for identifying the fields to graph.

Step 5 Depending on which fields you've added, you might see a dialog box that asks you to identify the fields that will be used as the labels. (If you've added only one text field, you won't see this dialog box.) Click the desired fields to use for the labels, then click `Next`.

Step 6 The next dialog box to appear asks for a title for your graph; by default, the title assigned is the same as the name of the underlying table or query. Enter a different title if desired, then click `Open` to open the form and view the graph or click `Design` to make changes to the graph's design. When you close the form containing the graph, Access will ask if you want to save the new form; if so, enter a title and the form containing the graph will be saved.

Creating graphs manually

You can create graphs manually without the aid of the FormWizard by opening a form and embedding a graph with the Graph tool on the Toolbox. This is a useful technique when you want to add a graph to an existing form. For example, you might have a form that displays data regarding each salesrep in a company, and you might want that form to display a graph showing recent performance for that salesrep. To create a graph manually, perform the following steps.

Step 1 If you are creating a graph within a new form, click the `Forms` button in the Database window, then click `New`. This causes the New Form dialog box to appear. If you want to insert a graph into an existing form, open the form in Design view, then skip ahead to step 3.

Step 2 In the Select a Table/Query list box, choose the table (or query) that will provide the data for the graph. Click the `Blank Form` button to display a blank form.

Step 3 If the Toolbox is not visible, choose `View/Toolbox` from the menus (or click the `Toolbox` button in the Toolbar) to display the Toolbox. Click the Graph tool in the Toolbox to select it.

Step 4 Click in the form at the upper-left corner where you want to place the graph, and drag down to the lower-right corner. Access inserts an empty graph frame in the form and displays a series of GraphWizard dialog boxes asking you for information about the graph; the first dialog box is shown in FIG. 6-36.

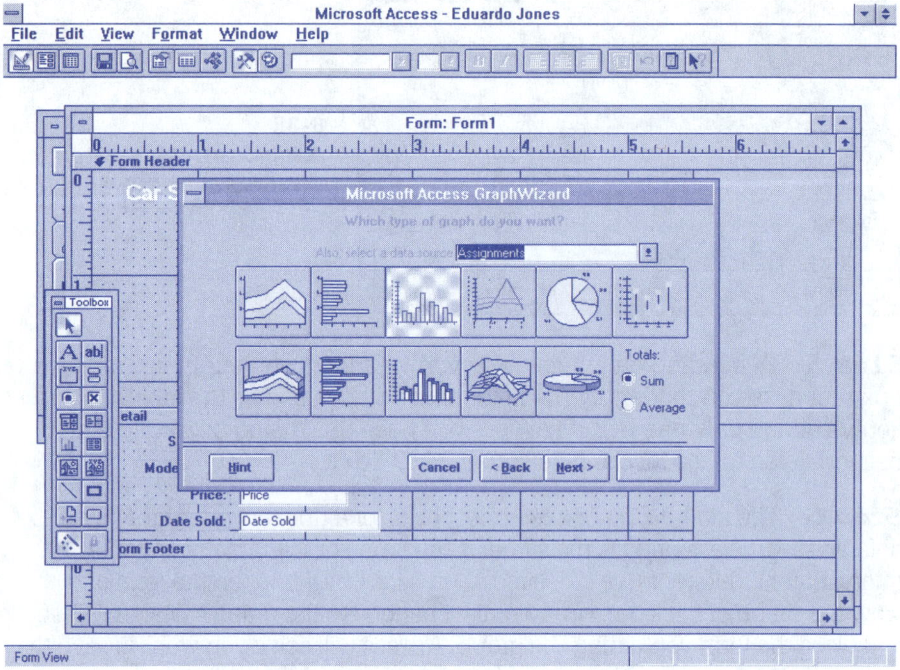

6-36
A dialog box used when creating the graphs manually.

You must provide the following: the data source (the name of the table or query supplying the data), the type of graph desired, the type of totals, the fields to graph and the fields to use for the labels, any desired grouping, any field used for linking multiple tables, and any desired title for the graph. After you have answered the prompts in the dialog boxes (which are similar to those used for creating graphs with the wizards, described earlier), an object containing the graph appears in the form, and you can switch between Design view and Form view to examine the graph.

Move and resize the graph as is necessary. The graph is an object, like any other object that you place in an Access form; you can click it to select it and use the sizing handles to resize the graph so that it fits in the desired area of your form. When you close the form containing the graph, Access will ask if you want to save the new form; if so, enter a title and the form containing the graph will be saved.

Note: When you embed a graph within a form, you might see a slowed response time whenever you open the form. This is due to the fact that Access creates graphs using a Windows application, MS Graph, as an *object server*. In a nutshell, this means that each time Access draws a graph, it must call a separate program (which is included with the purchase of Access, Word for Windows, or Excel) and run that program to create the graph. This causes a drop in response time, so it takes longer to open the form.

7 Working with reports

For many users, creating reports is what database management is all about. You can readily perform queries to gain immediate answers to specific questions, but much of your work with Access probably will involve generating reports. Detailed reports are easy to produce with Access thanks to the ReportWizards, which can quickly produce many different styles of reports. You can combine the reports produced by the wizards with selective queries to obtain reports of specific data.

Access provides several ways to design and print reports. You can design and print plain reports by opening a table in the Datasheet view and choosing `File/Print` from the menus. As mentioned, you can use the ReportWizards to quickly design a report. You can use the sophisticated report design options present in Access to create customized reports. You can print form letters or mailing labels. Reports that you design in Access can be divided into two overall groups: reports that use the wizards and custom reports. As with forms, reports that are created with the wizards involve your answering a few questions about the fields to be used and the style desired for the report. Once you answer these questions, Access creates the report, and you can save it or further modify it manually. The field names supplied during the table or query design phase are used as headings or labels for the fields in the report.

Custom reports, by comparison, are reports that you create or modify to better fit your specific needs. Custom reports that you design can contain any data you desire from the fields of the database. They can include numeric information, such as totals or other calculations based on numeric fields. Reports also can include headings that contain the specified title of the report, the date (as determined by the PC's clock), and the page number for each page. Such headings are commonly used with group-oriented reports. Figure 7-1 shows an example of a *group-oriented report*. Group-oriented reports contain the data arranged in groups of columns. Figure 7-2 shows an example of a report in a *single-column layout*. Single-column layouts often resemble paper-based forms.

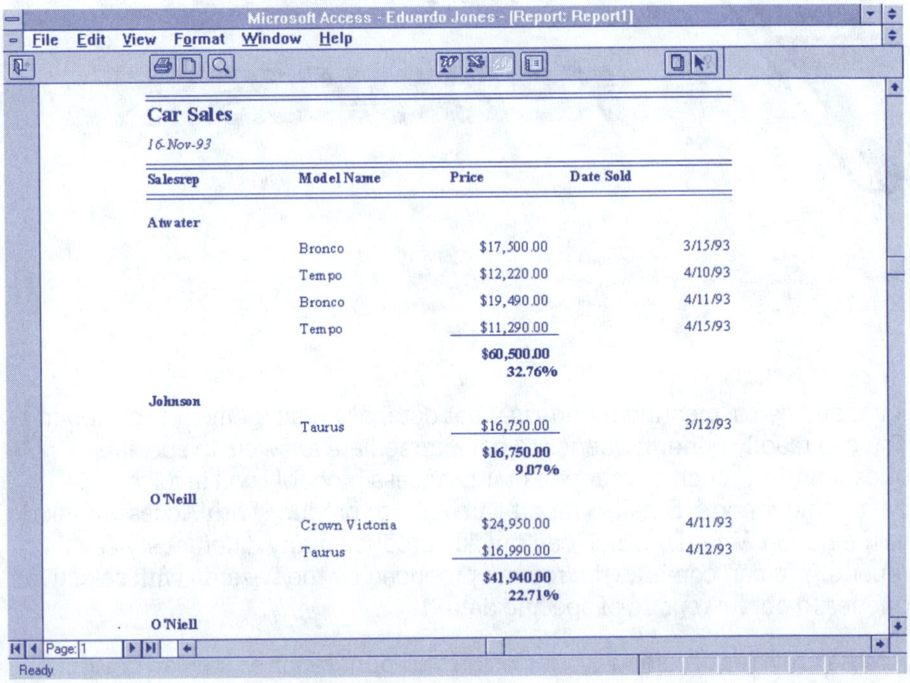

7-1
A group-oriented report.

As with forms, you also can save time when designing reports by combining the two methods. You can use the ReportWizards to create the report initially, then proceed to modify that design as you want, deleting fields, moving the location of fields, changing headings, or adding other text or graphics.

Creating reports with the Quick Report Button

By far, the fastest way to create a report is with the use of the Quick Report button on the Toolbar. (If you are using a version of Access prior to version 2.0, you will not have this feature.) The `Quick Report` button creates a single-column oriented style of report for whatever table or query is selected or active at the time you click the button. The table (or query) can be the open, active window, or you can click the desired table or query in the Database window to select it. With the desired table or query selected or active, just click the `Quick Report` button in the Toolbar. Access creates

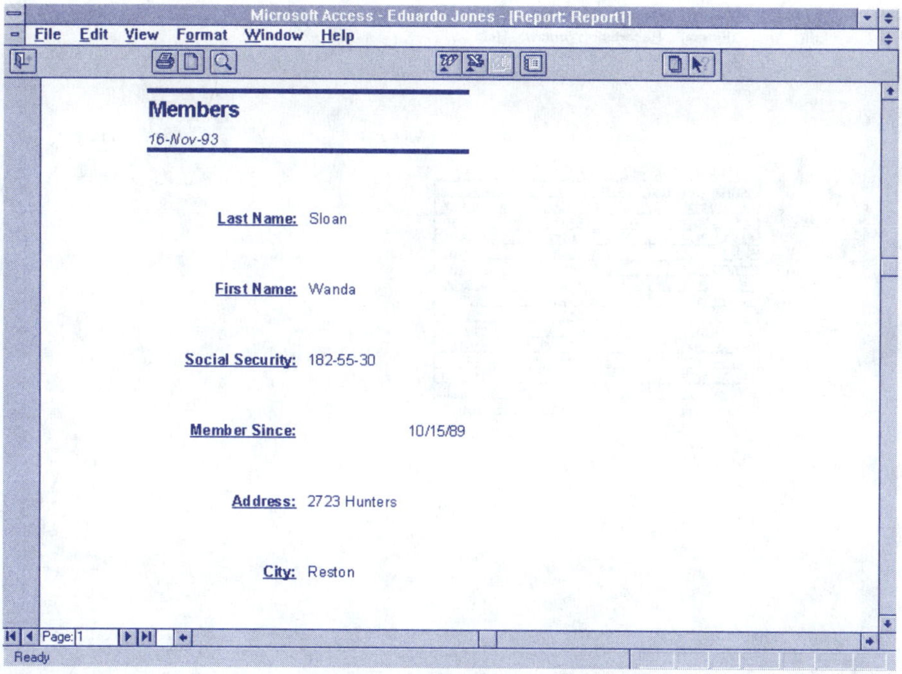

7-2 *A single-column-oriented report.*

and opens a report in Print Preview mode, without asking any questions about it's design. As an example, if you open the Earth Aware database provided on the sample disk, click the `Tables` button in the Database window and click `Members` to highlight it, then click the `Quick Report` button in the Toolbar, Access creates the report shown earlier, in FIG. 7-2.

Getting a fast report by printing a table

One of the fastest ways to obtain a report is to simply open a table or a query in Datasheet view, and choose `File/Print` from the menus. This method provides a quick-and-dirty listing of your data, although it does suffer from offering the least in the way of formatting options. Because queries in Access are so flexible, you first can create a query to filter your data in precisely the fashion that you need it, then choose `File/Print` to print the report. Change any options that you want to change in the Print dialog box that appears, then click `OK` to print the report. (For more about these options, see "About the Print dialog box" later in this chapter.) The report that is produced when you use this technique resembles the print preview shown in FIG. 7-3.

As you can see from the figure, what you get with this technique is a simple, columnar report, with the field names appearing as headers above each column. If you want a report in a format other than columnar or with totals or other design elements such as graphics, you will have to resort to designing the report manually or with the aid of the wizards.

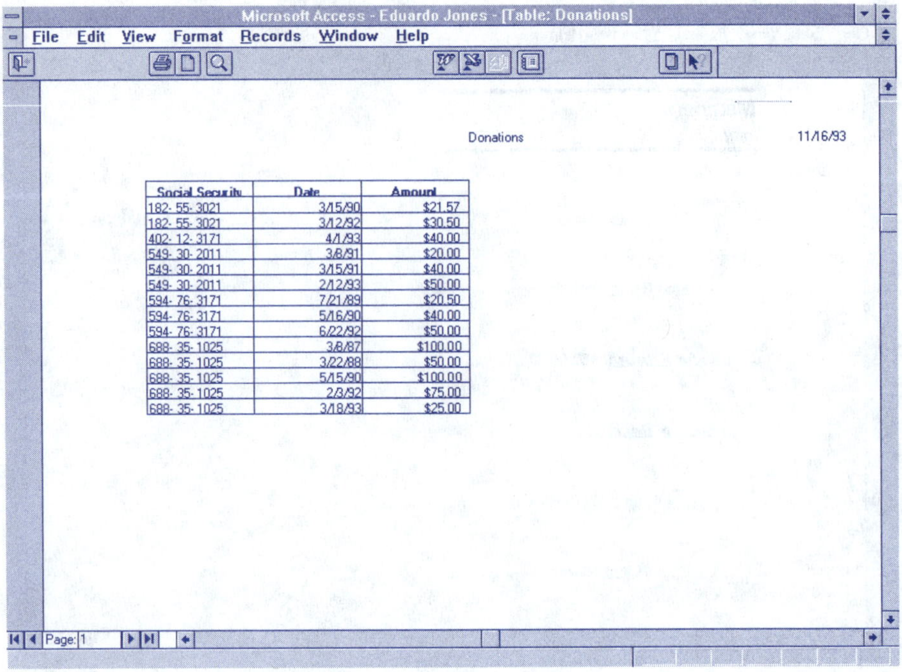

Social Security	Date	Amount
182- 55- 3021	3/15/90	$21.57
182- 55- 3021	3/12/92	$30.50
402- 12- 3171	4/1/93	$40.00
549- 30- 2011	3/8/91	$20.00
549- 30- 2011	3/15/91	$40.00
549- 30- 2011	2/12/93	$50.00
594- 76- 3171	7/21/89	$20.50
594- 76- 3171	5/16/90	$40.00
594- 76- 3171	6/22/92	$50.00
688- 35- 1025	3/8/87	$100.00
688- 35- 1025	3/22/88	$50.00
688- 35- 1025	5/15/90	$100.00
688- 35- 1025	2/3/92	$75.00
688- 35- 1025	3/18/93	$25.00

7-3
A Print Preview of report produced by printing a table's datasheet.

About the Print dialog box

Whenever you print any report, whether by using a report that you've saved earlier or by opening a table or query and choosing File/Print, Access first displays the Print dialog box shown in FIG. 7-4.

You can use the options in the Print Range portion of the dialog box to specify a range of pages to print or to print all pages of a report. To print all pages, click the All button if it is not already selected (this is the default). To specify a range of pages, click the Pages button. Then, enter a starting page number in the From text box and an ending number in the To text box. To print from the first page to a specific page, you can leave the From box empty and just enter a number in the To box. To print a single page, just enter the same page number in both boxes. If you have selected one or more records within the table or query, you can print just the selection by clicking the Selection option. (See chapter 4 for techniques on selecting records.)

TIP

The Print Range options can be useful for reprinting part of a large table after a paper jam. You can specify just those pages of the report that you need and avoid reprinting the entire report.

Use the Print Quality option to select your choice of print quality: high, medium, or low. (Your printer must support these options for this choice to take effect.) Use the Copies option to change the number of copies that you want printed; the default is one. If you are printing more than one copy of a report, leave the Collate Copies box checked if you want multiple copies

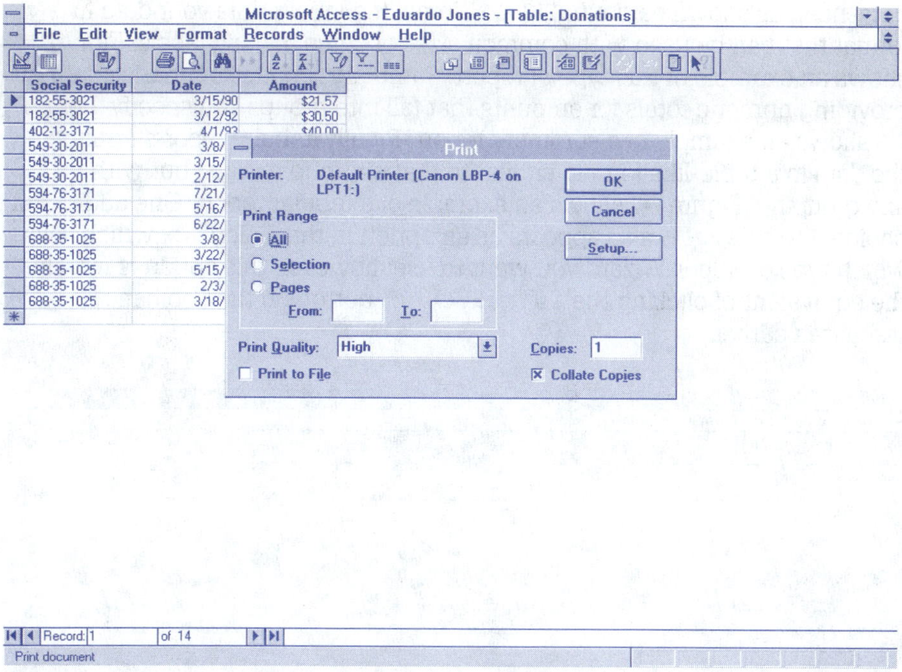

7-4
The Print dialog box.

to be collated into sets. The Print To File check box can be checked to print the report to a disk file.

After you have set all the options as you want them, click OK. A status message appears in a dialog box labeled "Printing" while Access sends the report to the Windows Print Manager. You can choose Cancel from this dialog box at any time to stop sending the report.

TIP

Once the Printing dialog box vanishes, it is too late to cancel a report within Access. However, you still might be able to cancel part or all of the report by switching to the Windows Print Manager by pressing Ctrl–Esc, choosing Print Manager from the Task List, selecting the print job by name, and choosing Delete.

Creating reports with the ReportWizards

You can quickly design a report with the use of the ReportWizards. This feature of Access helps you create a report by asking you questions about the report (such as what type of report you desire and which fields should appear on the report). Once you answer the questions, the ReportWizard automatically creates the report. You can use ReportWizards to create single-column reports, group reports, mailing labels, summary reports, or tabular reports. The report shown earlier (in FIG. 7-1) is an example of a single-column report. In such reports, one column displays all the fields in a single column at the left side of the report with each field appearing on a single line. A group report displays your data in a table-like format, similar to that of a datasheet, as shown earlier in FIG. 7-2. A mailing label prints your data in a format that can be used with common sizes of office mailing labels. Figure 7-5 shows an example of this type of report. Summary reports summarize data by providing numeric totals for amounts that fall into groups you specify. Figure 7-6 shows an example of a summary report. Finally, tabular reports arrange the data in a table-like format, similar to that of group reports, but without any grouping. Figure 7-7 shows an example of a tabular report. One additional choice, `AutoReport`, also appears as an option in the dialog box which asks which type of ReportWizard you want to use; however, this option is merely the equivalent of clicking the `Quick Report` button on the Toolbar, discussed earlier.

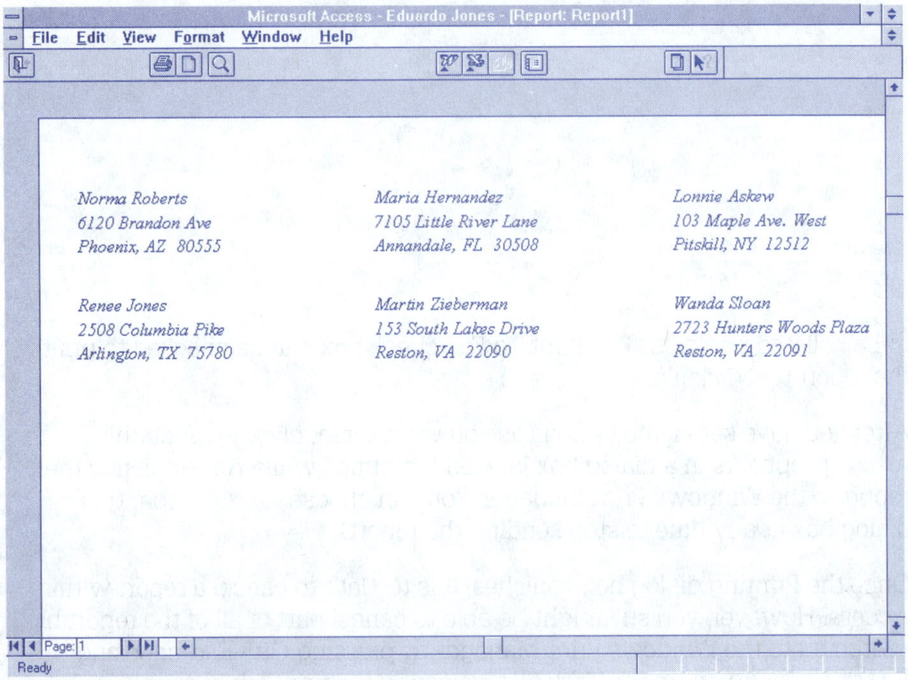

7-5 *An example of a report for producing mailing labels.*

To create a report with a ReportWizard, perform the following steps.

Step 1 In the Database window, click the `Report` button. Click `New`. The New Report dialog box appears (FIG. 7-8).

Step 2 Click the down arrow beside the Select A Table/Query text box to open the list box, and click the name of the table (or query) that is to serve at the basis for the report. (If the data that you want to use is in one table, choose that table by name. If the data is stored in more than one table, you'll need to use a query as the basis for the report. See chapter 5 for details on creating and saving queries.)

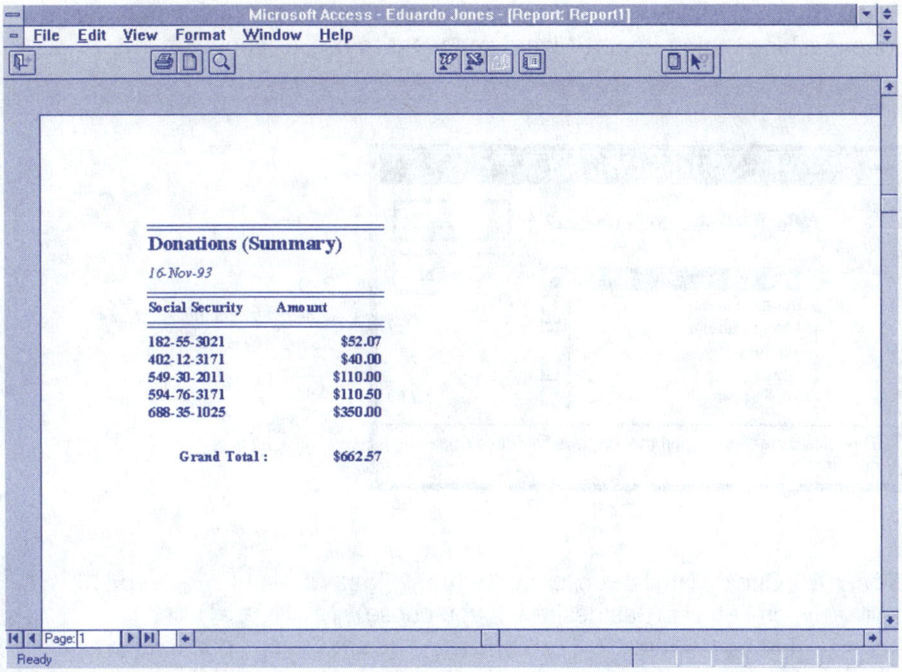

7-6
An example of a summary report.

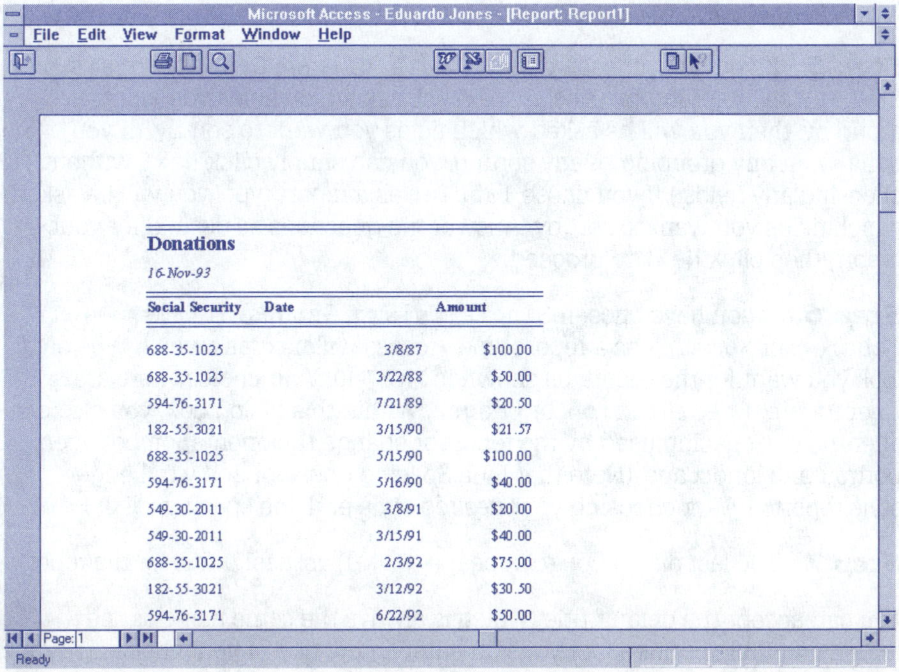

7-7
An example of a tabular report.

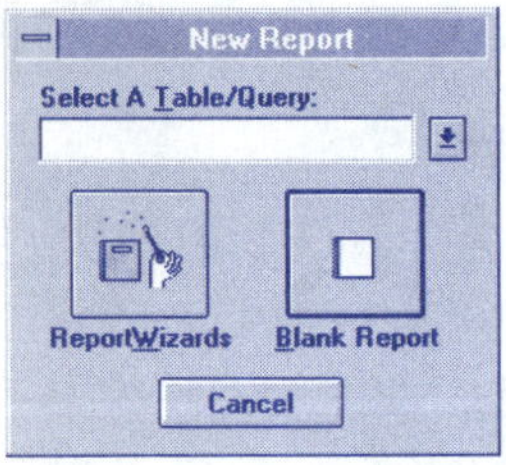

7-8 *The New Report dialog box.*

Step 3 Click the `ReportWizards` button. This causes a dialog box to appear asking which ReportWizard you want to use, as shown in FIG. 7-9.

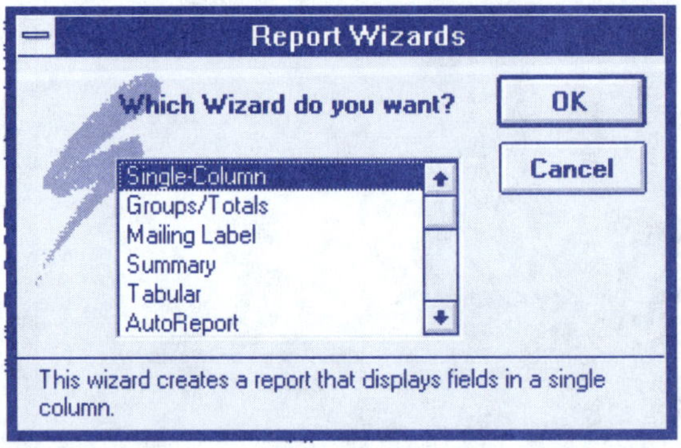

7-9 *The ReportWizard dialog box.*

Step 4 Click `Single-column`, `Groups/Totals`, `Mailing Label`, `Summary`, or `Tabular`, as desired. If you chose `Single-column`, `Groups/Totals`, `Summary`, or `Tabular`, the next dialog box to appear asks which fields you want included on the report. If you chose `Mailing Labels`, you next are asked how the fields should appear on the label (see "Creating mailing labels" later in this chapter for more details on this dialog box.) Answer the questions asked for your particular type of report, then click `Next` to proceed.

Step 5 If you have chosen either `Single-column`, `Groups/Totals`, or `Summary` as a report type, Access next will ask which fields you want to group by, then you will be asked which fields you want to sort by. (If you don't want any grouping or any sorting, you can simply click `Next` without choosing any fields.) If you chose `Tabular` as a report type, you will be asked which fields you want to sort by. Answer the questions as desired for your report, then click `Next` to proceed.

Step 6 If you have chosen `Single-column`, `Groups/Totals`, `Tabular`, or `Summary` as a report type, Access will next ask which type of look you want for the report, as shown in FIG. 7-10. Your choices here are `Executive`, `Presentation`, or `Ledger`. Within this dialog box, you also can alter the line spacing used by the report or change the orientation between portrait and landscape. (Note that Line Spacing does not apply to Ledger-style reports.) After choosing your desired style and line spacing, click `Next`.

Step 7 The last dialog box to appear (FIG. 7-11) asks for a title for the report.

You can accept the default title (which is always the same name as the underlying table or query), or you can enter a new title of your choosing. (This

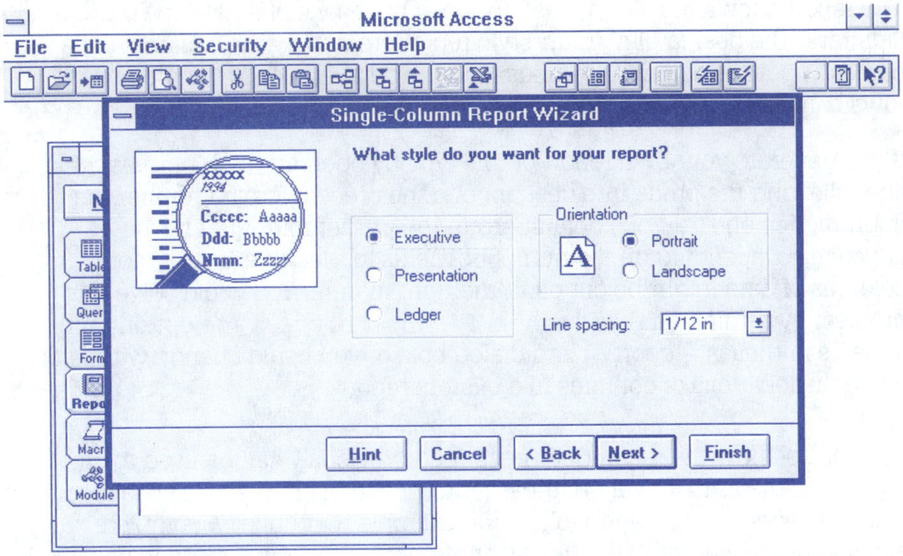

7-10
A dialog box for the desired report look.

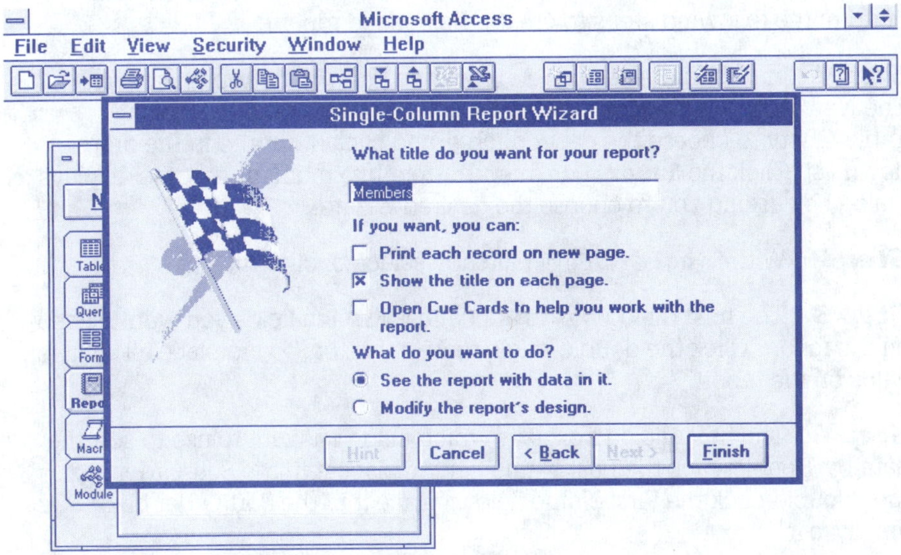

7-11
A dialog box for the report title.

title will appear at the top of the completed report.) Then, click "See the report with data in it" to open the report in Print Preview mode, or click "Modify the report's design" to open the report in Design mode (where you can make additional changes to the report manually, if desired).

The report shown in FIG. 7-1 was produced by means of a ReportWizard. It illustrates the design of a group-style report created by the wizards. Field names appear as column headings, and the data appears in single-spaced rows beneath the headings.

If you generate your own report of this type by opening the Members table and following the procedure described in the preceding paragraphs, you might notice one trait of a default group report that might not be very appealing. Depending on the number of fields in the table, one or more columns of data might be cut off at the right margin. You could solve this problem by turning on the `Fit All Fields on One Page` option that appears in the last ReportWizard dialog box, or you could change widths or move the locations of columns in a custom report.

Hands-on practice: creating reports

You can see how the techniques described previously can be used to create reports for the Earth Aware database introduced in chapter 4. These reports will be needed if you plan to follow the example that builds a complete application in chapter 9. For the second report in this example, you will need the Names and Donations query created in the hands-on example in chapter 5. If you have not yet created that query, do so before proceeding with this example. Open the EARTH.MDB database if it is not already open, and perform the following steps to create the needed reports.

Step 1 In the Database window, click the `Report` button, then click `New`. The New Report dialog box appears. Click the arrow under Select a Table/Query to choose the desired table, and click `Members` in the drop-down list. Click the `ReportWizards` button. In a moment, Access displays a dialog box asking you to choose the desired wizard.

Step 2 With `Single-column` already selected, click `OK`.

Step 3 The next dialog box to appear asks which fields you want placed on the report. Click the double-angle bracket button (`>>`) to place all available fields on the report.

Step 4 The next dialog box asks which field you want to use to sort the data by. Double-click the Last Name field to place it in the Sort Order box, then double-click the First Name field to place it in the Sort Order box. Finally, click `Next`.

Step 5 The next dialog box to appear asks what kind of look you want for the report. Click `Presentation`, then click `Next`.

Step 6 The next dialog box to appear asks for a title for the report; by default, the title `Members` appears in the text box. Click the `Design` button to accept the title and open the report in Design view. Click at the top of the page footer (where the mouse pointer changes to the shape of a double-headed arrow), and drag the footer down roughly one-half inch. Doing so will add a small amount of space between the records of the report, so that they do not run together on the page.

Step 7 Choose File/Save to save the new report. When prompted for a title, enter Members for a report name, then click OK. Press Ctrl–F4 to close the new report.

Next, continue with the following steps to produce the report for the member donations.

Step 1 In the Database window, click the Report button, then click New. The New Report dialog box appears. Click the arrow under Select a Table/Query to choose the desired table, and click Names and Donations in the drop-down list. (If you do not see a query by this name, you did not create the needed query earlier; see chapter 5 for details on how you can create the Names and Donations query.)

Step 2 Click the ReportWizards button. In a moment, Access displays a dialog box asking you to choose the desired wizard. Click Groups/Totals to select it, then click OK.

Step 3 The next dialog box to appear asks which fields you want placed on the report. Click the double-angle bracket button (>>) to place all available fields on the report, then click Next.

Step 4 The next dialog box asks which field you want to use to group the data by. Double-click the Last Name field to place it in the Group Order box, then click Next.

Step 5 The next dialog box asks how you want to group the data in each field. The default is acceptable in this case, so click Next to bypass this question.

Step 6 The next dialog box asks which field that you want to use to sort the data by. Because the grouping by last name also will sort on that field, you can click Next to bypass this question.

Step 7 The next dialog box to appear asks what kind of look you want for the report. Click Presentation, then click Next.

Step 8 The next dialog box to appear asks for a title for the report; by default, the title Names and Donations appears in the text box. Click the Design button to accept the title and open the report in Design view. Choose File/Save to save the new report. When prompted for a title, enter Donations for a report name, then click OK.

Step 9 Press Ctrl–F4 to close the new report. You can try printing data using either of the reports. First, click the desired report in the Database window to select it, then choose `File/Print` from the menus. Click `OK` in the dialog box that appears to begin printing.

Designing custom reports

When you prefer to place fields in various locations, add custom headers and footers, add graphics, and change formatting attributes, you can design custom reports. Depending on how complex your needs are, the precise steps involved in the report's design will vary in complexity. The description that follows illustrates the basic process in creating a custom report with a columnar format. To create a custom report, perform the following steps.

Step 1 In the Database window, click the `Report` button. Click `New`. The New Report dialog box appears.

Step 2 Click the down arrow beside the Select A Table/Query text box to open the list box, and click the name of the table (or query) that is to serve at the basis for the report. (If the data that you want to use is in one table, choose that table by name. If the data is stored in more than one table, you'll need to use a query as the basis for the report. See chapter 5 for details on creating and saving queries.)

Step 3 Click the `Blank Report` button. Access displays the report in Design view, as shown in FIG. 7-12. Place the desired objects (fields, text, and

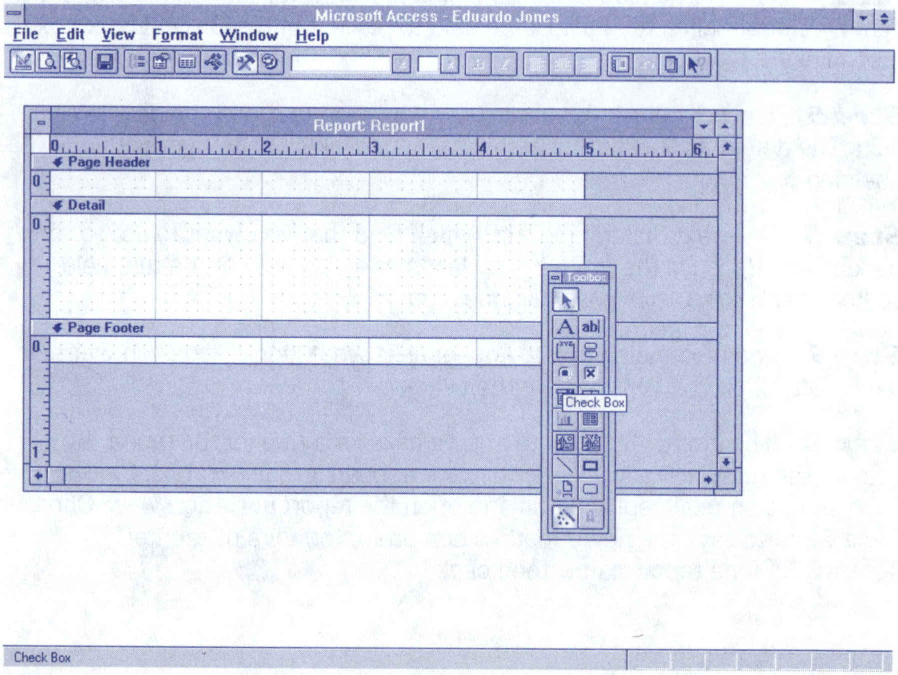

7-12 *A blank report in design view.*

any graphics) on the report, and add any necessary bands for sorting or grouping. Then, save the report by choosing `File/Save`. The placement of objects on a blank report is covered in more detail in the pages that follow.

Keep in mind that you often can save time by using a wizard to create a report that is close to what you desire. Then, open the report, click the Design View icon of the Toolbar to enter design view and make the desired changes to the report.

TIP

Design View window & report views

When you begin designing a report, you are placed in the Design View window, further detailed in FIG. 7-13. You can think of this window as a drawing area where you can lay out your desired report. When you are designing a report, the Toolbar takes on the appearance shown in the figure. Note that the Toolbar contains a `Print Preview` button near the far left; you can click this button to leave Design View and see what your printed report will look like.

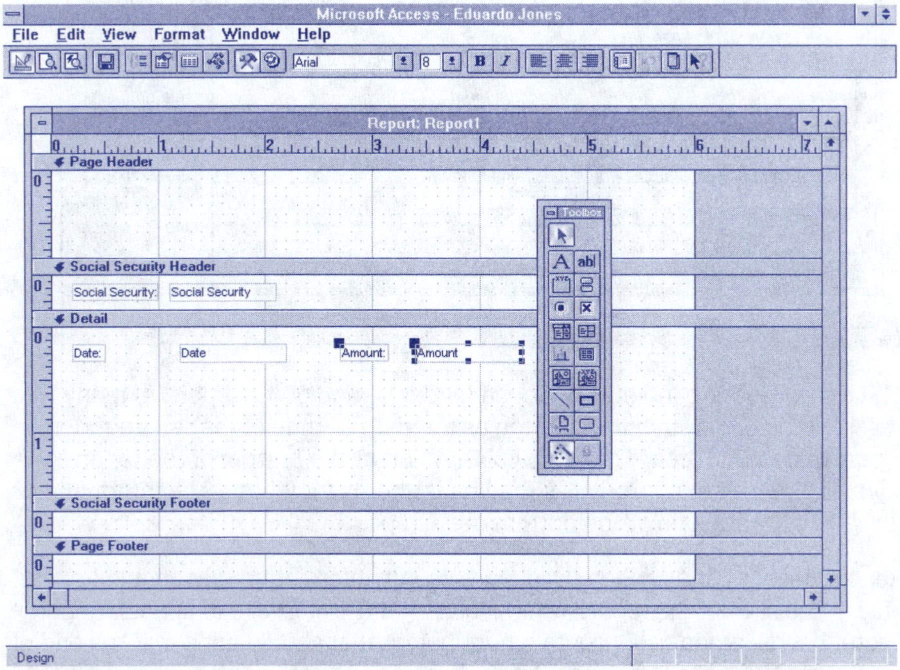

7-13 *The Design View window for reports.*

In addition to the `Print Preview` button, the Toolbar also contains buttons for adding, deleting, or changing levels of grouping, viewing properties of a selected object, displaying a list of fields you can drag to your report, and displaying the Palette that can be used to change the appearance of an object.

Before you begin designing reports, remember the use of `Edit/Undo` from the menus. If you make a change or an addition to a report and you don't like the change, in most cases you can choose `Edit/Undo` to reverse the action.

TIP

The report layout

The report's layout is made up of several parts, as illustrated in FIG. 7-14. Different portions of the report appear in horizontal areas known as *report bands*. Every report contains a Page Header band, a Page Footer band, and a Detail band. There also can be an optional Report Header band or Report Footer band, and there can be optional Group bands. In the figure, the band containing the name of a field, Social Security, is a Group band.

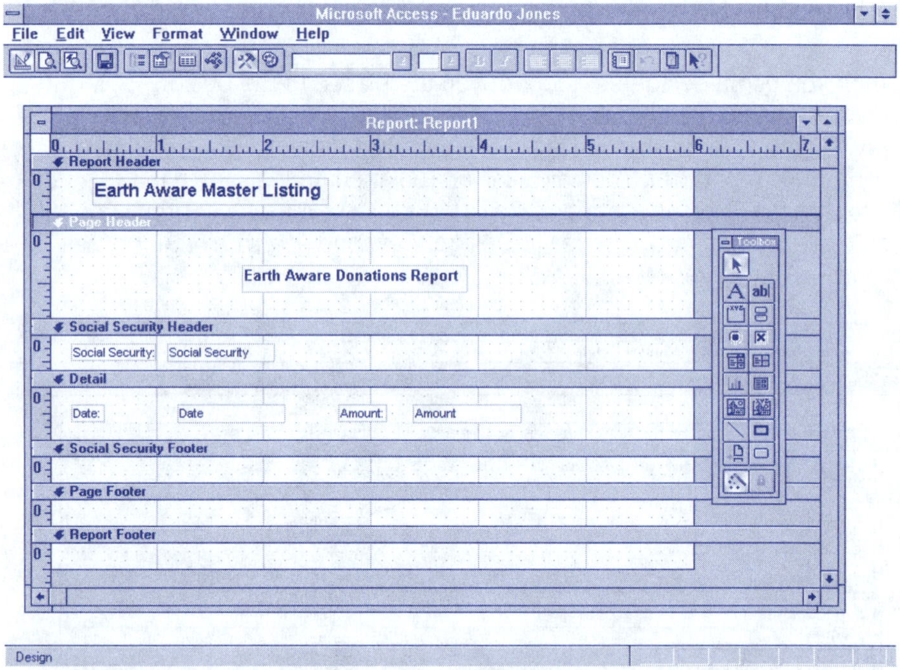

7-14 *Parts of a report layout.*

The Page Header band appears once for each page of the report. In many cases, you'll place such information as the date or time of the report and a report title in this area. The Page Footer band at the bottom of the report layout has the same purpose as the header but is for footers, the information that typically appears at the bottom of each page.

Report Header bands, when used, contain any information that should appear only at the start of the report (as opposed to at the start of each page). Report Footer bands, when used, contain information that should appear at the end of the report. You usually will use Report Footer bands for totals of numeric fields.

The Detail band is used to define the actual information (usually fields) that will appear in the body of the report. The values in the Detail band are represented by rectangular frames containing the name of the field or expression. While fields are most common, expressions also can be used; such expressions might contain a function representing the current date or a calculated value based on a numeric field.

Group bands, which are optional, are printed once for each group of records in a report. Group bands provide a means of grouping records in a report. Such grouping often includes some type of header identifying the group, along with subtotals of numeric data. You might or might not want to group records in a report. As an example of grouping, you might decide to print a list of members of the membership table by state. If you decide to include groups, Access lets you add an unlimited number of groups to a single report.

Using controls within reports

Once the report layout appears on the screen, you can use the Toolbar, the Toolbox, and various options of the menus to add, rearrange, or remove fields; to add lines, text, or graphics; to increase or decrease spacing between bands; and to change the layout or format of the report in general. As with forms, you place controls throughout your report as desired. Much of the information that follows is detailed more thoroughly in the previous chapter, "Working with Forms." It is provided in more summarized form in this chapter as a convenience (so you don't need to flip back to the prior chapter for information). However, if you have not yet become familiar with how you can manipulate controls in forms, you might want to consider the prior chapter.

Placing controls bound to fields You place *bound controls* or controls that are bound to a field in a table or query to display data in your reports. To add bound controls to a report, you drag them from the *field list* to the desired location on the form. To add a field to the report, first click the `Field` button in the Toolbar. (Doing so causes the field list to appear.) Then, click the desired field within the list, and drag it to the desired location on the report. Figure 7-15 shows a blank report after five fields (Last Name, First Name, Member Since, Date, and Amount) were dragged from the field list into the detail band of the report.

To select and place multiple adjacent fields at one time, click the first field in the group, hold the Shift key and click the last field in the group. Then, click and drag the fields (as a group) to the desired location on the report and release the mouse button to place the fields. To select all the fields in the list at once, double-click the title bar of the field list.

Selecting controls Before you can make changes to a control—such as resizing or moving it—you first must select the control. To select a control, click anywhere in the control. When you do so, the control becomes surrounded by handles, indicating that it has been selected, as shown in the case of the Last Name field in FIG. 7-16.

Note that, with many controls (such as the text box shown here), the handles include *move handles* and *sizing handles*. Most controls, including text boxes, also have two parts, as shown here: a *label* and the text box itself.

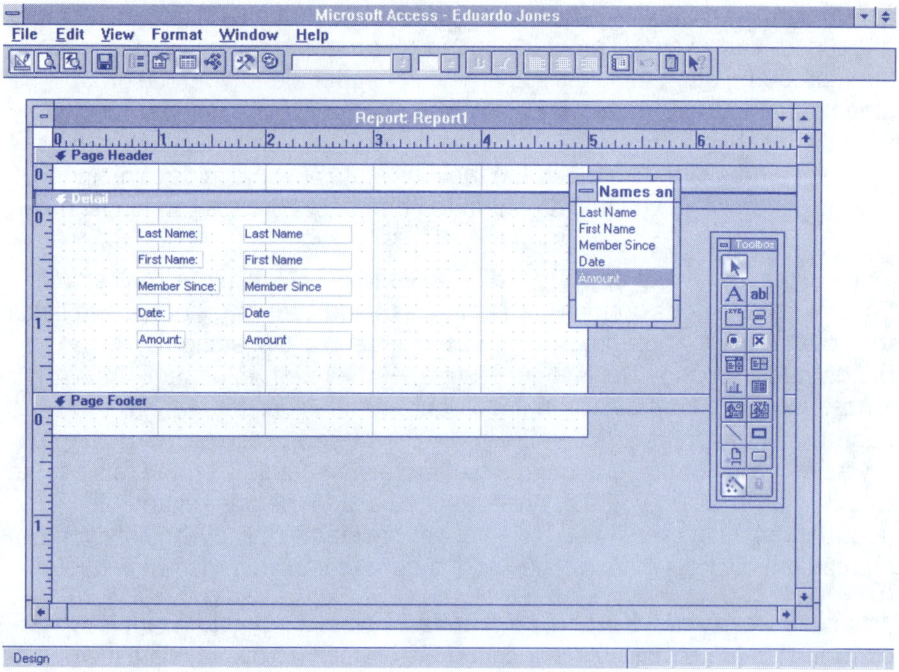

7-15

A blank report with the controls added from the field list.

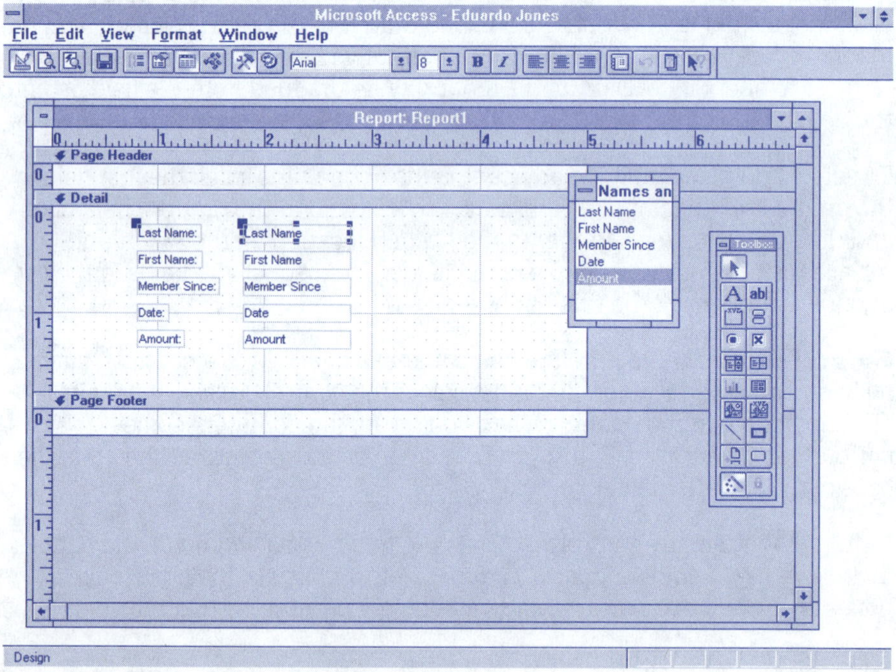

7-16

A control with selection handles.

Selecting adjacent controls To select a group of adjacent controls, first place the pointer at any point outside the top or bottom control in the group. Then, click and drag the pointer around or through the desired controls.

Selecting nonadjacent or overlapping controls To select nonadjacent controls (ones that are not next to each other) or controls that overlap, hold the Shift key, while clicking each control that you want to select.

Selecting all controls You can quickly select every control on a report by choosing `Edit/Select All` from the menus. (Note that you can deselect all selected controls by just clicking anywhere outside of a control.)

Moving and sizing controls To move a control, first select it, as detailed earlier. Then, move the pointer to the border of the control. When the pointer changes into the shape of a palm, click and drag the control to the desired location.

To move a control separately from any attached label, first select the control (or the label) by clicking it. Then, place the pointer on the move handle (it's in the upper-left corner of the control), and click and drag the control to the desired location.

To resize a control, first select the control. Then, move the pointer to any of the control's sizing handles and click and drag the control to the desired size.

Aligning controls You can maintain the alignment of controls as you move them with the use of the Shift key. Whenever you hold the Shift key while moving a control, the control moves either horizontally or vertically in whatever direction you started, but not in both directions. Hence, if you wanted to maintain vertical alignment of a control while moving it horizontally, you would select the control, hold the Shift key, and click and drag the control horizontally.

Copying controls At times, you might find it helpful to make duplicates of a control for use elsewhere in the report. To copy a control, first select the desired control. (If the control consists of a label attached to a text box, make sure you select the text box; otherwise, you will copy only the label.) With the control selected, choose `Edit/Duplicate` from the menus. Access will create a duplicate of the control, and you can use the movement methods described earlier to move the copy of the control to the desired location in the report.

Deleting controls To delete a control, first select the control, then press the Del key (or choose `Edit/Delete` from the menus). If you want to delete only the label, make sure that you have the label selected, and not the text box (click on the label to select it).

Changing labels If you want to change a label, first click the label to select it, then click the label again. When you click for the second time, the mouse pointer changes to the shape of an I-beam and an insertion pointer appears within the text of the label. You then can use the Backspace or Del keys as necessary to delete existing text and type the new text.

Creating controls with the Toolbox

To add *unbound controls* to a form, such as decorative graphics, descriptive text, lines and rectangles, or to add *calculated controls*, you use the Toolbox (FIG. 7-17). The Toolbox is explained in more detail in chapter 6; refer to that chapter for a complete explanation of each tool in the Toolbox.

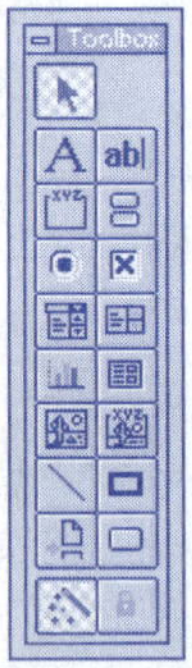

7-17 *The Toolbox.*

If you are working in Design View and the Toolbox is not visible, choose `View Toolbox` (or click the Toolbox button in the Toolbar) to display it. To create a tool using the Toolbox, you perform the following steps.

Step 1 Click the tool for the desired type of control.

Step 2 Point to the place on the form where you want the upper-left corner of the control to begin, and click and drag down to the lower right corner.

You can use the Text Box tool to create a text box that is bound to a field; however, because this is the default control of the Toolbox, it is not necessary for you to use it before dragging a field from the Fields List to the form.

Previewing the report

You can preview the report at any time during the design process. To do so, choose `File/Print Preview` or click the `Print Preview` button on the Toolbar. With either method, you see a window containing the report as it will look when printed, similar to the example shown in FIG. 7-18.

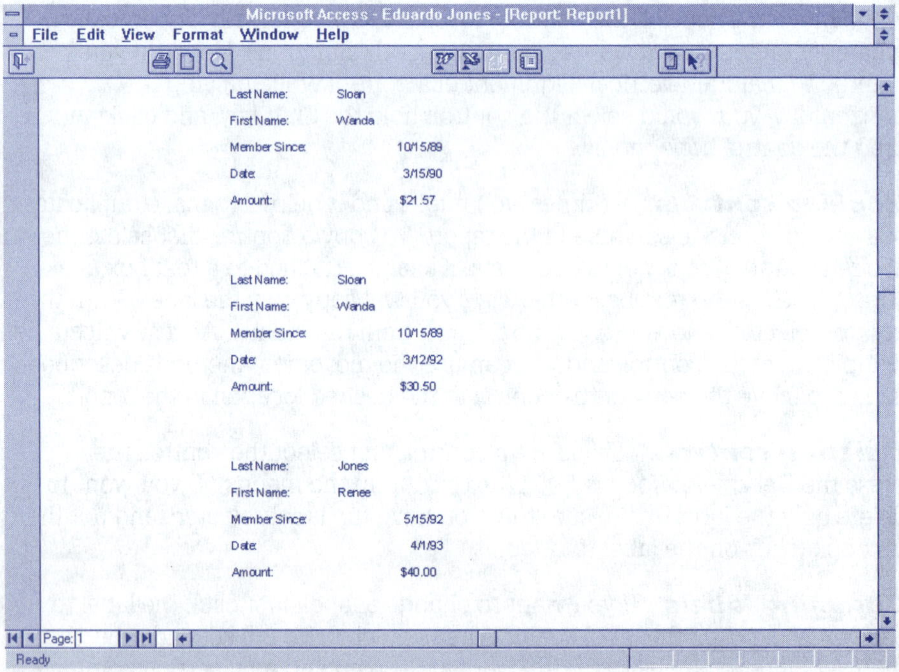

7-18 *An example of Print Preview.*

Use the scroll bars or the PgUp and PgDn keys to view additional portions of the report. You can click the arrows at the bottom of the window to view other pages in the report: click the left-pointing arrow to view the prior page and click the right-pointing arrow to view the next page. While in the Print Preview mode, three buttons appear at the left center of the Toolbar: `Print`, `Page Setup`, and `Zoom`. You can click the `Print` button to send the report to the printer. Clicking the `Page Setup` button causes the Print Setup dialog box to appear (FIG. 7-19). You can change any of the desired setup options for your printer, such as orientation, paper size, margins, and the type of printer used.

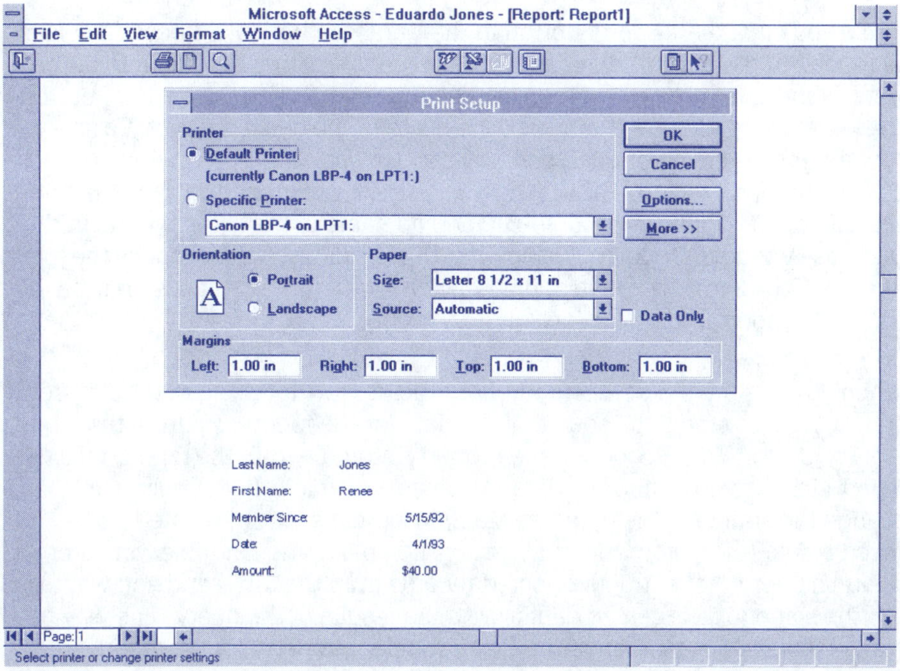

7-19
The Print Setup dialog box.

Click the `Zoom` button in the Toolbar to alternately zoom in or out in the preview. (Note that you also can zoom in or out by placing the pointer in any area of the report where it changes shape to a magnifying glass and clicking.) Finally, when you are done previewing the report, click the `Close` button (at the far left edge of the Toolbar) to return to the Design View.

Saving the report

Saving a report is much like saving any other object in Access. You can choose `File/Save` from the menus and supply a name (if asked) for the report, then you can close the form by pressing Ctrl–F4 or clicking on the window's close icon. You first can press Ctrl–F4 to close the window (or double-click the Close icon in the window), then answer `Yes` to the prompt when asked if you want to save changes. If you are saving a report for the first time, Access also will ask you to supply a name for the report. With either method, the report is saved to the current database.

Modifying a saved report

To modify a saved report, click the `Report` button in the Database window. Then, click `Design`. The report will open in a Design View window, and you can make the necessary changes.

Printing reports

To print a report, click the `Report` button in the Database window, then choose `File/Print`. Change any desired options in the Print dialog box that appears, then click `OK` to print the report. (You also can print a report from within the Print Preview mode of the report design process, by clicking the `Print` button in the Toolbar.)

Opening an existing report

When you click the `Report` button in the Database window, Access displays all reports in the current database. You can open existing reports in Design view, or in Print Preview. To open an existing report, click the `Report` button in the Database window, then click the name of the desired report. To see how a printed version of the report will appear, click the `Print Preview` button. To modify the report's design, click the `Design` button. Note that you also can open a report by double-clicking its name in the list of reports in the Database window. Double-clicking with the left mouse button opens the report in Print Preview, while double-clicking with the right mouse button opens the report in Design view.

Where's the data?

When you design and save a report (whether it is with the aid of the Wizards or not), Access stores the source of the data for the report as part of the report's design. The RecordSource property, stored within the report, tells the report where to go to find the data. At times, you might find it helpful to change the source of the data; for example, perhaps you've created and saved a detailed custom report that is based on a particular table, you later design a query that extracts selected records from the table, and you want to use the same report created earlier with the results of the query. One way to handle this need is to change the RecordSource property for the report. Changing the RecordSource property, in effect, changes the underlying table or query used for the report. To change a report's RecordSource property, you perform the following steps.

Step 1 While in Design view for the report, open the property window by choosing `View/Properties`, or clicking on the `Properties` button in the Toolbar.

Step 2 In the RecordSource property box, select or type the name of the table or query you want to use as the source of data for the report.

Those who are experienced with the SQL language should note that you also can type SQL statements directly into the RecordSource property box. The SQL statement will be used as a basis for record selection when the report runs.

Adding sorting

You can add levels of sorting to your reports. (Keep in mind that there are other ways to sort data. If you base reports on queries that include sorting, there is no need to sort the report as well.) To specify a sort order for a report, perform the following steps.

Step 1 While in the Design View for the report, choose `View/Sorting and Grouping` from the menus (or click the `Sorting and Grouping` button on the Toolbar). This causes the Sorting and Grouping dialog box to appear (FIG. 7-20).

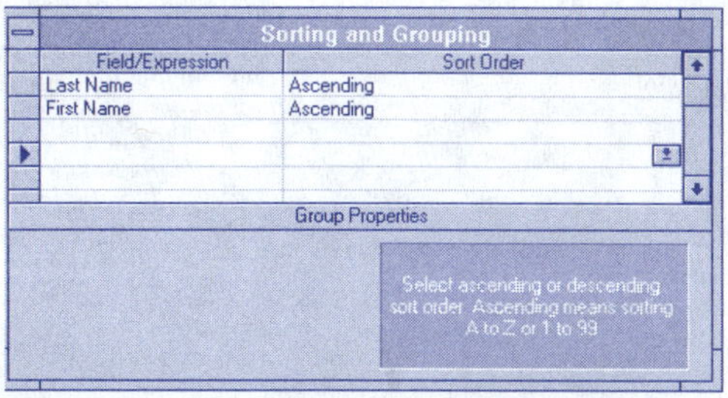

7-20
The Sorting and Grouping dialog box.

Step 2 Click the Field/Expression box, then click the down arrow to open the list box. Select the desired field to sort on from the list box. If desired, click in the Sort Order box, and choose `Descending` (ascending is the default sort order).

Step 3 Repeat step 2 for any additional fields that you want to sort by.

As an example, if you wanted to sort a report that produces mailing labels by State, then by City, then by Last Name, you would place the State field in the first row of the dialog box, the City field in the second row, and the Last Name field in the third row, as shown in FIG. 7-21. When you print the report, Access sorts the data in the order requested.

TIP

It's a wise idea to add sorting to the mailing labels that you create, because mailings often are grouped by postal codes to save on mailing costs.

Adding grouping

Access also lets you add groupings of records to a report. You probably will need to arrange your reports to be broken down by groups. For example, you might need to see all members divided into groups by state of residence. Using the Sorting and Grouping dialog box shown earlier, you can define multiple levels of grouping. While many more than two or three levels of groups might seem like overkill to some, it is nice to know that Access is accommodating when you must base a complex report on a large number of subgroups; up to 10 levels of grouping can be included in a report. Multiple groupings can be quite common in business applications. In something as simple as a national mailing list, for example, you might need to see records by groups of states, within each state group by city, and within each city

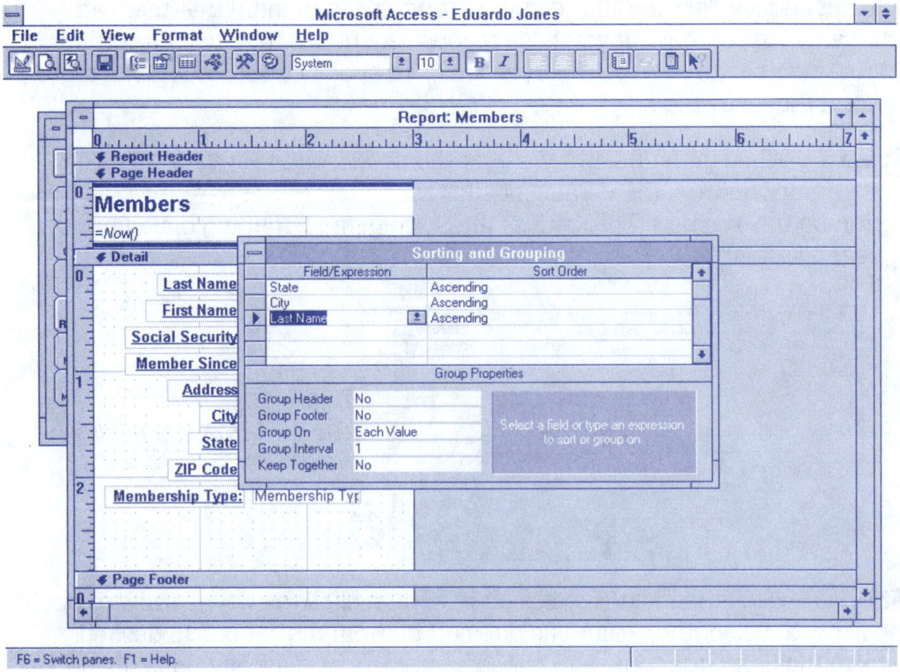

7-21
A dialog box with the levels of sorting added.

group by ZIP code. That represents three levels of grouping alone. Cut the data in the table more specifically—by other categories like income levels, for example—and you can quickly come to appreciate Access's ability to perform effective grouping.

Because any group of data implies sorting, you must tell Access to sort the data that the group will be based on. For example, if you print a report of customers in groups by state and, within each state, in groups by city, you must sort the report by state and where the state is the same, by city. You use the same technique as described previously in choosing the fields to use for the sort from the Sorting and Grouping dialog box. The only difference is that, with grouping, you also must turn on the group header and group footer options, as desired, in the Sorting and Grouping dialog box. To add grouping to a report, you would perform the following steps.

Step 1 While in the Design View for the report, choose `View/Sorting and Grouping` from the menus (or click the `Sorting and Grouping` button on the Toolbar). This causes the Sorting and Grouping dialog box to appear, as shown previously.

Step 2 Click the Field/Expression box, then click the down arrow to open the list box. Select the desired field to sort (and base the group on) from the list box.

Step 3 If desired, click in the Sort Order box, and choose `Descending` (ascending is the default sort order).

Step 4 To add a group header, click the Group Header text box, then click the arrow and choose `Yes` from the list.

Step 5 To add a group footer, click the Group Footer text box, then click the arrow and choose `Yes` from the list.

Step 6 If you want to add additional subgroups, repeat steps 2 and 3 for the additional fields that you want to base the groups on.

By way of example, if you wanted to add grouping for a report of customers by State, you would place the State field in the Field/Expression column of the dialog box. In the Group Properties portion of the dialog box, you would choose `Yes` for Group Header if you wanted a header and `Yes` for Group Footer if you desired a footer, as shown in FIG. 7-22.

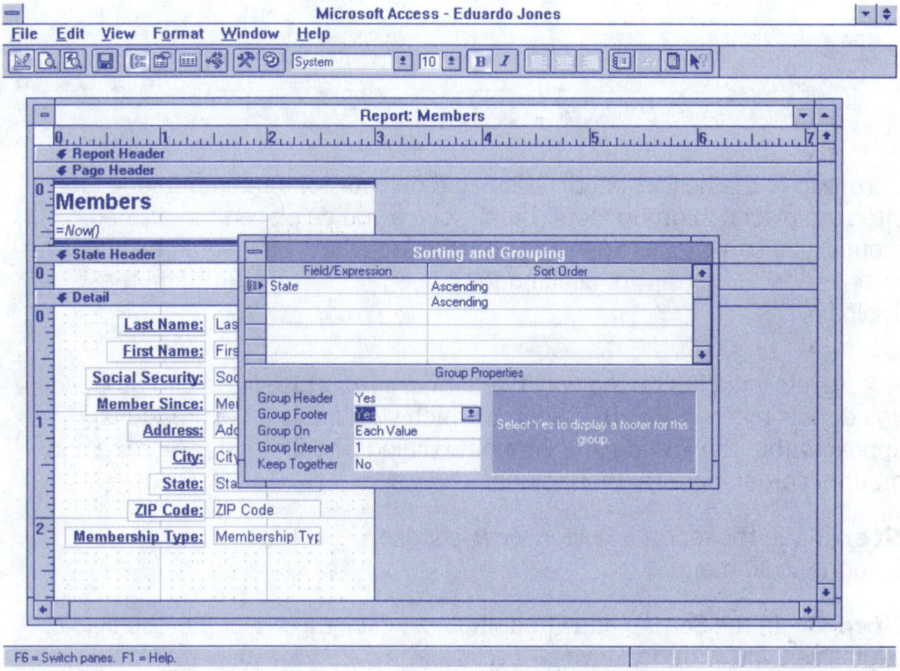

7-22
A dialog box with the level of grouping added.

After choosing these options and putting away the dialog box, the report's design will contain the new header and footer bands, as shown in FIG. 7-23.

You then can proceed to add any desired fields or other design elements to the new bands. In most cases, you will want to add the field that identifies

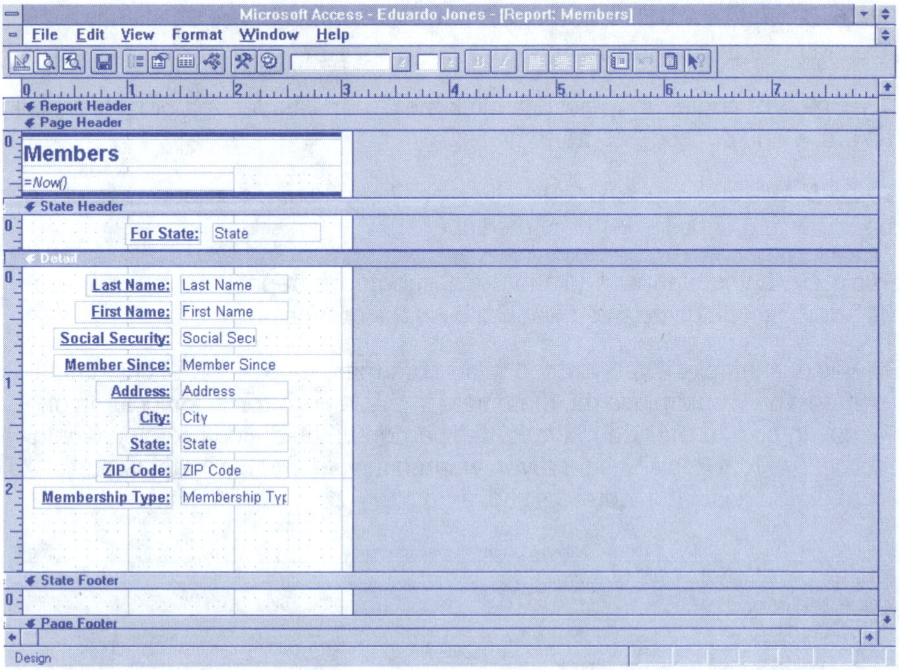

7-23
A report with the level of grouping added.

the group to the header band. Calculated objects containing numeric totals often are placed in group footer bands. Once you've placed the desired groups, you can check to see if the results are what you wanted by choosing `File/Print Preview` or clicking the `Print Preview` button in the Toolbar.

Changing sorting & grouping order

Access lets you change the way the data in a report is sorted and grouped. You do this by changing the order in which your fields (or expressions) appear within the Sorting and Grouping dialog box. To change sorting and grouping order, perform these steps.

Step 1 In the report's Design view, choose `Sorting and Grouping` from the View menu.

Step 2 In the Sorting and Grouping box, click the selector of the field or expression you want to move.

Step 3 Click the selector again, and drag the row to a new location in the list.

If headers and footers have been assigned to the groups that you rearrange, Access automatically moves the headers, footers, and controls within them to the new positions.

Adding headers & footers

The ReportWizards automatically add various types of headers and footers to a report, depending on the options that you choose while using the Wizards. If you design your own reports manually, you'll need the ability to add headers and footers on your own. Once in Design mode for any report, you can add or remove report, page, or group headers or footers. Note that when you remove a header and footer, you also remove all controls associated with that header and footer. To add or remove a report header and footer, choose `Report Header/Footer` from the Format menu. To add or remove a page header and footer, choose `Page Header/Footer` from the Format menu.

To add or remove a group header or footer, choose `Sorting and Grouping` from the View menu, or click the `Sorting and Grouping` button on the toolbar. In the Sorting and Grouping dialog box that appears, click the field name, or type the expression that you want to use to create the header or footer. Finally, to add the group header or footer, set the GroupHeader or GroupFooter property to `Yes`. Note that you can remove a group header or footer by setting these properties to `No`.

Adding the current date or time

You can easily add the current date or time, as measured by the PC's clock, to a report. You do this by creating a text box, then defining (within the text box) an expression that provides the date or the time. To add the current date or time to a form or report, perform these steps.

Step 1 Open the report in Design view, and add a text box to the section where you want the date or time to appear.

Step 2 With the text box selected, choose `View/Properties` to open the Property window for the text box.

Step 3 In the ControlSource property, type an equal sign followed by an expression using the Now function or the Date function. As an example, you would enter `=Date()` to display the current date, or you would enter `=Now()` to display the current time.

Step 4 As an option, you can use the Format property to display a date in a predefined format. For example, to show the date using a format like 5-May-92, you would change the Format property to `Medium Date`.

Adding page breaks

You can add page breaks to a report with the Page Break control of the Toolbox. To place a page break, first click the Page Break tool in the Toolbox to select it. Then, with the report open in Design view, click in the section where you want to place the page break. A small dotted line appears, indicating the presence of the page break in the report.

Note that where the new pages print in the report will be determined by where you place the page break. If you place a page break at the end of the detail section, a new page will print for each record. If you place the page break in a group header band, a new page will print each time data begins for a new group.

Adding page numbers to a form or report

You can include the current page number, or the total number of pages in a report by using the Page and Pages properties. Use the Page property to show the current page number, and use the Pages property to show the total number of pages in a report. To add page numbers to a report, perform these steps.

Step 1 In Design view, add a text box to the section (usually the page header or footer) where you want the page number to appear.

Step 2 Open the property sheet for the text box.

Step 3 In the ControlSource property box, type a page number expression. As an example, `=Page` in a text box would give the current page number. The expression `="Page " & Page` would give the page number preceded by the word "Page," as in "Page 1," "Page 2," and so on. The following expression:

```
="Page " & Page & " of " & Pages
```

would, on page 23 of a 26-page report, provide the text "Page 23 of 26."

Adding line controls

One type of control that is more common to reports than to forms is the *line control*. The line control lets you add straight lines to a report. The lines can be horizontal, vertical, or at any desired angle. To add a line control to a form, use these steps.

Step 1 Open the desired report in Design view. Click the Line Tool in the Toolbox.

Step 2 Place the mouse pointer where the line is to begin, and click and drag to where you want the line to end. *Note*: If you hold the Shift key while you drag, you will force the line to be perfectly horizontal or vertical.

As with other controls added to reports, where you place the line control determines where the lines appear. If a line control is added to a group header, the line will appear within the report's group header. A line placed in a group footer will appear once at the end of each group.

Combining text values from multiple fields

At times, you will need to combine text values from multiple fields into a single expression within a report. A common example is that of a person's name. Rather than displaying the contents of a last name field, followed by the contents of a first name field, you might prefer to have a single field in a report that shows the first name, followed by a space, then the last name.

This type of task can be accomplished by combining values from multiple fields, through the use of expressions. To combine text values using an expression, perform these steps.

Step 1 Open the report in Design view, and add a text box to the section where you want the expression to appear.

Step 2 With the text box selected, choose `View/Properties` to open the Property window for the text box.

Step 3 In the ControlSource property, type an equal sign followed by an expression that combines the fields. As an example, assuming you had fields in the table named "Last Name" and "First Name," you could enter an expression like `=[First Name] & " " & [Last Name]` to provide the desired results.

Adding calculations

As with forms, you can add text boxes to reports that display data based on a calculation. You can include any of the Access functions in expressions that you place in calculations. You can find a complete list of Access functions in your Access Language Reference manual or in the Access help screens; however, for your reference, some of the functions commonly used in reports are:

Function	Use
Date()	Provides current date
Time()	Provides current time
Now()	Provides current date and time
Avg(*value*)	Provides average of a value
Min(*value*)	Provides minimum value in the set of records
Max(*value*)	Provides maximum value in the set of records
Sum(*value*)	Provides a sum (total) of the values

As an example, you might want to display a calculation that represents the amount in a Quantity field, multiplied by the amount in a Price field. To create a text box that displays a calculation, you would perform the following steps.

Step 1 Click the Text Box tool in the Toolbar to select it. Click in the report at the upper-left corner where you want the text box to begin, and drag to the lower-right corner.

Step 2 Click in the text box, and type the desired expression, starting with an equal symbol. For example, if you want the text box to display the contents of a field named "Quantity" multiplied by a field named" "Price," you would enter `=[Quantity] * [Price]` in the text box.

As another example, you could use the Access SUM() function to display the total of a numeric or currency field in a report. This function is commonly used in the Group Footer or Report Footer bands of a report. When placed in a

Group Footer, it provides a sum for all the records in a group. When placed in the Report Footer, it provides a sum for all the records in the report. If, for example, you wanted to display the sum of a field called "Sales," you could place a text box in the Group Footer or the Report Footer band, and you would enter `=Sum([Sales])` in the text box.

Calculating totals in reports

You can include calculations to provide a total for a single record, a group of records, or for all the records in a report. To calculate a total, you include a text box with an expression that provides the values that you want to use in computing the total. How Access calculates the total depends on where the control is placed within the report. To calculate a total for one record, perform these steps.

Step 1 In the report's Design view, add a text box to the detail section.

Step 2 Display the property sheet for the control.

Step 3 In the ControlSource property box, type an appropriate expression.

As an example, the following expression:

```
=[Quantity]*[Unit Price]
```

would calculate the sale amount for each product in a report based on a product sales table.

Calculating running sums

A very common use for calculated fields in reports is to calculate running sums, or sums that keep a running total of numeric amounts.

You can calculate a running total in a report by using a text box containing an expression that forms the basis for the calculation. As an example, in the report footer section of a report, you might include an expression such as `=Count([Order ID])` or `=Sum([Salary])`. In the first case, a running count is kept of the number of orders; in the second case, a running sum total is kept of the Salary field. The running total can be for the records in each group or for all the records in a report, depending on where you place the text box (in the group header or footer, or in the report header or footer). To calculate running sums, perform these steps.

Step 1 In the report's Design view, add a bound text box or a calculated text box. Place the text box in the detail section to calculate a record-by-record total, or place the text box in a group header or group footer to calculate a group-by-group total.

Step 2 Open the property sheet for the text box, and set the text box's RunningSum property according to the type of running total you want. Choose `Over Group` to create a running total that resets to 0 at the beginning of each higher group level, or choose `Over All` to create a running total that accumulates until the end of the report.

Adding a graphic

You can use the cut-and-paste techniques inherent in Windows to add graphics to your reports. Figure 7-24 shows an example of a report containing a graphic. Such graphics can be created within drawing programs like Windows Paintbrush or Corel DRAW!

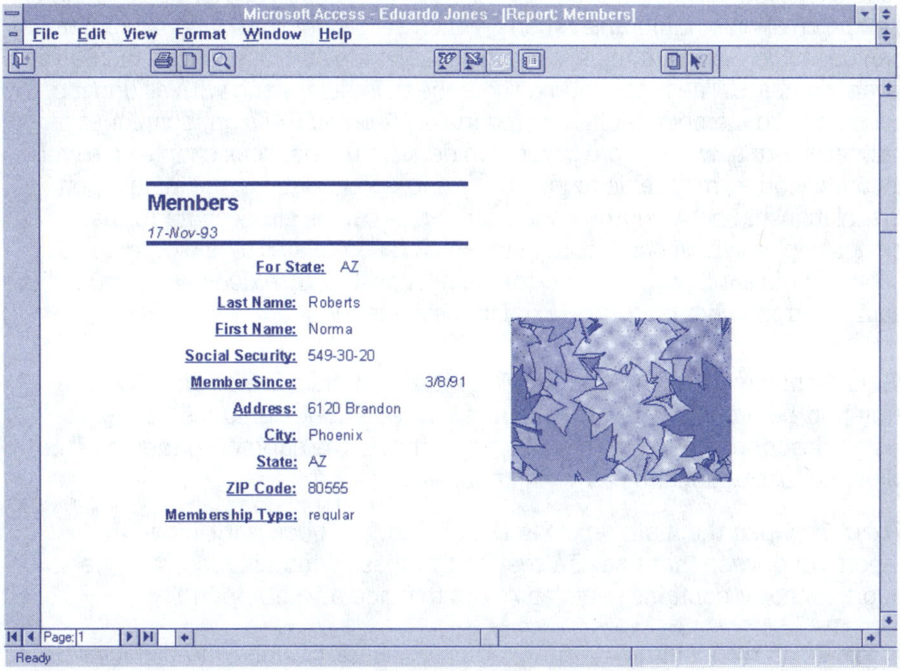

7-24
A report containing a graphic.

To add a graphic to a report, you can use the following steps.

Step 1 Open the desired report in Access, and get into Design View.

Step 2 Start your graphics program under Windows (you can press Ctrl–Esc to switch from Access to the Windows Program Manager), and design or load the graphics image that you want to use.

Step 3 Using Windows selection techniques applicable to your package, select the portion of the graphic you want to place in the form in Access. Choose `Edit/Copy` from the application's menus.

Step 4 Press Ctrl–Esc to bring up the Windows Task Switcher, and choose Microsoft Access from the list.

Step 5 From the menus in Access, choose `Edit/Paste`. When you do so, the graphic appears in the report.

Step 6 Using the move and sizing techniques detailed earlier, place the graphic in the desired location on the report.

TIP

Once a graphic has been placed, you can modify it in the original application by double-clicking the graphic, assuming the original application you used to create the graphic supports Windows OLE (object linking and embedding).

Creating multitable reports with subreports

Access lets you design reports within reports. A common use for this technique is in the creation of multitable reports, which are reports with records from more than one table. As an example, a report could be created for use with the Earth Aware database. The report would show the members, along with all donations made for each member. Multitable reports use the same design techniques as multitable forms, which were covered in detail in the previous chapter. As with multitable forms, multitable reports use a subreport bound to the main report. The relationship between the underlying tables can be either a one-to-many relationship, in which one record in the main report relates to one or more records in the subreport, or a one-to-one relationship, in which one record in the main report matches only one record in the subreport.

When manually creating a multitable report, you must create and save the subreport before designing the main report. Use the techniques for report design described earlier in this chapter to create the subreport, then use the following instructions to create the multitable report.

Step 1 Open the main report in Design view. (If necessary, move the Report window so that you can see the Database window. Also, size the report so that it contains sufficient room to place the subreport.)

Step 2 In the Database window, click the `Report` button to display the list of reports.

Step 3 In the list box, find the report that you want to use as a subreport, and click and drag it from the Database window to the main report. When you release the mouse button, a subreport control appears within the main report, as shown in FIG. 7-25. Move the subreport as desired to its location in the main report.

Step 4 With the subreport selected, choose `View/Properties` from the menus (or click the `Properties` button in the Toolbar) to open the Properties window for the subreport.

Step 5 Click the LinkMasterFields property. If it contains an entry already, verify that Access has created the relational link on the fields that you had in mind. If Access has not established a link, you must type the name of the field in the main report that will be used as a link to the records shown in the subreport.

Step 6 Close the report and save it when prompted, using the methods described earlier in the chapter. When you open the report in print preview, the records for the table that you've used for the main report appear, and the associated records from the related table appear within the subreport. Figure 7-26 shows a print preview of a report designed using these steps.

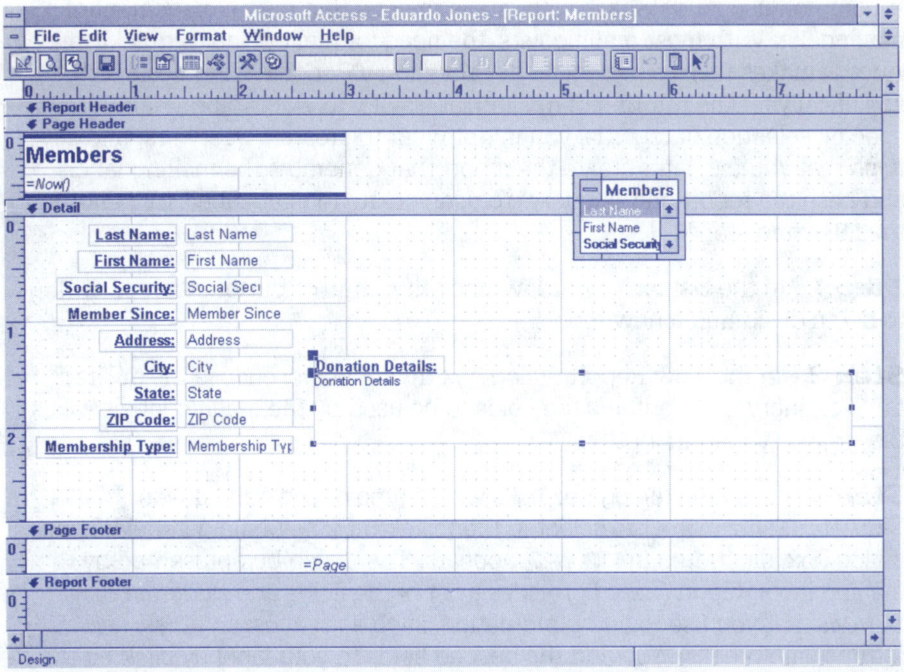

7-25
A subreport control in a main report.

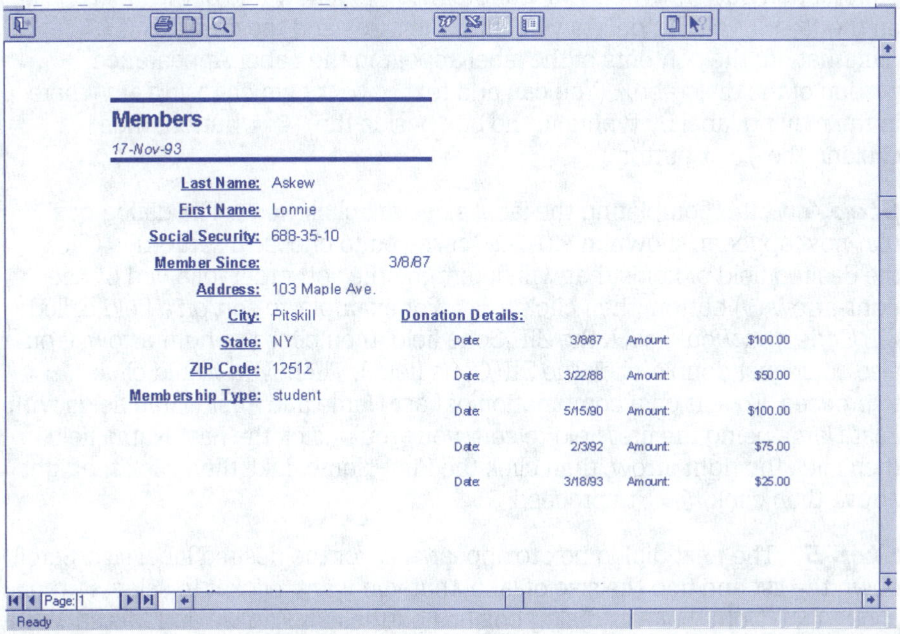

7-26
An example of a report containing a subreport.

Creating mailing labels

A common use for database software is the creation and management of a mailing list. With most mailing lists, the need for mailing labels quickly arises. Access makes this a simple task by providing a ReportWizard designed specifically for the printing of mailing labels. If you want to print labels for a specific selection of records, you might want to create a query first and save it, so that you can later create the report that generates the mailing labels and base the report on the query. You can create mailing labels by performing the following steps.

Step 1 In the Database window, click the `Report` button, then click `New` to begin designing a new report.

Step 2 In the New Report dialog box that appears, choose the desired table or query that contains the fields to be used by the mailing labels. Click the `ReportWizards` button.

Step 3 The next dialog box asks which type of wizard you want to use. Click `Mailing Label` to select it, then click `OK`. The Mailing Label Wizard dialog box, illustrated in FIG. 7-27, appears. The dialog box presented by the mailing label ReportWizard provides a list of the fields and *punctuation buttons* that you use to add punctuation, such as spaces, commas, and returns (line breaks). You add the desired fields to your label by clicking the field name in the list of fields to select it, followed by the right arrow (`>`) button. To add punctuation such as a space or a comma, click on the desired punctuation button. When you want to move to a new line of the label, click on the `New Line` button. As you enter the fields and the desired punctuation, the contents of the label appear in the Label Appearance portion of the dialog box. (You can add text of your own choosing anywhere in the mailing label by typing in the box beside the `Text` button, then clicking the `Text` button.)

Step 4 After completing the label's design, click `Next`. The dialog box that now appears, shown in FIG. 7-28, asks you to choose a sort order. Click the desired field or fields that will determine the sort order followed by the right-arrow (`>`) button, then click `Next`. For example, to sort on a field called ZIP Code, you would click the ZIP Code field, then click the right arrow. (You also could just double-click the ZIP Code field.). Then, you would click `Next` to proceed. To sort on a combination of Last Name and First Name fields with Last Name being the first field to sort, you would click the Last Name field, then click the right arrow, then click the First Name field, then click the right arrow, then click `Next` to proceed.

Step 5 The next dialog box to appear asks for the desired label size. Scroll down the list and find the size of label that you want, click it to select it, then click `Next`. Note that this dialog box has buttons for English and Metric. With

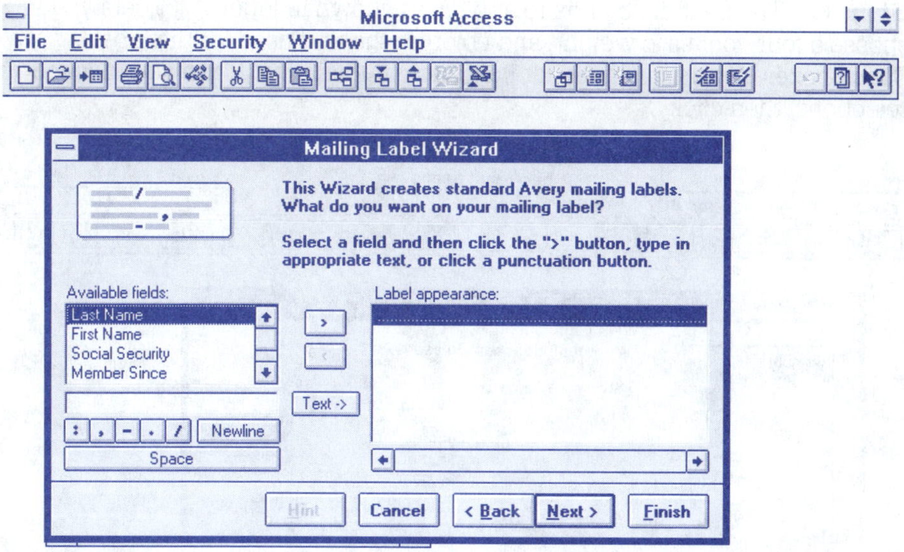

7-27
The Mailing Label Wizard dialog box.

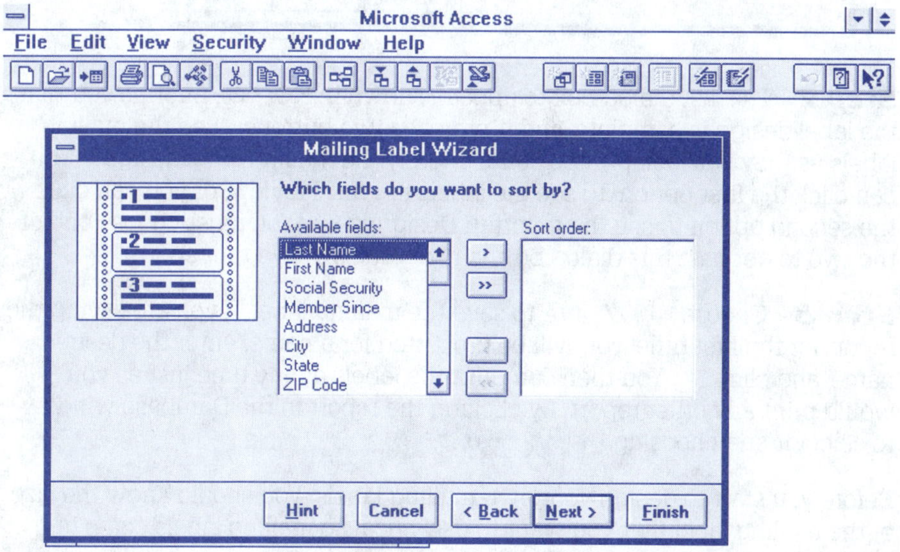

7-28
The Mailing Label Wizard sort dialog box.

the default of English selected, you see various labels that are measured in inches. If you click `Metric`, you will see common metric label sizes. Under Label Type, choose `Sheet Feed` or `Continuous`, as desired.

Step 6 The next dialog box to appear, as shown in Figure 7-29, lets you choose a font, font size, weight, and color for the text used for the labels. Check boxes also are included for italics and underlining. Make your desired selections, then click `Next`.

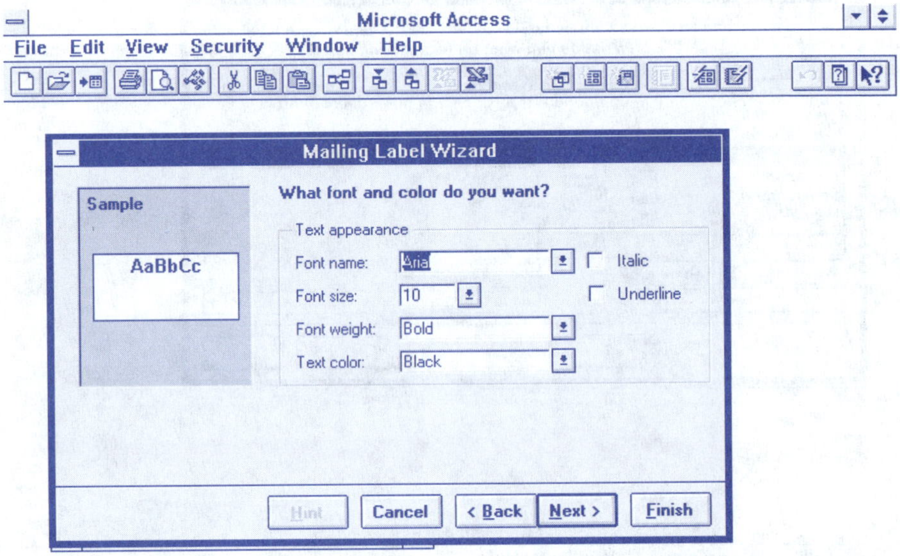

7-29
The Mailing Label Wizard font dialog box.

Step 7 The last dialog box to appear, shown in FIG. 7-30, informs you that the label design is complete, and it provides two buttons: "See the mailing labels as they will look printed" and "Modify the mailing label design." You can click the first option to see the labels in Print Preview, or you can click the second option to see the report in Design view. (You must choose one of the two to get past this dialog box so that you can save the report.)

Step 8 Choose `File/Save` to save the mailing label. If you are saving the report for the first time, you will be prompted for a name; enter the desired name, and click `OK`. You then can print the labels at any time just as you would print any other report, by clicking the report in the Database window to select it and choosing `File/Print`.

Before you start to design your own mailing labels, you should know the size of the mailing label that you want to use, because mailing labels come in such a wide variety of sizes. The ReportWizards in Access make this easier by including the common Avery mailing label numbers in the choices. If you are not using Avery mailing labels and are unsure of the label dimensions, check the side of the box of labels to see if there is an equivalent Avery number. You also should be sure to use the correct type of labels designed for your printer. Labels designed for laser printers usually don't feed well into

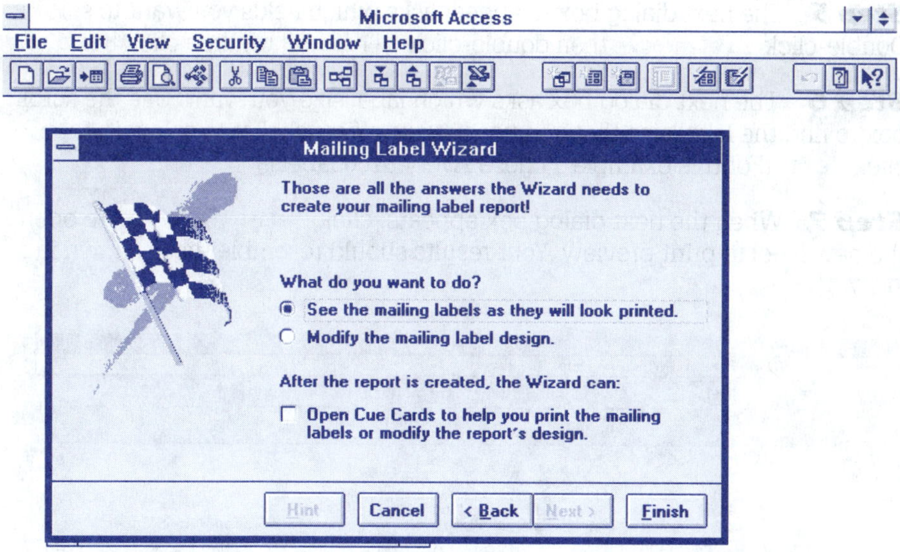

7-30
The Completed Label dialog box.

dot-matrix printers, and labels designed for dot-matrix printers might damage laser printers.

Hands-on practice: creating mailing labels

If you want to see how you can use the techniques described earlier to create a report that produces mailing labels, you can use a report along with the Members table created in chapter 4. Open the EARTH.MDB database if it is not already open, and perform the following steps.

Step 1 In the Database window, click `Report`, then click `New`. The New Report dialog box appears. Click the arrow in the Select A Table/Query list box, and choose `Members` from the list. Then, click the `ReportWizards` button.

Step 2 The next dialog box to appear asks which wizard you want to use. Click `Mailing Label`, then click `OK`.

Step 3 The next dialog box to appear asks what you want to put on the mailing label. Double-click `First Name`, then click `Space`, then double-click `Last Name`. Click the `New Line` button in the dialog box (this causes the label to begin a new line).

Step 4 Double-click the Address field, then click the `New Line` in the dialog box. Double-click `City`, then click `Comma`, then click `Space`, then double-click `State`, then click `Space`, then double-click `ZIP Code`, then click `Next`.

Step 5 The next dialog box to appear asks which fields you want to sort by. Double-click `Last Name`, then double-click `First Name`, then click `Next`.

Step 6 The next dialog box asks which label size you want. Use the scroll box to find the label size that you use in your office, click it to select it, then click `Next`. (For this example, I chose Avery 5160 labels.)

Step 7 When the next dialog box appears, click `Print Preview` to open the new label in print preview. Your results should resemble those shown in FIG. 7-31.

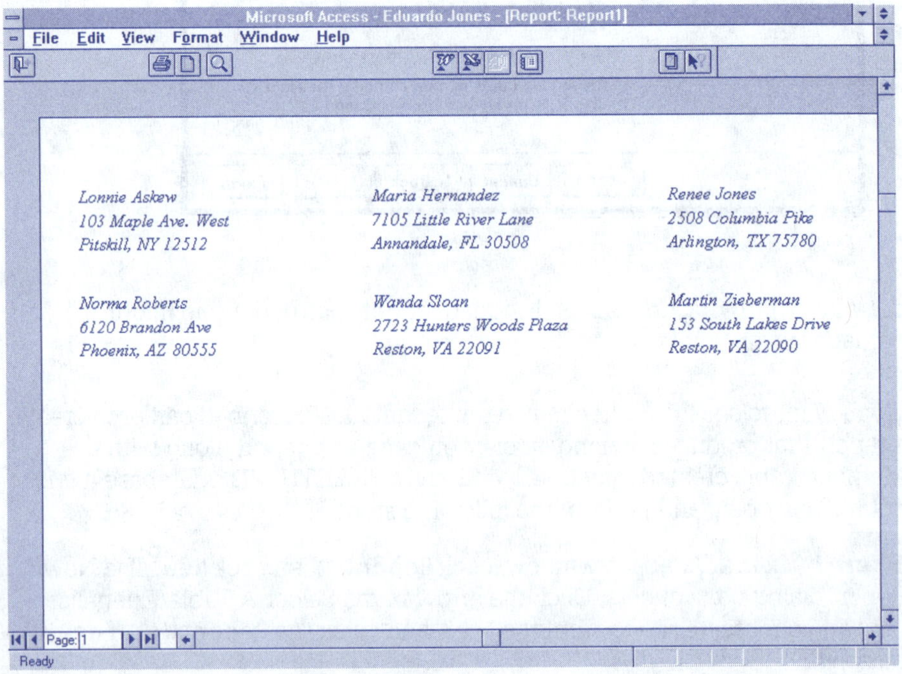

7-31
A Print Preview of mailing labels.

Step 8 From the menus, choose `File/Save`. When prompted for a name, enter `Mailing Labels`, then click `OK`. Press Ctrl–F4 to close the report.

Using pictures & desktop publishing

With the capabilities present in Access, it is a simple matter to add a "desktop-published" presentation quality to your reports. You can add graphics or pictures to reports and can make use of the various fonts, the Palette, and the Toolbox tools to add graphics, lines, rectangles, labels, and other design elements to the reports that you create. Lines and rectangles can help greatly in separating data into visually definable groups. In FIG. 7-32, the report shown uses a thin double line to separate a member's name from the member's donations and a thicker single line to separate one member from another. Also, a decorative rectangle has been placed around the member names.

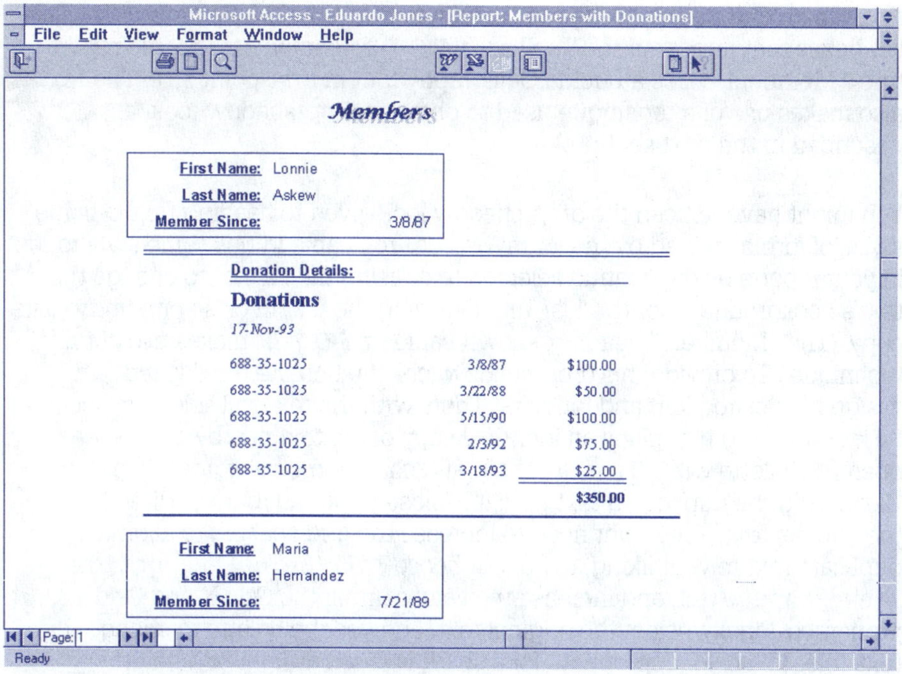

7-32
A report with lines added.

Drawing lines & rectangles

To draw a line while in the report in Design view, click the Line tool in the Toolbar, click where you want the line to begin, then drag to where you want the line to end. If you want to draw a line that is perfectly horizontal or perfectly vertical, hold the Shift key, then click and drag. If you want to draw the line at an angle, don't hold down the Shift key. To draw a rectangle, click the Rectangle tool in the Toolbox, then click where you want to place the upper-left corner of the rectangle and drag down to the lower-right corner.

Once you have placed lines or rectangles, you can vary the thickness used to draw them by selecting the desired line or rectangle, choosing `View/Properties` to open the Properties window and changing the Border Width property. To change the color of the line or rectangle, click the line or rectangle to select it, then choose `View/Palette` to open the Palette and choose the desired color.

Note that, by default, rectangles cover any other objects they are placed over. If you want to put a rectangle as a decorative item around a group of fields, add the rectangle in the desired location. Then, with the rectangle still selected, choose `Layout/Send To Back` from the menus. (Doing this will move the rectangle underneath the objects that it covers.)

Using different fonts

Remember that you can use the wealth of fonts and font sizes available under Windows to embellish the text used throughout your report. Headings in particular often benefit from the use of an attractive font and font size. To change the font or font size for any text, first select the object containing the text. Then, choose the desired font and font size from the Font and Font Size list boxes that appear in the Toolbar. In FIG. 7-32 (shown earlier), the report's title, "Members," uses a Lucida Calligraphy font in a 14-point size. The text also makes use of a technique used to obtain a drop-shadow look, as described in the next section.

Adding the drop-shadow look

You might have noticed the drop-shadow look given to heading text in some styles of forms created by the FormWizards. You can add this same style to text in your reports by duplicating selected text, using the Palette to change the text's background color to Clear, and dragging the text in close proximity to its copy. (The "Members" heading, shown earlier in FIG. 7-32, makes use of this technique.) To provide this drop-shadow look, first create the desired text and assign it a desired font and font size. Then, with the text still selected, choose `Edit/Duplicate` to place an identical copy of the text nearby. Select the copy, open the Palette with `View/Palette`, and change the background color to Clear. Drag the duplicated text until it is closely aligned (but not directly over) the original text. You might need to increase the grid spacing to align the duplicate text to your liking; to do so, choose `Edit/Select Report`, then `View/Properties`, and increase the values under the Grid X and Grid Y properties. Finally, select the original text, and use the Palette to change the text color to a color appropriate for a shadow (such as light or dark gray).

Adding graphics or pictures

You can easily add graphics or pictures as design elements in a report. Any graphics that are stored in OLE fields of a table can be used as fields of the report, and you can place and size those fields just as you would place or size any other type of field. In addition, pictures or graphics can be inserted as design elements from your favorite graphics or photo package (such as Corel Draw! or Harvard Graphics for Windows) or from Windows Paintbrush. You can perform the following steps to use your graphics as design element in a report.

TIP

If you are running Access and your graphic program simultaneously, one easy way to switch between them is to press Ctrl–Esc to display the Windows Task List. Then, choose the desired application from the list.

Step 1 Open the desired report in Access, and get into Design View.

Step 2 Start your graphics program under Windows, and design or load the graphics image that you want to use. Using Windows selection techniques applicable to your package, select the portion of the graphic that you want to place in the report in Access. Choose `Edit/Copy` from the application's menus.

Step 3 Press Ctrl–Esc to bring up the Windows Task List, and choose Microsoft Access from the list.

Step 4 From the menus in Access, choose `Edit/Paste`. When you do so, the graphic appears in the report.

Step 5 Using the move and sizing techniques detailed earlier, place the graphic in the desired location on the report.

Figure 7-33 shows a printed report that makes use of both graphics as a design element and an OLE field in a table containing graphics. This figure shows one page of a catalog from a tropical fish supplier. In the table, each record contains an OLE field that is used to store a picture of a particular species of fish. For each record in the report, fields containing the name, price, and picture of the fish are shown. In addition, a design element consisting of a Windows Paintbrush picture of an aquarium has been added in the page header. Figure 7-34 shows the same report in Design view.

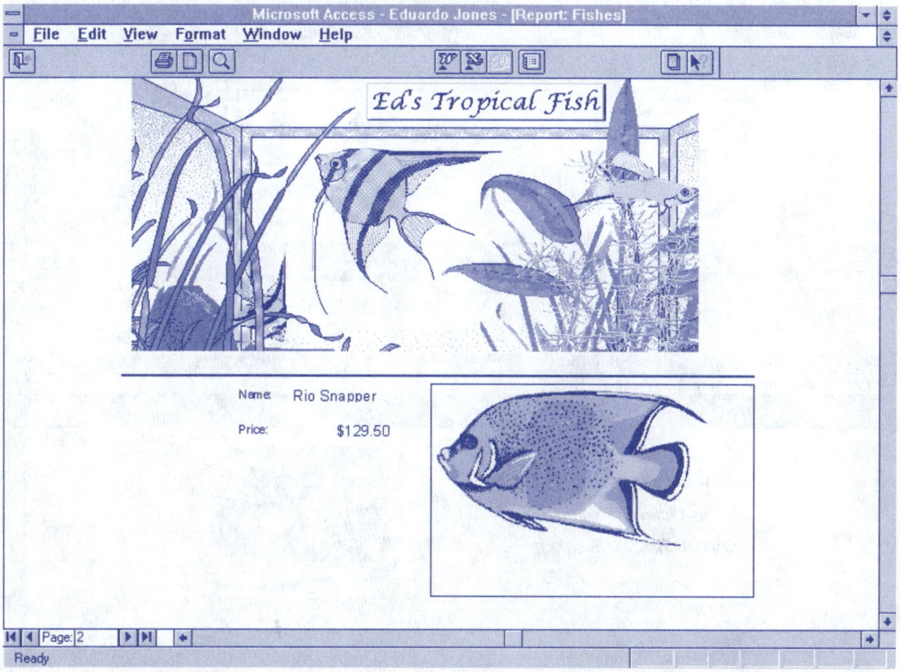

7-33
A report using graphics as design elements and within fields.

Creating form letters

You can create an Access report that serves as a form letter. Once you grow accustomed to the technique, this often is faster than exporting names and addresses to a word processor and performing a mail-merge in the word processor. Also, an advantage of using an Access report for your form letters is that you can include Access objects, such as pictures stored in OLE fields, within your form letters. Figure 7-35 shows a print preview of a form letter, created entirely within Access. Figure 7-36 shows the Design view for the same letter.

To create this type of report, it usually is best to begin with a blank report, rather than using the ReportWizards. In the Page Header band, you can add any descriptive text (such as the letterhead design shown in the figure). In the Detail band, you can add the desired fields, along with the text. (Use the

7-34
A graphical report in Design view.

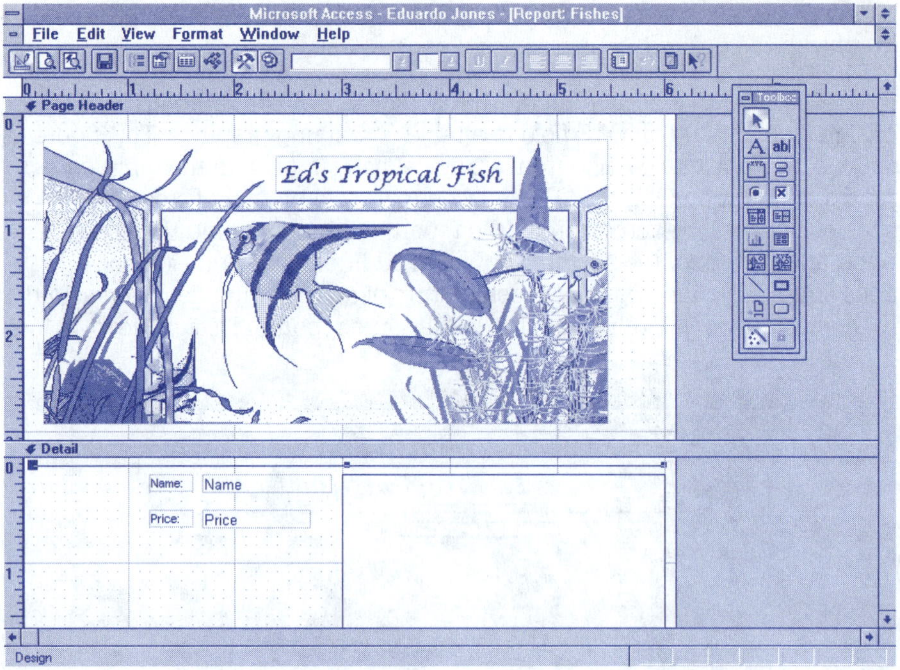

7-35
A form letter in Print Preview.

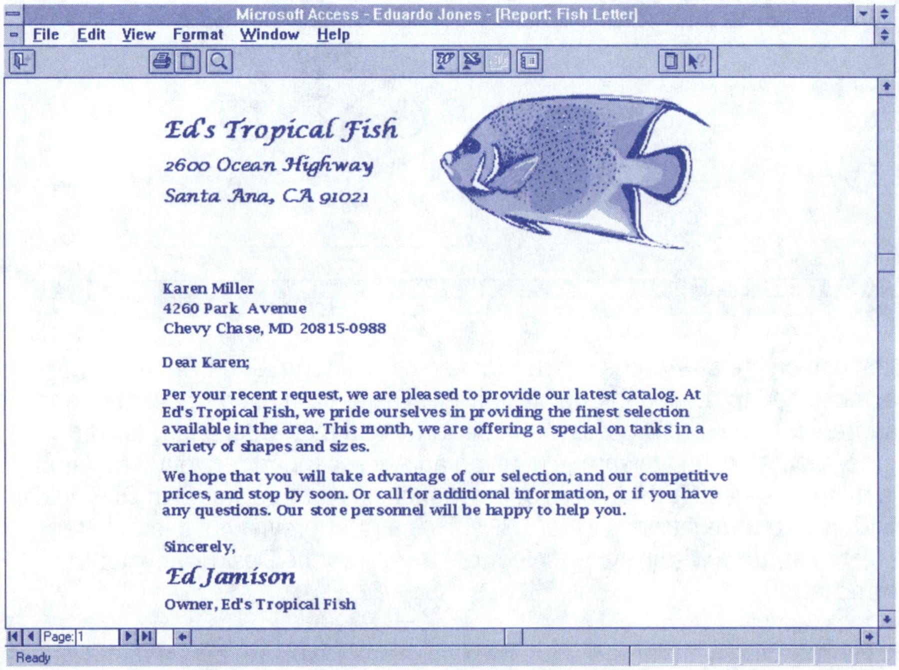

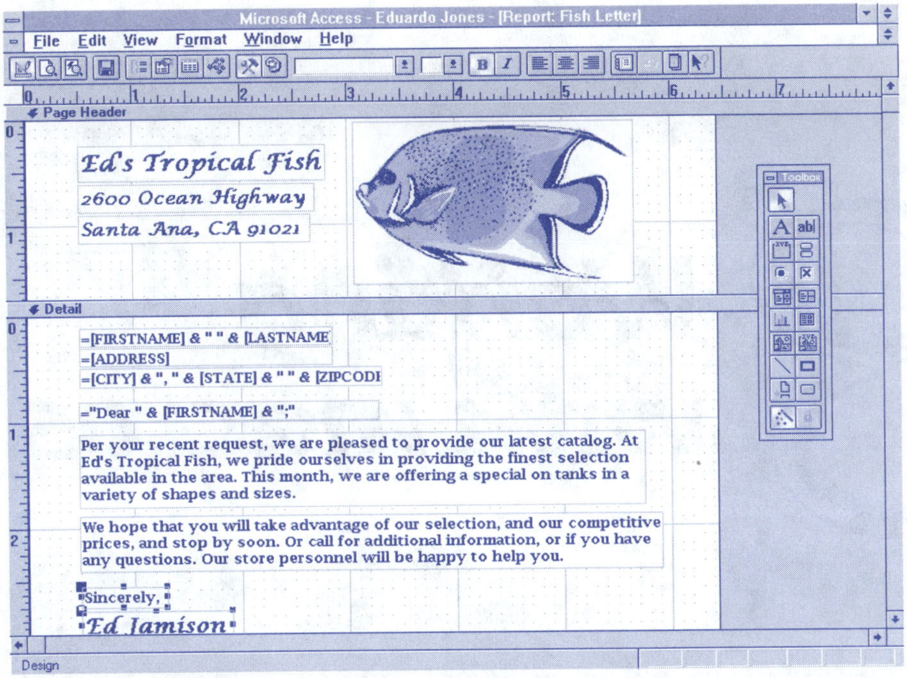

7-36
A form letter in Design view.

Label tool of the Toolbox to add text. Remember to choose a desired font and font size before you start typing.) Note that, when you are typing a paragraph of text, you must use Ctrl–Enter at the end of a line to begin a new line within the same label box. Also, keep in mind that Access limits the contents of a label box to 2048 characters, so you might need to use multiple text boxes for multiple paragraphs. In the figure, the first and second paragraphs are stored in separate label boxes.

If you want to print a first and last name separated by a space, you will need to use the Text Box tool of the Toolbox to add a text box, click in the text box, and type the desired expression. An expression like `=[First Name] & " " & [Last Name]` is sufficient, assuming your fields are called "First Name" and "Last Name." To combine a City, State, and ZIP Code field, you can use an expression like `=[City] & ", " & [State] & " " & [ZIP Code]`. Finally, at the bottom of the page, add a Page Break (use the Page Break tool of the Toolbox), so that each letter prints on its own page.

A note about relational reports

Designing reports to retrieve data from more than one table is a simple matter, because you can base your reports on tables or on queries. The easiest way to design relational reports in Access is to use the ReportWizards and base the report on a query that retrieves the data from the desired tables. (See chapter 5 for details on designing relational queries.)

8 Working with macros

This chapter introduces *macros*, a fundamental part of your work in creating applications in Access. Macros can be used for a wide variety of tasks in Access; they can help you automate routine operations and make better use of your tables, queries, forms, and reports. Macros are the key to providing complete applications, as they can provide complete menu-driven systems that will shield novice users from the complexities of Access. How you can use macros to design and build such systems is detailed in chapter 9; this chapter details the basics of macro use.

What's a macro?

In Access, a macro is a list of actions that you specify in advance. When you run the macro, Access carries out the list of actions for you. As an example, perhaps you routinely open two forms and three reports and work most often with these throughout your day. You can create a macro that automatically opens the desired forms and reports and places them on your screen in the desired locations. If you routinely run a query and export the results of that query to an Excel spreadsheet, you can create a macro that handles this task.

If you have used macros with other software products, you might be accustomed to the concept of *macro recorders*, where you activate a "recording" capability of the software, then carry out a group of actions (such as a series of menu selections). Later, when you play back the macro, it duplicates the actions that you recorded. If this is your idea of macros, be warned that Access is very different in its approach to macros. There is no "recorder" feature. With Access macros, you must specifically tell the macro what actions you want performed by choosing actions in a macro window. While this initially might sound more complicated to some, the benefits of the Access approach go far beyond any apparent added complexities. It is this ability to specify a wide range of actions in an Access macro that gives macros the power to manipulate your database in so many different ways.

Where you can use macros

When considering ways to use macros, think about the routine tasks that you normally perform in Access and how you would like to perform them with less effort. Some candidates for the use of macros might include the following:

- Automatically open often-used objects—You can use a macro to automatically open and arrange the tables, forms, and reports that you use most often.
- Add convenience to your forms and reports—You can add command buttons to forms and reports that let you easily perform common tasks, such as printing or moving to another record.
- Validating data—You can use a macro to validate data that's entered into a form with greater flexibility than can be provided with the validation rules available in table design.
- Automate transfer of data—A macro can automatically import or export data between Access and other software packages.
- Provide a custom user interface for an application—As shown in the following chapter, Access macros can provide custom menus and dialog boxes designed to manage a specific application.

Creating a macro

To create a macro, click the `Macro` button in the Database window, then click `New`. (Note that you also can choose `File/New/Macro` from the menus to create a new macro.) Using either of these methods causes a new Macro window to open. An example of a macro window is shown in FIG. 8-1.

About the Macro window

The Macro window can be divided into two areas: an upper portion, which contains *actions* and *comments*, and a lower portion, which displays *action arguments*, as shown in the FIG. 8-1. (If others have been using Access on your computer, you also might see columns in the upper portion titled *Conditions* and *Macro Names*. If you see these columns, you can ignore them for now; their use will be detailed later in the chapter.)

In the upper portion of the Macro window within the Action column, you select or list the *actions* that you want the macro to perform; how to do so is described shortly. In the Comment column, you can enter a comment describing what the macro does. Such comments are purely optional and provide a reference to help you remember how your macros operate.

About the Macro window Toolbar

When the Macro window is active, the Macro window Toolbar appears, as shown in FIG. 8-2. As shown, the Macro window Toolbar contains buttons titled `Save`, `Macro Names`, `Conditions`, `Run`, `Single-Step`, `Show Database Container`, `Invoke Builder`, `Undo`, `Cue Cards`, and `Help`.

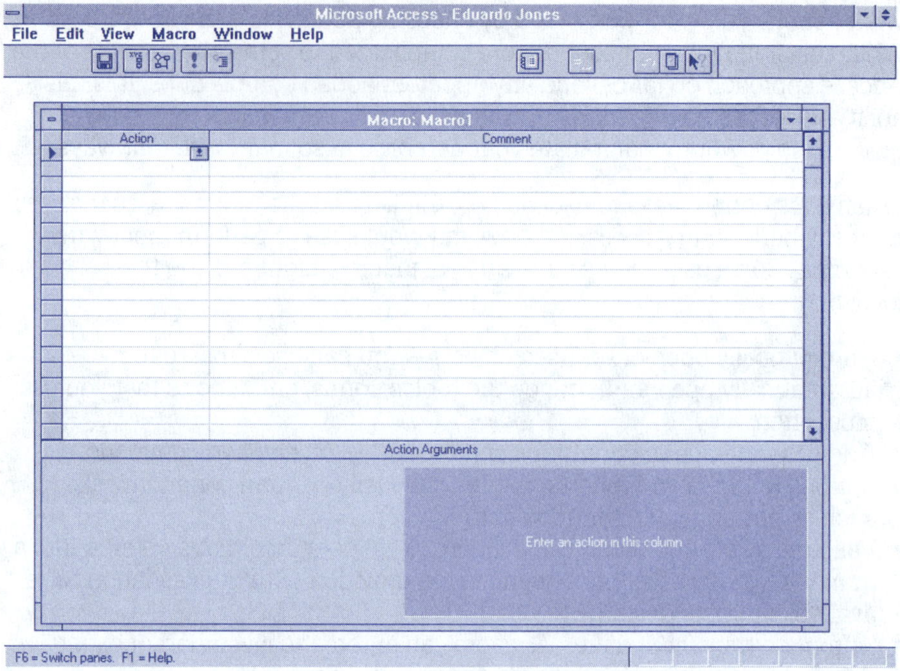

8-1
A macro window.

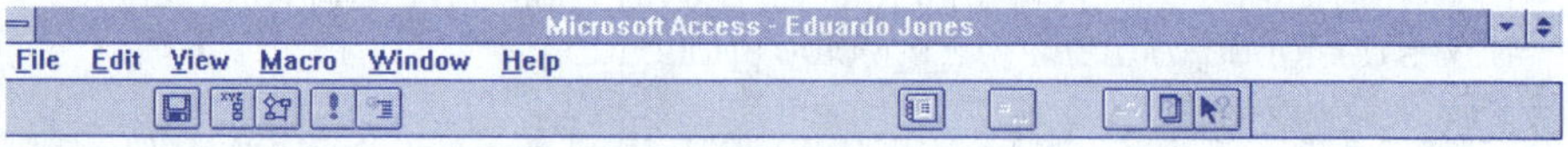

8-2
The macro window Toolbar.

Save This button saves the current macro; it is a fast equivalent to choosing `File/Save` from the menus when a macro is open.

Macro Names This button lets you show or hide a column that displays macro names. You'll use macro names when you store multiple macros as a group within a single macro window.

Conditions This button lets you show or hide a column that displays conditions. You'll use the Conditions column if you want to include conditions that a macro must evaluate before performing the actions specified in the macro.

Run This button runs the macro. (The Toolbar's `Run` button is just one way of running a macro; this chapter highlights many others.)

Single-Step This button can be used to move through a macro, performing one action at a time.

Show Database Container This button causes the Database window to be placed in front of any other open windows.

Invoke Builder This button displays an expression builder that can be used as an aid in entering expressions into the Condition column.

Undo This button lets you undo your most recent action.

Cue Cards Use this button to display Cue Cards that aid in explaining a task.

Help Use this button to open a Help window explaining the use of the Macro window.

Specifying actions

Much of your work in designing macros will consist of telling the macro what you want Access to do by means of *actions*. Actions simply are instructions that tell Access what type of task to perform. An action might be the opening of a particular form, the running of a query, or the selection of a series of menu commands. While actions are named using a specific syntax, you need not worry about the precise syntax, because you can choose the desired actions from a pull-down list. You specify the actions that you want the macro to perform in the Action column of the macro window. To specify an action, you perform the following steps.

Step 1 In the Macro window, click the first empty cell in the Action column. Click the down arrow, or press Alt–down arrow to display the action list.

Step 2 Choose the desired action from the list. (Note that you also can type the name of the action you want to add.) If desired, type an optional comment for the action in the Comment column.

Step 3 In the bottom portion of the window, specify the arguments for the action (if any are required).

Most macro actions have arguments that apply to the action. Arguments can be thought of as specific definitions for an action. As an example, the OpenQuery action, which opens a query, requires the name of the desired query as an argument. A few macro actions, such as Maximize and Minimize, have no arguments. Table 8-1 shows the available macro actions, their uses, and their arguments.

Table 8-1
Table of Macro Actions.

Macro action	Purpose
AddMenu	Adds a drop-down menu to a custom menu bar.
ApplyFilter	Applies a filter, a query, or an SQL WHERE clause to a form or report to filter or sort the records from the form's or report's underlying table or query.
Beep	Sounds a beep using the computer's speaker.
CancelEvent	Cancels the event that caused Access to run the macro containing the action.

Table 8-1 Continued.

Macro action	Purpose
CloseAction	Closes either a specified window or closes the active window if none is specified.
CopyObject	Copies the selected database object to a different Access database or to the same database under a different name.
DoMenuItem	Carries out a menu command.
Echo	Determines whether Access updates the computer screen while a macro runs.
FindNext	Finds the next record that meets the criteria specified by the last FindRecord action or in the Find dialog box of the Find command.
FindRecord	Finds the first record following the current record that meets the criteria specified by the arguments.
GoToControl	Moves the insertion pointer to the specified field or control on the open form, datasheet, or query dynaset.
GoToPage	Moves the insertion pointer in the active form to the first field on a specified page.
GoToRecord	Makes the specified record the current record in an open table, form, or query dynaset.
Hourglass	Changes the mouse pointer to an hourglass while the macro is running.
Maximize	Enlarges the active window so that it fills the Access application window.
Minimize	Reduces the active window to an icon at the bottom of the Access application window.
MoveSize	Moves or resizes the active window.
MsgBox	Displays a message box containing a warning or an informational message.
OpenForm	Opens a form in Form view, Design view, Print Preview, or Datasheet view.
OpenQuery	Opens a select query in Datasheet view, Design view, or Print Preview.
OpenReport	Opens a report in Design view or Print Preview or prints the report.
OpenTable	Opens a table in Datasheet view, Design view, or Print Preview.
Print	Prints the active object.
Quit	Exits Access.
Rename	Renames the selected database object.
RepaintObject	Finishes any pending screen updates for the specified object or for the active database object if none is specified.
Requery	Updates the data in a specified control on the active object by requerying the source of the control.

Restore	Restores a maximized or minimized window to its prior size.
RunApp	Runs a Windows or a DOS application.
RunCode	Executes an Access Basic procedure.
RunMacro	Runs another macro.
RunSQL	Runs an action query using the corresponding SQL statement.
SelectObject	Selects the specified object.
SendKeys	Sends keystrokes directly to Access or to an active Windows-based application.
SetValue	Sets the value of a field, control, or property on a form, a form datasheet, or a report.
SetWarnings	Turns system messages on or off.
ShowAllRecords	Removes any applied filter from the active form and displays all records in the form's underlying table or query.
StopAllMacros	Stops all macros that currently are running.
StopMacro	Stops the currently running macro.
TransferDatabase	Imports or exports data between the current Access database and another database.
TransferSpreadsheet	Imports or exports data between the current Access database and a spreadsheet file.
TransferText	Imports or exports text between the current Access database and a text file.

As a simple example, perhaps you want a macro to open the Members form (created in chapter 6) and maximize the form so that it fills the Access window. In the first empty cell of the Action column, you would click the down arrow and choose `OpenForm` from the list box. You then could enter an optional comment such as "open the members form" in the Comment column. Then, in the Action Arguments area at the bottom of the macro window, you could click in the Form Name text box and type `Members` or click the down arrow and select the form name, `Members`, from the list box. This would complete the first action required by the macro.

Because the macro needs one more action, that of maximizing the form to full-size in the window, you would click in the next empty cell of the Action column, click the down arrow, and choose `Maximize` from the list. (Again, you could add a comment if desired, but remember that comments are optional.) At this point, your macro window might resemble the example shown in FIG. 8-3.

If you then save the macro (by choosing `File/Save` from the menus) and run the macro (by clicking the `Run` button in the Toolbar), you'll see that the macro performs the specified actions. The Members form is opened and

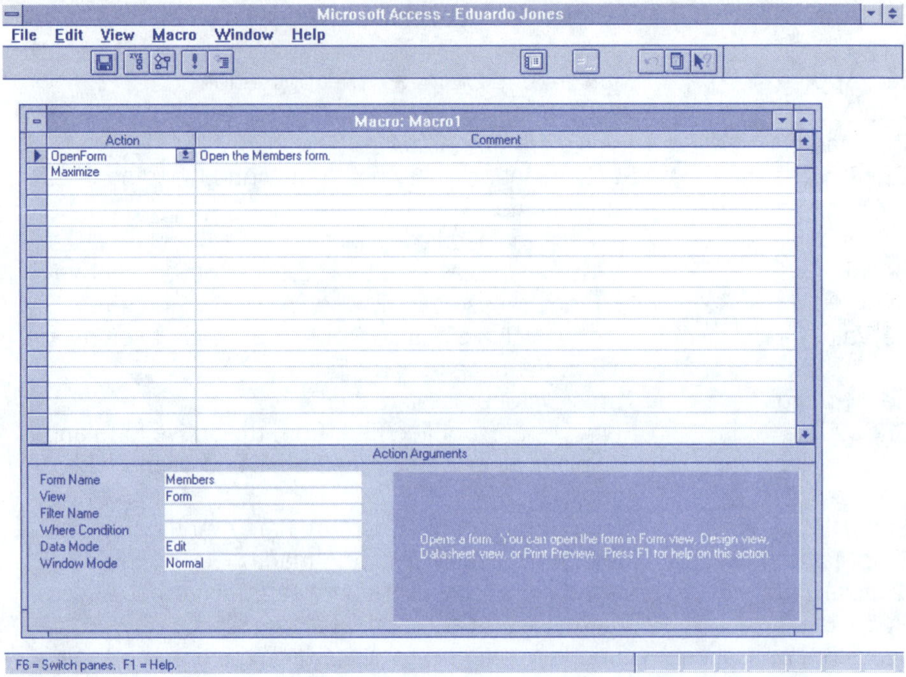

8-3
An example of a macro.

maximized to fill the Access window. (For more on saving and running macros, see "Saving macros" and "Running macros" in this chapter.)

Using drag-and-drop to specify actions

As illustrated earlier, one way to specify actions is to choose them from the list box. Another way is to use a method called *drag-and-drop*, in which you click and drag an object from the Database window into the Action column of the Macro window. While you cannot use this method for all types of actions, you can use it to perform actions that open any database object (such as a table, form, query, or report). To specify a macro action using drag-and-drop, perform the following steps.

Step 1 Move and size the Macro window and the Database window so that you can see them both at the same time. (One quick way to make both windows visible is to choose Window/Tile from the menus.)

Step 2 In the Database window, click the button for the kind of object that you want the macro to open. As an example, if you want your macro to open a report, you would click the `Report` button in the Database window.

Step 3 Locate the desired object by name, and drag the object to a cell in the Action column of the Macro window.

As an example, consider FIG. 8-4. In the figure, the report named "Members" has been dragged into the Action column of a new macro. As a result, Access has automatically entered "OpenReport" as an action. Within the

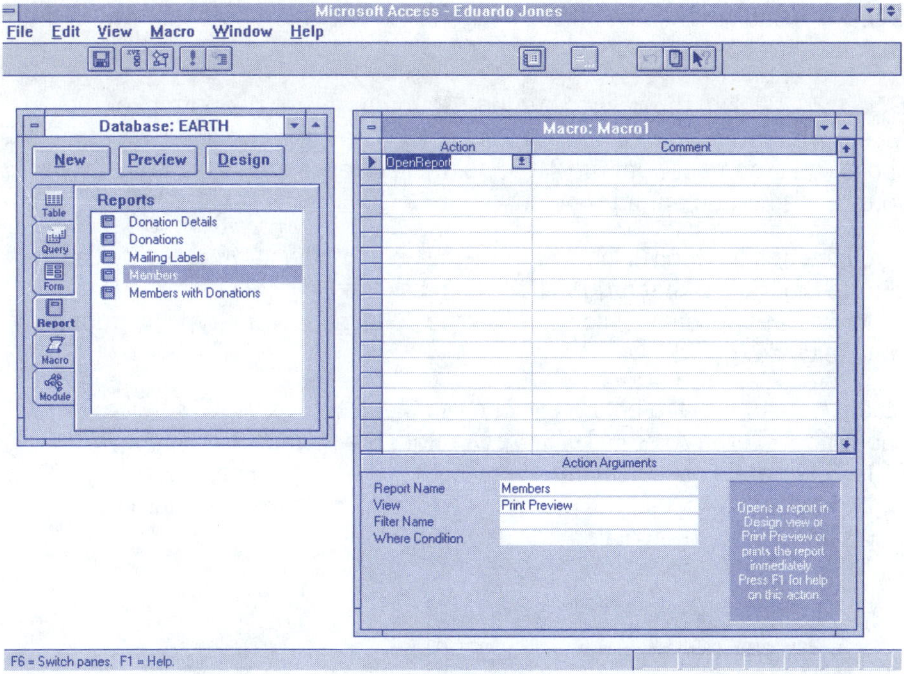

8-4
The results of drag-and-drop in a macro window.

Action Arguments portion of the Macro window, Access has entered "Members" as the report name and chosen "Print Preview" as a default view.

TIP

You can use drag-and-drop to have one macro run another macro. Whenever you drag an existing macro to the Action column of a macro window, Access adds an action that runs the existing macro as part of the new macro.

Moving & deleting actions

If you decide to change the actions that a macro uses, you can easily do so without starting all over again. Access lets you move or delete actions in a macro. To move an action, first click the row selector at the left edge of the Macro window to select the row containing the desired action, then click again and drag the row to the new desired location. To delete an action, select the desired row by clicking the row selector at the left edge of the window, then press the Del key (or choose `Edit/Delete`).

Adding arguments

Most macro actions include *arguments*, which provide additional information needed by Access to handle the task exactly as you prefer. For example, a macro action might tell Access to open a form, but Access does not inherently know which form should be opened. The argument provides the name of the desired form. Arguments often also provide additional information. For example, in the case of a form, arguments can indicate whether the form should be opened in form view, in design view, or in print preview and whether the form should allow editing or be used in a display-only ("read-only") mode of operation. You can assign or change the arguments for any actions with the following steps.

Step 1 Click in the row for the desired action to make sure that row is the currently selected row in the macro.

Step 2 Click in the desired Action Argument row at the bottom of the Macro window. If a down arrow appears, you can click on the arrow, then choose an argument from the list. If no down arrow appears, you must type your desired argument into the box.

TIP

If you are unsure about what response is needed to an argument, you can click in the row for that argument, then press the Help (F1) key. The Help window that appears will contain specific details about the type of argument you are working with.

Saving macros

Macros must be saved before you can run them. You can save a macro by choosing `File/Save` or `File/Save As` from the menus. If you choose `File/Save` and you are saving the macro for the first time or if you choose `File/Save As`, Access will prompt you for the name for the macro by displaying the Save As dialog box (FIG. 8-5).

8-5
The Save As dialog box.

You can enter any name of up to 64 characters, including spaces. Click `OK`, and the macro will be saved.

If you attempt to close a Macro window containing a new macro that you haven't saved, Access will warn you that the macro has not been saved and will ask if you want to save it. If you click `Yes`, Access displays the Save As dialog box, and you can enter the desired name for the macro and click `OK` to save it.

Running macros

There are a number of ways that you can run a macro. As the next chapter will detail, one way that's common with applications is to attach the macro to a command button so that the macro runs when the user clicks a button on a form. You also can design custom menus and attach your macros to commands on those menus. This topic also is detailed in the following chapter. To run a macro directly, use any of these methods you prefer:

- *To run a macro from the Database window:* In the Database window, click the `Macro` button to display all your macros. Click the desired macro by name, then click `Run`. Note that you also can double-click the desired macro by name in the Database window; double-clicking is the same as clicking a macro name to select it, then clicking the `Run` button.
- *To run a macro from the Macro window:* If the Macro window is the active window, click the `Macro` button in the Toolbar or choose `Macro/Run` from the menus.

- *To run a macro from any other window:* Choose `File/Run Macro` from the menus. In the list box that appears, choose the desired macro by name, then click `OK`.

Copying & deleting macros

You can copy and delete existing macros. Copying macros saves time when you want to create a macro that is similar in design to an existing macro. Rather than creating the new macro from scratch, copy the macro to a new name, then make the desired changes to the new macro. To copy a macro, perform the following steps.

Step 1 In the Database window, click the `Macro` button to display all your macros. Click the desired macro that you want to copy.

Step 2 Choose `Edit/Copy` from the menus (or press Ctrl–C). Choose `Edit/Paste` from the menus (or press Ctrl–V).

Step 3 In the Paste As dialog box that appears, type a name for the new macro, then click `OK`.

TIP

You can copy macros from one database to another. To do so, use the previous instructions; however, before performing step 4, close the current database and open the database where you want to copy the macro to.

To delete an existing macro, in the Database window, click the `Macro` button to display all your macros. Click the desired macro that you want to delete, then press the Del key and click `OK` in the confirmation box that appears.

Adding macros to forms & reports

A common use for macros in Access (and one that is emphasized heavily throughout the applications in Part 2 of this book) is to attach them to forms or reports. Macros can be dragged from the Database window onto the design surface of a form to add a command button. When the user clicks the button in the completed form, the macro runs. Macros also can be attached to forms or reports by naming the macros in various properties of the form or report. As an example, you might want a macro to run when a certain event occurs, such as the opening of a report. The macro might provide a confirmation box that the user would have to accept before printing of a report would begin. Another common use is in the validation of data; you might want a macro to validate data that is entered into a particular field of a form. Access recognizes events for forms, controls on a form, reports, and report sections. You can attach a macro to a form or report with the following steps.

Step 1 Open the desired form or report in Design view.

Step 2 Choose `View/Properties` to open the Properties window, and type or choose the macro name in the appropriate property (see TABLE 8-2). The property determines when Access runs the macro.

Table 8-2
Properties for running macros.

Property	Runs macro when–
OnOpen	Before opening a form or report
OnClose	Before closing a form or report
BeforeUpdate	Before saving a record
AfterUpdate	After saving a record
OnCurrent	Before displaying a different record (or the first record when opening the form or report)
OnInsert	Before inserting a new record
OnDelete	Before deleting a record
For controls on forms	
BeforeUpdate	Before saving data in the control
AfterUpdate	After saving data in the control
OnEnter	Before entering the control
OnExit	Before leaving the control
OnDblClick	When you double-click the control
OnPush	When you click a command button
For report sections	
OnFormat	Before setting page layout for printing.
OnPrint	Before printing the section

One excellent way to get an idea of how macros can be attached to forms or reports is to examine examples of applications. Those provided on the disk (and detailed in Part 2 of this book) further illustrate how you can attach macros to your forms and reports.

Note: If you are attaching a macro in a macro group to a property, be sure to include the name of the macro, along with the name of the macro. In such cases, you would enter `macrogroupname.macroname` in the Property text box.

Adding macros to forms & reports with drag-and-drop

One common use for macros in applications involves adding command buttons for everyday tasks to forms. As an example, you might design a macro to print the current record in a form. You then could add a command button to the form, so a user could click on the button to easily print the current record. You can use the following steps to add any macro you've designed to a form.

Step 1 Open the desired form in design mode.

Step 2 In the Database window, click the `Macro` button to display the list of macros. Move and size the windows so that both the Database window and the form design window are visible at the same time. (You can choose `Window/Tile` from the menus to do this quickly.)

Step 3 In the Database window, click the desired macro to select it.

Step 4 With the macro selected, click it again and drag it into an empty area of the form design window, then release the mouse button. When you do so, a button with the name of the macro appears.

Step 5 Use the techniques detailed in chapters 6 and 7 to move and size the button as desired, then save the form by choosing `File/Save` from the menus. When the form is opened, clicking on the button will cause the macro to run. For examples of how these techniques can be applied, see the following chapter or any of the chapters in Part 3 of this book. All the applications detailed in this book make use of this technique to add command buttons to various forms.

Synchronizing forms using macros

One important ability of Access macros is to synchronize two forms. With this technique, you can show a record or records on one form and, at the same time, display related records on another form. (Another way to handle this kind of task is by designing a form that contains a subform, as detailed in chapter 6.) However, when for one reason or another, you prefer to use separate forms, you must use this technique of synchronizing them with a macro. As an example of this type of task, you might have one form that shows customer names and addresses. Each time that you display a different customer, you might want another form to show all orders (stored in an orders table) placed by that customer. You can synchronize two forms by performing these steps.

Step 1 Create a macro that contains an OpenForm action. Use this action to open the second form that you want synchronized to the first form.

Step 2 In the Where Condition action argument of the OpenForm action, specify the value of a control on the second form equal to the value of the same control on the first form. As an example, if the common field is named Customer ID and the first form is named Customers, you might enter an expression like this:

```
[Customer ID] = Forms![Customers]![Customer ID]
```

Attach the macro to the first form, using the OnPush property. When you click the command button, the second form will appear with the matching records displayed.

With this technique, the Where Condition argument that you specify in the macro is the key to synchronizing the forms. In the example described earlier, the Customer ID control on the second form is set to the value of the Customer ID control on the first form. When opened, the two forms show the record for the same customer.

Using conditions in a macro

Access lets you use conditional expressions in macros, to determine whether the macro is carried out. By adding a condition, you force the macro to follow one of two paths, depending on whether a specified condition is true or false. As an example, you might have a macro attached to a form that contains fields for addresses. If you entered the expression `[City] = "Dallas"` in the Condition box of the macro, the macro would run only when `Dallas` was entered into the City field of the form. You can enter a conditional expression in a macro by performing the following steps.

Step 1 From the menus, choose `View/Conditions` (or click the `Conditions` button on the Toolbar). This causes the Condition column to appear in the macro.

Step 2 In the Condition column, enter an expression in the row where you want to place the condition.

Step 3 In the Action column, choose the desired action that you want Access to perform when the specified condition is true.

TIP

If a macro action has a long argument or condition, remember that you can display it in the Zoom box by clicking the desired cell in the Macro window and pressing Shift–F2.

The expressions that you enter can contain operators, literals, functions, and/or identifiers. Operators identify the operations to be performed on the other parts of the expression. In a conditional expression, you can use the math operators (`+ - * /`), the comparison operators (`= <> < > <= >=`), the concatenation operator (`&`), the logical operators (`AND`, `NOT`, `OR`), and other operators (`BETWEEN`, `IN`, `LIKE`). (For a complete description of operators allowed in Access, refer to your Microsoft Access Language Reference.)

Identifiers can be used to refer to controls within forms and reports. Identifiers contain object names, separated by exclamation marks. You use the format, `Forms![form-name]![control-name]`, to refer to a control within a form, and you use the format, `[Reports![report-name]![control-name]`, to refer to a control within a report. As an example, perhaps you want a macro to run if a value entered into the Salary field of a form named Employees is greater than $20.50. In such a case, you might use an expression like the following in the Conditions column of the macro:

```
Forms![Employees]![Salary] > 20.50
```

Literals are literal values and can be characters, dates, or numeric values. Character strings must be enclosed in quotes, and number signs (#) must be used around dates, as shown in the following expressions:

```
Forms![Orders]![Payment] = "VISA"
Forms![Employees]![Hire Date] > = #01/01/92#
```

How conditional macros execute

When a macro runs, Access checks the Condition column for an expression. If none is present, the macro runs. If a condition is present, Access first evaluates the condition, and if the condition is true, the macro runs. Access continues to perform any additional actions within the macro, as long as an ellipsis is present in the Condition column for the additional actions. If Access encounters a blank entry in the Condition column, another expression, or the end of the macro, execution of the macro stops.

If the condition is false, Access skips ahead to the next blank row in the Condition column, to the next entry (other than an ellipsis), or to the next macro name. As an example, consider the macro shown in FIG. 8-6.

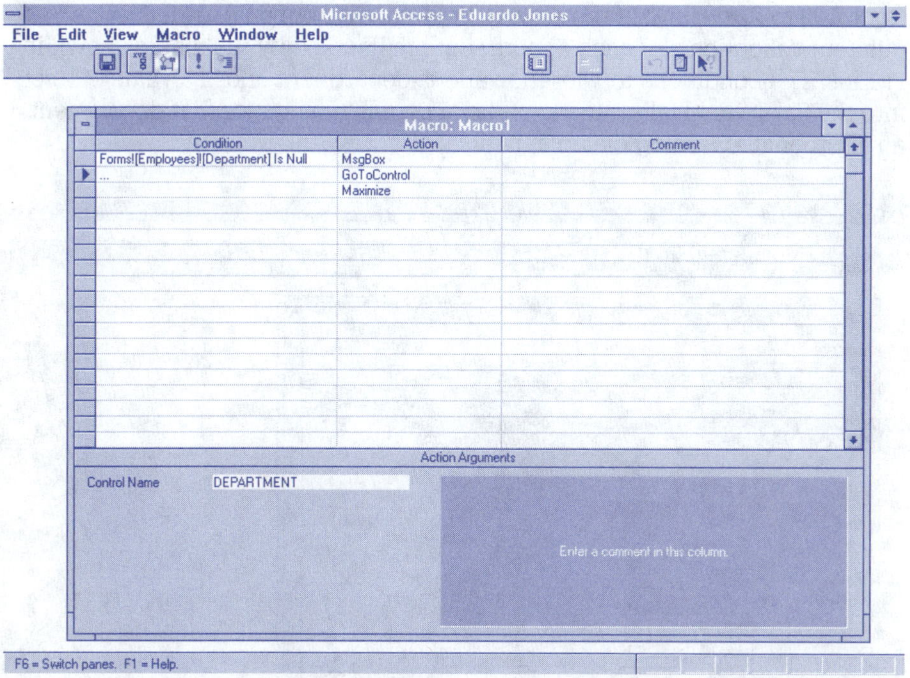

8-6
An example of a conditional macro.

If the condition shown in the Condition box `Forms![Employees]![Department] Is Null` is true, a message box containing a warning message is displayed and the insertion pointer is moved to the Department field of the form. If the condition is false, only the last action of the macro, that of maximizing the form, is performed.

Using macros for data validation

One useful task for macros is that of data validation in a form. As shown in chapters 4 and 6, you can add validation rules to tables or to the fields that you place in a form. However, there might be times when you need a more complex type of validation than is possible with the validation rules present in tables and forms. As an example, perhaps a Salary field in a table of employees has different acceptable ranges, depending on which department an employee is assigned to. This type of validation cannot be handled with validation rules in a table or a form, but you can handle this task with macros.

In the Condition column of the macro, you enter the desired condition that will validate the data. To call the macro, you name the macro within the On Exit or Before Update property of the control. If you always want the entry validated (even when there is no change to the data), use the On Exit property. If you want to validate data only after it has been changed, use the Before Update property. As an example, consider the form shown in FIG. 8-7. In this example, there are multiple ranges of allowable salary amounts. Salaries for employees in the Admin department can range from 6.50 to 15.00; in the Manufacturing department from 4.50 to 18.00; in the Sales department from 7.00 to 22.00; and in the Service department from 6.00 to 20.00. The different validations for each department are handled by the macro shown in FIG. 8-8. The conditions test for the various department and, if a value entered into the Salary field falls outside of the acceptable range for that department, an appropriate warning dialog appears.

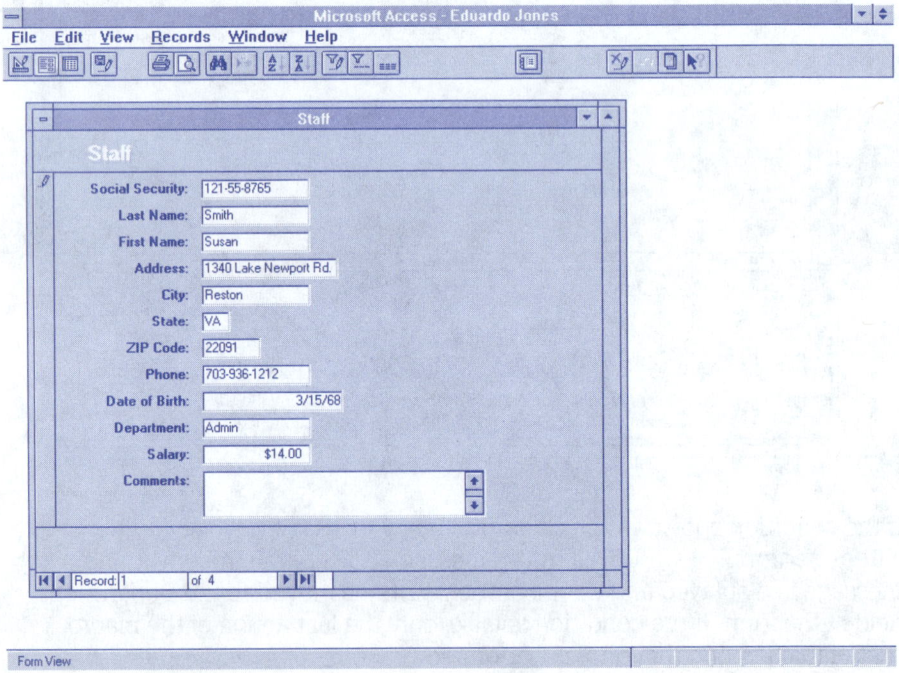

8-7 *A form containing Department and Salary fields.*

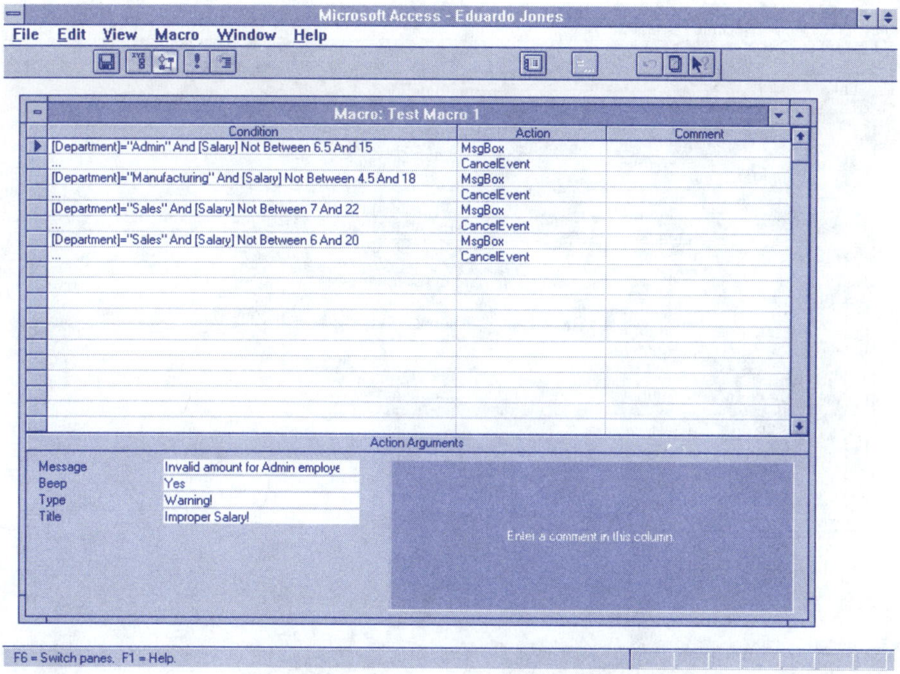

8-8
A Macro to evaluate conditions for salaries.

The macro shown is named in the Before Update property of the Salary field in the form shown earlier in FIG. 8-7. If a user enters an amount that is outside of the acceptable range, the CancelEvent action in the macro cancels the update made by the user. Figure 8-9 shows the dialog box that appears when an invalid amount is entered.

Creating macro groups

As you grow proficient with designing macros, you will find that the collection of macros in the Macro window can grow quite large. This is particularly so when you begin designing complete applications, because you might have a collection of macros used for common tasks, such as manipulating forms, moving to various records, and running different queries. To keep your collections of macros from getting out of hand, you can group related macros together.

Any number of macros can be stored in a *macro group*. A macro group is simply a macro window that contains more than one macro. You identify each macro by providing it with its own title in the Macro Name column of the Macro window. (By default, this column does not appear, but you can show and hide it at will by clicking the `Macro Names` button in the Toolbar or by choosing `View/Macro Names` from the menus.) Note that it normally is not a good idea to group together macros that you want to run directly from the Database window, because running the desired macro gets a little more complex, as detailed shortly. You normally will use this technique of placing multiple macros in a macro group when you want to run the macros from

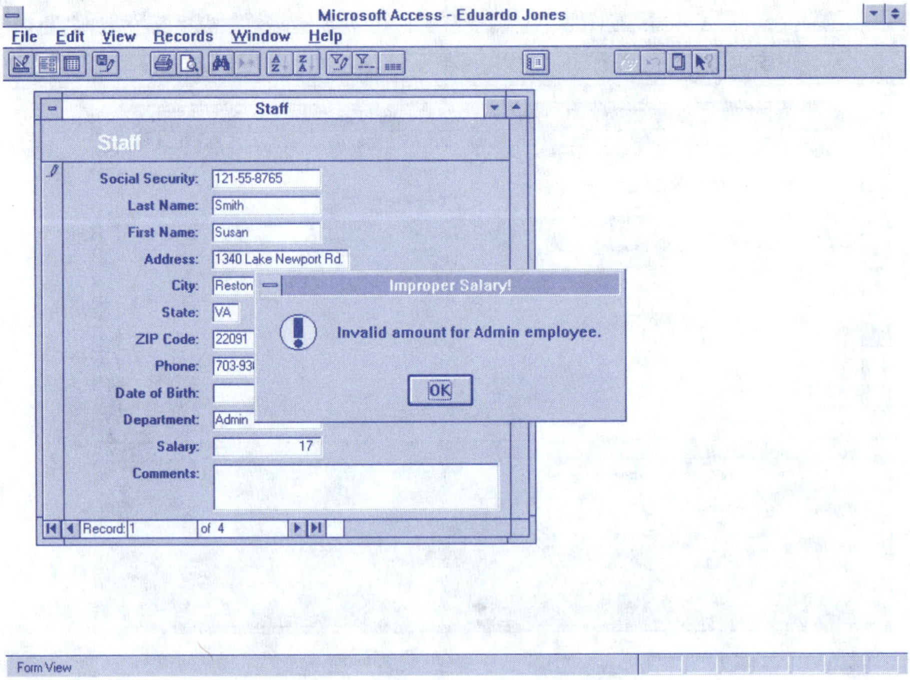

8-9
A dialog box response to an improper amount.

command buttons or menu options within an application. You can create a macro group by performing the following steps.

Step 1 Click the `Macro` button in the Database window, then click `New` to open a new Macro window.

Step 2 If the Macro Names column is not visible in the window, click the `Macro Names` button on the Toolbar or choose `View/Macro Names` to display the Macro Names column.

Step 3 In the Macro Names column, enter a macro name of your choosing for each set of actions that make up a macro. Whenever a macro contains more than one action, you should include the macro name only beside the first action. Leave the macro name column beside the other actions blank.

As an example, consider FIG. 8-10. In the figure, the Macro window contains three separate macros. Each macro is identified by its name in the Macro Name column. The Members Form macro opens the membership form and maximizes it, the Donations Form macro does the same for the donations form, and the Donations Report macro opens and prints the donations report.

Running a macro in a macro group

Running a macro that's stored in a macro group is somewhat different, because you need to identify which of the macros stored in the group should be run. You do this by referring to the macro by the macro group name, followed by a period, followed by the macro name. As an example, in FIG. 8-10,

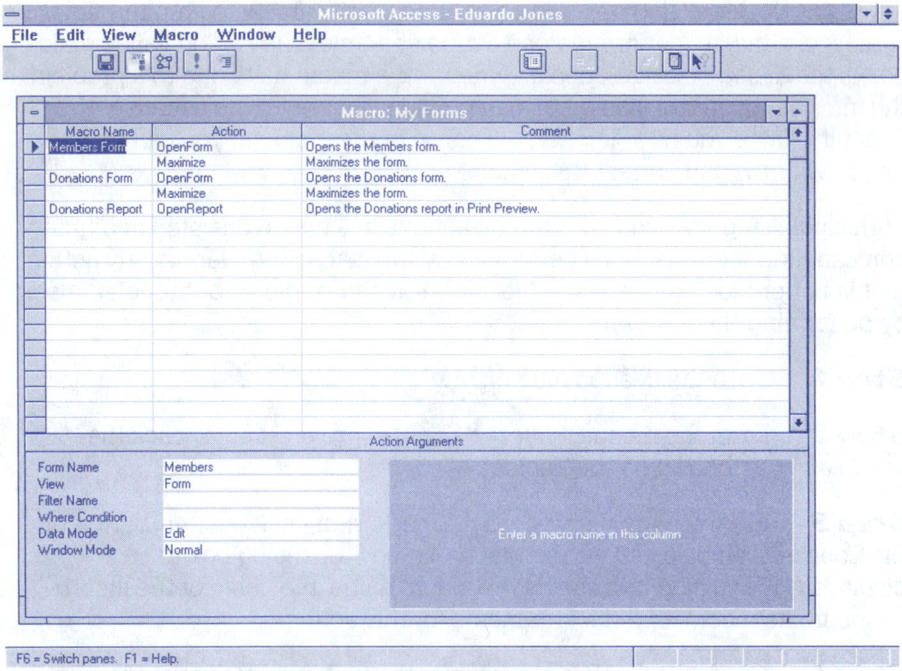

8-10
An example of a macro group.

the macro group is named "My Forms." If you wanted to run the macro named "Donations Form," you would need to use the title `My Forms.Donations Form` to refer to the macro name.

Note: When necessary, you can run a macro in a macro group directly, by choosing `File/Run Macro` from the menus. In the Run Macros dialog box that appears, type the name of the macro group, followed by a period, followed by the name of the desired macro. *Don't* use the `Run` button in the Macro Toolbar to run a macro that's in a macro group; the `Run` button will run the first macro stored in the macro window, regardless of which macro you actually might want to run.

As mentioned, macro groups are most commonly used when you are creating a number of controls or menu options to manage a complete application. The following chapters will detail how you can use macro groups to store macros that are used for common tasks, such as finding data and printing various reports.

When things go wrong

Because so much of the work in developing applications is performed using Access macros, it stands to reason that many problems in the logic or the flow of an application are going to occur in your macros. Even the most expert programmers spend significant amounts of time debugging programs, and the complex macros that you create can be considered a kind of a program, because they tell Access what steps to take. Access offers two tools that can help you locate any problems in macro design: single stepping and the Action Failed dialog box. *Single stepping* is the ability to step through the actions of a macro, performing one action at a time. The Action Failed dialog box is the dialog box that appears whenever a macro halts due to a problem; the information in the dialog box can provide clues as to the source of the difficulty. Once you have located the cause of the problem, you can go to the Macro window and correct the actions.

Single stepping

With single stepping, you can run the actions in a macro one step at a time. You can monitor the actions performed by the macro and identify any action that is not producing the desired results. You can single step through a macro by performing the following steps.

Step 1 Open the desired macro.

Step 2 From the menus, choose `Macro/Single Step` or click the `Single Step` button on the Toolbar.

Step 3 From the menus, choose `Macro/Run` or click the `Run` button on the Toolbar. Doing so causes the Macro Single Step dialog box to be displayed. This dialog box shows the macro name, the name of the first action in the macro, and the arguments for this action.

Step 4 Choose the desired buttons in the dialog box to move through the macro. `Step` runs the action shown in the dialog box, `Halt` stops the running of the macro, and `Continue` runs the rest of the macro.

About the Action Failed dialog box

When an error occurs while a macro is running, Access displays an error message. When you click `OK`, Access displays the Action Failed dialog box (FIG. 8-11).

The dialog box shows the name of the macro, the name of the action where the problem occurred, and the arguments for the action. You can choose `Halt` and return to the Macro window where you can (hopefully) correct the cause of the error. Many errors in your macros are likely to be syntactical in nature; look for missing punctuation marks or misspellings as a prime cause of unexpected halts in your macros.

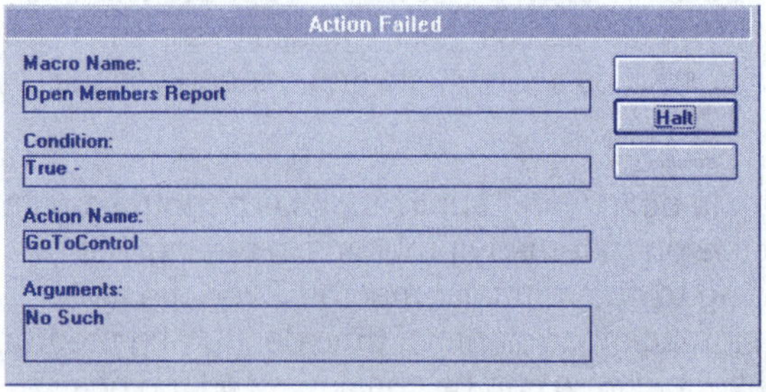

8-11
The Action Failed dialog box.

9 Creating applications with macros

The previous chapter provided an introduction to the power of Access macros and what they can do for you. This chapter will carry that theme further, showing how you can design your applications using Access macros. The primary intent of a completed application is to make common tasks easier for the user. For example, if others in your office must manage the data in an Access database, it would be time-consuming to teach everyone how to use all the menu options within Access to perform tasks such as adding, editing, and printing reports.

With databases in the business world, custom applications are routinely designed for use by novice users. Such applications routinely provide main menus with clearly-defined user options and various prompts or dialog boxes guide users through the various tasks. How you can design this type of application in Access is the overall premise of this book. If you think of the objects covered in earlier chapters—the tables, queries, forms, and reports—as building blocks of a complete application, you can consider the kinds of macros presented in this chapter as the glue that holds an application together.

This chapter will show how you can create various objects, such as custom menus, custom toolbars, and dialog boxes, that can be used as part of an application. Using the Earth Aware database (created in the previous chapters and stored on the accompanying disk) as an example, you will see how these objects can simplify the use of a database. These same techniques will be used to develop the different applications throughout Part 3 of this book, which follows this chapter. The objects that you can add to an application include the following:

- *Switchboards*—Forms containing buttons for performing common tasks. Switchboards routinely are used as menus in an application. If you open the Time and Billing or the Assignment Tracking database on the accompanying disk or open the Northwind Traders database included with Access by Microsoft, you were greeted with a main menu in the form of a switchboard. Figure 9-1 shows the switchboard that is part of the Assignment Tracking System; this application, included on the disk, is detailed in chapter 16.

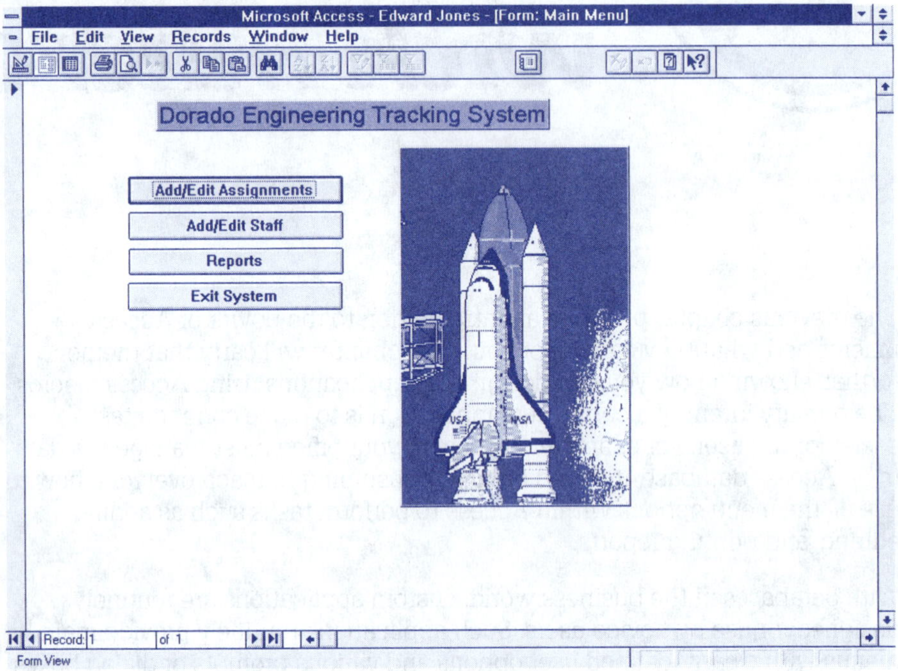

9-1
The switchboard used by the Assignment Tracking system.

- *Custom menus*—Menu bars with pull-down menu options that you can use to replace the standard menu bar that Access provides.
- *Custom dialog boxes*—Forms designed to resemble dialog boxes. You can use dialog boxes to ask users for specialized input or for confirmation before performing an action (such as printing a report). You also could use custom dialog boxes for special funtions, such as the entry of a password.
- *Custom toolbars*—Forms containing buttons purposely designed to resemble a toolbar. The buttons can perform tasks not normally available through the Access menus. For example, you could design a toolbar with

buttons that would display the Windows Calculator or Calendar when pressed.

- *Autoexec macros*—Macros that automatically run as soon as a database is opened. Whenever you open a database and a switchboard immediately appears, it is the result of an Autoexec macro stored as part of the database. As an example, you might use an Autoexec macro to open a switchboard containing command buttons and to hide the Database window and the Toolbar so that a novice user does not get into trouble with them.

This chapter provides tips and techniques for designing all of these objects, and you can use these techniques for your own databases or with any of the applications detailed in Part 2 of this text.

Creating switchboards

Switchboards are simply blank forms that contain buttons that are used to perform the desired tasks (such as opening a form or printing a report). Because the buttons that you place on the switchboard call macros, you also will need to create the macros that respond to the buttons. Switchboard design generally is easier if you first create the needed macros, because once they exist, you can easily create the buttons using the drag-and-drop method detailed shortly. (In a nutshell, you click on the macro name in the Database window and drag the name to the switchboard to create the button.) To create a switchboard, you will need to perform the following steps.

Step 1 Create a macro for each button that you plan to include on the switchboard. For example, if you want to include a button for adding a new record through a form, you will need to create a macro that opens the desired form and moves to the blank record at the end of the table. (When you name your macros, try to give them the same names as you would like to appear on the buttons in the switchboard. Doing so will save you the effort of editing the names within the buttons later, assuming you use the drag-and-drop method of creating the buttons.

Step 2 In the Database window, click the `Form` button, then click `New` to create a new form.

Step 3 In the New Form dialog box that appears, leave the Select A Table/Query box empty, and click the `Blank Form` button to open a blank form in design view. Move and size the form window so that you can see both the form and the Database window at the same time.

Step 4 In the Database window, click the `Macro` button to display your macros.

Step 5 Click a desired macro in the list box, and drag over to the blank form. When you release the mouse button, a button appears in the form that will call the macro. (Users of version 2.0 might see a dialog box warning that the Button Wizard can't be used to modify existing buttons; you can click `OK` to ignore this dialog box.) Using the moving and sizing techniques detailed in chapter 6, place the button in the desired location on the form and resize it if desired.

Step 6 Repeat step 5 for every button that you want to place on the switchboard.

Step 7 Add any desired text, graphics, colors, or shading to the switchboard, to improve its appearance. (Remember, the switchboard is no more than a blank form, so you can use the form techniques detailed in chapter 6 to enhance the form's appearance.)

Hands-on practice: creating an example switchboard

To consider a simple example (which will grow in complexity as the chapter progresses), start with a menu for the Earth Aware application. Figure 9-2 shows the appearance of this switchboard.

At first, you want to provide a switchboard with choices for adding new members, editing existing members, adding donations, editing donations, and printing reports. To create the macro for adding and editing the records in the Members table, try the following steps.

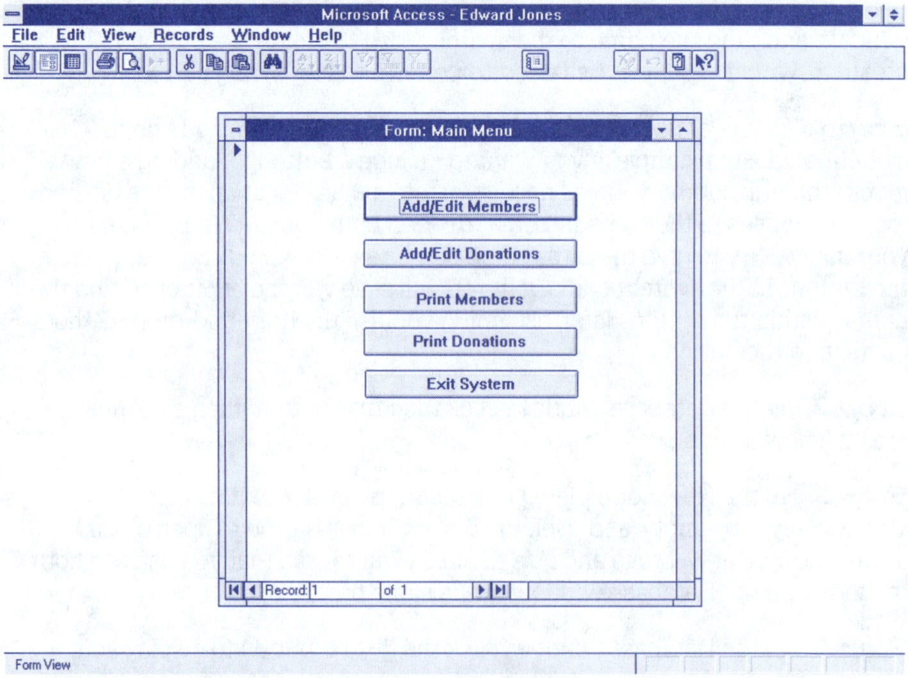

9-2
An example switchboard.

Step 1 In the Database window, click the `Macro` button, then click `New`. Move and resize the macro window that appears so that you can see both the Database window and the Macro window at the same time. Click the `Form` button, then click on `Members` in the list box and drag over to the first column under Action in the macro window. As a result, OpenForm appears in the Action column with the form name (Members) shown in the Action Arguments portion of the macro window (FIG. 9-3).

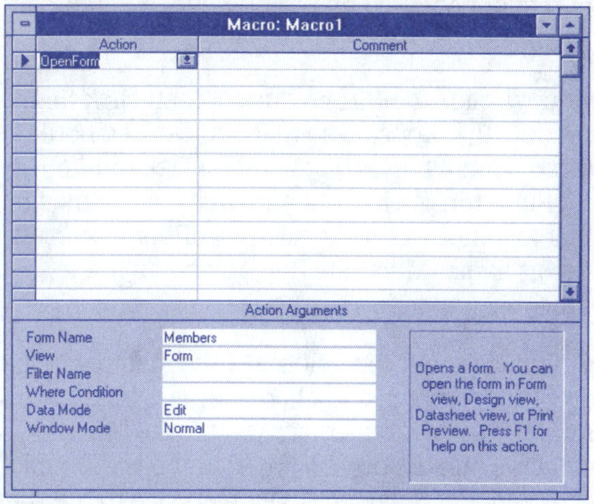

9-3
The Members macro with the OpenForm action added.

Step 2 Click in the second line of the Action column of the macro window. Click the arrow to open the drop-down menu, and choose `Maximize` from the list. Double-click the Close box of the Macro window. Answer `Yes` in response to the "Save changes" prompt that appears. When prompted for a name, call the macro `Add/Edit Members`.

Step 3 In the Database window, click the `Macro` button, then click `New`. Move and resize the macro window that appears so that you can see both the Database window and the Macro window at the same time. Click the `Form` button, then click on Donations in the list box and drag over to the first column under Action in the macro window. As a result, OpenForm appears in the Action column with the form name (Donations) shown in the Action Arguments portion of the macro window (FIG. 9-4).

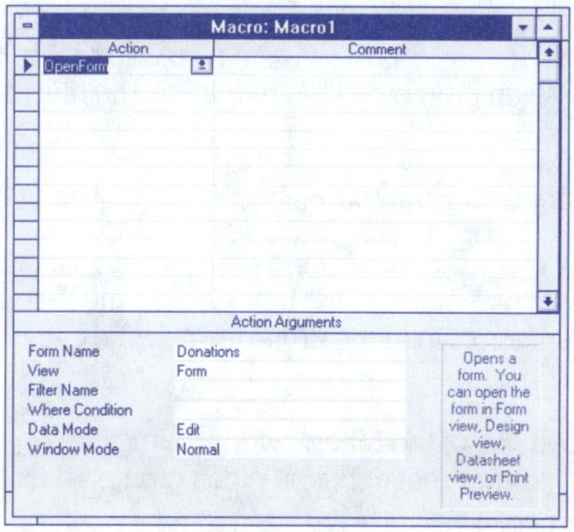

9-4
The Donations macro with the OpenForm action added.

Step 4 Click in the second line of the Action column of the macro window. Click the arrow to open the drop-down menu, and choose `Maximize` from the list. Double-click the Close box of the Macro window. Answer `Yes` in response to the "Save changes" prompt that appears. When prompted for a name, call the macro `Add/Edit Donations`.

Step 5 In the Database window, click the `Macro` button, then click `New`. Move and resize the macro window that appears so that you can see both the Database window and the Macro window at the same time. Click the `Report` button, then click on Members Report in the list box and drag over to the first column under Action in the macro window. As a result, OpenReport appears in the Action column with the report name (Members Report) shown in the Action Arguments portion of the macro window.

Step 6 Click in the second line of the Action column of the macro window. Click the arrow to open the drop-down menu, and choose `Print` from the list. Click in the third line of the Action column of the macro window. Click the arrow to open the drop-down menu, and choose `Close` from the list. Double-click the Close box of the Macro window. Answer `Yes` in response to the "Save changes" prompt that appears. When prompted for a name, call the macro `Print Members`.

Step 7 In the Database window, click the `Macro` button, then click `New`. Move and resize the macro window that appears so that you can see both the Database window and the Macro window at the same time. Click the `Report` button, then click on Donations Report in the list box and drag over to the first column under Action in the macro window. As a result, OpenReport appears in the Action column with the report name (Donations Report) shown in the Action Arguments portion of the macro window.

Step 8 Click in the second line of the Action column of the macro window. Click the arrow to open the drop-down menu, and choose `Print` from the list. Click in the third line of the Action column of the macro window. Click the arrow to open the drop- down menu, and choose `Close` from the list. Double-click the Close box of the Macro window. Answer `Yes` in response to the "Save changes" prompt that appears. When prompted for a name, call the macro `Print Donations`.

Step 9 In the Database window, click the `Macro` button, then click `New`.

Step 10 Click in the first row of the Action column of the macro. Open the drop-down list box, and choose `Close` from the list box. Click in the second row of the Action column of the macro. Open the drop-down list box, and again choose `Close` from the list box.

Step 11 Double-click the Close box of the Macro window. Answer `Yes` in response to the "Save changes" prompt that appears. When prompted for a name, call the macro `Exit System`.

With the macros created, you can proceed to create the form that will serve as the Switchboard for the application. Perform the following steps to create the switchboard.

Step 1 In the Database window, click the `Form` button, then click `New`. When the New Form dialog box appears, leave the Select a Table/Query text box blank. Click the `Blank Form` button to open a blank form that is not associated with any table.

Step 2 Increase the size of the drawing area on the form by dragging the lower-right corner until it is at least 4 × 4", then use the scroll bars to get back to the upper-left corner of the drawing area. Move and resize the form so that you can see both the form and the Database window at the same time.

Step 3 In the Database window, click the `Macros` button to display all the macros you have created. Click `Add/Edit Members`, and drag it over to a position roughly 1" from the left edge and ½" below the top of the form. When you release the mouse button, a button appears that will call the macro. (Users of version 2.0 might see a dialog box warning that the Button Wizard can't be used to modify existing buttons; you can click `OK` to ignore this dialog box.) Place the mouse pointer over the right edge of the button until it changes shape to a double-pointed arrow. Click and drag to the right until the button is roughly 2" in length. When you do so, the entire title of the macro, "Add/Edit Members," should be visible within the button.

Step 4 In the Database window, click `Add/Edit Donations`, and drag it over to a position roughly ¼" below the existing button. When you release the mouse button, a button appears that will call the macro. (If you see the Button Wizard warning dialog box, click `OK` to ignore it.) Place the mouse pointer over the right edge of the button until it changes shape to a double-pointed arrow. Click and drag to the right until the button is the same size as the previous button. When you do so, the entire title of the macro, "Add/Edit Donations," should be visible within the button.

Step 5 Move the mouse pointer over the button until it changes to the shape of a hand, then click and drag the button as necessary until it is aligned ¼" directly underneath the first button. (If you are nearing the bottom of the form, you might want to use the vertical scroll bar to scroll the form upwards so that you will have sufficient room to place the remaining buttons.)

Step 6 In the Database window, click `Print Members`, and drag it over to a position roughly ¼" below the `Add/Edit Donations` button. (If you see the Button Wizard warning dialog box, click `OK` to ignore it.) Place the mouse pointer over the right edge of the new button until it changes shape to a double-pointed arrow. Click and drag to the right until the button is the same size as the other buttons. When you do so, the entire title of the macro, "Print Members," should be visible within the button. Move the mouse pointer over the button until it changes to the shape of a hand, then click and drag the button as necessary until it is aligned ¼" directly underneath the second button.

Step 7 In the Database window, click `Print Donations`, and drag it over to a position roughly ¼" below the `Print Members` button. (If you see the Button Wizard warning dialog box, click `OK` to ignore it.) Place the mouse pointer over the right edge of the new button until it changes shape to a double-pointed arrow. Click and drag to the right until the button is the same size as the other buttons. When you do so, the entire title of the macro, "Print Donations," should be visible within the button. Move the mouse pointer over the button until it changes to the shape of a hand, then click and drag the button as necessary until it is aligned ¼" directly underneath the third button.

Step 8 In the Database window, click `Exit System`, and drag it over to a position roughly ¼" below the `Print Donations` button. (If you see the Button Wizard warning dialog box, click `OK` to ignore it.) Place the mouse pointer over the right edge of the new button until it changes shape to a double-pointed arrow. Click and drag to the right until the button is the same size as the other buttons. When you do so, the entire title of the macro, "Exit System," should be visible within the button. Move the mouse pointer over the button until it changes to the shape of a hand, then click and drag the button as necessary until it is aligned ¼" directly underneath the fourth button.

Step 9 Double-click the `Close` button of the Form window to close it. When Access asks if you want to save the form, click `Yes`. When prompted for a name for the form, enter `Main Menu`.

To use the switchboard, open it as you would open any form, and click on the desired button. In response, the macro that corresponds to the button executes. For example, if you open the form and click on the `Print Members` button, the Members Report macro causes the Members report to open and begin printing.

Note that, while the drag-and-drop method of creating buttons for the switchboard was used in this example, this is not the only way to create buttons for switchboards. You also could create the buttons manually by using the Button tool on the Toolbox to add the buttons. If you manually create your buttons, you must tell Access what to do when the button is pressed by opening the Properties for each button (click the button, then choose `View/Properties`) and specifying a macro name in the OnPush property of the button.

Using one switchboard to call another

You can use one switchboard to call another; that is, you can design a macro to open a switchboard and drag that macro onto another switchboard to create a button. The button, when clicked by the user, will cause the second switchboard to appear. This technique is common in menu design for many applications, because most applications contain too many options to place on a single menu. As an example, a `Print` button on a switchboard could cause another switchboard to appear; the second switchboard could contain buttons for printing a variety of different reports.

To have one switchboard call another, design the second switchboard, using the design techniques outlined previously, and save the second switchboard under the desired name. Next, create a macro that opens the second switchboard. Finally, open (in Design view) the first switchboard, move and size the windows so that you can see both the form containing the switchboard and the macro window, and click and drag the macro that opens the second switchboard onto the first switchboard. The command button that appears as a result can be used in the application to open the second switchboard.

If your application requires a number of switchboards, you probably will want to store your macros in macro groups, rather than storing each macro individually. Storing the macros in macro groups holds down the clutter in the Database window and keeps your macros better organized. (See chapter 8 for details on storing macros in macro groups.)

Keep in mind that the use of multiple switchboards is not the only way to handle numerous menu options in an application. You also can create custom menus that replace the usual Access menus when your application runs. For more on this topic, see "Creating custom menus" later in this chapter.

Starting an application with Autoexec macros

Once your application has been completed and tested, you probably will want to automatically start the application's main menu switchboard whenever the database is opened. This can easily be accomplished by means of an *autoexec* macro. An autoexec macro is nothing more than a macro saved under the name Autoexec. Whenever Access opens a database, it looks for a macro named Autoexec. If that macro exists, it is run automatically. To automatically start your application, first design the switchboard that will serve as the main menu for the application, as detailed earlier in this chapter, then create a new macro and place a single OpenForm action inside that macro. You also might want to add a Minimize action before the OpenForm action to minimize the Database window before opening the form; doing so gives the display a cleaner appearance. Under Form Name in the action arguments, choose the form that serves as your switchboard. Close the macro, and when prompted for a name, call the macro `Autoexec`. From that point on, whenever you open the database, the switchboard will appear.

TIP

You can disable an autoexec macro by holding the Shift key while you open the database.

Hiding the database window

If you want to clean up your screen area as an application runs, you probably will want to hide the Database window. You can easily do so by writing a macro that chooses `Window/Hide` from the menus, while the Database window is the active window. It normally makes sense to do this immediately after opening the database, because the Database window is always the active window right after the database has been opened. Create a new macro, and in the Action column, choose `DoMenuItem`. Under Action Arguments, set the arguments as shown in TABLE 9-1.

Table 9-1
How the arguments should be set.

Argument	Setting
Menu Bar	Database
Menu Name	Window
Command	Hide

Save the macro under your desired name (such as "Hide Database Window"). Then, open your form that serves as the main menu switchboard, enter design mode, open the Properties window for the form, and set the On Open property to the name of your macro that hides the Database window.

TIP

After hiding a Database window, remember that you can redisplay it at any time by pressing F11. If, for some reason, you want to redisplay the Database window under the control of your application, you can create a macro that simulates pressing the F11 key. Create the macro, and in the Action column, choose SendKeys as the action, choose Keystrokes under Argument, and enter `{F11}` as a setting. (Remember to include the curly braces around the key name.)

Creating custom menus

When your application runs, you might prefer to replace the usual Access menus with a custom menu bar of your own design. (This is one way to provide a user with choices in an Access application; the technique of switchboards, described earlier in this chapter, is another.) Figure 9-5 shows an example of a custom menu bar in an application. This menu bar is used by the Order Entry System detailed in chapter 12.

9-5 *An example of the custom menu bar.*

You can add custom menus to your applications with the following steps.

Step 1 Create a macro group that will display the menu bar. The only actions in this macro group will be AddMenu actions; you must add one AddMenu action for each menu name that appears in the menu bar. Under the Action Arguments for each Add Menu action in the Menu Name text box, enter the menu name (the name that you want the option to have on the menu bar). Precede any letter in this name by an ampersand if you want the letter to be used as an optional hot key to open the menu. In the Menu Macro Name text box, enter the name of the macro that contains the choices for that drop-down menu, as detailed in step 2.

Step 2 Create a macro group for each drop-down menu that the menu bar provides. The macros within the macro group will perform the desired actions when the command is chosen from the drop-down menu.

Step 3 Open a form that will serve as the opening display to your application (this could be a blank form with no more on it than the name of the company or a logo of some sort). In Design view, choose `Edit/Select Form`, then choose `View/Properties` to open the Properties window for the form. Click in the OnMenu property, and choose the macro that displays your menu bar (the one created in step 1).

As an example, consider FIG. 9-6. Two macro groups are visible in this figure: one called Main Menu and the other called Orders. The Main Menu macro group

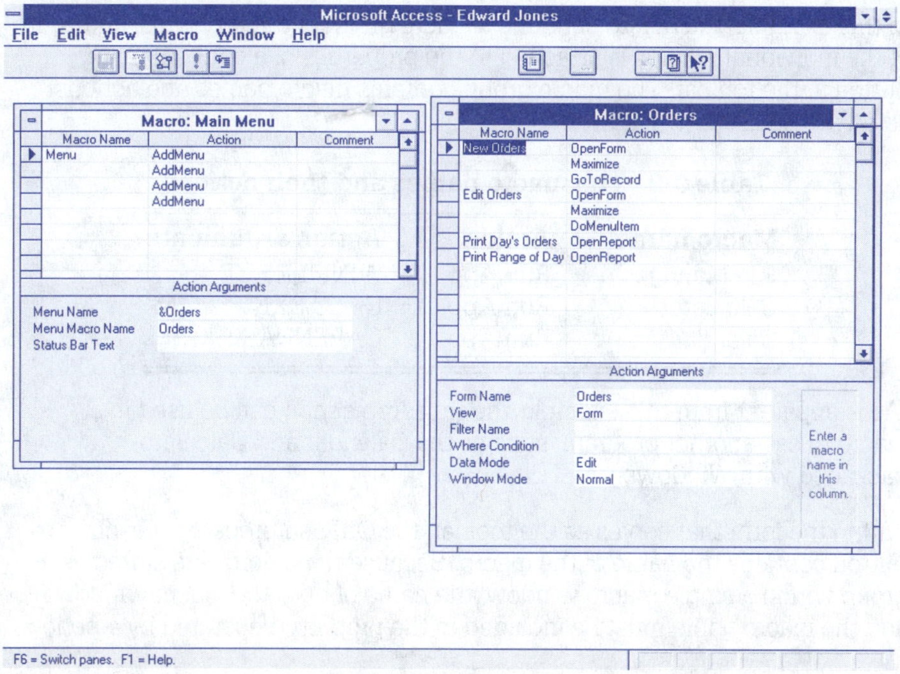

9-6 *The macro groups used as part of the menu bar.*

contains the AddMenu actions that cause the menu bar for the application (shown in FIG. 9-5) to be displayed. The first choice on the menu bar is Orders; hence, under Action Arguments, the menu name of `&Orders` causes the menu bar to display "Orders" as an option, and the user can press Alt–O as a hot key to open the drop-down menu. The second macro group, called Orders, contains the macros that provide each of the commands on the Orders drop-down menu. The macro names (New Orders, Edit Orders, Print Day's Orders, and Print Range of Days) become the available commands on the Orders drop-down menu. For a step-by-step description of how the macros are designed to produce this menu, see the section "Developing the application" in chapter 12.

Creating custom toolbars

You can create custom toolbars to perform specialized tasks by first creating macros that will perform the desired tasks, then by creating buttons that will call the macros. The buttons then can be placed on a blank form that is sized to resemble a toolbar. In the properties for the blank form, you set the Pop-Up property to `Yes`, the Modal property to `No`, the Scroll Bars property to `Neither`, and the Record Selectors property to `No`. Size the form as desired so that the form takes on the desired shape for your toolbar. As an example, consider the toolbar shown in FIG. 9-7.

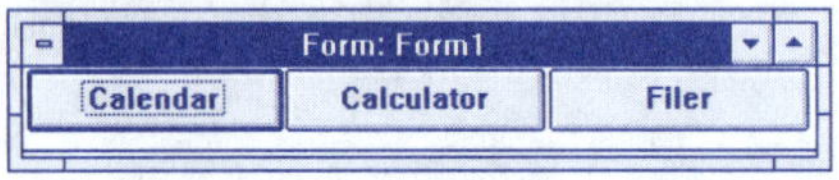

9-7
A custom toolbar.

Figure 9-8 shows the same toolbar in design mode, along with a macro window containing the macros that respond to the toolbar buttons.

In this example, the macro contains a macro group of three macros, and each of the individual macros is attached to the properties of a corresponding button in the toolbar. The macro group contains macro names and actions listed in TABLE 9-2.

Table 9-2 The macro names and their actions.

Macro name	Action	Action arguments
File Manager	Run App	WINFILE.EXE
Calculator	Run App	CALC.EXE
Calendar	Run App	CALENDAR.EXE

(As is apparent from this example, the Run App action can be used in a macro to call another program, such as the Calendar and Calculator packaged with Windows.)

Within the form that serves as the toolbar, the OnPush property of each button contains the name of the macro. Because the macros are stored as a group within a single macro window, the name of both the macro window and the macro name must be included in the property, separated by a period.

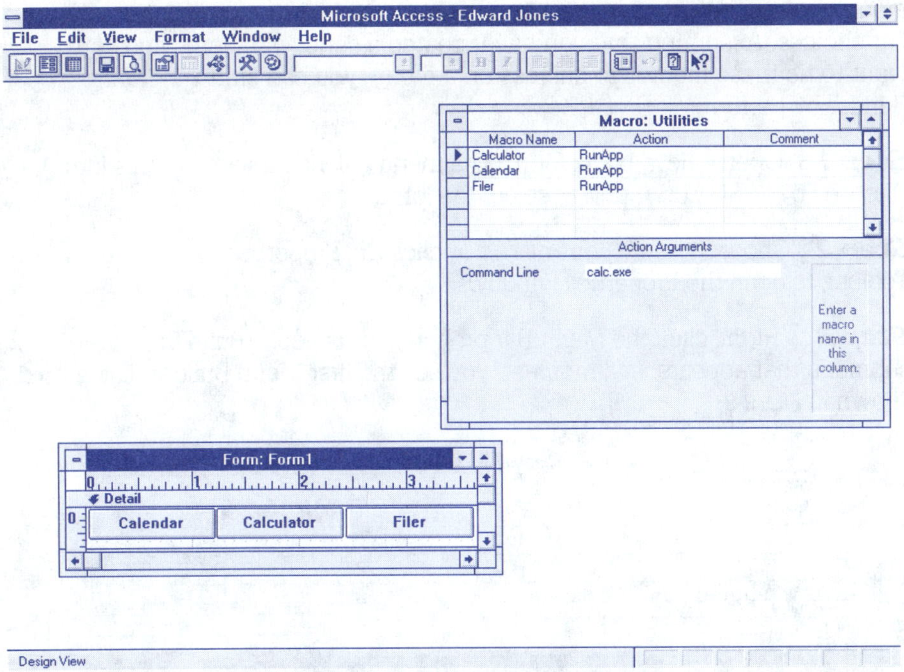

9-8
A custom toolbar in design view.

In this example, getting into form design mode, clicking on the `Filer` button, then choosing `View/Properties` to open the Properties window reveals this in the OnPush property:

```
Utilities.File Manager
```

where `Utilities` refers to the name of the macro containing the macro group and `File Manager` identifies the individual macro within the macro group. While this example uses the Run App macro action to call other Windows applications, you are by no means limited to this type of use of a custom toolbar. You can attach any macro actions that are appropriate to your application. For example, you might attach an Open Form action to a toolbar button to open an often-used form, or you might attach a Print action to a toolbar button to print a currently active table or query.

Creating menus with the Menu Builder

Another way to create menus in Access is to use the Menu Builder, a feature added to Access version 2.0. With the Menu Builder, you define the menus and commands that you want on the menu bar, and the menu builder creates the macros needed. The end result is the same as if you had created the macros manually, as described in the previous section of this chapter. Before using the Menu Builder, it helps to know the names of the macros that the menu options will run. The list boxes within the Menu Builder do not display the names of all available macros, so you might want to write down the macro names before running the Menu Builder. Also note that the menu builder can create menus that do more than run macros in response to the menu choices. You also can run Access Basic code or perform standard menu bar choices. Assuming that you have created a series of macros and you want to tie these macros to choices on a menu, you can start the Menu Builder by performing these steps.

Step 1 Open a new, blank form. (The menu will be attached to this form.) Choose `Edit/Select Form` to select the form.

Step 2 Choose `View/Properties` or click the Properties icon in the Toolbar, to open the Properties window.

Step 3 Right-click the Menu Bar property, and choose Build from the submenu that appears. In a moment, you see the first Menu Builder dialog box, shown in FIG. 9-9.

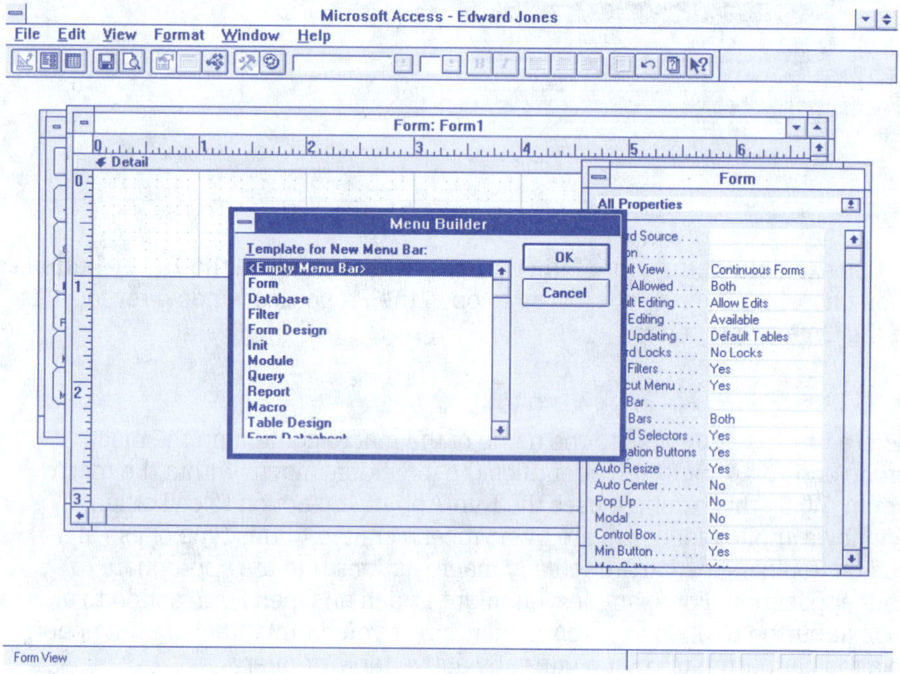

9-9
A dialog box and macro that print selected records.

Step 4 With Empty Menu Bar selected in the list box, click `OK`. (The remaining choices let you use existing Access menus as templates for a new menu.)

When you click `OK`, the Menu Builder dialog box that now appears (FIG. 9-10) is used in the construction of the menu. You use the options in this dialog box to define the captions for your menus and what actions should be taken by each of the menu choices that you add.

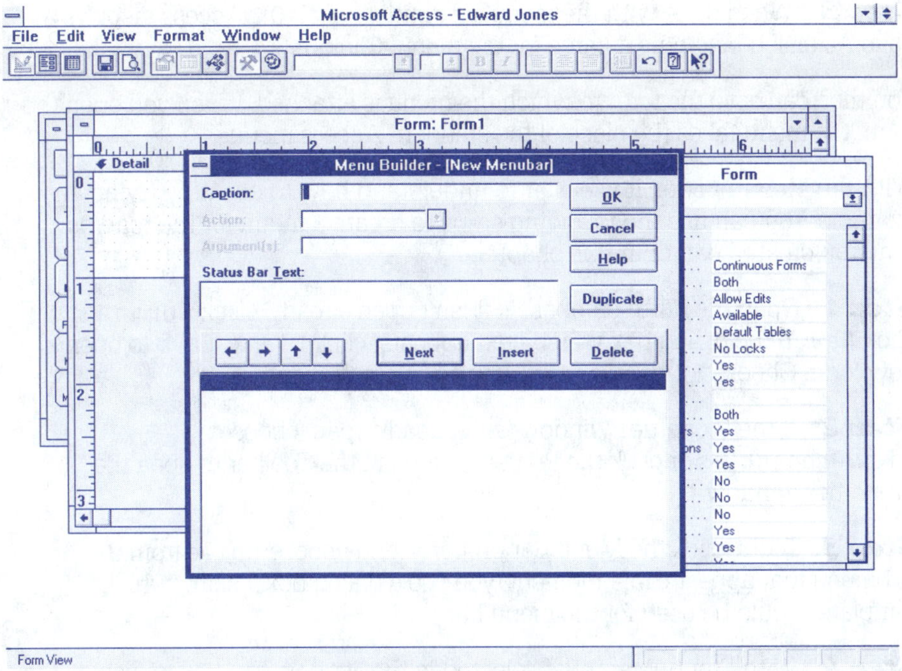

9-10
A Menu Builder dialog box for entering menus and actions..

In the Caption portion of the Menu Builder dialog box, you enter the menu name or the command name as you want it to appear on the menu bar. Under Action and Arguments, you enter the actions that you want the command to carry out, plus any appropriate arguments. In the Status Bar Text box, you can enter optional text that appears in the Status Bar when the menu option is highlighted.

The lower half of the dialog box shows all the menus and command that will appear on the menu bar. You can use the left and right arrows to indent and un-indent items as you add them, and you use the up and down arrows to move among the available menu items in the lower half of the dialog box. Items that are flush left in the dialog box will appear as menu items at the top of the menu bar. Items that are indented to one level will appear as choices underneath a menu; and items that are indented to two or more levels become submenus of the prior menu.

To define the menu, you perform these steps.

Step 1 Fill in the caption for a menu or a menu item in the Caption box, then click `Next`. Repeat this step for all menu items.

Step 2 Indent the items that are to represent commands on the menus. For each indented command, choose an action and fill in any needed arguments. The available menu actions are DoMenuItem (which runs a standard Access menu command), RunMacro (to run a macro), or RunCode (to run an Access Basic procedure).

Step 3 When done with the menu's definition, click `OK`. Access displays a Save As dialog box; type a name for the menu. Click `OK`.

You then can save the form to which the menu is attached. When you open the form, the menu takes the place of the standard Access menus.

An example of the use of the Menu Builder

With the Menu Builder, it is easier to understand how to use it by trying an example. You can use the following steps to create a menu for the macros that you created earlier in this chapter.

Step 1 Open the Earth database if it isn't open already. Click `Form`, then click `New`. In the dialog box which next appears, click `Blank Form` to open a new form. Choose `Edit/Select Form`, to select the form.

Step 2 If the Properties window isn't already open, choose `View/Properties` or click the Properties icon in the Toolbar to open the Properties window.

Step 3 Right-click the Menu Bar property, and choose `Build` from the submenu that appears. In a moment, you see a dialog box, asking which template should be used for the menu bar.

Step 4 With Empty Menu Bar selected in the list box, click `OK` to display the Menu Builder dialog box.

Step 5 In the Caption box, do the following steps: Enter `Records`, then click `Next`. Enter `Add/Edit Members`, then click `Next`. Enter `Add/Edit Donations`, then click `Next`. Enter `Printing`, then click `Next`. Enter `Print Members`, then click `Next`. Enter `Print Donations`, then click `Next`. Enter `Exit`, then click `Next`. Enter `Exit System`, then click `Next`.

Step 6 In the lower half of the dialog box, click `Add/Edit Members` to select it, then click the right-arrow button to indent it.

Step 7 Click `Add/Edit Donations` to select it, then click the right-arrow button to indent it.

Step 8 Click `Print Members` to select it, then click the right-arrow button to indent it.

Step 9 Click `Print Donations` to select it, then click the right-arrow button to indent it.

Step 10 Click `Exit System` to select it, then click the right-arrow button to indent it. At this point, your menu's design should resemble the one shown in FIG. 9-11.

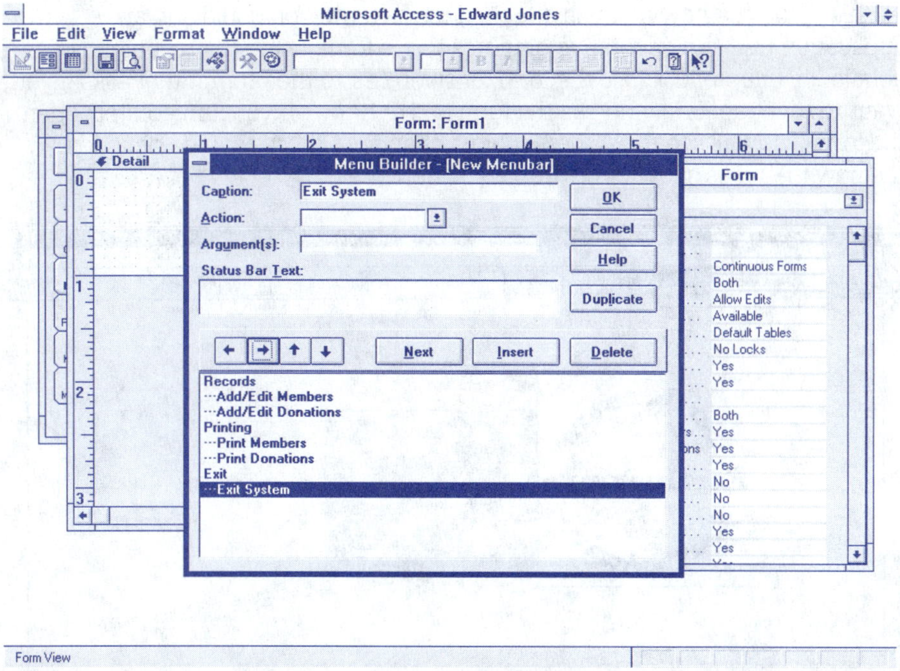

9-11
A Menu Builder dialog box with menu nqmes filled in.

The captions that you've added will create the menus and the choices for each of the menus. Now, perform the steps that follow to link those choices to the appropriate macros.

Step 1 In the lower half of the dialog box, click `Add/Edit Members` to select it. In the Action list box, choose `Run Macro`. Click in the Arguments text box, and enter `Add/Edit Members` as the name of the macro to run.

Step 2 Click `Add/Edit Donations` to select it. In the Action list box, choose `Run Macro`. Click in the Arguments text box, and enter `Add/Edit Donations` as the name of the macro to run.

Step 3 Click `Print Members` to select it. In the Action list box, choose `Run Macro`. Click in the Arguments text box, and enter `Print Members` as the name of the macro to run.

Step 4 Click `Print Donations` to select it. In the Action list box, choose `Run Macro`. Click in the Arguments text box, and enter `Print Donations` as the name of the macro to run.

Step 5 Click `Exit System` to select it. In the Action list box, choose `Run Macro`. Click in the Arguments text box, and enter `Exit System` as the name of the macro to run.

Step 6 Click `OK` in the dialog box. A Save As dialog box appears, asking for a name for the menu. Enter `Main Menu` in the Save As dialog box, then click `OK`.

At this point, the new menu is attached to the form. You could add an application title and decorative graphics to the form, using the techniques detailed in chapter 6. Close the form (answer `Yes` to the prompt that asks if you want to save the form, and call the form `Main Menu`). If you immediately open the form, you will see the Access menus change to those that are defined by the new menu, as shown in FIG. 9-12.

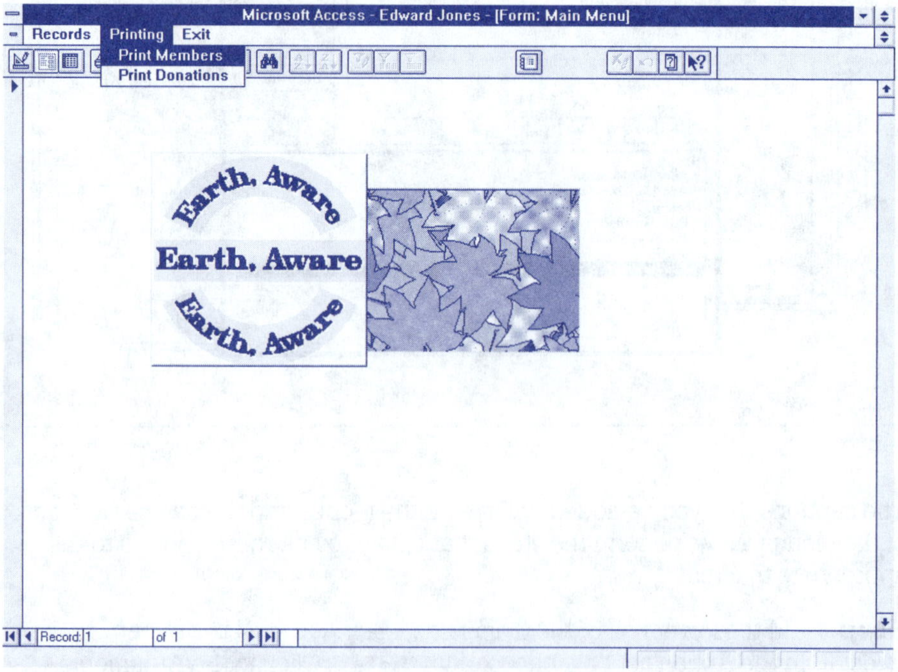

9-12
The results of the new menu design.

Creating custom dialog boxes

You also can use blank forms to create custom dialog boxes. These can be used to query your users for specific information that's needed at a given time. For example, often in printing reports, you might need to ask for criteria that will limit the records printed. As discussed in chapter 5, one way that you can do this by means of *parameter queries*, which cause a query, when run, to stop and ask the user for information. However, you might want dialog boxes with a more attractive appearance or more detailed explanations than can be provided by parameter queries. You can create forms that serve as dialog boxes, and the responses typed into those forms can be used within the action arguments of a macro.

The dialog boxes that you create should be *modal*, and *pop-up*. When you design the form, open the Properties window, and set the Pop-Up property to `Yes`, the Modal property to `Yes`, the Record Selectors property to `No`, the Navigation Buttons property to `No`, and the Scroll Bars property to `Neither`. Giving the form a modal property means that all other objects on the screen will be unavailable until you close the form, which is what normally is desired for a dialog box of any sort. Normally, you'll want to include one or more command buttons in the form with captions like `Print`, `OK`, or `Cancel`. You can use the following steps to create dialog boxes.

Step 1 Create the form that will serve as the dialog box. Using the techniques outlined in chapter 6, add the controls that will be needed in the dialog box.

Step 2 Create a new macro, and add the desired macro actions that will respond to the buttons in the dialog box. Save the macro.

Step 3 Open the form in design view, open the properties for the form, and in the OnPush property, type the name of the macro that should run.

As an example of a dialog box, consider the form shown in FIG. 9-13. This form serves as a dialog box that asks the user to enter a starting date and an ending date in preparation for running a report. Once the user enters the information and clicks on the `OK` button, the report is printed with records based on the range of dates provided.

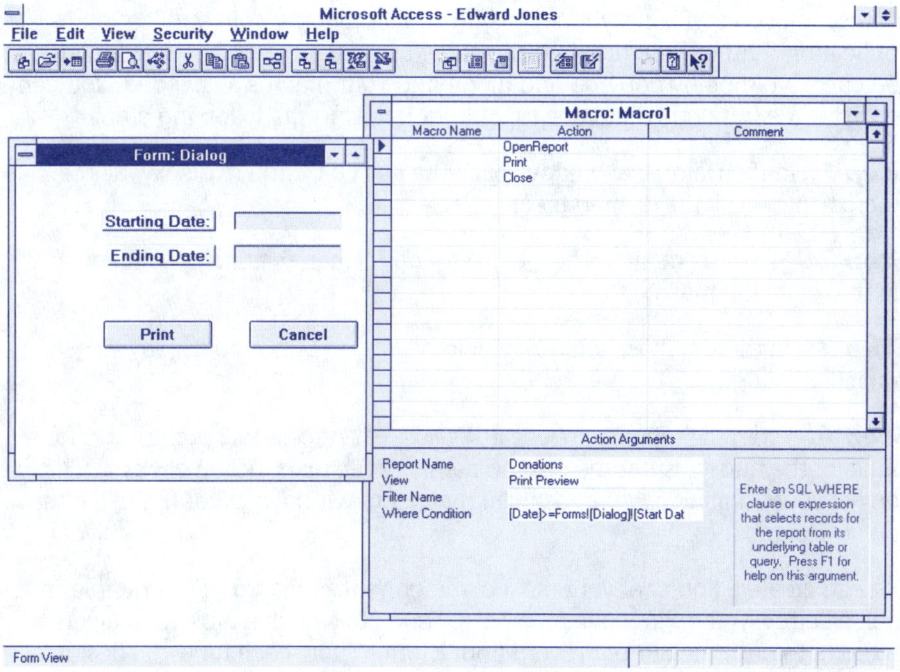

9-13
A dialog box and macro that print selected records.

The unbound text boxes that will contain the starting and ending dates typed by the user are named (in this example) Start Date and Ending Date, respectively. The desired macro name, "Print from Dialog," is entered In the OnPush property for the `Print` button; therefore, when this button is clicked, the macro named "Print Donations" executes. This macro also is visible in the figure. The macro actions contained in this macro are OpenReport, Print, and Close. Under the OpenReport macro action, a Where condition is specified that uses the values entered into the form. In this case, the Where condition stored in the macro is as follows:

```
[Date]>=Forms![Dialog]![Start Date] And [Date]<=Forms!
[Dialog]![Ending Date]
```

This condition is the key to obtaining the information from the dialog box. Once the user types the data into the dialog box and clicks `OK`, Access uses the information to set the condition in the report shown, and print the specific records.

You can activate the dialog box when needed with a OpenForm action in an appropriate macro. For example, a `Print` button on a switchboard might have an OpenForm action attached to it; the OpenForm action would open the dialog box you designed, and an `OK` button within the dialog box could call the actual report that then would be printed.

Copying macros to other databases

If it is your job to construct applications on a company-wide basis or for other clients, you soon will find yourself using similar macros from application to application. Rather than creating the same or similar macros over and over, you can save time by copying and modifying your macros as needed. You can copy macros from one database to another by using the following steps.

Step 1 In the Database window, click the `Macro` button to display all the macros, then click the desired macro to select it.

Step 2 From the menus, choose `Edit/Copy`. Open the database that you want to copy the macro into.

Step 3 In the Database window, click the `Macro` button to display all macros.

Step 4 From the menus, choose `Edit/Paste`. Access will prompt you for a name for the macro. Enter the desired name for the macro, then click `OK`. The copy of your original macro appears in the macro window, under the name that you've assigned.

You can create a library of your most commonly-used macros. For example, in such a library, you might have macros designed to search a table for a given record or to print the current record from a form. Then, each time you design a new application, you can copy macros from your library as needed to handle these common tasks in the new application.

part 3

The Access applications

10 Introduction to Access Basic

Relational databases that approach Access in terms of capability usually have built-in programming languages, and so does Access. The programming language built into Access is known as Access Basic, and it is similar in design to some other languages used by Microsoft products. In particular, users of Microsoft's Visual Basic and Word Basic (built into Word for Windows) will find Access Basic to be familiar. If you have developed applications using any of the xBASE dialects (like dBASE or FoxPro) or using the PAL language built into Borland's Paradox, you will find some aspects of programming in Access Basic to be similar. The major area in which Access Basic differs from programming in other database managers is that many tasks that require writing code can be handled in Access by the properties that are attached to an object or through the use of macros. As a result, programming in Access Basic tends to be used for specialized tasks. As is evident in the prior chapter, you can design and implement the average database application without writing a single line of code in Access Basic. However, for specialized tasks, such as custom user-defined functicns that can perform unique calculations or for jobs like dialing a phone through a modem, you'll need to resort to Access Basic.

Modules vs. procedures

Programs written in Access Basic are stored in *procedures*. One or more procedures can be stored in a *module*. Modules can be thought of as containers that hold your procedures, and you can think of the procedures as the programs themselves. In Access, you run your programs, or procedures, by attaching them to Access objects or by calling them as actions within macros. Users of xBASE dialects should note this significant difference between Access and the xBASE variants. In any dialect of xBASE, a program is a text file of sequential instructions, and you run the program with the DO command. If the program is the main menu for a complete application, the program governs how the application operates. In Access, the structure of the application is determined by macros (as outlined in the previous chapter), and your procedures are called by parts of the application as they are needed.

Creating a module

To create a module, in the Database window, click the `Module` button, then click `New`. Access opens a window containing the new module, similar to the example shown in FIG. 10-1.

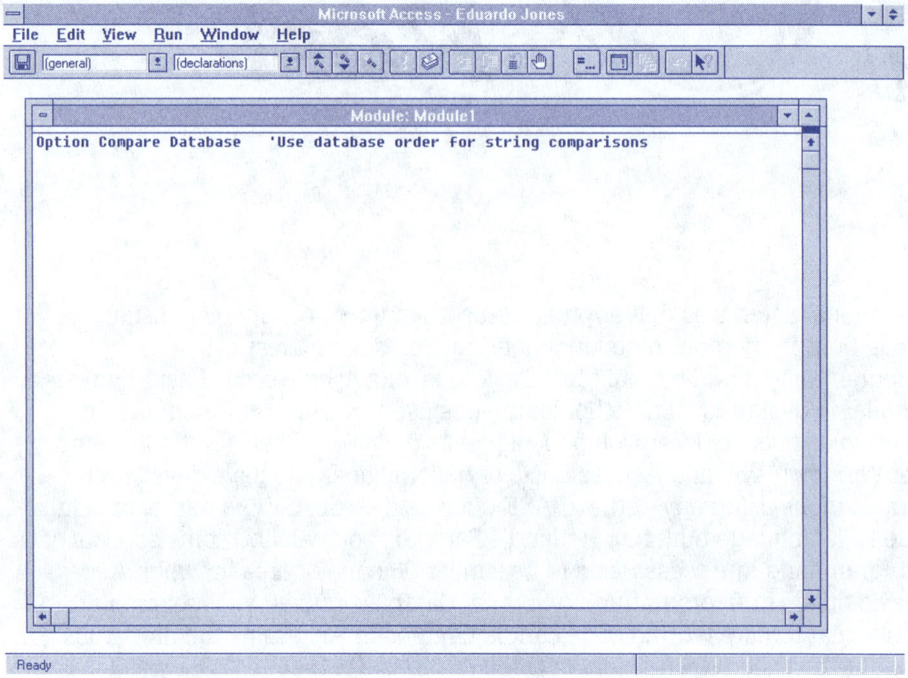

10-1
A new module in its window.

At the start of the module appears the *declaration section*. This section initially contains the declaration, "Option Compare Database - Use database order for string comparisons." You can leave this at its default value, or you can replace it with "Option Compare Text" (meaning text strings are compared without regard to upper or lower case) or with "Option Compare Binary" (meaning text strings are compared with binary values, so case is significant).

Viewing existing modules

You can open existing modules in a manner similar to that of opening other objects in Access; you click the desired button in the Database window (in this case,the `Module` button) to display all the modules. Then, click the desired module to select it, and click `Design` (or just double-click the desired module). The module opens in a window, and you see the declarations portion of the module.

As an example, if you open the CONTACTS.MDB database provided on the accompanying disk and hold the Shift key while opening the database, it will open without starting the Autoexec macro. Click the `Module` button in the Database window, and open the Dial My Number module that appears in the list (by selecting it and clicking the `Design` button), you see the declarations portion of this module, similar to the example shown earlier in FIG. 10-1.

Creating a procedure

Creating a new procedure is a simple matter, as Access automatically starts a new procedure when you begin typing in the module window. All procedures begin with `Sub` or with `Function`, followed by the name of the procedure and any optional arguments (surrounded by parenthesis) used by the procedure. (Procedure names can be up to 40 characters in length and must begin with a letter.) You type `Sub` or `Function` to indicate whether your procedure is a *sub procedure* or a *function procedure*. Function procedures are like the functions built into Access in that they return a value. Sub procedures do not return a value. Which type of procedure that you create depends entirely on what you want the procedure to accomplish. Sub procedures are called by function procedures. (You cannot use sub procedures in an expression elsewhere in Access.)

As soon as you type the first line of the procedure and press Enter, Access automatically places the line that you typed into a procedure window and adds an End Function statement two lines below your line of text, as shown in FIG. 10-2. You can type the text of your desired procedure between the Function and End Function statements (or between the Sub Function and End Sub statements).

If you want to begin another procedure within the same module, just start a new line past the End statement and type a new Function or a Sub statement. When you press Enter, Access will automatically place the new procedure you are typing on its separate page.

Examining existing procedures

While a module can contain multiple procedures, Access normally shows only one procedure in the module at a time. You can switch between multiple procedures of the same module by pressing the PgUp or PgDn keys, by choosing `View/Previous Procedure` and `View/Next Procedure` from the menus, or by clicking the `Previous Procedure` and `Next Procedure` buttons in the Toolbar.

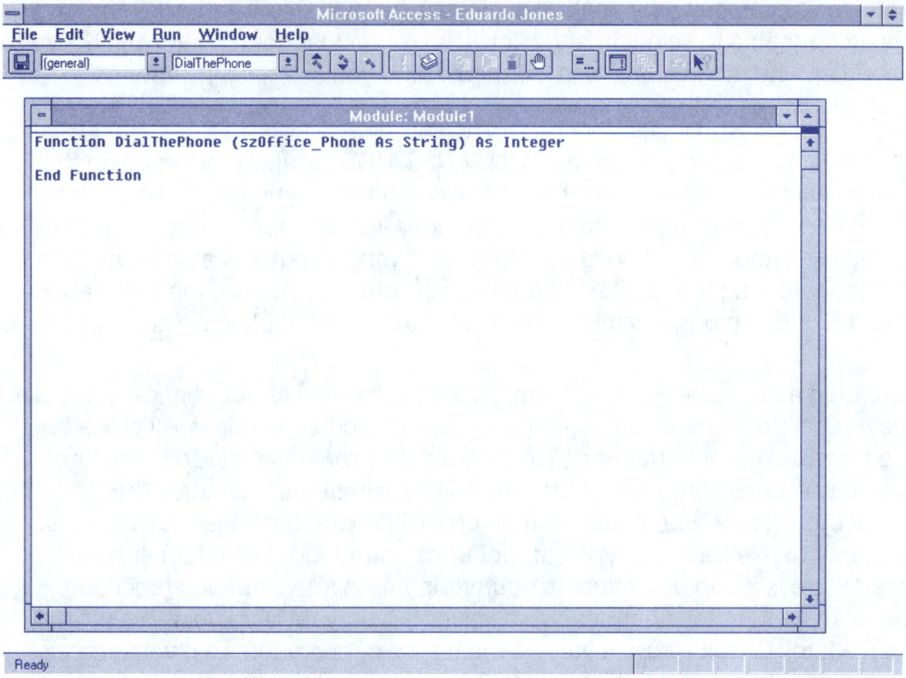

10-2 *The Function and End Function statements in procedure window.*

As an example, if you have opened the Dial My Number module as outlined earlier, press the PgDn key. You should see a procedure that begins with the line:

```
Function MyDialerOnPush (doOffice_Phone As String) As
Integer
```

as shown in FIG. 10-3. Because there is only one procedure in this module, continuing to press the PgDn key returns you to the declarations statement in the module window.

Using a procedure

Once you have saved your procedures, you can use them by attaching them to properties within forms or reports or to actions or conditions within macros. With forms and reports, you can specify the procedures by name in the same places where you would use one of the built-in Access functions. For example, if the Default Value property for a field of a given form contains the `Date()` function, you could replace that function with a custom function of your own design, called `BizDay()`, which might be designed to return the next business day closest to the current date.

In the case of macros, you can attach your procedures to macro actions. To run one of your procedures as a macro action, open the macro in Design view, click in the Action column and choose RunCode as the action, then under Action Arguments enter the name of the function in the Function Name argument.

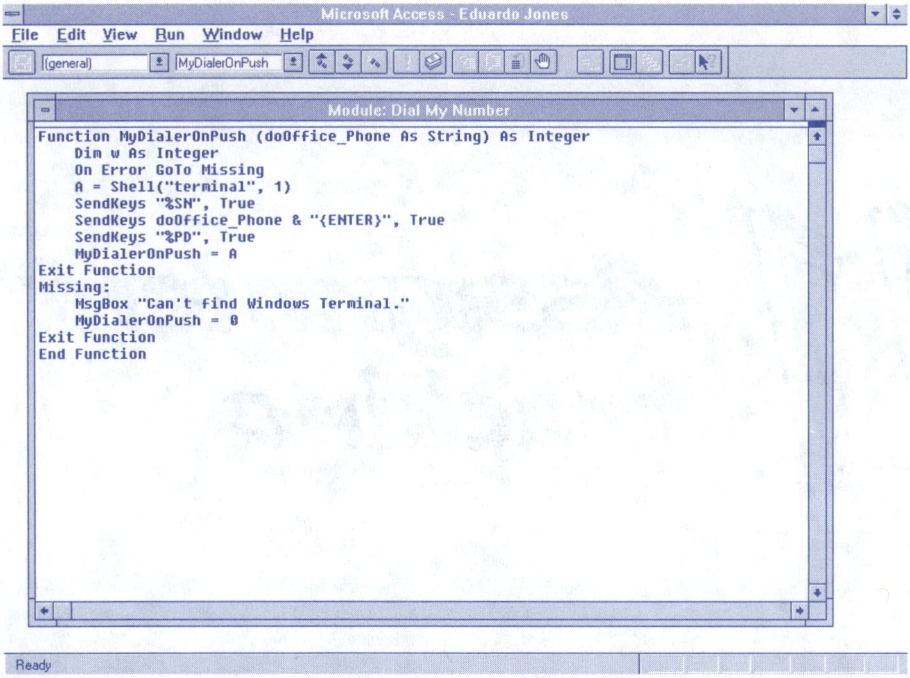

10-3
The Dial My Phone Procedure stored in CONTACTS database.

As an example of the use of a procedure, chapter 18 of this book attaches the procedure shown in FIG. 10-3 to a button on a form. (The form is named "Contacts," and the field containing the phone number to dial is named "Office Phone.") When pressed, the button dials the phone by using the Access Basic code stored in the procedure to send a set of keystrokes to the Windows Terminal program. In the button that is added to the form, the following expression is stored in the OnPush property for the button:

```
=MyDialerOnPush(Forms![Contacts]![Office Phone])
```

When the button is pushed, the value stored in the Office Phone field of the Contacts form is passed to the function. The function then uses the Shell function and the SendKeys function (both of which are built-in Access functions) to call the Windows Terminal program and to pass the keystrokes necessary to dial the phone using the Terminal program. For a complete description of how to create and use this procedure to dial a phone, refer to the step-by-step instructions in chapter 18.

Where to go from here

As mentioned earlier, this chapter is meant to serve as a brief introduction to Access Basic. Access Basic is a rich programming environment and to cover it in depth is the subject of a book in itself. The *Access Basic Reference* included with your Access documentation includes more details on programming in Access Basic. Other references, such as *Microsoft Access Programming* (which also is available from Windcrest), can teach you the specifics of programming in Access.)

11 Assignment tracking

Many corporate settings require the tracking of assignments given to various employees; this task commonly arises within architectural or engineering firms, law firms, consultant agencies, and other organizations that assign teams of individuals to handle a particular client's project. (A similar requirement for such organizations is the management of time and billing. See chapter 13 for details on how you can build an application that manages time and billing.) The files used by the Assignment Tracking System presented in this chapter can be found on the accompanying disk in the TRACKING database; use the Windows File Manager or DOS commands to copy this database into your Microsoft Access directory. Figure 11-1 shows the appearance of the main menu for the Assignment Tracking System.

By intent, this application is the least complex of all those presented within Part 3 of this book. If you are new to Access and to applications design, you might want to consider working through the steps outlined to create this application from scratch. By doing so, you will become more familiar with the techniques that you can use in implementing your own database applications.

Creating the database & tables

The Assignment Tracking System requires two tables: one named Staff and another named Assignments. The Staff table contains a record with the vital statistics for each employee. It is assigned a key field called Social Security, which serves to provide a unique identifier for every employee. The

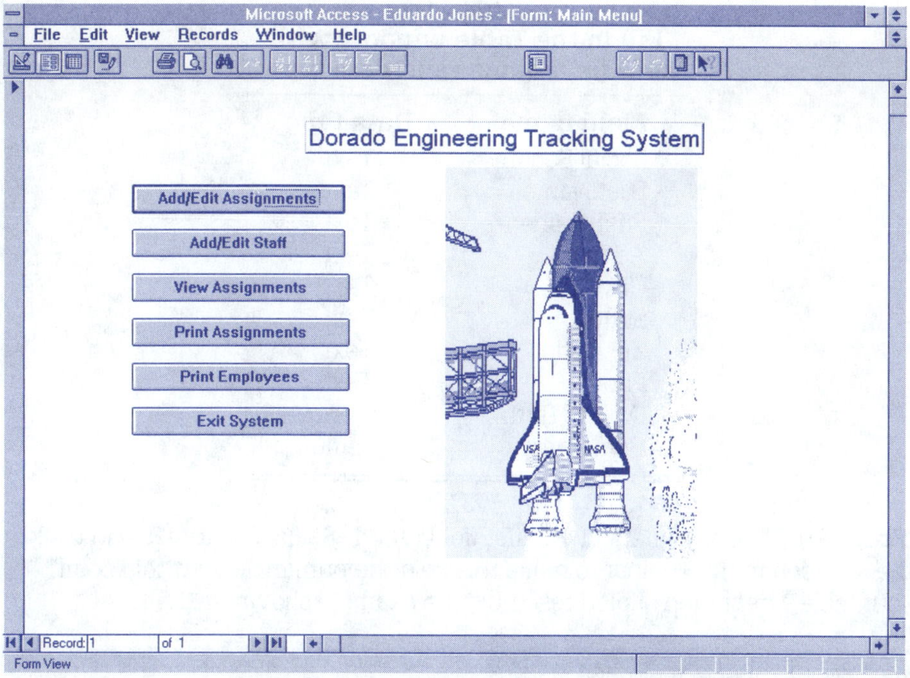

11-1
The Main menu for the Assignment Tracking database.

Assignments table contains the details of the assignments as they are given to the employees. Because each employee might have a number of assignments over a period of time, there is no unique aspect of the records in the Assignment table, so a counter field has been added to the end of the table to provide a key field. To create the database and its required tables, first start Access in the usual manner, then perform the following steps.

Step 1 Choose `File/New Database` to open the New Database dialog box. (If you want to store the new database in a different directory, use the Directory list box to locate the desired directory now. Click on the desired directory, and Access will store the new database in that directory.)

Step 2 Enter `TRACKING` in the File Name text box as a name for the database, then click `OK`. (remember, in Access, database names must be 8 characters or less, with no spaces.) Access creates the database file on your hard disk, and the Database window appears, as shown in FIG. 11-2.

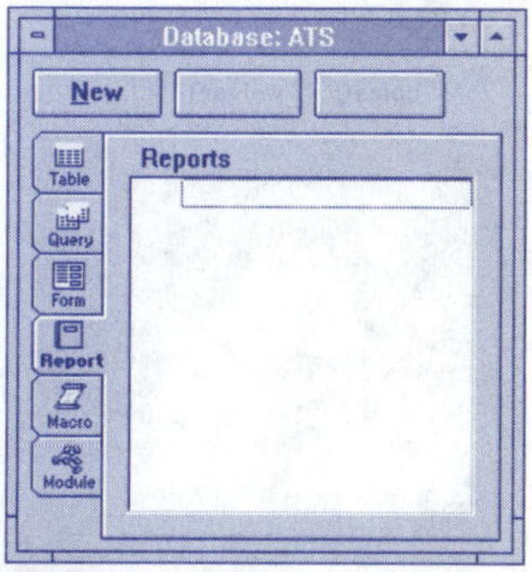

11-2
The Database window.

Step 3 In the Database window, click the `Table` button, then click `New`. In the New Table dialog box that appears, click `New Table`. The Table window appears. Fill in the Table window with the field names and data types for the fields shown in TABLE 11-1.

Table 11-1
Fill in the Table window with these field names and data types.

Field name	Data type
Social Security	Text
Last Name	Text
First Name	Text
Address	Text
City	Text
State	Text
ZIP Code	Text
Phone	Text
Date of Birth	Date/Time
Comments	Memo

Step 4 Click anywhere in the first field (titled "Social Security"), and click the Key icon in the Toolbar to make this field the primary key. At this point, your table's definition should resemble the example shown in FIG. 11-3.

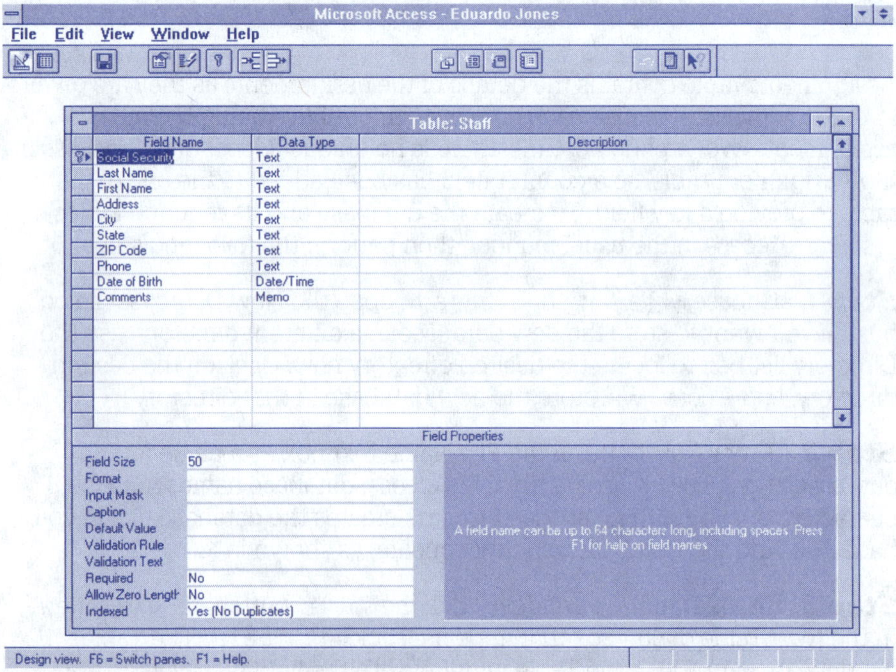

11-3
The completed definition of the Staff table.

Step 5 When you are done defining the fields, choose `File/Save` to save the table. When prompted for a table name, enter `Staff` as the name and click `OK`. Press Ctrl–F4 to close the Table window. The new table, Staff, now appears in the Database window.

Step 6 In the Database window, again click `New`. In the New Table dialog box that appears, click `New Table`. The Table window again appears. Fill in the Table window with the field names and data types for the fields shown in TABLE 11-2.

Table 11-2
Fill in the Table window with these field names and data types.

Field name	Data type
Social Security	Text
Date Assigned	Date/Time
Date Due	Date/Time
Hours Projected	Number
Client	Text
Matter	Text
Task Description	Text
In Charge	Text
Completed?	Yes/No
Completed When	Date/Time
Evaluation	Memo
Comments	Memo
Record ID	Counter

Step 7 While the insertion pointer is within the last field (titled "Record ID"), click the Key icon in the Toolbar to make this field the primary key. At this point, your table's definition should resemble the example shown in FIG. 11-4.

Step 8 When you are done defining the fields, choose `File/Save` to save the table. When prompted for a table name, enter `Assignments` as the name and click `OK`. Press Ctrl–F4 to close the Table window. The new table, Assignments, now appears in the Database window.

If you haven't copied the database from the disk provided with this book, you will need to enter data into the completed tables. You can use the sample data provided on the disk or enter data of your own choosing. (See chapter 4 for more details on adding data to a table).

Creating the forms

The database will require three forms: one will be used for adding new employees, the second will be used for adding new assignments, and the third will provide a means of viewing each employee with his or her related assignments. To create the needed forms, perform the following steps.

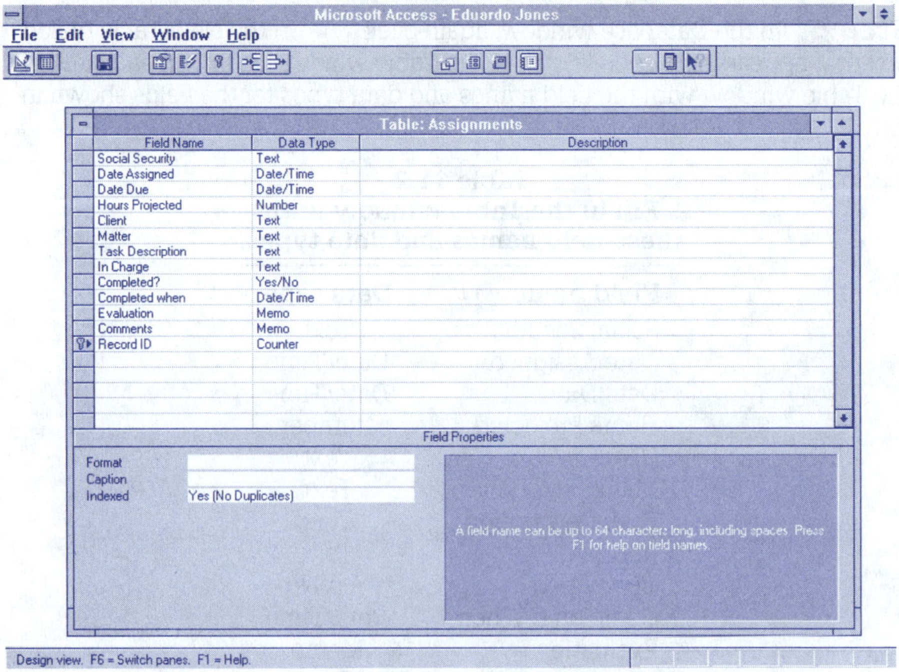

11-4 *The completed definition of the Assignment table.*

Step 1 In the Database window, click the `Form` button, then click `New`. The New Form dialog box appears, as shown in FIG. 11-5. Click the arrow under Select a Table/Query to choose the desired table, and click on Assignments in the drop-down list. Click the `FormWizards` button. In a moment, Access displays a dialog box asking you to choose the desired wizard, as shown in FIG. 11-6. With Single-column already selected, click `OK`.

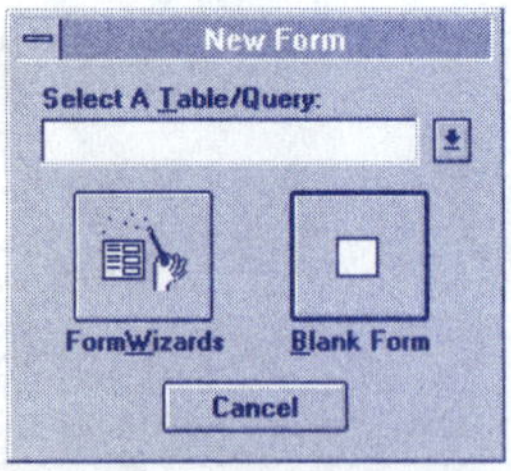

11-5 *The New Form dialog box.*

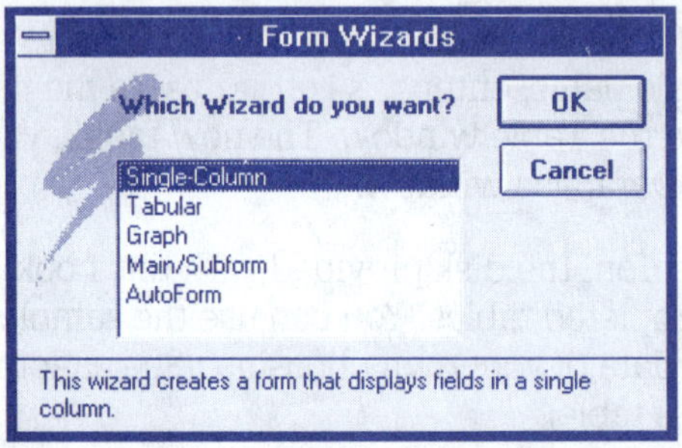

11-6 *The FormWizard dialog box.*

Step 2 The next dialog box to appear (FIG. 11-7) asks which fields you want selected on the form. Click the double-angle bracket button (`>>`) to place all available fields on the form, then click `Next`.

Step 3 The next dialog box to appear asks what kind of look you want for the form. Click `Shadowed`, then click `Next`.

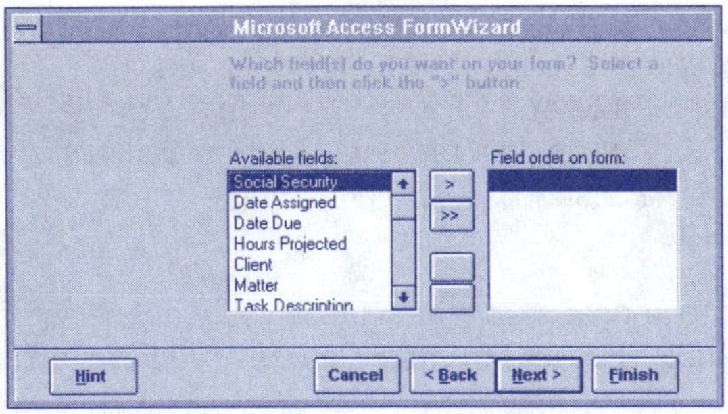

11-7
A dialog box to select the desired fields.

Step 4 The next dialog box to appear asks for a title for the form. By default, the title `Assignments` appears in the text box. Click the `Open` button to accept the title and open the form. Your new form should resemble the example shown in FIG. 11-8.

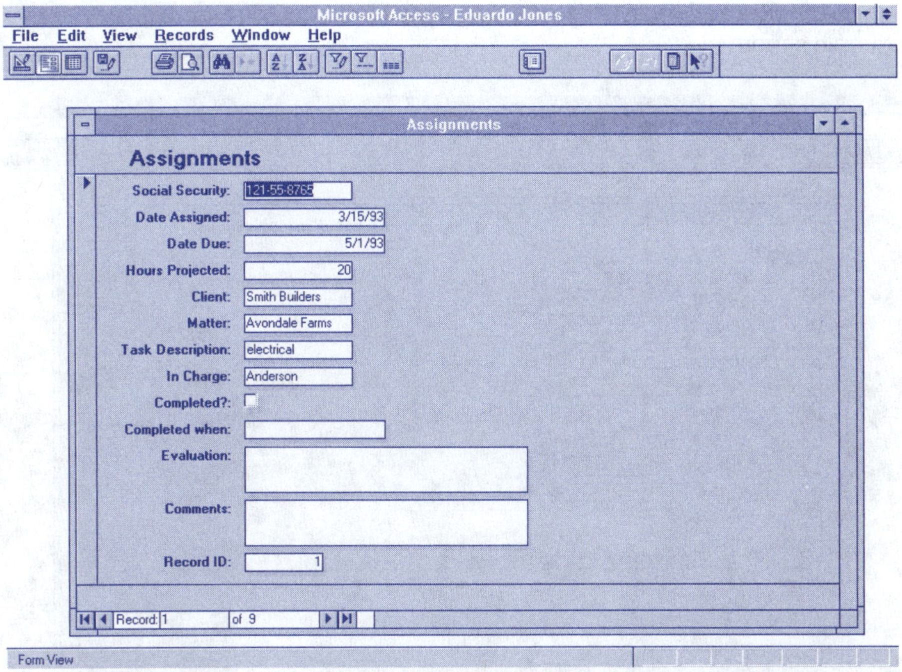

11-8
The completed form for the Assignments table.

At this point, you could add data; however, the other two forms still must be created for later use. Press Ctrl–F4 to close the new form (click `Yes` in the dialog box that appears asking if you want to save your changes to the form). When prompted for a name, enter `Assignments` as the name for the form and click `OK`. Next, perform the following steps to create the form needed for the employees.

Step 1 In the Database window, with the `Form` button still selected, click `New`. The New Form dialog box appears. Click the arrow under Select a Table/Query to choose the desired table, and click on `Staff` in the drop-down list. Click the `FormWizards` button. In a moment, Access displays a dialog box asking you to choose the desired wizard. With Single-column already selected, click `OK`.

Step 2 The next dialog box to appear asks which fields you want selected on the form. Click the double-angle bracket button (`>>`), to place all available fields on the form, then click `Next`.

Step 3 The next dialog box to appear asks what kind of look you want for the form. Click `Shadowed`, then click `Next`.

Step 4 The next dialog box to appear asks for a title for the form. By default, the title `Staff` appears in the text box. Click the `Open` button to accept the title and open the form. Your new form should resemble the example shown in FIG. 11-9.

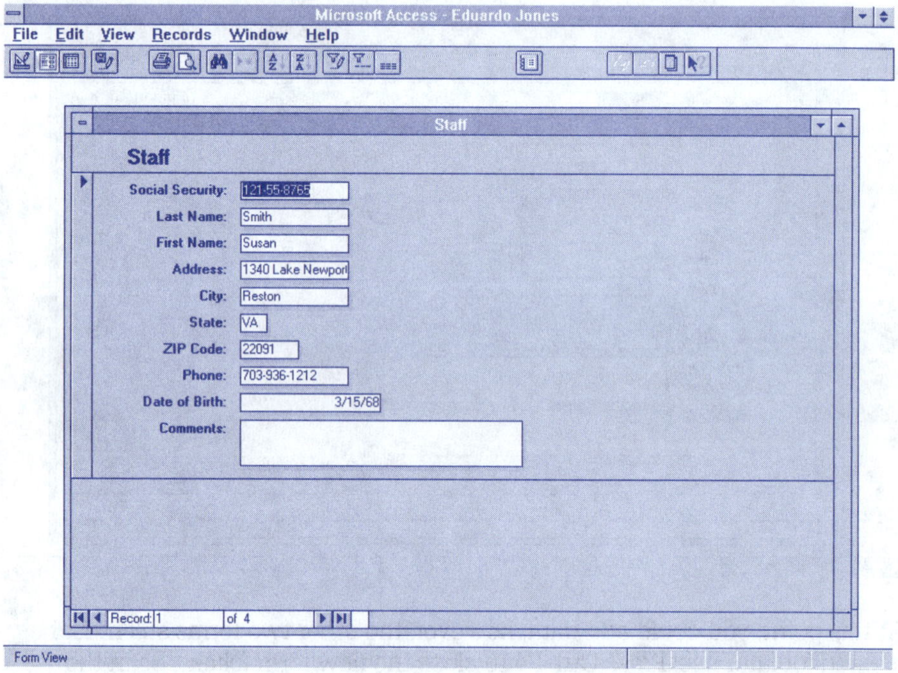

11-9 *The completed form for the Staff table.*

This form will be used for the addition of employees, but one form remains to be created. Press Ctrl–F4 to close the new form (click `Yes` in the dialog box that appears asking if you want to save your changes to the form). When prompted for a name, enter `Staff` as the name for the form and click `OK`. Next, perform the following steps to create the form needed for viewing each employee's assignments.

Step 1 In the Database window, with the `Form` button still selected, click `New`. The New Form dialog box appears. Click the arrow under Select a Table/Query to choose the desired table, and choose `Staff` from the drop-down list. Click the `FormWizards` button. In a moment, Access displays a dialog box asking you to choose the desired wizard. Click `Main/Subform`, then click `OK`. The next dialog box to appear (FIG. 11-10) asks which table contains the data for the subform. Click `Assignments`, then click `Next`.

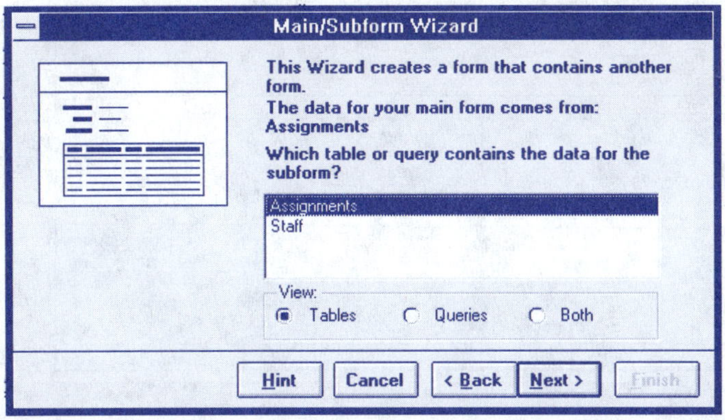

11-10
A dialog box to identify a table for a subform.

Step 2 The next dialog box to appear asks which fields you want to add to the main form. Double-click the First Name field to add it to the main form, then double-click the Last Name field to add it to the main form. Then, click `Next`.

Step 3 The next dialog box to appear asks which fields you want to include on the subform. Double-click each of the following fields to add them to the form: Date Assigned, Date Due, Hours Projected, Client, Task Description, and Completed When. Then, click `Next`.

Step 4 The next dialog box to appear asks what kind of look you want for the form. Click `Shadowed`, then click `Next`.

Step 5 The next dialog box to appear asks for a title for the form. By default, the title `Staff` appears in the text box. Type `View Assignments` in the form title text box now, then click the `Open` button to accept the title and open the form. Access will display a dialog box warning you that you must save the subform before saving the main form; click `OK` in this dialog box. In the Save As dialog box that next appears, enter `View Assignments` as a title and click `OK`. Your new form should resemble the example shown in FIG. 11-11.

Step 6 Press Ctrl–F4 to close the new form (click `Yes` in the dialog box that appears asking if you want to save the form). When prompted for a name, enter `Edit Assignments` as the name for the form.

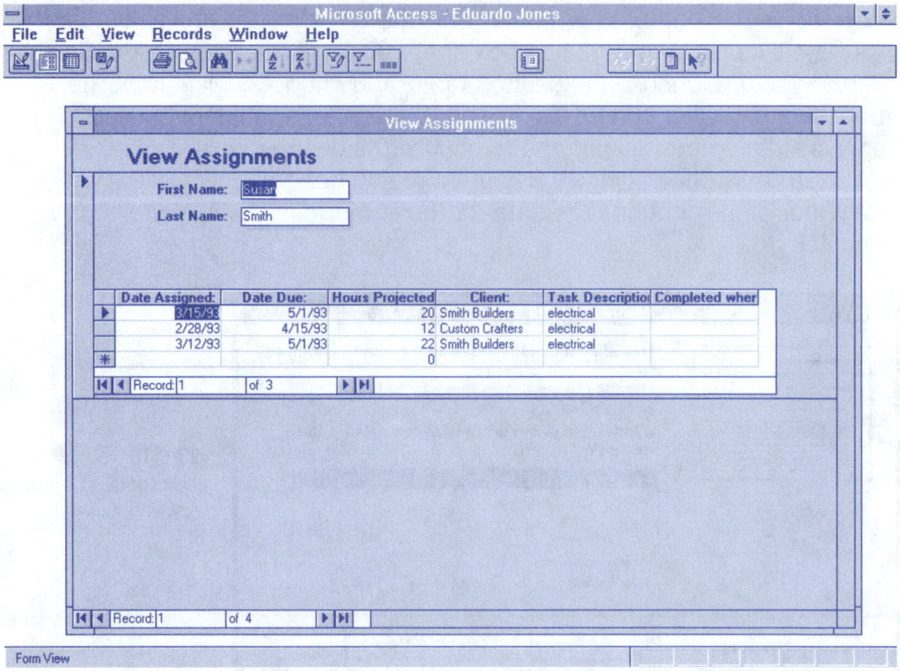

11-11
A completed form for viewing assignments.

Creating the relational query

To support the reports used by the Assignment Tracking application, a relational query will be needed. Perform the following steps to create the query.

Step 1 In the Database window, click the `Query` button, then click `New`. In the New Query dialog box which appears, click `New Query`. The Add Table dialog box appears, as shown in FIG. 11-12.

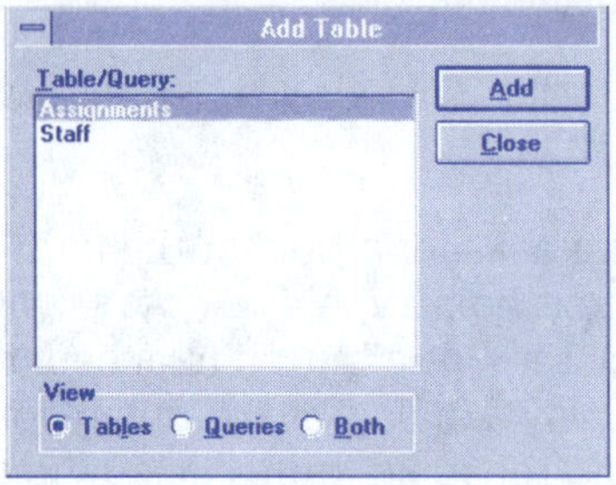

11-12
The Add Table dialog box.

Step 2 In the Table/Query list box, click `Assignments`, then click `Add`. Next, click `Staff`, then click `Add` again. Finally, click `Close`. This causes the list boxes with the fields from both tables to appear in the Select Query window, as shown in FIG. 11-13.

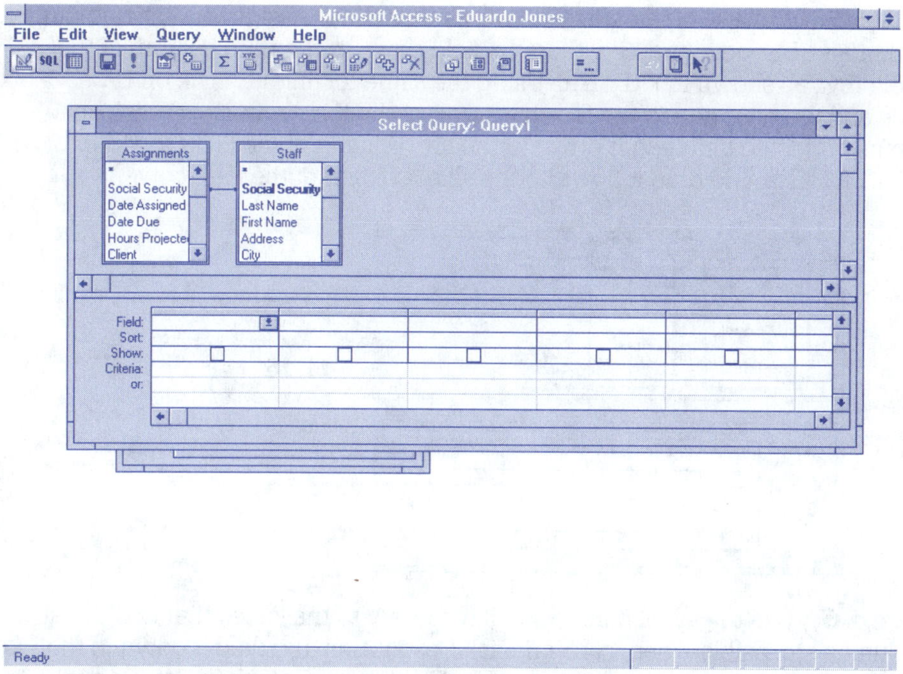

11-13
The Select Query window with list boxes for the Assignments and Staff tables.

Step 3 If a line automatically appears between the Social Security fields of both tables, skip to the next step. If a line does not appear between the fields, then in the Assignments list box, click the Social Security field. While holding the mouse button depressed, drag over to the Social Security field within the Staff list box. (In earlier versions of Access, this step establishes the relationship between the tables; in version 2.0, the relationship is automatically established.)

Step 4 In the Staff list box, click on Last Name. While holding the mouse button depressed, drag the field down to the first column of the Field row, as shown in FIG. 11-14. Using the same technique, click on First Name and drag it down to the second column of the Field row.

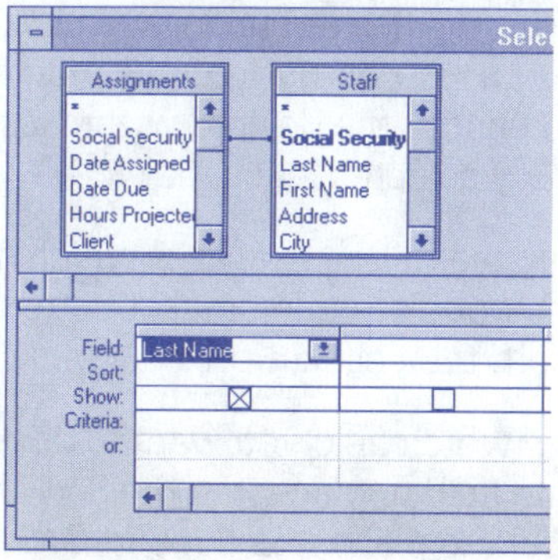

11-14
Selection of Last Name field.

Step 5 In the Assignments list box, click on Date Assigned. While holding the mouse button depressed, drag the field down to the third column of the Field row, as shown in FIG. 11-15. Using the same technique, click on Date Due and drag it down to the fourth column of the Field row. Next, click on Hours Projected and drag it down to the fifth column of the Field row. Next, click on Client and drag it down to the sixth column of the Field row.

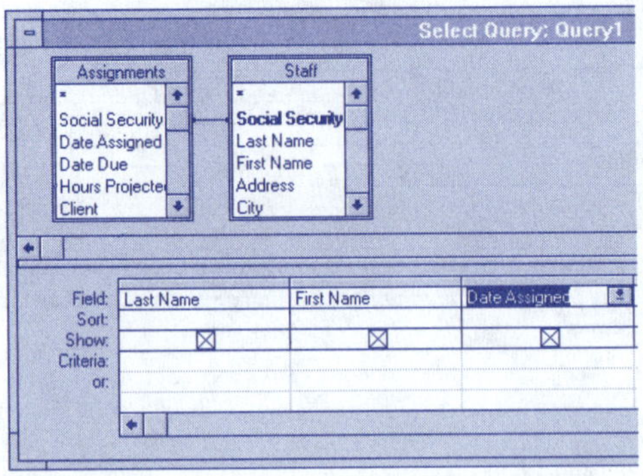

11-15 *Selection of Date Assigned field.*

Step 6 Use the scroll bars to scroll the query to the left so that additional columns are visible. Then, click on Task Description and drag it down to the next empty column of the Field row. Finally, click on Completed When and drag it down to the next empty column of the Field row. Choose `File/Save`. Access will prompt you for a name for the query; enter `Relational Tracking` and click `OK`.

Step 7 Press Ctrl–F4 to close the Select Query window. The new query appears by name in the Database window,

Creating the reports

Two reports are needed for the application. One will list the statistics for each staff member; the other will list assignments grouped by staff members. Perform the following steps to create the reports.

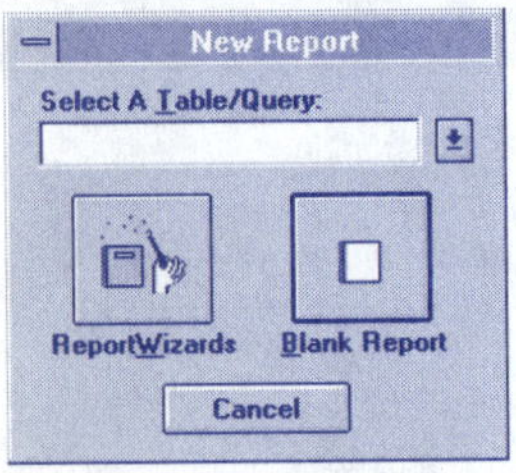

11-16 *The New Report dialog box.*

Step 1 In the Database window, click the `Report` button, then click `New`. The New Report dialog box appears, as shown in FIG. 11-16. Click the arrow under Select a Table/Query to choose the desired table, and click `Staff` in the drop-down list. Click the `ReportWizards` button. In a moment, Access displays a dialog box asking you to choose the desired wizard, as shown in FIG. 11-17. With Single-column already selected, click `OK`.

Step 2 The next dialog box to appear (FIG. 11-18) asks which fields you want placed on the report. Click the double-angle bracket button (`>>`) to place all available fields on the report, then click `Next`.

Step 3 The next dialog box asks which field you want to use to sort the data by. Double-click the Last Name field to place it in the Sort Order box, then double-click the First Name field to place it in the Sort Order box. Finally, click `Next`.

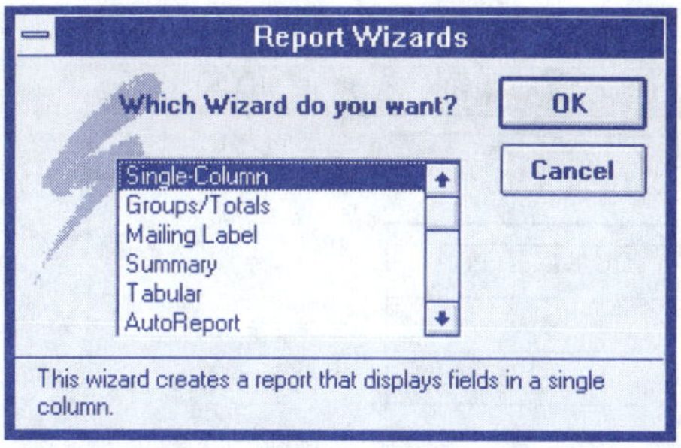

11-17
The ReportWizard dialog box.

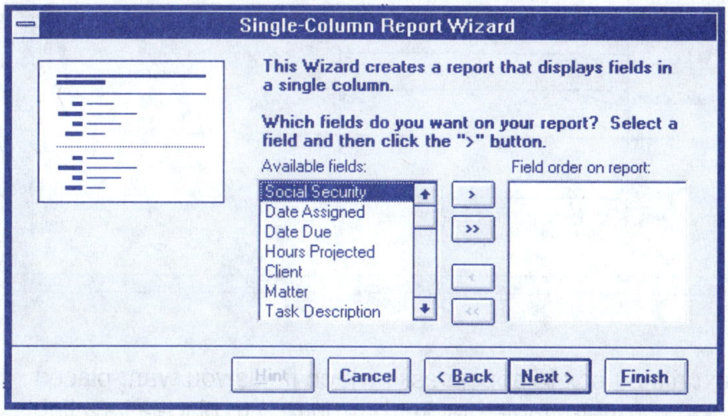

11-18
A dialog box to select the desired fields.

Step 4 The next dialog box to appear asks what kind of look you want for the report. Click `Ledger`, then click `Next`.

Step 5 The next dialog box to appear asks for a title for the form. By default, the title `Staff` appears in the text box. Click the `Print Preview` button to accept the title and display the report. If you are using the sample data from the disk, your new report should resemble the example shown in FIG. 11-19. Choose `File/Save` to save the new report. When prompted for a title, enter `Staff Listing` for a report name, then click `OK`.

Step 6 Press Ctrl–F4 to close the new report.

Next, perform the following steps to create the report needed for the assignments.

Step 1 In the Database window, with the `Report` button still selected, click `New`. The New Report dialog box appears. Click the arrow under Select a Table/Query to choose the desired table, and click `Relational Tracking` in the drop-down list. Click the `ReportWizards` button. In a moment, Access displays a dialog box asking you to choose the desired wizard. Click `Groups/Totals`, then click `OK`.

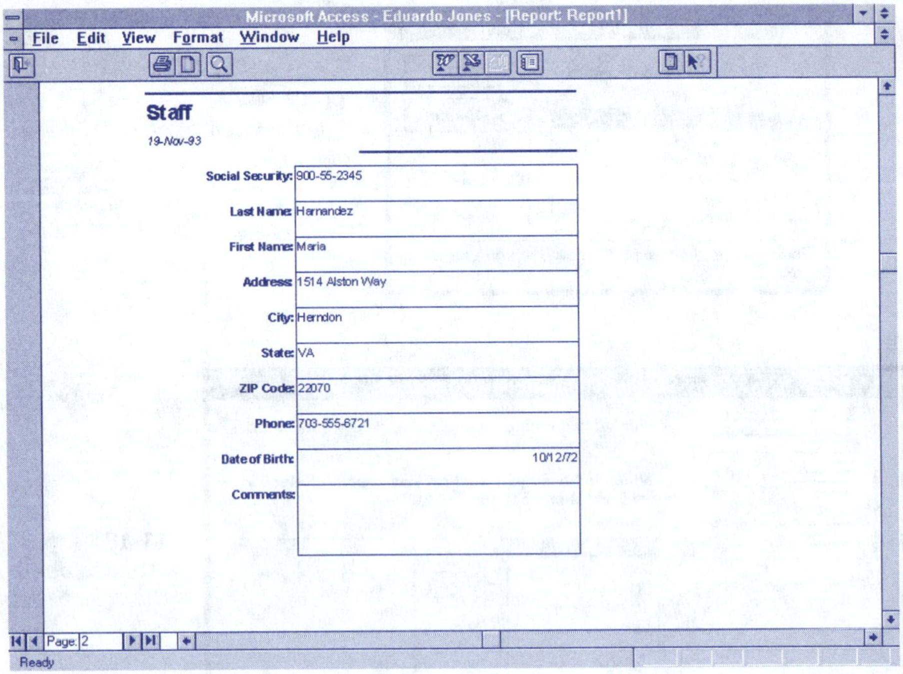

11-19
A completed Report for the Staff table.

Step 2 The next dialog box to appear asks which fields you want placed on the report. Click the double-angle bracket button (>>) to place all available fields on the report, then click `Next`.

Step 3 The next dialog box to appear asks which fields you want to group the report by. Double-click the Date Due field, then click `Next`. In the next dialog box which appears, you are asked whether the dates should be grouped normally, or by year, quarter, month, week, or day. With the default of `Normal` selected, click `Next`.

Step 4 The next dialog box asks which field you want to use to sort the data by. Double-click the Last Name field to place it in the Sort Order box, then double-click the First Name field to place it in the Sort Order box. Finally, click `Next`.

Step 5 The next dialog box to appear asks what kind of look you want for the report. Click `Ledger`, then click `Next`.

Step 6 The next dialog box to appear asks for a title for the report. By default, the title `Relational Tracking` appears in the text box. Click the `Print Preview` button to accept the title and display the report. If you are using the sample data supplied on the disk, your new report should resemble the example shown in FIG. 11-20. Choose `File/Save` to save the new report. When prompted for a title, enter `Relational Tracking` for a report name, then click `OK`.

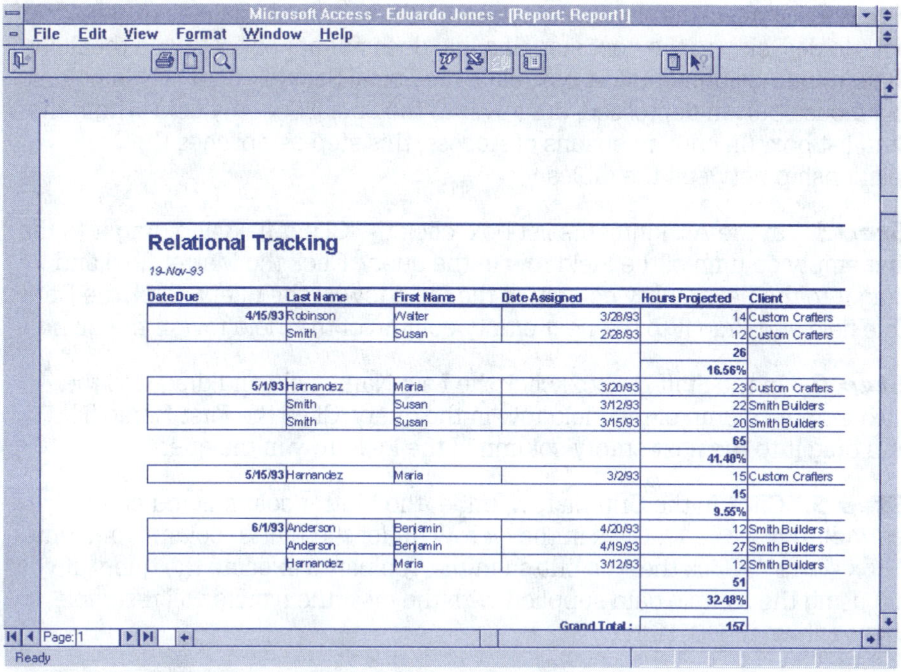

11-20
A completed Relational Report.

Step 7 Press Ctrl–F4 to close the new report.

Adding & editing data

Before you can experiment with queries and reporting, you will need to add data to the tables in the Tracking System database. You can use the files that are on the disk provided with this book, or you can enter your own examples of data.

To add new employees, click the `Form` button in the Database window, then click `Staff`, then click `Open`, and enter the new records as desired. To add new assignments for an employee, click the `Form` button in the Database window, then click `Assignments`, then click `Open`. For additional details on adding data to a table, refer to chapter 4.

An example query

As one example of data that might be needed from this database, perhaps a manager needs to know the due dates for all assignments at two housing developments named Woodburn Lakes and Fox Farm. The following steps would provide the needed query.

Step 1 Click the `Query` button in the Database window, then click `New`. When the New Query dialog box appears, click `New Query`. The Add Table dialog box appears. Click `Assignments`, then click `Add`. Next, click `Staff`, then click `Add`. Finally, click `Close`.

Step 2 If a line automatically appears between the Social Security fields of both tables, skip to the next step. If a line does not appear between the fields, then in the Assignments list box, click the Social Security field. While holding the mouse button depressed, drag over to the Social Security field within the Staff list box. (In earlier versions of Access, this step establishes the relationship between the tables.)

Step 3 In the Assignments list box, click the Client field and drag it to the first empty column of the Field row in the query. Click the Matter field and drag it to the next empty column of the Field row in the query. Click the Date Due field and drag it to the next empty column of the Field row in the query.

Step 4 In the Staff list box, click the Last Name field and drag it to the next empty column of the Field row in the query. Click the First Name field and drag it to the next empty column of the Field row in the query.

Step 5 Click in the Criteria row, under the Matter column, and enter `"Woodburn Lakes"`. Click in the Or row under the Matter column, and enter `"Fox Farm"`. Click the `Run` button in the Toolbar to execute the query. If you are using the sample data supplied with the disk, the results will resemble those shown in FIG. 11-21.

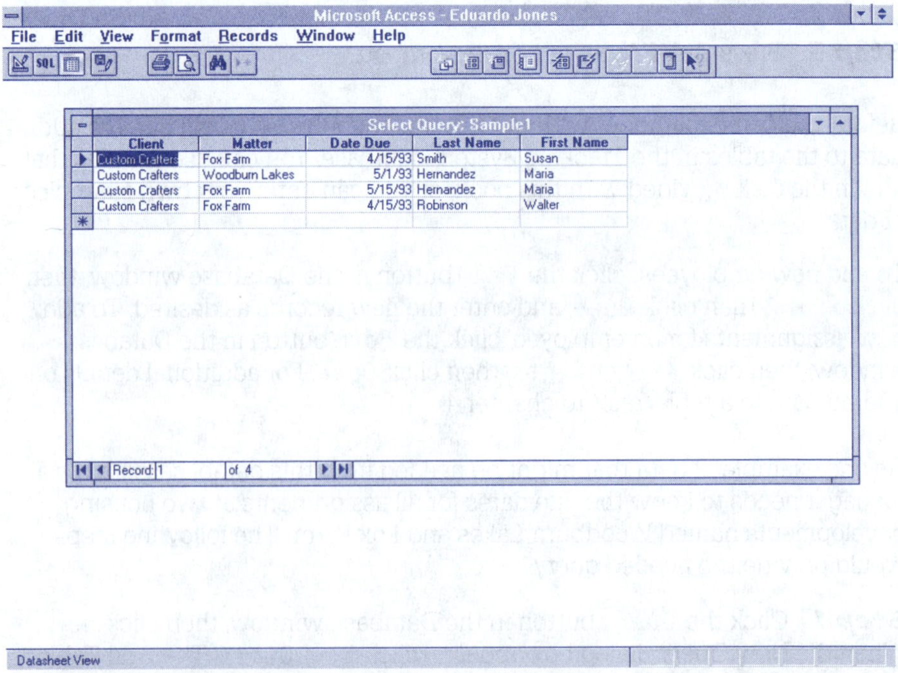

11-21
A sample query.

When you are done with the query, double-click the Close box of the Query window to close it. You can answer `No` to the prompt that asks if you wish to save the query, as it will not be needed for the application.

Developing the application

The application requires a series of macros that provide the menu choices for performing database operations and the actions that should occur in response to those menu choices. Perform the following steps to create the macros required for the application.

Perform the following steps to create the macro for adding and editing the records in the staff table.

Step 1 In the Database window, click the `Macro` button, then click `New`. Move and resize the macro window that appears so that you can see both the Database window and the Macro window at the same time. Click the `Form` button, then click on `Staff` in the list box and drag it over to the first column under Action in the macro window. As a result, OpenForm appears in the Action column with the form name (Staff) shown in the Action Arguments portion of the macro window, as shown in FIG. 11-22.

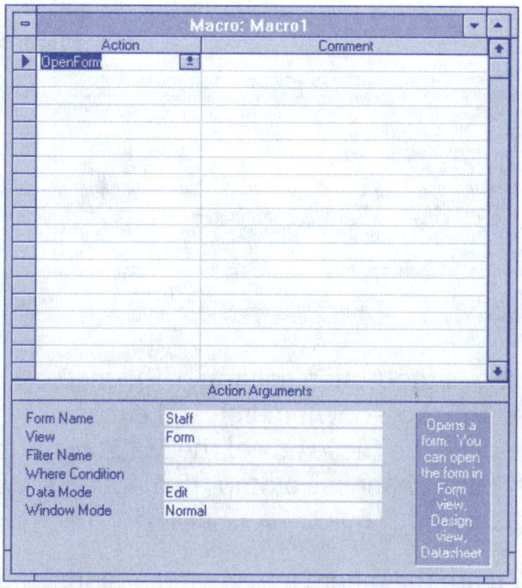

11-22
A macro for adding and editing records to the Staff table.

Step 2 Click in the second line of the Action column of the macro window. Click the arrow to open the drop-down menu, and choose `Maximize` from the list. Double-click the Close box of the Macro window. Answer `Yes` in response to the "Save changes" prompt that appears. When prompted for a name, call the macro `Add/Edit Staff`.

Perform the following steps to create the macro for adding and editing records to the assignment table.

Step 1 In the Database window, click the `Macro` button, then click `New`. Move and resize the macro window that appears so that you can see both the Database window and the Macro window at the same time. Click the `Form` button, then click on `Assignments` in the list box and drag it over to the first column under Action in the macro window. As a result, OpenForm appears in the Action column, with the form name (Assignments) shown in the Action Arguments portion of the macro window, as shown in FIG. 11-23.

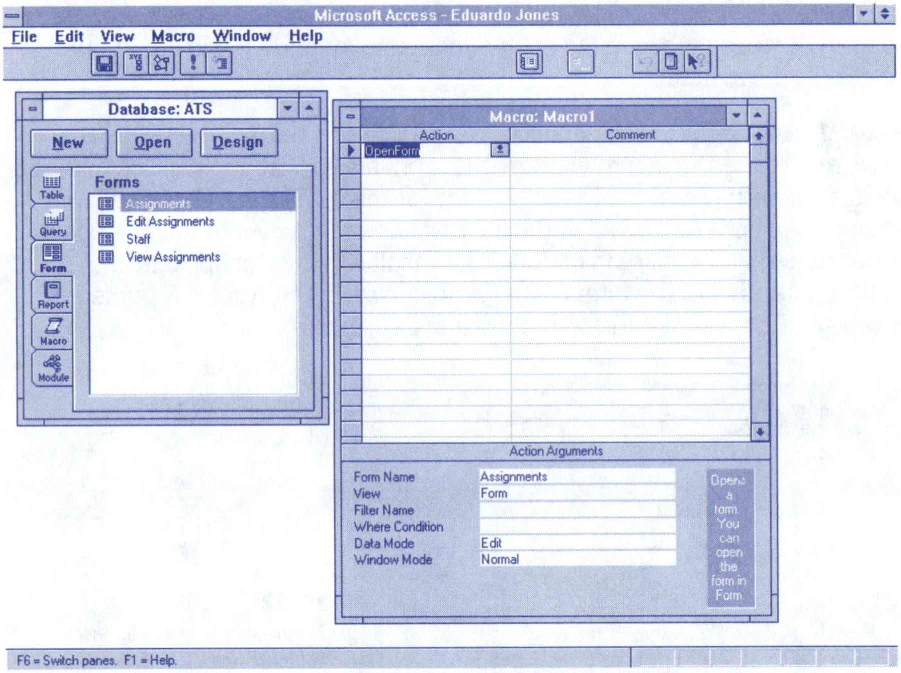

11-23
A macro for adding and editing records to the Assignment table.

Step 2 Click in the second line of the Action column of the macro window. Click the arrow to open the drop-down menu, and choose `Maximize` from the list. Double-click the Close box of the Macro window. Answer `Yes` in response to the "Save changes" prompt that appears. When prompted for a name, call the macro `Add/Edit Assignments`.

Perform the following steps to create the macro for viewing assignments for an employee.

Step 1 In the Database window, click the `Macro` button, then click `New`. Move and resize the macro window that appears so that you can see both the Database window and the Macro window at the same time. Click the `Form` button, then click on `Edit Assignments` in the list box and drag it over to the first column under Action in the macro window. As a result, OpenForm appears in the Action column, with the form name (Edit Assignments) shown in the Action Arguments portion of the macro window.

Step 2 Click in the second line of the Action column of the macro window. Click the arrow to open the drop-down menu, and choose `Maximize` from the list. At this point, your macro should resemble the example shown in FIG. 11-24. Double-click the Close box of the Macro

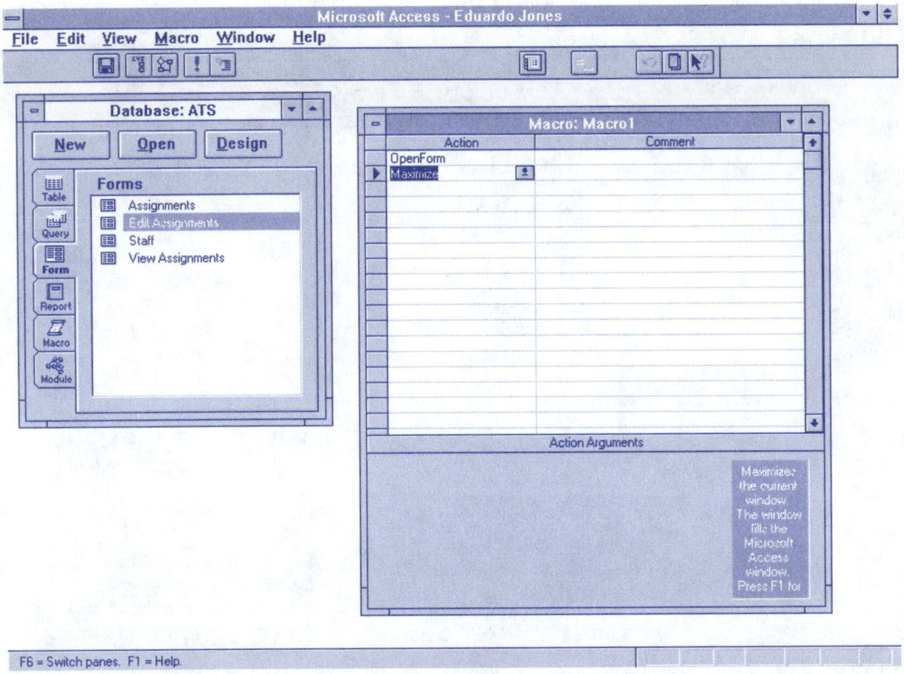

11-24
A macro for viewing records in the Assignment table.

window. Answer `Yes` in response to the "Save changes" prompt that appears. When prompted for a name, call the macro `View Assignments`.

Perform the following steps to create the macro for printing the records in the assignment table.

Step 1 In the Database window, click the `Macro` button, then click `New`. Move and resize the macro window that appears so that you can see both the Database window and the Macro window at the same time. Click the `Report` button, then click on `Relational Tracking` in the list box and drag it over to the first column under Action in the macro window. As a result, OpenReport appears in the Action column, with the report name (Relational Tracking) shown in the Action Arguments portion of the macro window.

Step 2 Click in the second line of the Action column of the macro window. Click the arrow to open the drop-down menu, and choose `Print` from the list. Click in the third line of the Action column of the macro window. Click the arrow to open the drop-down menu, and choose `Close` from the list. At this point, your macro should resemble the example shown in FIG. 11-25.

Step 3 Double-click the Close box of the Macro window. Answer `Yes` in response to the "Save changes" prompt that appears. When prompted for a name, call the macro `Print Assignments`.

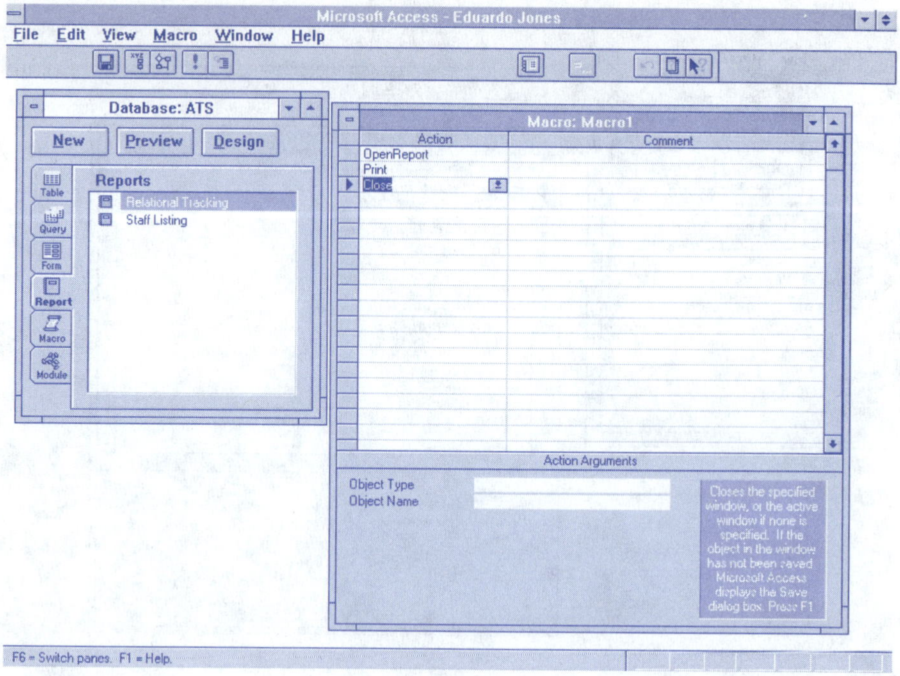

11-25
A macro for printing records in the Assignment table.

Perform the following steps to create the macro for printing a list of the employees.

Step 1 In the Database window, click the `Macro` button, then click `New`. Move and resize the macro window that appears so that you can see both the Database window and the Macro window at the same time. Click the `Report` button, then click on `Staff Listing` in the list box and drag it over to the first column under Action in the macro window. As a result, OpenReport appears in the Action column, with the report name (Staff Listing) shown in the Action Arguments portion of the macro window.

Step 2 Click in the second line of the Action column of the macro window. Click the arrow to open the drop-down menu, and choose `Print` from the list. Click in the third line of the Action column of the macro window. Click the arrow to open the drop-down menu, and choose `Close` from the list.

Step 3 Double-click the Close box of the Macro window. Answer `Yes` in response to the "Save changes" prompt that appears. When prompted for a name, call the macro `Print Employees`.

Perform the following steps to create a macro for finding a record.

Step 1 In the Database window, click the `Macro` button, then click `New` to create another macro. Click in the Action column of the first row, and choose `DoMenuItem` from the list box.

Step 2 Under Action Arguments, click in the Command box, open the list box, and choose `Find`. Press Ctrl–F4 to close the macro. Answer `Yes` when asked if you want to save the macro. For a name, call the macro `Search`.

Perform the following steps to create a macro for deleting a record.

Step 1 In the Database window, with the `Macro` button still selected, click `New`. Click in the first row of the Action column of the macro. Open the drop-down list box, and choose `DoMenuItem`. Under Action Arguments, click in the Command text box, and choose `Select Record` from the list.

Step 2 Click in the second row of the Action column of the macro. Open the drop-down list box, and choose `DoMenuItem`. Under Action Arguments, click in the Command text box, and choose `Delete` from the list. Press Ctrl–F4. Answer `Yes` in response to the "Save changes" prompt that appears. When prompted for a name, call the macro `Delete`.

Perform the following steps to create a macro for closing a form.

Step 1 In the Database window, with the `Macro` button still selected, click `New`. Click in the first row of the Action column of the macro. Open the drop-down list box, and choose `Close` from the list box.

Step 2 Press Ctrl–F4. Answer `Yes` in response to the "Save changes" prompt that appears. When prompted for a name, call the macro `Close`.

Perform the following steps to create the macro for exiting from the application.

Step 1 In the Database window, with the `Macro` button still selected, click `New`. Click in the first row of the Action column of the macro. Open the drop-down list box, and choose `Close` from the list box.

Step 2 Click in the second row of the Action column of the macro. Open the drop-down list box, and again choose `Close` from the list box. Press Ctrl–F4. Answer `Yes` in response to the "Save changes" prompt that appears. When prompted for a name, call the macro `Exit System`.

Next, the form that will serve as the main menu of the application is needed. Perform the following steps to create the main menu.

Step 1 In the Database window, click the `Form` button, then click `New`. When the New Form dialog box appears, leave the Select a Table/Query text box blank. Click the `Blank Form` button to open a blank form that is not associated with any tables. Increase the size of the drawing area on the form by dragging the lower-right corner until it is at least 8 × 8", then use the scroll bars to get back to the upper-left corner of the drawing area. Move and resize the form so that you can see both the form and the Database window at the same time.

Step 2 In the Database window, click the `Macro` button to display all the macros that you have created. Click `Add/Edit Assignments`, and drag it over to a position roughly 1" from the left edge and 1" below the top of the form. (*Note*: Upon doing this, users of Access 2.0 might see a dialog box warning that Wizards can't be used with existing buttons. If you see this dialog box, just click `OK` each time it appears to bypass it.) When you release the mouse button, a button appears that will call the macro. Place the mouse pointer over the right edge of the button until it changes shape to a double-pointed arrow. Click and drag to the right until the button is roughly 2" in length. When you do so, the entire title of the macro, "Add/Edit Assignments," should be visible within the button.

Step 3 In the Database window, click `Add/Edit Staff` and drag it over to a position roughly ¼" below the existing button. When you release the mouse button, a button appears that will call the macro. Place the mouse pointer over the right edge of the button until it changes shape to a double-pointed arrow. Click and drag to the right until the button is the same size as the previous button. When you do so, the entire title of the macro, "Add/Edit Staff," should be visible within the button. Move the mouse pointer over the button until it changes to the shape of a hand, then click and drag the button as necessary until it is aligned ¼" directly underneath the first button. (If you are nearing the bottom of the form, you might want to use the vertical scroll bar to scroll the form upwards so that you will have sufficient room to place the remaining buttons.)

Step 4 In the Database window, click `View Assignments` and drag it over to a position roughly ¼" below the previous button. When you release the mouse button, a button appears that will call the macro. Place the mouse pointer over the right edge of the button until it changes shape to a double-pointed arrow. Click and drag to the right until the button is the same size as the previous button. When you do so, the entire title of the macro, "View Assignments," should be visible within the button. Move the mouse pointer over the button until it changes to the shape of a hand, then click and drag the button as necessary until it is aligned ¼" directly underneath the previous button. (If you are nearing the bottom of the form, you might want to use the vertical scroll bar to scroll the form upwards so that you will have sufficient room to place the remaining buttons.)

Step 5 In the Database window, click `Print Assignments` and drag it over to a position roughly ¼" below the `View Assignments` button. Place the mouse pointer over the right edge of the new button until it changes shape to a double-pointed arrow. Click and drag to the right until the button is the same size as the other buttons. When you do so, the entire title of the macro, "Print Assignments," should be visible within the button. Move the mouse pointer over the button until it changes to the shape of a hand, then click and drag the button as necessary until it is aligned ¼" directly underneath the previous button.

Step 6 In the Database window, click `Print Employees` and drag it over to a position roughly ¼" below the `Print Assignments` button. Place the mouse pointer over the right edge of the new button until it changes shape to a double-pointed arrow. Click and drag to the right until the button is the same size as the other buttons. When you do so, the entire title of the macro, "Print Employees," should be visible within the button. Move the mouse pointer over the button until it changes to the shape of a hand, then click and drag the button as necessary until it is aligned ¼" directly underneath the previous button.

Step 7 In the Database window, click `Exit System` and drag it over to a position roughly ¼" below the `Print Employees` button. Place the mouse pointer over the right edge of the new button until it changes shape to a double-pointed arrow. Click and drag to the right until the button is the same size as the other buttons. When you do so, the entire title of the macro, "Exit System," should be visible within the button. Move the mouse pointer over the button until it changes to the shape of a hand, then click and drag the button as necessary until it is aligned ¼" directly underneath the previous button.

Step 8 Click the form's `Maximize` button so that you can see the entire form. If the Toolbar is not already visible, choose `View/Toolbox` to display the Toolbox. Click the Label tool in the Toolbox, and click in the form at a point roughly 1" below the top of the form and 4" to the right. Type a desired name for the application; in this example, I used the name "Dorado Engineering Tracking System." Click at the edge of the text that you just typed to select the text object. In the Toolbar, use the Font and Font Size list boxes to change the font to another font that you desire (such as Arial) and to change to a larger font size (such as 16 point). Then, choose `Format/Size/To Fit` from the menus, and reposition the text box to a centered location of your choice on the form.

Step 9 With the text box still selected, click the `Palette` button in the Toolbar. When the palette appears, change the appearance to raised (click the `Raised` button in the Palette) and click on a wider width for the border (you can change the fill colors for the text, if desired, by clicking a color of your choice in the Back Color column). Then, double-click the Palette's `Close` button to put away the Palette.

As an option, you can add a graphic to the form. If you want to do so, use standard Windows techniques to switch to Windows Paintbrush (or your desired graphics package) and open the desired art. Capture the desired portion of the art, using the standard Windows techniques for your graphics package, then choose `Edit/Copy`. Use standard Windows techniques to switch back to Access, and choose `Edit/Paste`. Resize and position the graphic as desired on the form. At this point, your form should resemble the example shown in FIG. 11-26.

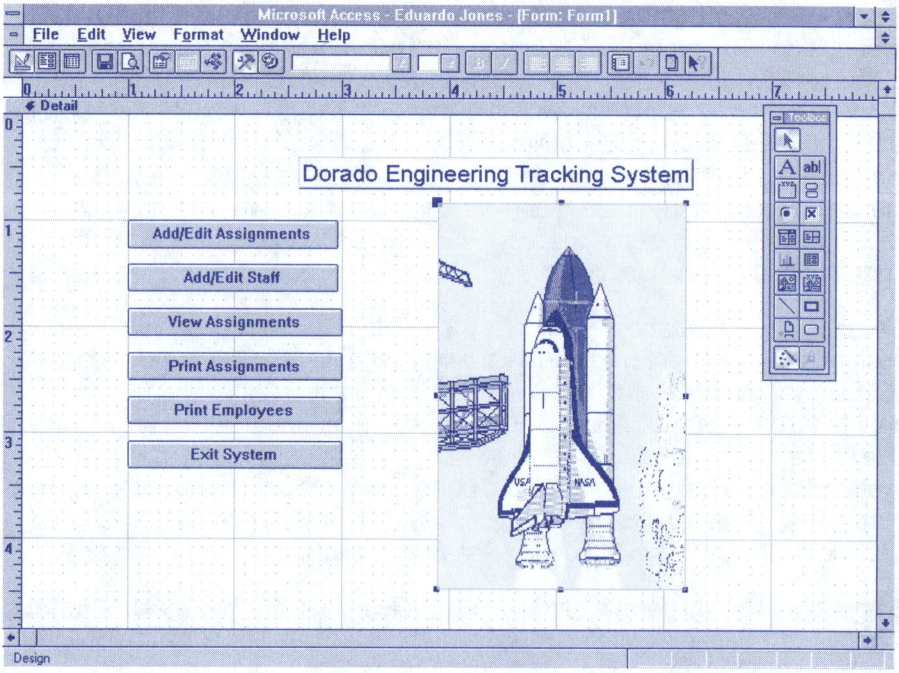

11-26
A form design for the main menu.

Step 10 Press Ctrl–F4 to close the form. When Access asks if you want to save the form, click `Yes`. When you are prompted for a name for the form, enter `Main Menu`.

Step 11 In the Database window, click the `Form` button, then click `Staff`, then click `Design`. Move or resize the form window so that you can see both the Database window and the Form window at the same time.

Step 12 In the Database window, click the `Macro` button, then click the Search macro, and drag the macro over to a blank space anywhere within the header of the form (but leave room to the right of the button to add two buttons of the same size). Center the button vertically as desired within the header.

Step 13 In the Database window, click the Delete macro and drag the macro to the space to the right of the `Search` button. If necessary, move the `Delete` button so that is aligned horizontally and vertically, and just to the right of the `Search` button.

Step 14 In the Database window, click the Close macro and drag the macro to the space to the right of the `Delete` button. If necessary, move the `Close` button so that is aligned horizontally and vertically and just to the right of the `Delete` button. Press Ctrl–F4 to close the form (click `Yes` in the dialog box that appears asking if you want to save your changes to the form).

Step 15 In the Database window, click the Form button, then click Assignments, then click Design. Move or resize the form window so that you can see both the Database window and the Form window at the same time.

Step 16 In the Database window, click the Macro button, then click the Search macro, and drag the macro over to a blank space just to the right of the Assignments title in the header of the form (but leave room to the right of the button to add two buttons of the same size). Center the button vertically as desired within the header.

Step 17 In the Database window, click the Delete macro and drag the macro to the space to the right of the Search button. If necessary, move the Delete button so that is aligned horizontally and vertically and just to the right of the Search button.

Step 18 In the Database window, click the Close macro and drag the macro to the space to the right of the Delete button. If necessary, move the Close button so that is aligned horizontally and vertically and just to the right of the Delete button. Press Ctrl–F4 close the form (click Yes in the dialog box that appears asking if you want to save your changes to the form).

At this point, all that is needed is the macro that will automatically start the application when the database is opened. In Access, any macro named "Autoexec" will run automatically when the database is opened. Use these steps to create the macro.

Step 1 In the Database window, click Macro, then click New. Move and resize the macro window that appears so that you can see both the Database window and the Macro window at the same time.

Step 2 In the Database window, click the Form button, then click on Main Menu and drag it over to the first line of the Action column.

Step 3 Click in the second line of the Action column of the macro window. Click the arrow to open the drop-down menu, and choose Maximize from the list.

Step 4 Press Ctrl–F4 to close the macro window. When Access asks if you want to save the macro, click Yes. When prompted for a name for the macro, enter Autoexec.

At this point, the application is complete. Double-click the `Close` button of the Database window to close it. Then, to try running the application, choose `File/Open Database`. When the Open Database dialog box appears, double-click `TRACKING` to reopen the database. Because you added the Autoexec macro, when the database opens, the form containing the menu for the application opens automatically, as shown earlier in FIG. 11-1. You can test the application by adding and editing data and printing the desired reports. Use the techniques detailed in this chapter to add any additional reports or specialized queries (and corresponding menu option buttons) to refine the application so it precisely suits your needs.

12 Order-entry system

The tracking of orders based on a given inventory and a customer list is not only one of the most common applications for relational database managers, it also is one of the more challenging to design. Such an application must make use of a minimum of three tables, and often more. This straightforward example of an order-entry and inventory tracking system makes use of four tables to store orders, customer data, and inventory data. Any supply firm that ships products to a single address for each individual customer can make use of a system like this one to manage the task of order entry and inventory control. Figure 12-1 shows the Order-Entry System in use.

This application is different than most others in this section of the book in one respect: its user interface makes use of pull-down menus, instead of command buttons, for choosing the various options of the application. If your application must contain a large number of menu choices or if you simply prefer to imitate the Windows style of menu design in your applications, you can use the techniques demonstrated in this chapter to develop applications with pull-down menus.

Creating the database & tables

The Order-Entry System requires four tables: one named Orders, the second named Order Details, the third named Customers, and the last named Inventory. Much of the data manipulated by the application is stored in the Orders and Order Details tables. The Orders table contains a unique order number (which serves as a key and a means of identifying orders), a customer

12-1
The Order Entry system in use.

number, the date of the order, and the method of shipping. The Order Details table contains details about each order, including the order number, the stock number, and the quantity of each item ordered. The Customer table contains the names and shipping addresses of all customers placing orders, and the Inventory table contains the details regarding each item that is sold, such as the stock number (which serves to identify the item within the inventory), the description, the price, and its location within the warehouse. To create the database and its required tables, first start Access in the usual manner, then perform the following steps.

Step 1 Choose `File/New Database` to open the New Database dialog box.

TIP

If you want to store the new database in a different directory, use the Directory list box to locate the desired directory now. Click on the desired directory, and Access will store the new database in that directory.

Step 2 Enter `ORDERS` in the File Name text box as a name for the database, then click `OK`. (Remember, in Access, database names must be 8 characters or less, with no spaces.) Access creates the database file on your hard disk, and the Database window appears.

Step 3 In the Database window, click the `Table` button, then click `New`. In the New Table dialog box which appears, click `New Table`. The Table window appears. Fill in the Table window with the field names and data types for the fields shown in TABLE 12-1. Click anywhere in the first field

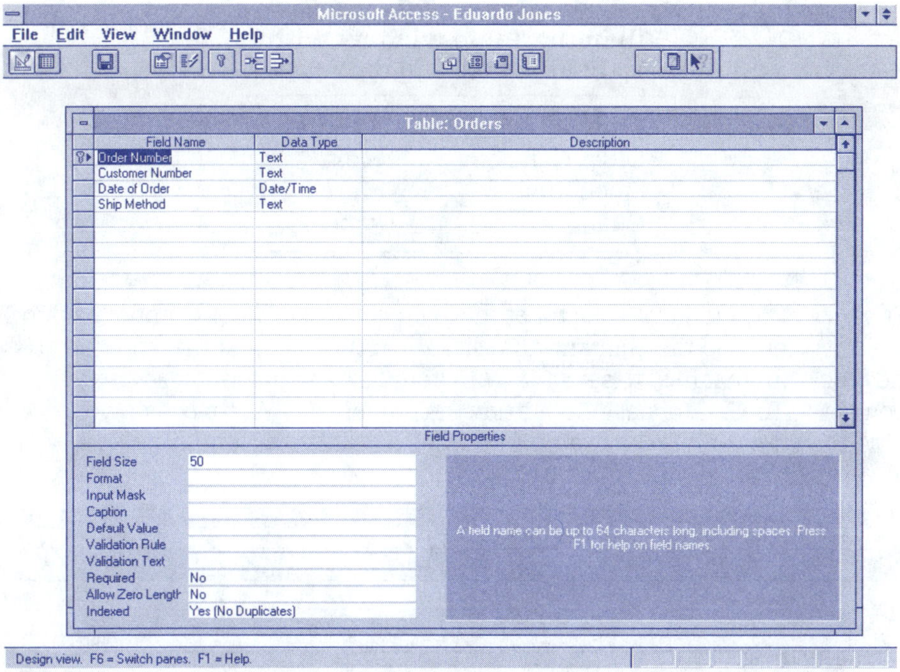

12-2
The completed Orders table.

(titled "Order Number"), and click the Key icon in the Toolbar to make this field the primary key. At this point, your table should resemble the example shown in FIG. 12-2.

Table 12-1
Fill in the Table window with these field names and data types.

Field name	Data type
Order Number	Text
Customer Number	Text
Date of Order	Date/Time
Ship Method	Text

Step 4 When done defining the fields, choose `File/Save` to save the table. When prompted for a table name, enter `Orders` as the name, and click `OK`. Press Ctrl–F4 to close the Table window. The new table, Orders, now appears in the Database window.

Step 5 In the Database window, with the `Table` button still selected, click `New`. In the New Table dialog box that appears, click `New Table`. The Table window again appears. Fill in the Table window with the field names and data types for the fields shown in TABLE 12-2.

Table 12-2
Fill in the Table window with these field names and data types.

Field name	Data type
Order Number	Text
Stock Number	Text
Quantity	Number

Step 6 Click the row selector at the left edge of the Order Number field to select it, then hold the Shift key and click the row selector at the left edge of the Stock Number field to select it. With both fields selected, click the Key icon in the Toolbar to make both fields the primary key. At this point, your table should resemble the example shown in FIG. 12-3.

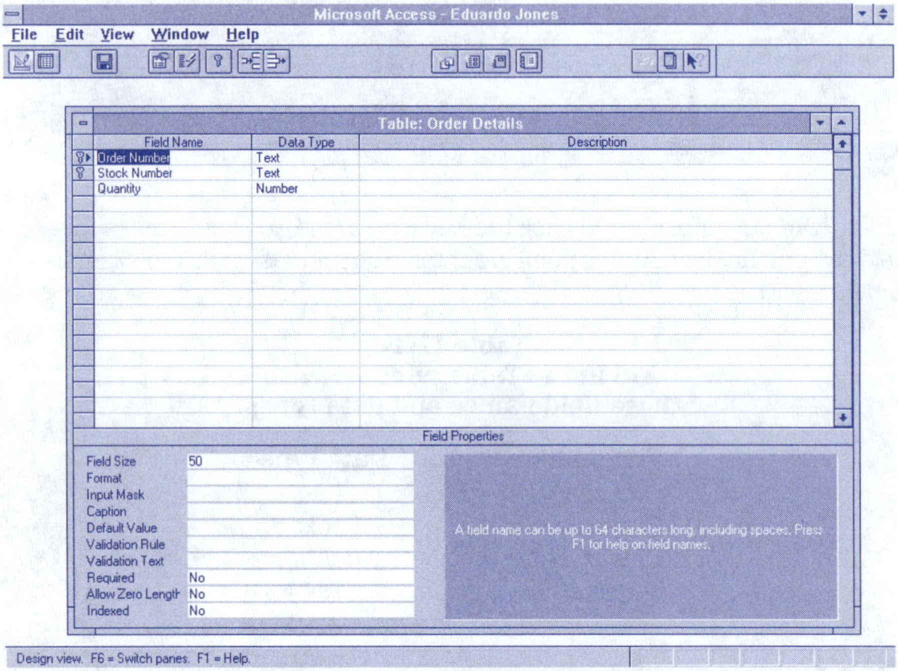

12-3
The completed Order Details table.

Step 7 When you are done defining the fields, choose `File/Save` to save the table. When you are prompted for a table name, enter `Order Details` as the name, and click `OK`. Press Ctrl–F4 to close the Table window. The new table, Order Details, now appears in the Database window.

Step 8 In the Database window, with the `Table` button already selected, click `New`. In the New Table dialog box that appears, click `New Table`. The Table window again appears. Fill in the Table window with the field names

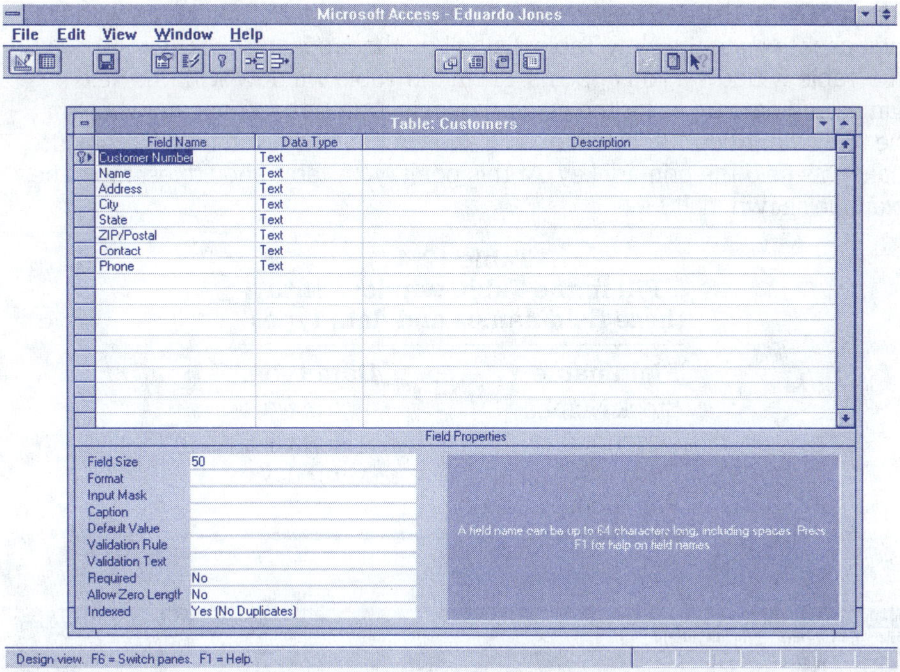

12-4
The completed Customers table.

and data types for the fields shown in TABLE 12-3. Click anywhere in the first field (titled "Customer Number"), and click the Key icon in the Toolbar to make this field the primary key. At this point, your table should resemble the example shown in FIG. 12-4.

Table 12-3
Fill in the Table window with these field names and data types.

Field name	Data type
Customer Number	Text
Name	Text
Address	Text
City	Text
State	Text
Zip/Postal	Text
Contact	Text
Phone	Text

Step 9 When you are done defining the fields, choose `File/Save` to save the table. When you are prompted for a table name, enter `Customers` as the name, and click `OK`. Press Ctrl–F4 to close the Table window. The new table, Customers, now appears in the Database window.

Step 10 In the Database window, with the `Table` button still selected, then click `New`. In the New Table dialog box that appears, click `New Table`. The Table window again appears. Fill in the Table window with the field names and data types for the fields shown in TABLE 12-4. Click anywhere in the first field (titled "Stock Number"), and click the Key icon in the Toolbar to make this field the primary key. At this point, your table should resemble the example shown in FIG. 12-5.

Table 12-4
Fill in the Table window with these field names and data types.

Field name	Data type
Stock Number	Text
Description	Text
Price	Currency
Warehouse Location	Text

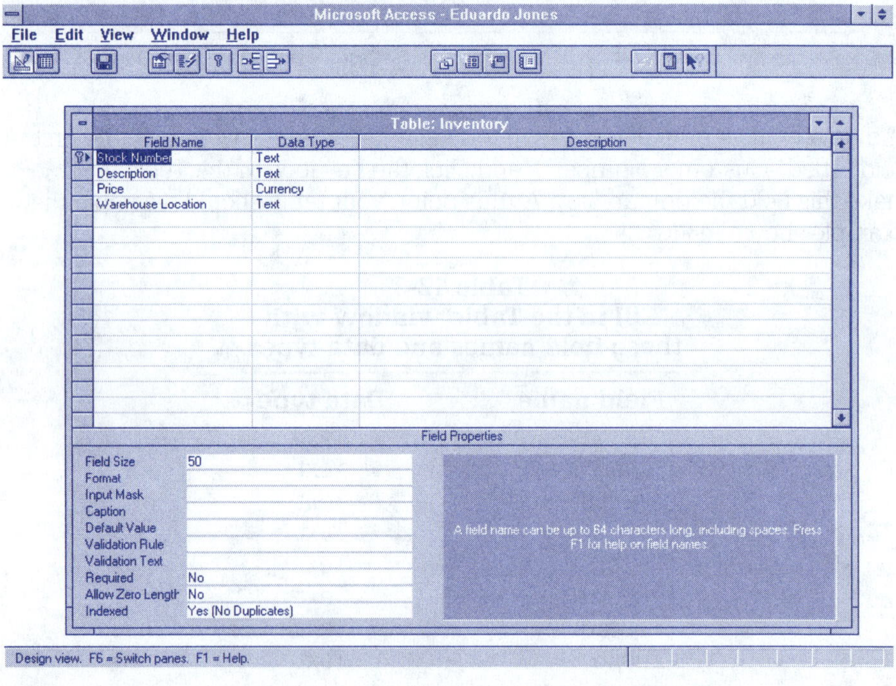

12-5
The completed Inventory table.

Step 11 When you are done defining the fields, choose `File/Save` to save the table. When you are prompted for a table name, enter `Inventory` as the name, and click `OK`. Press Ctrl–F4 to close the Table window. The new table, Inventory, now appears in the Database window.

Creating the details-&-items query

Before you create the needed forms, one query will be needed that will support the viewing of all items associated with a particular order. Perform the following steps to create this query.

Step 1 In the Database window, click `Query`, then click `New`. In the New Query dialog box that appears, click `New Query`.

Step 2 In the Add Table dialog box that appears, click `Order Details`, then click `Add`, then click `Inventory`, then click `Add`, then click `Close`. If a line does not automatically appear between the Stock Number fields in the list boxes, click the Stock Number field in the Order Details list, and drag over to the Stock Number field in the Inventory list, then release the mouse button to establish the relational link.

Step 3 One by one, click and drag the following fields from the Order Details list to the empty cells of the Field row in the Query grid: Order number, Stock number, and Quantity.

Step 4 One by one, click and drag the Description and Price fields from the Inventory list to the empty cells of the Field row in the Query grid. At this point, your query should resemble the example shown in FIG. 12-6.

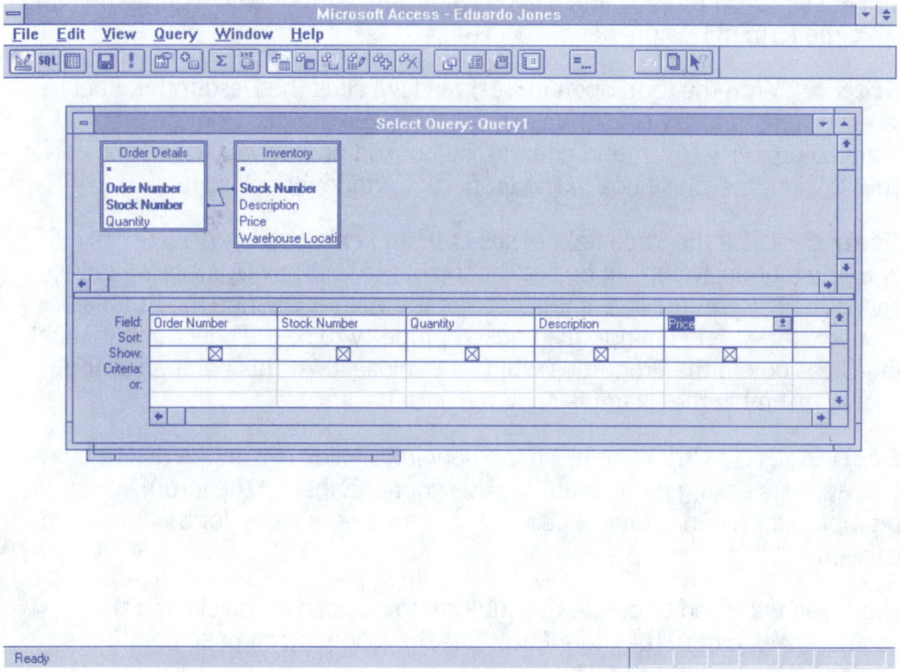

12-6 *The Details and Items query.*

Step 5 Press Ctrl–F4. Answer `Yes` to the question that asks if you want to save the query. Enter `Details and Items` as a name for the query.

Creating the forms

The database will require four forms. One will be used for adding new orders, the second for editing existing orders, the third to display and edit the records in the customer table, and the fourth to add or edit records in the inventory table. To create the subform for displaying the detail items, perform the following steps.

Step 1 In the Database window, click the Form button, then click New. The New Form dialog box appears. Click the arrow under Select a Table/Query to choose the desired table, and click on Details and Items in the drop-down list. Click the FormWizards button. In a moment, Access displays a dialog box asking you to choose the desired wizard. Click Tabular in the dialog box, then click OK.

Step 2 The next dialog box to appear asks which fields you want selected on the form. Click the double-angle bracket button (>>), to place all available fields on the form, then click Next.

Step 3 The next dialog box to appear asks what kind of look you want for the form. Choose Standard, and click Next.

Step 4 The next dialog box to appear asks for a title for the form. By default, the title Details and Items appears in the text box. Change this title to Items Ordered, and click the Design button to accept the title and open the form in Design view.

Step 5 With the form open in Design view, click the Description field to select it and choose View/Properties from the menus. Change the Enabled property to No, and change the Locked property to Yes. Then, double-click the Close box in the Properties window to close it.

Step 6 Click the Price field to select it, and choose View/Properties from the menus. In the list box at the top of the window (Access 2.0 only), choose All Properties if it is not already visible. Change the Enabled property to No, and change the Locked property to Yes. Then, double-click the Close box in the Properties window to close it. At this point, your form should resemble the example shown in FIG. 12-7.

Step 7 Press Ctrl–F4 to close the new form (click Yes in the dialog box that appears asking if you want to save your changes to the form). When prompted for a name, enter Items Ordered as the name for the form, and click OK.

Next, you will need to create the subform to be used for displaying the customers as part of the order form. Use the following steps to create the subform.

Step 1 In the Database window, click the Form button, then click New. The New Form dialog box appears. Click the arrow under Select a

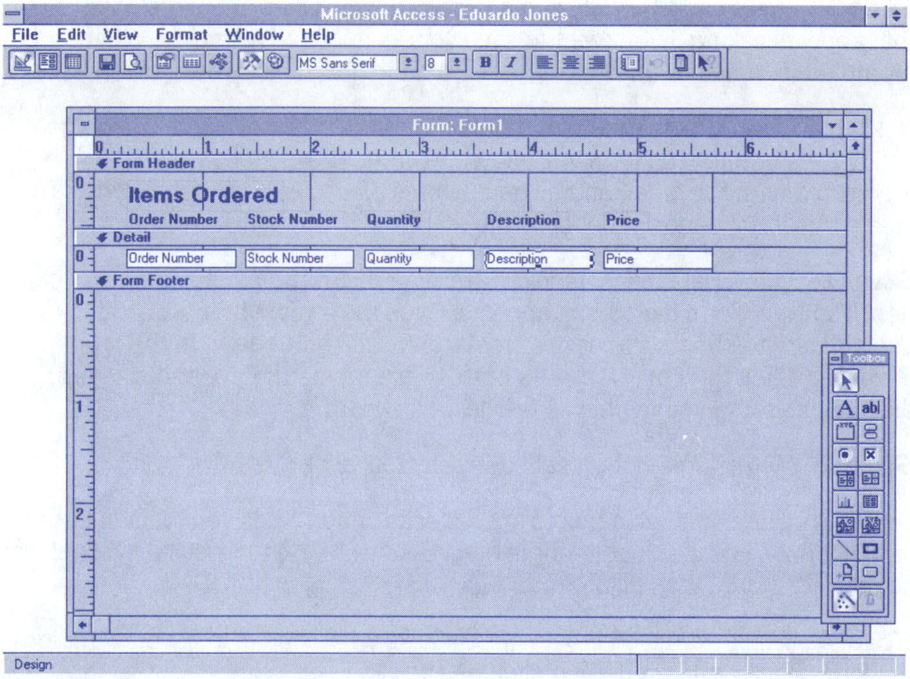

12-7
The completed Items Ordered form.

Table/Query to choose the desired table, and click on Customers in the drop-down list. Click the `FormWizards` button. In a moment, Access displays a dialog box asking you to choose the desired wizard.

Step 2 With `Single-column` already selected in the dialog box, click `OK`.

Step 3 The next dialog box to appear asks which fields you want selected on the form. Click the double-angle bracket button (`>>`) to place all available fields on the form, then click `Next`.

Step 4 The next dialog box to appear asks what kind of look you want for the form. Check `Standard`, and click `Next`.

Step 5 The next dialog box to appear asks for a title for the form. By default, the title `Customers` appears in the text box. Change this title to `Ship To`:, and click the `Design` button to accept the title and open the form in Design view.

Step 6 Choose `Edit/Select Form` from the menus, then choose `View/Properties` to open the Properties window for the form. In the list box at the top of the window (Access 2.0 only), choose `All Properties` if it is not already visible. Change the Allow Editing properties to `Unavailable`, and change the Scroll Bars property to `Neither`. Then, double-click the Close box in the Properties window to close it.

Step 7 Press Ctrl–F4 to close the new form (click `Yes` in the dialog box that appears asking if you want to save your changes to the form). When prompted for a name, enter `Ship To` as a name for the form, and click `OK`.

Next, you'll need to create the multitable form that will be used for adding and editing orders. The form will show the order, the customer name associated with the order, and all detail items placed as part of that order. To create this form, perform the following steps.

Step 1 In the Database window, with the `Form` button still selected, click `New`. The New Form dialog box appears. Click the arrow under Select a Table/Query to choose the desired table, and click on `Orders` in the drop-down list. Click the `FormWizards` button. In a moment, Access displays a dialog box asking you to choose the desired wizard.

Step 2 With Single-column already selected, click `OK`.

Step 3 The next dialog box to appear asks which fields you want selected on the form. Click the double-angle bracket button (`>>`) to place all available fields on the form, then click `Next`.

Step 4 The next dialog box to appear asks what kind of look you want for the form. Click `Embossed`, then click `Next`.

Step 5 The next dialog box to appear asks for a title for the form. By default, the title `Orders` appears in the text box. Click the `Design` button to accept the title and open the form in Design view.

Step 6 Using the techniques detailed in chapter 6, click and drag the right border of the form until the design area of the form is roughly 7" in width, and click and drag the form footer until the detail area is at least 3" deep. (Doing so provides sufficient room to place the subforms.)

Step 7 If necessary, move and size the windows so that you can see both the form window and the Database window at the same time.

Step 8 Click the `Form` button in the Database window, and click and drag the Ship To form from the Database window onto the right side of the form you are designing. Use the techniques covered in chapter 6 to move the subform so that it is just below the start of the Detail band and to the right of the existing fields from the Orders table.

Step 9 With the Ship To subform still selected, choose `View/Properties` from the menus. In the list box at the top of the window (Access 2.0 only), choose `All Properties` if it is not already visible. Click in the Link Child Fields property, and enter `Customer Number` as a field name, then do the same for the Link Master Fields property. Change the Enabled property to `No`, and change the Locked property to `Yes`. Then, double-click the Property window's close icon to put away the Property window.

Step 10 If necessary, scroll the form upward so that you will have sufficient room at the bottom to place the Items Ordered subform. Then, click the `Form` button in the Database window, and click and drag the Items Ordered form from the Database window onto the bottom of the form you are designing. Use the techniques covered in chapter 6 to move the subform so that it is just below the Customers subform and ½" from the left edge of the form. Then, resize the form (stretch it vertically) so that it is as deep as is possible within the main form. At this point, your form should resemble the example shown in FIG. 12-8.

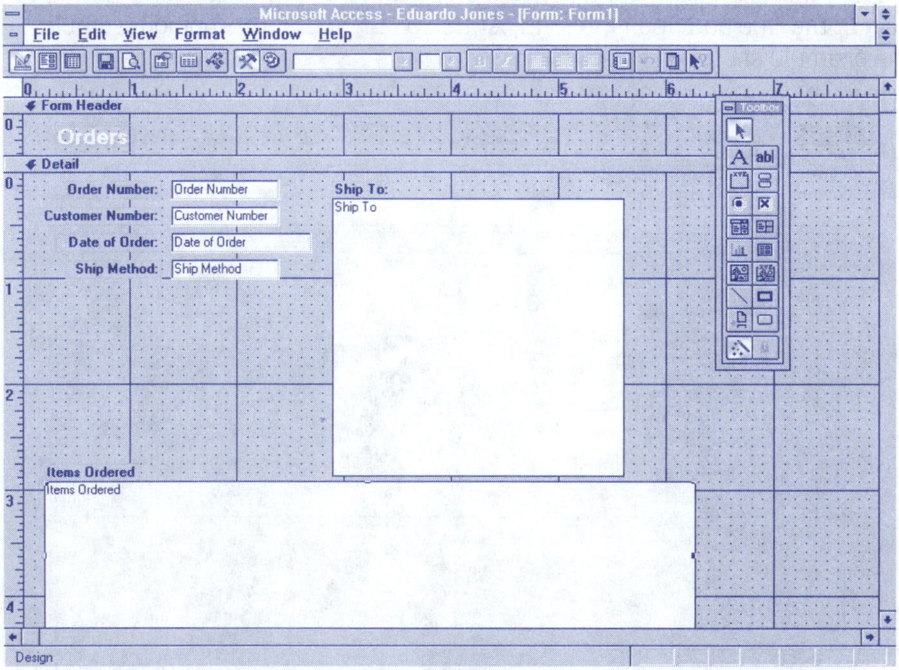

12-8
The completed Orders form.

Step 11 Press Ctrl–F4 to close the new form (click `Yes` in the dialog box that appears asking if you want to save your changes to the form). When prompted for a name, enter `Orders` as the name for the form, and click `OK`.

With the form for the orders created, you can proceed to create the forms that will be used for adding and editing records in the Customer and Inventory tables. Perform the following steps to create these forms.

Step 1 In the Database window, click the `Form` button, then click `New`. The New Form dialog box appears. Click the arrow under Select a Table/Query to choose the desired table, and click on Customers in the drop-down list. Click the `FormWizards` button. In a moment, Access displays a dialog box asking you to choose the desired wizard.

Step 2 With Single-column already selected in the dialog box, click `OK`.

Step 3 The next dialog box to appear asks which fields you want selected on the form. Click the double-angle bracket button (`>>`) to place all available fields on the form, then click `Next`.

Step 4 The next dialog box to appear asks what kind of look you want for the form. Click `Embossed`, and click `Next`.

Step 5 The next dialog box to appear asks for a title for the form. By default, the title `Customers` appears in the text box. Click the `Open` button to accept the title and open the form. At this point, your form should resemble the example shown in FIG. 12-9.

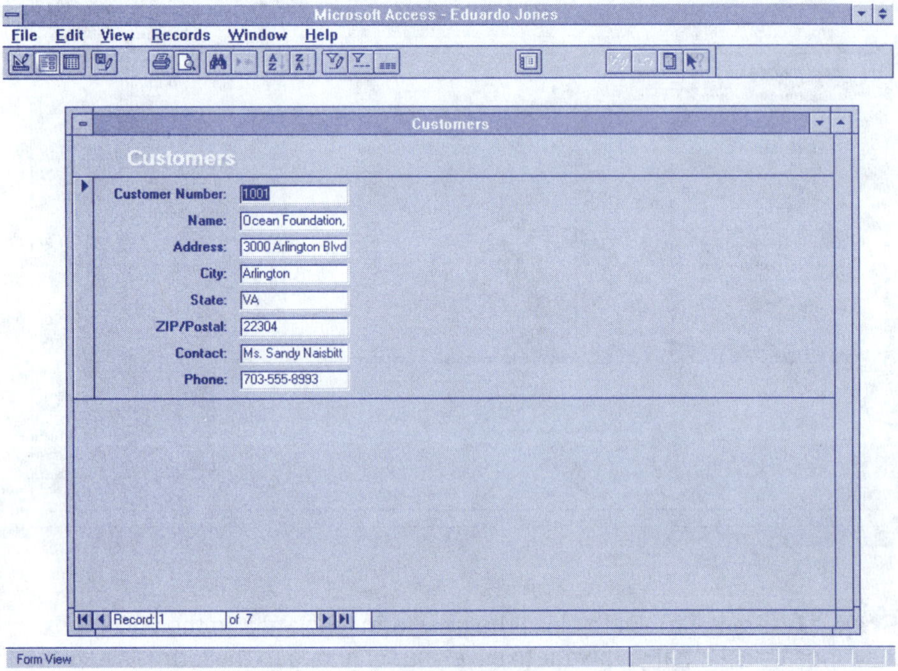

12-9 *The completed Customers form.*

Step 6 Press Ctrl–F4 close the new form (click `Yes` in the dialog box that appears asking if you want to save your changes to the form). When prompted for a name, enter `Customers` as the name for the form, and click `OK`.

Step 7 In the Database window, with the `Form` button still selected, click `New`. The New Form dialog box appears. Click the arrow under Select a Table/Query to choose the desired table, and click on Inventory in the drop-down list. Click the `FormWizards` button. In a moment, Access displays a dialog box asking you to choose the desired wizard.

Step 8 With Single-column already selected in the dialog box, click OK.

Step 9 The next dialog box to appear asks which fields you want selected on the form. Click the double-angle bracket button (>>) to place all available fields on the form, then click Next.

Step 10 The next dialog box to appear asks what kind of look you want for the form. Click Embossed, and click Next.

Step 11 The next dialog box to appear asks for a title for the form. By default, the title Inventory appears in the text box. Click the Design button to accept the title and open the form in Design view.

Step 12 Using the sizing techniques covered in chapter 6, widen the Description field until it is roughly 2" in length. Then, widen the form until it is slightly wider than the edge of the Description field. At this point, your form should resemble the example shown in FIG. 12-10.

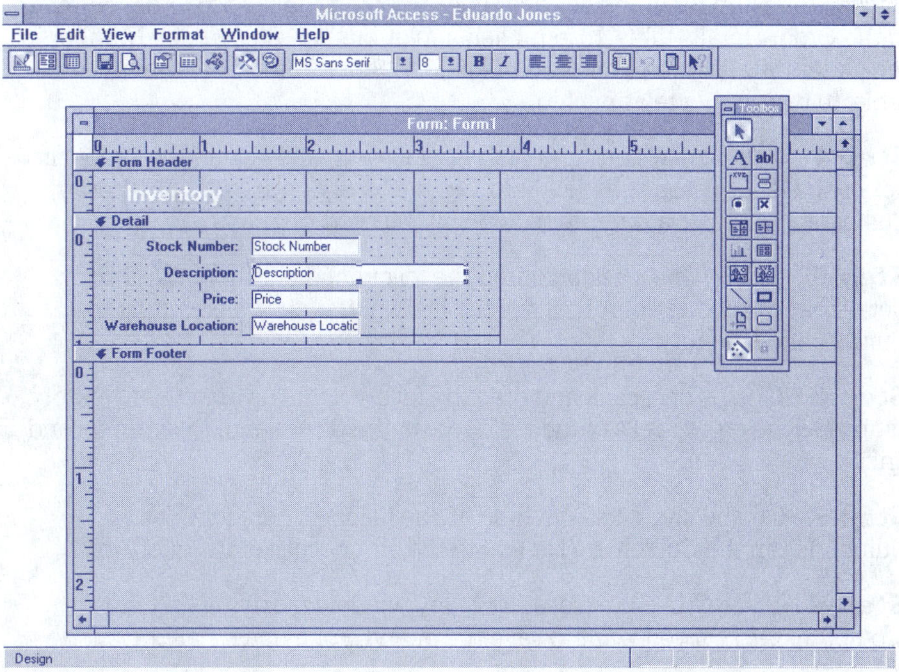

12-10 *The completed Inventory form.*

Step 13 Press Ctrl–F4 to close the new form (click Yes in the dialog box that appears asking if you want to save your changes to the form). When prompted for a name, enter Inventory as the name for the form, and click OK.

Creating the queries

Three additional queries will be needed to support the printing of reports. One will retrieve a single order based on the order number, the second will retrieve all orders for a given day, and the third will retrieve all orders within a given range of dates. You can quickly create all three queries by creating one query and basing the others on the first. Perform the following steps to create the queries.

Step 1 In the Database window, click the `Query` button, then click `New`. In the New Query dialog box that appears, click `New Query`. A new query appears, with the Add Table dialog box above it.

Step 2 In the Add Table dialog box, click `Customers`, then click `Add`, then click `Orders`, then click `Add`, then click `Order Details`, then click `Add`, then click `Inventory`, then click `Add`. Finally, click `Close` to put away the dialog box. If lines indicating relationships appear between the field lists (as with Access 2.0), skip to step 4. If you are using an earlier version of Access, perform step 3.

Step 3 Click Customer Number in the Customers table, and drag the field to Customer Number in the Orders table to establish a relationship. Click Order Number in the Orders table, and drag the field to Order Number in the Order Details table, to establish a relationship. Click Stock Number in the Order Details table, and drag the field to Stock Number in the Inventory table, to establish a relationship.

Step 4 One by one, click and drag the following fields from the Orders list box to the empty cells of the Field row in the Query grid: Order number, Customer number, Date of Order, and Ship Method.

Step 5 One by one, click and drag the following fields from the Order Details list box to the empty cells of the Field row in the Query grid: Stock Number and Quantity.

Step 6 One by one, click and drag the following fields from the Inventory list box to the empty cells of the Field row in the Query grid: Description and Price.

Step 7 One by one, click and drag all the fields (except for Customer Number) from the Customers list box to the empty cells of the query grid.

Step 8 Press Ctrl–F4 to close the query window (answer `Yes` to the prompt that asks if you want to save the query). For a name, call the query `All records`.

Step 9 In the Database window, click `All Records`, then choose `Edit/Copy` from the menus. Next, choose `Edit/Paste`. In the Paste As dialog box that appears, enter `One Day` as a name for the copied query, and click `OK`.

Step 10 In the Database window, click `All Records`, then choose `Edit/Copy` from the menus. Next, choose `Edit/Paste`. In the Paste As dialog box that appears, enter `Range of Days` as a name for the copied query, and click `OK`.

Step 11 In the Database window, click `One Day`, then click `Design` to open the query in Design view. Click in the Criteria row, under the Date of Order field, and enter this parameter:

```
[Enter the date for the orders:]
```

then press Ctrl–F4 and answer `Yes` to the prompt that asks if you want to save the changes.

Step 12 In the Database window, click `Range of Days`, then click `Design` to open the query in Design view. Click in the Criteria row, under the Date of Order field, and enter this parameter:

```
between [Enter the starting date:] and [Enter the ending
date:]
```

then press Ctrl–F4 and answer `Yes` to the prompt that asks if you want to save the changes.

Creating the reports

Four reports are needed for the application. One report will print a group of orders processed in a given day. Another report will produce a summary of all orders within a range of dates. Reports will be included to provide listings of current inventory and of customers. Perform the following steps to create the reports.

Step 1 In the Database window, click the `Report` button, then click `New`. The New Report dialog box appears. Click the arrow under Select a Table/Query to choose the desired table, and click `One Day` in the drop-down list. Click the `ReportWizards` button. In a moment, Access displays a dialog box asking you to choose the desired wizard. Click `Groups/Totals`, then click `OK`.

Step 2 The next dialog box to appear asks which fields you want placed on the report. Click the Name field, then click the angle bracket (>) to place the Name field on the report. Repeat this step for the Date of Order, Quantity, Description, and Price fields, then click `Next`.

Step 3 The next dialog box asks which field you want to use to group the data by. Click the Name field, then click the angle bracket (>), then click `Next`.

Step 4 The next dialog box asks how you want to group the data in each field. The default value is fine here, so just click `Next`.

Step 5 The next dialog box asks which fields you want to use to sort the data by. Double-click the Date of Order field to place it in the Sort Order box, then click `Next`.

Step 6 The next dialog box to appear asks what kind of look you want for the report. Click `Ledger`, then click `Next`.

Step 7 The next dialog box to appear asks for a title for the form. By default, the title `One Day` appears in the text box. Change this title to `Daily Orders Report`. Click the Fit All Fields on One Page check box to turn it on, turn off the Calculate Percent of Total option, then click the `Design` button to open the report. At this point, your report should resemble the example shown in FIG. 12-11. Choose `File/Save` to save the new report. When you are prompted for a title, enter `Daily Orders Report` for a report name, then click `OK`.

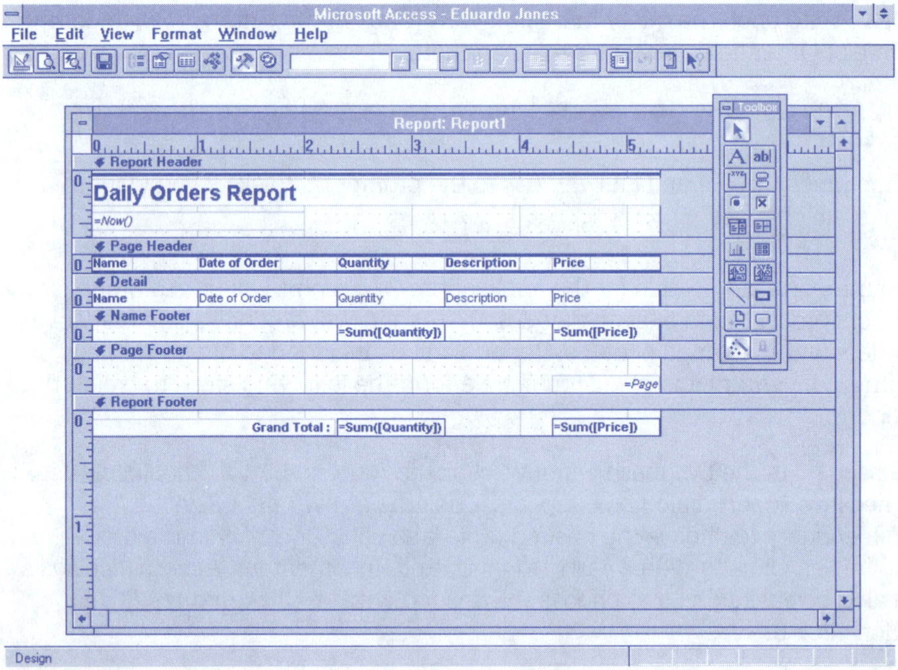

12-11 *The completed Daily Orders report.*

Step 8 Press Ctrl–F4 to close the new report.

You can quickly create a report that shows orders for a range of dates by copying the report that you just created and changing the source of the records. Perform the following steps to do this.

Step 1 In the Database window, click Daily Orders Report to select it.

Step 2 From the menus, choose `Edit/Copy`, then choose `Edit/Paste`. In the Paste As dialog box that appears, enter `Range of Days Report` as a name for the new report. Click Range of Days to select the report, then click `Design` to open the report in Design view.

Step 3 From the menus, choose View/Properties. Change the Record Source property to Range of Days.

Step 4 Press Ctrl–F4. Answer Yes to the prompt that asks if you want to save the changes.

Next, perform the following steps to create the report needed for the Customer List.

Step 1 In the Database window, click New. The New Report dialog box appears. Click the arrow under Select a Table/Query to choose the desired table, and click Customers in the drop-down list. Click the ReportWizards button. In a moment, Access displays a dialog box asking you to choose the desired wizard.

Step 2 With Single-column already selected, click OK.

Step 3 The next dialog box to appear asks which fields you want placed on the report. Click the double-angle bracket (>>) to place all fields on the report, then click Next.

Step 4 The next dialog box asks which fields you want to use to sort the data by. Double-click the Name field to place it in the Sort Order box, then click Next.

Step 5 The next dialog box to appear asks what kind of look you want for the report. Click Ledger, then click Next.

Step 6 The next dialog box to appear asks for a title for the report. By default, the title Customers appears in the text box. Leave this title as is, and click the Design button to open the report in Design view. Use the vertical scroll bar to scroll towards the bottom of the report, and click and drag the page footer down by about ¼". (Doing so will create a clean break between records when the report prints.)

Step 7 Choose File/Save to save the new report. When prompted for a title, enter Customers for a report name, then click OK.

Step 8 Press Ctrl–F4 to close the new report.

Next, perform the following steps to create the report needed for the Inventory List.

Step 1 In the Database window, click New. The New Report dialog box appears. Click the arrow under Select a Table/Query to choose the desired table, and click Inventory in the drop-down list. Click the ReportWizards button. In a moment, Access displays a dialog box asking you to choose the desired wizard. Click Groups/Totals, then click OK.

Step 2 The next dialog box to appear asks which fields you want placed on the report. Click the double-angle bracket (`>>`) to place all fields on the report, then click `Next`.

Step 3 The next dialog box asks which fields you want to use to group the data by. Click `Next` to bypass this question, as it is not relevant for the Inventory table.

Step 4 The next dialog box asks which fields you want to use to sort by. Double-click the Stock Number field, then click `Next`.

Step 5 The next dialog box to appear asks what kind of look you want for the report. Click `Ledger`, then click `Next`.

Step 6 The next dialog box to appear asks for a title for the report. By default, the title `Inventory` appears in the text box. Leave this title as is, and click the `Print Preview` button to open the report.

Step 7 Choose `File/Save` to save the new report. When prompted for a title, enter `Inventory` for a report name, then click `OK`. Press Ctrl–F4 to close the new report.

Developing the application

The application requires a series of macros that provide the main menu bar and the associated drop-down menus and the actions that should occur in response when a user chooses a menu option. Perform the following steps to create the macros required for the application.

To create the macro that will display the menu bar of the main menu, perform these steps.

Step 1 In the Database window, click the `Macro` button, then click `New`. If the Macro Name column is not visible, choose `View/Macro Names` from the menu so that you can see the Macro Names column. Click in the first row of the Macro Name column, and enter `Menu` as a macro name.

Step 2 Click in the first row of the Action column, open the list box, and choose AddMenu as an action. Click in Menu Name under Action Arguments, and enter `&Orders` as the entry. Press Tab once or click directly underneath, in the Menu Macro Name entry, and enter `Orders`.

Step 3 Click in the second row of the Action column, open the list box, and choose AddMenu as an action. Click in Menu Name under Action Arguments, and enter `&Customers` as the entry. Press Tab once or click directly underneath, in the Menu Macro Name entry, and enter `Customers`.

Step 4 Click in the third row of the Action column, open the list box, and choose AddMenu as an action. Click in Menu Name under Action

Arguments, and enter `&Inventory` as the entry. Press Tab once or click directly underneath, in the Menu Macro Name entry, and enter `Inventory`.

Step 5 Click in the fourth row of the Action column, open the list box, and choose AddMenu as an action. Click in Menu Name under Action Arguments, and enter `&Exit` as the entry. Press Tab once or click directly underneath, in the Menu Macro Name entry, and enter `Exit`.

Step 6 Press Ctrl–F4. Answer `Yes` to the prompt that asks if you want to save the macro; for a name, enter `Main Menu`.

To create the drop-down menu for the Orders choices on the menu bar, perform the following steps.

Step 1 In the Database window, with the `Macro` button still selected, click `New`. If the Macro Name column is not visible, choose `View/Macro Names` from the menu so that you can see the Macro Names column.

Step 2 Click in the first row of the Macro Name column, and enter `New Orders` as a name for the first macro in this group. Click in the first row of the Action column, open the list box, and choose `OpenForm` as an action.

Step 3 Under Action Arguments, click the `Form Names` entry, and choose `Orders` from the list of forms.

Step 4 Click in the second row of the Action column, and choose `Maximize` from the list. Click in the third row of the action column, and choose `GoToRecord` from the list.

Step 5 Under Action Arguments, click `Record`, and choose `New` from the list.

Step 6 Click in the Macro Name column in the fourth row of the macro, and enter `Edit Orders` as a title for the second macro in this group. Click the Action column in the fourth row of the macro (beside the macro name you just entered), open the list box, and choose `OpenForm` as an action.

Step 7 Under Action Arguments, click the `Form Names` entry, and choose Orders from the list of forms. Click in the fifth row of the Action column, and choose `Maximize` from the list. Click in the sixth row of the action column, and choose `DoMenuItem` from the list.

Step 8 Under Action Arguments, click `Command`, and choose `Find` from the list. Click in the Macro Name column in the seventh row of the macro, and enter `Print Day's Orders` as a title for the third macro in this group.

Step 9 Click the Action column in the seventh row of the macro (beside the macro name you just entered), open the list box, and choose `OpenReport` as an action.

Step 10 Under Action Arguments, click the Report Name entry, and choose `Daily Orders Report` from the list of reports. Leave the View entry set to `Print Preview`. Click in the Macro Name column in the eighth row of the macro, and enter `Print Range of Days` as a title for the last macro in this group.

Step 11 Click the Action column in the eighth row of the macro (beside the macro name you just entered), open the list box, and choose `OpenReport` as an action.

Step 12 Under Action Arguments, click the Report Name entry, and choose `Range of Days Report` from the list of reports. Leave the View entry set to `Print Preview`.

Step 13 Press Ctrl–F4. Answer `Yes` when you are asked if you want to save the new macro. When you are prompted, enter `Orders` as the name for the macro.

To create the macro that builds the drop-down menu for the Customers choices on the menu bar, perform the following steps.

Step 1 In the Database window, with the `Macro` button still selected, click `New`. If the Macro Name column is not visible, choose `View/Macro Names` from the menu so that you can see the Macro Names column.

Step 2 Click in the first row of the Macro Name column, and enter `New Customers` as a name for the first macro in this group. Click in the first row of the Action column, open the list box, and choose `OpenForm` as an action.

Step 3 Under Action Arguments, click the `Form Name` entry, and choose `Customers` from the list of forms. Click in the second row of the Action column, and choose `Maximize` from the list. Click in the third row of the action column, and choose `GoToRecord` from the list.

Step 4 Under Action Arguments, click `Record` and choose `New` from the list. Click in the Macro Name column, in the fourth row of the macro, and enter `Edit Customers` as a title for the second macro in this group. Click the Action column in the fourth row of the macro (beside the macro name you just entered), open the list box, and choose `OpenForm` as an action.

Step 5 Under Action Arguments, click the `Form Name` entry, and choose `Customers` from the list of forms. Click in the fifth row of the Action column, and choose `Maximize` from the list. Click in the sixth row of the action column, and choose `DoMenuItem` from the list.

Step 6 Under Action Arguments, click `Command`, and choose `Find` from the list. Click in the Macro Name column, in the seventh row of the macro, and enter `Print Customer Lists` as a title for the last macro in this group. Click the Action column in the seventh row of the macro (beside the macro name you just entered), open the list box, and choose `OpenReport` as an action.

Step 7 Under Action Arguments, click the `Report Name` entry, and choose `Customers` from the list of reports. Leave the View entry set to `Print Preview`.

Step 8 Press Ctrl–F4. Answer `Yes` when asked if you want to save the new macro. When prompted, enter `Customers` as the name for the macro.

To create the macro that builds the drop-down menu for the Inventory choices on the menu bar, perform the following steps.

Step 1 In the Database window, with the `Macro` button still selected, click `New`. If the Macro Name column is not visible, choose `View/Macro Names` from the menu so that you can see the Macro Names column. Click in the first row of the Macro Name column, and enter `Add to Inventory` as a name for the first macro in this group. Click in the first row of the Action column, open the list box, and choose `OpenForm` as an action.

Step 2 Under Action Arguments, click the `Form Name` entry, and choose `Inventory` from the list of forms. Click in the second row of the Action column, and choose `Maximize` from the list. Click in the third row of the action column, and choose `GoToRecord` from the list.

Step 3 Under Action Arguments, click `Record`, and choose `New` from the list. Click in the Macro Name column, in the fourth row of the macro, and enter `Edit Inventory` as a title for the second macro in this group. Click the Action column in the fourth row of the macro (beside the macro name you just entered), open the list box, and choose `OpenForm` as an action.

Step 4 Under Action Arguments, click the `Form Name` entry, and choose `Inventory` from the list of forms. Click in the fifth row of the Action column, and choose `Maximize` from the list. Click in the sixth row of the action column, and choose `DoMenuItem` from the list.

Step 5 Under Action Arguments, click `Command`, and choose `Find` from the list. Click in the Macro Name column, in the seventh row of the macro, and enter `Print Inventory` as a title for the last macro in this group. Click the Action column in the seventh row of the macro (beside the macro name you just entered), open the list box, and choose `OpenReport` as an action.

Step 6 Under Action Arguments, click the `Report Name` entry, and choose `Inventory` from the list of reports. Leave the View entry set to `Print Preview`.

Step 7 Press Ctrl–F4. Answer `Yes` when asked if you want to save the new macro. When prompted, enter `Inventory` as the name for the macro.

To create the macro that builds the drop-down menu for the Exit choices on the menu bar, perform the following steps.

Step 1 In the Database window, with the Macro button still selected, click New. If the Macro Name column is not visible, choose View/Macro Names from the menu so that you can see the Macro Names column.

Step 2 Click in the first row of the Macro Name column, and enter Exit System as a name for the macro. Click in the first row of the Action column, open the list box, and choose Close as an action. Click in the second row of the Action column, open the list box, and again choose Close as an action.

Step 3 Press Ctrl–F4. Answer Yes when asked if you want to save the new macro. When you are prompted, enter Exit as the name for the macro.

The forms used by the application will need command buttons that can be used to close the forms and return to the main menu when done. Perform the following steps to create a macro for closing forms and to add it to the required forms.

Step 1 In the Database window, with the Macro button still selected, click New. Click in the first row of the Action column of the macro. Open the drop-down list box, and choose Close from the list box.

Step 2 Press Ctrl–F4. Answer Yes in response to the "Save changes" prompt that appears. When you are prompted for a name, call the macro Close.

Step 3 In the Database window, click Form, then click Orders, then click Design to open the Orders form in Design view. Size the form so that you will have room to work, and move the windows so that both the Database window and the form are visible.

Step 4 In the Database window, click the Macro button to display the macros. Click the Close macro, and drag it to a location within the header of the form, roughly 4" from the left edge of the form. (*Note*: If you see a dialog box warning you that Wizards cannot be used on existing buttons, click OK to ignore it and ignore any more buttons like this that you see.) Use the movement techniques outlined in chapter 6 to center the button vertically.

Step 5 Press Ctrl–F4. Answer Yes to the prompt that asks if you want to save the changes to the form.

Step 6 In the Database window, click Form, then click Customers, then click to open the Customers form in Design view. Size the form so that you will have room to work, and move the windows so that both the Database window and the form are visible.

Step 7 In the Database window, click the `Macro` button to display the macros. Click the Close macro, and drag it to a location within the header of the form, roughly 2" from the left edge of the form. Use the movement techniques outlined in chapter 6 to center the button vertically.

Step 8 Press Ctrl–F4. Answer `Yes` to the prompt that asks if you want to save the changes to the form.

Step 9 In the Database window, click `Form`, then click `Inventory`, then click `Design` to open the Inventory form in Design view. Size the form so that you will have room to work, and move the windows so that both the Database window and the form are visible.

Step 10 In the Database window, click the `Macro` button to display the macros. Click the Close macro, and drag it to a location within the header of the form, roughly 2" from the left edge of the form. Use the movement techniques outlined in chapter 6 to center the button vertically.

Step 11 Press Ctrl–F4. Answer `Yes` to the prompt that asks if you want to save the changes to the form.

Finally, you will create a blank form that fills the window and presents the main menu of the application. Perform the following steps.

Step 1 In the Database window, click the `Form` button, then click `New`. When the New Form dialog box appears, leave the Select a Table/Query text box blank. Click the `Blank Form` button to open a blank form that is not associated with any tables. Increase the size of the drawing area on the form by dragging the lower-right corner until it is at least 8 × 8", then use the scroll bars to get back to the upper-left corner of the drawing area.

Step 2 From the menus, choose `Edit/Select Form`. Then, choose `View/Properties` to open the Properties window for the form.

Step 3 In the Properties window, select All Properties in the list box at the top of the window (Access 2.0 only) if it is not already selected. Then, click in the Menu Bar property (or with versions 1.0 and 1.1 of Access, the On Menu property), and choose `Main Menu.Menu` from the list of macros. Click in the Allow Editing property, and set the property to `Unavailable`. Click in the Scroll Bars property, and set the property to `Neither`. Then, double-click the Close icon in the Property window to close the window.

Step 4 If the Toolbox is not already visible, choose `View/Toolbox` to display the Toolbox. Click the Text tool in the Toolbox, and click in the form at a point roughly 1" below the top of the form and 3" to the right. Type a desired name for the application. In this example, I used the name "Nova Technologies, Inc." Click at the edge of the text that you just typed to select the text object. In the Toolbar, use the Font and Font Size list boxes to change the font to another font that you desire (such as Lucida Calligraphy) and to a larger font size (such as 16 point). Then, choose Layout/Size To Fit from the menus and reposition the text box to a centered location of your choice on the form.

Step 5 With the text box still selected, click the Palette button in the Toolbar. When the palette appears, change Appearance to Raised and click on a wider width for the border (you can change the fill colors for the text, if desired, by clicking a color of your choice in the Back Color column). Then, double-click the Palette's Close button to put away the Palette.

Step 6 As an option, you can add a graphic to the form. If you want to do so, use standard Windows techniques to switch to Windows Paintbrush (or your desired graphics package) and open the desired art. Capture the desired portion of the art, using the standard Windows techniques for your graphics package, then choose Edit/Copy. Use standard Windows techniques to switch back to Access, and choose Edit/Paste. Resize and position the graphic as desired near the center of the form. At this point, your form might resemble the example shown in FIG. 12-12.

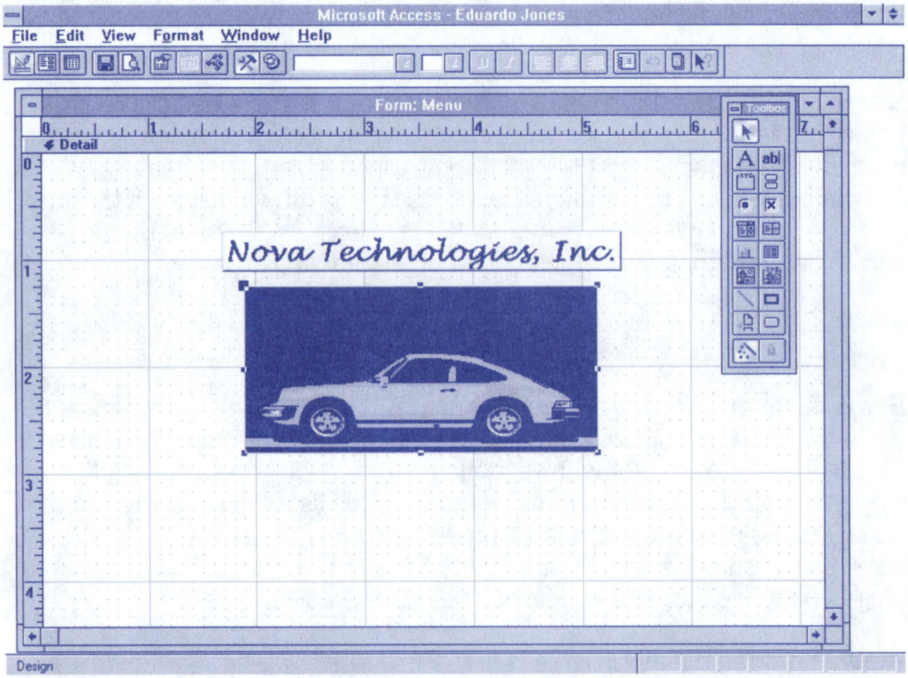

12-12
The Completed Menu form.

Step 7 Press Ctrl–F4. Answer Yes to the prompt that asks if you want to save the form. When prompted, enter Menu as a name for the form.

Step 8 In the Database window, click the `Macro` button, then click `New` to open a new macro. Click in the Action column in the first row of the macro, and choose `OpenForm` from the list.

Step 9 Under Action Arguments, click in `Form Name`, and choose `Menu` from the list of forms. Click in the Action column in the second row of the macro, and choose `Maximize` from the list.

Step 10 Press Ctrl–F4. Answer `Yes` to the prompt that asks if you want to save the macro. When you are prompted, enter `Autoexec` as a name for the macro.

At this point, the application is complete. Double-click the `Close` button of the Database window to close it. Then, to try running the application, choose `File/Open Database`. When the Open Database dialog box appears, double-click `ORDERS` to reopen the database. Because you added the Autoexec macro, when the database opens, the main menu appears automatically, as shown earlier in FIG. 12-1. You can test the application by adding and editing data and printing the desired reports. Additional queries, reports, and macros can be added as needed to increase the functionality of the application.

13 Professional time & billing

Professionals know all too well the importance of the saying, "Time is money." Professionals bill their expertise to those willing to pay at an hourly rate. If those hours are not carefully tracked, the bills are inaccurate and the professionals wind up being short-changed when it comes to income. Those who bill for their time—attorneys, designers, consultants, accountants, and members of dozens of other professional occupations—can use Access to track hourly charges and to send out bills on a regular basis.

The approach described in this chapter uses a report that serves as an itemized bill. The report is printed after all records for a particular client and a particular time period (usually one month) have been selected by means of a query. The files used by the Time-and-Billing System presented in this chapter can be found on the accompanying disk within the BILLING.MDB database; use the Windows File Manager or DOS commands to copy this database into your Microsoft Access directory. Figure 13-1 shows the main menu for the Time-and-Billing System.

Creating the database & tables

The Time-and-Billing System requires two tables: one named Clients and another named Time. The Clients table contains a Clients identification number, Clients name and address, the phone number of the Clients, and a contact name (preferably the person who gets the bills). To keep things simple, the application uses a three-letter alphabetical abbreviation to identify Clients. The Time table contains fields for the Clients identification

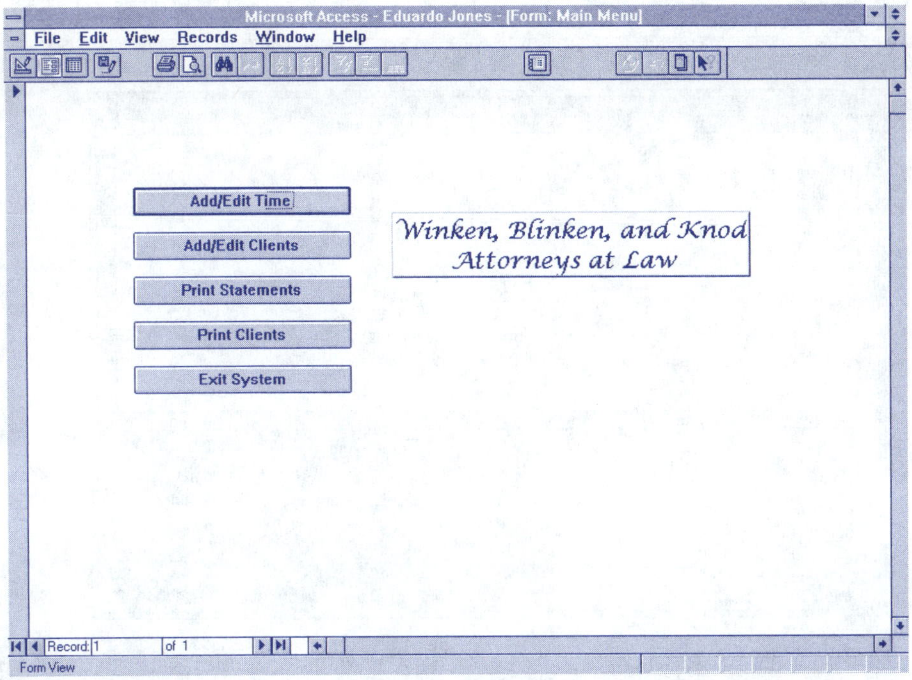

13-1
The Main menu for the Time and Billing database.

code, the date the work was performed, the name of the staff member who did the work, the billing rate, the number of hours worked, the hourly fee charged, and a description of the work.

To create the database and its required tables, first start Access in the usual manner, then perform the following steps.

Step 1 Choose `File/New Database` to open the New Database dialog box.

TIP

If you want to store the new database in a different directory, use the Directory list box to locate the desired directory now. Click on the desired directory, and Access will store the new database in that directory.

Step 2 Enter `BILLING` in the File Name text box as a name for the database, then click `OK`. (Remember, in Access, database names must be 8 characters or less, with no spaces.) Access creates the database file on your hard disk, and the Database window appears.

Step 3 In the Database window, click the `Table` button, then click `New`. In the New Table dialog box that appears, click `New Table`. The Table window appears. Fill in the Table window with the field names and data types for the fields shown in TABLE 13-1. Click anywhere in the first field (titled "Client ID"), and click the Key icon in the Toolbar to make this field the

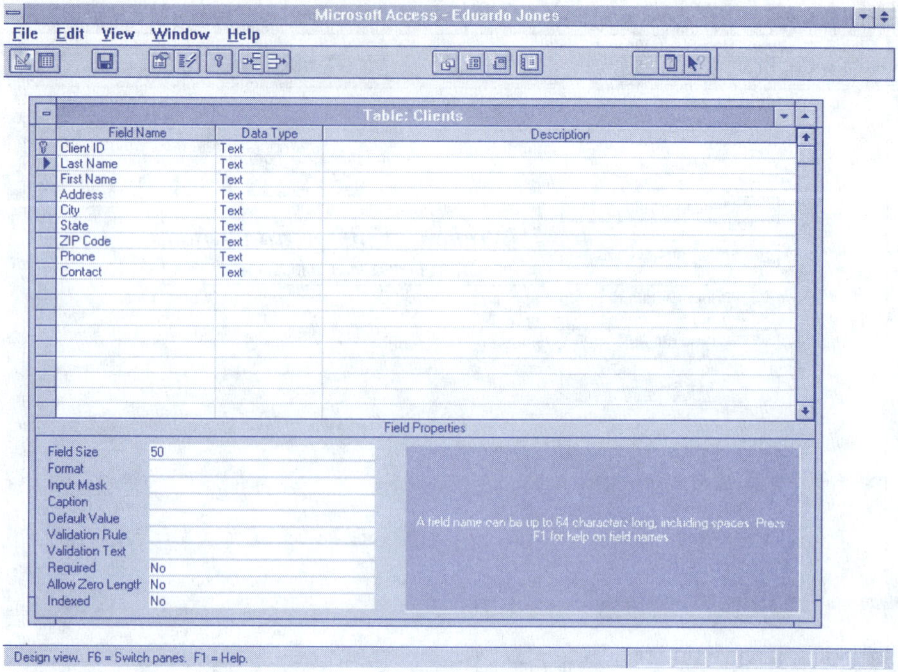

13-2 *The completed Clients table.*

primary key. At this point, your table should resemble the example shown in FIG. 13-2.

Table 13-1 Fill in the Table window with these field names and data types.

Field name	Data Type
Client ID	Text
Last Name	Text
First Name	Text
Address	Text
City	Text
State	Text
ZIP Code	Text
Phone	Text
Contact	Text

Step 4 When you are done defining the fields, choose `File/Save` to save the table. When prompted for a table name, enter `Clients` as the name, and click `OK`.

Step 5 Press Ctrl–F4 to close the Table window. The new table, Clients, now appears in the Database window.

Step 6 In the Database window, click `New`. In the New Table dialog box that appears, click `New Table`. The Table window again appears. Fill in the Table window with the field names and data types for the fields shown in TABLE 13-2. Click and drag through the record selectors of the first three rows to select all three fields, then click the Key icon in the Toolbar to make the combination of these fields the primary key. At this point, your table should resemble the example shown in FIG. 13-3.

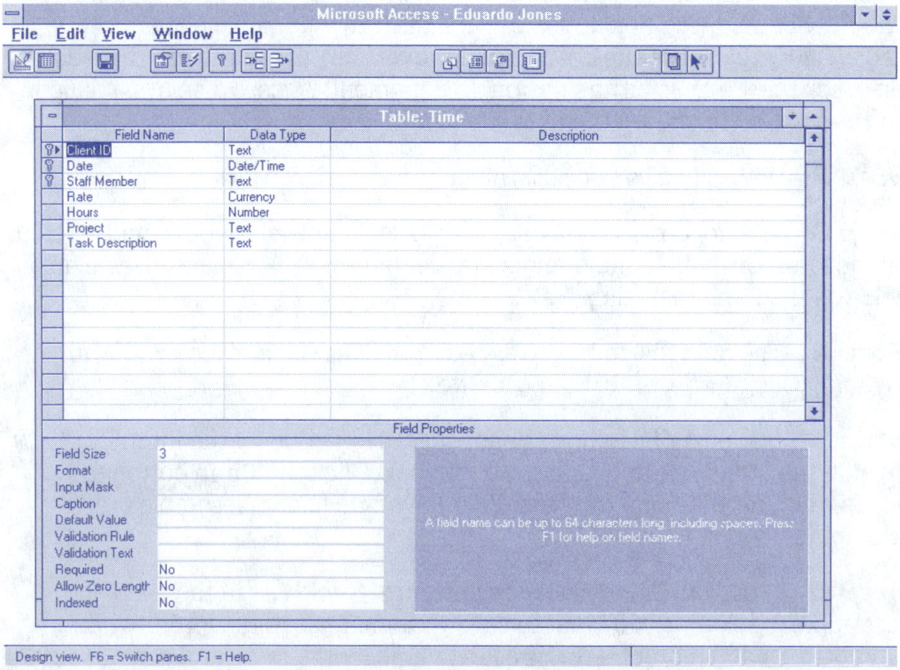

13-3
The completed Time table.

Table 13-2 Fill in the Table window with these field names and data types.

Field name	Data Type
Client ID	Text
Date	Date/Time
Staff Member	Text
Rate	Currency
House	Number
Project	Text
Task Description	Text

Step 7 When you are done defining the fields, choose `File/Save` to save the table. When prompted for a table name, enter `Time` as the name, and click `OK`.

Step 8 Press Ctrl–F4 to close the Table window. The new table, Time, now appears in the Database window.

Creating the forms

The database will require three forms: one will be used for adding and editing clients, the second will be used for adding and editing records in the Time table, and the third will provide a means of viewing each client along with the related time spent. To create the needed forms, perform the following steps.

Step 1 In the Database window, click the `Form` button, then click `New`. The New Form dialog box appears. Click the arrow under Select a Table/Query to choose the desired table, and click on `Time` in the drop-down list. Click the `FormWizards` button. In a moment, Access displays a dialog box asking you to choose the desired wizard.

Step 2 With `Single-column` already selected, click `OK`.

Step 3 The next dialog box to appear asks which fields you want selected on the form. Click the double-angle bracket button (`>>`) to place all available fields on the form, then click `Next`.

Step 4 The next dialog box to appear asks what kind of look you want for the form. Click `Embossed`, then click `Next`.

Step 5 The next dialog box to appear asks for a title for the form. By default, the title `Time` appears in the text box. Click the `Open` button to accept the title and open the form. Your new form should resemble the example shown in FIG. 13-4.

Step 6 Press Ctrl–F4 to close the new form (click `Yes` in the dialog box that appears asking if you want to save your changes to the form). When prompted for a name, enter `Time` as the name for the form, and click `OK`.

Next, perform the following steps to create the form needed for the clients.

Step 1 In the Database window, click `New`. The New Form dialog box appears. Click the arrow under Select a Table/Query to choose the desired table, and click on `Clients` in the drop-down list. Click the `FormWizards` button. In a moment, Access displays a dialog box asking you to choose the desired wizard.

Step 2 With `Single-column` already selected, click `OK`.

Step 3 The next dialog box to appear asks which fields you want selected on the form. Click the double-angle bracket button (`>>`), to place all available fields on the form, then click `Next`.

Step 4 The next dialog box to appear asks what kind of look you want for the form. Click `Embossed`, then click `Next`.

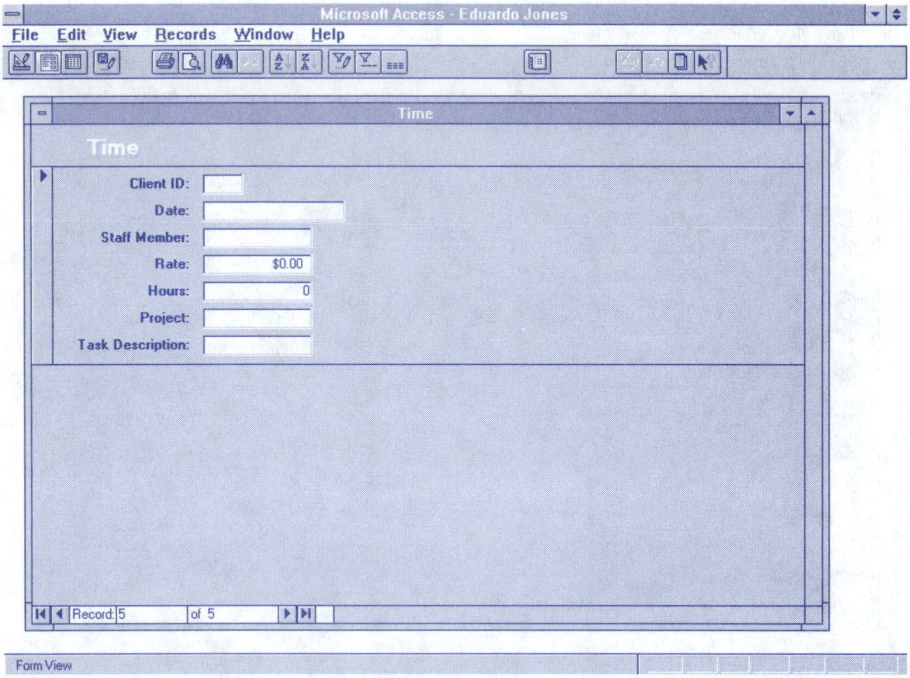

13-4
The completed Time form.

Step 5 The next dialog box to appear asks for a title for the form. By default, the title `Clients` appears in the text box. Click the `Open` button to accept the title and open the form. Your new form should resemble the example shown in FIG. 13-5.

Step 6 Press Ctrl–F4 to close the new form (click `Yes` in the dialog box that appears asking if you want to save your changes to the form). When you are prompted for a name, enter `Clients` as the name for the form, and click `OK`.

Next, perform the following steps to create the form needed for viewing each client's billable time.

Step 1 In the Database window, click `New`. The New Form dialog box appears. Click the arrow under Select a Table/Query to choose the desired table, and choose `Clients` from the drop-down list. Click the `FormWizards` button. In a moment, Access displays a dialog box asking you to choose the desired wizard. Click `Main/Subform`, then click `OK`. The next dialog box to appear asks which table contains the data for the subform. Click `Time`, then click `Next`.

Step 2 The next dialog box to appear asks which fields you want to add to the main form. Double-click the following fields in this order: First Name, Last Name, City, then State. Then, click `Next`.

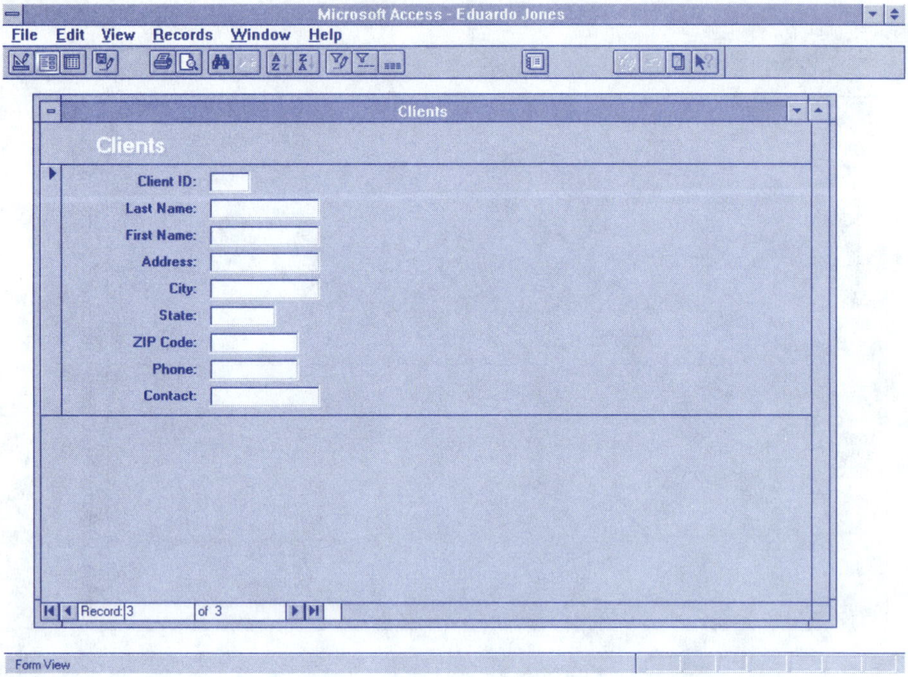

13-5
The completed Clients form.

Step 3 The next dialog box to appear asks which fields you want to include on the subform. Double-click the following fields in this order: Date, Project, Hours, Rate, then Task Description. Then, click `Next`.

Step 4 The next dialog box to appear asks what kind of look you want for the form. Click `Shadowed`, then click `Next`.

Step 5 The next dialog box to appear asks for a title for the form. By default, the title Clients appears in the text box. Type `View Time` in the form title text box now, then click the `Design` button to accept the title and open the form in Design view. Access will display a dialog box warning you that you must save the subform before saving the main form; click `OK` in this dialog box. In the Save As dialog box that next appears, enter `Time Spent` as a title.

Step 6 When the form opens in Design view, choose `Edit/Select Form` from the menus, then choose `View/Properties` to open the Properties window for the form. If All Properties is not already selected in the list box at the top of the form (Access 2.0 only), select it now. Click in the Default Editing property, and change it from `Allow Edits` to `Read-Only`. Then, double-click the Close icon in the Property window to close it. At this point, your form should resemble the example shown in FIG 13-6.

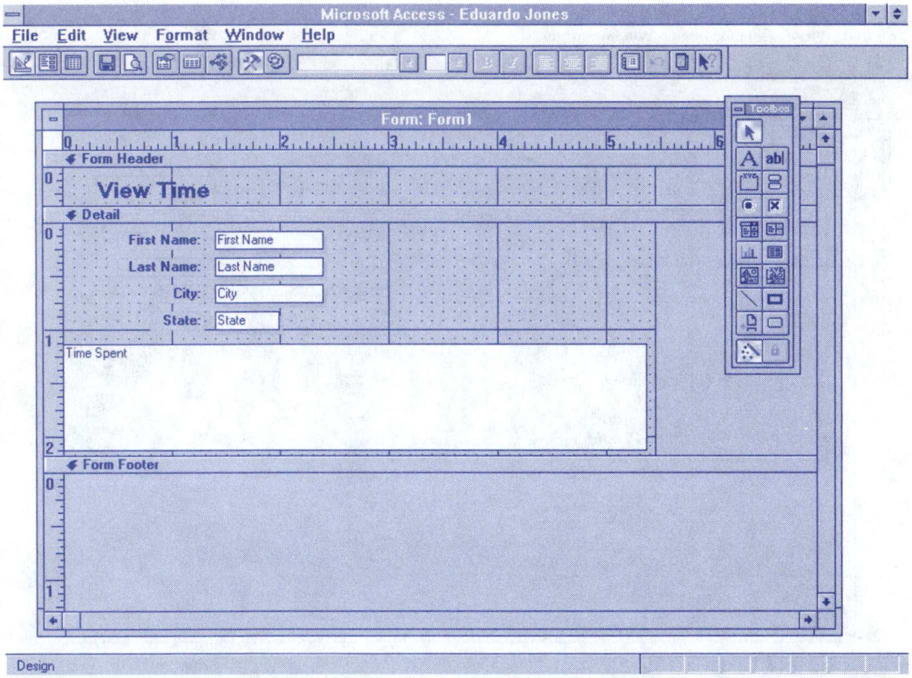

13-6 *The completed View Time form.*

Step 7 Press Ctrl–F4 to close the new form (click `Yes` in the dialog box that appears asking if you want to save the form). When you are prompted for a name, enter `View Client Time` as the name for the form.

Establishing the relationship

Because this application makes a straightforward use of a simple one-to-many relation (one client with many time records), the relationship can be easily established with the `Edit/Relationships` command; this will make later construction of queries a simpler matter. Perform these steps to define the relationship.

Step 1 From the menus, choose `Edit/Relationships`. Doing so causes the Relationships dialog box to appear, with the Add Table dialog box open above it.

Step 2 In the Add Table dialog box, click `Clients`, then click `Add`, then click `Time`, then click `Add`. Finally, click `Close`.

Step 3 In the Clients list box, click the `Client ID` field, and drag over to the `Client ID` field in the Time list box. When you release the mouse button, a Relationships dialog box appears. Click `Create` in this dialog box to create the relationship. At this point, your screen should resemble that shown in FIG. 13-7.

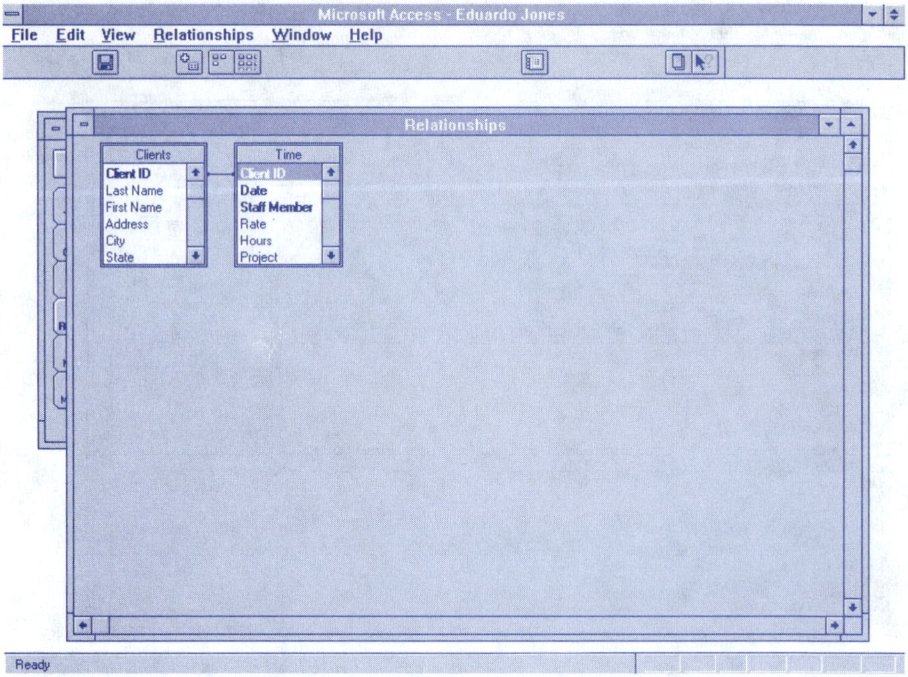

13-7
The Relationships dialog box.

Step 4 Press Ctrl–F4 to close the Relationships dialog box. Answer 'Yes' to the dialog box that asks if you want to save the changes to the relationship.

Creating the relational query

To support the reports used by the time-and-billing application, a relational query will be needed. Perform the following steps to create the query.

Step 1 In the Database window, click the `Query` button, then click `New`. In the New Query dialog box that appears, click `New Query`. The Add Table dialog box appears.

Step 2 In the Table/Query list box, click `Time`, then click `Add`. Next, click `Clients`, then click `Add`. Finally, click `Close`. This causes list boxes with the fields from both tables to appear in the Select Query window. Because a relationship has been already established, a link appears automatically between Client ID field in the Clients and Time field lists.

Step 3 In the Clients list box, click on `Last Name`. While holding the mouse button, drag the field down to the first column of the Field row. Use the same technique to drag the First Name, Address, City, State, ZIP Code, and Contact fields down to the adjacent empty columns of the Field row.

Step 4 In the Time list box, click on `Date`. While holding the Shift key, click on the last field in the list box.

Step 5 With all of the fields (except for Client ID) in the Time list box now selected, click on any of the fields and drag the fields down to the next adjacent empty column of the Field row.

Step 6 Choose `File/Save`. Access will prompt you for a name for the query. Enter `Billing Query`, and click `OK`. Press Ctrl–F4 to close the Select Query window. The new query appears by name in the Database window.

Creating the reports

Two reports are needed for the application. One will list the details for each Client; the other will provide billing statements for the clients, containing a summary of the work performed for a given time period. Perform the following steps to create the reports.

Step 1 In the Database window, click the `Report` button, then click `New`. The New Report dialog box appears. Click the arrow under Select a Table/Query to choose the desired table, and click `Billing Query` in the drop-down list. Click the `ReportWizards` button. In a moment, Access displays a dialog box asking you to choose the desired wizard. Click `Groups/Totals`, then click `OK`.

Step 2 The next dialog box to appear asks which fields you want placed on the report. Scroll down the list box and click the Date field, then click the angle bracket (>) to place the Date field on the report. Repeat this step for the Hours, Project, Task Description, and Rate fields, then click `Next`.

Step 3 The next dialog box asks which field you want to use to group the data by. Click the Rate field, then click the angle bracket (>), then click `Next`.

Step 4 The next dialog box asks how you want to group the data in each field. The default is fine here, so just click `Next`.

Step 5 The next dialog box asks how you want to sort the data. Click the Date field, then click the angle bracket (>), then click `Next`.

Step 6 The next dialog box to appear asks what kind of look you want for the report. Click `Ledger`, then click `Next`.

Step 7 The next dialog box to appear asks for a title for the form. By default, the title `Billing Query` appears in the text box. Replace the default title by typing `Statement` in the report title box, and turn off the "Calculate Percentage of Total" option. Then, click the `Design` button to accept the title and open the report in Design view.

Step 8 If the Toolbox is not visible, choose `View/Toolbox`. Click the Text Box tool in the Toolbox. Next, click at a blank spot in the report's header, roughly 3" from the left edge of the report, and drag until the text box is roughly ⅛" high and 2" wide. Click in the text box, and type the following expression (don't forget the equal symbol):

```
=[First Name] & " " & [Last Name]
```

Step 9 In the rate footer, find the text box containing the expression, `=Sum([Hours])`. Click within the expression, and change the expression to `=Sum([Hours]*[Rate])`.

Step 10 In the report footer, find the text box containing the same expression, `=Sum([Hours])`. Again, click within the expression, and change the expression to `=Sum([Hours]*[Rate])`. At this point, your report should resemble the example shown in FIG. 13-8.

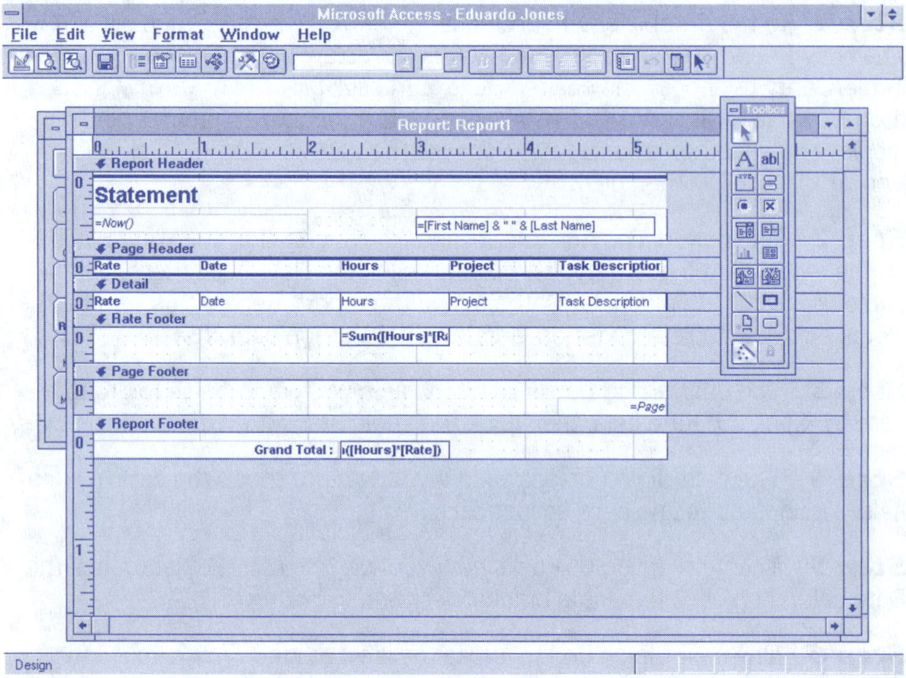

13-8
The completed Statements report.

Step 11 Choose `File/Save` to save the new report. When you are prompted for a title, enter `Statements` for a report name, then click `OK`. Press Ctrl–F4 to close the new report.

Next, perform the following steps to create the report needed for printing a listing of the clients.

Step 1 In the Database window, click the `Report` button, then click `New`. The New Report dialog box appears. Click the arrow under Select a Table/Query to choose the desired table, and click `Clients` in the drop-down list. Click the `ReportWizards` button. In a moment, Access displays a dialog box asking you to choose the desired wizard.

Step 2 With Single-column already selected, click OK.

Step 3 The next dialog box to appear asks which fields you want placed on the report. Click the double-angle bracket button (>>) to place all available fields on the report, then click Next.

Step 4 The next dialog box asks which field you want to use to sort the data by. Double-click the State field to place it in the Sort Order box, then double-click the City field to place it in the Sort Order box. Finally, click Next.

Step 5 The next dialog box to appear asks what kind of look you want for the report. Click Executive, then click Next.

Step 6 The next dialog box to appear asks for a title for the form. By default, the title Clients appears in the text box. Click the Design button to accept the title and open the report in Design view. At this point, your report should resemble the example shown in FIG. 13-9.

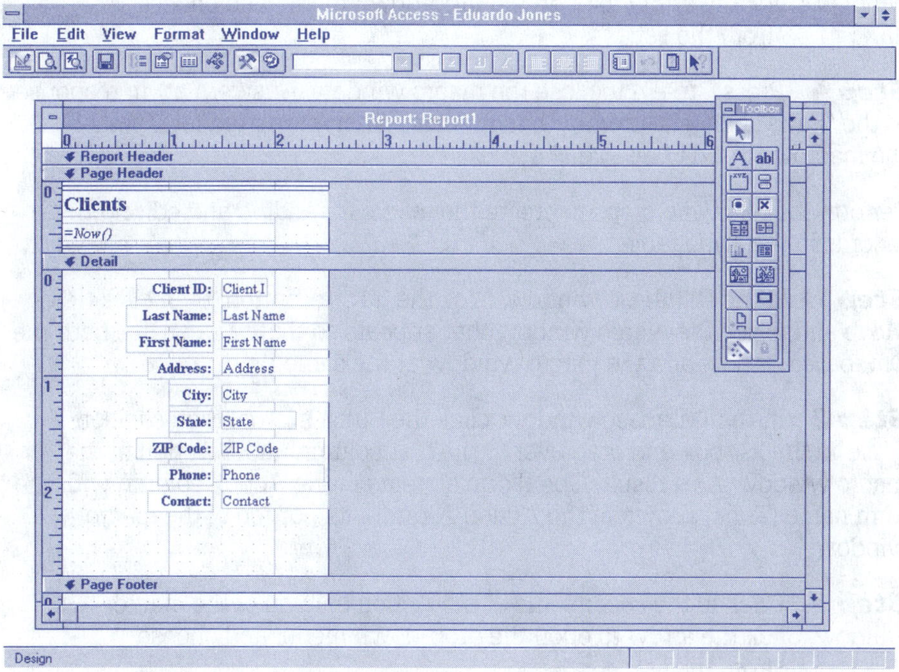

13-9
The completed Clients report.

Step 7 Choose File/Save to save the new report. When you are prompted for a title, enter Clients for a report name, then click OK. Press Ctrl–F4 to close the new report.

Developing the application

The application requires a series of macros that provide the menu choices for performing database operations and the actions that should occur in response to those menu choices. Perform the following steps to create the macros required for the application.

Perform the following steps to create the macro for adding and editing the records in the Clients table.

Step 1 In the Database window, click the `Macro` button, then click `New`. Move and resize the macro window that appears so that you can see both the Database window and the macro window at the same time.

Step 2 In the Database window, click the `Form` button, then click on `Clients` in the list box and drag over to the first column under Action in the macro window. As a result, OpenForm appears in the Action column with the form name (Clients) shown in the Action Arguments portion of the macro window.

Step 3 Click in the second line of the Action column of the macro window. Click the arrow to open the drop-down menu, and choose `Maximize` from the list.

Step 4 Press Ctrl–F4 to close the macro window. Answer `Yes` in response to the "Save changes" prompt that appears. When prompted for a name, call the macro `Add/Edit Clients`.

Perform the following steps to create the macro for adding and editing the records in the Time table.

Step 1 In the Database window, click the `Macro` button, then click `New`. Move and resize the macro window that appears so that you can see both the Database window and the macro window at the same time.

Step 2 In the Database window, click the `Form` button, then click on `Time` in the list box and drag over to the first column under Action in the macro window. As a result, OpenForm appears in the Action column with the form name (Time) shown in the Action Arguments portion of the macro window.

Step 3 Click in the second line of the Action column of the macro window. Click the arrow to open the drop-down menu, and choose `Maximize` from the list.

Step 4 Press Ctrl–F4 to close the macro window. Answer `Yes` in response to the "Save changes" prompt that appears. When prompted for a name, call the macro `Add/Edit Time`.

Perform the following steps to create the macro for printing the statements.

Step 1 In the Database window, click the `Macro` button, then click `New`. Move and resize the macro window that appears so that you can see both the Database window and the macro window at the same time.

Step 2 In the Database window, click the `Report` button, then click on `Statements` in the list box and drag over to the first column under Action in the macro window. As a result, OpenReport appears in the Action column with the report name (Statements) shown in the Action Arguments portion of the macro window.

Step 3 Press Ctrl–F4 to close the macro window. Answer `Yes` in response to the "Save changes" prompt that appears. When you are prompted for a name, call the macro `Print Statements`.

Perform the following steps to create the macro for printing a list of the clients.

Step 1 In the Database window, click the `Macro` button, then click `New`. Move and resize the macro window that appears so that you can see both the Database window and the macro window at the same time.

Step 2 In the Database window, click the `Report` button, then click on `Clients` in the list box and drag over to the first column under Action in the macro window. As a result, OpenReport appears in the Action column with the report name (Clients) shown in the Action Arguments portion of the macro window.

Step 3 Press Ctrl–F4 to close the macro window. Answer `Yes` in response to the "Save changes" prompt that appears. When you are prompted for a name, call the macro `Print Clients`.

Perform the following steps to create a macro for finding a record.

Step 1 In the Database window, click `Macro`, then click `New` to create another macro. Click in the Action column of the first row, and choose `DoMenuItem` from the list box.

Step 2 Under Action Arguments, click in the Command box, open the list box, and choose `Find`.

Step 3 Press Ctrl–F4 to close the macro. Answer `Yes` when you are asked if you want to save the macro. For a name, call the macro `Search`.

Perform the following steps to create a macro for closing a form.

Step 1 In the Database window, click the `Macro` button, then click `New`.

Step 2 Click in the first row of the Action column of the macro. Open the drop-down list box, and choose `Close` from the list box.

Step 3 Press Ctrl–F4 to close the macro window. Answer `Yes` in response to the "Save changes" prompt that appears. When you are prompted for a name, call the macro `Close`.

Perform the following steps to create a macro for deleting a record.

Step 1 In the Database window, click the `Macro` button, then click `New`. Click in the first row of the Action column of the macro. Open the drop-down list box, and choose `DoMenuItem`. Under Action Arguments, click in the Command text box and choose `Select Record` from the list.

Step 2 Click in the second row of the Action column of the macro. Open the drop-down list box, and choose `DoMenuItem`. Under Action Arguments, click in the Command text box and choose `Delete` from the list.

Step 3 Press Ctrl–F4 to close the macro window. Answer `Yes` in response to the "Save changes" prompt that appears. When you are prompted for a name, call the macro `Delete`.

Perform the following steps to create the macro for exiting from the application.

Step 1 In the Database window, click the `Macro` button, then click `New`. Click in the first row of the Action column of the macro. Open the drop-down list box, and choose `Close` from the list box.

Step 2 Click in the second row of the Action column of the macro. Open the drop-down list box, and again choose `Close` from the list box.

Step 3 Press Ctrl–F4 to close the macro window. Answer `Yes` in response to the "Save changes" prompt that appears. When you are prompted for a name, call the macro `Exit System`.

Next, the form that will serve as the main menu of the application is needed. Perform the following steps to create the main menu.

Step 1 In the Database window, click the `Form` button, then click `New`. When the New Form dialog box appears, leave the Select a Table/Query text box blank. Click the `Blank Form` button to open a blank form that is not associated with any tables. Increase the size of the drawing area on the form by dragging the lower-right corner until it is at least 8 × 8", then use the scroll bars to get back to the upper-left corner of the drawing area. Move and resize the form so that you can see both the form and the Database window at the same time.

Step 2 In the Database window, click the `Macro` button to display all the macros you have created. Click `Add/Edit Time`, and drag it over to a position roughly 1" from the left edge and 1" below the top of the form. When you release the mouse button, a button appears that will call the macro.

(*Note*: If you see a dialog box warning you that wizards cannot be used with existing buttons, click `OK` to ignore it, and ignore any other dialog boxes like this that you see later.) Place the mouse pointer over the right edge of the button until it changes shape to a double-pointed arrow. Click and drag to the right until the button is roughly 2" in length. When you do so, the entire title of the macro, "Add/Edit Time," should be visible within the button.

Step 3 In the Database window, click `Add/Edit Clients`, and drag it over to a position roughly ¼" below the existing button. When you release the mouse button, a button appears that will call the macro. Place the mouse pointer over the right edge of the button until it changes shape to a double-pointed arrow. Click and drag to the right until the button is the same size as the previous button. When you do so, the entire title of the macro, "Add/Edit Clients," should be visible within the button. Move the mouse pointer over the button until it changes to the shape of a hand, then click and drag the button as necessary until it is aligned ¼" directly underneath the first button. (If you are nearing the bottom of the form, you might want to use the vertical scroll bar to scroll the form upwards so that you will have sufficient room to place the remaining buttons.)

Step 4 In the Database window, click `Print Statements`, and drag it over to a position roughly ¼" below the `Add/Edit Clients` button. Place the mouse pointer over the right edge of the new button until it changes shape to a double-pointed arrow. Click and drag to the right until the button is the same size as the other buttons. When you do so, the entire title of the macro, "Print Statements," should be visible within the button. Move the mouse pointer over the button until it changes to the shape of a hand, then click and drag the button as necessary until it is aligned ¼" directly underneath the second button.

Step 5 In the Database window, click `Print Clients` and drag it over to a position roughly ¼" below the `Print Statements` button. Place the mouse pointer over the right edge of the new button until it changes shape to a double-pointed arrow. Click and drag to the right until the button is the same size as the other buttons. When you do so, the entire title of the macro, "Print Clients," should be visible within the button. Move the mouse pointer over the button until it changes to the shape of a hand, then click and drag the button as necessary until it is aligned ¼" directly underneath the previous button.

Step 6 In the Database window, click `Exit System` and drag it over to a position roughly ¼" below the `Print Employees` button. Place the mouse pointer over the right edge of the new button until it changes shape to a double-pointed arrow. Click and drag to the right until the button is the same size as the other buttons. When you do so, the entire title of the macro, "Exit System," should be visible within the button. Move the mouse pointer over the button until it changes to the shape of a hand, then click and drag the button as necessary until it is aligned ¼" directly underneath the previous button.

Step 7 Click the form's `Maximize` button so that you can see the entire form. If the Toolbar is not already visible, choose `View/Toolbox` to display the Toolbox. Click the Label tool in the Toolbox, and click in the form at a point roughly 1" below the top of the form and 4" to the right. Type a desired name for the application. Click at the edge of the text you just typed to select the text object. In the Toolbar, use the Font and Font Size list boxes to change the font to another font that you desire (such as Times New Roman) and to a larger font size (such as 14 point). Then, choose `Layout/Size To Fit` from the menus, and reposition the text box to a centered location of your choice on the form.

Step 8 With the text box still selected, click the `Palette` button in the Toolbar. When the palette appears, change the appearance to raised (click the `Raised` button in the Palette) and click on a wider width for the border (you can change the background colors for the text, if desired, by clicking a color of your choice in the Back column). Then, double-click the Palette's `Close` button to put away the Palette. As an option, you can add a graphic to the form. If you want to do so, use standard Windows techniques to switch to Windows Paintbrush (or your desired graphics package) and open the desired art. Capture the desired portion of the art, using the standard Windows techniques for your graphics package, then choose `Edit/Copy`. Use standard Windows techniques to switch back to Access, and choose `Edit/Paste`. Resize and position the graphic as desired on the form. At this point, your form might resemble the example shown in FIG. 13-10.

Step 9 Double-click the `Close` button of the Form window to close it. When Access asks if you want to save the form, click `Yes`. When you are prompted for a name for the form, enter `Main Menu`.

Step 10 In the Database window, click the `Form` button, then click `Clients`, then click `Design`. Move or resize the form window so that you can see both the Database window and the Form window at the same time.

Step 11 In the Database window, click the `Macro` button, then click the Search macro and drag the macro over to a blank space anywhere within the header of the form. (However, leave room to the right of the button to add two buttons of the same size. You might need to widen the form to provide room for the buttons. If so, do so by dragging the right edge of the form further to the right.) Center the button vertically as desired within the header.

Step 12 In the Database window, click the Delete macro and drag the macro to the space to the right of the `Search` button. If necessary, move the `Delete` button so that it is aligned horizontally and vertically and just to the right of the `Search` button.

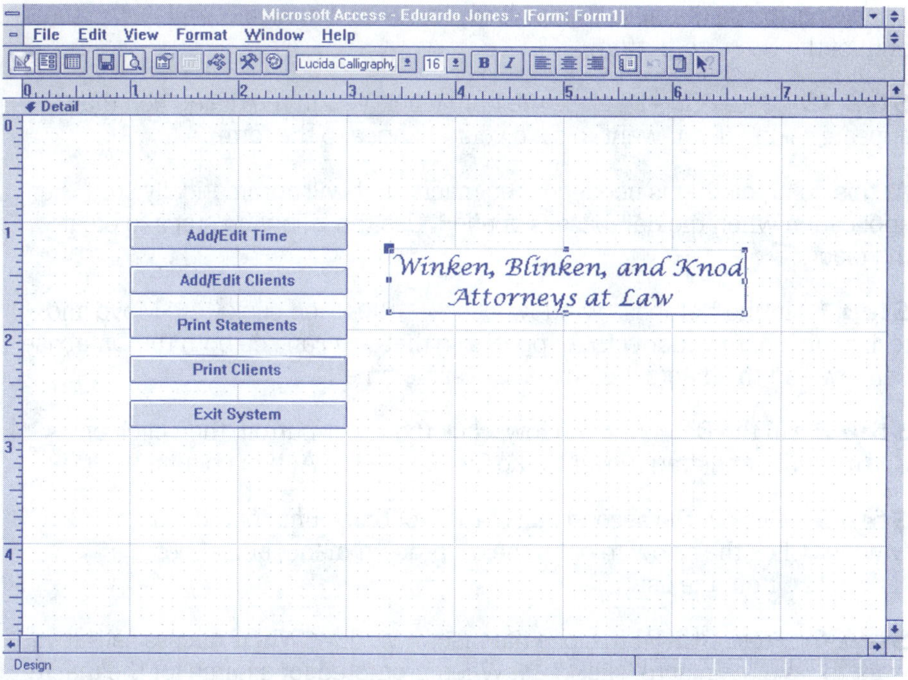

13-10
The completed Main Menu form.

Step 13 In the Database window, click the Close macro and drag the macro to the space to the right of the `Delete` button. If necessary, move the `Close` button so that it is aligned horizontally and vertically and just to the right of the `Delete` button.

Step 14 Press Ctrl–F4 close the form (click `Yes` in the dialog box that appears asking if you want to save your changes to the form).

Step 15 In the Database window, click the `Form` button, then click `Time`, then click `Design`. Move or resize the form window so that you can see both the Database window and the Form window at the same time.

Step 16 In the Database window, click the `Macro` button, then click the Search macro and drag the macro over to a blank space anywhere within the header of the form (but leave room to the right of the button to add two buttons of the same size). Center the button vertically as desired within the header.

Step 17 In the Database window, click the Delete macro and drag the macro to the space to the right of the `Search` button. If necessary, move the `Delete` button so that it is aligned horizontally and vertically and just to the right of the `Search` button.

Step 18 In the Database window, click the Close macro and drag the macro to the space to the right of the `Delete` button. If necessary, move the

Close button so that it is aligned horizontally and vertically and just to the right of the Delete button.

Step 19 Press Ctrl–F4 close the form (click Yes in the dialog box that appears asking if you want to save your changes to the form).

At this point, all that is needed is the macro that will automatically start the application when the database is opened. Use the following steps to create the macro.

Step 1 In the Database window, click Macro, then click New. Move and resize the macro window that appears so that you can see both the Database window and the macro window at the same time.

Step 2 In the Database window, click the Form button, then click on Main Menu, and drag it over to the first line of the Action column.

Step 3 Click in the second line of the Action column of the macro window. Click the arrow to open the drop-down menu, and choose Maximize from the list.

Step 4 Press Ctrl–F4 to close the macro window. When Access asks if you want to save the macro, click Yes. When prompted for a name for the macro, enter Autoexec.

At this point, the application is complete. Double-click the Close button of the Database window to close it. Then, to try running the application, choose File/Open Database. When the Open Database dialog box appears, double-click BILLING to reopen the database. Because you added the Autoexec macro, when the database opens, the form containing the menu for the application opens automatically, as shown earlier in FIG. 13-1. You can test the application by adding and editing data and printing the desired reports. Use the techniques detailed in this chapter to add any additional reports or specialized queries (and corresponding menu option buttons) to refine the application so it precisely suits your needs.

14 Real estate home showcase

Designed to meet the needs of house-hunting clients who visit the typical real estate office, the Home-Showcase System presented in this chapter is an example of an application that makes use of graphics within forms to present important information. The Home-Showcase System requires two tables: one named Homes and another named Agents. The Homes table contains a record with the vital statistics for each house offered, including a photo of the home. A field called MLS number, commonly used by real estate agents, serves to provide a unique identifier for every employee. The Agents table contains the details of the real estate agents who offer the homes for sale. To keep things simple, the key for the Agents table is based on a combination of the last name and first name fields. (Such a scheme would be unworkable with a large number of names; however, considering the fact that the average real estate office has a limited number of agents, the design suffices for this type of application.) Figure 14-1 shows the Home-Showcase System.

Creating the database & tables

To create the database and its required tables, first start Access in the usual manner, then perform the following steps.

Step 1 Choose `File/New Database` to open the New Database dialog box.

TIP

If you want to store the new database in a different directory, use the Directory list box to locate the desired directory now. Click on the desired directory, and Access will store the new database in that directory.

14-1
The Home Showcase database in use.

Step 2 Enter `HOMES` in the File Name text box as a name for the database, then click `OK`. (Remember, in Access, database names must be 8 characters or less with no spaces.) Access creates the database file on your hard disk, and the Database window appears.

Step 3 In the Database window, click the `Table` button, then click `New`. In the New Table dialog box which appears, click `New Table`. The Table window appears. Fill in the Table window with the field names and data types for the fields shown in TABLE 14-1. Click anywhere in the first field (titled "MLS Number"), and click the Key icon in the Toolbar to make this field the primary key. At this point, your table should resemble the example shown in FIG. 14-2.

Table 14-1
Fill in the Table window with these field names and data types.

Field name	Data type
MLS Number	Text
Owners	Text
Street Address	Text
City	Text
State	Text
ZIP/Postal	Text
Phone	Text

County	Text
City/Town Taxes	Text
Subdivision	Text
Price	Currency
Square Footage	Number
Year Built	Text
Description	Memo
Agent Last name	Text
Agent First Name	Text
Photo	Object

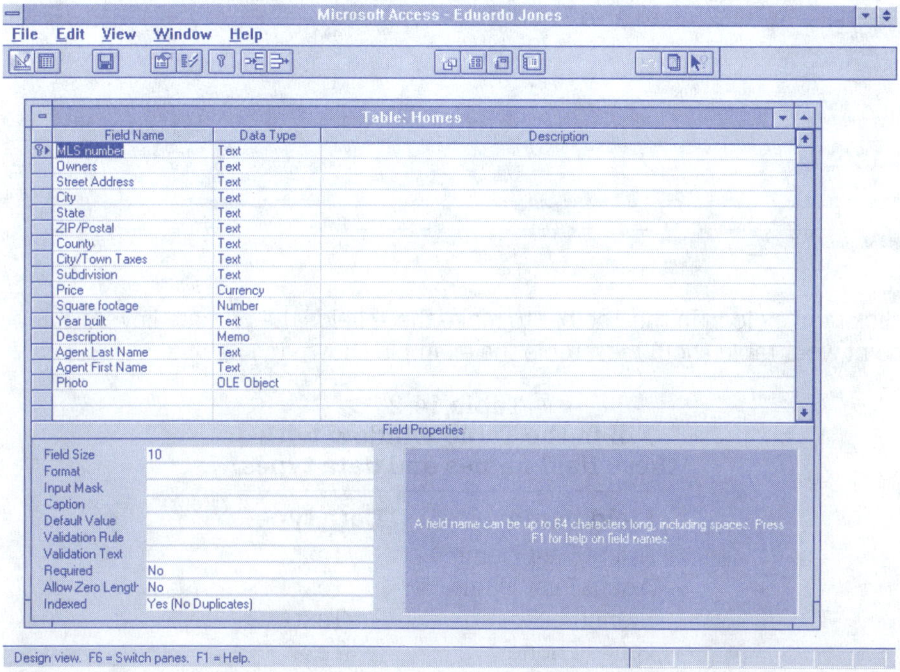

14-2
The completed Homes table.

Step 4 When you are done defining the fields, choose File/Save to save the table. When you are prompted for a table name, enter Homes as the name, and click OK. Press Ctrl–F4 to close the Table window. The new table, Homes, now appears in the Database window.

Step 5 In the Database window, with the Table button still selected, click New. In the New Table dialog box that appears, click New Table. The Table window again appears. Fill in the Table window with the field names and data types for the fields shown in TABLE 14-2. Click the Record Selector beside the Agent Last Name field to select it. Then, while holding the Shift key, do the same for the Agent First Name field so that both fields are selected. Then,

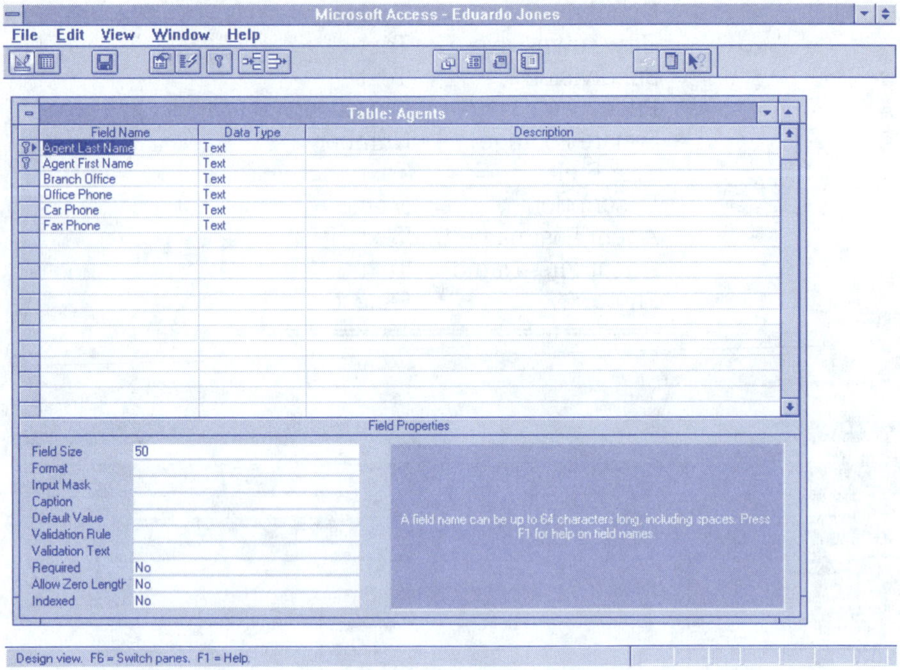

14-3
The completed Agents table.

click the Key icon in the Toolbar to make these fields the primary key. At this point, your table should resemble the example shown in FIG. 14-3.

Table 14-2
Fill in the Table window with these field names and data types.

Field name	Data type
Agent Last Name	Text
Agent First Name	Text
Branch Office	Text
Office Phone	Text
Home Phone	Text
Car Phone	Text
FAX Phone	Text

Step 6 When you are done defining the fields, choose File/Save to save the table. When you are prompted for a table name, enter Agents as the name, and click OK. Press Ctrl–F4 to close the Table window. The new table, Agents, now appears in the Database window.

Creating the forms

The database will require two forms. One serves as the main form used throughout the application and displays the particulars, including the photo, of a particular home. The other form displays data on the agents assigned to the office. To create the needed forms, perform the following steps.

Step 1 In the Database window, click the `Form` button, then click `New`. The New Form dialog box appears. Click the arrow under Select a Table/Query to choose the desired table, and click on `Homes` in the drop-down list. Click the `FormWizards` button. In a moment, Access displays a dialog box asking you to choose the desired wizard.

Step 2 With `Single-column` already selected, click `OK`.

Step 3 The next dialog box to appear asks which fields you want selected on the form. Click the double-angle bracket button (`>>`) to place all available fields on the form, then click `Next`.

Step 4 The next dialog box to appear asks what kind of look you want for the form. Click `Embossed`, then click `Next`.

Step 5 The next dialog box to appear asks for a title for the form. By default, the title `Homes` appears in the text box. Click the `Design` button to accept the title and open the form in Design view. Maximize the window containing the form so that you have room to work, and click and drag the right edge of the drawing area until the drawing area of the form is at least 7" in width.

Step 6 Click the Photo field to select it (you might need to scroll the form downwards to find the field). With the field selected, move the mouse pointer near the edge until it changes into the shape of a hand, and click and drag the field to the upper right corner of the form.

Step 7 Delete the objects currently in the header area of the form (the "Homes" title and the shadow boxes) by clicking them to select them, and pressing Del.

Step 8 If the Toolbox is not visible, choose `View/Toolbox` from the menus. Click the Label tool in the Toolbox, and click in the header at a point roughly 2" from the left edge of the form. Type a desired name for the application. In this example, I used the name "Lakeside Homes Showcase."

Step 9 Click at the edge of the text that you just typed to select the text object. In the Toolbar, use the Font and Font Size list boxes to change the font to another font that you desire (such as Lucida Calligraphy) and to a larger font size (such as 14 point). Then, choose `Format/Size/To Fit` from the menus, and reposition the text box to a centered location of your choice on the form.

Step 10 With the text box still selected, click the `Palette` button in the Toolbar. When the palette appears, change the appearance to sunken (click the Sunken button in the Palette) and click on a wider width for the border. Then, double-click the Palette's Close button to put away the Palette. At this point, your form should resemble the example shown in FIG. 14-4.

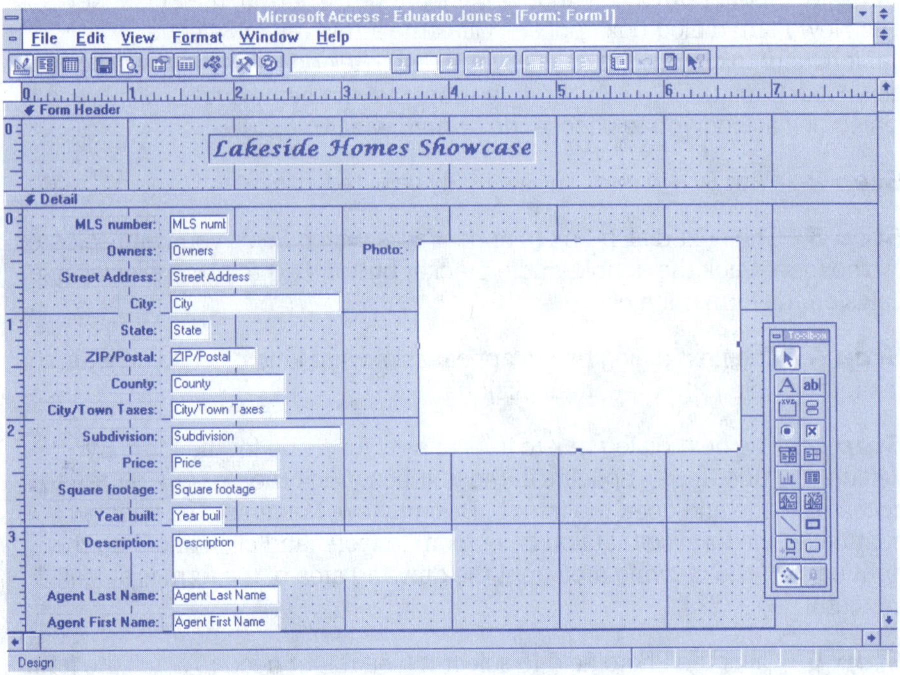

14-4 *The completed Homes form.*

Step 11 Press Ctrl–F4 to close the new form (click Yes in the dialog box that appears asking if you want to save your changes to the form). When you are prompted for a name, enter Homes as the name for the form and click OK.

Next, perform the following steps to create the form needed for the agents.

Step 1 In the Database window, click the Form button, then click New. The New Form dialog box appears. Click the arrow under Select a Table/Query to choose the desired table, and click on Agents in the drop-down list. Click the FormWizards button. In a moment, Access displays a dialog box asking you to choose the desired wizard.

Step 2 With Single-column already selected, click OK.

Step 3 The next dialog box to appear asks which fields you want selected on the form. Click the double-angle bracket button (>>), to place all available fields on the form, then click Next.

Step 4 The next dialog box to appear asks what kind of look you want for the form. Click Shadowed, then click Next.

Step 5 The next dialog box to appear asks for a title for the form. By default, the title Agents appears in the text box. Click the Open button to accept the title and open the form. At this point, your form should resemble the example shown in FIG. 14-5.

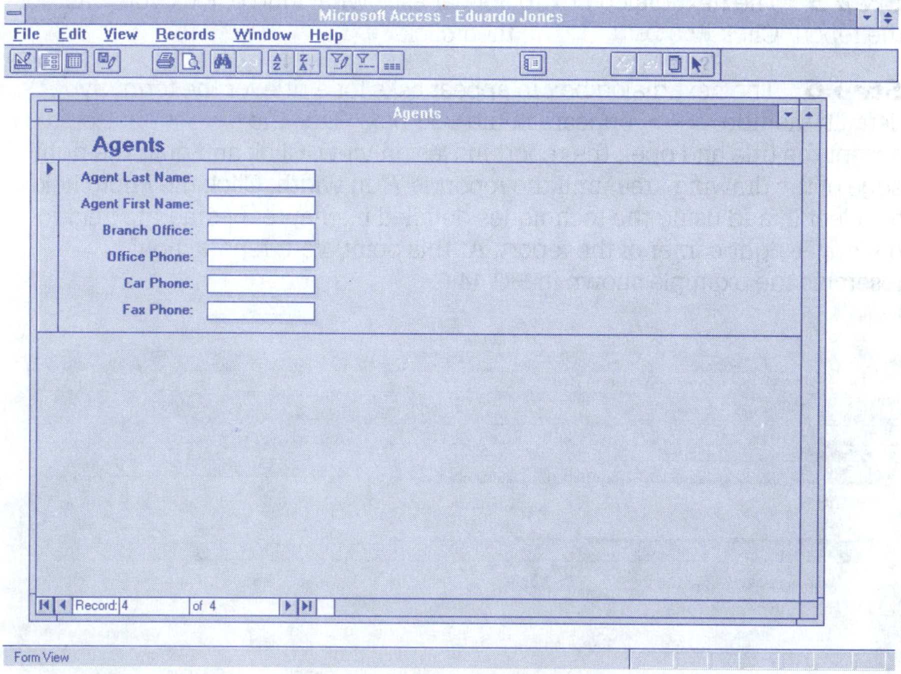

14-5 *The completed Agents form.*

Press Ctrl–F4 to close the new form (click Yes in the dialog box that appears asking if you want to save your changes to the form). When you are prompted for a name, enter Agents as the name for the form, and click OK.

Creating the reports

Two reports are needed for the application. One will provide potential buyers with a list of houses of interest; the other will provide a list of all agents in the office. Perform the following steps to create the reports.

Step 1 In the Database window, click the Report button, then click New. The New Report dialog box appears. Click the arrow under Select a Table/Query to choose the desired table, and click Homes in the drop-down list. Click the ReportWizards button. In a moment, Access displays a dialog box asking you to choose the desired wizard.

Step 2 With Single-column already selected, click OK.

Step 3 The next dialog box to appear asks which fields you want placed on the report. Click the double-angle bracket button (>>) to place all available fields on the report, then click `Next`.

Step 4 The next dialog box asks which field you want to use to sort the data by. Double-click the State field to place it in the Sort Order box, then double-click the City field to place it in the Sort Order box. Finally, click `Next`.

Step 5 The next dialog box to appear asks what kind of look you want for the report. Click `Presentation`, then click `Next`.

Step 6 The next dialog box to appear asks for a title for the form. By default, the title `Homes` appears in the text box. Click the `Design` button to accept the title and open the report in Design view. Click and drag the right edge of the drawing area until the report is 7" in width. Click the Photo field to select it, and using the techniques detailed in chapter 6, drag the field to the upper-right corner of the report. At this point, your report should resemble the example shown in FIG. 14-6.

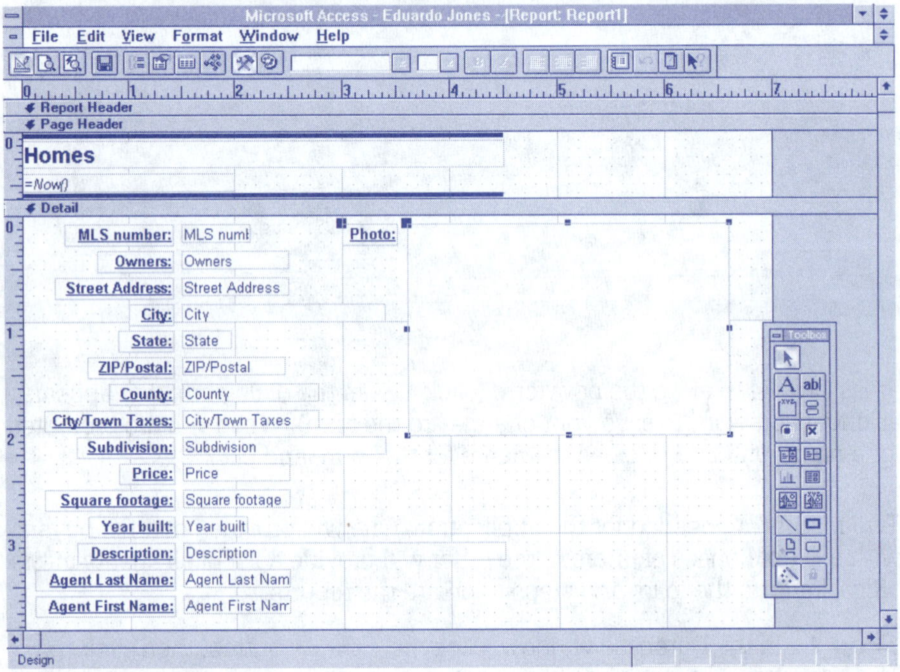

14-6
The completed Homes Listing report.

Step 7 Choose `File/Save` to save the new report. When you are prompted for a title, enter `Homes listing` for a report name, then click `OK`. Press Ctrl–F4 to close the new report.

Next, perform the following steps to create the report needed for the listing of the agents.

Step 1 In the Database window, click the `Report` button, then click `New`. The New Report dialog box appears. Click the arrow under Select a Table/Query to choose the desired table, and click `Agents` in the drop-down list. Click the `ReportWizards` button. In a moment, Access displays a dialog box asking you to choose the desired wizard. Click `Groups/Totals`, then click `OK`.

Step 2 The next dialog box to appear asks which fields you want placed on the report. Click the double-angle bracket button (>>) to place all available fields on the report, then click `Next`.

Step 3 The next dialog box to appear asks which fields you want to group the report by. Double-click the Branch Office field, then click `Next`. When the next dialog box appears, click `Next` to bypass this dialog box.

Step 4 The next dialog box asks which field you want to use to sort the data by. Double-click the Last Name field to place it in the Sort Order box, then double-click the First Name field to place it in the Sort Order box. Finally, click `Next`.

Step 5 The next dialog box to appear asks what kind of look you want for the report. Click `Presentation`, then click `Next`.

Step 6 The next dialog box to appear asks for a title for the form. By default, the title `Agents` appears in the text box. Click the `Design` button to accept the title and open the report in Design view. At this point, your report should resemble the example shown in FIG. 14-7.

Step 7 Choose `File/Save` to save the new report. When prompted for a title, enter `Agents Listing` for a report name, then click `OK`. Press Ctrl–F4 to close the new report.

Developing the application

The Home Showcase application uses the "event-driven" style of user interface similar to that used by the Clients Contact system in chapter 11, where data in the main table (in this case, "Homes") is visible within a form at all times and command buttons placed on the form let the user perform different tasks, including accessing data in the related Agents table. Macros are attached to the command buttons to perform the desired database operations. Perform the following steps to create the macros required for the application.

Perform the following steps to create the macro that will display the Homes form (and allow for adding and editing records).

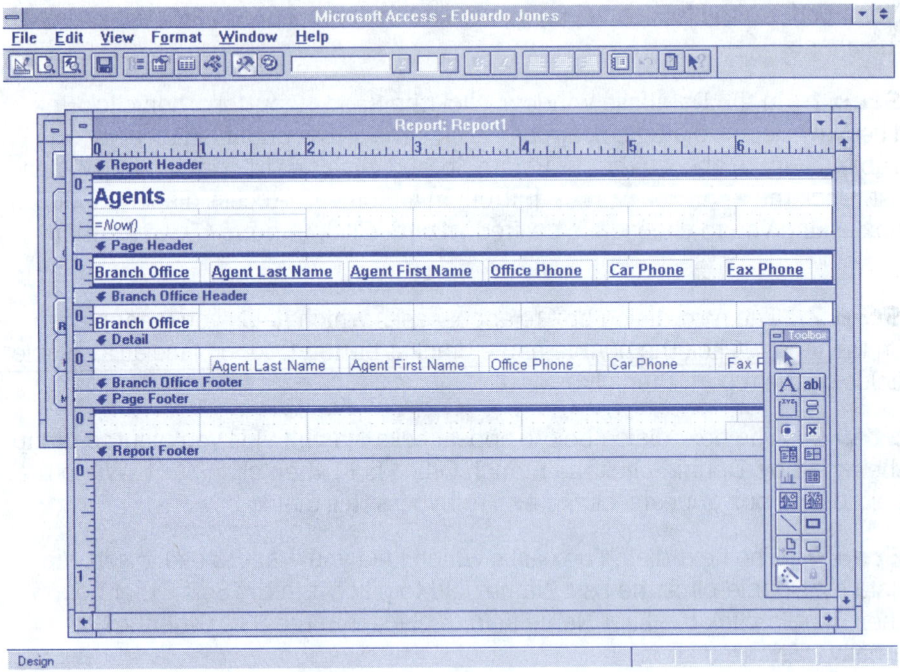

14-7
The completed Agents Listing report.

Step 1 In the Database window, click the `Macro` button, then click `New`. Move and resize the macro window that appears so that you can see both the Database window and the Macro window at the same time.

Step 2 In the Database window, click the `Form` button, then click on `Homes` in the list box and drag over to the first column under Action in the macro window. As a result, OpenForm appears in the Action column with the form name (Homes) shown in the Action Arguments portion of the macro window.

Step 3 Click in the second line of the Action column of the macro window. Click the arrow to open the drop-down menu, and choose `Maximize` from the list.

Step 4 Press Ctrl–F4. Answer `Yes` in response to the "Save changes" prompt that appears. When you are prompted for a name, call the macro `Autoexec`. (Assigning the name "Autoexec" to the macro will cause it to run automatically as soon as the database is opened within Access.)

Perform the following steps to create the macro for adding and editing the records in the Agents table.

Step 1 In the Database window, click the `Macro` button, then click `New`. Move and resize the macro window that appears so that you can see both the Database window and the Macro window at the same time.

Step 2 In the Database window, click the Form button, then click on Agents in the list box and drag over to the first column under Action in the macro window. As a result, OpenForm appears in the Action column with the form name (Agents) shown in the Action Arguments portion of the macro window.

Step 3 Press Ctrl–F4. Answer Yes in response to the "Save changes" prompt that appears. When you are prompted for a name, call the macro Agents.

Perform the following steps to create a group of macros for navigating within the Homes table.

Step 1 In the Database window, click the Macro button, then click New. Click in the Action column of the first row, and choose GoToRecord from the list box.

Step 2 Under Action Arguments, click in the Record box, open the list box, and choose New.

Step 3 Press Ctrl–F4 to close the macro. Answer Yes when you are asked if you want to save the macro. For a name, call the macro New.

Step 4 In the Database window, click New to create another macro. Click in the Action column of the first row, and choose DoMenuItem from the list box.

Step 5 Under Action Arguments, click in the Command box, open the list box, and choose Find.

Step 6 Press Ctrl–F4 to close the macro. Answer Yes when you are asked if you want to save the macro. For a name, call the macro Search.

Perform the following steps to create the macro for printing the records in the Homes table.

Step 1 In the Database window, click the Macro button, then click New. Move and resize the macro window that appears so that you can see both the Database window and the Macro window at the same time.

Step 2 In the Database window, click the Report button, then click on Homes Listing in the list box and drag over to the first column under Action in the macro window. As a result, OpenReport appears in the Action column with the report name (Homes Listing) shown in the Action Arguments portion of the macro window.

Step 3 Click in the second line of the Action column of the macro window. Click the arrow to open the drop-down menu, and choose Print from the list.

Step 4 Click in the third line of the Action column of the macro window. Click the arrow to open the drop-down menu, and choose `Close` from the list.

Step 5 Press Ctrl–F4. Answer `Yes` in response to the "Save changes" prompt that appears. When you are prompted for a name, call the macro `Print Homes`.

Perform the following steps to create the macro for printing a list of the agents.

Step 1 In the Database window, click the `Macro` button, then click `New`. Move and resize the macro window that appears so that you can see both the Database window and the Macro window at the same time.

Step 2 In the Database window, click the `Report` button, then click on Agents Listing in the list box and drag over to the first column under Action in the macro window. As a result, OpenReport appears in the Action column with the report name (Agents Listing) shown in the Action Arguments portion of the macro window.

Step 3 Click in the second line of the Action column of the macro window. Click the arrow to open the drop-down menu, and choose `Print` from the list.

Step 4 Click in the third line of the Action column of the macro window. Click the arrow to open the drop-down menu, and choose `Close` from the list.

Step 5 Press Ctrl–F4. Answer `Yes` in response to the "Save changes" prompt that appears. When you are prompted for a name, call the macro `Print Agents`.

Perform the following steps to create a macro for closing the Agents form.

Step 1 In the Database window click the `Macro` button, then click `New`.

Step 2 Click in the first row of the Action column of the macro. Open the drop-down list box, and choose `Close` from the list box.

Step 3 Press Ctrl–F4. Answer `Yes` in response to the "Save changes" prompt that appears. When you are prompted for a name, call the macro `Close`.

Perform the following steps to create the macro for exiting from the application.

Step 1 In the Database window, click the `Macro` button, then click `New`.

Step 2 Click in the first row of the Action column of the macro. Open the drop-down list box, and choose `Close` from the list box.

Step 3 Click in the second row of the Action column of the macro. Open the drop-down list box, and again choose `Close` from the list box.

Step 4 Press Ctrl–F4. Answer `Yes` in response to the "Save changes" prompt that appears. When you are prompted for a name, call the macro `Exit System`.

Next, you will need to add the command buttons to the Homes form. You can do this by dragging the macros from the Database window onto the form. Perform the following steps to do this.

Step 1 In the Database window, click the `Form` button, then click `Homes`, then click `Design` to open the Homes form in Design view. Size the form so that you will have room to work, and move the windows so that both the Database window and the form are visible.

Step 2 In the Database window, click the `Macro` button to display the macros. Click the `New` button, and drag it to a location roughly ¼" below the bottom center of the photo field. When you release the mouse, a command button titled `New` appears. (*Note*: If you see a dialog box warning you that Wizards cannot be used on existing buttons, click `OK` to ignore it, and ignore any more buttons like this that you see.) When clicked by the user, this command button will call the New macro, causing movement to a new record. By dragging the remaining macros to the form in a similar manner, you will add command buttons for the remaining tasks.

Step 3 In the Database window, click the Search macro, and drag it to a point roughly ¼" below the `New` button. Using the techniques covered in chapter 6, move the button until it is aligned underneath the `New` button.

Step 4 In the Database window, click the Agents macro, and drag it to a point roughly ¼" below the `New` button. Using the techniques covered in chapter 6, move the button until it is aligned underneath the `Search` button.

Step 5 In the Database window, click the Print Homes macro, and drag it to a point roughly ¼" below the `Agents` button. Using the techniques covered in chapter 6, move the button until it is aligned underneath the `Agents` button.

Step 6 In the Database window, click the Print Agents macro, and drag it to a point roughly ¼" below the `Print Homes` button. Using the techniques covered in chapter 6, move the button until it is aligned underneath the `Print Homes` button.

Step 7 In the Database window, click the Exit System macro, and drag it to a point roughly ¼" below the `Print Agents` button. Using the techniques covered in chapter 6, move the button until it is aligned underneath the `Print Agents` button.

Step 8 Press Ctrl–F4 close the form (click `Yes` in the dialog box that appears asking if you want to save your changes to the form).

Step 9 In the Database window, click the `Form` button, then click `Agents`, then click `Design`. Move or resize the form window so that you can see both the Database window and the Form window at the same time.

Step 10 In the Database window, click the `Macro` button, then click the Search macro and drag the macro over to a blank space anywhere within the header of the form (but leave sufficient space to put another button of the same size to the right of it).

Step 11 In the Database window, click the Close macro, and drag the macro to the space to the right of the `Search` button. If necessary, move the `Close` button so that it is aligned horizontally and just to the right of the `Search` button.

Step 12 Press Ctrl–F4 close the form (click `Yes` in the dialog box that appears asking if you want to save your changes to the form).

At this point, the application is complete. Double-click the `Close` button of the Database window to close it. Then, to try running the application, choose `File/Open Database`. When the Open Database dialog box appears, double-click `HOMES` to reopen the database. Because you added the Autoexec macro, when the database opens, the form containing the menu for the application opens automatically, as shown earlier in FIG. 14-1. You can test the application by adding and editing data and printing the desired reports. Use the techniques detailed in this chapter to add any additional reports or specialized queries (and corresponding menu option buttons) to refine the application so it precisely suits your needs.

15 Mailing list management

Businesses, political and social organizations, schools, and private individuals often need to keep track of names and addresses of customers, voters, members, friends and relatives, and numerous others. For this reason, mailing lists have been a popular database applications for as long as database software has existed for computers. The Mailing List Management System presented in this chapter is designed to handle the task of tracking names and addresses and printing of mailing labels for those names and addresses. Figure 15-1 shows the Mailing List Management System in use.

The files used by the Mailing List Management System presented in this chapter can be found on the accompanying disk in the MAILER database. Use the Windows File Manager or DOS commands to copy this database into your Microsoft Access directory.

Creating the database & table

The Mailing List Management System requires only one table, obviously used to store the names and addresses. This straightforward use of Access in a nonrelational sense makes the task of database design a simple one; however, the application offers much in the way of demonstrating applications design as it offers a wide variety of menu options. In any system that manages a mailing list, reporting needs are going to be of prime importance. Such a system must be able to "cut the data" in a variety of ways (such as by ZIP code or by State) and produce detail reports and mailing labels in the needed sizes.

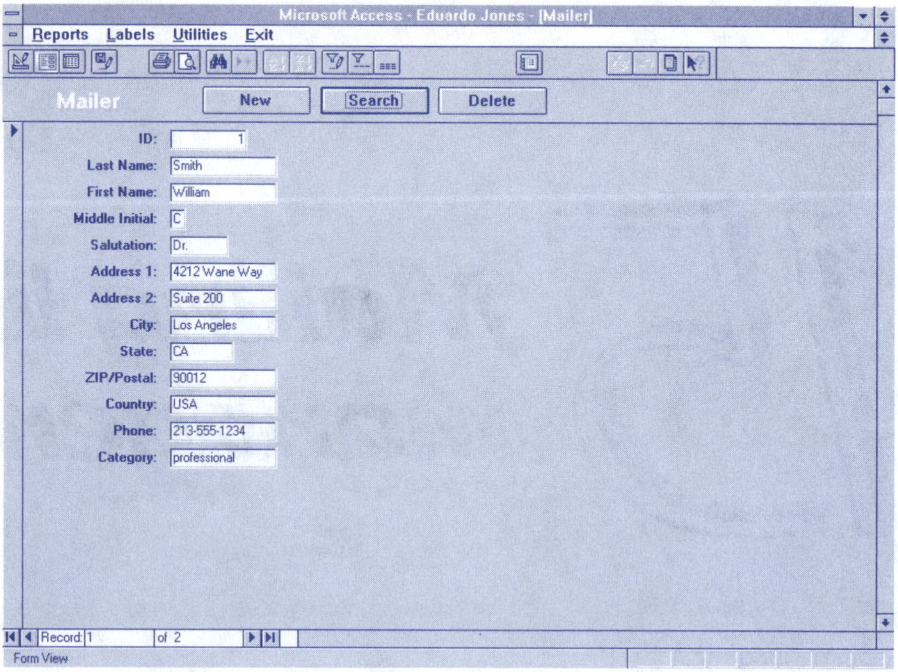

15-1
The Mailing List Management system in use.

To create the database and the table, first start Access in the usual manner, then perform the following steps.

Step 1 Choose `File/New Database` to open the New Database dialog box.

TIP

If you want to store the new database in a different directory, use the Directory list box to locate the desired directory now. Click on the desired directory, and Access will store the new database in that directory.

Step 2 Enter `MAILER` in the File Name text box as a name for the database, then click `OK`. (Remember, in Access, database names must be 8 characters or less with no spaces.) Access creates the database file on your hard disk, and the Database window appears.

Step 3 In the Database window, click the `Table` button, then click `New`. When the New Table dialog box appears, click `New Table`. The Table window appears. Fill in the Table window with the field names and data types for the fields shown in TABLE 15-1.

Step 4 When done defining the fields, choose `File/Save` to save the table. When prompted for a table name, enter `Mailer` as the name and click `OK`. Access will warn you that there is no primary key defined for the table, then click `Yes` in the dialog box to let Access add a counter field that will serve as a primary key. At this point, your table should resemble the example shown in FIG. 15-2.

Table 15-1
Fill in the Table window with these field names and data types.

Field name	Data type
Last Name	Text
First Name	Text
Middle Initial	Text
Salutation	Text
Address 1	Text
Address 2	Text
City	Text
State	Text
Zip/Postal	Text
Country	Text
Phone	Text
Category	Text

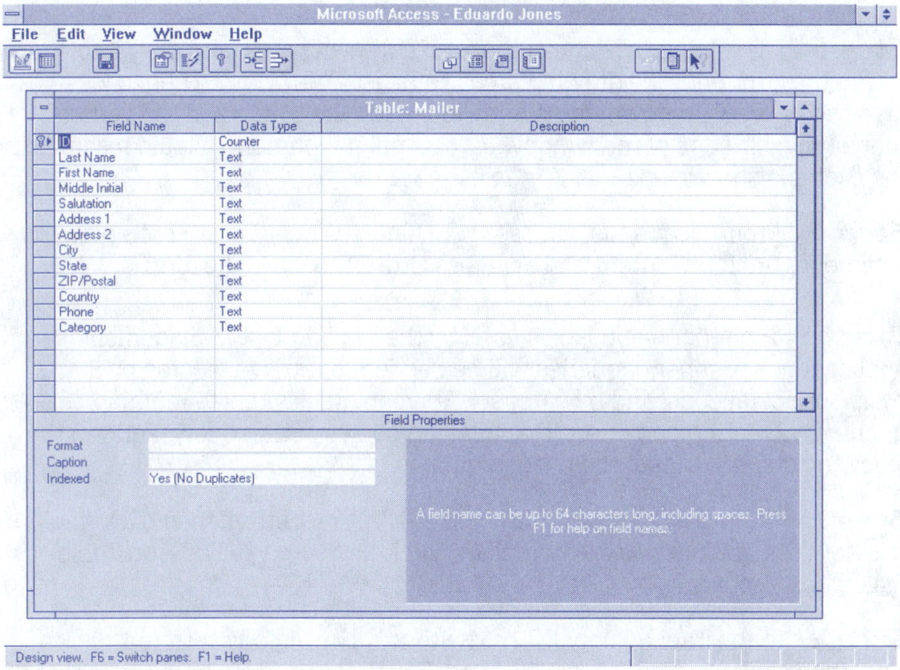

15-2
The completed Mailer table.

Step 5 Press Ctrl–F4 to close the Table window. The new table, Mailer, now appears in the Database window.

Creating the form

One advantage of a single-table, or "flat-file," database such as this one is that only one form is necessary for the adding and editing of records. To create the needed form, perform the following steps.

Step 1 In the Database window, click the `Form` button, then click `New`. The New Form dialog box appears. Click the arrow under Select a Table/Query to choose the desired table, and click on `Mailer` in the drop-down list. Click the `FormWizards` button. In a moment, Access displays a dialog box asking you to choose the desired wizard. With `Single-column` already selected, click `OK`.

Step 2 The next dialog box to appear asks which fields you want selected on the form. Click the double-angle bracket button (`>>`), to place all available fields on the form, then click `Next`.

Step 3 The next dialog box to appear asks what kind of look you want for the form. Click `Embossed`, then click `Next`.

Step 4 The next dialog box to appear asks for a title for the form. By default, the title `Mailer` appears in the text box. Click the `Design` button to accept the title and open the form in Design view.

Step 5 Click the right edge of the form's drawing area, and drag it to widen the form until the drawing area is at least 7" in width. Then, click and drag the form footer downwards until you reach the 5" mark in the vertical ruler at the left edge of the window. At this point, your form should resemble the example shown in FIG. 15-3.

Step 6 From the menus, choose `File/Save`. When you are prompted for a name for the form, enter `Mailer`. Press Ctrl–F4 to close the form.

Creating the needed queries

To support the reports and labels used by the Mailing List Management application, a number of queries will be needed to retrieve records by State, by ZIP or postal code, and by category. You can quickly create multiple queries by creating one query, then making copies of that query. Perform the following steps to create the needed queries.

Step 1 In the Database window, click the `Query` button, then click `New`. In the New Query dialog box that appears, click `New Query`. The Add Table dialog box appears.

Step 2 In the Table/Query list box with `Mailer` already selected, click `Add`, then click `Close`. This causes a list box with the fields from the table to appear in the Select Query window. Click the ID field in the list box, then scroll to the last field in the list. While holding the Shift key, click the last field (Category) in the list to select all the fields.

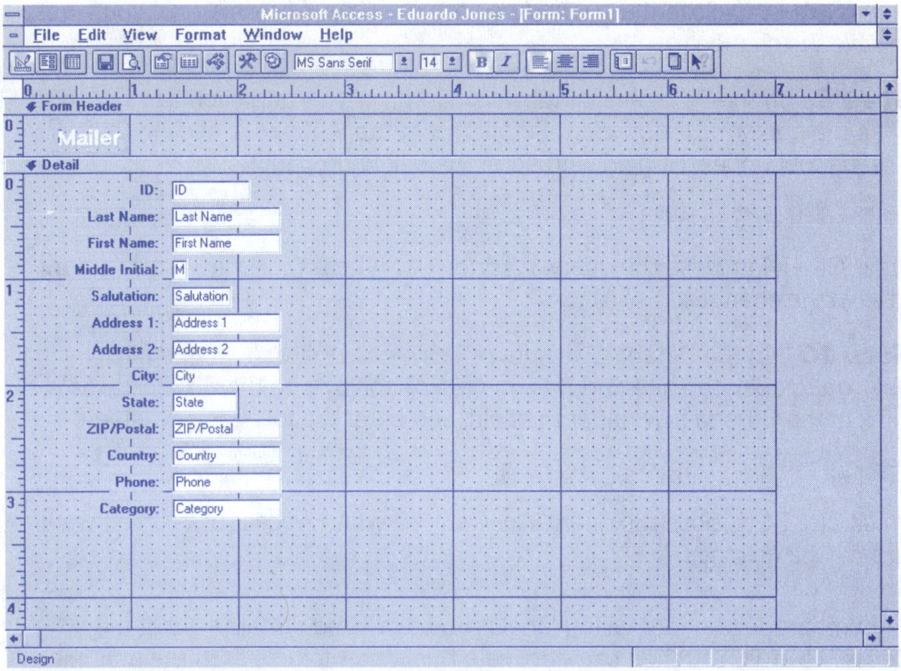

15-3
The completed Mailer form.

Step 3 With all fields selected, click any field in the list and drag it to the first empty cell of the Field row in the query grid. Doing so causes all the fields to be placed in the query grid.

Step 4 Choose `File/Save`. Access will prompt you for a name for the query; enter `All Records` and click `OK`. Press Ctrl–F4 to close the Select Query window. The new query appears by name in the Database window.

Step 5 With the All Records query still selected in the Database window, choose `Edit/Copy` from the menus, and again choose `Edit/Paste`. In the Paste As dialog box that appears, enter `By State` and click `OK`.

Step 6 With the All Records query still selected in the Database window, choose `Edit/Copy` from the menus, and again choose `Edit/Paste`. In the Paste As dialog box that appears, enter `By ZIP/Postal` and click `OK`.

Step 7 With the All Records query still selected in the Database window, choose `Edit/Copy` from the menus, and again choose `Edit/Paste`. In the Paste As dialog box that appears, enter `By Category` and click `OK`.

Step 8 In the Database window, click `By Category`, and click `Design` to open the query in Design view. Scroll over to the Category field, click in the Criteria row under the field, and enter the following parameter:

```
[Enter the category:]
```

Press Ctrl–F4 to close the query. Answer Yes when Access asks if you want to save the changes.

Step 9 In the Database window, click By State, and click Design to open the query in Design view. Scroll over to the State field, click in the Criteria row under the field, and enter the following parameter:

```
[Enter the State:]
```

Press Ctrl–F4 to close the query. Answer Yes when Access asks if you want to save the changes.

Step 10 In the Database window, click By ZIP/Postal, and click Design to open the query in Design view. Scroll over to the ZIP/Postal field, click in the Criteria row under the field, and enter the following parameter:

```
[Enter ZIP or Postal code:]
```

Press Ctrl–F4 to close the query. Answer Yes when Access asks if you want to save the changes.

Creating the reports

A report in the form of mailing labels can be created with the aid of the ReportWizards. You then can duplicate this report for use with the multiple queries created earlier. Perform the following steps to create the report that will produce mailing labels.

Step 1 In the Database window, click Report, then click New. The New Report dialog box appears. Click the arrow in the Select A Table/Query list box, and choose All Records from the list. Then, click the ReportWizards button.

Step 2 The next dialog box to appear asks which wizard you want to use. Click Mailing Label, then click OK.

Step 3 The next dialog box to appear, shown in FIG. 15-4, asks what you want to put on the mailing label. Double-click Salutation, then click Space, then double-click First Name, then click Space, then double-click Middle Initial, then click Space, and finally double-click Last Name.

Step 4 Click the New Line button in the dialog box (this causes the label to begin a new line). Double-click the Address 1 field, then click the New Line button in the dialog box. Double-click the Address 2 field, then click the New Line button in the dialog box. Double-click City, then click Comma, then click Space, then double-click State, then click Space, then double-click ZIP/Postal, then click Next.

Step 5 The next dialog box to appear asks which fields you want to sort by. Double-click Last Name, then double-click First Name, then click Next.

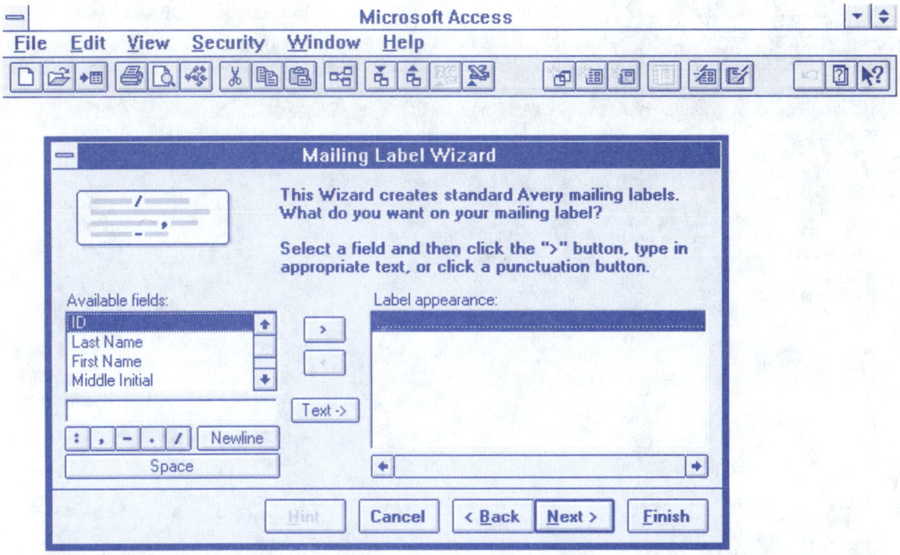

15-4
The Mailing Label dialog box.

Step 6 The next dialog box asks which label size you want. Use the scroll box to find the label size that you use in your office, and click it to select it, then click `Next`. (For this example, I chose Avery 5160 labels.)

Step 7 The next dialog box asks for a font size and style. Change the font size to 10 (this allows all four lines to fit in the label size chosen, if you use the Avery 5160 size labels), then click `Next`.

Step 8 When the next dialog box appears, click `Design` to open the new label in Design view. At this point, your report should resemble the example shown in FIG. 15-5.

Step 9 From the menus, choose `File/Save`. When you are prompted for a name, enter `All Labels`, then click `OK`. Press Ctrl–F4 to close the report.

Step 10 With `All Labels` still selected in the Database window, choose `Edit/Copy` from the menus, and choose `Edit/Paste`. In the Paste As dialog box that appears, enter `By Category` and click `OK`.

Step 11 With `All Labels` still selected in the Database window, choose `Edit/Copy` from the menus, and again choose `Edit/Paste`. In the Paste As dialog box that appears, enter `By State` and click `OK`.

Step 12 With `All Labels` still selected in the Database window, choose `Edit/Copy` from the menus, and again choose `Edit/Paste`. In the Paste As dialog box that appears, enter `By ZIP/Postal` and click `OK`.

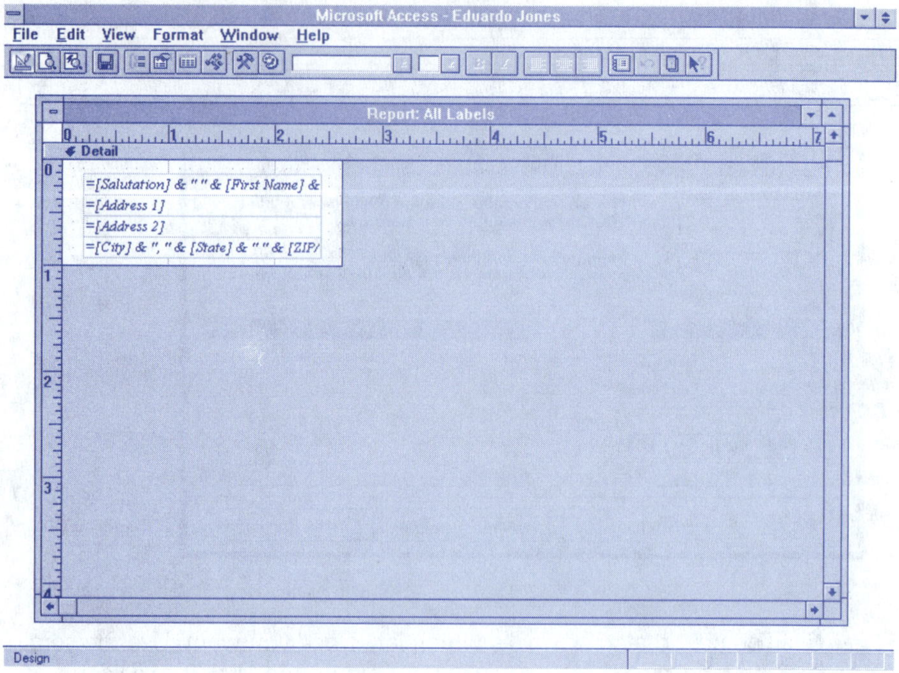

15-5
The completed All Labels report.

Step 13 In the Database window, click `By Category`, and click `Design` to open the report in Design view. From the menus, choose `Edit/Select Report`, then choose `View/Properties`. If All Properties is not visible in the list box at the top of the Properties window that opens (Access 2.0 only), select it now. In the Properties window, change the Record Source to `By Category`. Press Ctrl–F4 to close the report. Answer `Yes` to the "Save Changes" prompt that appears.

Step 14 In the Database window, click `By State`, and click `Design` to open the report in Design view. Because the Properties window still was open when you closed the last report, it will open by default in this report. In the Properties window, change the Record Source to `By State`. Press Ctrl–F4 to close the report. Answer `Yes` to the "Save Changes" prompt that appears.

Step 15 In the Database window, click `By ZIP/Postal`, and click `Design` to open the report in Design view. In the Properties window which opens, change the Record Source to `By ZIP/Postal`. Press Ctrl–F4 to close the report. Answer `Yes` to the "Save Changes" prompt that appears.

Next, perform the following steps to create the report needed for printing a listing of the names and addresses.

Step 1 In the Database window, click the `Report` button, then click `New`. The New Report dialog box appears. Click the arrow under Select a Table/Query to choose the desired table, and click `All Records` in the drop-down list. Click the `ReportWizards` button. In a moment, Access displays a dialog box asking you to choose the desired wizard. With `Single-column` already selected, click `OK`.

Step 2 The next dialog box to appear asks which fields you want placed on the report. Click the double-angle bracket button (>>) to place all available fields on the report. Then, scroll back up in the Field Order on Report list box and find the ID field, click it to select it, and click the single left angle bracket (<) to remove just the ID field from the list, then click `Next`.

Step 3 The next dialog box asks which field you want to use to sort the data by. Double-click the Last Name field to place it in the Sort Order box, then double-click the First Name field to place it in the Sort Order box. Finally, click `Next`.

Step 4 The next dialog box to appear asks what kind of look you want for the report. Click `Presentation`, then click `Next`.

Step 5 The next dialog box to appear asks for a title for the report. By default, the title `All Records` appears in the text box. Click the `Design` button to accept the title and open the report in Design view. Click at the top of the page footer (where the mouse pointer changes to the shape of a double-headed arrow), and drag the footer until it is roughly ½" from the last field. At this point, your report should resemble the example shown in FIG. 15-6.

Step 6 Choose `File/Save` to save the new report. When prompted for a title, enter `All Records` for a report name, then click `OK`. Press Ctrl–F4 to close the new report.

Step 7 In the Database window, click `All Records` to select it, choose `Edit/Copy` from the menus, then choose `Edit/Paste`. In the Paste As dialog box that appears, enter `Records By Category` and click `OK`.

Step 8 With `All Records` still selected in the Database window, choose `Edit/Copy` from the menus, and again choose `Edit/Paste`. In the Paste As dialog box that appears, enter `Records By State` and click `OK`.

Step 9 With `All Records` still selected in the Database window, choose `Edit/Copy` from the menus, and again choose `Edit/Paste`. In the Paste As dialog box that appears, enter `Records By ZIP/Postal` and click `OK`.

Step 10 In the Database window, click `Records By Category`, and click `Design` to open the report in Design view. (If the Properties window is not visible, choose `Edit/Select Report`, then choose `View/Properties`.) In the Properties window, change the Record Source to `By Category`. Press

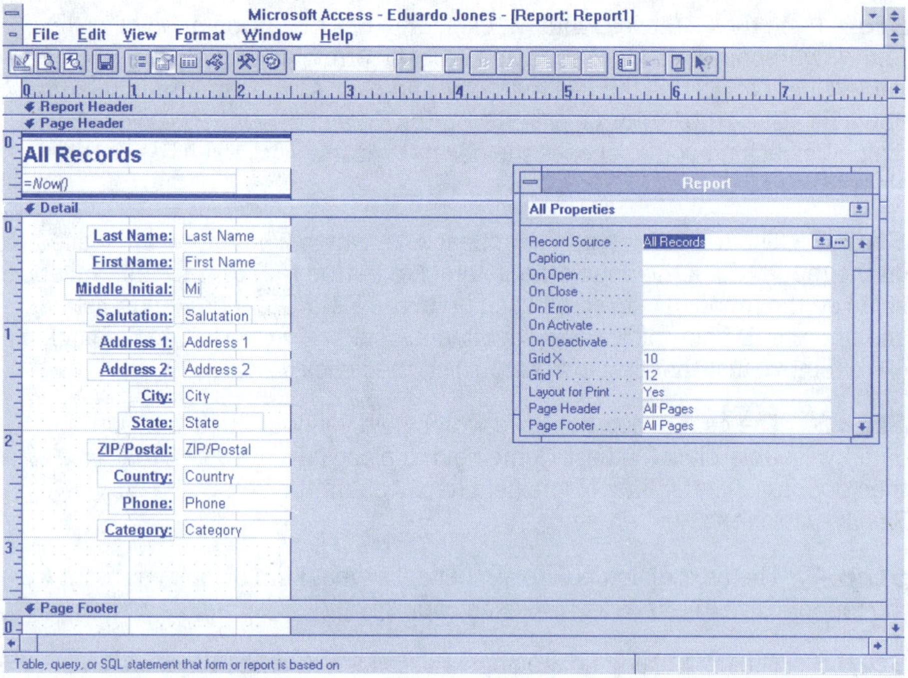

15-6
The completed All Records report.

Ctrl–F4 to close the report. Answer Yes to the "Save Changes" prompt that appears.

Step 11 In the Database window, click Records By State, and click Design to open the report in Design view. In the Properties window, change the Record Source to By State. Press Ctrl–F4 to close the report. Answer Yes to the "Save Changes" prompt that appears.

Step 12 In the Database window, click Records By ZIP/Postal, and click Design to open the report in Design view. In the Properties window, change the Record Source to By ZIP/Postal. Press Ctrl–F4 to close the report. Answer Yes to the "Save Changes" prompt that appears.

Developing the application

The application requires a series of macros that provide the menu choices for performing database operations and the actions that should occur in response to those menu choices. Perform the following steps to create the macros required for the application.

To create the macro that will display the menu bar of the main menu, perform these steps.

Step 1 In the Database window, click the Macro button, then click New. If the Macro Name column is not visible, choose View/Macro Names from the menu so that you can see the Macro Names column. Click in the first row of the Macro Name column, and enter Menu as a macro name.

Step 2 Click in the first row of the Action column, open the list box, and choose `AddMenu` as an action.

Step 3 Click in Menu Name under Action Arguments, and enter `&Reports` as the entry. Press Tab once or click directly underneath, in the `Menu Macro Name` entry, and enter `Reports`. Click in the second row of the Action column, open the list box, and choose `AddMenu` as an action.

Step 4 Click in Menu Name under Action Arguments, and enter `&Labels` as the entry. Press Tab once or click directly underneath, in the `Menu Macro Name` entry, and enter `Labels`. Click in the third row of the Action column, open the list box, and choose `AddMenu` as an action.

Step 5 Click in Menu Name under Action Arguments, and enter `&Utilities` as the entry. Press Tab once or click directly underneath, in the `Menu Macro Name` entry, and enter `Utilities`. Click in the fourth row of the Action column, open the list box, and choose `AddMenu` as an action.

Step 6 Click in Menu Name under Action Arguments, and enter `&Exit` as the entry. Press Tab once or click directly underneath, in the `Menu Macro Name` entry, and enter `Exit System`.

Step 7 Press Ctrl–F4. Answer `Yes` to the prompt that asks if you want to save the macro. For a name, enter `Main Menu`.

To create the drop-down menu for the Labels choices on the menu bar, perform the following steps.

Step 1 In the Database window, click `New`. If the Macro Name column is not visible, choose `View/Macro Names` from the menu so that you can see the Macro Names column. Click in the first row of the Macro Name column, and enter `All Records` as a name for the first macro in this group.

Step 2 Click in the first row of the Action column, open the list box, and choose `OpenReport` as an action. Under Action Arguments, click the `Report Names` entry, and choose `All Labels` from the list of reports. Then, click the `View` entry, and change it from `Print Preview` to `Print`.

Step 3 Click in the Macro Name column in the next row of the macro, and enter `By Category` as a title for the second macro in this group. Click the Action column (beside the macro name that you just entered), open the list box, and choose `OpenReport` as an action.

Step 4 Under Action Arguments, click the `Report Names` entry, and choose `By Category` from the list of reports. Then, click the `View` entry, and change it from `Print Preview` to `Print`. Click in the Macro Name column in the third row of the macro, and enter `By State` as a title for the third macro in this group.

Step 5 Click the Action column (beside the macro name that you just entered), open the list box, and choose OpenReport as an action.

Step 6 Under Action Arguments, click the Report Names entry, and choose By State from the list of reports. Then, click the View entry, and change it from Print Preview to Print. Click in the Macro Name column in the fourth row of the macro, and enter By ZIP/Postal as a title for the fourth macro in this group.

Step 7 Click the Action column (beside the macro name you just entered), open the list box, and choose OpenReport as an action.

Step 8 Under Action Arguments, click the Report Names entry, and choose By ZIP/Postal from the list of reports. Then, click the View entry, and change it from Print Preview to Print.

Step 9 Press Ctrl–F4. Answer Yes when you are asked if you want to save the new macro. When you are prompted, enter Labels as the name for the macro.

To create the drop-down menu for the Reports choices on the menu bar, perform the following steps.

Step 1 In the Database window, click Macro, then click Labels to select the macro that you just created. From the menus, choose Edit/Copy, then choose Edit/Paste. In the dialog box that appears, enter Reports as a name for the new macro, and click OK.

Step 2 In the Database window, click the Reports macro to select it, then click Design.

Step 3 Click in the first row of the macro, in the Action column. Then, under Action Arguments, click in the Report Name text box, and change the report name to All Records.

Step 4 Click in the second row of the macro, in the Action column. Then, under Action Arguments, click in the Report Name text box, and change the report name to Records by Category.

Step 5 Click in the third row of the macro, in the Action column. Then, under Action Arguments, click in the Report Name text box, and change the report name to Records by State.

Step 6 Click in the fourth row of the macro, in the Action column. Then, under Action Arguments, click in the Report Name text box, and change the report name to Records by ZIP/Postal.

Step 7 Press Ctrl–F4. Answer Yes when you are asked if you want to save the new macro.

To create the drop-down menu for the Utilities choices on the menu bar, perform the following steps.

Step 1 In the Database window, click `New`. If the Macro Name column is not visible, choose `View/Macro Names` from the menu so that you can see the Macro Names column.

Step 2 Click in the first row of the Macro Name column, and enter `Calendar` as a name for the first macro in this group. Click in the first row of the Action column, open the list box, and choose `Run App` from the list. Under Action Arguments, enter `CALENDAR.EXE` in the Command Line text box.

Step 3 Click in the second row of the Macro Name column, and enter `Calculator` as a name for the first macro in this group. Click in the second row of the Action column, open the list box, and choose `Run App` from the list. Under Action Arguments, enter `CALC.EXE` in the Command Line text box.

Step 4 Click in the third row of the Macro Name column, and enter `Filer` as a name for the last macro in this group. Click in the third row of the Action column, open the list box, and choose `Run App` from the list. Under Action Arguments, enter `WINFILE.EXE` in the Command Line text box.

Step 5 Press Ctrl–F4. Answer `Yes` when you are asked if you want to save the new macro. When prompted, enter `Utilities` as the name for the macro.

To create the macro that builds the drop-down menu for the Exit choices on the menu bar, perform the following steps.

Step 1 In the Database window, click the `Macro` button, then click `New`. If the Macro Name column is not visible, choose `View/Macro Names` from the menu so that you can see the Macro Names column.

Step 2 Click in the first row of the Macro Name column, and enter `Exit System` as a name for the macro.

Step 3 Click in the first row of the Action column, open the list box, and choose `Close` as an action.

Step 4 Click in the second row of the Action column, open the list box, and again choose `Close` as an action.

Step 5 Press Ctrl–F4. Answer `Yes` when you are asked if you want to save the new macro. When you are prompted, enter `Exit System` as the name for the macro.

The application also will need command buttons for finding records and for moving to a new record. To create the needed macros, perform the following steps.

Step 1 In the Database window, click `Macro`, then click `New` to create another macro. Click in the Action column of the first row, and choose `DoMenuItem` from the list box. Under Action Arguments, click in the Command box, open the list box, and choose `Find`. Press Ctrl–F4 to close the macro; answer `Yes` when you are asked if you want to save the macro. For a name, call the macro `Search`.

Step 2 In the Database window, click `New` to create another macro. Click in the Action column of the first row, and choose `DoMenuItem` from the list box. Under Action Arguments, click in the Menu Name box, open the list box and choose `Records`. Under Action Arguments, click in the Command box, open the list box, and choose `GoTo`. Under Action Arguments, click in the Subcommand box, open the list box, and choose `New`. Press Ctrl–F4 to close the macro; answer `Yes` when you are asked if you want to save the macro. For a name, call the macro `New`.

Step 3 In the Database window, click the `Macro` button, then click `New`. Click in the first row of the Action column of the macro. Open the drop-down list box, and choose `DoMenuItem`. Under Action Arguments, click in the Command text box and choose `Select Record` from the list. Click in the second row of the Action column of the macro. Open the drop-down list box, and choose `DoMenuItem`. Under Action Arguments, click in the Command text box and choose `Delete` from the list.

Step 4 Press Ctrl–F4. Answer `Yes` in response to the "Save changes" prompt that appears. When you are prompted for a name, call the macro `Delete`.

An Autoexec macro is needed to open and maximize the form when the database is first opened. Perform these steps to create this macro.

Step 1 In the Database window, click `Macro`, then click `New`.

Step 2 Click in the first row in the Action column of the new macro. Open the list box, and choose `OpenForm` from the list. Click in Form Name under Action Arguments, and choose `Mailer` from the list of forms.

Step 3 Click in the second row in the Action column of the macro. Open the list box, and choose `Maximize` from the list.

Step 4 Press Ctrl–F4. Answer `Yes` when you are asked if you want to save the macro. When you are prompted for a name, enter `Autoexec` in the dialog box.

Finally, you need to modify the form's properties so that the main menu is called when the form is opened. Also, the command buttons must be placed on the form. Perform the following steps.

Step 1 In the Database window, click `Form`. With `Mailer` selected, click `Design` to open the Customers form in Design view. (If the Properties window for the form does not open, choose `Edit/Select Form`, then choose `View/Properties`.) Click the MenuBar property (or in versions of Access prior to 2.0, the OnMenu property), open the list box, and choose `Main Menu.Menu` from the list of macros. Then, double-click the Close box in the Property window to close it.

Step 2 Size the form so that you will have room to work, and move the windows so that both the Database window and the form are visible.

Step 3 In the Database window, click the `Macro` button to display the macros. Click the New macro, and drag it to a location within the header of the form, roughly 2" from the left edge of the form. (*Note*: If you see a dialog box warning you that Wizards cannot be used on existing buttons, click `OK` to ignore it, and ignore any more buttons like this that you see.) Use the movement techniques outlined in chapter 6 to center the button vertically.

Step 4 In the Database window, click the Search macro, and drag it to a location within the header of the form to the immediate right of the New button. If necessary, move the `Search` button so that it is aligned horizontally and vertically and just to the right of the `New` button.

Step 5 In the Database window, click the Delete macro, and drag the macro to the space to the right of the `Search` button. If necessary, move the

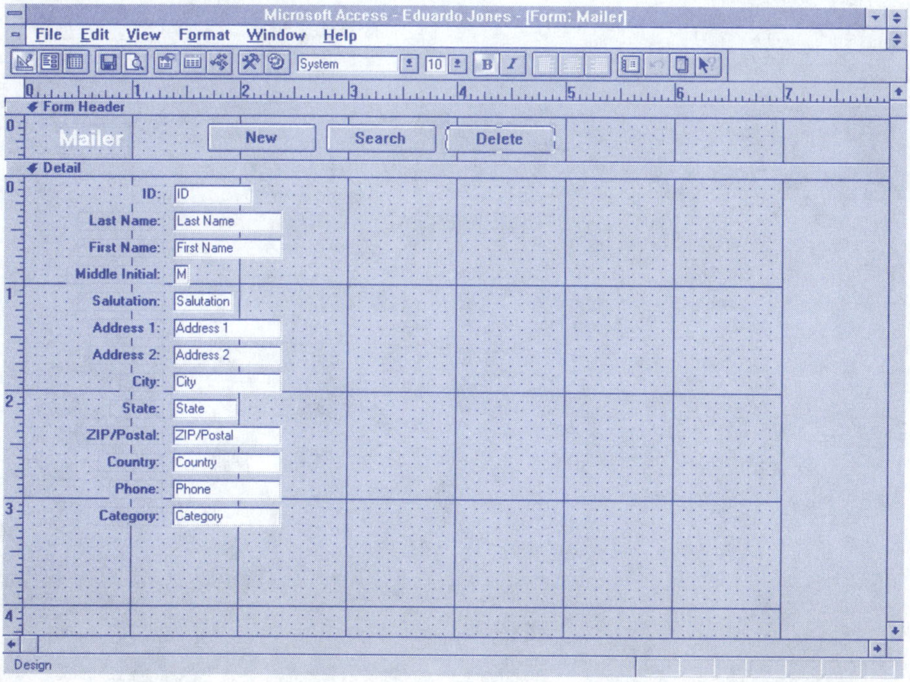

15-7
The Mailer form with the command buttons added.

Delete button so that it is aligned horizontally and vertically and just to the right of the Search button. At this point, your form should resemble the example shown in FIG. 15-7.

Step 6 Press Ctrl–F4. Answer Yes when you are asked if you want to save the changes to the form.

At this point, the application is complete. Double-click the Close button of the Database window to close it. Then, to try running the application, choose File/Open Database. When the Open Database dialog box appears, double-click MAILER to reopen the database. Because you added the Autoexec macro, when the database opens, the form containing the menu for the application opens automatically, as shown earlier in FIG. 15-1. You can test the application by adding and editing data and printing the desired mailing labels or reports. Use the techniques detailed in this chapter to add any additional reports or specialized queries (and corresponding menu options or command buttons) to refine the application so it precisely suits your needs.

16 Personnel Tracking System

The Personnel Tracking System detailed in this chapter is designed to handle statistics for the personnel department of a typical mid-sized business. Common personnel data, such as names and addresses, job title and department, employee ID, and supervisor data are compiled in a personnel table. The application also makes use of a photo field, which is used to display a picture of each employee. Figure 16-1 shows the Personnel Tracking System in use.

The files used by the Personnel Tracking System presented in this chapter can be found on the accompanying disk in the STAFF database. Use the Windows File Manager or DOS commands to copy this database into your Microsoft Access directory.

Creating the database & table

To create the database and its required table, first start Access in the usual manner, then perform the following steps.

Step 1 Choose `File/New Database` to open the New Database dialog box.

TIP

If you want to store the new database in a different directory, use the Directory list box to locate the desired directory now. Click on the desired directory, and Access will store the new database in that directory.

Step 2 Enter `STAFF` in the File Name text box as a name for the database, then click `OK`. (Remember, in Access, database names must be 8 characters

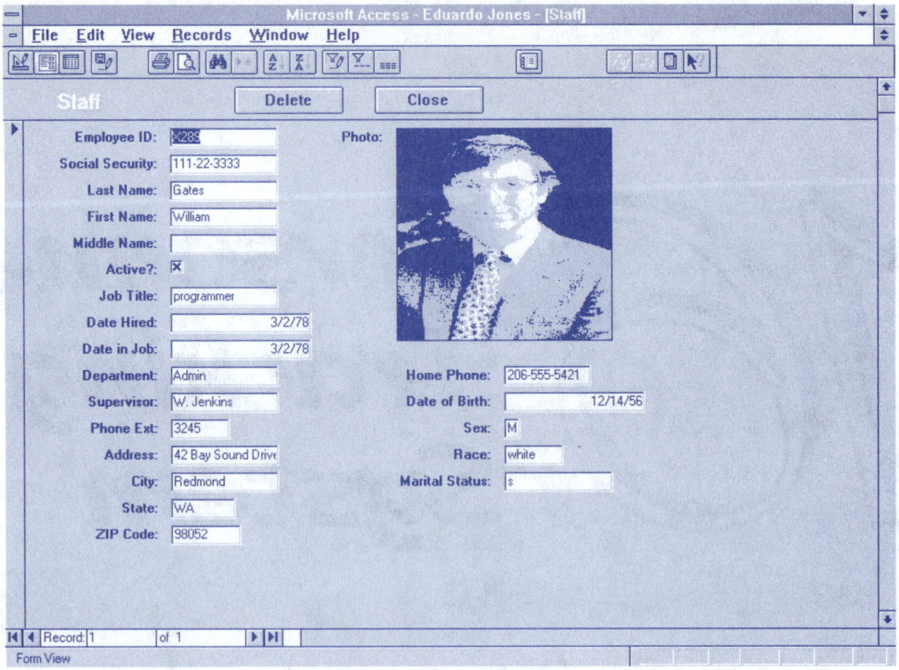

16-1
The Personnel Tracking system in use.

or less with no spaces.) Access creates the database file on your hard disk, and the Database window appears.

Step 3 In the Database window, click the `Table` button, then click `New`. In the New Table dialog box that appears, click `New Table`. The Table window appears. Fill in the Table window with the field names and data types for the fields shown in TABLE 16-1. *Note*: if your organization uses social security numbers as an employee ID field, you can save time by omitting the Employee ID field and using the Social Security field as a key field.

Table 16-1
Fill in the Table window with these field names and data types.

Field name	Data type
Employee ID	Text
Social Security	Text
Last Name	Text
First Name	Text
Middle Name	Text
Active?	Yes/No
Job Title	Text
Date Hired	Date
Date in Job	Date
Department	Text

Supervisor	Text
Phone Ext	Text
Address	Text
City	Text
State	Text
ZIP Code	Text
Home Phone	Text
Date of Birth	Date/Time
Sex	Text
Race	Text
Marital Status	Text
Photo	OLE Object

Step 4 Click anywhere in the first field (titled "Employee ID"), and click the Key icon in the Toolbar to make this field the primary key. At this point, your table should resemble the example shown in FIG. 16-2.

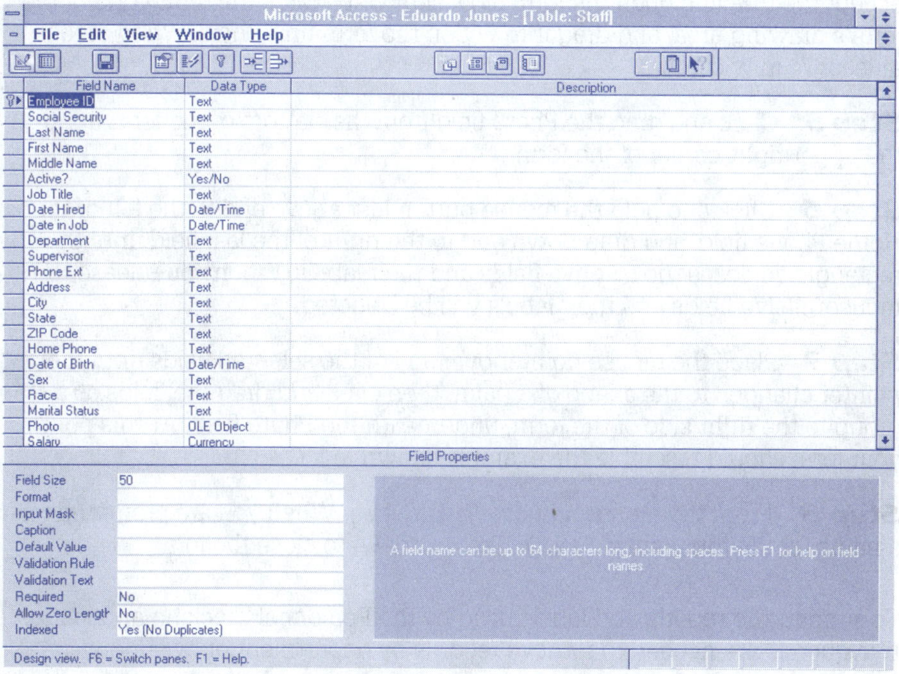

16-2
The completed Staff table.

Step 5 When you are done defining the fields, choose `File/Save` to save the table. When you are prompted for a table name, enter `Staff` as the name, and click `OK`. Press Ctrl–F4 to close the Table window. The new table, Staff, now appears in the Database window.

Creating the form

To create the form that will be used for adding and editing personnel records, perform the following steps.

Step 1 In the Database window, click the `Form` button, then click `New`. The New Form dialog box appears. Click the arrow under Select a Table/Query to choose the desired table, and click on `Staff` in the drop-down list. Click the `FormWizards` button. In a moment, Access displays a dialog box asking you to choose the desired wizard. With `Single-column` already selected, click `OK`.

Step 2 The next dialog box to appear asks which fields you want selected on the form. Click the double-angle bracket button (`>>`) to place all available fields on the form, then click `Next`.

Step 3 The next dialog box to appear asks what kind of look you want for the form. Click `Embossed`, then click `Next`.

Step 4 The next dialog box to appear asks for a title for the form. By default, the title `Staff` appears in the text box. Click the `Design` button to accept the title and open the form in Design view. Click the right edge of the form's drawing area, and drag it to widen the form until the drawing area is at least 7" in width.

Step 5 Click and drag the Photo field from the bottom of the form up to the upper-right corner of the form.

Step 6 Click and hold the mouse button just above and to the left of the Home Phone field, and drag down and to the right of the last field until the rectangle encloses the last five fields and their labels. When you release the mouse, all five fields and their labels will be selected.

Step 7 Place the mouse pointer over any of the selected fields until the pointer changes to the shape of a palm, then click and drag the fields as a group to the right side of the form, underneath the Photo field. At this point, your form should resemble the example shown in FIG. 16-3.

Step 8 From the menus, choose `File/Save`. When you are prompted for a name for the form, enter `Staff`. Press Ctrl–F4 to close the form.

Creating the needed queries

To support the reports and labels used by the Personnel Tracking application, two queries are needed to retrieve records by department or by supervisor name. Perform the following steps to create the needed queries.

Step 1 In the Database window, click the `Query` button, then click `New`. In the New Query dialog box that appears, click `New Query`. The Add Table dialog box appears.

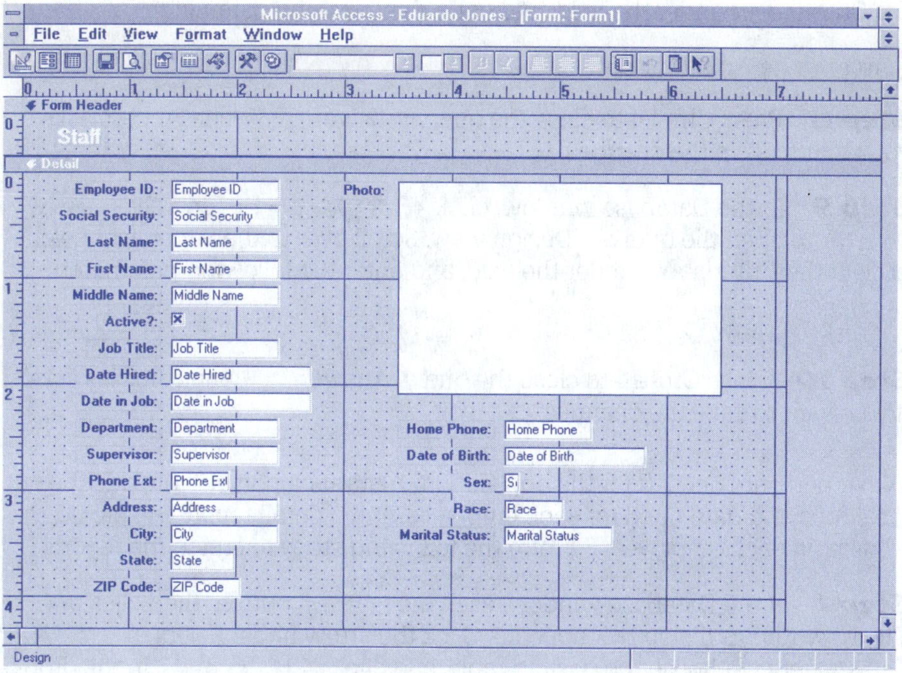

16-3
The completed Staff form.

Step 2 In the Table/Query list box, with `Staff` already selected, click `Add`, then click `Close`. This causes a list box with the fields from the table to appear in the Select Query window. Click the Employee ID field in the list box. (If you omitted this field during the design stage, click the Social Security field instead.) Then, scroll to the last field in the list. While holding the Shift key, click the last field (Photo) in the list to select all the fields.

Step 3 With all fields selected, click any field in the list and drag it to the first empty cell of the Field row in the query grid. Doing so causes all the fields to be placed in the query grid.

Step 4 Choose `File/Save`. Access will prompt you for a name for the query; enter `All Records` and click `OK`. Press Ctrl–F4 to close the Select Query window. The new query appears by name in the Database window.

Step 5 With the `All Records` query still selected in the Database window, choose `Edit/Copy` from the menus, and choose `Edit/Paste`. In the Paste As dialog box that appears, enter `By Department` and click `OK`.

Step 6 With the `All Records` query still selected in the Database window, choose `Edit/Copy` from the menus, and again choose `Edit/Paste`. In the Paste As dialog box that appears, enter `By Supervisor` and click `OK`.

Step 7 In the Database window, click `By Department`, and click `Design` to open the query in Design view. Scroll over to the Department field, click in the Criteria row under the field, and enter the following parameter:

```
[Enter the department:]
```

Step 8 Press Ctrl–F4 to close the query. Answer `Yes` when Access asks if you want to save the changes.

Step 9 In the Database window, click `By Supervisor`, and click `Design` to open the query in Design view. Scroll over to the Supervisor field, click in the Criteria row under the field, and enter the following parameter:

```
[Enter Supervisor Name:]
```

Step 10 Press Ctrl–F4 to close the query. Answer `Yes` when Access asks if you want to save the changes.

Creating the reports

Two reports are needed for the application. A status report will provide the job status and date hired for each employee, and a detail report will provide all data on each employee. Perform the following steps to create the reports.

Step 1 In the Database window, click the `Report` button, then click `New`. The New Report dialog box appears. Click the arrow under Select a Table/Query to choose the desired table, and click `All Records` in the drop-down list. Click the `ReportWizards` button. In a moment, Access displays a dialog box asking you to choose the desired wizard.

Step 2 With `Single-column` already selected, click `OK`.

Step 3 The next dialog box to appear asks which fields you want placed on the report. Click the double-angle bracket button (`>>`) to place all available fields on the report, then click `Next`.

Step 4 The next dialog box asks which field you want to use to sort the data by. Double-click the Last Name field to place it in the Sort Order box, then double-click the First Name field to place it in the Sort Order box. Finally, click `Next`.

Step 5 The next dialog box to appear asks what kind of look you want for the report. Click `Presentation`, then click `Next`.

Step 6 The next dialog box to appear asks for a title for the report. By default, the title `All Records` appears in the text box. Change this title to `Detail Report`, then click the `Design` button to accept the title and open the report in Design view. Click at the top of the page footer (where the mouse pointer changes to the shape of a double-headed arrow), and drag the footer up roughly ½". At this point, your report should resemble the example shown in FIG. 16-4.

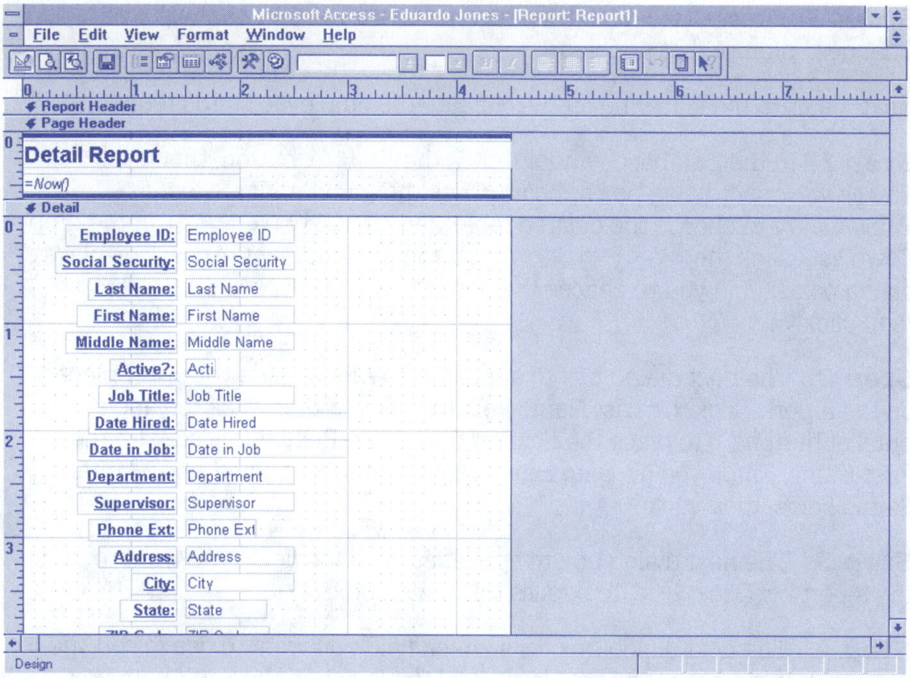

16-4
The completed Detail Report.

Step 7 Choose `File/Save` to save the new report. When prompted for a title, enter `Detail Report` for a report name, then click `OK`. Press Ctrl–F4 to close the new report.

Step 8 With `Detail Report` still selected in the Database window, choose `Edit/Copy` from the menus, and again choose `Edit/Paste`. In the Paste As dialog box that appears, enter `Detail by Department` and click `OK`.

Step 9 With `Detail Report` still selected in the Database window, choose `Edit/Copy` from the menus, and again choose `Edit/Paste`. In the Paste As dialog box that appears, enter `Detail by Supervisor` and click `OK`.

Step 10 In the Database window, click `Detail by Department`, and click `Design` to open the report in Design view. (If the Properties window is not visible, choose `Edit/Select Report`, then choose `View/Properties`.) If All Properties is not visible in the list box at the top of the Properties window that opens (Access 2.0 only), select it now. In the Properties window, change the Record Source to `By Department`.

Step 11 Press Ctrl–F4 to close the report. Answer `Yes` to the "Save Changes" prompt that appears.

Step 12 In the Database window, click `Detail by Supervisor`, and click `Design` to open the report in Design view. In the Properties window, change the Record Source to `By Supervisor`.

Step 13 Press Ctrl–F4 to close the report. Answer `Yes` to the "Save Changes" prompt that appears.

Next, perform the following steps to create the employee status report.

Step 1 In the Database window, click the `Report` button, then click `New`. The New Report dialog box appears. Click the arrow under Select a Table/Query to choose the desired table, and click `All Records` in the drop-down list. Click the `ReportWizards` button. In a moment, Access displays a dialog box asking you to choose the desired wizard. Click `Groups/Totals`, then click `OK`.

Step 2 The next dialog box to appear asks which fields you want placed on the report. Click the Last Name field to select it, then click the angle bracket button (>) to place the field on the report. Repeat this step for the First Name, Employee ID, Date Hired, Department, Sex, Race, and Marital Status fields, then click `Next`.

Step 3 The next dialog box to appear asks which fields you want to group the report by. Click `Next` to bypass this dialog box.

Step 4 The next dialog box asks which field you want to use to sort the data by. Double-click the Last Name field to place it in the Sort Order box, then double-click the First Name field to place it in the Sort Order box. Finally, click `Next`.

Step 5 The next dialog box to appear asks what kind of look you want for the report. Click `Presentation`, then click `Next`.

Step 6 The next dialog box to appear asks for a title for the form. By default, the title `All Records` appears in the text box. Enter `Status Report` as a new title for the report, then click the `Design` button to open the report in Design view. At this point, your report should resemble the example shown in FIG. 16-5.

Step 7 Choose `File/Save` to save the new report. When prompted for a title, enter `Status Report` for a report name, then click `OK`. Press Ctrl–F4 to close the new report.

Step 8 In the Database window, click `Status Report` to select it, choose `Edit/Copy` from the menus, then choose `Edit/Paste`. In the Paste As dialog box that appears, enter `Status by Department` and click `OK`.

Step 9 With `Status Report` still selected in the Database window, choose `Edit/Copy` from the menus, and again choose `Edit/Paste`. In the Paste As dialog box that appears, enter `Status by Supervisor` and click `OK`.

Step 10 In the Database window, click `Status by Department`, and click `Design` to open the report in Design view. (If the Properties window is

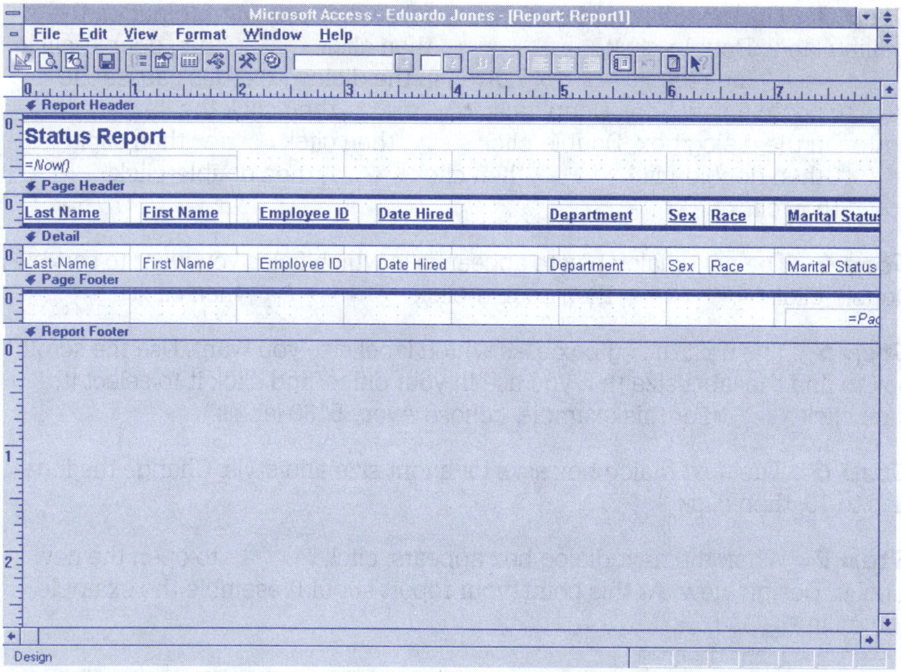

16-5
The completed Status Report.

not visible, choose Edit/Select Report, then choose View/Properties.) If All Properties is not visible in the list box at the top of the Properties window that opens (Access 2.0 only), select it now. In the Properties window, change the Record Source to By Department.

Step 11 Press Ctrl–F4 to close the report. Answer Yes to the "Save Changes" prompt that appears.

Step 12 In the Database window, click Status by Supervisor, and click Design to open the report in Design view. In the Properties window, change the Record Source to By Supervisor.

Step 13 Press Ctrl–F4 to close the report. Answer Yes to the "Save Changes" prompt that appears.

Perform the following steps to create the report that will produce mailing labels for the employees.

Step 1 In the Database window, click Report, then click New. The New Report dialog box appears. Click the arrow in the Select A Table/Query list box, and choose All Records from the list. Then, click the ReportWizards button.

Step 2 The next dialog box to appear asks which wizard you want to use. Click Mailing Label, then click OK.

Step 3 The next dialog box to appear asks what you want to put on the mailing label. Double-click `First Name`, then click `Space`, then double-click `Last Name`. Click the `New Line` button in the dialog box (this causes the label to begin a new line). Double-click `Address`, then click the `New Line` button in the dialog box. Double-click `City`, then click `Comma`, then click `Space`, then double-click `State`, then click `Space`, then double-click `ZIP Code`, then click `Next`.

Step 4 The next dialog box to appear asks which fields you want to sort by. Double-click `Last Name`, then double-click `First Name`, then click `Next`.

Step 5 The next dialog box asks which label size you want. Use the scroll box to find the label size that you use in your office, and click it to select it, then click `Next`. (For this example, I chose Avery 5160 labels.)

Step 6 The next dialog box asks for a font size and style. Change the font size to 10, then click `Next`.

Step 7 When the next dialog box appears, click `Design` to open the new label in Design view. At this point, your report should resemble the example shown in FIG. 16-6.

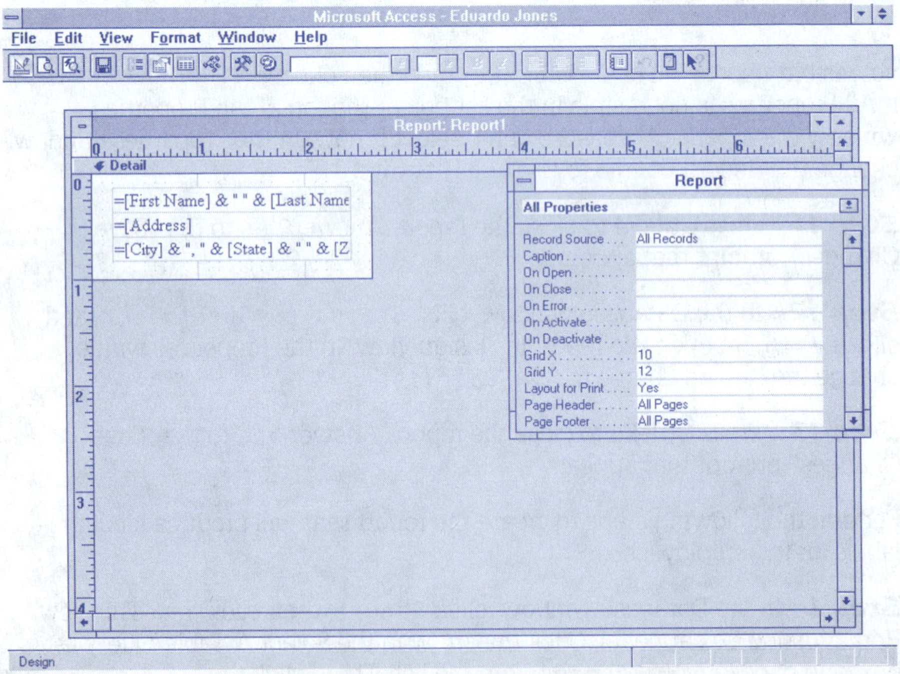

16-6 *The completed Mailing Labels.*

Step 8 From the menus, choose `File/Save`. When prompted for a name, enter `All Labels`, then click `OK`. Press Ctrl–F4 to close the report.

Step 9 In the Database window, click `All Labels` to select it, choose `Edit/Copy` from the menus, then choose `Edit/Paste`. In the Paste As dialog box that appears, enter `Labels by Department` and click `OK`.

Step 10 With `All Labels` still selected in the Database window, choose `Edit/Copy` from the menus, and again choose `Edit/Paste`. In the Paste As dialog box that appears, enter `Labels by Supervisor` and click `OK`.

Step 11 In the Database window, click `Labels By Department`, and click `Design` to open the report in Design view. Because the Properties window still was open when you closed the last report, it will open by default in this report. In the Properties window, change the Record Source to `By Department`.

Step 12 Press Ctrl–F4 to close the report. Answer `Yes` to the "Save Changes" prompt that appears.

Step 13 In the Database window, click `Labels By Supervisor`, and click `Design` to open the report in Design view. In the Properties window, change the Record Source to `By Supervisor`.

Step 14 Press Ctrl–F4 to close the report. Answer `Yes` to the "Save Changes" prompt that appears.

Developing the application

The application requires a series of macros that provide the main menu bar and the associated drop-down menus and the actions that should occur in response when a user chooses a menu option. Perform the following steps to create the macros required for the application.

To create the macro that will display the menu bar of the main menu, perform these steps.

Step 1 In the Database window, click the `Macro` button, then click `New`. If the Macro Name column is not visible, choose `View/Macro Names` from the menu so that you can see the Macro Names column.

Step 2 Click in the first row of the Macro Name column, and enter `Menu` as a macro name. Click in the first row of the Action column, open the list box, and choose `AddMenu` as an action. Click in `Menu Name` under Action Arguments, and enter `&Staff` as the entry. Press Tab once or click directly underneath, in the Menu Macro Name entry, and enter `Staff`.

Step 3 Click in the second row of the Action column, open the list box, and choose `AddMenu` as an action. Click in `Menu Name` under Action Arguments, and enter `&Reports` as the entry. Press Tab once or click directly underneath, in the Menu Macro Name entry, and enter `Reports`.

Step 4 Click in the third row of the Action column, open the list box, and choose `AddMenu` as an action. Click in `Menu Name` under Action Arguments, and enter `&Labels` as the entry. Press Tab once or click directly underneath in the Menu Macro Name entry, and enter `Labels`.

Step 5 Click in the fourth row of the Action column, open the list box, and choose `AddMenu` as an action. Click in `Menu Name` under Action Arguments, and enter `&Tools` as the entry. Press Tab once or click directly underneath in the Menu Macro Name entry, and enter `Tools`.

Step 6 Click in the fifth row of the Action column, open the list box, and choose `AddMenu` as an action. Click in `Menu Name` under Action Arguments, and enter `&Exit` as the entry. Press Tab once or click directly underneath in the Menu Macro Name entry, and enter `Exit System`.

Step 7 Press Ctrl–F4. Answer `Yes` to the prompt that asks if you want to save the macro. For a name, enter `Main Menu`.

To create the drop-down menu for the Update choices on the menu bar, perform the following steps.

Step 1 In the Database window, click the `Macro` button, then click `New`. If the Macro Name column is not visible, choose `View/Macro Names` from the menu so that you can see the Macro Names column. Click in the first row of the Macro Name column, and enter `New Employees` as a name for the first macro in this group. Click in the first row of the Action column, open the list box, and choose `OpenForm` as an action.

Step 2 Under Action Arguments, click the `Form Names` entry, and choose `Staff` from the list of forms. Click in the second row of the Action column, and choose `Maximize` from the list. Click in the third row of the action column, and choose `GoToRecord` from the list.

Step 3 Under Action Arguments, click `Record`, and choose `New` from the list. Click in the Macro Name column, in the fourth row of the macro, and enter `Edit Employees` as a title for the second macro in this group. Click the Action column in the fourth row of the macro (beside the macro name you just entered), open the list box, and choose `OpenForm` as an action.

Step 4 Under Action Arguments, click the `Form Names` entry, and choose `Staff` from the list of forms. Click in the fifth row of the Action column, and choose `Maximize` from the list. Click in the sixth row of the action column, and choose `DoMenuItem` from the list.

Step 5 Under Action Arguments, click `Command`, and choose `Find` from the list.

Step 6 Press Ctrl–F4. Answer `Yes` when asked if you want to save the new macro. When prompted, enter `Staff` as the name for the macro.

To create the macro that builds the drop-down menu for the Reports choices on the menu bar, perform the following steps.

Step 1 In the Database window, click the `Macro` button, then click `New`. If the Macro Name column is not visible, choose `View/Macro Names` from the menu so that you can see the Macro Names column. Click in the first row of the Macro Name column, and enter `Detail Report` as a name for the first macro in this group. Click in the first row of the Action column, open the list box, and choose `OpenReport` as an action.

Step 2 Under Action Arguments, click the `Report Names` entry, and choose `Detail Report` from the list of reports. Then, click in the `View` entry, and change it from `Print Preview` to `Print`. Click in the second row of the Macro Name column, and enter `Detail by Department` as a name for the second macro in this group. Click in the second row of the Action column, open the list box, and choose `OpenReport` as an action.

Step 3 Under Action Arguments, click the `Report Names` entry, and choose `Detail by Department` from the list of reports. Then, click in the `View` entry, and change it from `Print Preview` to `Print`. Click in the third row of the Macro Name column, and enter `Detail by Supervisor` as a name for the third macro in this group. Click in the third row of the Action column, open the list box, and choose `OpenReport` as an action.

Step 4 Under Action Arguments, click the `Report Names` entry, and choose `Detail by Supervisor` from the list of reports. Then, click in the `View` entry, and change it from `Print Preview` to `Print`. Click in the fourth row of the Macro Name column, and enter `Status Report` as a name for the first macro in this group. Click in the fourth row of the Action column, open the list box, and choose `OpenReport` as an action.

Step 5 Under Action Arguments, click the `Report Names` entry, and choose `Status Report` from the list of reports. Then, click in the `View` entry, and change it from `Print Preview` to `Print`. Click in the fifth row of the Macro Name column, and enter `Status by Department` as a name for the fifth macro in this group. Click in the fifth row of the Action column, open the list box, and choose `OpenReport` as an action.

Step 6 Under Action Arguments, click the `Report Names` entry, and choose `Status by Department` from the list of reports. Then, click in the `View` entry, and change it from `Print Preview` to `Print`. Click in the sixth row of the Macro Name column, and enter `Status by Supervisor` as a name for the last macro in this group. Click in the sixth row of the Action column, open the list box, and choose `OpenReport` as an action.

Step 7 Under Action Arguments, click the `Report Names` entry, and choose `Status by Supervisor` from the list of reports. Then, click in the `View` entry, and change it from `Print Preview` to `Print`.

Step 8 Press Ctrl–F4. Answer `Yes` when asked if you want to save the new macro. When prompted, enter `Reports` as the name for the macro.

To create the macro that builds the drop-down menu for the Labels choices on the menu bar, perform the following steps.

Step 1 In the Database window, click the `Macro` button, then click `New`. If the Macro Name column is not visible, choose `View/Macro Names` from the menu so that you can see the Macro Names column. Click in the first row of the Macro Name column, and enter `All Employees` as a name for the first macro in this group. Click in the first row of the Action column, open the list box, and choose `OpenReport` as an action.

Step 2 Under Action Arguments, click the `Report Names` entry, and choose `All Labels` from the list of reports. Then, click in the `View` entry, and change it from `Print Preview` to `Print`. Click in the second row of the Macro Name column, and enter `Labels by Department` as a name for the second macro in this group. Click in the second row of the Action column, open the list box, and choose `OpenReport` as an action.

Step 3 Under Action Arguments, click the `Report Names` entry, and choose `Labels By Department` from the list of reports. Then, click in the `View` entry, and change it from `Print Preview` to `Print`. Click in the third row of the Macro Name column, and enter `Labels by Supervisor` as a name for the third macro in this group. Click in the third row of the Action column, open the list box, and choose `OpenReport` as an action.

Step 4 Under Action Arguments, click the `Report Names` entry, and choose `Labels by Supervisor` from the list of reports. Then, click in the `View` entry, and change it from `Print Preview` to `Print`.

Step 5 Press Ctrl–F4. Answer `Yes` when asked if you want to save the new macro. When prompted, enter `Labels` as the name for the macro.

To create the drop-down menu for the Tools choices on the menu bar, perform the following steps:

Step 1 In the Database window, click `New`. If the Macro Name column is not visible, choose `View/Macro Names` from the menu so that you can see the Macro Names column.

Step 2 Click in the first row of the Macro Name column, and enter `Clock` as a name for the first macro in this group. Click in the first row of the Action column, open the list box, and choose `Run App` from the list. Under Action Arguments, enter `CLOCK.EXE` in the Command Line text box.

Step 3 Click in the second row of the Macro Name column, and enter `Calendar` as a name for the first macro in this group. Click in the second row of the Action column, open the list box, and choose `Run App` from the list. Under Action Arguments, enter `CALENDAR.EXE` in the Command Line text box.

Step 4 Click in the third row of the Macro Name column, and enter `Notepad` as a name for the last macro in this group. Click in the third row of the Action column, open the list box, and choose `Run App` from the list. Under Action Arguments, enter `NOTEPAD.EXE` in the Command Line text box.

Step 5 Click in the fourth row of the Macro Name column, and enter `Calculator` as a name for the last macro in this group. Click in the fourth row of the Action column, open the list box, and choose `Run App` from the list. Under Action Arguments, enter `CALC.EXE` in the Command Line text box.

Step 6 Press Ctrl–F4. Answer `Yes` when you are asked if you want to save the new macro. When you are prompted, enter `Tools` as the name for the macro.

To create the macro that builds the drop-down menu for the Exit choices on the menu bar, perform the following steps.

Step 1 In the Database window, click the `Macro` button, then click `New`. If the Macro Name column is not visible, choose `View/Macro Names` from the menu so that you can see the Macro Names column.

Step 2 Click in the first row of the Macro Name column, and enter `Exit System` as a name for the macro. Click in the first row of the Action column, open the list box, and choose `Close` as an action.

Step 3 Click in the second row of the Action column, open the list box, and again choose `Close` as an action.

Step 4 Press Ctrl–F4. Answer `Yes` when you are asked if you want to save the new macro. When you are prompted, enter `Exit System` as the name for the macro.

The forms used by the application will need command buttons that can be used to delete records and to close the forms and return to the main menu when done. Perform the following steps to create the macros and to add them to the required forms.

Step 1 In the Database window, click the `Macro` button, then click `New`. Click in the first row of the Action column of the macro. Open the drop-down list box, and choose `Close` from the list box. Press Ctrl–F4. Answer `Yes` in response to the "Save changes" prompt that appears. When you are prompted for a name, call the macro `Close`.

Step 2 In the Database window, click the `Macro` button, then click `New`. Click in the first row of the Action column of the macro. Open the drop-down list box, and choose `DoMenuItem`. Under Action Arguments, click in the

Command text box, and choose `Select Record` from the list. Click in the second row of the Action column of the macro. Open the drop-down list box, and choose `DoMenuItem`. Under Action Arguments, click in the Command text box, and choose `Delete` from the list. Press Ctrl–F4. Answer `Yes` in response to the "Save changes" prompt that appears. When you are prompted for a name, call the macro `Delete`.

Step 3 In the Database window, click `Form`, then click `Staff`, then click `Design` to open the Orders form in Design view. Size the form so that you will have room to work, and move the windows so that both the Database window and the form are visible.

Step 4 In the Database window, click the `Macro` button to display the macros. Click the Delete macro, and drag it to a location within the header of the form, roughly 2" from the left edge of the form. *Note*: If you see a dialog box warning you that Wizards cannot be used on existing buttons, click `OK` to ignore it, and ignore any more buttons like this that you see. Use the movement techniques outlined in chapter 6 to center the button vertically.

Step 5 In the Database window, click the Close macro and drag the macro to the space to the right of the `Delete` button. If necessary, move the `Close` button so that it is aligned horizontally and vertically and just to the right of the `Delete` button.

Step 6 Press Ctrl–F4. Answer `Yes` to the prompt that asks if you want to save the changes to the form.

Finally, you will create a blank form that fills the window and presents the main menu of the application. Perform the following steps.

Step 1 In the Database window, click the `Form` button, then click `New`. When the New Form dialog box appears, leave the Select a Table/Query text box blank. Click the `Blank Form` button to open a blank form that is not associated with any tables.

Step 2 Increase the size of the drawing area on the form by dragging the lower-right corner until it is at least 8 × 8", then use the scroll bars to get back to the upper-left corner of the drawing area.

Step 3 From the menus, choose `Edit/Select Form`. Then, choose `View/Properties` to open the Properties window for the form.

Step 4 In the Properties window, click in the `Menu Bar` property (or in versions of Access prior to 2.0, the `On Menu` property), and choose `Main Menu.Menu` from the list of macros. Click in the `Allow Editing` property, and set the property to `Unavailable`. Click in the Scroll Bars property, and set the property to Neither. Then, double-click the Close icon in the Property window to close the window.

Step 5 If the Toolbar is not already visible, choose `View/Toolbox` to display the Toolbox.

Step 6 Click the Label tool in the Toolbox, and click in the form at a point roughly 1" below the top of the form and 3" to the right. Type a desired name for the application. In this example, I used the name `The Personnel Director`.

Step 7 Click at the edge of the text that you just typed to select the text object. In the Toolbar, use the Font and Font Size list boxes to change the font to another font you desire (such as Lucida Handwriting) and to a larger font size (such as 16 point). Then, choose `Format/Size/To Fit` from the menus, and reposition the text box to a centered location of your choice on the form.

Step 8 With the text box still selected, click the `Palette` button in the Toolbar. When the palette appears, change the appearance to raised (click the `Raised` button in the Palette) and click on a wider width for the border (you can change the background colors for the text, if desired, by clicking a color of your choice in the Back Color column). Then, double-click the Palette's `Close` button to put away the Palette.

Step 9 As an option, you can add a graphic to the form. If you want to do so, use standard Windows techniques to switch to Windows Paintbrush (or your desired graphics package) and open the desired art. Capture the desired portion of the art using the standard Windows techniques for your graphics package, then choose `Edit/Copy`. Use standard Windows techniques to switch back to Access, and choose `Edit/Paste`. Resize and position the graphic as desired near the center of the form. At this point, your form might resemble that shown in FIG. 16-7.

Step 10 Press Ctrl–F4. Answer `Yes` to the prompt that asks if you want to save the form. When prompted, enter `Menu` as a name for the form.

Step 11 In the Database window, click the `Macro` button, then click `New` to open a new macro. Click in the Action column in the first row of the macro, and choose `OpenForm` from the list.

Step 12 Under Action Arguments, click in `Form Name`, and choose `Menu` from the list of forms. Click in the Action column in the second row of the macro, and choose `Maximize` from the list.

Step 13 Press Ctrl–F4. Answer `Yes` to the prompt that asks if you want to save the macro. When prompted, enter `Autoexec` as a name for the macro.

At this point, the application is complete. Double-click the `Close` button of the Database window to close it. Then, to try running the application, choose `File/Open Database`. When the Open Database dialog box appears,

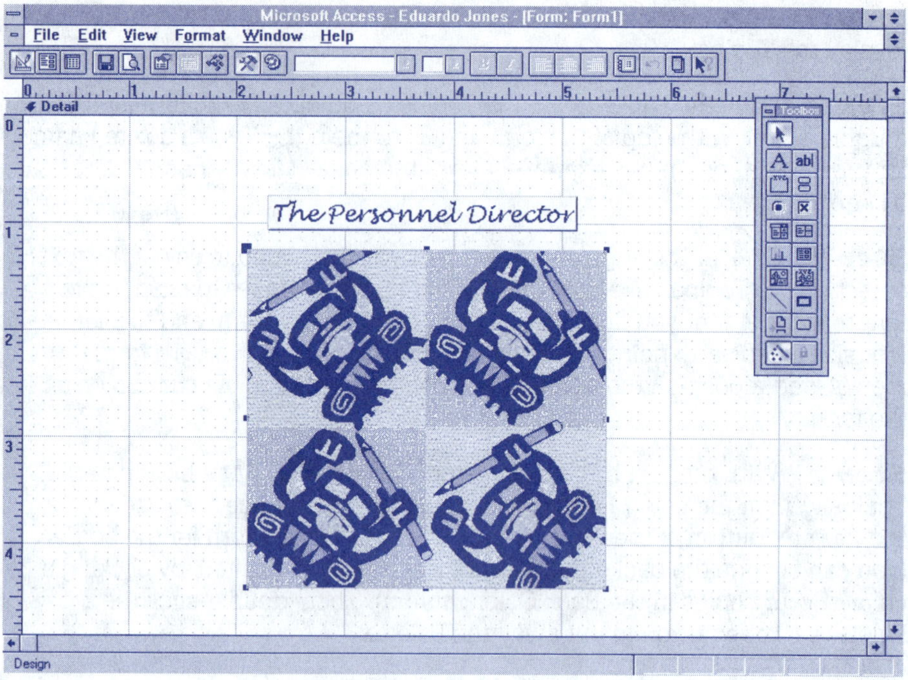

16-7 *The completed Personnel Tracking form.*

double-click STAFF to reopen the database. Because you added the Autoexec macro, when the database opens, the main menu appears automatically, as shown earlier in FIG. 16-1. You can test the application by adding and editing data and printing the desired reports. Additional queries, reports, and macros can be added as needed to increase the functionality of the application.

17 Payroll processing

Few tasks take on the importance at most offices of meeting the payroll. To put it simply, if the payroll is not managed effectively, people don't get paid correctly or on time. While a complete payroll system that handles specialized taxes for specific municipalities is somewhat beyond the scope of this book, the system outlined in this chapter can effectively handle payroll calculations for gross pay and can be used as a basis for a more complex system that will deal with the particular taxes in your area. The files used by the Payroll Processing System presented in this chapter can be found on the accompanying disk in the PAYROLL database. Use the Windows File Manager or DOS commands to copy this database into your Microsoft Access directory. Figure 17-1 shows the Payroll Processing System in use.

Creating the database & tables

The Payroll Processing System requires two tables: one named Employees and another named Time. The Employee table contains a record with the vital statistics for each employee. It is assigned a key field called Social Security, which serves to provide a unique identifier for every employee. The Time table contains the regular and overtime hours worked for any given employee during the week. Each week, a new record for each employee is entered into the Time table based on the time card handed in by the employee. To create the database and its required tables, first start Access in the usual manner, then perform the following steps.

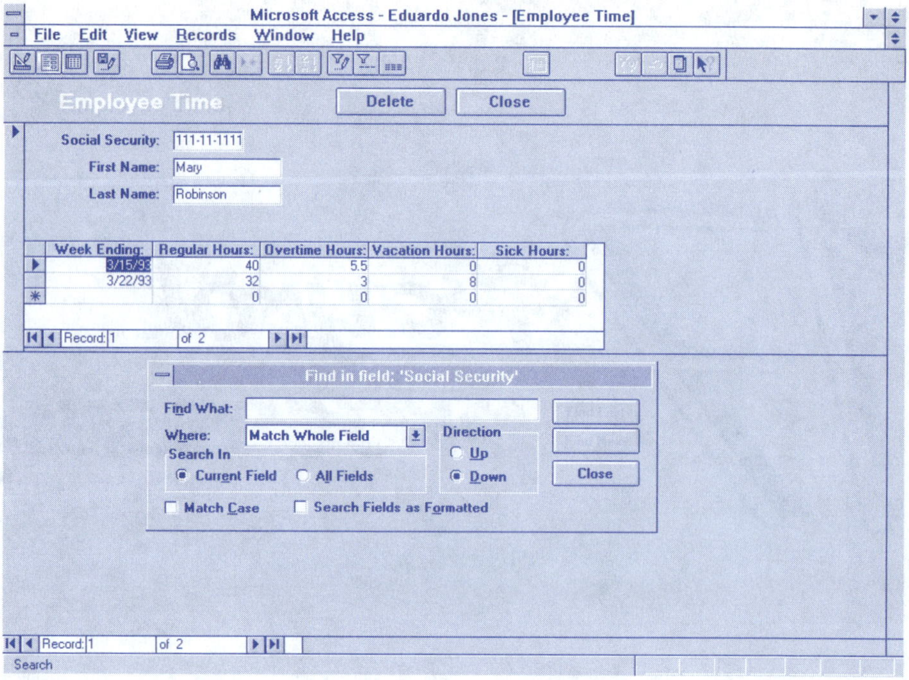

17-1
The Payroll Processing system in use.

Step 1 Choose `File/New Database` to open the New Database dialog box.

TIP

If you want to store the new database in a different directory, use the Directory list box to locate the desired directory now. Click on the desired directory, and Access will store the new database in that directory.

Step 2 Enter `PAYROLL` in the File Name text box as a name for the database, then click `OK`. (Remember, in Access, database names must be 8 characters or less with no spaces.) Access creates the database file on your hard disk, and the Database window appears.

Step 3 In the Database window, click `New`. In the New Table dialog box that appears, click `New Table`. The Table window appears. Fill in the Table window with the field names and data types for the fields shown in TABLE 17-1. Click anywhere in the first field (titled "Social Security"), and click the Key icon in the Toolbar to make this field the primary key. At this point, your table should resemble the example shown in FIG. 17-2.

Step 4 When you are done defining the fields, choose `File/Save` to save the table. When you are prompted for a table name, enter `Employees` as the name and click `OK`. Press Ctrl–F4 to close the Table window. The new table, Employees, now appears in the Database window.

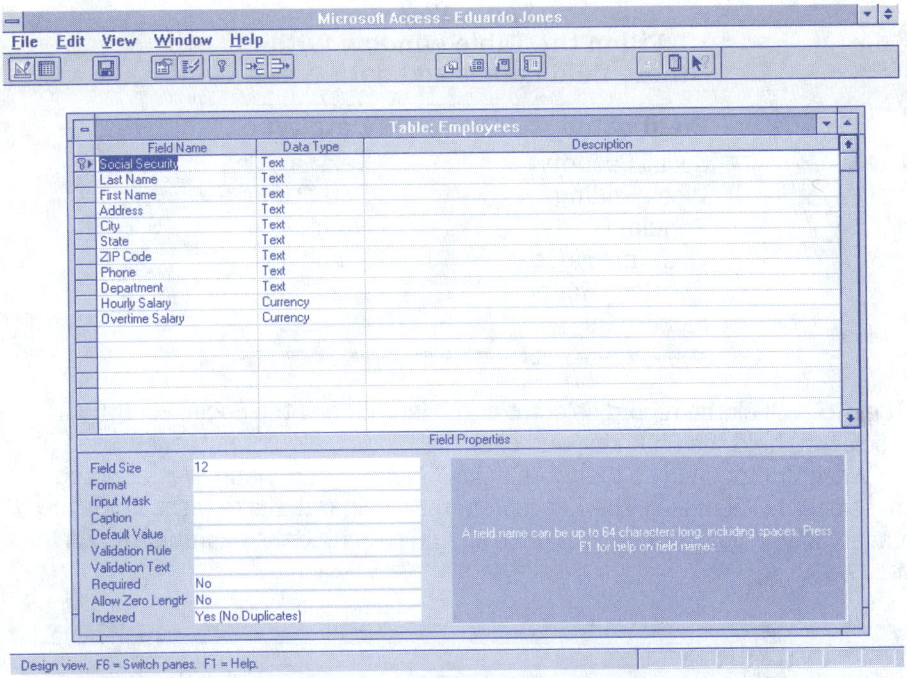

17-2
The completed Employees table.

Table 17-1
Fill in the Table window with these field names and data types.

Field name	Data type
Social Security	Text
Last Name	Text
First Name	Text
Address	Text
City	Text
State	Text
ZIP Code	Text
Phone	Text
Department	Text
Hourly Salary	Currency
Overtime Salary	Currency

Step 5 In the Database window, click `New`. In the New Table dialog box that appears, click `New Table`. The Table window again appears. Fill in the Table window with the field names and data types for the fields shown in TABLE 17-2.

Table 17-2
Fill in the Table window with these field names and data types.

Field name	Data type
Social Security	Text
Week Ending	Date/Time
Regular Hours	Number
Overtime Hours	Number
Vacation Hours	Number
Sick Hours	Number

Step 6 Click the record selector at the left edge of the Social Security field to select it, hold the Shift key, and click the record selector at the left edge of the Week Ending field so that both fields (Social Security and Week Ending) are selected. Then, click the Key icon in the Toolbar to make these fields the primary key. At this point, your table should resemble the example shown in FIG. 17-3.

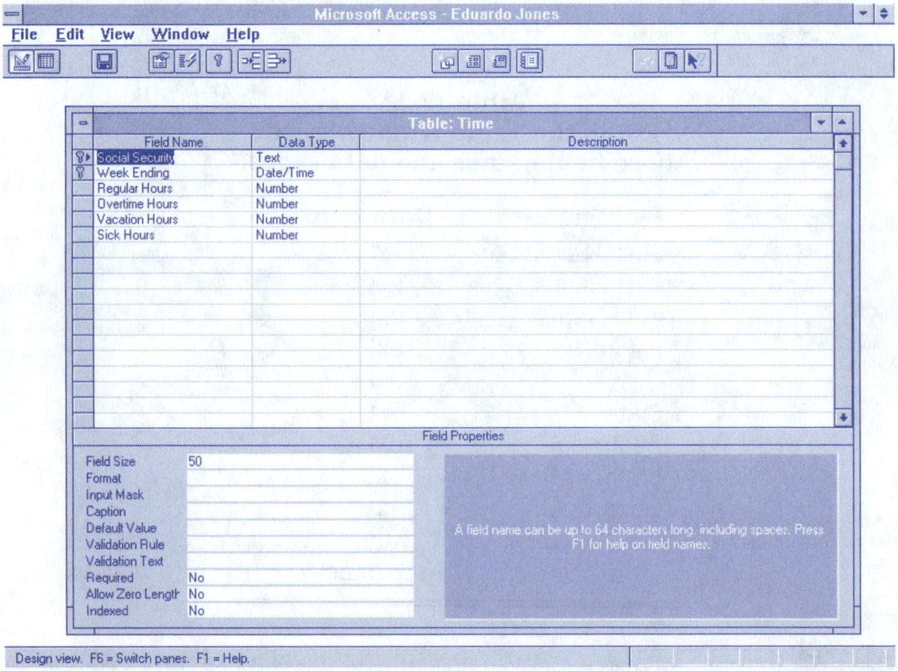

17-3
The completed Time table.

Step 7 When you are done defining the fields, choose `File/Save` to save the table. When you are prompted for a table name, enter `Time` as the name and click `OK`.

Step 8 Press Ctrl–F4 to close the Table window. The new table, Time, now appears in the Database window.

Creating the forms

The database will require three forms. One will be used for adding new employees, the second will be used for adding and editing weekly entries in the Time table, and the third will provide a means of viewing each employee with his or her related Time. To create the needed forms, perform the following steps.

Step 1 In the Database window, click the `Form` button, then click `New`. The New Form dialog box appears. Click the arrow under Select a Table/Query to choose the desired table, and click on `Time` in the drop-down list. Click the `FormWizards` button. In a moment, Access displays a dialog box asking you to choose the desired wizard.

Step 2 With `Single-column` already selected, click `OK`.

Step 3 The next dialog box to appear asks which fields you want selected on the form. Click the double-angle bracket button (`>>`) to place all available fields on the form, then click `Next`.

Step 4 The next dialog box to appear asks what kind of look you want for the form. Click `Embossed`, then click `Next`.

Step 5 The next dialog box to appear asks for a title for the form. By default, the title `Time` appears in the text box. Click the `Open` button to accept the title and open the form. At this point, your form should resemble the example shown in FIG. 17-4.

Step 6 From the menus, choose `File/Save Form`. When prompted for a name, enter `New Time` as the name for the form, then click `OK`. Press Ctrl–F4 to close the new form.

Next, perform the following steps to create the form needed for adding and editing employee records.

Step 1 In the Database window, with the `Form` button still selected, click `New`. The New Form dialog box appears. Click the arrow under Select a Table/Query to choose the desired table, and click on `Employees` in the drop-down list. Click the `FormWizards` button. In a moment, Access displays a dialog box asking you to choose the desired wizard.

Step 2 With `Single-column` already selected, click `OK`.

Step 3 The next dialog box to appear asks which fields you want selected on the form. Click the double-angle bracket button (`>>`) to place all available fields on the form, then click `Next`.

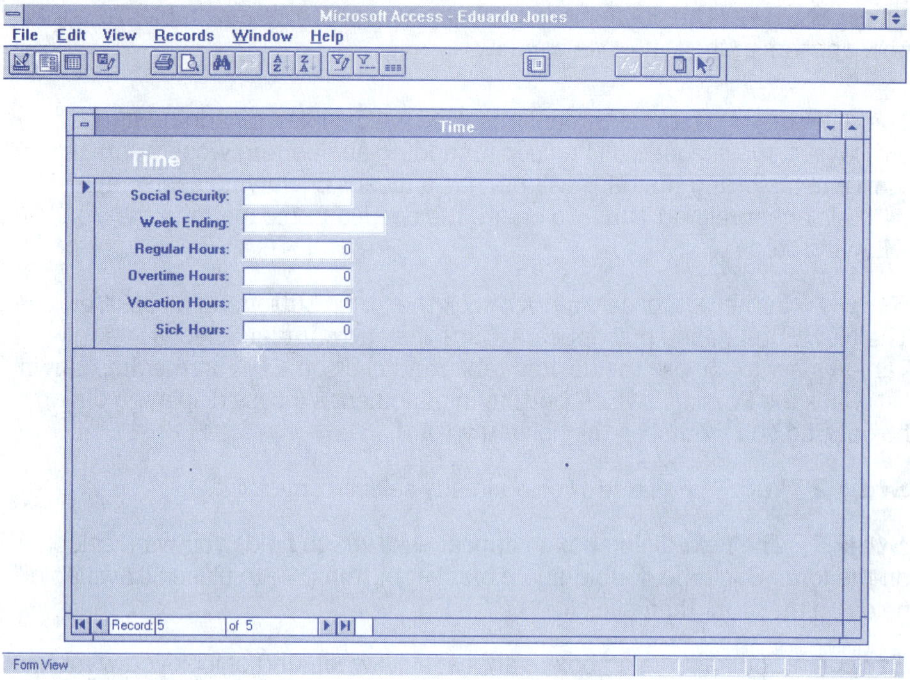

17-4
The completed New Time form.

Step 4 The next dialog box to appear asks what kind of look you want for the form. Click `Embossed`, then click `Next`.

Step 5 The next dialog box to appear asks for a title for the form. By default, the title `Employees` appears in the text box. Click the `Open` button to accept the title and open the form. At this point, your form should resemble the example shown in FIG. 17-5.

Step 6 From the menus, choose `File/Save Form`. When prompted for a name, enter `Employees` as the name for the form, then click `OK`. Press Ctrl–F4 to close the new form.

Next, perform the following steps to create a main/subform that will be used for editing existing time records for an employee.

Step 1 In the Database window, with the `Form` button still selected, click `New`. The New Form dialog box appears. Click the arrow under Select a Table/Query to choose the desired table, and choose `Employees` from the drop-down list. Click the `FormWizards` button. In a moment, Access displays a dialog box asking you to choose the desired wizard. Click `Main/Subform`, then click `OK`. The next dialog box to appear asks which table contains the data for the subform. Click `Time`, then click `Next`.

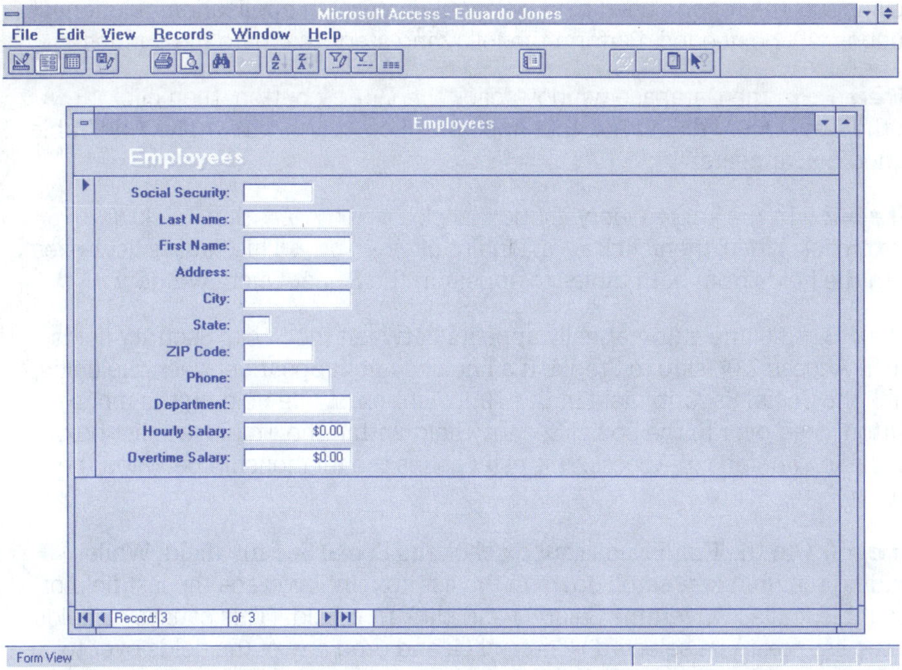

17-5
The completed Employees form.

Step 2 The next dialog box to appear asks which fields you want to add to the main form. Double-click the Social Security field to add it to the main form, then double-click the First Name field to add it to the main form, then double-click the Last Name field to add it to the main form. Then, click `Next`.

Step 3 The next dialog box to appear asks which fields you want to include on the subform. Double-click each of the following fields to add them to the form: Week Ending, Regular Hours, Overtime Hours, Vacation Hours, and Sick Hours. Then, click `Next`.

Step 4 The next dialog box to appear asks what kind of look you want for the form. Click `Embossed`, then click `Next`.

Step 5 The next dialog box to appear asks for a title for the form. By default, the title `Employees` appears in the text box. Type `Employee Time` in the form title text box now, then click the `Open` button to accept the title and open the form. Access will display a dialog box warning you that you must save the subform before saving the main form; click `OK` in this dialog box. In the Save As dialog box which next appears, enter `Employee Time` as a title, and click `OK`.

Step 6 Press Ctrl–F4 to close the new form (click `Yes` in the dialog box that appears asking if you want to save the form). When prompted for a name, enter `Edit Time` as the name for the form.

Creating the relational queries

To support the reports used by the Payroll Processing application, relational queries will be needed. Perform the following steps to create the queries.

Step 1 In the Database window, click the `Query` button, then click `New`. In the New Query dialog box that appears, click `New Query`. The Add Table dialog box appears.

Step 2 In the Table/Query list box, click `Employees`, then click `Add`. Next, click `Time`, then click `Add`. Finally, click `Close`. This causes list boxes with the fields from both tables to appear in the Select Query window.

Step 3 If a line automatically appears between the Social Security fields (as in Access 2.0), skip to Step 4. If a line does not appear between the fields, click the Social Security field in the Time list box. While holding the mouse button, drag over to the Social Security field within the Employees list box. (In earlier versions of Access, this establishes the relationship between the tables.)

Step 4 In the Employees list box click the Social Security field. While holding the Shift key, scroll down in the list box until you see the last field of the table (called "Overtime Salary") and click that field. (This causes all fields in the list box to be selected.) Then, click and drag any of the fields over to the first empty cell in the Field row of the query grid to place all the fields in the query.

Step 5 Using the Scroll bars, scroll the query grid to the right until you can again see the first empty cell of the grid.

Step 6 In the Time list box, click the Week Ending field. While holding the Shift key, click the Sick Hours field in the list box to cause all remaining fields in the list box to be selected. Then, click and drag any of the fields over to the first empty cell in the Field row of the query grid to place all the fields in the query.

Step 7 Choose `File/Save`. Access will prompt you for a name for the query. Enter `All Payroll Records` and click `OK`. Press Ctrl–F4 to close the Select Query window. The new query appears by name in the Database window.

Step 8 With the `All Payroll Records` query selected in the Database window, choose `Edit/Copy` from the menus, then choose `Edit/Paste`. When you are prompted for a name for the newly copied query, enter `Weekly Payroll` and click `OK`.

Step 9 With the `All Payroll Records` query still selected in the Database window, choose `Edit/Copy` from the menus, then choose `Edit/Paste`. When you are prompted for a name for the newly copied query, enter `Payroll for One Employee` and click `OK`.

Step 10 Click the `Weekly Payroll` query to select it, then click `Design`. Click in the Criteria row, in the Week Ending column, and enter the following parameter:

```
[Enter week ending date:]
```

Press Ctrl–F4 to close the query. Answer `Yes` when you are asked if you want to save the changes to the query.

Step 11 Click the Payroll for One Employee query to select it, then click `Design`. Click in the Criteria row in the Social Security column, and enter the following parameter:

```
[Enter social security number:]
```

Press Ctrl–F4 to close the query. Answer `Yes` when you are asked if you want to save the changes to the query.

Creating the reports

Perform the following steps to create the report needed for printing the payroll statements for each employee.

Step 1 In the Database window, click the `Report` button, then click `New`. The New Report dialog box appears. Click the arrow under Select a Table/Query to choose the desired table, and click `Weekly Payroll` in the drop-down list. Click the `ReportWizards` button. In a moment, Access displays a dialog box asking you to choose the desired wizard.

Step 2 With `Single-column` already selected, click `OK`.

Step 3 The next dialog box to appear asks which fields you want placed on the report. Double-click the following fields in the order shown to place them in the report: Social Security, Last Name, First Name, Address, City, State, ZIP Code, Week Ending, Regular Hours, Overtime Hours, Vacation Hours, and Sick Hours. Then, click `Next`.

Step 4 The next dialog box asks which field you want to sort by. Double-click `Social Security`, then click `Next`.

Step 5 The next dialog box asks which kind of look you want for the report. Click `Presentation`, then click `Next`.

Step 6 The next dialog box displays a title of `Weekly Payroll` for the report. Click the `Design` button to accept this title and open the report in Design view. Maximize the report's window so that you will have room to work. Click the right edge of the drawing area, and drag it out to the 6" mark on the horizontal ruler.

Step 7 If necessary, scroll down in the window until the page footer is visible. Click at the top of the page footer, and drag the footer down roughly 1".

Step 8 Click near the vertical ruler at the left edge of the window just above the top of the Week Ending field, and drag until the rectangle that appears surrounds the last five fields of the form. Then, release the mouse. When you do so, all five fields and their labels should be selected. Place the mouse pointer over the selected fields until the pointer changes to the shape of a hand, and click and drag the fields as a group down by roughly ½". Then, click anywhere outside of the fields to deselect them.

Step 9 Click the Sick Hours field to select it (be sure to click the field and not the label to the left). From the menus, choose Edit/Copy, then choose Edit/Paste. As a result, a copy of the field appears on the form. Drag the copy of the field to a point roughly ⅛" below the existing field and aligned with the existing field. Click in the text label for the new field, and change the text from Sick Hours to Total Salary.

Step 10 Click the field to select it, and choose View/Properties to open the Properties window for the field. Click the Control Source property, and press Shift–F2 to open a Zoom window into the property. Delete the existing entry, Sick Hours, and enter the following expression:

```
=([Regular Hours]*[Hourly Salary]) + ([Overtime Hours]*
[Overtime Salary]) + ([Vacation Hours]*[Hourly Salary])
+ ([Sick Hours]* [Hourly Salary])
```

When you are done entering the expression, click OK to close the Zoom box.

Step 11 Click the Format Property, and change it to Currency. Then, click the Decimal Places property, and change it from Auto to 2. Finally, double-click the Close box in the Properties window to close it.

Step 12 If the Toolbox is not visible, choose View/Toolbox. Then, click the Page Break tool in the Toolbox to select it. Then, click below the Total Salary field and just above the footer to place a page break. At this point, your report should resemble the example shown in FIG. 17-6.

Step 13 From the menus, choose File/Save to save the report. When you are prompted for a name, enter Payroll, and click OK. Press Ctrl–F4 to close the report.

Next, perform the following steps to create the report needed for printing a listing of the employees.

Step 1 In the Database window, with the Report button still selected, click New. The New Report dialog box appears. Click the arrow under Select a Table/Query to choose the desired table, and click Employees in the drop-down list. Click the ReportWizards button. In a moment, Access displays a dialog box asking you to choose the desired wizard.

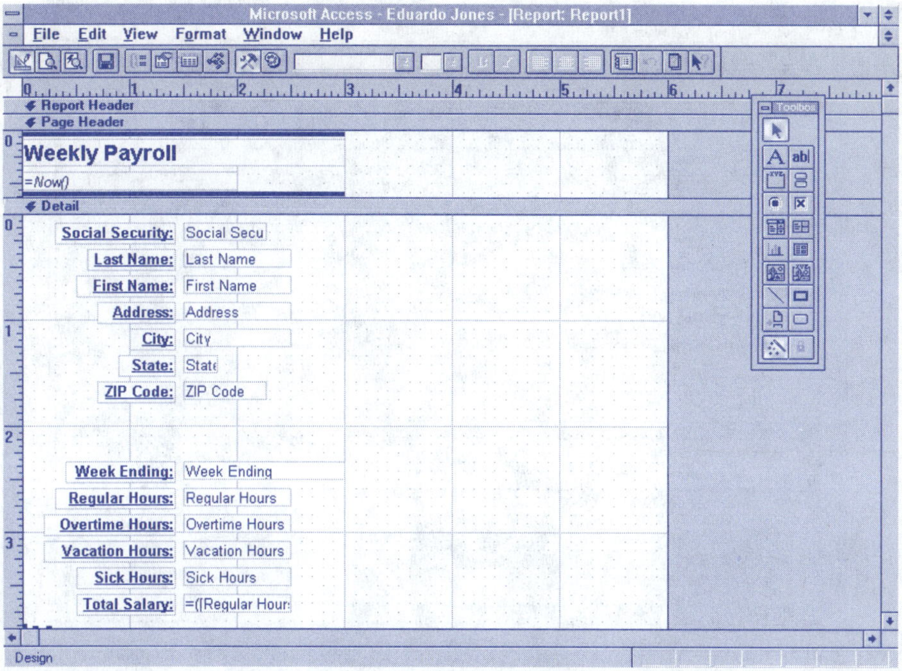

17-6
The Payroll report.

Step 2 With `Single-column` already selected, click `OK`.

Step 3 The next dialog box to appear asks which fields you want placed on the report. Click the double-angle bracket button (`>>`) to place all available fields on the report, then click `Next`.

Step 4 The next dialog box asks which field you want to use to sort the data by. Double-click the Department field to place it in the Sort Order box, then click `Next`.

Step 5 The next dialog box to appear asks what kind of look you want for the report. Click `Executive`, then click `Next`.

Step 6 The next dialog box to appear asks for a title for the form. By default, the title `Employees` appears in the text box. Click the `Design` button to accept the title and open the report in Design view. Scroll down in the report's window until the page footer is visible. Click at the top of the page footer (where the mouse pointer changes to the shape of a double-headed arrow), and drag the footer down roughly ½". At this point, your report should resemble the example shown in FIG. 17-7.

Step 7 Choose `File/Save` to save the new report. When prompted for a title, enter `Employees` for a report name, then click `OK`. Press Ctrl–F4 to close the new report.

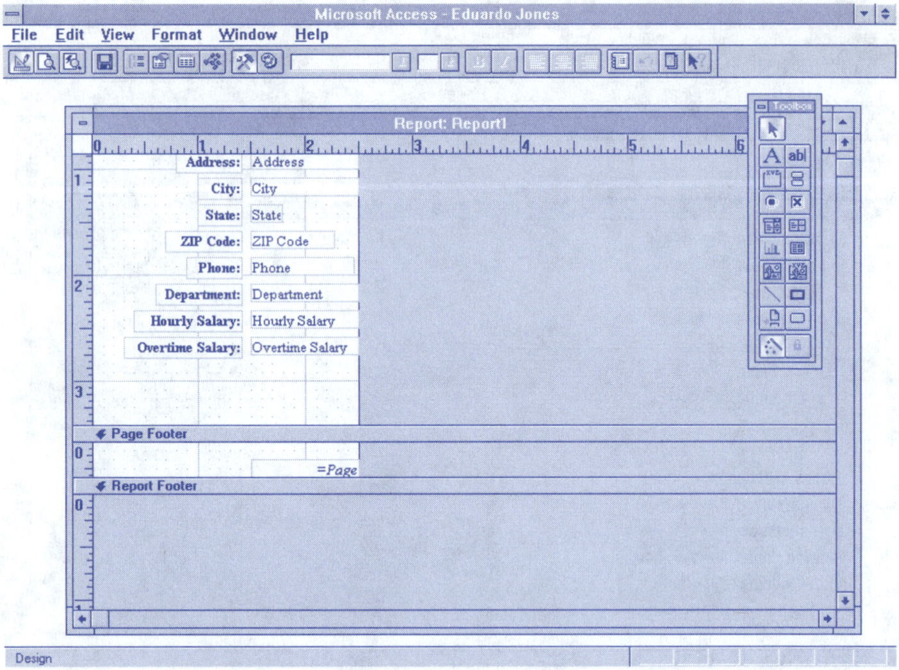

17-7
The Employees report.

Finally, perform the following steps to create the report needed for printing all time associated with a single employee.

Step 1 In the Database window, click the `Report` button, then click `New`. The New Report dialog box appears. Click the arrow under Select a Table/Query to choose the desired table, and click `Payroll for One Employee` in the drop-down list. Click the `ReportWizards` button. In a moment, Access displays a dialog box asking you to choose the desired wizard. Click `Groups/Totals`, then click `OK`.

Step 2 The next dialog box to appear asks which fields you want placed on the report. Double-click the following fields in the order shown: Social Security, Week Ending, Regular Hours, Overtime Hours, Vacation Hours, and Sick Hours. Then, click `Next`.

Step 3 The next dialog box asks which field you want to use to group the data by. Double-click the Social Security field to place it in the Group Order box, then click `Next`.

Step 4 The next dialog box asks how you want to group the data in each field. Click `Next` to bypass this question.

Step 5 The next dialog box asks which field you want to use to sort the data by. Double-click the `Week Ending` to place it in the Sort Order box, then click `Next`.

Step 6 The next dialog box to appear asks what kind of look you want for the report. Click `Executive`, then click `Next`.

Step 7 The next dialog box to appear asks for a title for the form. By default, the title `Payroll for One Employee` appears in the text box. Change this title to `Employee Time`, turn off the "Calculate Percent of Total" option, then click the `Design` button to accept the title and open the report in Design view.

Step 8 If the list of fields is not visible, choose `View/Field List` from the menus to display it. Click Last Name in the field list, and drag the field into the Social Security header, beside the existing Social Security field. Align the field vertically, if necessary. Click First Name in the field list, and drag the field into the Social Security header, beside the existing Last Name field. Align the field vertically, if necessary. At this point, your report should resemble the example shown in FIG. 17-8.

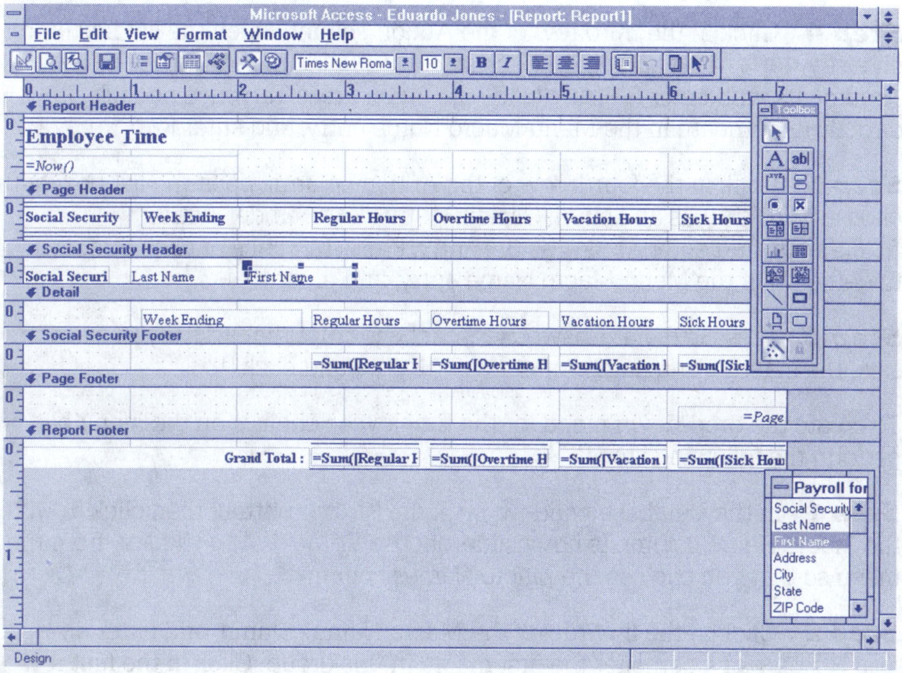

17-8
The Employee Time report.

Step 9 Choose `File/Save` to save the new report. When prompted for a title, enter `Employee Time` for a report name, then click `OK`. Press Ctrl–F4 to close the new report.

Developing the application

The application requires a series of macros that provide the main menu bar and the associated drop-down menus and the actions that should occur in response when a user chooses a menu option. Perform the following steps to create the macros required for the application.

To create the macro that will display the menu bar of the main menu, perform these steps.

Step 1 In the Database window, click the Macro button, then click New. If the Macro Name column is not visible, choose View/Macro Names from the menu so that you can see the Macro Names column.

Step 2 Click in the first row of the Macro Name column, and enter Menu as a macro name. Click in the first row of the Action column, open the list box, and choose AddMenu as an action. Click in Menu Name under Action Arguments, and enter &Employees as the entry. Press Tab once or click directly underneath in the Menu Macro Name entry, and enter Employees.

Step 3 Click in the second row of the Action column, open the list box, and choose AddMenu as an action. Click in Menu Name under Action Arguments, and enter &Time Cards as the entry. Press Tab once or click directly underneath in the Menu Macro Name entry, and enter Time Cards.

Step 4 Click in the third row of the Action column, open the list box, and choose AddMenu as an action. Click in Menu Name under Action Arguments, and enter &Reports as the entry. Press Tab once or click directly underneath in the Menu Macro Name entry, and enter Reports.

Step 5 Click in the fourth row of the Action column, open the list box, and choose AddMenu as an action. Click in Menu Name under Action Arguments, and enter &Exit as the entry. Press Tab once or click directly underneath in the Menu Macro Name entry, and enter Exit.

Step 6 Press Ctrl–F4. Answer Yes to the prompt that asks if you want to save the macro. For a name, enter Main Menu, and click OK.

To create the drop-down menu for the Employees choices on the menu bar, perform the following steps.

Step 1 In the Database window, click the Macro button, then click New. If the Macro Name column is not visible, choose View/Macro Names from the menu so that you can see the Macro Names column.

Step 2 Click in the first row of the Macro Name column, and enter New Employees as a name for the first macro in this group. Click in the first row of the Action column, open the list box, and choose OpenForm as an action.

Step 3 Under Action Arguments, click the Form Name entry, and choose Employees from the list of forms. Click in the second row of the Action column, and choose Maximize from the list. Click in the third row of the action column, and choose GoToRecord from the list.

Step 4 Under Action Arguments, click `Record`, and choose `New` from the list. Click in the Macro Name column in the fourth row of the macro, and enter `Edit Employees` as a title for the second macro in this group. Click the Action column in the fourth row of the macro (beside the macro name you just entered), open the list box, and choose `OpenForm` as an action.

Step 5 Under Action Arguments, click the `Form Name` entry, and choose `Employees` from the list of forms. Click in the fifth row of the Action column, and choose `Maximize` from the list. Click in the sixth row of the action column, and choose `DoMenuItem` from the list.

Step 6 Under Action Arguments, click `Command`, and choose `Find` from the list.

Step 7 Press Ctrl–F4. Answer `Yes` when you are asked if you want to save the new macro. When you are prompted, enter `Employees` as the name for the macro.

To create the macro that builds the drop-down menu for the Time Cards choices on the menu bar, perform the following steps.

Step 1 In the Database window, click the `Macro` button, then click `New`. If the Macro Name column is not visible, choose `View/Macro Names` from the menu so that you can see the Macro Names column.

Step 2 Click in the first row of the Macro Name column, and enter `Enter Time` as a name for the first macro in this group. Click in the first row of the Action column, open the list box, and choose `OpenForm` as an action.

Step 3 Under Action Arguments, click the `Form Name` entry, and choose `New Time` from the list of forms. Click in the second row of the Action column, and choose `Maximize` from the list. Click in the third row of the action column, and choose `GoToRecord` from the list.

Step 4 Under Action Arguments, click `Record`, and choose `New` from the list. Click in the Macro Name column in the fourth row of the macro, and enter `Edit Time` as a title for the second macro in this group. Click the Action column in the fourth row of the macro (beside the macro name you just entered), open the list box, and choose `OpenForm` as an action.

Step 5 Under Action Arguments, click the `Form Name` entry, and choose `Edit Time` from the list of forms. Click in the fifth row of the Action column, and choose `Maximize` from the list. Click in the sixth row of the action column, and choose `DoMenuItem` from the list.

Step 6 Under Action Arguments, click `Command`, and choose `Find` from the list.

Step 7 Press Ctrl–F4. Answer `Yes` when you are asked if you want to save the new macro. When you are prompted, enter `Time Cards` as the name for the macro.

To create the macro that builds the drop-down menu for the Reports choices on the menu bar, perform the following steps.

Step 1 In the Database window, click the `Macro` button, then click `New`. If the Macro Name column is not visible, choose `View/Macro Names` from the menu so that you can see the Macro Names column.

Step 2 Click in the Macro Name column in the first row of the macro, and enter `Run Payroll` as a title for the first macro in this group. Click the Action column in the first row of the macro (beside the macro name you just entered), open the list box, and choose `OpenReport` as an action.

Step 3 Under Action Arguments, click the `Report Name` entry, and choose `Payroll` from the list of reports. Leave the View entry set to `Print Preview`. Click in the Macro Name column, in the second row of the macro, and enter `Employee List` as a title for the next macro in this group. Click the Action column in the second row of the macro (beside the macro name you just entered), open the list box, and choose `OpenReport` as an action.

Step 4 Under Action Arguments, click the `Report Name` entry, and choose `Employees` from the list of reports. Leave the View entry set to `Print Preview`. Click in the Macro Name column in the third row of the macro, and enter `Employee Time` as a title for the last macro in this group. Click the Action column in the third row of the macro (beside the macro name you just entered), open the list box, and choose `OpenReport` as an action.

Step 5 Under Action Arguments, click the `Report Name` entry, and choose `Employee Time` from the list of reports. Leave the View entry set to `Print Preview`.

Step 6 Press Ctrl–F4. Answer `Yes` when you are asked if you want to save the new macro. When you are prompted, enter `Reports` as the name for the macro.

To create the macro that builds the drop-down menu for the Exit choices on the menu bar, perform the following steps.

Step 1 In the Database window, click the `Macro` button, then click `New`. If the Macro Name column is not visible, choose `View/Macro Names` from the menu so that you can see the Macro Names column.

Step 2 Click in the first row of the Macro Name column, and enter `Exit System` as a name for the macro.

Step 3 Click in the first row of the Action column, open the list box, and choose `Close` as an action.

Step 4 Click in the second row of the Action column, open the list box, and again choose `Close` as an action.

Step 5 Press Ctrl–F4. Answer `Yes` when you are asked if you want to save the new macro. When you are prompted, enter `Exit` as the name for the macro.

The forms used by the application will need command buttons that can be used to close the forms and return to the main menu when done. Perform the following steps to create a macro for closing forms and to add it to the required forms.

Step 1 In the Database window, click the `Macro` button, then click `New`. Click in the first row of the Action column of the macro. Open the drop-down list box, and choose `Close` from the list box. Press Ctrl–F4. Answer `Yes` in response to the "Save changes" prompt that appears. When you are prompted for a name, call the macro `Close`.

Step 2 In the Database window, click the `Macro` button, then click `New`. Click in the first row of the Action column of the macro. Open the drop-down list box, and choose `DoMenuItem`. Under Action Arguments, click in the Command text box, and choose `Select Record` from the list. Click in the second row of the Action column of the macro. Open the drop-down list box, and choose `DoMenuItem`. Under Action Arguments, click in the Command text box, and choose `Delete` from the list. Press Ctrl–F4. Answer `Yes` in response to the "Save changes" prompt that appears. When prompted for a name, call the macro `Delete`.

Step 3 In the Database window, click `Form`, then click `Employees`, then click `Design` to open the Employees form in Design view. Size the form so that you will have room to work, and move the windows so that both the Database window and the form are visible. Click the right edge of the drawing area, and widen the drawing area by roughly 2" more.

Step 4 In the Database window, click the `Macro` button to display the macros. Click the Delete macro, and drag it to a location within the header of the form, roughly 2" from the left edge of the form. *Note*: If you see a dialog box warning you that Wizards cannot be used on existing buttons, click `OK` to ignore it, and ignore any more buttons like this that you see. Use the movement techniques outlined in chapter 6 to center the button vertically.

Step 5 In the Database window, click the Close macro and drag it to a location within the header of the form to the immediate right of the `Delete` button. Use the movement techniques outlined in chapter 6 to center the button vertically.

Step 6 Press Ctrl–F4. Answer Yes to the prompt that asks if you want to save the changes to the form.

Step 7 In the Database window, click Form, then click New Time, then click Design to open the New Time form in Design view. Size the form so that you will have room to work, and move the windows so that both the Database window and the form are visible.

Step 8 In the Database window, click the Macro button to display the macros. Click the Close macro, and drag it to a location within the header of the form, roughly 1" from the left edge of the form. Use the movement techniques outlined in chapter 6 to center the button vertically.

Step 9 Press Ctrl–F4. Answer Yes to the prompt that asks if you want to save the changes to the form.

Step 10 In the Database window, click Form, then click Edit Time, then click Design to open the Edit Time form in Design view. Size the form so that you will have room to work, and move the windows so that both the Database window and the form are visible.

Step 11 In the Database window, click the Macro button to display the macros. Click the Delete macro, and drag it to a location within the header of the form, roughly 3" from the left edge of the form. Use the movement techniques outlined in chapter 6 to center the button vertically.

Step 12 In the Database window, click the Macro button to display the macros. Click the Close macro, and drag it to a location within the header of the form, to the immediate right of the Delete button. Use the movement techniques outlined in chapter 6 to center the button vertically.

Step 13 Press Ctrl–F4. Answer Yes to the prompt that asks if you want to save the changes to the form.

Finally, you will create a blank form that fills the window and presents the main menu of the application. Perform the following steps.

Step 1 In the Database window, click the Form button, then click New. When the New Form dialog box appears, leave the Select a Table/Query text box blank. Click the Blank Form button to open a blank form that is not associated with any tables.

Step 2 Increase the size of the drawing area on the form by dragging the lower-right corner until it is at least 8 × 8", then use the scroll bars to get back to the upper-left corner of the drawing area.

Step 3 From the menus, choose Edit/Select Form. Then, choose View/Properties to open the Properties window for the form.

Step 4 In the Properties window, click in the `Menu Bar` property (or in earlier versions of Access, the `On Menu` property) and choose `Main Menu.Menu` from the list of macros. Click in the Allow Editing property, and set the property to `Unavailable`. Click in the Scroll Bars property, and set the property to `Neither`. Then, double-click the Close icon in the Property window to close the window.

Step 5 If the Toolbox is not already visible, choose `View/Toolbox` to display the Toolbox. Click the Label tool in the Toolbox, and click in the form at a point roughly 1" below the top of the form and 3" to the right. Type a desired name for the application. In this example, I used the name `The Payroll Manager`. Click at the edge of the text you just typed to select the text object. In the Toolbar, use the Font and Font Size list boxes to change the font to another font you desire (such as Lucida Calligraphy) and to a larger font size (such as 24 point). Then, choose `Layout/Size To Fit` from the menus, and reposition the text box to a centered location of your choice on the form.

Step 6 With the text box still selected, click the `Palette` button in the Toolbar. When the palette appears, change the appearance to raised (click the `Raised` button in the Palette) and click on a wider width for the border (you can change the background colors for the text, if desired, by clicking a color of your choice in the Back Color column). Then, double-click the Palette's `Close` button to put away the Palette.

Step 7 As an option, you can add a graphic to the form. If you want to do so, use standard Windows techniques to switch to Windows Paintbrush (or your desired graphics package) and open the desired art. Capture the desired portion of the art using the standard Windows techniques for your graphics package, then choose `Edit/Copy`. Use standard Windows techniques to switch back to Access, and choose `Edit/Paste`. Resize and position the graphic as desired near the center of the form.

Step 8 Press Ctrl–F4. Answer `Yes` to the prompt that asks if you want to save the form. When you are prompted, enter `Menu` as a name for the form.

Step 9 In the Database window, click the `Macro` button, then click `New` to open a new macro. Click in the Action column in the first row of the macro, and choose `OpenForm` from the list.

Step 10 Under Action Arguments, click in `Form Name`, and choose `Menu` from the list of forms. Click in the Action column in the second row of the macro, and choose `Maximize` from the list.

Step 11 Press Ctrl–F4. Answer `Yes` to the prompt that asks if you want to save the macro. When you are prompted, enter `Autoexec` as a name for the macro.

At this point, the application is complete. Double-click the `Close` button of the Database window to close it. Then, to try running the application, choose `File/Open Database`. When the Open Database dialog box appears, double-click `PAYROLL` to reopen the database. Because you added the Autoexec macro, when the database opens, the main menu appears automatically. You can test the application by adding and editing data and printing the desired reports. Additional queries, reports, and macros can be added as needed to increase the functionality of the application.

18 Client Contacts Management

In business, databases often are used to track activity between a company and its clients whenever phone calls are made. Many commercial programs, falling under the general heading of "contact management," exist for the purpose of keeping up with phone calls made to clients. The Client Contacts Management system outlined in this chapter is designed to address this common business need. The files used by the Clients Contacts Management System presented in this chapter can be found on the accompanying disk in the CONTACTS database. Use the Windows File Manager or DOS commands to copy this database into your Microsoft Access directory. Figure 18-1 shows the Clients Contacts System in use.

Creating the database & tables

The Clients Contact System requires three tables: one named Contacts, the second named Calls, and the last named Tickler. The Contacts table serves as the main table used by the application. It contains details about each contact (such as the name and address and all phone numbers). The Contacts table uses a counter field as its key field; the application makes use of the unique value stored in the counter field to link to related records in the other tables. The Calls table contains the log of all contacts (phone calls) made to each person in the Contacts table, and the Tickler table contains the "tickler" file of all events that are related to a person in the Contacts table.

To create the database and its required tables, first start Access in The usual manner, then perform the following steps.

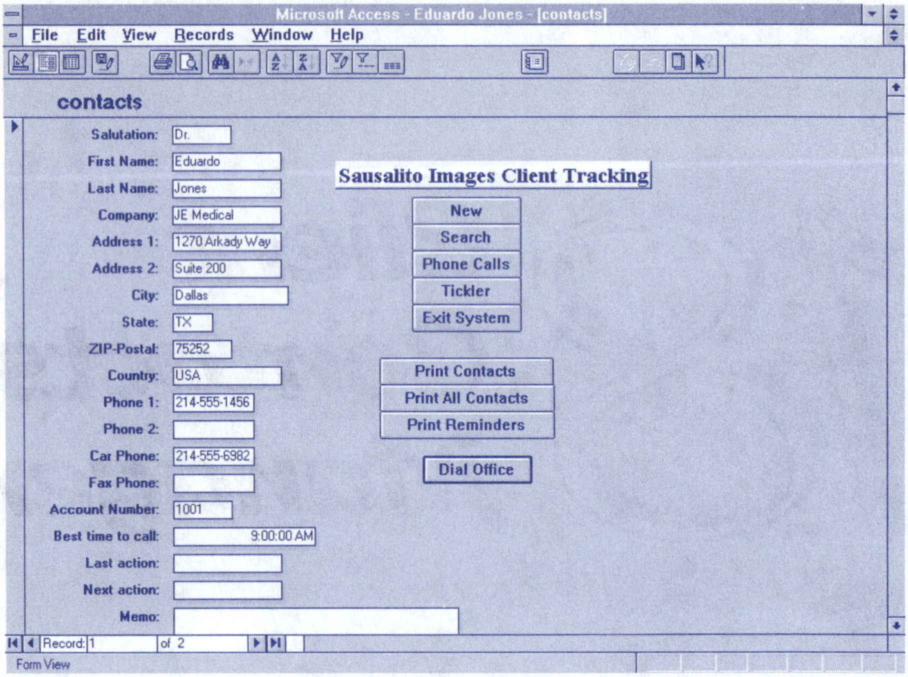

18-1
The Clients Contact system in use.

Step 1 Choose `File/New Database` to open the New Database dialog box.

TIP

If you want to store the new database in a different directory, use the Directory list box to locate the desired directory now. Click on the desired directory, and Access will store the new database in that directory.

Step 2 Enter `CONTACTS` in the File Name text box as a name for the database, then click `OK`. (Remember, in Access, database names must be eight characters or less with no spaces.) Access creates the database file on your hard disk, and the Database window appears.

Step 3 In the Database window, click the `Table` button, then click `New`. In the New Table dialog box that appears, click `New Table`. The Table window appears. Fill in the Table window with the field names and data types for the fields shown in TABLE 18-1.

Step 4 With the insertion pointer anywhere in the last field (titled "Account Number"), click the Key icon in the Toolbar to make this field the primary key. At this point, your table should resemble the example shown in FIG. 18-2.

Step 5 When you are done defining the fields, choose `File/Save` to save the table. When prompted for a table name, enter `Contacts` as the name, and

Table 18-1
Fill in the Table window with these field names and data types.

Field name	Data type
Salutation	Text
Last Name	Text
First Name	Text
Company	Text
Address 1	Text
Address 2	Text
City	Text
State	Text
ZIP/Postal	Text
Country	Text
Office Phone	Text
Home Phone	Text
Car Phone	Text
Fax Phone	Text
Best time to call	Date/time
Last action	Text
Next action	Text
Memo	Memo
Account Number	Text

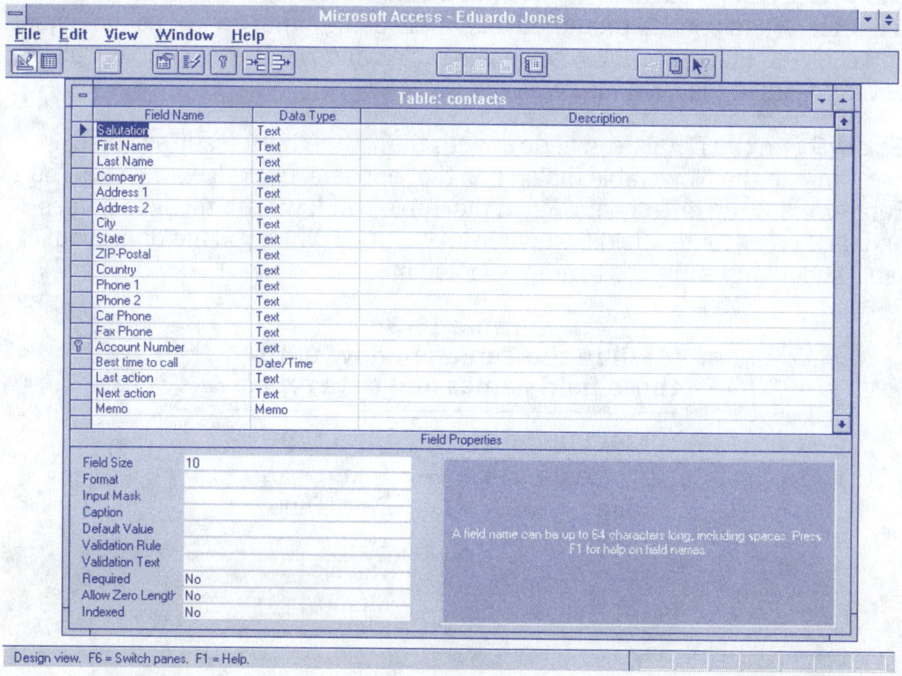

18-2
The completed Contacts table.

click OK. Press Ctrl–F4 to close the Table window. The new table, Contacts, now appears in the Database window.

Step 6 In the Database window, with the Table button still selected, click New. In the New Table dialog box that appears, click New Table. The Table window again appears. Fill in the Table window with the field names and data types for the fields shown in TABLE 18-2.

Table 18-2
Fill in the Table window with these field names and data types.

Field name	Data type
Account number	Text
Date of call	Date/Time
Time of call	Date/Time
Status	Text
Comments	Memo

Step 7 Click and drag through the record selectors (at the left edge of the table) for the account number, date of call, and time of call fields to select all three fields. Then, click the Key icon in the Toolbar to make all three fields a combined primary key. At this point, your table should resemble the example shown in FIG. 18-3.

Step 8 When you are done defining the fields, choose File/Save to save the table. When you are prompted for a table name, enter Calls as the name, and click OK. Press Ctrl–F4 to close the Table window. The new table, Calls, now appears in the Database window.

Step 9 In the Database window, with the Table button still selected, click New. In the New Table dialog box that appears, click New Table. The Table window again appears. Fill in the Table window with the field names and data types for the fields shown in TABLE 18-3. When you are done, your table should resemble the example shown in FIG. 18-4.

Table 18-3
Fill in the Table window with these field names and data types.

Field name	Data type
Account number	Text
Date	Date/Time
Action	Text
Done?	Yes/No
Notes	Memo

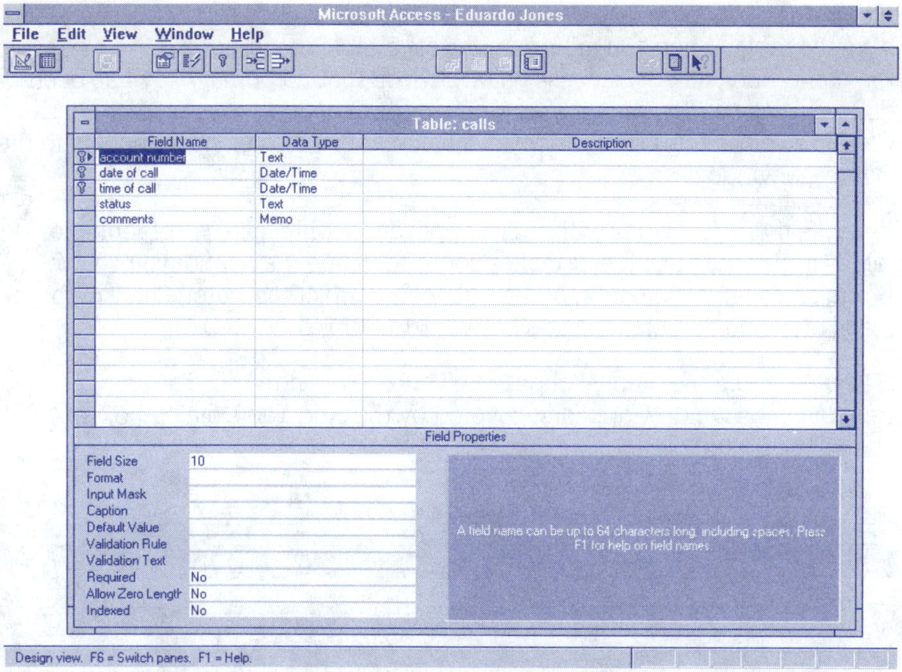

18-3
The completed Calls table.

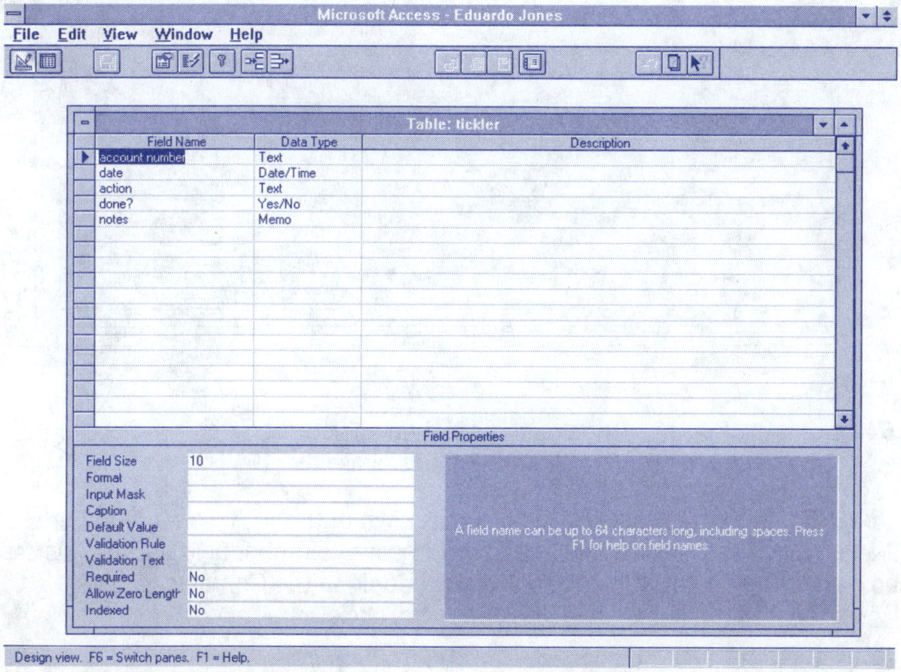

18-4
The completed Tickler table.

Step 10 When you are done defining the fields, choose `File/Save` to save the table. When you are prompted for a table name, enter `Tickler` as the name, and click `OK`. Access will warn you that no primary key has been defined. Answer `No` when it asks if you want to define a primary key. Press Ctrl–F4 to close the Table window. The new table, Tickler, now appears in the Database window.

Defining the relationships

Because many functions within this application will make use of multiple tables in a related fashion, it makes sense to define the relationships now. Doing so will make creation of the queries a simpler task later. Perform these steps to define the relationships between the tables.

Step 1 From the menus, choose `Edit/Relationships`. The Relationships window appears, covered by the Add Table dialog box, as shown in FIG. 18-5.

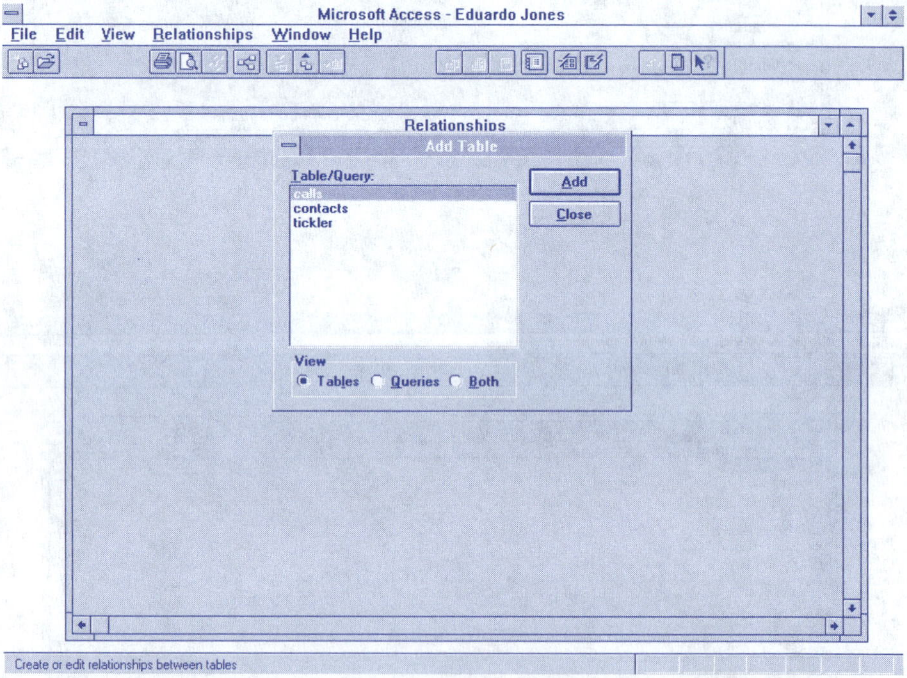

18-5 *The Relationships dialog box.*

Step 2 Click `Calls`, then click `Add`, then click `Contacts`, then click `Add`, then click `Tickler`, then click `Add`. Finally, click `Close`.

Step 3 In the Contacts list box, scroll down until the Account Number field comes into view. Then, click in the Account Number field in the Calls list box, and drag over to the Account Number field in the Contacts list box. When the Relationships dialog box appears, click `Create`.

Step 4 Click in the Account Number field in the Tickler list box, and drag over to the Account Number field in the Contacts list box. When the Relationships dialog box appears, click `Create`.

Step 5 Press Ctrl–F4 to close the Relationships window and store the relationship. Answer "Yes" to the prompt that asks if you want to save the changes.

Creating the forms

The database will require three forms: one will be used for adding and editing contacts, the second will be used to display and edit the records in the calls table, and the third will be used to add or edit records in the tickler file. To create the needed forms, perform the following steps.

Step 1 In the Database window, click the `Form` button, then click `New`. The New Form dialog box appears. Click the arrow under Select a Table/Query to choose the desired table, and click on `Contacts` in the drop-down list. Click the `FormWizards` button. In a moment, Access displays a dialog box asking you to choose the desired wizard.

Step 2 With `Single-column` already selected, click `OK`.

Step 3 The next dialog box to appear asks which fields you want selected on the form. Click the double-angle bracket button (`>>`) to place all available fields on the form, then click `Next`.

Step 4 The next dialog box to appear asks what kind of look you want for the form. Click `Shadowed`, then click `Next`.

Step 5 The next dialog box to appear asks for a title for the form. By default, the title `Contacts` appears in the text box. Click the `Design` button to accept the title and open the form in Design view.

Step 6 Click the form's `Maximize` button so that you can see the entire form. If the Toolbar is not already visible, choose `View/Toolbox` to display the Toolbox. Click the right edge of the drawing area, and drag to the right until the drawing area is 7" wide.

Step 7 Click the Text tool in the Toolbox, and click in the form at a point roughly 1" below the top of the form and 4" to the right. Type a desired name for the application. In this example, I used the name `Sausalito Images Client Tracking`.

Step 8 Click at the edge of the text that you just typed to select the text object. In the Toolbar, use the Font and Font Size list boxes to change the font to another font that you desire (such as New Times Roman) and to a larger font size (such as 14 point). Then, choose `Layout/Size to Fit` from the menus and reposition the text box to a centered location of your choice on the form.

Step 9 Click the `Palette` button in the Toolbar. When the palette appears, change `Appearance` to `Raised` and click on a wider width for the border (you can change the fill colors for the text, if desired, by clicking a color of your choice in the Fill column). Then, double-click the Palette's `Close` button to put away the Palette.

Note: As an option, you can add a graphic to the form. If you want to do so, use standard Windows techniques to switch to Windows Paintbrush (or your desired graphics package) and open the desired art. Capture the desired portion of the art using the standard Windows techniques for your graphics package, then choose `Edit/Copy`. Use standard Windows techniques to switch back to Access, and choose `Edit/Paste`. Resize and position the graphic as desired on the form. At this point, your form should resemble the example shown in FIG. 18-6.

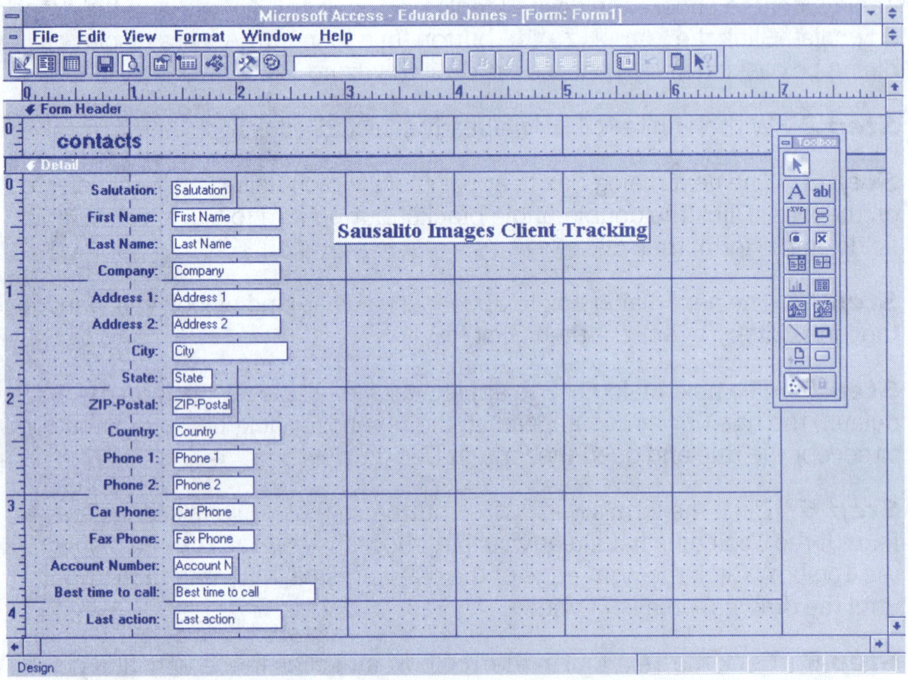

18-6 *The completed Contacts form.*

Step 10 Press Ctrl–F4 to close the new form (click `Yes` in the dialog box that appears asking if you want to save your changes to the form). When you are prompted for a name, enter `Contacts` as the name for the form and click `OK`.

Next, you'll need to create a multitable form to be used for adding and editing phone calls. The form will show the contact name within the main form and all phone calls associated with that contact in the subform. To create this form, perform the following steps.

Step 1 In the Database window, click the `Form` button, then click `New`. The New Form dialog box appears. Click the arrow under Select a Table/Query to choose the desired table, and click on `Calls` in the drop-down list. Click the `FormWizards` button. In a moment, Access displays a dialog box asking you to choose the desired wizard.

Step 2 With `Single-column` already selected, click `OK`.

Step 3 The next dialog box to appear asks which fields you want selected on the form. Click the Date of Call field to select it, then click the single-angle bracket button (>), to place the Date of Call field on the form. Repeating this step, place the Time of Call, Status, and Comment fields on the form. Then, click `Next`.

Step 4 The next dialog box to appear asks what kind of look you want for the form. Click `Standard`, then click `Next`.

Step 5 The next dialog box to appear asks for a title for the form. By default, the title `Calls` appears in the text box. Change this title to `Phone Calls`. Click the `Open` button to accept the title and open the form. At this point, your form should resemble the example shown in FIG. 18-7.

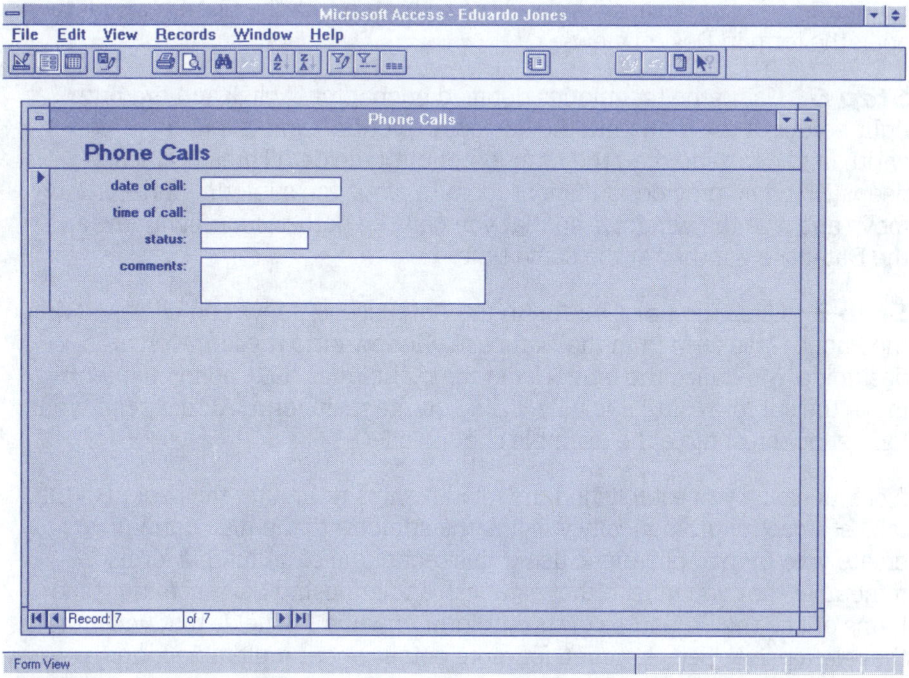

18-7
The completed Phone Calls form.

Step 6 Press Ctrl–F4 to close the new form (click `Yes` in the dialog box that appears asking if you want to save your changes to the form). When you are prompted for a name, enter `Phone calls` as the name for the form, and click `OK`.

Next, perform the following steps to create the main form that will contain the subform that you created.

Step 1 In the Database window, click the `Form` button, then click `New`. The New Form dialog box appears. Click the arrow under Select a Table/Query to choose the desired table, and click on `Contacts` in the drop-down list. Click the `FormWizards` button. In a moment, Access displays a dialog box asking you to choose the desired wizard.

Step 2 With `Single-column` already selected, click `OK`.

Step 3 The next dialog box to appear asks which fields you want selected on the form. Click the First Name field to select it, then click the single-angle bracket button (>) to place the First Name field on the form. Repeating this step, place the Last Name, Company, City, and State fields on the form. Then, click `Next`.

Step 4 The next dialog box to appear asks what kind of look you want for the form. Click `Standard`, then click `Next`.

Step 5 The next dialog box to appear asks for a title for the form. By default, the title `Contacts` appears in the text box. Change this title to `Contact Calls`. Then, click the `Design` button (*not* the `Open` button!) to open the form in Design view.

Step 6 Using the techniques detailed in chapter 6, click and drag the right border of the form until the design area of the form is roughly 7" in width, and click and drag the form footer until the detail area is at least 3" deep. (Doing so provides sufficient room to place the subform.) If necessary, move and size the windows so that you can see both the form window and the Database window at the same time.

Step 7 Click the `Form` button in the Database window, and click and drag the Phone Calls form from the Database window onto the form you are designing. Maximize the form. Using the techniques detailed in chapter 6, move the subform until it is fully visible on the main form. At this point, your form should resemble the example shown in FIG. 18-8.

Note: Because you established the relationships right after the design of the tables, Access automatically will link the subform to the main form. If you create your own applications using this technique of multitable forms, remember that you must either establish a relationship before creating the forms or use the Properties of the subform to name the fields that will provide the relationship. See chapter 6 for more details about multitable forms.

Step 8 Press Ctrl–F4 to close the new form (click `Yes` in the dialog box that appears asking if you want to save your changes to the form). When you are prompted for a name, enter `Contact calls` as the name for the form and click `OK`.

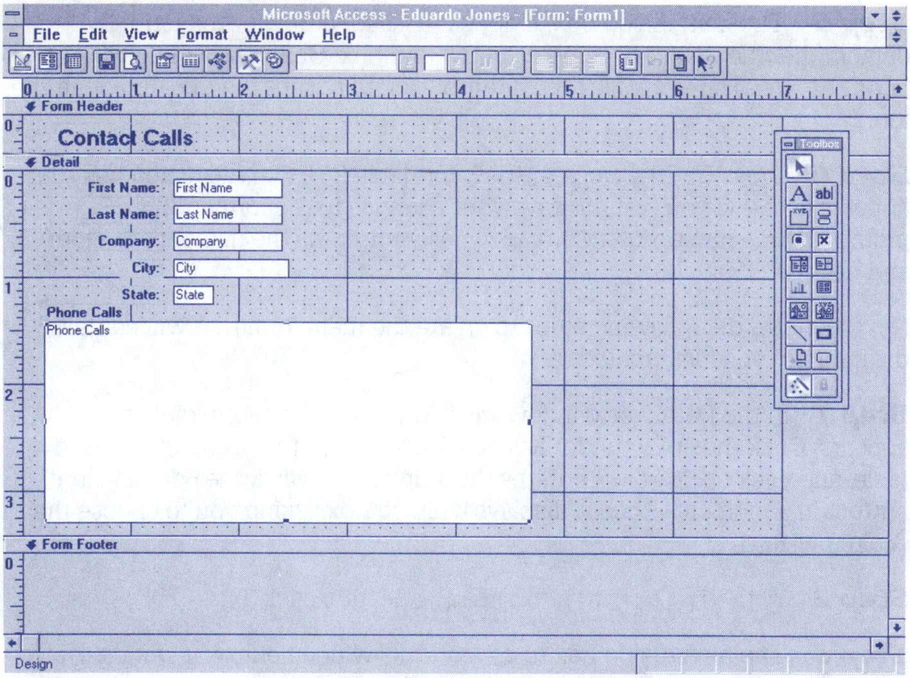

18-8
The completed Contacts Calls form.

With the form for the phone calls of each contact created, you will perform a similar process to create the form that will be needed for the tickler file. As with the phone calls, the relationship between the contacts table and the tickler table is a one-to-many relationship. For each contact, there might be many reminders, or ticklers. A multitable form will show the contact name and the associated ticklers for that contact. Perform the following steps to create the form.

Step 1 In the Database window, click the `Form` button, then click `New`. The New Form dialog box appears. Click the arrow under Select a Table/Query to choose the desired table, and click on `Tickler` in the drop-down list. Click the `FormWizards` button. In a moment, Access displays a dialog box asking you to choose the desired wizard.

Step 2 With `Single-column` already selected, click `OK`.

Step 3 The next dialog box to appear asks which fields you want selected on the form. Click the Date field to select it, then click the single-angle bracket button (>) to place the Date field on the form. Repeating this step, place the Action, Done, and Notes fields on the form. Then, click `Next`.

Step 4 The next dialog box to appear asks what kind of look you want for the form. Click `Standard`, then click `Next`.

Step 5 The next dialog box to appear asks for a title for the form. By default, the title Tickler appears in the text box. Change this title to Contact Reminders. Click the Open button to accept the title and open the form.

Step 6 Press Ctrl–F4 close the new form (click Yes in the dialog box that appears asking if you want to save your changes to the form). When prompted for a name, enter Contact reminders as the name for the form, and click OK.

Next, perform the following steps to create the main form that will contain the subform you just created.

Step 1 In the Database window, click New. The New Form dialog box appears. Click the arrow under Select a Table/Query to choose the desired table, and click on Contacts in the drop-down list. Click the FormWizards button. In a moment, Access displays a dialog box asking you to choose the desired wizard.

Step 2 With Single-column already selected, click OK.

Step 3 The next dialog box to appear asks which fields you want selected on the form. Click the First Name field to select it, then click the single-angle bracket button (>), to place the First Name field on the form. Repeating this step, place the Last Name, Company, City, and State fields on the form. Then, click Next.

Step 4 The next dialog box to appear asks what kind of look you want for the form. Click Standard, then click Next.

Step 5 The next dialog box to appear asks for a title for the form. By default, the title Contacts appears in the text box. Change this title to Tickler. Then, click the Design button (*not* the Open button!) to open the form in Design view.

Step 6 Using the techniques detailed in chapter 6, click and drag the right border of the form until the design area of the form is roughly 7" in width, and click and drag the form footer until the detail area is at least 3" deep. (Doing so provides sufficient room to place the subform.) If necessary, move and size the windows so that you can see both the form window and the Database window at the same time.

Step 7 Click the Form button in the Database window, and click and drag the Contact Reminders form from the Database window onto the form you are designing. Maximize the form. Using the techniques detailed in chapter 6, move the subform until it is fully visible on the main form.

Step 8 Press Ctrl–F4 close the new form (click `Yes` in the dialog box that appears asking if you want to save your changes to the form). When you are prompted for a name, enter `Tickler` as the name for the form, and click `OK`.

Creating the queries

To support the reports used by the Calls report, a parameter query that retrieves all calls for a specific contact will be needed. Perform the following steps to create the query.

Step 1 In the Database window, click the `Query` button, then click `New`. In the New Query dialog box that appears, click `New Query`. The Add Table dialog box appears.

Step 2 In the Table/Query list box, click `Contacts`, then click `Add`. Next, click `Calls`, then click `Add`. Finally, click `Close`. This causes list boxes with the fields from both tables to appear in the Select Query window.

Step 3 In the Contacts list box click the Salutation field. While holding the Shift key, scroll down in the list box until you see the last field of the table (called "Memo") and click that field. (This causes all fields in the list box to be selected.) Then, click and drag any of the fields over to the first empty cell in the Field row of the query grid to place all the fields in the query.

Step 4 Using the Scroll bars, scroll the query grid to the right until you can again see the first empty cell of the grid.

Step 5 In the Calls list box, click the Date of Call field. While holding the Shift key, click the Comments field in the list box to cause all fields in the list box to be selected. Then, click and drag any of the fields over to the first empty cell in the Field row of the query grid to place all the fields in the query.

Step 6 Using the Scroll bars, scroll the query grid to the left until you can again see the leftmost fields of the query grid. Click in the Criteria row underneath the First Name field, and type the following parameter (including the angle brackets):

```
[Enter the first name:]
```

Click in the Criteria row underneath the Last Name field, and type the following parameter (including the angle brackets):

```
[Enter the last name:]
```

Choose `File/Save`. Access will prompt you for a name for the query. Enter `Contacts Query`, and click `OK`.

Step 7 Press Ctrl–F4 to close the Select Query window. The new query appears by name in the Database window.

To support the reports used by the Reminders report, a parameter query that retrieves all reminders for a specific contact will be needed. Perform the following steps to create the query.

Step 1 In the Database window, click the `Query` button, then click `New`. In the New Query dialog box that appears, click `New Query`. The Add Table dialog box appears.

Step 2 In the Table/Query list box, click `Contacts`, then click `Add`. Next, click `Tickler`, then click `Add`. Finally, click `Close`. This causes list boxes with the fields from both tables to appear in the Select Query window.

Step 3 In the Contacts list box, click the Salutation field. While holding the Shift key, scroll down in the list box until you see the last field of the table (called "Memo") and click that field. (This causes all fields in the list box to be selected.) Then, click and drag any of the fields over to the first empty cell in the Field row of the query grid, to place all the fields in the query.

Step 4 Using the Scroll bars, scroll the query grid to the right until you can again see the first empty cell of the grid.

Step 5 In the Tickler list box, click the Date field. While holding the Shift key, click the Notes field in the list box to cause all fields in the list box to be selected. Then, click and drag any of the fields over to the first empty cell in the Field row of the query grid, to place all the fields in the query.

Step 6 Using the Scroll bars, scroll the query grid to the left until you can again see the leftmost fields of the query grid.

Step 7 Click in the Criteria row underneath the First Name field, and type the following parameter (including the angle brackets):

```
[Enter the first name:]
```

Click in the Criteria row underneath the Last Name field, and type the following parameter (including the angle brackets):

```
[Enter the last name:]
```

Step 8 Choose `File/Save`. Access will prompt you for a name for the query. Enter `Reminders Query`, and click `OK`. Press Ctrl–F4 to close the Select Query window. The new query appears by name in the Database window.

One more query will be needed to support the "All Reminders" report. This report will provide a listing of all reminders in the tickler table for a given period of time. Perform the following steps to create this query.

Step 1 In the Database window, with the `Query` button still selected, click `New`. In the New Query dialog box that appears, click `New Query`. The Add Table dialog box appears.

Step 2 In the Table/Query list box, click `Contacts`, then click `Add`. Next, click `Tickler`, then click `Add`. Finally, click `Close`. This causes list boxes with the fields from both tables to appear in the Select Query window.

Step 3 In the Contacts list box, click the Salutation field and drag it to the first empty cell of the Field row in the query grid. Repeating this step, drag the Last name and Company fields to the next empty cells of the Field row.

Step 4 In the Tickler list box, click the Date field. While holding the Shift key, click the Notes field in the list box to cause all fields in the list box to be selected. Then, click and drag any of the fields over to the first empty cell in the Field row of the query grid to place all the fields in the query.

Step 5 Click in the Criteria row underneath the Date field, and type the following parameter (including the angle brackets):

```
between [Enter the starting date:] and [Enter the ending
date:]
```

Step 6 Choose `File/Save`. Access will prompt you for a name for the query. Enter `All Reminders`, and click `OK`. Press Ctrl–F4 to close the Select Query window. The new query appears by name in the Database window.

Creating the reports

Four reports are needed for the application. The Contact Report will be based on the Contacts Query and will print all calls for a given contact. The Tickler Report will be based on the Reminders Query and will print all reminders for a given contact. The All Reminders Report will be based on the All Reminders Query and will print all reminders within a given time span. Finally, the All Contacts report will print all information stored in the Contacts table. Perform the following steps to create the reports.

Step 1 In the Database window, click the `Report` button, then click `New`. The New Report dialog box appears. Click the arrow under Select a Table/Query to choose the desired table, and click `Contacts Query` in the drop-down list. Click the `ReportWizards` button. In a moment, Access displays a dialog box asking you to choose the desired wizard. Click `Groups/Totals`, then click `OK`.

Step 2 The next dialog box to appear asks which fields you want placed on the report. Click the First name field, then click the angle bracket (>) to place the field on the report, then click `Next`. Repeat this step for the Last Name and Company fields.

Step 3 Using the scroll box, scroll down to the bottom of the fields list. Then, click the Date of Call field, and click the angle bracket (>) to place the field on the report, then click Next. Using this same technique, place the Time of Call, Status, and Comments fields on the report. Then, click Next.

Step 4 The next dialog box asks which field you want to use to group the data by. Click the Company field, then click the angle bracket (>), then click Next.

Step 5 The next dialog box asks how you want to group the data in each field. The default value is fine here, so just click Next.

Step 6 The next dialog box asks which fields you want to use to sort the data by. Double-click the Last Name field to place it in the Sort Order box, then double-click the First Name field to place it in the Sort Order box. Finally, click Next.

Step 7 The next dialog box to appear asks what kind of look you want for the report. Click Ledger, then click Next.

Step 8 The next dialog box to appear asks for a title for the form. By default, the title Contacts Query appears in the text box. Change this title to Contacts Report. Click the Fit All Fields on One Page check box to turn it on, turn off the Calculate Percent of Total option, then click the Design button to open the report in Design view. At this point, your form should resemble the example shown in FIG. 18-9.

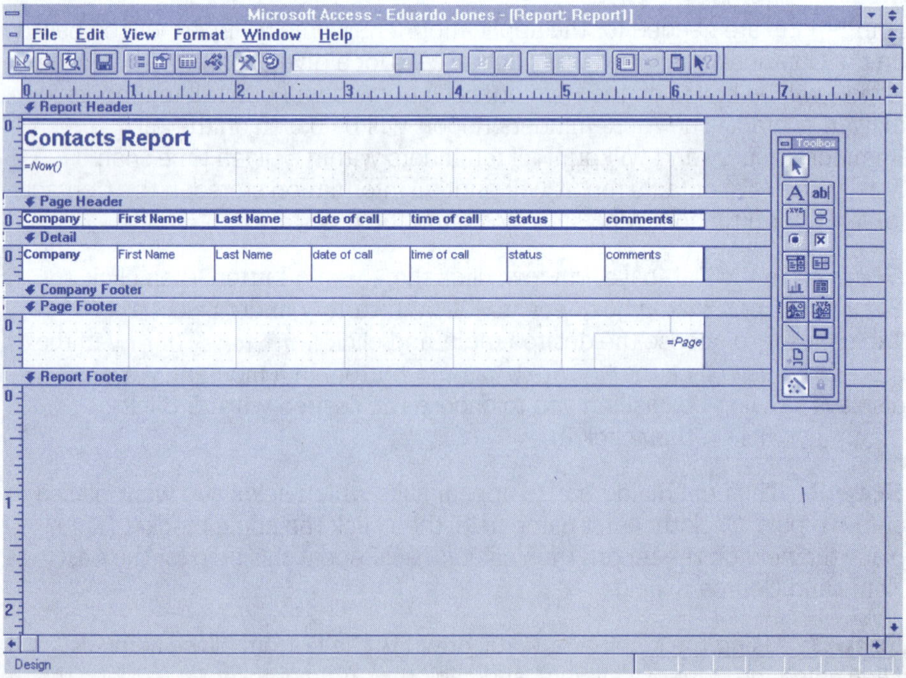

18-9 *The completed Contacts report.*

Step 9 Choose File/Save to save the new report. When you are prompted for a title, enter Contacts Report for a report name, then click OK. Press Ctrl–F4 to close the new report.

Next, perform the following steps to create the report needed for the Reminders.

Step 1 In the Database window, click New. The New Report dialog box appears. Click the arrow under Select a Table/Query to choose the desired table, and click Reminders Query in the drop-down list. Click the ReportWizards button. In a moment, Access displays a dialog box asking you to choose the desired wizard. Click Groups/Totals, then click OK.

Step 2 The next dialog box to appear asks which fields you want placed on the report. Click the First name field, then click the angle bracket (>) to place the field on the report, then click Next. Repeat this step for the Last Name and Company fields.

Step 3 Using the scroll box, scroll down to the bottom of the fields list. Then, click the Date field, and click the angle bracket (>) to place the field on the report, then click Next. Using this same technique, place the Action, Done, and Notes fields on the report. Then, click Next.

Step 4 The next dialog box asks which field you want to use to group the data by. Click the Company field, then click the angle bracket (>), then click Next.

Step 5 The next dialog box asks how you want to group the data in each field. The default value is fine here, so just click Next.

Step 6 The next dialog box asks which fields you want to use to sort the data by. Double-click the Last Name field to place it in the Sort Order box, then double-click the First Name field to place it in the Sort Order box. Finally, click Next.

Step 7 The next dialog box to appear asks what kind of look you want for the report. Click Ledger, then click Next.

Step 8 The next dialog box to appear asks for a title for the form. By default, the title Reminders Query appears in the text box. Change this title to Reminders Report. Click the Fit All Fields on One Page check box to turn it on, turn off the Calculate Percent of Total option, then click the Design button to open the report in Design view. At this point, your report should resemble the example shown in FIG. 18-10.

Step 9 Choose File/Save to save the new report. When you are prompted for a title, enter Reminders Report for a report name, then click OK. Press Ctrl–F4 to close the new report.

Next, perform the following steps to create the All Contacts report.

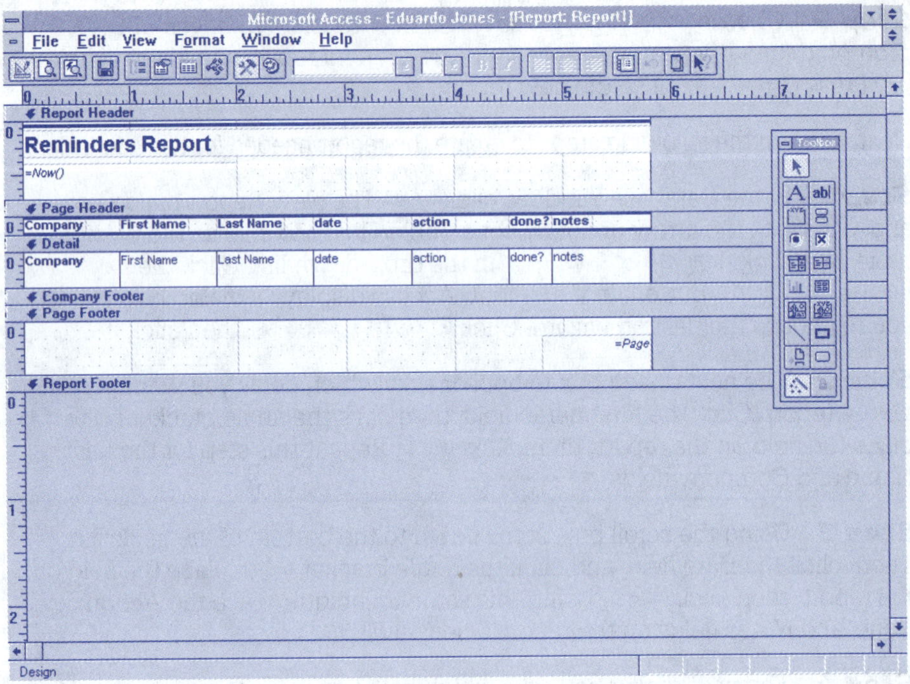

18-10
The completed Reminders report.

Step 1 In the Database window, click New. The New Report dialog box appears. Click the arrow under Select a Table/Query to choose the desired table, and click Contacts in the drop-down list. Click the ReportWizards button. In a moment, Access displays a dialog box asking you to choose the desired wizard.

Step 2 With Single-column already selected, click OK.

Step 3 The next dialog box to appear asks which fields you want placed on the report. Click the double-angle bracket (>>) to place all fields on the report, then click Next.

Step 4 The next dialog box asks which fields you want to use to sort the data by. Double-click the Last Name field to place it in the Sort Order box, then double-click the First Name field to place it in the Sort Order box. Finally, click Next.

Step 5 The next dialog box to appear asks what kind of look you want for the report. Click Ledger, then click Next.

Step 6 The next dialog box to appear asks for a title for the report. By default, the title Contacts appears in the text box. Leave this title as-is, and click the Design button to open the report in Design view.

Step 7 Use the vertical scroll bar to scroll towards the bottom of the report, and click and drag the page footer down by about ¼". (Doing so will create a clean break between records when the report prints.) At this point, your report should resemble the example shown in FIG. 18-11.

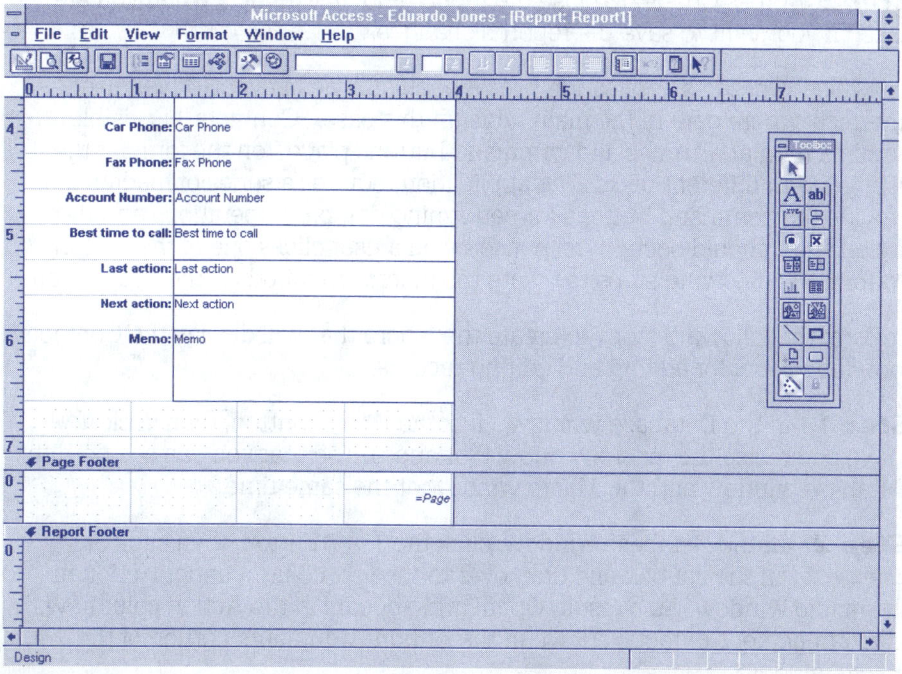

18-11
The completed All Contacts report.

Step 8 Choose `File/Save` to save the new report. When you are prompted for a title, enter `All Contacts` for a report name, then click `OK`. Press Ctrl–F4 to close the new report.

One more report is needed to print all reminders for a given date. You can easily create this report by copying the Reminders Report you created earlier and changing its record source to the "All Reminders" query. Perform the following steps to do so.

Step 1 In the Database window, click the `Reminders Report` to select it, then choose `Edit/Copy` from the menus. Choose `Edit/Paste` from the menus. When you do so, the Paste As dialog box appears.

Step 2 Enter `All Reminders` as the name for the new report, then click `OK`. The new report, titled "All Reminders," appears in the Database window.

Step 3 Click All Reminders to select it, then click `Design` to open the report in Design view.

Step 4 Choose View/Properties (or click the Properties button in the Toolbar). When the Properties window for the report opens, click in the Record Source property, and click the down arrow to change the source from Reminders Query to All Reminders.

Step 5 Press Ctrl–F4 to close the report, and answer Yes when you are asked if you want to save the report's changes.

Developing the application

The Client Contacts application uses a popular style of event-driven user interface, where data in the main table (in this case, "Contacts") is visible within a form at all times and command buttons placed on the form let the user perform different tasks. The application requires a series of macros that provide the command buttons for performing database operations and the actions that should occur in response when a user clicks one of the buttons. Perform the following steps to create the macros required for the application.

Perform the following steps to create the macro that will display the Contacts form (and allow for adding and editing records).

Step 1 In the Database window, click the Macro button, then click New. Move and resize the macro window that appears so that you can see both the Database window and the Macro window at the same time.

Step 2 In the Database window, click the Form button, then click on Contacts in the list box and drag over to the first column under Action in the macro window. As a result, OpenForm appears in the Action column with the form name (Contacts) shown in the Action Arguments portion of the macro window.

Step 3 Click in the second line of the Action column of the macro window. Click the arrow to open the drop-down menu, and choose Maximize from the list.

Step 4 Press Ctrl–F4. Answer Yes in response to the "Save changes" prompt that appears. When you are prompted for a name, call the macro Autoexec. (Assigning the name "Autoexec" to the macro will cause it to run automatically, as soon as the database is opened within Access.)

Perform the following steps to create the macro for adding and editing the records in the Calls table.

Step 1 In the Database window, click the Macro button, then click New. Move and resize the macro window that appears so that you can see both the Database window and the Macro window at the same time.

Step 2 In the Database window, click the Form button, then click on Contact Calls in the list box and drag over to the first column under Action in the macro window. As a result, OpenForm appears in the Action column with the form name (Contact Calls) shown in the Action Arguments portion of the macro window.

Step 3 Press Ctrl–F4. Answer `Yes` in response to the "Save changes" prompt that appears. When you are prompted for a name, call the macro `Phone Calls`.

Perform the following steps to create the macro for adding and editing the records in the Tickler table.

Step 1 In the Database window, click the `Macro` button, then click `New`. Move and resize the macro window that appears so that you can see both the Database window and the Macro window at the same time.

Step 2 In the Database window, click the `Form` button, then click on `Tickler` in the list box and drag over to the first column under Action in the macro window. As a result, OpenForm appears in the Action column with the form name (Tickler) shown in the Action Arguments portion of the macro window.

Step 3 Press Ctrl–F4. Answer `Yes` in response to the "Save changes" prompt that appears. When you are prompted for a name, call the macro `Tickler`.

Perform the following steps to create a group of macros for navigating within the Contacts table.

Step 1 In the Database window, click the `Macro` button, then click `New`. Click in the Action column of the first row, and choose `GoToRecord` from the list box. Under Action Arguments, click in the Record box, open the list box, and choose `New`.

Step 2 Press Ctrl–F4 to close the macro. Answer `Yes` when you are asked if you want to save the macro. For a name, call the macro `New`.

Step 3 In the Database window, click `New` to create another macro. Click in the Action column of the first row, and choose `DoMenuItem` from the list box. Click in the Command box, open the list box, and choose `Find`.

Step 4 Press Ctrl–F4 to close the macro. Answer `Yes` when you are asked if you want to save the macro. For a name, call the macro `Search`.

Perform the following steps to create the macro for printing the records in the Contacts table.

Step 1 In the Database window, click the `Macro` button, then click `New`. Move and resize the macro window that appears so that you can see both the Database window and the Macro window at the same time.

Step 2 In the Database window, click the Report button, then click on All Contacts in the list box and drag over to the first column under Action in the macro window. As a result, OpenReport appears in the Action column with the report name (All Contacts) shown in the Action Arguments portion of the macro window.

Step 3 Click in the second line of the Action column of the macro window. Click the arrow to open the drop-down menu, and choose Print from the list.

Step 4 Click in the third line of the Action column of the macro window. Click the arrow to open the drop-down menu, and choose Close from the list.

Step 5 Press Ctrl–F4. Answer Yes in response to the "Save changes" prompt that appears. When you are prompted for a name, call the macro Print All Contacts.

Perform the following steps to create the macro for printing all contacts for a particular person.

Step 1 In the Database window, click the Macro button, then click New. Move and resize the macro window that appears so that you can see both the Database window and the Macro window at the same time.

Step 2 In the Database window, click the Report button, then click on Contacts Report in the list box and drag over to the first column under Action in the macro window. As a result, OpenReport appears in the Action column with the report name (Contacts Report) shown in the Action Arguments portion of the macro window.

Step 3 Click in the second line of the Action column of the macro window. Click the arrow to open the drop-down menu, and choose Print from the list.

Step 4 Click in the third line of the Action column of the macro window. Click the arrow to open the drop-down menu, and choose Close from the list.

Step 5 Press Ctrl–F4. Answer Yes in response to the "Save changes" prompt that appears. When you are prompted for a name, call the macro Print Contacts.

Perform the following steps to create the macro for printing all reminders for a particular person.

Step 1 In the Database window, click the Macro button, then click New. Move and resize the macro window that appears so that you can see both the Database window and the Macro window at the same time.

Step 2 In the Database window, click the `Report` button, then click on `Reminders Report` in the list box and drag over to the first column under Action in the macro window. As a result, OpenReport appears in the Action column with the report name (Reminders Report) shown in the Action Arguments portion of the macro window.

Step 3 Click in the second line of the Action column of the macro window. Click the arrow to open the drop-down menu, and choose `Print` from the list.

Step 4 Click in the third line of the Action column of the macro window. Click the arrow to open the drop-down menu, and choose `Close` from the list.

Step 5 Press Ctrl–F4. Answer `Yes` in response to the "Save changes" prompt that appears. When you are prompted for a name, call the macro `Print Reminders`.

Perform the following steps to create a macro for closing the tickler or phone calls forms.

Step 1 In the Database window, click the `Macro` button, then click `New`.

Step 2 Click in the first row of the Action column of the macro. Open the drop-down list box, and choose `Close` from the list box.

Step 3 Press Ctrl–F4. Answer `Yes` in response to the "Save changes" prompt that appears. When you are prompted for a name, call the macro `Close`.

Perform the following steps to create the macro for exiting from the application.

Step 1 In the Database window, click the `Macro` button, then click `New`.

Step 2 Click in the first row of the Action column of the macro. Open the drop-down list box, and choose `Close` from the list box.

Step 3 Click in the second row of the Action column of the macro. Open the drop-down list box, and again choose `Close` from the list box.

Step 4 Press Ctrl–F4. Answer `Yes` in response to the "Save changes" prompt that appears. When you are prompted for a name, call the macro `Exit System`.

Next, you will need to add the command buttons to the Contacts form. You can do this by dragging the macros from the Database window onto the form. Perform the following steps to do this.

Step 1 In the Database window, click the `Form` button, then click `Contacts`, then click `Design` to open the Contacts form in Design view. Size the form so that you will have room to work, and move the windows so that both the Database window and the form are visible.

Step 2 In the Database window, click the `Macro` button to display the macros. Click the `New` button, and drag it to a location roughly 3" to the right of the left edge of the form and roughly 1" below the top of the detail band. When you release the mouse, a command button titled `New` appears. *Note*: If you see a dialog box warning you that Wizards cannot be used on existing buttons, click `OK` to ignore it, and ignore any more buttons like this that you see. When the user clicks this button, it will call the New macro, causing movement to a new record. By dragging the remaining macros to the form in a similar manner, you will add command buttons for the remaining tasks.

Step 3 In the Database window, click the Search macro and drag it to a point roughly ⅛" below the `New` button. Using the techniques covered in chapter 6, move the button until it is aligned underneath the `New` button.

Step 4 In the Database window, click the Phone Calls macro and drag it to a point roughly ⅛" below the `Search` button. Using the techniques covered in chapter 6, move the button until it is aligned underneath the `Search` button.

Step 5 In the Database window, click the Tickler macro and drag it to a point roughly ⅛" below the `Phone Calls` button. Using the techniques covered in chapter 6, move the button until it is aligned underneath the `Phone Calls` button.

Step 6 In the Database window, click the Exit System macro and drag it to a point roughly ⅛" below the `Tickler` button. Using the techniques covered in chapter 6, move the button until it is aligned underneath the `Tickler` button.

Step 7 In the Database window, click the Print Contacts macro and drag it to a point roughly 1" below the `Exit System` button. Using the techniques covered in chapter 6, move the button until it is aligned underneath the `Exit System` button. Then, resize the button until it is wide enough to display its full name, `Print Contacts`.

Step 8 In the Database window, click the Print Contacts Data macro and drag it to a point roughly ⅛" below the `Tickler` button. Using the techniques covered in chapter 6, move the button until it is aligned underneath the `Print Contacts` button. Then, resize the button until it is wide enough to display its full name, `Print Contacts Data`.

Step 9 In the Database window, click the Print Reminders Data macro and drag it to a point roughly ⅛" below the `Tickler` button. Using the techniques covered in chapter 6, move the button until it is aligned underneath the `Print Contacts Data` button. Then, resize the button until it is wide enough to display its full name, `Print Reminders`.

Next, you will create a module containing a small Access Basic program. The program will be used to dial the phone using a modem. If no modem is installed in your computer and you don't want this capability in the application, you can press Ctrl–F4 to save the form now and skip ahead to the end of this chapter. Otherwise, perform the following steps.

Step 1 In the Database window, click the `Module` button. Then, click `New` to open a window where you can design a new module. In the window that appears, you will see a line like this:

```
Option Compare Database  'Use database order for string
comparisons
```

Step 2 Access automatically places this line as the first line of any module that you create. The insertion pointer should be flashing just below this line at the start of a new line. On the new line, type the following:

```
Function MyDialerOnPush (szOffice_Phone As String) As
Integer
```

When you finish typing the line and press Enter, you will note that Access automatically places a line with the text `End Function` below, and the insertion pointer now appears between the line that you just typed and the `End Function` line. Because you started the module with a function, Access assumes that an `End Function` statement is needed at the end of the module, because all functions end this way.

Step 3 Now, leave the insertion pointer where it is (above the `End Function` line) and type these lines as shown here, pressing Enter after each line.

```
    Dim w As Integer
    On Error GoTo Missing
    w = Shell("terminal", 1)
    SendKeys "%SN", True
    SendKeys szOffice_Phone & "{ENTER}", True
    SendKeys "%PD", True
    MyDialerOnPush = w
Exit Function
Missing:
    MsgBox "Can't find Windows Terminal."
    MyDialerOnPush = 0
 Exit Function
```

At this point, all of this text should appear between the first `Function` line that you typed and the last `End Function` line that was inserted by Access.

Step 4 Check your work for errors, then choose `File/Save` from the menus. When you see the "Save As" dialog box, type `Dial My Number` as a name for the module, then click `OK`. Press Ctrl–F4 to close the module window.

Next, you need to add a button to the form that will call the module that you just wrote. Perform the following steps to add the button to the Contacts form.

Step 1 Click within the Contacts form to make it the active window. If the Toolbox is not visible, choose `View/Toolbox` from the menus to display the Toolbox.

Step 2 Click the Control Wizards icon (the lowest button on the left side) to turn off the Control Wizards. Then, click the Command Button icon in the Toolbox to select it (remember, it's in the right-hand row, second from furthest button down).

Step 3 Click and hold down the mouse button in a blank area of the form beside the Office Phone field, and drag down and to the right until you have a button roughly ¼" deep and 1" in length. Click in the button, and click and drag through the existing text to select it all, then press Del to delete it. Type the words `Dial Office` to replace the existing text.

Step 4 Click anywhere outside the button to deselect the text in the button. Then, place the mouse pointer near the corner of the button and click the button to select it. (When the button is selected, there will be handles—small boxes—surrounding the button.)

Step 5 Choose `View/Properties` from the menus. A Command Button dialog box will open for the button. In the Control Name box, delete the existing entry, and type `Dial Office`.

Step 6 Click in the OnClick box of this window to place the insertion pointer there, and type the following, then press Tab after completing this entry:

```
=MyDialerOnPush(Forms![Contacts]![Office Phone])
```

Step 7 Double-click the Close icon at the upper-left corner of the properties window to close this window. Press Ctrl–F4 close the form (click `Yes` in the dialog box that appears asking if you want to save your changes to the form).

Step 8 In the Database window, click the `Form` button, then click `Contact Calls`, then click `Design`. Move or resize the form window so that you can see both the Database window and the Form window at the same time.

Step 9 In the Database window, click the `Macro` button, then click the Search macro and drag the macro over to a blank space anywhere within the header of the form (but leave sufficient space to put another button of the same size to the right of it).

Step 10 In the Database window, click the Close macro and drag the macro to the space to the right of the `Search` button. If necessary, move the `Close` button so that it is aligned horizontally and just to the right of the `Search` button.

Step 11 Press Ctrl–F4 close the form (click `Yes` in the dialog box that appears asking if you want to save your changes to the form).

Step 12 In the Database window, click the `Form` button, then click `Tickler`, then click `Design`. Move or resize the form window so that you can see both the Database window and the Form window at the same time.

Step 13 In the Database window, click the `Macro` button, then click the Search macro and drag the macro over to a blank space anywhere within the header of the form (but leave sufficient space to put another button of the same size to the right of it).

Step 14 In the Database window, click the Close macro and drag the macro to the space to the right of the `Search` button. If necessary, move the `Close` button so that it is aligned horizontally and just to the right of the `Search` button.

Step 15 Press Ctrl–F4 close the form (click `Yes` in the dialog box that appears asking if you want to save your changes to the form).

At this point, the application is complete. Double-click the `Close` button of the Database window to close it. Then, to try running the application, choose `File/Open Database`. When the Open Database dialog box appears, double-click `CONTACTS` to reopen the database. Because you added the Autoexec macro, when the database opens, the form displaying the contacts opens automatically. You can test the application by adding and editing data and printing the desired reports. Additional queries, reports, and macros can be added as needed to increase the functionality of the application.

Appendix

Installation

Access comes with several disks that you will use to install the program on your PC's hard disk. Before starting installation, it is a wise idea to make backup copies of your program disks. (If you are unfamiliar with how to make backup copies of disks, refer to your DOS or Windows documentation for details.)

Your computer must meet certain minimum hardware requirements to use Microsoft Access. The following are the minimum requirements:

- IBM-compatible computer capable of running Windows (minimum 386SX or better processor; a 386DX/33 or better is highly recommended for performance reasons)
- A hard disk or network file server with 13Mb of free space
- 4Mb of memory or more (8Mb or more is highly recommended)
- IBM-compatible EGA, VGA, or other graphics card compatible with Microsoft Windows, version 3.0 or above
- Microsoft Mouse or other compatible pointing device
- MS-DOS or PC-DOS, version 3.1 or above
- Microsoft Windows, version 3.0 or above

Perform the following steps to install Access on your computer:

Step 1 Start Windows in the usual manner. (On most PCs, you can do this by typing `WIN` at the DOS prompt.)

Step 2 Insert the Microsoft Access Setup Disk in your floppy disk drive.

Step 3 Open the Windows File menu (press Alt–F), and choose `Run`.

Step 4 In the Run dialog box that appears, enter `A:SETUP` (if the setup disk is in drive A:) or `B:SETUP` (if the setup disk is in drive B:), then press Enter.

The installation process will begin, and you can follow the directions that appear on the screen to complete the installation. Some of the questions and prompts that you will see are covered in the following paragraphs.

Access will ask you to enter your name and the name of your company in a dialog box. If Access already was installed on another system using the same disks, you will see a warning box informing you of copyright regulations. Choose `Continue` from this dialog box to continue installation (or choose `Cancel Setup` to cancel the process).

Access will ask which directory you want to install the program in. By default, Access suggests C:\ACCESS as a directory name, although you can change this to any valid path name.

Access provides the opportunity to install all of the program, selective parts of the program ("custom installation"), or a minimum installation of the program. If you choose custom installation, you are presented with check boxes that let you decide which parts of the program you want to install. For example, you can choose to omit the tutorial. If you choose the complete installation, Access will require 13Mb of disk space to install the program. If you choose the minimum installation, Access will require 4Mb of disk space.

Access prompts for each additional disk as it is needed. When you are prompted, insert the specified disk in the drive and click `OK`.

Note: If you are installing Access on a network, you will see questions about the type of network that you are using. For additional details on installing Access on a network, refer to "Setting up Microsoft Access on a network" in your *Microsoft Access User's Guide*.

Once the installation process is complete, you are returned to the Windows desktop. A new program group containing Access will have been added to your desktop. You can open the program group and double-click the Microsoft Access icon within the group to start the program.

Index

About the author

Ed Jones is the author of over 25 computer books published by McGraw-Hill, including many bestsellers in the area of databases. He specializes in providing clear and understandable books at the novice and intermediate level. Jones also provides consulting, planning, software development, and training for federal government agencies, law firms, and corporate clients in the greater Washington, DC area. He has designed and provided personnel management software to an installed base of approximately 100 companies nationwide. Mr. Jones provides consulting services through the Computer Support Group of Annandale, Virginia. As a writer, Jones has published articles in *Lotus*, *Databased Adviser*, and *DBMS* magazines.

DISK WARRANTY

This software is protected by both United States copyright law and international copyright treaty provision. You must treat this software just like a book, except that you may copy it into a computer in order to be used and you may make archival copies of the software for the sole purpose of backing up our software and protecting your investment from loss.

By saying "just like a book," McGraw-Hill means, for example, that this software may be used by any number of people and may be freely moved from one computer location to another, so long as there is no possibility of its being used at one location or on one computer while it also is being used at another. Just as a book cannot be read by two different people in two different places at the same time, neither can the software be used by two different people in two different places at the same time (unless, of course, McGraw-Hill's copyright is being violated).

LIMITED WARRANTY

Windcrest/McGraw-Hill takes great care to provide you with top-quality software, thoroughly checked to prevent virus infections. McGraw-Hill warrants the physical diskette(s) contained herein to be free of defects in materials and workmanship for a period of sixty days from the purchase date. If McGraw-Hill receives written notification within the warranty period of defects in materials or workmanship, and such notification is determined by McGraw-Hill to be correct, McGraw-Hill will replace the defective diskette(s). Send requests to:

Customer Service
Windcrest/McGraw-Hill
13311 Monterey Lane
Blue Ridge Summit, PA 17294-0850

The entire and exclusive liability and remedy for breach of this Limited Warranty shall be limited to replacement of defective diskette(s) and shall not include or extend to any claim for or right to cover any other damages, including but not limited to, loss of profit, data, or use of the software, or special, incidental, or consequential damages or other similar claims, even if McGraw-Hill has been specifically advised of the possibility of such damages. In no event will McGraw-Hill's liability for any damages to you or any other person ever exceed the lower of suggested list price or actual price paid for the license to use the software, regardless of any form of the claim.

McGRAW-HILL, INC. SPECIFICALLY DISCLAIMS ALL OTHER WARRANTIES, EXPRESS OR IMPLIED, INCLUDING, BUT NOT LIMITED TO, ANY IMPLIED WARRANTY OF MERCHANTABILITY OR FITNESS FOR A PARTICULAR PURPOSE.

Specifically, McGraw-Hill makes no representation or warranty that the software is fit for any particular purpose and any implied warranty of merchantability is limited to the sixty-day duration of the Limited Warranty covering the physical diskette(s) only (and not the software) and is otherwise expressly and specifically disclaimed.

This limited warranty gives you specific legal rights; you may have others which may vary from state to state. Some states do not allow the exclusion of incidental or consequential damages, or the limitation on how long an implied warranty lasts, so some of the above may not apply to you.

If you need help with the enclosed disk . . .

The enclosed high-density 3½" disk contains the self-extracting file, BOOKDISK.EXE. This file contains 18 other programs in a compressed format.

Before you can access the programs contained in BOOKDISK.EXE, you must create a directory on your hard drive, copy BOOKDISK.EXE into the new directory, and run the BOOKDISK.EXE file. At the C> prompt, type:

`MD C:\directory_name`

(where *directory_name* is the name of the directory that you want to create) and press Enter. You have just created a directory on your hard drive to hold all of the programs contained in BOOKDISK.EXE. Now, place the companion diskette in drive A: and copy BOOKDISK.EXE to your newly created directory by typing:

`COPY A:\BOOKDISK.EXE C:\directory_name`

(where *directory_name* is the name of the directory that you created earlier) and press Enter. Now, you can safely run BOOKDISK.EXE to extract the other programs. Change to the directory that contains BOOKDISK.EXE by typing:

`CD directory_name`

at the C> prompt. To extract the files, type:

`BOOKDISK`

and press Enter. The program will list the name of each file as it is uncompressed and will return to the DOS prompt when all of the files have been uncompressed.

IMPORTANT

Read the Disk Warranty terms on the previous page before opening the disk envelope. Opening the envelope constitutes acceptance of these terms and renders this entire book-disk package nonreturnable except for replacement in kind due to material defect.